The Quality Management Sourcebook

The Quality Management Sourcebook

An international guide to materials and resources

Christine Avery and Diane Zabel

London and New York

First published 1997
by Routledge
11 New Fetter Lane, London EC4P 4EE
29 West 35th Street, New York, NY 10001

Typeset in Times by Florencetype Limited, Stoodleigh, Devon

Printed and bound in Great Britain by Clays Ltd, St. Ives plc

British Library Cataloguing in Publication Data
A catalogue record for this book is available from the British Library

Library of Congress Cataloging-in-Publication Data
Avery, Christine.
     The quality management sourcebook : an international guide to
materials and resources / Christine Avery and Diane Zabel.
        p.   cm.
     Includes indexes.
     alk. paper
     1. Total quality management—Bibliography. 2. Management–
Bibliography. I. Zabel, Diane. II. Title.
Z7164.07A95   1996
[HD62.15]
016.6585'62—dc20   96–8911
                                     CIP

ISBN 0–415–10831–4

Contents

Preface and Acknowledgments   vii

I   Introduction: General Sources for Information on Quality Management   1
    1   Internet resources   3
    2   Books   3
    3   Articles   10

II   Applications of TQM   17

III   Focus on Specific Aspects of Quality Management   123
    1   Teams   123
    2   Customers   126
    3   Analytical and statistical tools   131
    4   Corporate culture   140
    5   Leadership   149
    6   Training, human resource issues, and communication   156

IV   Quality in the Future: What Role Does ISO 9000 Play?   165
    1   Books on ISO 9000   168
    2   Articles on ISO 9000   170

V   Resource Materials   181
    1   Strategies for locating additional information   181
      i   Book publishers and distributors   181
      ii   Periodicals   183
      iii   Databases   187
      iv   Useful Library of Congress subject headings   188
    2   Training materials   189
      i   Audio-visual and interactive multimedia training resources   189
      ii   Software packages   211
      iii   Software finding aid   233
    3   Executive development programs   235
    4   Quality management consultants survey   251
    5   TQM associations   292
    6   Malcolm Baldrige National Quality Award   294

Glossary   297
Name index   303
Title index   310
Subject index   321

Preface

The quality management movement began in the manufacturing sector, but a growing concern with quality in other areas of the economy has led to its application in service industries, government, education, and other nonprofit agencies. In the past decade much has been published on this topic. Given the proliferation of interest in quality management, combined with our observation that much of the best material on quality is published by small presses, professional and trade associations, as well as consultants, we undertook the task of creating a handbook on the best sources of information on quality management. Although coverage has been restricted to English-language materials, the scope is international.

We believe this book will be of interest to people in industry, government, and academia; including management consultants, quality engineers, reference librarians, and information brokers. The handbook can serve as a desk reference for any organizations either implementing or actively involved in a quality management program. Additionally, an overview of the ISO 9000 registration process has been included. Students in academic courses with a quality management component will also find much useful information.

The types of materials covered include books, book chapters, journal articles, video, software, and other training materials. We have listed consultants with specialties in quality-related areas, organizations, publishers, Malcolm Baldrige Award winners, and professional short courses. Strategies for locating additional information are included as well as a glossary of terms.

Acknowledgments

We would like to acknowledge the support of the University Libraries at the Pennsylvania State University. In particular we would like to thank our colleagues in the General References section for their encouragement, and our excellent interlibrary loan department for their efforts on our behalf. We are grateful to the numerous consulting groups, associations, organizations, publishers and other companies that responded to our surveys, telephone calls, and other requests for information. Colville Wemyss, our editor at Routledge, was a pleasure to work with. Most of all we thank our families, especially our children (Julian and Carl and Zachary), for their patience.

1

Introduction: General Sources for Information on Quality Management

This chapter will provide a brief overview of the history of the quality movement and a summary of the basic concepts of total quality management. The rest of the chapter consists of annotations for both books and journals which can be used to identify useful sources of general information on quality management, as well as more specific sources of information on topics such as business process reengineering, making quality management programs more successful, and problems with TQM.

The modern quality movement has its roots in both Britain and America. British statisticians contributed seminal work which led to the development of techniques for statistical quality control, while the applied work of Walter A. Shewhart in 1924 (a physicist in the inspection department at Western Electric Company) was America's contribution. Shewhart suggested that better quality could be achieved at a lower cost if one moved from a system of inspecting products for defects, and instead looked at production processes. Monitoring and improving these processes would result in elimination of defects at the source, and thus result in lower costs.

Shewhart's book *Economic Control of Quality of Manufactured Products* was published in 1931, and his ideas played a direct role in the 1935 publication of the first British Standards Institute standard on quality control. Despite some heightened concern with industrial quality during World War II and the development of military procurement standards (the beginnings of ISO 9000) in both Great Britain and the United States, the next real marker on the road to quality didn't occur until 1950. In that year Armand V. Feigenbaum (who worked at General Electric) published *Total Quality Control*, W. Edwards Deming began working with the Japanese on quality improvement and developing his ideas on statistical process control, and in 1951 Joseph Juran published the *Quality Control Handbook*. At this point, the key ideas of quality management – continuous improvement, management responsibility, statistical controls, and organization-wide investment in quality – were all in place.

However, while these ideas took root and flourished in Japan, they were largely unknown in the rest of the industrialized world. British industry failed to develop a widespread interest in quality until the 1980s, although there was some sporadic activity over the years. American industry experienced a rapid expansion in the years following World War II, but it's probably safe to say that the quantity of goods produced was more important in the minds of most executives than quality. This changed sharply in the 1970s when serious problems with the quality of American goods as compared to Japanese products became evident. Moreover, it became apparent that the Japanese were producing goods at lower costs in less time than American manufacturers. As American consumers began to express a preference for foreign goods (European included) because the quality was superior, American companies began to experiment with methods of improving quality.

The first efforts at achieving a turnaround were based on the idea of participative management (borrowed from the Japanese) in which employees would be involved in improving work processes. Quality circles were tried beginning in the mid-1970s as a means of soliciting suggestions for improving quality and responding to competition from the Japanese. While extremely popular, quality circles were ultimately not particularly successful, for a number of reasons. However, the concepts of employee empowerment and teamwork introduced by quality circles were crucial in setting the stage for TQM. The widespread use of quality circles, the dawning understanding of the immense importance of customer satisfaction, and the sense of urgency centering around quality problems and economic competition gave TQM the opening it finally needed in the 1980s to break through in the western world.

Philip Crosby's book, *Quality is Free*, published in 1979, had much to do with focusing widespread attention on a different way of thinking about quality issues. Crosby developed a fourteen-step quality improvement program based on his belief that higher quality reduces costs and raises profits. Shortly thereafter, Americans "discovered" the other three management experts who had so much to do with the development of total quality management: W. Edwards Deming who by this time had developed a fourteen-point approach to improving quality (emphasizing a need to change organizational culture and making extensive use of statistical measures of quality), Joseph Juran and his ten-point approach to quality management (with a focus on reducing the cost of quality), and Armand Feigenbaum (with an emphasis on long-term commitment to quality as a way of managing an organization).

Since the early 1980s the terms total quality management (TQM), total quality control, quality assurance, and continuous quality improvement have all been used more or less interchangeably. These terms describe a management style aimed at improving the performance of an organization and meeting customer expectations through continual analysis and refinement of its processes for producing goods or services. The basic components of total quality management may be summarized as follows:

1 Processes need to be examined to determine ways to reduce complexity while providing a better service or producing a better product. The way work is done – not people – is most often the source of problems.
2 Satisfaction of customers, both internal and external, is paramount.
3 Management must provide leadership and foster commitment to quality.
4 The empowerment of employees is crucial. Employees must understand the business of their organization, and must have an understanding of how their activities contribute to the organization. Employee participation is critical in identifying root problems and finding solutions to such problems; employees should be encouraged to control, manage, and improve processes for which they are responsible.
5 Total quality management is built around the concept of using teamwork to accomplish change. Teams need to be trained in using problem-solving techniques aimed at quality improvement. Teams typically function with a leader, employees with a stake in the work being performed, and a facilitator.
6 Tools and techniques are important and must be integrated into an organization's routine. Processes are brought under control through consistent application of a quality improvement methodology. Measurement of quality indicators and collection of data, as opposed to use of anecdotal evidence, is emphasized. A cycle of progress followed by feedback and assessment leads to continual improvement.
7 Long-term commitment is critical. TQM is based on the concept of incremental change, which leads to a gradual change in organizational culture. As the organization institutionalizes a philosophy of quality management, the areas where changes occur increase until the entire organization has been transformed into a more effective entity.

A 1994 survey revealed TQM to be the top workplace trend in the United States. *Training* magazine's "1994 Industry Report" (October 1994) indicated that 58 percent of the more than 2300 companies responding to the survey reported that they were pursuing TQM initiatives. Other interesting results were that 44 percent were making a transition to a team-based structure, 34 percent were partnering with suppliers and customers, 31 percent were downsizing, and 31 percent were reengineering. While TQM has sometimes been criticized for not producing the desired impact on a company's bottom line, an interesting experiment does suggest that quality pays off in higher stock prices. *Training* (April 1995, p. 18) reports that the National Institute of Standards and Technology has built a model which compares the return on investment for Baldrige Award winners' stock to the market in general. Companies with a tie to the Baldrige Award (winner, or subsidiary of a winner) clearly enjoy a substantially higher rate of return (three to six times).

TQM will continue to develop and evolve. Companies are learning to apply quality concepts in ways that best suit their needs. This ultimately means there are several routes to quality. Many organizations feel the pace of change has been too slow while practicing TQM. This has led to new techniques such as reengineering (which actually has much in common with TQM) and reorganization; the idea being to combine continuous improvement with periods of greater change in hopes of making faster quality and productivity advances. A February 1995 survey by Pitney Bowes Management Services found that 83 of the 100 Fortune 500 companies they surveyed had introduced reengineering initiatives. (*HR FOCUS*, February 1995, p. 24). The effect of massive downsizing in corporations has to be factored into changes in quality management as well.

However, the widespread acceptance of most of the basic tenets of TQM mean that quality has become a central theme and will remain with us in some form, even if it's not called TQM. As Jeremy Main said in the conclusion of his book *Quality Wars* (pp. 316–317):

> In spite of the criticism, the obstacles, the difficulties, and the many failures and disappointments, quality improvement has, in the dozen or so years since Americans began taking it seriously, had an enormous impact on the way we work and run our businesses and other organizations . . . we are creating a new way to work and it is better.

1 Internet resources

The fastest growing area for information on quality management could well be the World Wide Web. The number of quality-related resources on the Web is too extensive and changes too rapidly to make a listing of sites feasible. The following two citations are for articles on the topic of quality in cyberspace. Both provide a good start for novice Web searchers. The articles describe resources including information sites (such as the sites developed by the American Society for Quality Control and the American National Standards Institute Online) and discussion lists (for example QUALITY, which deals with application of TQM in the manufacturing and service industries; and ISO 9000 which is for those individuals interested in sharing information about the ISO 9000 quality standards).

Clauson, Jim
"Cyberquality: Quality Resources on the Internet." *Quality Progress* 28, no.1 (January 1995): 45–48.

Dusharme, Dirk
"Quality in Cyberspace." *Quality Digest* 16, no. 3 (March 1996): 22–28.

2 Books

Brown, Mark Graham, Darcy E. Hitchcock, and Marsha L. Willard
Why TQM Fails and What to Do About It. Burr Ridge, IL: Irwin Professional Publishing, 1994.

The authors believe that TQM is even more critical as an organizational philosophy now than it was ten years ago. They acknowledge that while many TQM efforts may not have delivered the expected results, there are common causes for such failures. The book focuses on three phases of TQM involvement (start-up, alignment, and integration) and separate chapters address the reasons for failure at each stage. Among the problems discussed are lack of executive commitment, pursuing TQM as a short-cut to profitability, implementing training incorrectly, failure to integrate TQM into the corporate culture, collecting the wrong kind of data or using it incorrectly, failure to empower teams, and rigid organizational structures. The authors make suggestions in each case for ways to overcome the problems they identify (methods for building interest in TQM, pacing the implementation of TQM in a way that increases employee participation, etc.)

and provide useful examples from various organizations.

Cole, Robert E. (ed.)
The Death and Life of the American Quality Movement. New York: Oxford University Press, 1995.

Cole's assumption is that the quality movement in the United States needs to be re-energized, especially since the move toward quality is more important than ever for U.S. firms competing in a global marketplace. Although quality performance has improved across a wide range of industries and thousands of companies are using the Malcolm Baldrige Award criteria for self-assessment, many companies' quality efforts seem to have plateaued and many firms appear to be at a loss as to how to proceed further. This book, which brings together eleven papers by a diverse group of experts, provides suggestions for ways out of the current impasse. Contributors from small, medium, and large-sized manufacturing and service firms are represented. Among the critical issues addressed are the role of employee participation, reconciling quality with downsizing, the relationship between restructuring/reengineering and quality, the relation between process and results orientations, the role marketing plays in quality, and the special challenges that small high-tech companies face when attempting to improve quality.

Cole, William E., and John W. Mogab
The Economics of Total Quality Management: Clashing Paradigms in the Global Market. Oxford: Blackwell Business, 1995.

The authors are concerned with the underlying economic logic of the shift from the dominant paradigm of this century, "Mass Production-Scientific Management" to the new paradigm of "Total Quality Management and the Continuous Improvement Firm." After describing both paradigms, Cole and Mogab discuss historical changes in the way labor and management interact (with emphasis on the disappearance of the line between those who think and those who do) and the economic implications of this change. They then look at productivity, cost of production, customer demand and competition in the continuous improvement firm model. Final chapters look at international variants of

continuous improvement in firms and the future of TQM.

Cound, Dana M.
A Leader's Journey to Quality. New York: Marcel Dekker, 1992.

Cound asserts the belief that quality improvement requires more than the application of statistical tools. He firmly believes change is a constant for all organizations and that leadership is of paramount importance in managing change successfully. Success depends upon a corporate vision and the ability to communicate a basic philosophy, a clear mission, and strategies for achieving the mission. Cound discusses the basic components of a quality improvement process and presents methods for structuring, reporting, and analyzing quality costs. Additionally, basic statistical techniques are discussed.

Crosby, Philip B.
Quality is Free: The Art of Making Quality Certain. New York: New American Library, 1979.

Crosby advances the theory that higher quality reduces costs and raises profits and that it costs nothing to do things right the first time; i.e. "quality is free." Crosby provides a detailed explanation of the fourteen-step quality improvement program he developed. The program focuses on changing an organization through securing management commitment to quality improvement, developing organization-wide quality awareness, making extensive use of teams, evaluating the cost of quality, continuously refining processes, and setting goals.

Crosby, Philip B.
Quality Without Tears: The Art of Hassle-Free Management. New York: New American Library, 1984.

This book is useful when used in conjunction with Crosby's book *Quality is Free*. Crosby uses the themes he established in *Quality is Free* as a starting point, and discusses the implementation of the various elements. Organizational change as a result of following his fourteen-step program is illustrated.

Dale, Barrie G. (ed.)
Managing Quality, 2nd edn. New York: Prentice Hall, 1994.

Managing Quality is a comprehensive source of information on managing a process of continuous quality improvement throughout an organization. The contributors, drawn from academia, industry, and management consulting, are all UK-based. Background information on the development of quality management is followed by chapters dealing with the relationship between quality management and product liability, quality and the design process, reliability engineering, and the cost of quality. Another major section covers issues such as managing service quality, quality policies, and barriers to quality. The largest section of the book includes separate chapters on quality management systems, management audits, detailed information on quality management tools and techniques (flowcharts, checksheets, graphs, Pareto analysis, cause and effect diagrams, etc.), quality function deployment, Taguchi methods, failure mode and effects analysis, statistical process control (including construction of control charts), benchmarking, and teams. The last section of the book provides case studies of quality management at three different firms (a bank, a chemical company, and a supplier to the automotive market). Each study describes how the organization started TQM, what approach was used, the types of difficulties encountered, the benefits achieved, and plans for the future.

Deming, W. Edwards
Out of the Crisis. Cambridge, MA: Massachusetts Institute of Technology, Center for Advanced Engineering Study, 1986.

Deming advances the theory that quality improves productivity and an organization's competitive position. He contends that the goal of quality improvement is to reduce variation, and advocates a highly statistical approach to evaluating quality. His approach also focuses on the need for management to work toward changing an organization's culture. Deming discusses his fourteen-point approach to improving quality which involves embracing a philosophy of quality and becoming competitive economically, eliminating the need for inspection, minimizing costs, continuously improving, providing training, instituting leadership, breaking down barriers between departments, driving out fear, eliminating slogans and quotas, and removing barriers that interfere with pride of workmanship.

Dobyns, Lloyd, and Clare Crawford-Mason
Thinking about Quality: Progress, Wisdom, and the Deming Philosophy. New York: Times Books, 1994.

The authors provide an overview of quality in the United States. They contend that relatively few managers in either the public or private sector have successfully adopted quality methods; but quality management is needed more than ever. The shift in management attitudes which has occurred in the twentieth century is examined, along with resistance to change among managers. Dobyns and Crawford-Mason discuss Deming's philosophy and theories and follow this with an examination of two companies that adopted Deming's principles and effected corporate turnarounds. One company was ultimately successful, while the other later filed for bankruptcy. The authors also explore some of the differences between the Baldrige Award criteria and Deming's fourteen points (they serve differing purposes but can be seen as complementary). Other chapters include a history of the Baldrige Award, and applications of Deming's principles in areas such as health care, education, and government.

Ebel, Kenneth E.
Achieving Excellence in Business: A Practical Guide to the Total Quality Transformation Process. Milwaukee, WI: ASQC Quality Press; New York: Marcel Dekker, 1991.

Ebel has written a practical guide to implementing TQM. It can be used by any type of organization, and does not assume that readers have much previous knowledge of total quality management. In addition to the overview of TQM, the author has provided two highly useful appendices. The first is an excellent summary of the basic problem-solving techniques used by teams. Topics include brainstorming, Pareto analysis, graphs, fishbone diagrams, and charts. The second appendix consists of examples of annual strategic plans that address quality improvement.

Hammer, Michael, and James Champy
Reengineering the Corporation: A Manifesto for Business Revolution. New York: HarperBusiness, 1993.

Hammer and Champy have written a thorough introduction to the concept of business reengineering. The authors define reengineering as a rethinking and redesign of business processes which aims to produce dramatic improvements in performance measures such as cost, quality, service, and speed. Hammer and Champy contend that when responsibility for an entire process becomes fragmented, major performance problems for organizations result (in the form of errors that go undetected, delays that cost time and money, unnecessary work, etc.). Solving such problems involves redesigning processes from a customer's perspective, with the goal of being more responsive. The authors discuss management systems that result from reengineering, how information technology relates to reengineering, how to identify those processes which should be reengineered, techniques for reengineering teams, and dealing with major organizational change. Case studies are provided.

Harrington, H. James
Total Improvement Management: The Next Generation in Performance Improvement. New York: McGraw-Hill, 1995.

Harrington has developed a fifteen-step model which can be used by organizations to improve quality. The author has melded aspects of TQM, total cost management, total productivity management, and other quality approaches to provide a hybrid approach to quality management. Among the topics addressed are the importance of securing a commitment to change from senior management, creating business plans that help an organization focus its activities, recognition and reward systems, and balancing team and individual efforts. Harrington's model has been used and tested by Ernst & Young's total improvement management team.

Hodgetts, Richard M
Implementing TQM in Small & Medium-Sized Organizations: A Step-By-Step Guide. New York: AMACOM, 1995.

Hodgetts has written a hands-on book that will help any type of small or medium-sized organization implement quality management. The author has developed quality training programs for many small and medium-sized organizations. His strategy involves seven steps: developing a quality focus by creating a vision and/or mission statement; identifying customer needs; designing an organizational structure that helps implement a quality-driven strategy; training staff in the necessary tools and techniques (such as checklists, Pareto analysis, cause-and-effect diagrams, and brainstorming); getting feedback from internal and external customers; developing an effective recognition and reward system; and creating the necessary climate for making continuous improvement efforts. Examples of questionnaires, worksheets, and dozens of real-world examples contribute to the book's usefulness.

Hunt, V. Daniel
Managing for Quality: Integrating Quality and Business Strategy. Homewood, IL: Business One Irwin, 1993.

Hunt reviews the importance of quality management in a global business environment and the need for organizations to become more flexible and adapt quickly to change. He then provides an overview of TQM which is followed by a discussion of different quality strategies (Crosby, Deming, Juran) with a comparative assessment. Hunt includes chapters dealing with self-assessment of quality, how to use TQM to improve quality, TQM tools and techniques for improving processes (cost estimation, graphs, cost of quality, quality function deployment, etc.), quality awards (Baldrige, Deming, and the European Quality Award), case studies of successful quality management, and integrating TQM with organizational functions (such as marketing and sales, product design, facilities management, and distribution).

Jablonski, Joseph R.
Implementing TQM: Competing in the Nineties Through Total Quality Management, 2nd edn. Albuquerque, NM: Technical Management Consortium, 1992.

Jablonski, a consultant specializing in TQM design and implementation, examines the foundations of TQM, explains the criteria and application process for the Malcolm Baldrige

National Quality Award and introduces ISO 9000. The bulk of the book is concerned with Jablonski's five-step approach to implementing TQM: preparation, planning, assessment, implementation, and diversification (bringing other units such as suppliers and vendors into the quality improvement process). He also devotes chapters to TQM implementation scheduling, resource estimating, and the state of the American quality movement.

Juran, Joseph M.

Juran on Planning for Quality. New York: Free Press, 1988.

Juran focuses on quality improvement goals such as increased conformance and decreased cost of quality in this book. A companion volume dealing with the role of top management in implementing quality is entitled *Juran on Leadership for Quality: An Executive Handbook* (Free Press, 1989). Juran advocates a three-pronged approach to improving quality: one program to deal with sporadic problems an organization encounters, another to deal with chronic problems, and a third program to develop overall quality management policies in an organization. He discusses two kinds of quality management which need to operate in tandem: breakthroughs which attack chronic problems, and control techniques which attack sporadic problems. Jurans's *Quality Control Handbook* (first published in 1951) is a classic in quality control.

Kaydos, Will

Measuring, Managing, and Maximizing Performance: What Every Manager Needs to Know About Quality and Productivity to Make Real Improvements in Performance. Cambridge, MA: Productivity Press, 1991.

Kaydos presents clear discussions of techniques that organizations can use to measure performance, deal with problems, and improve processes. Kaydos stresses the importance of collecting data as the basis for effective decision-making. He includes a chapter on effective presentation of statistics through use of graphs and charts. Kaydos encourages readers to match techniques appropriately to problems; many problems can be handled with relatively simple methodologies. The author also emphasizes his belief that an organization must effect a substantial cultural shift before quality improvement can be truly successful.

Latzko, William J., and David M. Saunders

Four Days with Dr. Deming: A Strategy for Modern Methods of Management. Reading, MA: Addison-Wesley, 1995.

The authors have provided an introduction to Deming's management theory by summarizing the content of lectures delivered by Dr. Deming in the 1980s. The structure of the book mimics an actual four day seminar. On the "first day" American industry and its problems are discussed along with "quick fixes." This is followed by an explanation of why a different philosophy is needed and a discussion of Deming's ideas relative to quality and the need for continual improvement. Lectures on subsequent "days" expand on his philosophy, deal with threats to quality, overcoming obstacles, and discuss topics such as leadership, management and training, and measurement issues.

Levit, Steve

Quality is Just the Beginning: Managing for Total Responsiveness. New York: McGraw-Hill, 1994.

Levit believes that response-based organizations capable of responding quickly to changes in the marketplace are the wave of the future. He offers a ten-step model for guiding a business' transformation to a response-managed organization. Examples and answers to likely questions are provided. Levit discusses the barriers likely to be faced by organizations in attempting to respond to changes. Suggestions for dealing with problems as well as advice on topics such as fostering teamwork and rebuilding are included.

Main, Jeremy

Quality Wars: The Triumphs and Defeats of American Business. New York: Free Press, 1994.

Main does an excellent job of chronicling the problems with American industry that eventually led to America's involvement in the quality movement. He includes interviews with workers and managers illustrating the lack of concern with quality, inefficient management, and resistance to change that made it possible for Japan to overwhelm American industry with the quality and pricing of its goods. Main traces the evolution of thinking about quality, the first attempt to make a change and do something about the quality of American goods (quality circles), and the realization that quality must focus on customers which led to the emergence of TQM in the 1980s. Main includes an interesting chapter on how different companies have used (and misused) quality management tools and also discusses topics such as the relationship between Just-in-Time inventories and quality, benchmarking (stealing shamelessly!), and measuring quality (often measuring the wrong things).

The second part of the book takes an in-depth look at the experiences of several industries (automotive, electronic, rail, service, government, and professional services). In addition a chapter on "the fumblers" is included: good companies that somehow just can't get TQM right. Main refers to this chapter as "cautionary tales" for anyone who thinks TQM is easy to do well or sustain. He concludes by discussing some of the fairly harsh criticism leveled at TQM, but sums up the profound impact TQM has had. While TQM will surely evolve over time, it has changed the way organizations work and the basic tenets will remain with us.

Oakland, John S., and Leslie J. Porter
Cases in Total Quality Management. Oxford: Butterworth Heinemann, 1994.

This book contains seventeen case studies of the implementation of TQM in organizations in the UK; complete with data, exhibits, and results. The companies (of varying sizes) are drawn from a range of industries and are closer to the "average" organization in the extent to which they measure up to quality ideals. In other words, each case presents opportunities for improvement. The companies discussed are also at varying stages in their progress with TQM. The cases presented are suitable for discussion as part of continuing education or training programs.

Roberts, Lon
Process Reengineering: The Key to Achieving Breakthrough Success. Milwaukee, WI: ASQC Quality Press, 1994.

Roberts examines the philosophy behind process reengineering and discusses the basic concepts involved, problems posed, and payoffs to be had through implementing a structured approach to process reengineering. Processes and sub-processes are defined. The author focuses on a company's business operations as the prime candidates for reengineering (as opposed to production operations). Roberts is of the opinion that business functions offer the best opportunities for fast reduction of waste and inefficiency. Production processes are usually in better shape. Additionally, he contends that customers are more forgiving of product defects than they are of poor business practices. TQM tools and techniques are included as applicable to reengineering projects. Human resource factors are addressed as well.

Schmidt, Warren H., and Jerome P. Finnegan
The Race Without a Finish Line: America's Quest for Total Quality. San Francisco: Jossey-Bass, 1992.

Schmidt and Finnegan provide a clear overview of TQM. They include an excellent chapter on the evolution of the TQM movement. In addition to placing TQM in a historical context in terms of the development of management theory, they also discuss some of the management approaches that are clearly incompatible with a total quality organization. The authors discuss planning for change, leadership commitment needed if TQM is to be successful, and offer five key strategies for making TQM work: establishing supportive organizational structures; using the proper tools; making a long-term investment in training; creating a meaningful recognition and award system; and encouraging communication. Additionally, they provide material on practices of Baldrige Award recipients which other organizations will be able to learn from.

Shecter, Edwin S.
Managing for World-Class Quality: A Primer for Executives and Managers. New York: Marcel Dekker; Milwaukee, WI: ASQC Quality Press, 1992.

The intent of this book is to introduce managers to the basic concepts of quality. Shecter begins by identifying twenty-five general points that lead to excellence in performance, and follows with definitions of quality that can be measured (conformance, fitness for use, reliable, and of a certain yield). The chapters which follow explain the mechanics of making better products at lower costs (reporting and analyzing quality costs); the fundamentals of control charts, sampling, quality audits, controlling vendor supplied items; and tools such as Pareto distributions, histograms, and design of experiments. None of the chapters are technically oriented, all are aimed at general readers.

Spechler, Jay W.

Managing Quality in America's Most Admired Companies. San Francisco: Berrett-Koehler; Norcross, GA: Industrial Engineering and Management Press, 1993.

Spechler is a senior examiner for the Malcolm Baldrige National Quality Award and a judge for the Sterling Quality and Productivity Award for the state of Florida. The first part of the book presents some guidelines for implementing quality management. Spechler examined the successful approaches of a number of companies (winners of the Baldrige Award or finalists, companies singled out by the *Economist* as providing the greatest added value for their customers, etc.) and subsequently identified ten critical success factors for implementing quality management and continuous improvement. The steps are to: create a vision and values statement; integrate strategic quality goals into the corporate strategic business planning process; select a total quality management model; develop an organization structure to implement quality improvement; establish a design team to tailor quality process implementation to the company's culture; design training for quality improvement efforts; prepare a communications plan for quality; determine key business processes for cross-functional analysis and improvement; develop quality performance measures for all business processes; and benchmark operations against world class companies.

The second part of the book contains case studies of quality management in thirty-two leading companies written by managers responsible for quality at those organizations. Industries represented include beverages, chemicals, communications, computers and electronics, hotels, insurance, retail, and others. The last part of the book consists of several useful appendices: text of the actual quality themes of several leading companies, a matrix showing the parts of the Baldrige Award criteria that were covered by each of the case studies in the book, job descriptions for quality-related personnel, and the 1993 Baldrige Award criteria.

Svenson, Ray, Guy Wallace, Karen Wallace, and Bruce Wexler

The Quality Roadmap: How to Get Your Company on the Quality Track – and Keep It There. New York: AMACOM, 1994.

This book is aimed at companies which have just begun a quality improvement journey, as well as those whose efforts have been unsuccessful. The authors believe that most companies practicing TQM have failed to target their efforts (and attempt to improve everything – large and small – at once), know little about the area of human performance technology (a systematic analysis of organization and individual performance followed by redesign to improve performance), and have pursued quality without linking it to business goals. The book is designed as a guide to planning and implementing quality effectively.

Talley, Dorsey

Total Quality Management: Performance and Cost Measures: The Strategy for Economic Survival. Milwaukee, WI: ASQC Quality Press, 1991.

Talley provides a very clear and concise introduction to TQM. The basic philosophy and techniques of total quality management are discussed. The book includes many highly illustrative examples from industry in discussing the importance of leadership and the costs of "unquality" in organizations. Also included are lists of quality measures for specific functions of an organization (such as facilities, finance, and marketing).

Townsend, Patrick L., and Joan E. Gebhardt

Quality in Action: 93 Lessons in Leadership, Participation, and Measurement. New York: Wiley, 1992.

The stated goal of this book is to take the mystery out of quality. The authors look at leadership, participation, and measurement because these are the three main issues that impact the success of quality processes. Each "lesson" illuminates some particular aspect of one of the three issues, and is followed by an axiom summarizing the point of the lesson. Townsend and Gebhardt's book is useful in coming to terms with what a variety of quality concepts really mean, and ultimately leaves the reader with a more balanced sense of what quality and quality improvement should mean to an organization.

Waterman, Robert H.
What America Does Right: Learning From Companies That Put People First. New York: W.W. Norton & Co., 1994.

This book provides an in-depth look at the strategic and organizational reasons for success in a selection of American businesses, as well as a school and a clinic. Waterman believes that the organizations he studied are better organized to meet the needs of people they employ. They recognize that people want a certain amount of self-direction, need to believe that their organization stands for something important, want challenges, need recognition, and need the opportunity to keep learning. The organizations discussed in the book are also better organized to meet customers' needs, are continually innovating, and make a sustained effort to keep costs low. Waterman provides numerous examples as he discusses the evidence for his beliefs. The relationship between quality and the success of organizations is also examined, with a particularly interesting chapter on Motorola.

Articles

"A Total Quality Special Issue." *Academy of Management Review* 19, no.3 (July 1994): 390–618.

This special issue is aimed at stimulating the development of theory on total quality. Articles examine areas such as the relationship between TQM and traditional management theory in various domains (leadership, human resources, customer satisfaction, etc.); the evolution of definitions of quality and implications of differences observed; how total quality management relates to various models of organization; a proposed theory of quality management based on the Deming management method; the contributions TQM has made to a theory of work performance; predicting conditions under which use of different aspects of TQM will be more or less effective; and a theory of why change efforts (such as TQM) often fail.

Becker, Selwyn W., William A.J. Golomski, and Daniel C. Lory
"TQM and Organization of the Firm: Theoretical and Empirical Perspectives." *Quality Management Journal* 1, no.2 (January 1994): 18–24.

Thirty companies known to be actively involved with total quality management were surveyed. Data on revenues, supervision methods, incentive systems, supplier relationships, teams, and participation in strategic planning was collected for a "before TQM" period and a "during TQM" period. Findings indicate that adoption of TQM leads to flatter organizations with larger spans of control in supervision; more cross-functional problem-solving teams; a decrease in number of employees with an increase in output (as measured by revenues); a shift in incentive systems from emphasis on the individual to group reward; more frequent involvement in planning by lower-level employees; and more open communication (for example, sharing information with suppliers, benchmarking, and joint ventures with competitors). The authors believe the results indicate more efficient functioning is related to the implementation of TQM and hope their results will be used as a benchmark.

Bishop-Gains, Lynn
"Policy Deployment: A Key To TQM Implementation." *Annual Quality Congress Transactions* 46 (1992): 564–569.

This article summarizes some of the differences between policy deployment and traditional management methods. Policy deployment is a means of implementing TQM throughout an organization and integrating TQM with everyday operations. This gets around the problem faced by many organizations in which TQM is perceived as a "project" or as only applicable to specific situations. Policy deployment is an interactive process that aligns the operational activities of an organization around its vision for the future and strategic plan. At each level within an organization there is an appraisal of what is currently being done which is linked to targets for what can be achieved. However, the appraisals and targets at one level are also directly influenced by activities at levels above and below. In other words, the process ensures a back-and-forth as well as up-and-down flow of information which facilitates buy-in throughout the organization, alignment of activities, and the support needed to achieve continuous improvement within an entire organization.

Davenport, Thomas H.

"Need Radical Innovation and Continuous Improvement? Integrate Process Reengineering and TQM." *Planning Review* 21 (May/June 1993): 6–12.

Davenport discusses the trend in organizational change programs from TQM in the 1980s to reengineering in the 1990s. He contends that the best change programs are a meld of contributions from both approaches. The author discusses similarities and differences between continuous improvement programs and reengineering, and discusses four approaches, which can be used singly or together, to integrate continuous improvement with more radical change (reengineering or process innovation). The first is to sequence change initiatives, or to alternate between improvement and innovation. The idea is to initiate a fairly radical change, then continuously improve it, and repeat that pattern. The second involves creating a portfolio of process change programs, which involves looking at all processes and categorizing them by the type of change needed. When rapid change is needed then a program of restructuring or reengineering might be most appropriate; but other problems might be more amenable to continuous process improvement. This allows a matching of problem to technique. The third approach is to limit the scope of work design to higher-level processes and leave the more specific details to those actually doing the work so that when work is reengineered the benefits of employee involvement (more associated with TQM) can be preserved. The fourth approach is to undertake improvement through innovation, or to combine short-term improvements in a longer-term redesign effort.

Davenport also deals with the infrastructure necessary to integrate TQM and reengineering, and in a sidebar summarizes the role of information technology in process reengineering.

Dodson, Robert L.

"Speeding The Way To Total Quality." *Training and Development* 45 (June 1991): 35–42.

The author discusses resistance to total quality management programs within companies, and discusses the importance of employee attitudes in a successful TQM effort. Based on the idea that employee satisfaction is the key to customer satisfaction, Dodson explores the concept of managers and employees as either internal customers or suppliers (depending upon whether one is looking at the flow of work or the traditional management chain) and the need to develop a measure of internal quality to guide efforts to optimize employee support for TQM. The internal quality audit is discussed along with what to do with the findings. Dodson makes the case that internal quality audits are a necessary step in transforming managers and employees into an effective team, the basis for achieving results from TQM.

Gilbert, James D.

"TQM Flops: A Chance To Learn From The Mistakes Of Others." *National Productivity Review* 11, no.4 (Autumn 1992): 491–499.

Three case studies are presented in which TQM was applied in response to major problems with production. The problems experienced in all three cases provide valuable insight. In the first case a company failed despite implementing a TQM program, due to a combination of poor management, TQM efforts that didn't go far enough in getting managers involved with TQM, and training that came too late. In the second case a combination of poor management and insufficient training in TQM led to a program that didn't manage to save the company. In the third case, the time and support a TQM program received was enough to save a company that was experiencing problems just as severe as those in the first two cases. Gilbert offers several lessons for managers as a result, which include managing by walking around, listening to workers, training managers in TQM methods first – then workers, screening TQM consultants carefully, being patient and not trying to solve all problems at once, removing fear from the workplace, and making employees look good.

Goodman, John A., Scott M. Broetzman, and Dianne S. Ward
"Preventing TQM Problems: Measured Steps Toward Customer-Driven Quality Improvement." *National Productivity Review* 12, no.4 (Autumn 1993): 555–571.

Many organizations have spent a great deal of time and money on TQM programs, yet have little to show in terms of tangible results. The authors attribute this to a failure to focus on a limited number of customer-driven problem areas and lack of an ongoing customer-oriented measurement program that focuses on results. Goodman *et al.* advocate a definition of quality based on customer expectations. A customer-driven model of quality improvement involves consistently meeting or exceeding customer needs and expectations. Using examples, the authors discuss the impact of problems on customer loyalty and the payback gained through effective response to such problems, including the issue of quantification of results. Problems that organizations encounter in setting quality-improvement priorities are discussed (such as relying on intuition instead of empirical data from customers, or failure to integrate data from different internal sources in a meaningful analysis). Problems with follow-up measurement of progress and criteria for designing an effective tracking system with examples are presented.

Gordon, Jack
"An Interview with Joseph M. Juran." *Training* 31 (May 1994): 35–41.

In an interview, Juran discusses shortcomings in the direction and progress of the American quality movement, but indicates that he feels many companies have "gotten it right." He also talks about the need for senior executives to be firmly connected with the work and goals of quality in their companies. Juran contends that the constantly evolving Baldrige Award criteria are the best list available for defining total quality management. When asked about ISO 9000, Juran advances the opinion that Europeans will be in for a letdown if they don't pay attention to continuous improvement, employee empowerment, and leadership issues after achieving certification. He also believes that resistance to TQM in the service sector is more cultural resistance than reflection of a problem with applicability of TQM to such

organizations. One of his last points is that process reengineering is just a new label for quality improvement.

Greising, David
"Quality: How to Make It Pay." *Business Week*, no.3384 (August 8, 1994): 54–59.

This article looks at some of the mixed results experienced by companies that implemented total quality programs. Quality efforts are well-intentioned but frequently misguided; thus the new emphasis on getting a return on quality and making sure that the "quality" offered matches the "quality" actually desired by customers. Examples of companies employing this technique are provided. Federal Express (a 1990 Baldrige Award winner) ended up rethinking its original quality goals. They initially stressed speed over accuracy, but fixing a soaring number of mistakes became expensive. An investment in new equipment apparently brought them both speed and accuracy. Requiring quality programs to generate positive financial results tends to keep them on track. The author advises companies to start with an effective quality program, calculate the cost of current quality initiatives and measure them against revenue returns, determine the factors that retain customers (and also what drives them away), focus on the quality efforts most likely to improve customer satisfaction at a reasonable cost, pilot-test programs and scrap those that don't have much impact, and improve programs continually.

Harari, Oren
"Ten Reasons Why TQM Doesn't Work." *Management Review* 82, no.1 (January 1993): 33–38.

The author examines the primary reasons for the failure of a majority of the TQM programs implemented. The points made are that: TQM often fails to focus on external results; TQM focuses on minimum standards; it develops a cumbersome bureaucracy; quality is often delegated to experts instead of being the responsibility of everyone; TQM doesn't deal with the need for organizational reform; TQM does not demand a relationship between quality and management compensation levels; there is no tie between TQM and a company's relationships with outside partners; TQM appeals to those who like quick fixes;

innovation within organizations is put at a disadvantage by the standardization and routinization favored by TQM; and it's hard to feel an emotional tie to the step-by-step methods of TQM.

Holpp, Lawrence

"10 Reasons Why Total Quality Is Less Than Total." *Training* 26 (October 1989): 93–103.

This article presents a concise summary of some of the most common reasons total quality improvement programs fail and suggests ways to avoid them. The problems are: vision statements that read like textbooks instead of realistic goals people understand; poor objectives that lead to separate groups fighting for resources; people who use quality programs to build an empire as well as people who disparage TQM (answer is to hold empire-builders accountable to measurable outcomes while the disparagers should get a kick in the pants and some responsibility for tracking quality indicators that will eventually co-opt them); demoralized teams with no sense of direction and supervisors who have no idea what their subordinates are doing (answer is to find new duties for supervisors if they're redundant and to make managers responsible for keeping teams engaged in productive work); difficulties with statistical thinking (invest in training in deductive thinking skills); cynicism toward new programs (don't treat it as a "program"); ineffective training (make it relevant and reinforce it with performance measures); competitive cross-functional management (pay serious attention to teaching people how to work with people they can't control); remote managers (management must be involved in total quality); and expecting changes in attitudes overnight.

Juran, Joseph M.

"Made in U.S.A.: A Renaissance in Quality." *Harvard Business Review* 71 (July/August 1993): 42–50.

Juran debunks the myth that had he and W. Edwards Deming not given lectures in Japan in the 1950s, Japanese goods would still be of inferior quality. Juran contends that consumer products were shoddy in Japan because most of Japan's energy and resources had previously gone toward military initiatives. The shock produced in Japan by their defeat in World War II had the effect of encouraging the Japanese to see the need for change; and thus the willingness to listen to western business experts. However, CEOs (with the ability to make changes happen) were Juran's audience in Japan (as opposed to engineers and quality control managers in the U.S.). Juran relays his experiences in running into organizational barriers in attempting to improve quality in U.S. industry, and discusses the way Japan proceeded to avoid such barriers. He examines the early success of Xerox and its later brush with death as a result of competition from Japanese manufacturers. The resurgence of Xerox has given Juran new confidence in the ability of manufacturers to succeed in quality improvement initiatives, despite the failure of many quality efforts. Juran believes the active participation of senior managers in quality leadership is critical.

Keiningham, Timothy L., Roland T. Rust, and M. Marshall Weems

"The Bottom Line On Quality." *Financial Executive* 10, no.5 (September/October 1994): 50–52.

Customer satisfaction and quality improvement efforts undertaken by corporations do not automatically translate into profits. Companies need to determine if their quality programs have been profitable, because resources allocated to quality should yield a return comparable to other available investment alternatives. The authors discuss companies that invested heavily in quality initiatives and saw dramatic increases in customer satisfaction as well as quality of goods, but which suffered financially due to a failure to link quality to overall profitability. In the long run, quality programs that cost too much or programs that fail to concentrate on the most cost effective improvement alternatives will fail or substantially underperform. Processes which lower a company's costs while improving customer satisfaction and customer retention are likely to be among the most successful quality-improvement efforts. Verification of quality costs, reliable estimates of profitability increases, testing of quality programs for results, and continuous monitoring of program progress and financial returns are presented as keys to success.

Kolesar, Peter J.
"What Deming Told the Japanese in 1950." *Quality Management Journal* 2, no.1 (Fall 1994): 9–24.

This article summarizes and analyzes the content of a series of quality control lectures W. Edwards Deming delivered in Japan in 1950. Although Deming spent most of his time discussing statistical process control, his opening remarks contained the beginnings of the philosophy for which he later became famous. The article discusses the people and events that helped shape Deming's early thinking about statistics and quality (for example, his experiences at Western Electric, his personal relationship with Walter Shewhart, and his involvement in training the U.S. military in the use of statistical quality control methods). Kolesar believes that many elements of what is known as "Japanese-style companywide quality control" are not contained in the 1950 lectures and considers it likely that other sources and developers of these ideas were at work.

Morgan, Chris
"TQM and BPR Compared." In *Examining Business Process Re-engineering: Current Perspectives and Research Directions* (London: Kogan Page, 1995), 186–191.

Morgan looks at the relationships and differences between business process reengineering (BPR) and total quality management. He provides a table comparing the two in three basic areas. In each of the areas (the philosophy's impact on management and management systems, impact on operational organization, and impact on employees) specific features are contrasted. For example, the main control measure with TQM is the cost of quality, while with BPR it's the cost of a process. Similarly, the potential for promotion is only marginally changed with TQM, but BPR results in fewer opportunities. Morgan feels the areas of agreement are fairly limited but suggests that it is too soon to assume that management theories such as TQM, BPR, Just-in-Time, and Kaizen are truly independent. The success with which some theories have worked together may indicate the gradual evolution of a new management system.

Sissell, Kara
"Sustaining the gains: Pivotal Role for Quality." *Chemical Week* 157, no.10 (September 20, 1995): 31–42.

Sissell takes a look at TQM now, after several years of both success and challenges. TQM is still important to manufacturers, but it has been scaled down somewhat. The premise of achieving small continuous improvement in quality and customer satisfaction has been shaken by the notion of reengineering. Reengineering urges companies to make breakthrough improvements that reestablish how a company does business; the results are to be great leaps forward. However, many companies have been more likely to experience transformation as a result of downsizing. The author contends that TQM is more important than ever. Transformation through downsizing or reengineering means that a company needs its quality programs to sustain the benefits of drastic change and re-energize them. Keeping TQM focused on bottom line results is crucial. This means making sure the company is doing the right things and improving productivity, but also realizing that cost-cutting has its limits and growth has to occur. The author thinks that while TQM has helped companies remain competitive during downsizing, the new challenge will be how to make the same tools work in corporate acquisitions. That is, when dealing with different corporate cultures and business processes as well as intensified pressure to produce a financial return. The author feels that opportunity exists to make system-wide improvements. Sissell believes that reengineering has been good for TQM in the sense that it has moved quality beyond the status quo to bolstering the effectiveness of new ways of doing business.

Thomas, Michael
"What You Need to Know About: Business Process Re-Engineering." *Personnel Management* 26, no.1 (January 1994): 28–31.

Thomas looks at business process reengineering and provides a "plain person's guide" to the concept. He discusses different definitions of processes and core processes, and concludes that business process reengineering entails a "radical scrutiny, questioning, redefinition and redesign of business processes with the aim of eliminating all activities not central to the process goals" and perhaps "automating all activities not requiring human judgmental input, or facilitating that judgment at reduced cost" (p.29). Thomas describes the mythology developing around process reengineering, particularly the notion that technology is driving such reengineering (he believes some skepticism is healthy here). He contends that business process reengineering does not necessarily empower staff as is often the case, and offers examples. Thomas also examines some of the assumptions shared by both TQM and process reengineering (getting control over processes, same language of change management, etc.). In looking at examples of reengineering in the UK, Thomas contends that many aren't actually transformations of existing people and practices, but rather represent new start-ups for existing organizations. He discusses implications of this finding for human resources.

Walker, Terry

"Creating Total Quality Improvement That Lasts." *National Productivity Review* 11, no.4 (Autumn 1992): 473–478.

Five reasons for the failure or underachievement of TQM programs are discussed: many organizations rely on slogans and motivational hype instead of dedicating the needed resources to programs and education; failure to link tools and techniques to specific and important problems affecting customers and the larger goals of an organization; viewing TQM in the context of separate projects instead of effecting a fundamental change in an organization's culture and thinking about quality; bad experiences earlier with quality circles left many managers with the idea that quality problems are the fault of workers, not processes, and impeded an understanding of teamwork, as well as the need for management support for TQM; and increasing testing and inspection to resolve problems instead

of involving the workforce in perfecting processes. Many organizations are also guilty of confusing the elements of TQM with the objectives of TQM and thus do a better job of teaching the tools of TQM than they do of achieving results through the application of TQM to important problems. Educating employees on the objectives of an organization and the challenges it faces, and incorporating a reward system into a TQM program are discussed as two means of increasing program effectiveness.

Yavas, Burhan F.

"Quality Management Practices Worldwide: Convergence or Divergence?" *Quality Progress* 28, no.10 (October 1995): 57–61.

This article reports on a study comparing quality perceptions of U.S. and Asian managers. Earlier studies indicated differences, with U.S. managers tending to think costs increase with quality and Japanese believing the opposite after considering the effects of rework. However, more recent evidence points toward a convergence. This study examined attitudes of middle managers in the electronics industry in Japan, Hong Kong, Singapore, Taiwan, and the United States. The evidence was somewhat mixed but evidence for a convergence in attitudes is apparently increasing. U.S. and Asian managers had similar opinions regarding the level of managerial commitment to quality in their respective firms, the extent to which quality is a problem in their company, and a zero-defects philosophy. On the other hand, more Asian managers believe the concept of quality is the same throughout their organization, more U.S managers feel confident about making quality improvement suggestions, and more Asian managers feel responsibility for quality can be assigned to a particular department like manufacturing.

II

Applications of TQM

The Standard Industrial Classification (SIC) code, a widely used system of classifying products and services, has been used to categorize the following articles and books about TQM applications. The SIC code was developed by the United States government more than fifty years ago and the government uses it to collect and publish business data. Every economic activity is assigned a code. All retail businesses have an SIC code beginning with a 5, all service industries have an SIC code beginning with a 7. Each industry code has four digits. For example, 7011 is the code for hotels and motels. Whenever businesses or business activities are listed, counted, sorted, or compared, the SIC code is likely to be used. It is used by both governmental and private publishers in the United States to disseminate industry information. Readers should keep in mind that this section is not a comprehensive inventory of all the published literature on TQM in manufacturing and nonmanufacturing industries. It is a selection of some of the best and most useful writings about specific TQM applications.

SIC 1500: Construction industry

Kubal, Michael T.
Engineered Quality in Construction: Partnering and TQM. New York: McGraw-Hill, 1994.

Kubal's premise is that TQM will only work in the construction industry if the project team satisfies the customer's (that is, the building owner's) interests. The construction industry refers to this teaming as partnering. All the players involved with a building project must work as a team to improve quality in all phases of construction. This includes the owner, the architects, the engineers, the contractor, trade contractors, manufacturers, suppliers, code officials, and unions. Kubal shows how partnering and TQM can be integrated to improve quality in any construction project. The author is an experienced practitioner, having worked as a project manager on multimillion dollar building projects. His book will be valuable to architects, engineers, contractors, and construction managers.

SIC 2082: Malt beverages

Rammes, William L., and Lee J. Waltemade
"Anheuser-Busch: The Strength of Tradition, the Power of People." In *Managing Quality in America's Most Admired Companies* (San Francisco: Berrett-Koehler Publishers; Norcross, GA: Industrial Engineering and Management Press, 1993), 95–101.

The authors, both vice presidents at Anheuser-Busch, describe the Anheuser-Busch company's philosophy of quality. A commitment to quality was established more than a century ago by Adolphus Busch, the company's founder. Anheuser-Busch's philosophy of quality involves three central themes. The first, is that steady growth over a long-term period (years and decades) is more important than quarterly earnings. The second critical idea is the importance of customers. The third basic idea is that quality control means doing things the right way even if it's not the most efficient or cost effective way. Anheuser-Busch uses a traditional brewing process to produce their beer because it feels that this is the right way to make beer, even if it is the most expensive way of producing beer. In addition, Anheuser-Busch is committed to providing a high-quality workplace for its employees since the company believes that empowered employees enable Anheuser-Busch to produce a quality product.

SIC 2099: Food preparations, not elsewhere classified

Golomski, William A.
"Total Quality Management and the Food Industry: Why is it Important?" *Food Technology* 47, no.5 (May 1993): 74–79.

Golomski defines total quality management, provides a history of quality management, and explains why TQM is relevant to the food industry. He also explains why TQM is different from related concepts, such as quality assurance. His article is an excellent introduction to TQM and would benefit professionals outside the food industry.

Keiser, Thomas C., and Douglas A. Smith
"Customer-Driven Strategies: Moving From Talk to Action." *Planning Review* 21, no.5 (September/October 1993): 25–32.

This is an interesting article because it is a case study of a company whose first quality efforts failed. The company featured is Kraft General Foods Canada (KGFC) and its failure is not unique. It is among the 80 percent of companies whose initial efforts at implementing TQM fail. KGFC's efforts failed for several reasons. One primary reason was that TQM was not part of the fabric of the organization. TQM was not given the priority it needed in order to be successful. There was no organizational vision to provide the context for TQM. TQM was simply viewed as a fad by many managers. However, KGFC's goal is to be recognized as a "leading food company in the world by 1996." In order to achieve this, KGFC intends to use the following six strategies: develop superior value brands; implement new product ideas and improvements faster than KGFC's competitors; develop world-class manufacturing capabilities; focus on the customer; take advantage of information technology; and create an organizational climate where everyone in the company is empowered to satisfy customers.

O'Reilly, Anthony J.
"Leading a Global Strategic Change." *Journal of Business Strategy* 12 (July/August 1991): 10–13.

H. J. Heinz, the ketchup giant, is a highly diversified company based in Pittsburgh, Pennsylvania. TQM has been an important management strategy. TQM training has been organization-wide. By reducing the cost of waste and rework, and by meeting or exceeding customers' specifications, the company believes it can save at least $200 million annually by the mid-1990s.

SIC 2211: Textile mills

Proske, Robert J.
"The Quality Quandary." *Financial Executive* 8 (May/June 1992): 35–39.

The author, CFO of Craftex Mills, Inc., a textile mill located in Blue Bell, Pennsylvania, is convinced that TQM works. A quality improvement team has traced the cause of one of the mill's most serious production flaws to a machine maintenance program. This led to a half-million dollar capital improvement project with a return on investment of more than 100 percent. Other improvements resulting from this TQM initiative have saved money. For example, a pilot project studying machine set up time led to improvements saving several hours of set-up time. This improvement added $5\frac{1}{2}$ percent capacity to the plant, an achievement that would typically require one million dollars of capital investment.

Walton, Wayne, and Steve Melton
"Doran Textiles, Inc. – A Case Study in Turnaround and Revival." *National Productivity Review* 12 (Autumn 1993): 491–501.

The managers of Doran Textiles Inc. used TQM to revive a failing firm. TQM helped turn Doran Textiles around, making it a leader again in the textile industry. An outside firm, Organizational Dynamics Inc., helped develop Doran's quality plan. Doran's quality plan included the following components: a measurement system; an education and training program beginning with top management; the formation of initial quality action teams to solve the two problem areas of machine breakdown and work environment; a participative style of management; a long-range strategic plan for employee training; development of a recognition and rewards system; and development of a gain-sharing program. Doran has reaped many benefits from its quality plan including the following: increased sales; a yearly reduction of failure costs; reductions in off-quality products; a large reduction in consumer complaints; a reduction in absenteeism and turnover rates; a safer work environment (resulting in fewer workers' compensation claims); and a more participative management environment.

Woods, Robert

"Springs Industries, Inc: Quality Through Improved Use of Human Resources." In *Managing Quality in America's Most Admired Companies* (San Francisco: Berrett-Koehler Publishers; Norcross, GA: Industrial Engineering and Management Press, 1993), 241–250.

Springs Industries, Inc. is one of the largest manufacturers of home furnishings and finished industrial fabrics in the United States. Springs began a quality improvement initiative in 1989, one which would involve the training of 20,000 employees (virtually all of Springs' workforce). Woods describes the quality process at one of Springs' plants, the Katherine Plant. The Katherine Plant, located in Chester, South Carolina, has been involved in a quality improvement process since 1990. It is one of Springs' most modern weaving facilities. The quality process has been successful at the Katherine Plant due to training, a team-oriented work environment, the establishment of achievement teams to address special concerns, wide employee participation, effective two-way communication, and an effective recognition and rewards system. The results have been positive at the Katherine Plant. Absenteeism has been reduced, turnover has decreased, quality has improved, productivity has improved, and the overall work environment is more positive as reflected by employee attitude survey results.

SIC 2519: Household furniture, not elsewhere classified

Maya, Victor F., and Charles D. Carpenter

"Total Quality Management in the Furniture Industry." *Annual Quality Congress Transactions* 46 (1992): 570–576.

Henredon Furniture Industries, a manufacturer of home furnishings, in Morganton, North Carolina, was introduced to TQM by Coopers & Lybrand Management Consulting Services. Henredon Furniture was motivated to try TQM when one of its plants, Plant 6, was faced with closing. Henredon worked with Coopers & Lybrand to create a TQM model tailored for the furniture industry. Henredon's TQM program consisted of six phases: developing a vision; gathering customer feedback; implementing "Design for Excellence", a process that bridges the gap between the customer and the product; using quality improvement teams; establishing standard operating practices; and developing an effective measurement system. Although the TQM system is still in its infancy, benefits have already been seen in terms of Henredon's balance sheet and the attitudes of its employees.

SIC 2621: Paper mills

Ingman, Lars C.

"Seeing the Forest and the Trees." *Pulp & Paper* 66 (March 1992): 203–205.

Most paper and pulp mills in North America use some type of statistical process control (SPC). A few mills have created quality matrices which relate charted outputs to quality attributes and customer satisfaction. Although some mills have moved to automated charting, pulp and paper mills lag behind the chemical and petrochemical companies in the area of online SPC.

SIC 2711: Newspapers: publishing, or publishing and printing

Weber, Carol A.

"Knight-Ridder, Inc: The End of an Error." In *Managing Quality in America's Most Admired Companies* (San Francisco: Berrett-Koehler Publishers; Norcross, GA: Industrial Engineering and Management Press, 1993), 325–330.

Weber describes how one newspaper, the *Tallahassee Democrat* (Talahassee, Florida) used teamwork to eliminate advertising errors and improve service to their advertisers. The newspaper was motivated to improve the quality of its advertising service since it was losing more than

$100,000 a year in billing adjustments (that is, running corrected ads free of charge). The *Democrat* created a customer service department which enabled advertisers to deal with a single employee. A cross-functional team of sales-people, designers, typesetters, printers, and employees from other units (such as finance) was formed. The team traced the reasons for adver-tising errors. Although they found that most of the errors were due to carelessness, they identi-fied practical solutions. The *Democrat's* approach has been adopted by more than a dozen other Knight-Ridder newspapers.

SIC 2731: Book publishing

Hicks, Jennifer
"Large Plant Management: The Adaptability Factor." *American Printer* 209, no.6 (September 1992): 59–62.

This case study of TQM in the printing industry features Port City Press in Pikesville, Maryland. Pike City Press publishes short-to-medium-run texts, directories, and manuals for legal and asso-ciation clients. Judd's Inc., Port City's parent company, adopted TQM in 1991 and Port City began to implement TQM in January 1992. Although this article was written while the TQM initiative was in its early stages, this management change is transforming the way this book publisher does business. A team-oriented philos-ophy has been implemented from the executive level down. Typesetters, proofreaders, and pasteup artists share responsibilities rather than performing one task. Because of this flexibility Port City is now able to process jobs faster and better, while satisfying customers. The use of adaptable equipment has also speeded up the printing process. TQM has helped Port City become more competitive while increasing service. Their new flexibility allows them to handle delays when customers miss a·deadline.

SIC 2752: Commercial printing, lithographic

Roth, Jill
"A Tradition of Service: TQM Philosophy Helps Meet Customer Needs." *American Printer* 211 (July 1993): 46–48.

Imperial Litho/Graphics Inc. is a $20 million dollar printing service with 200 employees, located in Phoenix, Arizona. Although the company has always maintained a strong customer focus, the firm implemented a formal TQM program in the early 1990s. One of Imperial's customers was a Malcolm Baldrige Award winner that sponsored TQM training for its suppliers, which included Imperial. Imperial formed IQ (Imperial Quality) teams that have addressed issues such as absenteeism, safety procedures, and the development of on-demand printing services. Imperial's commitment to quality and customer satisfaction has paid off. In 1992, sales exceeded expectations and Imperial was able to establish offices in Tucson and Albuquerque.

SIC 2816: Inorganic pigments

"Quality Systems and TQM in the Tioxide Group Ltd." In *Cases in Total Quality Manage-ment* (Oxford (England): Butterworth-Heinemann, 1994), 63–75.

The Tioxide Group is the second largest producer of titanium pigments and related chem-ical products. Tioxide has been a leader in the quality movement since the mid-1980s. One of the Tioxide Group's sites, the Greatham Plant, was the first chloride titanium dioxide plant in the world to be registered to BS 5750: Part 2/ISO 9002. This was followed by other Tioxide site registrations to BS 5750, ISO 9002, and AFNOR (the French standards). All of Tioxide's European plants have quality systems in place.

SIC 2819: Industrial inorganic chemicals, not elsewhere classified

Askey, J. M., and G. R. Turner, eds
Total Quality in the Chemical Industry. Cambridge (England): Royal Society of Chemistry, 1992.

This volume is a compilation of the edited pro-ceedings of a 1991 symposium on total quality management in the chemical industry, a confer-ence emphasizing the chemical industry in Europe. The symposium was sponsored by the Royal Society of Chemistry and the Society of

Chemical Industry. There are eleven papers in total addressing issues such as organizational change, the role of the European Foundation for Quality Management, quality tools, customer service, and ISO 9000. The authors are experienced practitioners from a wide range of companies. Different sizes and different types of companies are represented. Among the companies represented are Shell Chemicals UK Ltd., Hoechst UK Ltd., Akzo Chemicals Ltd., Exxon Chemical International Marketing, International Biosynthetics Ltd., and Baxenden Chemicals Ltd.

"Customer Satisfaction, Quality Improvement and the Use of SPC Tools at Charter Chemicals." In *Cases in Total Quality Management* (Oxford (England): Butterworth-Heinemann, 1994), 92–105.

Charter Chemicals manufactures polyethylene, polypropylene, and polyvinyl chloride, products that are the raw material for a wide range of plastic goods. One of Charter's customers asked Charter to produce data relating to process capability since it was reviewing the capability of all its suppliers. This case study describes how Charter used statistical process control (SPC) to monitor its manufacturing process. Charter found that implementing SPC is not easy and it requires a willingness to devote resources for training at all levels of the organization.

"Goal Deployment in Exxon Chemical." In *Cases in Total Quality Management* (Oxford (England): Butterworth-Heinemann, 1994), 234–252.

This case study describes the goal deployment process used by Exxon Chemical. TQM and the Malcolm Baldrige Quality Award criteria influenced Exxon Chemical to implement a goal deployment process. Goal deployment process is a process by which strategic business plans are deployed throughout an organization. Goal deployment is characterized by the following elements: it focuses on results through improving the process; starts top-down but relies on bottom-up feedback processes; emphasizes team responsibility; establishes realistic measures, focuses on how an organization can improve; and emphasizes prioritization of goals and strategies.

Holmes, Jerry D., and David J. McCloskey
"Improving Research Using Total Quality Management." *Annual Quality Congress Transactions* 46 (1992): 531–537.

Eastman Chemical Company (ECC), a division of Eastman Kodak Company, manufactures and markets more than three hundred chemicals, three basic plastics, and two types of fibers with worldwide sales of almost $4 billion. It is also an extensive research organization whose mission is to provide new and improved products. In 1990, ECC's research unit implemented a quality management process to achieve improvement. As a result of this initiative, ECC's research organization doubled its output in one year without any substantial increase in resources. ECC's quality management process consisted of ten critical steps: reaching a consensus as to what research's main output was (the consensus was that it is new/improved product and process concepts); identifying the major processes that drive the main output; selecting the major processes to improve setting goals for the improvement of the main output and selected major processes; developing an improvement plan; allocating resources to support the improvement plan; using talented people to improve research's main output; conducting annual data based reviews, using the information to design the next year's improvement plan; and staying in touch with major customers and partners to ensure that improvements research was making were adding value.

Kelly, Janet
"Total Quality Management: ICI in the Lead." *Accountancy* 108 (November 1991): 107–109

ICI Chemicals & Polymers, which employs about 40,000 workers worldwide, began to implement TQM in the mid-1980s. It was the first company in the world to achieve ISO 9002 certification for its finance function. This article describes the quality assurance registration process undertaken by the finance department. The process took about eighteen months. As of late 1991, the company had achieved a total of 140 quality assurance registrations, more than any other company in the world.

"Quality '94: Offering the Best." *Chemical Marketing Reporter* 246, no.18 (October 31, 1994): SR3-SR6.

Quality initiatives are increasing in the chemical industry. However, more companies are focusing on the financial bottom line and are working to achieve a tangible return for their investment in quality. According to Joseph A. De

Feo of the Juran Institute, companies that are successful tend to dedicate 1–3 percent of their sales toward the implementation of their quality program. However, De Feo noted that the chemical industry has focused on quality more than many other sectors of the economy. One chemical company that has been a leader in the quality movement is Eastman Chemical. In fact, Eastman Chemical was the first chemical company in the United States to receive the Baldrige Award (in 1993). Other chemical companies such as BASF, Du Pont, and Reilly Industries have implemented quality improvement projects as part of their effort to achieve ISO 9000 certification. ISO 9000 registration can also produce significant cost savings. One chemical plant reported an annual savings of $2.4 million dollars due to its ISO 9000 implementation.

Thompson, Fred L.

"Monsanto: Employee Empowerment Through Total Quality Management." In *Managing Quality in America's Most Admired Companies* (San Francisco: Berrett-Koehler Publishers; Norcross, GA: Industrial Engineering and Management Press, 1993), 103–114.

The Chemical Group of Monsanto produces a series of materials that add quality and value to manufactured consumer goods ranging from sofas to automobiles. Several automobile manufacturers have asked Monsanto and other suppliers to improve the quality of goods and services that they supply to the automobile industry. This external pressure motivated Monsanto to develop a quality improvement process. Monsanto's total quality process is guided by three basic principles: a customer-focus; continuous improvement as a goal; and involving all employees in the process. Monsanto introduced a company-wide total quality improvement program in 1986. As a result of an extensive training program, all 15,000 employees of the Chemical Group have completed a one-day total quality improvement course. The Chemical Group uses teams extensively and teamwork has become an integral part of Monsanto's culture. The results have been impressive. The Chemical Group became the first Monsanto operation to achieve ISO 9001 certification and has received many preferred-supplier awards.

Wett, Ted

"Worthwhile Journey." *Chemical Marketing Reporter* 246, no.18 (October 31, 1994): SR7-SR8.

More than 3,000 companies in the United States are registered under the ISO 9000 standard. Chemical companies represent a significant portion of this total. ISO 9000 registration is not a stagnant process but a continuing process since firms have to pass a maintenance audit every six months and a reregistration audit every three years. One quality assurance manager interviewed for this article, Tom Kreinbrook from Monsanto's plant in Sauget (Illinois), admitted that his company wasn't prepared for the amount of documentation required for registration, or for the depth of the audits. Monsanto's Sauget plant is the first chemical unit to be registered in the United States. However, the work done for the original ISO certification, made it easier for Monsanto to achieve certifications at twenty sites around the world. Many chemical companies have reported that the internal audits required by the ISO process are particularly valuable since they can detect shortcomings in a company's TQM system.

SIC 2834: Pharmaceutical preparations

D'Angelo, Elizabeth B., Susan D. Alatary, and Timothy C. Gau

"Total Quality Management in the Pharmaceutical Clinical Research Environment: A Challenge." *Proceedings of the Project Management Institute Annual Seminar Symposium* (1991): 558–562.

ICI (Imperial Chemical Industries) is a British company with several divisions, including pharmaceuticals. ICI decided to initiate a total quality program in order to reduce the time it takes to bring a drug to market. Getting a drug on the market three months ahead of schedule can result in several million dollars in additional sales. The firm's decision to implement TQM was also influenced by the growing importance of the ISO 9000 and BS 5750 standards. This article describes the first stages in ICI's total quality initiative. (Since the article appeared, ICI's pharmaceuticals division has been floated as a separate company, Zeneca.)

Gershon, M.
"Statistical Process Control for the Pharmaceutical Industry." *Journal of Parenteral Science and Technology* 45, no.1 (January-February 1991): 41–50.

This article provides an overview of total quality management and statistical process control (SPC). The author discusses the culture of problem solving and continuous improvement, the use of control charts, and Taguichi methods. Gershon identifies common mistakes that occur during the implementation of a TQM and SPC system, and provides specific recommendations for applications in the pharmaceutical industry.

Wood, Lindsey V., and David A. McCamey
"Implementing Total Quality in R & D." *Research Technology Management* 36 (July/August 1993): 39–41.

This article describes how Procter & Gamble integrated total quality in its Health and Personal Care Technology Division (H & PCTD) through the use of innovation teams. This case study demonstrates how health care research and development can be made more efficient and customer-focused through total quality management. Six critical success factors were identified by the authors: leadership by management; focusing improvement efforts on processes critical to the business; measurement; the use of innovation teams (some 60 innovation teams were established); training and rollout; and the creation of a steering team to maintain momentum. These changes have resulted in cost savings, reduced cycle time, better technology transfer, an increased net value of the division's drug development portfolio, and improved customer satisfaction.

SIC 2841: Soap and other detergents

Artzt, Edwin L.
"Customers Want Performance, Price, and Value." *Transportation & Distribution* 34 (July 1993): 32–34.

Procter & Gamble's success has been largely due to brand loyalty and consumer trust. The company markets more than 100 brands around the world and Procter & Gamble products are found in more than 95 percent of American households. Research has indicated that consumers expect both better quality and better price. Procter & Gamble re-evaluated its use of deep-discount promotions when it found that these deals were actually penalizing loyal customers. These short-term promotions also contributed to a costly and inefficient manufacturing and distribution system. Procter & Gamble changed its promotion and distribution logistics system in order to give customers more value. Frequent deep-discount promotions were replaced by value pricing, a strategy which resulted in reduced list prices for almost half of the Procter & Gamble products sold in the United States.

SIC 2860: Petrochemical industry

"TQM in the Research and Development Environment: A Balanced Approach Between 'Hard' and 'Soft' Quality: Esso Research Centre." In *Cases in Total Quality Management* (Oxford (England): Butterworth-Heinemann, 1994), 52–59.

The Esso Research Centre, located south of Oxford (UK), is part of the Exxon Corporation, the petrochemical giant. The Centre has two functions: the development of petroleum fuels and lubricant products for European use, and the development of specialty chemicals for use in finished fuels and lubricants. The petrochemical industry has recognized the importance of the concepts of TQM and the use of quality assurance standards since the mid-1980s. The Centre believes that TQM can be applied in an R & D environment and has developed a two-dimensional model of quality. It views its quality process as a mixture of "hard" quality (that is, business goals driving process control and improvement) and "soft" quality (values driving behavior and practices).

SIC 2869: Industrial organic chemicals, not elsewhere classified

Müller, Albrecht
"Applying Quality Management in Manufacturing." In *German Perspectives on Total Quality* (New York: The Conference Board, 1993), 13–20.

This is the edited transcript of a speech presented at the "Quality Management Forum", a 1993 symposium hosted by The Conference Board's European Council on Quality. Müller is a Divisional Managing Director of BASF. Müller describes the application of quality management within one of BASF's operating divisions, the division that manufactures textile and leather dyes and chemicals. Total quality management is referred to as BASF quality management within the company. BASF's definition of quality emphasizes lasting customer satisfaction.

SIC 2900: Petroleum products

McIntyre, Barry
"Supplier Service Quality: A Necessity in the 90's." *Management International Review* 33, no.1 (1993): 111–120.

This study of the petroleum industry in metropolitan Edmonton (Canada) indicates that petrochemical companies are demanding improved service from suppliers. Those suppliers not delivering quality service may lose business. In fact, over a five-year period, 400 suppliers were eliminated from a list of suppliers for local petrochemical firms. Those suppliers that have implemented TQM have received better performance ratings and are more likely to qualify for supplier partnerships. A supplier must have a performance rating in the upper 90 percent range, with on-time deliveries of 96 percent in order to quality for a supplier partnership.

SIC 3041: Hydraulic hoses

Zetie, John Sparrow, Alan Woodfield, and Tom Kilmartin
"Hydrapower Dynamics: Service Delivery Improvement in a Small Organization." In *Achieving Quality Performance: Lessons From British Industry* (London: Cassell, 1994), 55–78. Hydrapower Dynamics Limited, a small company based in Birmingham (UK), manufactures hydraulic hoses used in construction equipment, commercial vehicles, and the defense industry. They are a leading producer of hydraulic hoses in the UK, with a market share of approximately 40 percent. The company employs 25 workers. The experiences of Hydrapower Dynamics provides an interesting and important case study of implementing TQM in a small organization. The company's quality initiative, which began in 1990, has resulted in a number of immediate and long-term improvements. Some immediate payoffs have included the modernization of the telephone system, the investment in a networked computer system, and the renovation of the retail counter area. Some benefits over time have been improvements in three areas: the number of rejections, the percentage of products returned by customers, and the percentage of orders delivered late.

SIC 3312: Steel works, blast furnaces, and rolling mills

Majumdar, Amit, Megan Smolenyak, and Nancy Yencho
"Planting the Seeds of TQM." *National Productivity Review* 10 (Autumn 1991): 491–497.

The Steel Authority of India, Ltd. (SAIL) is one of the largest steel manufacturers in the world. SAIL has implemented a company-wide TQM program to improve the quality of products and services. This is an interesting case study of TQM in a developing country. There have been some unique challenges associated with implementing TQM in India. The possibility of downsizing is a particularly sensitive social issue, since any employees terminated would lose their housing as well as wages. Literacy is also an issue, since many workers do not speak, read, or write Hindi and/or English. SAIL is trying to remedy the situation by providing education for employees and their families. In TQM training, some instructors have used sketches in order to explain terms such as Pareto analysis and Ishikawa diagrams. Another challenge has been trying to implement TQM in a company that is dispersed across India. There are five plants and several specialty plants and some degree of consistency across all sites is desirable.

SIC 3334: Metals & metalworking industries

Lee, Sonja
"Industrial Engineers Help Quality Shine Through at Reynolds Metals." *Industrial Engineering* 25, no.3 (March 1993): 14–15.

Reynolds Metals Co., headquartered in Richmond, Virginia, is a leader in the vertically integrated aluminum business. It has been in business for more than seventy years and employs 31,000 workers. Within the metals and metal-working industries, it has been a pioneer in the implementation of TQM. The company introduced TQM in 1992. This article describes the critical role that industrial engineers have played in the company's TQM initiative.

SIC 3411: Metal cans and shipping containers

"Quality Systems in CarnaudMetalbox PLC, Foodcan UK, Perry Wood Factory." In *Cases in Total Quality Management* (Oxford (England): Butterworth-Heinemann, 1994), 76–82.

The CarnaudMetalbox Perry Wood Factory manufactures cans and containers. It is part of the Foodcan UK firm. In 1987 CarnaudMetalbox began to lose market share and customers were demanding more responsive and cost effective service. In order to become more competitive, CarnaudMetalbox decided to establish a quality management system and seek BS 5750/ISO 9000 certification. In 1988 the Perry Wood Factory was registered to BS 5750: Part 2. The next phase of the factory's quality improvement process focused on introducing statistical process control (SPC). Although SPC had been introduced earlier and had failed, this attempt was successful. SPC has encouraged teamwork and gave the factory's TQM program a boost. Other techniques, such as the failure mode and effect analysis, are being tested.

SIC 3462: Nuclear fuel fabrication and metal products

Arendt, Carl
"Westinghouse: TQM Targets the Bottom Line." In *Managing Quality in America's Most Admired Companies* (San Francisco: Berrett-Koehler Publishers; Norcross, GA: Industrial Engineering and Management Press, 1993), 221–232.

The Westinghouse Commercial Nuclear Fuel Division was a 1988 Baldrige Award winner. In this article, Arendt describes cost-time profiling, a technique used by Westinghouse to map, analyze, and chart the cost and time dimensions of any process. Cost-time profiling can be applied to a basic process such as responding to a customer complaint, or to a more complex process such as identifying company-wide product development and manufacturing strategies. Every cost-time profile has three components: purchased materials and supplies; labor or work performed; and wait times. The goal is to reduce both the cost and time required to perform a process. Westinghouse has applied cost-time methods to strategic planning, using this technique for determining decisions such as which businesses should grow, how much cash is required, and acceptable profit levels. This cost-time technique has also been used to select quality improvement projects and to quantify the impact of projects on cost and cycle time.

SIC 3563: Spray equipment, industrial

"Problem-Solving and the Use of Improvement Tools and Techniques at Hills Industries." In *Cases in Total Quality Management* (Oxford (England): Butterworth-Heinemann, 1994), 85–91.

Hills Industries, a subsidiary of a South Australian company, manufactures clothes dryers, other indoor and outdoor drying devices, and garden and industrial sprayers. It is based in Caerphilly, north of Cardiff. This case study focuses on Hills' use of quality tools to solve production problems related to the manufacturing of sprayers. In the 1980s Hills lost market share because of poor quality sprayers. Hills decided to initiate a TQM program in the early 1990s in order to regain lost market share and to achieve BS 5750 certification. However, Hills experienced a high rate of sprayer returns within eight months of initiating its TQM program. In order to determine the reasons for this increase in product returns, Hills assembled a problem-solving team. The team received training in the use of standard quality tools (brainstorming, fishbone diagrams, Pareto analysis, process flow diagrams, histograms, etc.) and was given a clear definition of the problem to be solved. By using these tools, the team was able to identify the root causes of the problem and recommend corrective actions.

SIC 3571: Computer industry

Bauer, Roy
"IBM Rochester: Market-Driven Quality." In *Managing Quality in America's Most Admired Companies* (San Francisco: Berrett-Koehler Publishers; Norcross, GA: Industrial Engineering and Management Press, 1993), 141–152.

IBM Rochester is responsible for developing and manufacturing the AS/400 computer system and hard disk storage devices for the AS/400 and RS/600 systems and the PS/2 computer. In 1990, the company received the Malcolm Baldrige National Quality Award. At IBM, quality is market-driven. IBM's market-driven quality cycle consists of six critical success factors: enhancing total product strategy and plans; improving the requirements definition process; implementing a Six-Sigma defect-level quality strategy; creating and deploying an excellence in education plan; enhancing and enabling employee involvement; and developing and implementing reductions in total cycle time. IBM Rochester has reduced rework by making sure that processes produce correct results the first time, and by improving education and employee involvement, productivity has increased and cycle time has been reduced.

Heller, Robert
"TQM: Not a Panacea But A Pilgrimage." *Management Today* (January 1993): 36–40.

Honeywell (UK) has zealously embraced TQM. Quality improvement projects have ranged from speeding up deliveries between Holland and the UK to introducing flexible, cellular manufacturing to reduce inventory and overhead. Honeywell's success can be partly attributed to its intensive training program. After a four-year period, TQM has become the norm, that is, part of Honeywell's culture.

The International Quality Study: Best Practices Report – An Analysis of Management Practices that Impact Performance. Cleveland, OH: Ernst Young; New York: American Quality Foundation, 1992.

The International Quality Study (IQS) was a study of the best management practices across four industries (health care, banking, automotive, and computer) within four industrialized countries (Canada, Germany, Japan, and the United States). This study was a joint project of Ernst & Young (one of the world's leading consulting firms) and the American Quality Foundation (an independent, nonprofit research organization established by the American Society of Quality Control). The results of the IQS has international significance since the findings serve as a benchmark for quality progress. The IQS was conducted using a self-administered questionnaire. The survey grouped questions into five major categories: business organization; product/ service development; delivery process and customer satisfaction; quality and strategic positioning; and culture. The IQS study found that these four industries have many common practices contributing to world class quality and service delivery. The IQS also demonstrated that industries can learn from unrelated industries. The IQS has analyzed more than 900 management practices in more than 500 organizations. Analysts found that some practices take longer to impact performance. The *Best Practices Report* identifies which management practices work. Earlier IQS reports included *The Top-Line Findings*, a report focusing on the ways businesses across all these industries and companies are managing the improvement process, and the four IQS industry reports detailing the specific findings for the health care, automotive, banking, and computer industries, All these reports may be obtained through the American Society for Quality Control.

Johns, Nick, and John Chesterton
"ICL Kidsgrove: Snapshot of a Changing Culture." In *Achieving Quality Performance: Lessons From British Industry* (London: Cassell, 1994): 81–109.

ICL PLC is one of Europe's leading information technology companies. It operates in more than 70 countries and employs more than 26,000 workers. This chapter describes the development of a quality management system at ICL's Kidsgrove Manufacturing Operations. The Kidsgrove site produces circuit boards for all ICL systems. Within ICL, the manufacturing division (which includes the Kidsgrove site and a plant in Ashton), has led the way in quality improvements. The Kidsgrove site achieved ISO 9002 registration in 1988 and was a finalist for the Perkins Award of the National Society for Quality Through Teamwork in 1992.

Kern, Jill Phelps

"Toward Total Quality Marketing." *Quality Progress* 26, no.1 (January 1993): 39–42.

Kern describes Digital Equipment Corporation's use of hoshin planning to direct marketing (defined by Digital as the development of new products). This planning tool includes the following key elements: continuous improvement of planning and implementation processes; a focus on critical systems to achieve strategic objectives; participation by and coordination between all levels and departments; planning driven by facts; and goals and tactical plans that involve the entire company. This approach helped Digital identify marketing's primary internal and external customers, improved the company's ability to work as a team; and strengthened relationships with sales and other customers by involving them in the improvement process.

Mitchell, Donald L.

"IBM's Quality Prescription for Improved Customer Satisfaction." In *Continuous Improvement In Action: Eight Original In-Depth Case Studies* (Dearborn, MI: Society of Manufacturing Engineers, 1993), 53–65.

Although IBM Rochester is a Baldrige Award winner (having received the award in 1990), the company is not resting on its laurels. In 1991, the company began a six-step process to help manage improvement of customer satisfaction. This case study outlines the process, using hardware quality as an example. The six-step process generates an action plan and tracks progress.

Pattison, Diane D., James M. Caltrider, and Robert Lutze

"Continuous Process Improvement at Brooktree." *Management Accounting* 74, no.8 (February 1993): 49–52.

Brooktree Corporation, a public company that employs more than 500 people worldwide, markets a broad family of computer chips used in computer graphics, imaging, and automotive test equipment. In 1989, Brooktree committed to a TQM approach. Brooktree also focused on improving the performance of its suppliers. Flowcharting and process analysis helped Brooktree improve the process of producing computer chip wafers by reducing the time required to obtain foundry commitments for wafers from fifteen to six working days. These techniques can be applied to any process and can form the basis of an activity-based cost accounting system.

Price, Michael J., and E. Eva Chen

"Total Quality Management in a Small, High-Technology Company." *California Management Review* 35 (Spring 1993): 96–117.

Many small high-tech companies have dismissed TQM as being too costly and complicated for small organizations. The authors explain how TQM can be adapted to meet the needs of small high-tech firms. Much of their advice is practical. For example, they recommend that TQM be adopted gradually, a process they term "growing into TQM". They identify some common errors that companies make in adopting TQM and explain how these mistakes can be avoided. This is an important article for managers of small high-tech companies since it demonstrates that many small companies have reaped significant benefits from the implementation of TQM.

SIC 3577: Computer peripheral equipment, not elsewhere classified

Miller, Thomas O.

"A Customer's Definition of Quality." *The Journal of Business Strategy* 13 (January/February 1992): 4–7.

The Norand Corporation, based in Cedar Rapids, Iowa, manufactures and markets portable computerized data collection systems and handheld radio frequency terminals. Concerned that annual customer surveys were not providing objective and thorough feedback, the company designed a formal customer feedback system. A research firm has conducted more than 1,000 in-depth interviews with customers chosen at random. Interviewees are asked to describe their opinions of Norand products and systems, software, personnel, delivery performance, invoicing, customer support programs, and overall company image. Specific customer complaints revealed in interviews are reported to the company within five days. These complaints are tracked until they are resolved. The data collected in these interviews is statistically tabulated and can be helpful in identifying trends. In addition to the customer surveys, Norand developed a customer profile data system that reflects details about the customer. Customer complaints registered by telephone are tracked through an online system that captures data such as name of caller, when the call was placed, why the call was placed, and the last action taken by Norand, and the present status of the complaint. Norand is even gathering customer feedback in its product presentations. All this separate data are compiled into a comprehensive customer database that is shared throughout the organization.

SIC 3632: Household refrigerators and home and farm freezers

Bartley, Robert E.
"Whirlpool Corporation: Leadership is the Critical Success Factor in a Quality Initiative." In *Managing Quality in America's Most Admired Companies* (San Francisco: Berrett-Koehler Publishers; Norcross, GA: Industrial Engineering and Management Press, 1993), 233–240.

The Whirlpool Corporation, founded in 1911, was a pioneer in the area of customer service. Whirlpool established a special task force on quality in the early 1950s to address the issue of customer satisfaction. In 1976, the company established a toll-free telephone service for consumers – at this time, such innovations were not common. Unlike many firms in other industries, Whirlpool did not implement a quality initiative in response to a loss of market share, global competition, or poor performance. Whirlpool's quality initiative was leader driven and leadership has been the critical success factor in Whirlpool's quality initiative.

SIC 3641: Electric lamp bulbs and tubes

Lee, Sang M., Fred Luthans, and Richard M. Hodgetts
"Total Quality Management: Implications for Central and Eastern Europe." *Organizational Dynamics* 20 (Spring 1992): 42–55.

The concept of quality is foreign to many managers of firms located in the former Communist bloc countries in Central and Eastern Europe. The authors believe that TQM can help turn these companies around and eventually make them competitive in the global marketplace. They promote some guidelines for implementing TQM in companies in Central and Eastern Europe. General Electric (GE) is one company that has introduced TQM to Eastern Europe. The authors describe TQM initiatives at Tungsram, the giant Hungarian light bulb factory. When General Electric bought Tungsram (an operation employing 18,000 workers), it found outdated office equipment, antiquated procedures, and bureaucratic rules. GE hoped that the introduction of TQM would help the company capture 12 percent of the European market by the mid-1990s, while reducing costs. This case study is important since there is a paucity of literature on the implication of TQM in Central and Eastern Europe. Two other TQM ventures in Central and Eastern Europe are described: the experiences of McDonald's and Polaroid.

SIC 3660: Communications and telecommunications industry

Endy, Sam
"Centex Telemanagement: Improving Client Service Through Leadership." In *Managing Quality in America's Most Admired Companies* (San Francisco: Berrett-Koehler Publishers; Norcross, GA: Industrial Engineering and Management Press, 1993), 115–122.

In 1985, Centex recruited Peter A. Howley as chief executive officer because of his reputation for focusing on customer service. He helped Centex establish a vision which was articulated in its mission statement. That goal, was to become "the most respected telecommunications management services firm in the industry". Howley introduced three guiding principles: all associates have to believe that client service is critical; associates need to control costs since clients are cost-conscious; and associates need to convey a sense of concern and hard work on their clients' behalf. The importance of client service is established by Howley's management style. Clients can contact him directly at all hours of the day. Client service is a regular agenda item at associate meetings. Examples of excellent client service are highlighted in memos sent out to all associates. Howley also sets the example for controlling costs. His attempts to pare travel expenses have become legends (one story reports that he almost missed a meeting with Wall Street analysts since he took a bus rather than a taxi in New York City). Centex has established a Total Client Satisfaction Program which focuses on three major areas: process improvement, human resources, and communications.

Hallmark, Clayton
"Does Total Quality Management Really Work?" *Telephony* 225 (July 12, 1993): 28, 30, 32.

TQM helped AT & T Network Systems' Transmission Systems unit turn around its forty-year-old factory at Merrimack Valley, Massachusetts. In fact, the company won the Malcolm Baldrige National Quality Award in 1992. The unit believes that leadership is the most critical success factor in a quality improvement process. Another success factor was the unit's ability to build a workable partnership with labor unions. The company has more than 800 quality teams. Participation is voluntary. Teams use a seven-step process to solve problems. These steps include the following: identifying a problem and the reason for improvement; selecting a problem and setting a target for improvement; identifying and verifying the root causes of the problem; planning and implementing countermeasures that will correct these root problems; confirming that the problem and its root causes have been decreased and the target for improvement has been set; preventing the problem and its root causes from recurring; and planning what to do about any remaining problems and evaluating the team's effectiveness. Several of the unit's projects have placed AT & T among the best-in-class manufacturer.

"Making a Success of TQEM." *Environmental Manager* 5, no.2 (September 1993): 7–11.

A team at AT & T's Columbus Works plant in Ohio applied total quality management to pollution control. Their goal was to identify incentives and barriers to reducing trichloroethane (TCA) emissions. The process led to the discovery of alternatives to TCA. One resource available to industries interested in implementing TQEM is a 1993 guide published by the Council of Great Lakes Industries. This ninety page guide, titled *TQEM Primer and Assessment Matrix* includes an adaptation of a TQM matrix originally developed by Eastman Kodak. The TQEM matrix has been reproduced in full for this article.

Miller, David E.
"Emphasize Quality." *Telephony* 225 (July 19, 1993): 12, 14, 16.

This article explains how TQM can be useful to telephone companies and the telecommunications network industry. TQM can help local carriers and networks reduce reroutes, retransmissions, redundancy, and overcapacity. Given the competitiveness of this industry, improved customer service can give a company a critical edge over competitors.

Moore, Beth Ann
"Octel Communications Corporation: Putting Metrics in Motion." In Managing Quality in America's Most Admired Companies (San Francisco: Berrett-Koehler Publishers; Norcross, GA: Industrial Engineering and Management Press, 1993), 123–133.

Octel Communications Corporation, founded in 1982, used Baldrige Award criteria and its core values to guide the development of its Total Quality Improvement process. Among Octel's core values are consistently achieving excellent financial results for shareholders, meeting customers' needs, establishing high-quality standards, strategically planning moves, valuing employees, and operating in an ethical manner. Customer feedback is provided through Octel user groups. Octel is developing a performance measurement process that will measure key performance areas from five perspectives: a financial perspective; a customer perspective; an internal business process perspective; an innovation and learning perspective; and an employee perspective.

"Organizing for Success at Pirelli Communication Cables." In *Cases in Total Quality Management* (Oxford (England): Butterworth-Heinemann, 1994), 177–183.

Pirelli Communication Cables designs, manufactures, and installs optical and copper communication/control cables in the UK and around the world. In 1989, Pirelli implemented a company-wide quality improvement process. This case study describes the five key components of Pirelli's process: the Total Quality Management Team; the Quality Improvement Process Manager; Quality Improvement Groups; Corrective Action Teams; and individual employees.

Seemer, Robert H.
"Winning More than the Malcolm Baldrige National Quality Award at AT & T Transmission Systems." *National Productivity Review* 12, no.2 (Spring 1993): 143–165.

In 1989, AT & T announced that it was restructuring the company into twenty business units. One of these units was AT & T's Transmission Systems Business Unit (TBU). TBU develops and manufactures systems for transporting voice and image data and serves a global market. The unit revamped its management system and used TQM to strengthen its position as a leader in this highly competitive industry. As a result of its efforts, TBU was awarded the coveted Malcolm Baldrige Award within two and a half years of implementing TQM.

SIC 3663: Radio and television broadcasting and communications equipment

Kumar, Sanjoy, and Yash P. Gupta
"Statistical Process Control at Motorola's Austin Assembly Plant." *Interfaces* 23, no.2 (March/April 1993): 84–92.

Motorola, a pioneer in the quality movement, implemented a total quality management system incorporating statistical process control (SPC) at its Austin semiconductor assembly plant in 1988. Six factors have been critical to its success: participative problem-solving teams; education and training programs; optimistic employee attitudes; improvement in communication among employees and between employees and management; a quality assurance certification program; and

creative design of experiments. SPC has helped Motorola improve the scrap rate, cycle time, and quality of product built at its Austin plant.

Yovovich, B. G.
"Motorola's Quest for Quality." *Business Marketing* 76 (September 1991): 14–16.

Motorola was one of the first Baldrige Award winners. As Motorola comes close to achieving its goal of Six Sigma (fewer than four defects per million parts), the company is paying more attention to the relationship between marketing and quality. This article describes how Motorola is changing its approach to market research, product development and design, advertising, and other marketing communications.

SIC 3678: Electronic connectors

Anderson, Doug N.
"3M: the Cultural Change at the Chico, California Plant." In *Managing Quality in America's Most Admired Companies* (San Francisco: Berrett-Koehler Publishers; Norcross, GA: Industrial Engineering and Management Press, 1993), 299–305.

3M used the Baldrige Award criteria as guidelines for developing a company-wide quality improvement program. 3M's quality initiative was given the name Q90. Each 3M organization develops its own quality action plan and uses Q90 tools such as statistical process control, quality function deployment, customer surveys, benchmarking, prioritization, high-performance teams, measurement, and time-compression. This article describes the quality process at one 3M organization, a 3M plant in Chico, California. The Chico plant manufactures high-speed data cables and assemblies used in computers, medical equipment, automatic testing equipment, and telecommunications systems. The plant had been acquired by 3M in the late 1980s and was plagued with productivity, quality, and safety problems. Within two years, 3M's Q90 process began to turn the Chico plant around. Employee attendance increased from 92 percent to 97 percent, on-time deliveries increased from 40 percent to 97.5 percent, in-process yields increased from 50 percent to 87 percent, and the Chico plant has become a model in the area of safety.

Craig, Robert J.
"From DuPont: A Step-By-Step Guide to Continuous Improvement." In *Continuous Improvement in Action: Eight Original In-Depth Case Studies* (Dearborn, MI: Society of Manufacturing Engineers, 1993), 109–131.

This case study demonstrates how the Connector Systems Division of the DuPont Company established and sustained a culture of continuous improvement. The Division found that continuous improvement required three key elements: a customer focus; employee empowerment and involvement; and structured problem solving. DuPont developed a step-by-step approach to continuous improvement. The steps in this process include the following: identifying an opportunity for improvement; describing the current process; determining possible causes; collecting data; analyzing data; taking action; verifying improvement efforts; holding the gains; and recognition and closure. DuPont believes that this structured approach can work in any company.

SIC 3711: Motor vehicles and passenger car bodies

Ingold, Tony, and Trevor Worthington
"Land Rover: Extraordinary Customer Satisfaction – the Road to Success." Chapter 5 in *Achieving Quality Performance: Lessons from British Industry* (London: Cassell, 1994), 113–141.

The Rover Group is Britain's largest motor vehicle manufacturer. It designs, manufactures, and markets small and medium-sized cars, vans, and four-wheel drive vehicles. It is the leading car producer and exporter in the UK. Land Rover is the marque name for the company's world-renowned four-wheel drive vehicles. The vehicles manufactured under this line include the Defender, Discovery, and Range Rover. All three are manufactured at a plant in Solihull that employs about 8,000 workers. In the early 1980s Land Rover saw its market share diminish with fierce competition from Japanese manufacturers. This chapter describes how quality improvement and a commitment to customer satisfaction turned Land Rover around.

The International Quality Study: Best Practices Report – An Analysis of Management Practices that Impact Performance. Cleveland, OH: Ernst & Young; New York: American Quality Foundation, 1992.

The International Quality Study (IQS) was a study of the best management practices across four industries (health care, banking, automotive, and computer) within four industrialized countries (Canada, Germany, Japan, and the United States). This study was a joint project of Ernst & Young (one of the world's leading consulting firms) and the American Quality Foundation (an independent, nonprofit research organization established by the American Society of Quality Control). The results of the IQS has international significance since the findings serve as a benchmark for quality progress. The IQS was conducted using a self-administered questionnaire. The survey grouped questions into five major categories: business organization; product/service development; delivery process and customer satisfaction; quality and strategic positioning; and culture. The IQS study found that these four industries have many common practices contributing to world class quality and service delivery. The IQS also demonstrated that industries can learn from unrelated industries. The IQS has analyzed more than 900 management practices in more than 500 organizations. Analysts found that some practices take longer to impact performance. The *Best Practices Report* identifies which management practices work. Earlier IQS reports included *The Top-Line Findings*, a report focusing on the ways businesses across all these industries and companies are managing the improvement process, and the four IQS industry reports detailing the specific findings for the health care, automotive, banking, and computer industries. All these reports may be obtained through the American Society of Quality Control.

Köster, Albrecht
"Quality as a Business Philosophy." In *German Perspectives on Total Quality* (New York: The Conference Board, 1993), 9–12.

This is the edited transcript of an address given at the "Quality Management Forum", a 1993 symposium hosted by The Conference Board's European Council on Quality. Köster was formerly senior vice president for quality assurance at Mercedes-Benz. He describes the TQM model at this German automobile company. At

Mercedes-Benz, TQM has three major components: quality planning, quality controlling, and
quality promotion.

Petersen, Donald E., and John Hillkirk
A *Better Idea: Redefining the Way Americans
Work*. Boston MA: Houghton Mifflin, 1991.

Petersen was president and chairman of the
Ford Motor Company in the 1980s. The authors
describe how Petersen turned Ford around
through participative management, worker
empowerment, employee involvement, and the
use of statistical process control. Petersen and
Hillkirk believe that these techniques (which are
based on Deming's philosophy) can be applied
to any company.

Rushwin, S. T.
"Winning the Canada Award for Business
Excellence in Quality Through Continuous
Improvement at Windsor Assembly Plant
Chrysler Corporation." In *Continuous Improve-
ment in Action: Eight Original In-Depth Case
Studies* (Dearborn, MI: Society of Manufacturing
Engineers, 1993), 13–32.

This case study features Chrysler's Minivan
assembly plant in Windsor, Ontario. The plant
received the Canada Award for Business
Excellence in Quality in 1991 (the Canadian
equivalent of the Malcolm Baldrige Award).
Rushwin describes how employees, customers,
and suppliers were folded into the plant's quality
improvement process. Over a three-year period,
absenteeism and employee grievances were
reduced more than 50 percent. Over the past six
years, manufacturing costs were reduced by more
than 20 percent.

Semple, Jack
"Why We Need TQM–PDQ." *Management
Today* (May 1992): 84–86.

According to Semple, TQM is essential to the
survival of British car manufacturers. Several UK
automobile manufacturers and carmakers that
manufacture cars in the UK have implemented
TQM programs, including Rover and Peugeot
Talbot. Those carmakers that have embraced
TQM report improved product quality and cite
an increase in exports to Europe. Exports to
Europe did increase dramatically from 1987 to
1991: in 1987, UK car manufacturers exported

248,577 cars to EC countries; in 1991, this figure
rose to 536,576.

Walklet, R. H.
"Cadillac Motor Car: Using Simultaneous
Engineering to Ensure Quality and Continuous
Improvement." In *Managing Quality in
America's Most Admired Companies* (San
Francisco: Berrett-Koehler Publishers; Norcross,
GA: Industrial Engineering and Management
Press, 1993), 293–298.

Cadillac was a 1990 Baldrige Award winner.
Walklet describes the simultaneous engineering
process that Cadillac introduced in 1985 to ensure
quality and continuous improvement. This
process requires individuals at all levels of the
organization to work together to design, engineer,
and manufacture a vehicle that meets pre-
determined objectives. Teamwork and communication are the factors that are critical to the
success of this model.

Wolak, Jerry
"Auto Industry Quality: What Are They Doing?"
Quality 32, no.1 (January 1993): 16–22.

Wolak reviews the quality efforts of General
Motors, Ford, and Chrysler. All three of these U.S.
automakers are focusing on customers. This customer focus has contributed to the use of cross-
functional teams in the U.S. auto industry. U.S.
automakers also use a variety of quality tools for
process improvement. The tool most often used
according to the *Automotive Industry Report*, a
study conducted by Ernst & Young in conjunction
with the American Quality Foundation, is SPC
charting. This is followed by Pareto analysis, business process improvement, histograms, quality
function deployment, cause-and-effect analysis,
brainstorming, design of experiments, failure
mode effects analysis, and scatter diagrams. The
big three automobile manufacturers are also working together to develop uniform practices for auto
industry supplier audits.

SIC 3721: Aircraft

"Performance Through Total Quality: The Shorts
Experience." In *Cases in Total Quality
Management* (Oxford (England): Butterworth-
Heinemann, 1994), 159–173.

Shorts Brothers PLC designs and manufactures civil and military aircraft, major components for other aerospace firms, and close air defense weapon systems. It is the largest industrial employer in Northern Ireland. In 1987 the company introduced a total quality management program. More than 1300 quality improvement projects have been completed. Shorts Brothers has been awarded a 1989 LTK National Training Award, the 1992 British Quality Award, and the 1992 Northern Ireland Quality Award. This case study describes the company's training program, major quality projects, performance improvements to date, and future plans for its TQM program.

Swart, Phillip J.
"A Successful Statistical Process Control (SPC) Program, So Far." In *Continuous Improvement in Action: Eight Original In-Depth Case Studies* (Dearborn, MI: Society of Manufacturing Engineers, 1993), 135–157.

This case study features the Boeing Commercial Airplane Group-Wichita Division (BCAG-Wichita Division). The BCAG-Witchita Division was having problems with the installation of CE-type rivets in the skin panels of models of its commercial jets. The Division used statistical process control (SPC) and design of experiments to solve this costly problem. As a result of this project, the Division has expanded SPC into other areas and SPC projects are becoming part of the Division's manufacturing culture.

SIC 3829: Measuring, analyzing, and controlling instruments, not elsewhere classified

Marion, Larry
"Changing the Culture at Teradyne." *Electronic Business* 19, no.1 (January 1993): 28–32.

Teradyne Corp., is a Boston-based manufacturer of automotive test equipment. The company was founded in 1960 by Nick de Wolf and Alexander d'Arbeloff. By the early 1980s, Teradyne was established as one of the leading manufacturers of automotive test equipment. However, fierce competition weakened Teradyne's position and the company suffered a serious financial crisis in 1986. In order to save

the company, d'Arbeloff instituted TQM. TQM, combined with a customer focus and better asset management transformed the company. Teradyne is once again an industry leader as a result of this radical change of corporate culture.

SIC 3841: Surgical and medical instruments and apparatus

Hohner, Gregory
"Quality Leadership at Baxter Healthcare Corporation." *Industrial Engineering* 25, no.1 (January 1993): 31–35.

Baxter Healthcare Corporation researches, designs, manufactures, and distributes more than 120,000 medical products, ranging from surgical gloves to dialysis equipment. Baxter initiated a quality leadership process (QLP) in the early 1980s. QLP encompasses all of Baxter's manufacturing, engineering, marketing, and sales functions. It is an approach that promotes the development of management, technical, and problem-solving skills to ensure that customer needs are understood and met every time. The value of Baxter's quality leadership process are fourfold: it focuses on prevention; it involves everyone; meeting customer requirements is fundamental; and it ensures that improvement activities produce results.

Smith, Valerie J.
"SpaceLabs Medical Inc: Using Policies, Values, and Measurement Systems to Ensure Quality." In *Managing Quality in America's Most Admired Companies* (San Francisco: Berrett-Koehler Publishers; Norcross, GA: Industrial Engineering and Management Press, 1993), 311–316.

SpaceLabs Medical Inc. manufactures products that are used to monitor patients. The company's commitment to customer service is articulated in three documents: its operating philosophy, company values, and its quality policy. Senior managers take responsibility for key hospital accounts and are involved in each phase of product development. An extensive customer service operation is in place to maximize customer satisfaction. A customer satisfaction survey program, conducted by an outside market research firm, measures the effectiveness of SpaceLabs Medical service activities.

SIC 3861: Photographic equipment and supplies

Aleo, Joseph P., Jr.
"Redefining the Manufacturer–Supplier Relationship." *Journal of Business Strategy* 13, no.5 (September/October 1992): 10–14.

In order to reduce manufacturing costs while maintaining quality, it is critical for manufacturers to develop partnerships with suppliers. Aleo maintains that these manufacturer–supplier partnerships may be the single most critical alliances for businesses in the 1990s. Eastman Kodak's system of evaluating supplier performance may be one model that other companies can follow. Kodak's Quality Leadership Process (QLP) is described in detail. Kodak developed three tools to objectively evaluate suppliers: a supplier performance rating system; a quality assurance audit; and a supplier team improvement process. As a result of this assessment program, the number of suppliers was reduced since those suppliers that were unable to meet Kodak's quality standards were eliminated. A smaller number of suppliers was easier and less costly to manage. In addition, Kodak's system resulted in other benefits: a reduction in overall manufacturing costs; shortened lead times (allowing Kodak to beat its competitors to the marketplace); and improved communications with suppliers.

Cooney, John F.
"Xerox: A Leadership Approach to Total Customer Satisfaction." In *Managing Quality in America's Most Admired Companies* (San Francisco: Berrett-Koehler Publishers; Norcross, GA: Industrial Engineering and Management Press, 1993), 135–140.

Xerox was a 1989 Baldrige Award winner. Senior executives at Xerox have guided the company's "Leadership Through Quality" program which began in the early 1980s. One of Xerox's earliest strategies was to benchmark Xerox performance against that of its Japanese affiliate, Fuji Xerox. Although Xerox's quality improvement process continues to be driven by senior management, an underlying theme is that quality is everyone's job. Senior managers serve on quality teams and act as quality role models. Customer satisfaction is Xerox's top priority and this priority drives Xerox's total quality process. Data about consumers is collected through market research, through Xerox's customer satisfaction measurement system (a monthly survey mailed to customers), from user groups, from benchmarking, from information collected in the product development process, and from sales, service, and administrative personnel who are in contact with customers. Customers can make their concerns known to Xerox by calling toll free numbers and hot lines, through follow-ups, and through working with employees who have been empowered to resolve customer issues. Over a five-year period, customer satisfaction has improved 42 percent and Xerox is regarded as the industry benchmark in customer satisfaction.

Gan, Gin T.
"Phonto-Sonics, Inc: Achieving Quality Results Through Vendor Site Surveys." In *Managing Quality in America's Most Admired Companies* (San Francisco: Berrett-Koehler Publishers; Norcross, GA: Industrial Engineering and Management Press, 1993), 307–309.

Photo-Sonics, Inc. is a leader in the area of imaging technology. The company produces a variety of cameras and photo-optical instrumentation for military, industrial, and scientific applications. It has been widely recognized for its product quality, having received an Oscar for the Acme Optical Printer and the Scientific and Engineering Award from the Academy of Motion Picture Arts and Sciences. The company's vendor relationships have been a key to its success. Gan describes the on-site vendor surveys that Photo-Sonics conducts prior to awarding a contract and during the performance of the contract.

Jacobson, Gary, and John Hillkirk
Xerox: American Samurai. New York: Macmillan, 1986.

This history of Xerox, written by two former newspapermen, chronicles Xerox's rise, decline, and rebirth. The authors describe how Xerox became more customer-oriented and turned itself around. Xerox's strategy was a ten-point system that included benchmarking, teamwork, and an emphasis on quality. Xerox also reduced costs and improved quality by dramatically reducing its number of vendors and by implementing better warehousing methods (using lessons it learned from L. L. Bean). In 1986, *Business Week* named this engrossing account as one of the year's best books about business and economics.

Kearns, David T., and David A. Nadler

Prophets in the Dark: How Xerox Reinvented Itself and Beat Back the Japanese. New York: HarperBusiness, 1992.

This is a case study of one corporate turnaround. In 1982, the Xerox Corporation was on the brink of collapse. In late 1989, Xerox was awarded the Malcolm Baldrige National Quality Award. Xerox's "Leadership Through Quality" program saved the company from extinction. This corporate history begins with the founding of Xerox and its development through the 1960s. While Xerox was one of the most successful companies of the 1960s, it faced stormy times in the 1970s and early 1980s. The second half of the book chronicles Xerox's quality story. In the final chapter, the authors identify ten sources of competitive decline, based upon the lessons that Xerox learned.

McCamus, David R.

"Critical Quality Levers." *Business Quarterly* 57 (Summer 1992): 99–104.

Xerox Canada, Inc. developed a total quality management program in the early 1980s in response to business pressures such as product maturity, foreign competition, rapidly changing markets, and rapidly changing technologies. The program was built according to its "Leadership Through Quality" blueprint. This blueprint has five elements that Xerox refers to as "critical levers for quality." These include company-wide training, use of statistical tools, consistent and constant communications, a system of recognition and rewards for teamwork and quality behavior, and changes in management behavior. This strategy has helped Xerox Canada increase customer satisfaction while controlling operating costs.

Sherer, Franz

"Winning the European Quality Award." In *German Perspectives on Total Quality* (New York: The Conference Board, 1993), 21–26.

This is a transcript of a presentation given at the "Quality Management Forum," a 1993 symposium hosted by The Conference Board's European Council on Quality. Sherer is the Managing Director of Rank Xerox Germany. Rank Xerox

Germany uses criteria established by the European Foundation for Quality Management as the basis for their TQM program. Rank Xerox was the recipient of the first European Foundation for Quality Management Award in 1992. Xerox has won every major quality award: Fuji Xerox received the Japanese Deming Prize in 1980 and Xerox was a Baldrige Award winner in 1989. Rank Xerox organized its quality improvement process around six major topics: management leadership; human resource management; process management; customer focus; quality support and tools; and business priorities/results. These elements were seen as the means for achieving four established priorities: long-term customer satisfaction; motivated employees; increased market share; and return on assets. Rank Xerox found that their employees were the most important part of their winning strategy.

SIC 3931: Musical instruments

Koenig, Daniel T.

"Quality Through an Artisan Work Ethic." In *Managing Quality in America's Most Admired Companies* (San Francisco: Berrett-Koehler Publishers; Norcross, GA: Industrial Engineering and Management Press, 1993), 317–323.

Steinway & Sons' goal is to ensure that no piano that is below standard be shipped to customers. Employees are regarded as artisans. Koenig describes three strategies used by Steinway & Sons to emphasize its quality philosophy: the Birthday Club (which brings together employees from all units of the company who have birthdays that month); quality improvement teams (teams are cross-functional and include employees at all levels of the organization); and the suggestion system (which pays employees for ideas that enhance quality).

SIC 3952: Lead pencils, crayons and artists' materials

Roberts, Joseph M., and Daniel W. Tretter

"Competing with Crayolas: Manufacturing as a Competitive Weapon at Binney & Smith." *National Productivity Review* 12 (Spring 1993): 183–191.

Binney & Smith is the manufacturer of Crayola crayons. In 1988, a major retailer asked Binney & Smith how fast the company could deliver an order. This question motivated Binney & Smith managers to analyze the company's manufacturing process. During the 1980s, Binney & Smith had explored several manufacturing techniques: Just-in-Time, total quality management, theory of constraints, and employee involvement. The company decided to pull these four techniques together in an improvement program called high velocity manufacturing (HVM). This article describes the development of Binney & Smith's HVM process. Binney & Smith defines HVM as "a process of ongoing improvement that is employee oriented and customer-focused". This HVM strategy has proved effective, resulting in double-digit growth for Binney & Smith.

SIC 3993: Signs and advertising specialties

Idstein, James R.
"Small Company TQM." *Management Accounting* 75, no.3 (September 1993): 39–40.

This case study demonstrates that although small companies don't have the resources to hire full-time quality managers or quality consultants, they can still successfully implement TQM. The Kane Graphical Corporation designs and manufactures signs, teller nameplates and badges, regulations, and other interior signage for banks, credit unions, and savings and loan associations. It employs forty-eight workers. A quality improvement effort was initiated after one of Kane's two owners attended a W. Edwards Deming seminar. All employees were surveyed about how Kane's manufacturing processes and customer service could be improved. Because the company is so small, only two teams of between five and eight employees were formed. The first team, the "Job Information Team," was formed to improve the clarity of forms used to process an order. The team completed its project and implemented changes. The second team (consisting entirely of volunteers) was formed to correct the problem of late deliveries. All employees are updated about the progress of teams through the company's newsletter. A system of recognition and rewards has also been developed.

SIC 4512: Air transportation, scheduled

Worth, Maurice W.
"Delta Air Lines, Inc: Excellent Service One Passenger at a Time." In *Managing Quality in America's Most Admired Companies* (San Francisco: Berrett-Koehler Publishers; Norcross, GA: Industrial Engineering and Management Press, 1993), 355–358.

Delta is one of the four largest airlines in the world. It operates 2,800 flights every day and has a staff of 80,000. Among major U.S. airlines, Delta ranks high in the area of customer satisfaction. According to Worth, the secret to Delta's success is its investment in staff. Delta's employment process is designed to identify applicants with a service orientation. Unlike many other airlines, Delta has a strong tradition of employment security. In addition, employees are compensated at salary levels that are at the top of the industry. Cross-utilization and mentoring are two strategies that help employees develop important skills.

SIC 4513: Package delivery services

Blueprints for Service Quality: The Federal Express Approach. New York: AMA Membership Publications Division, American Management Association, 1991.

In 1990, Federal Express, a leader in overnight air express, was a Baldrige Award winner. Federal Express was the first company to be awarded the Baldrige Award in the service category. This volume, part of the AMA Management Briefing series, shows how Federal Express established a quality-conscious culture. The American Management Association contracted independent researchers to spend time at Federal Express's headquarters in Memphis. These researchers pored through policy statements and interviewed managers. The briefing, which they wrote, presents detailed descriptions of Federal Express's policies and programs which can serve as blueprints for training programs, executive development, quality measurements, and customer research. Federal Express has always been open about its operations. Frederick W. Smith, chairman and CEO, noted during a keynote address that he delivered in 1990, that there are no secrets at Federal Express, since what Federal Express does "is all in the books". However, the AMA researchers found that these four characteristics set Federal Express apart: a clearly stated service quality goal of 100 percent customer satisfaction; a quantification of service failures to promote continuous quality improvement; empowered employees; and a corporate philosophy that puts people first. Smith has simplified Federal Express's philosophy to "people-service-profit", meaning that when people are placed first, they will deliver the highest level of service, which in turn generates customer satisfaction and profits.

"Culture Change Through Total Quality at Lynx." In *Cases in Total Quality Management* (Oxford (England): Butterworth-Heinemann, 1994), 3–9.

Lynx is a company that delivers small consignments and parcels to businesses in the United Kingdom and Europe. The corporate culture began to change at Lynx when Alan Soper became managing director in 1989. Soper found that the company was task-driven, not customer-driven. Lynx developed a mission statement that focused on meeting the expectations of customers. The cost of non-conformance was calculated. Two types of non-conformance were identified: company costs (lost consignments, damaged or misrouted parcels, damaged vehicles, late-entered data, lost customers) and customer costs (lost consignments, damaged parcels, late deliveries, and missed bookings). Over a two-year period, the climate began to change at Lynx. Permanent work teams were formed and a system of rewards and recognition was established. A number of non-conformance cost reductions were achieved during the two-year period. For example, lost consignments were reduced 40 percent, damaged parcels were reduced by 35 percent, and misrouted parcels were down by 15 percent.

Smith, Frederick W.
"Federal Express: the MBNQA is Our License to Practice." In *Managing Quality in America's Most Admired Companies* (San Francisco: Berrett-Koehler Publishers; Norcross, GA: Industrial Engineering and Management Press, 1993), 193–204.

Federal Express was a Malcolm Baldrige Award winner in 1990. Smith, who is chairman, president, and CEO, discusses the history of his company's quality improvement efforts, explains why Federal Express applied for the Baldrige Award, describes how Federal Express prepared for the site visit by Baldrige Award examiners, and outlines Federal Express's Quality Improvement Process (QIP). The objectives of the QIP are to achieve a 100 percent service level, increase profits, and make Federal Express a better place to work.

SIC 4911: Electric services

Hudiburg, John J.
Winning With Quality: The FPL Story. White Plains, NY: Quality Resources, 1991.

Florida Power & Light (FPL) is the fourth-largest and fastest-growing electric utility company in the United States. It serves about half the state of Florida and employs about 15,000 workers. Hudiburg is the former chairman and CEO of Florida Power & Light. According to many industry experts, his vision and leadership enabled FPL to become the first non-Japanese company to win the prestigious Deming Prize. Hudiburg also played a pivotal role in the national quality improvement movement. He was a driving force in the establishment of the Malcolm Baldrige Award. In the 1970s and early 1980s FPL was faced with several problems, including two oil crises, an unfavorable economic climate, increasing government regulation, and an increasing level of customer dissatisfaction. *Winning With Quality* is an insider's account of how TQM turned FPL around. FPL implemented a quality improvement process in 1985 and by 1989 the company became a leader in the quality arena. Hudiburg contends that TQM can work in any company, and in any country. This is an important account since many service companies have used FPL as a model.

Hultz, J. A.
"Ohio Edison Company: Quality Improvement Through Technical Staff Management." In *Managing Quality in America's Most Admired Companies* (San Francisco: Berrett-Koehler Publishers; Norcross, GA: Industrial Engineering and Management Press, 1993), 365–377.

The author describes quality improvements made over a three-year period at the W. H. Sammis Plant, Ohio Edison's largest coal-fired power plant. The plant needed to make some changes in order to become a more reliable and efficient producer of electricity. Hultz's article focuses on the changes and achievements of the technical support group at the Sammis plant.

Rutledge, Robert W.
"Life After the Deming Prize." *Business & Economic Review* 40, no.3 (April-June 1994): 26–31.

Rutledge describes Florida Power & Light's (FPL) quest for quality, the application process for the Deming Prize, and FPL's continued efforts to improve operations and earnings after becoming the first non-Japanese company to win the Deming Prize. After winning the Deming Prize, FPL restructured the company. This strategy eliminated more than 10 percent of FPL's workforce and reduced the layers of management from fourteen to five. Although FPL has not abandoned its commitment to quality, greater attention is being paid to competition and costs.

Seemer, Robert H.
"Keeping in Step with the Environment: Applying TQC to Energy Supply." *National Productivity Review* 9, no.4 (Autumn 1990): 439–455.

This article describes the implementation of Total Quality Control (TQC) at Florida Power & Light (FLP). FLP, the fastest growing and fourth-largest electric utility in the United States, introduced TQC in 1985. In 1989, FLP was awarded the Deming Prize, becoming the first non-Japanese company to win this prestigious quality award. FLP's TQC approach involved seven steps: determining what to improve; analyzing the current situation and developing a problem statement; analyzing the problem; developing measures to address the problem; tracking results; standardizing the process that effectively solved a problem; and ranking continuing plans for quality improvement.

SIC 4923: Natural gas transmission and distribution

Harmening, Thomas E., James Jannausch, and Deborah Love
"Michigan Consolidated Gas Company: Vision and Values Lead to Quality Service." In *Managing Quality in America's Most Admired Companies* (San Francisco: Berrett-Koehler Publishers; Norcross, GA: Industrial Engineering and Management Press, 1993), 359–363.

In 1989, senior managers of Michigan Consolidated Gas Company (Mich Con) held a retreat to discuss the future of the natural gas distribution industry. Although the purpose of the retreat was to develop a vision statement, Mich Con managers realized that there was room for improvement at the company and that employee participation was needed before a vision could be articulated. However, gathering employees together was problematic since Mich Con employees are scattered throughout Michigan at almost 100 facilities. Employees were brought together initially via satellite. The telecast was followed by more than 200 meetings held at Mich Con facilities. After the vision and values statement was completed, it was unveiled at one of Mich Con's smallest facilities to illustrate that even the smallest facilities would have to change.

"TQM Implementation in British Gas West Midlands." In *Cases in Total Quality Management* (Oxford (England): Butterworth-Heinemann, 1994), 204–221.

British Gas West Midlands, one of twelve regions within British Gas PLC, has 1.7 million customers and more than 6,000 employees. This case study describes British Gas West Midlands' implementation of TQM in 1989. The company's goal was to make British Gas West Midlands the leading region within British Gas within two years. The strategy that the company adopted was called "The Way Ahead." "The Way Ahead" consisted of five key elements: TQM, which was the central element that would bind activities together; a human resource development strategy that would give all employees the opportunity to develop their own potential; effective oral and written communications; a more active role in the West Midlands community; and information technology. In the four years since British Gas West

Midlands implemented TQM, a total of 142 quality teams have been established. It is estimated that quality projects have resulted in savings totaling (L)1 million per year.

SIC 5311: Department stores

Gennett, Michael
"Lazarus: Quality Control Committee Focuses on Customer Satisfaction." In *Managing Quality in America's Most Admired Companies* (San Francisco: Berrett-Koehler Publishers; Norcross, GA: Industrial Engineering and Management Press, 1993), 335–339.

Lazarus is a chain of department stores based in Cincinnati, Ohio. In 1988, its parent company (Federated) was acquired by the Campeau Corporation of Canada in a hostile takeover. Lazarus was plagued by serious customer service problems in the 1980s – in 1988 alone, there were more than 40,000 customer complaints. Most of them related to furniture, carpeting, and electronics. The takeover by Campeau forced Lazarus to address these problems, since the company feared that it would go out of business unless it was able to retain customers. Lazarus formed a quality control committee with the goal of reducing customer complaints by 50 percent. The committee was able to identify problems and solutions. Over a three-year period, the number of complaints has been drastically reduced.

SIC 5331: Variety stores

Rutherford, John
"Kmart Corporation: Partners for Quality." In *Managing Quality in America's Most Admired Companies* (San Francisco: Berrett-Koehler Publishers; Norcross, GA: Industrial Engineering and Management Press, 1993), 331–334.

Kmart is one of the largest retailers in the world. Customer satisfaction is measured through focus groups and data from the Kmart Customer Care Network, which includes a toll-free number for shoppers. Since one of the highest priorities is to have merchandise available when customers want it, Kmart has partnered with suppliers such as Procter & Gamble. Rutherford discusses the benefits that Kmart has reaped from partnering:

a better in-stock position, better turnaround time for goods, investment control, and reduced costs.

SIC 5734: Computer and computer software stores

Johnson, Patrice
"Intelligent Electronics, Inc. Building a Corporate Culture of Service Quality Excellence." In *Managing Quality in America's Most Admired Companies* (San Francisco: Berrett-Koehler Publishers; Norcross, GA: Industrial Engineering and Management Press, 1993), 153–159.

Intelligent Electronics, Inc., founded in 1982, is a multibillion dollar company that provides a range of products for offices. It is a leader in the retail and wholesale computer field and is recognized for its excellent customer service. Johnson describes how Intelligent Electronics has built a corporate culture committed to quality and excellence. The company has worked with IBM to develop an IE/IBM Six Sigma Program. Intelligent Electronics is also working with vendors since vendors are viewed as strategic partners. Employees are also regarded as strategic partners and are rewarded with stock options, bonuses, and other incentives.

SIC 5812: Eating places

Partlow, Charles G., and Fred E. Wencel
"Application of Total Quality Management in Contract Foodservice." *Journal of College & University Foodservice* 2, no.2 (1994): 3–14.

The authors studied quality improvement processes in six of the leading contract foodservice companies in the United States. They gathered comparative data in seven areas relating to TQM: leadership, data collection to support quality improvement, strategic quality planning, human resource development, management of quality process, operational results, and customer focus and satisfaction. All six companies cited a strong commitment to customer satisfaction. Four companies integrated TQM training into their orientation for new employees and one company introduced all employees to TQM. All but one company reported that quality was considered as a criteria in at least one of these areas:

performance reviews, recognition/awards, promotion, and compensation. All six companies indicated that TQM resulted in decreased food and labor costs. Each company had a customer feedback system in place (usually in the form of customer comment cards, customer surveys, and client surveys). However, since the application of TQM is in the beginning or early phases at these companies, it is too early to assess the overall effectiveness of TQM. The authors note that TQM often takes five or more years to implement, and none of the companies included in their study have been involved in TQM for that long. There is, however, a growing interest in TQM among contract foodservice companies.

SIC 5961: Catalog and mail-order houses

Anfuso, Dawn
"L. L. Bean's TQM Efforts Put People Before Processes." *Personnel Journal* 73 (July 1994): 72–76.

L.L. Bean, the Maine-based mail order company, applied for the Malcolm Baldrige National Quality Award in 1988 in the service category. Although it did not win the award, it was one of the two companies that qualified for a site visit. In fact, no Baldrige Award was given in 1988 in the service category. However, the company used feedback from the Baldrige committee to improve their total quality management process. The committee suggested that L. L. Bean (a company that has exemplary customer service) focus on ensuring that orders are processed correctly in the first place (rather than relying on its no-questions asked guaranteed policy) and that there be more employee involvement. L. L. Bean launched a company-wide TQM training program, created quality action teams, and gathered employee input through a feedback survey and feedback forums. L. L. Bean's efforts have won wide praise. Its manufacturing division won the Maine state quality awards and *Personnel Journal* awarded L. L. Bean the Personnel Journal Optimas Award for its management of change through a TQM approach.

Colacecchi, Mary Beth
"Quality Time: Catalogers Warming Up to Total Quality Programs." *Catalog Age* 9, no.12 (December 1992): 1, 34–35.

Mail order houses such as L. L. Bean, Gall's Inc., Sun Express, and The Music Stand are convinced that TQM is an effective strategy for improving customer satisfaction. TQM requires mail order houses to form partnerships with both customers and suppliers. L. L. Bean was one of the first large mail order companies to make a commitment to TQM. Smaller companies have also applied TQM to solve problems. Plow & Hearth, a cataloger with about $15 million in sales, has used TQM to reduce returns. Over a two-year period, the rate of returns decreased from 4.5 percent of gross sales to 3.1 percent. Other catalogers such as The Music Stand and the Brown & Jenkins Trading Co., have used some TQM methods such as cross-training so personnel can be easily shifted.

SIC 6021: National commercial banks

Lunt, Penny
"Ten Tips Toward Total Quality." *ABA Banking Journal* 86 (April 1994): 66, 69.

Henry Doss of First Union Bank and Oscar Foster of First Chicago are two bankers who have led quality improvement initiatives in their respective banks. Together, they offer ten practical pointers on implementing TQM in banking. The first tip is to ensure that management supports TQM. At both banks, quality awareness courses are taught by top-level managers. The second piece of advice is to eliminate unnecessary steps from employees workloads. Next, ask customers probing questions. The fifth tip is to ask customers why they left the bank. First Chicago has found that 40 percent of the customers who leave their bank do so for controllable reasons (that is, not because they've moved or died). Sixth, soothe irate customers. The next tip is to encourage employees to criticize themselves and their departments. The eighth pointer is to train employees in instalments. The ninth tip is to change the right things. The tenth and last tip is to acknowledge that TQM takes time.

White, M. L.
"Doing the Right Things Right the First Time."
Trusts & Estates 132 (September 1993): 30–37.

The Mellon Bank Corporation launched a quality improvement initiative in 1991. This article describes the work of one team charged with the task of reviewing all processes related to collective investment funds. The Collective Investment Funds Quality Improvement Team was composed of twelve members, ranging from junior officers to vice presidents, from eight different organizational units. The team reviewed the existing process for investing in these funds, identified areas of improvement, recommended solutions, and implemented these changes. As a result of their efforts, this process was streamlined, errors were reduced, information was disseminated more quickly, and staff were more aware of the specific details of this investing process.

SIC 6029: Commercial banks, not elsewhere classified

Boaden, R. J., and B. G. Dale
"Managing Quality Improvement in Financial Services: A Framework and Case Study." *The Service Industries Journal* 13, no.1 (January 1993): 17–39.

The authors describe a framework for managing quality improvement within the commercial banking industry. Their framework is based on research they conducted in the 1990s in one of the big four United Kingdom clearing banks. The bank employs more than 80,000 people and has more than 3,500 branches. The framework has four major components: organizing; changing the culture; using systems and techniques; and measurement and feedback. The authors drew the following conclusions from their research: a long-term strategy for quality improvement needs to be in place; TQM requires the introduction and acceptance of individual and organizational change; a number of quality tools that were developed in the manufacturing industry are transferable to the banking industry; a formal training program should be developed; market research can be used to obtain customer feedback to establish benchmarks, and an award ceremony or other types of recognition systems should be developed

to celebrate and commemorate success in quality service improvement efforts.

The International Quality Study: Best Practices Report – An Analysis of Management Practices that Impact Performance. Cleveland, OH: Ernst Young; New York: American Quality Foundation, 1992.

The International Quality Study (IQS) was a study of the best management practices across four industries (health care, banking, automotive, and computer) within four industrialized countries (Canada, Germany, Japan, and the United States). This study was a joint project of Ernst & Young (one of the world's leading consulting firms) and the American Quality Foundation (an independent, nonprofit research organization established by the American Society of Quality Control). The results of the IQS has international significance since the findings serve as a benchmark for quality progress. The IQS was conducted using a self-administered questionnaire. The survey grouped questions into five major categories: business organization; product/service development; delivery process and customer satisfaction; quality and strategic positioning; and culture. The IQS study found that these four industries have many common practices contributing to world class quality and service delivery. The IQS also demonstrated that industries can learn from unrelated industries. The IQS has analyzed more than 900 management practices in more than 500 organizations. Analysts found that some practices take longer to impact performance. The *Best Practices Report* identifies which management practices work. Earlier IQS reports included *The Top-Line Findings*, a report focusing on the ways businesses across all these industries and companies are managing the improvement process, and the four IQS industry reports detailing the specific findings for the health care, automotive, banking, and computer industries, All these reports may be obtained through the American Society for Quality Control.

Spagnola, Robert G., and Cynthia M. Spagnola
"Total Quality Management in Commercial Banking." *Journal of Commercial Lending* 75, no.6 (February 1993): 6–17.

The authors urge the U.S. banking and commercial lending industry to embrace TQM.

After providing an overview and history of TQM, they show how TQM can be applied to commercial lending. They argue that TQM can reduce costs, create loyal customers, and give commercial lenders an edge in the highly competitive banking industry.

SIC 6061: Credit unions

Haefner, Joseph L.
"TQM: Implement a Quality Evolution, Not Revolution." *Credit Union Executive* 33, no.5 (September/October 1993): 14–19.

This article explains how a credit union can implement TQM. TQM will have a greater chance of success if it follows these five guidelines: a credit union has to understand what TQM is and isn't; those involved need to have basic training in the seven quality tools and the seven-step improvement process; management needs to conduct an improvement project; learning has to be expanded to staff; and staff and management teams must be used to identify critical processes, and how to measure, stabilize, and standardize them. Haefner provides some good examples of possible pilot projects. For example, a credit union could use TQM to analyze loan application processing time or to reduce credit card application time.

SIC 6141: Personal credit institutions

Davis, Rob
"AT & T Universal Card Services: The Center of the Universe." In *Managing Quality in America's Most Admired Companies* (San Francisco: Berrett-Koehler Publishers; Norcross, GA: Industrial Engineering and Management Press, 1993), 213–219.

AT & T Universal Card Services (UCS) was a 1992 Malcolm Baldrige Award winner. UCS's philosophy is expressed in its corporate theme "Customers are the Center of Our Universe". UCS's strategy for building and maintaining customer relationships is based on determining the needs and expectations of customers, modifying existing products and services based on these needs and expectations, and evaluating and improving the business processes that impact

customers. By making customers satisfied, UCS became the third largest issuer of credit cards in the United States in only two years.

Goff, Heidi R.
"Master Card Division Masters the Quality Possibilities." *National Productivity Review* 11 (Winter 1991/92): 105–111.

Mastercard International's Mastercard Automated Point of Sale Program (MAPP) had been losing money in 1988. In an effort to turn the division around and save it from elimination, managers decided to undertake a series of quality initiatives. By 1990, MAPP had become one of the most profitable divisions of Mastercard International, returning a 14 percent net in 1990. In addition, a survey of employees found that 90 percent of employees were proud to work for MAPP and 92 percent of employees rated the MAPP senior management team as good or very good. This article chronicles the first four years of MAPP's quality program. As a result of MAPP's success, Mastercard launched Quality First, its own quality program in 1991.

SIC 6153: Diversified financial services

Hege-Kleiser, Carmen
"American Express Travel Services: A Human Resources Approach to Managing Quality." In *Managing Quality in America's Most Admired Companies* (San Francisco: Berrett-Koehler Publishers; Norcross, GA: Industrial Engineering and Management Press, 1993), 205–212.

Hege-Kleiser describes the Traveler's Check Group's (TCG) total quality approach which is based on three quality ordinals: prevention-based work processes and data systems; a commitment to train and empower employees to improve service and stop errors before they happen; and a commitment to customer service. Since 1987 TCG has increased the accuracy of telephone service in its claims processing group from 69.9 percent to 99.7 percent, increased accuracy of encashment assistance service from 76.2 percent to 99.9 percent, and reduced employee turnover in its operating center (which employs more than 80 percent of TCG's employees) from 24 percent to under 9 percent. During this same period, employee perception about TCG increased from

68 percent favorable to 85 percent favorable. These goals were achieved by TCG's strategy of "Becoming the Best Place to Work." This strategy emphasizes treating employees as customers, using employee input, measuring employee satisfaction, benchmarking, and incorporating best practices. TCG has been very innovative in implementing benefits and programs to help employees balance work and family responsibilities. Some of the programs that have been initiated include flexible benefits, flexible work arrangements, improved benefits for part-time employees, sabbaticals, a dependent care subsidy program, a child care subsidy program, family sick days, family leave, adoption assistance, a child care resource and referral service, an expanded employee assistance program, and health care and dependent care reimbursement plans.

Welch, James F.

"Service Quality Measurement at American Express Traveler's Cheque Group." *National Productivity Review* 11 (Autumn 1992): 463–471.

In 1982, the American Express Company (AMEXCO) Traveler's Cheque Group (TCG) had serious problems, including a declining market share, dissatisfied customers and employees, internal accounting problems, and escalating operating costs. In an effort to improve customer service, TCG developed a quality measurement tool called the Service Tracking Report (STR). The STR was designed to measure and report the expectations of three customer groups: sellers (institutions that offer AMEXCO traveler's checks to the public); purchasers (consumers who use AMEXCO checks); and acceptors (businesses that accept AMEXCO traveler's checks. Each group was surveyed about three aspects of TCG's customer service: accuracy, timeliness, and responsiveness. The STR has enabled TCG to monitor customers' satisfaction with service over time. TCG has STR data from 1983 on. TCG also developed a statistical process control that is used in conjunction with the Service Tracking Report. Like Motorola, TCG has adopted a Six-Sigma goal. TCG's Six-Sigma goal is 99.9997 percent compliance (three errors for every one million customer interactions).

SIC 6166: Mortgage bankers and loan correspondents

Fry, Darryl

"A Quest for Total Quality." *Mortgage Banking* 53, no.5 (February 1993): 83–91.

This is a case study of one mortgage company that has used the principles and tools of total quality management to improve efficiency, increase quality, and cut costs. Community West Mortgage, based in San Jose, California, initiated an "Opportunities for Improvement Project" that created teams, established a goal of continuous improvement, and led to a shared vision. The Project was successful and resulted in the company's commitment to the concepts of total quality management and quantitative efficiencies.

SIC 6311: Life insurance

"Assessing TQM Implementation in the Prudential Assurance Co Ltd, Life Administration Home Services Division." In *Cases in Total Quality Management* (Oxford (England): Butterworth-Heinemann, 1994), 10–51.

The Prudential Corporation is one of the largest financial services groups in the world. In the UK, Prudential's core business is conducted by the Home Service Division of the Prudential Assurance Co Ltd. The company's main lines of business are life insurance, pensions, savings, and general insurance. The Life Administration Group, with offices in Reading and Belfast, provides administrative support. In 1989, the Life Administration Group conducted market research as part of its planning process and concluded that customer service could be improved and productivity needed to increase. The Life Administration addresses these problems through a TQM program named the "Way of Life." This case study describes the "Way of Life" in detail. The program has resulted in productivity improvements, improved customer service, and savings in operation costs.

Gannon, Wynne
"New York Life: Increasing Productivity and Quality Through TQM." In *Managing Quality in America's Most Admired Companies* (San Francisco: Berrett-Koehler Publishers; Norcross, GA: Industrial Engineering and Management Press, 1993), 275–278.

New York Life initiated a total quality management process in 1988. The TQM process is based on three components: planning; quality improvement teams; and daily operations. New York Life has reaped many benefits from TQM. Teams have achieved the following: a 50 percent reduction in rejected mutual fund applications; a 42 percent reduction in life applications submitted incorrectly; $100,000 in annual tax savings for annuity policies; $100,000 annual reduction in expenses due to a quicker resolution of divident questions, and $100,000 in annual savings in the company's Canadian operations.

Messenger, Sally, and Stephen Tanner
"Prudential Insurance: The 'Way of Life' Programme." In *Achieving Quality Performance: Lessons From British Industry* (London: Cassell, 1994), 145–169.

Prudential Corporation PLC is one of the world's largest financial services groups. Prudential's major lines of business include life insurance and pensions, general insurance, life and general reinsurance, and investment management. The major division in the UK is the Home Services Division which offers life insurance, personal pensions, and general insurance. This division has approximately 13,000 agents in the field who are supported by Life Administration offices in Reading and Belfast. These offices employ about 1,500 workers. In 1989, the Life Administration began to undertake its "Way of Life" TQM program, in order to improve productivity and improve customer service. The Life Administration was motivated to try TQM since market trends indicated that first of all, the current staffing levels would not be supported unless productivity increased and secondly, customers were demanding speedy and friendly service. The "Way of Life" program included both "soft" objectives and "hard" objectives. Some examples of "soft" issues include changing the way people behave, reorganizing the organization, introducing a common language, involving everyone, and increasing customer focus. Some "hard" issues included improving accuracy, improving speed, meeting customer expectations, reducing costs, and improving morale. Life Administration developed a four-point quality strategy in order to achieve these goals. This strategy consisted of these main components: control of processes; a customer-focused culture; continuous improvement; and communication. The "Way of Life" program has resulted in improved efficiency, has led Prudential to become customer-focused, and has made staff more proactive. Prudential has won several awards for its quality initiative and the Industrial Branch of the firm has achieved BS 5750 registration in record time.

SIC 6321: Accident and health insurance

Raffio, Thomas
"Quality and Delta Dental Plan of Massachusetts." *Sloan Management Review* 34, no.1 (Fall 1992): 101–110.

This case study of TQM in the dental insurance industry features the Delta Dental Plan of Massachusetts (DDPMA). Quality improvement became a goal as early as 1987, DDPMA's first full year as a stand-alone operating company. Delta Dental Plan separated from Blue-Cross Blue Shield of Massachusetts in 1986. Delta Dental Plan's TQM program includes five major components: active employee involvement; a team structure; an integrated information system approach; service guarantees; and the use of the Malcolm Baldrige National Quality Award framework to assess strengths and weaknesses. The results have been impressive. Since 1987, the number of primary subscribers has increased, revenue has increased, more accounts are being retained, and overhead costs have decreased. DDPMA's set of service guarantees to all its customers has improved customer loyalty and distinguishes DDPMA from other dental plans. Raffio's article was awarded the Coopers & Lybrand/Sloan Management Review Quality Award.

SIC 6371: Pension, health, and welfare funds

Weiss, Daniela
"TIAA-CREF: Managing Quality at the World's Largest Pension System." In *Managing Quality in America's Most Admired Companies* (San Francisco: Berrett-Koehler Publishers; Norcross, GA: Industrial Engineering and Management Press, 1993), 341–354.

TIAA-CREF is one of the largest pension companies for professors, academic administrators, research scientists, and other educational employees. Employee feedback and staff development are a critical part of the company's quality efforts. Since the early 1980s, TIAA-CREF has used teams (first in the form of quality circles) to identify problems and solutions. Employee input is also obtained through TIAA-CREF's "Executive Interview Program" (which gives employees a chance to share ideas with managers from divisions other than their own) and the monthly Chairman's and President's Lunch (where twelve employees are randomly selected to sit down with the chairman and president to discuss concerns). TIAA-CREF has a practice of cultivating leadership from within the company. This is done through a program allowing junior level managers to work in the chairman's office for a five-month period. In addition, TIAA-CREF has a generous tuition reimbursement program (which pays for undergraduate programs, graduate programs, and certificate programs) and in-house continuing education.

SIC 6399: Insurance carriers, not elsewhere classified

Hall, Phil
"Living With TQM." *Risk Management* 39 (March 1992): 20, 22.

While a November 1989 survey conducted by *Time* magazine found that 87 percent of the largest U.S. industrial corporations were expanding their quality improvement programs, the insurance and risk management industries have only recently looked at TQM as a way to reduce overhead costs and improve customer service. However, insurance companies may want to give serious consideration to TQM, since an NBC Wall Street Journal poll found that 49 percent of the 2,000 Americans surveyed indicated that the quality of service provided by insurance companies has stagnated. The only line of business faring worse in the polls was gas stations. One insurance company that has been a pioneer in the area of quality control is the Zurich-American Insurance Group based in Schaumberg, Illinois. Its "Partners for Excellence" program maintains an eight-person department to continually monitor and improve operations within the corporate headquarters and at 40 other office locations.

Lenckus, Dave
"A Quality Solution to Improving Service." *Business Insurance* 27 (December 6, 1993): 19–20.

Some risk managers, especially those at large companies, have adopted TQM. Some risk management departments that have been pioneers in the area of TQM are those at Hallmark Cards Inc., the Weyerhaeuser Co., and the Xerox Corporation. The TQM tools most often used by risk managers include flowcharting, teamwork, and partnering (that is, team-building with other operations within the organization and with brokers, insurers, and consultants).

McDermott, Robert F.
"USAA: Employee Satisfaction Equals Customer Satisfaction." In *Managing Quality in America's Most Admired Companies* (San Francisco: Berrett-Koehler Publishers; Norcross, GA: Industrial Engineering and Management Press, 1993), 279–288.

USAA (United Services Automobile Association) was formed in 1922 to offer automobile insurance to military officers who were perceived to be higher risks. All commissioned officers (active, Reserve National Guard, or retired) are now eligible. Quality has been part of USAA's corporate culture for decades. Quality service was articulated as part of USAA's creed and mission as early as 1969. In 1981, USAA began to establish quality circles. The infrastructure for continuous improvement now includes an executive council, policy deployment committees, management action teams, and front-line teams. An effective employee recognition system has helped USAA produce dedicated and customer-focused employees. USAA's turnover rate is 7.1 percent (an industry low) and its rate of absenteeism is 2 percent.

SIC 6400: Employee benefits and compensation

Groff, Mary K.
"Using Continuous Improvement to Purchase Value in Health Care." *Employee Relations Today* 19, no.3 (Autumn 1992): 299–310.

The escalating cost of health care in the United States has created a financial burden for most corporations. Groff, a consultant for Iameter, Inc., helps corporations develop health care plans and/or purchase health care services. She outlines a twelve-step process, using continuous quality improvement tools, that can help corporations improve the quality and value of the health care services that they purchase. The following twelve steps can help corporations develop or redesign their current health care delivery system: becoming knowledgeable about the CQI process and establishing a commitment to CQI from top-level management; listing and prioritizing improvement projects; defining project goals and objectives; defining who will be a member of the decision-making team; defining process flow; analyzing customers needs; defining potential problems, their causes, and proactive measures to prevent these problems; designing a process monitoring and control system; implementation of the new program; checking the performance of the new program; developing and refining a monitoring system to evaluate performance; and identifying opportunities for improvement. This twelve-step process is most effective when used by an industry benefit staff, employee representatives, top managers, accounting staff, and other organizational groups that are potentially affected by the changes.

SIC 6531: Real estate agents and managers

Berger, Warren
"What's the Big Attraction of TQM?" *Real Estate Today* 27 (April 1994): 14–19.

The purpose of this article is to introduce real estate brokers to the concept of TQM. Although some experts believe that the real estate profession has lagged behind in its understanding and adoption of this management strategy, there is evidence that this is changing as brokers realize that quality of service is becoming increasingly important in this competitive profession. The author presents a reworking of Deming's fourteen principles: "TQM Principles with a Real Estate Twist". He also includes practical advice from brokers who have adopted a TQM approach.

Chalk, Mary Beth
"Measuring the Quality in Corporate Real Estate." *National Real Estate Investor* 36 (February 1994): 82 *et seq.*

After providing a historical overview of TQM and an introduction to its processes, Chalk presents examples of how corporate real estate groups have implemented the principles of TQM. For example, facility managers at Pacific Bell saved approximately $130,000 annually after revamping the oil filter replacement process. TQM has enabled Eastman Kodak to identify the core activities of its corporate real estate group and to form alliances with four service providers. Facility managers at the Lockheed Corporation use TQM to ensure customer satisfaction.

Smith, Anthony W., and Jeremy M. Sibler
"TQM Success – Or, It's the Process, Stupid!" *Journal of Property Management* 59, no.5 (September/October 1994): 12–17.

Smith and Sibler show how TQM can be implemented by property managers, using Robinson & Wetmore, Inc. as a case study. Robinson & Wetmore, a property management firm based in Virginia, manages approximately 3.5 million square feet of office and office/warehouse properties. In 1993, the company began to implement TQM. Six quality teams have been formed to address issues ranging from the budget process to vendor qualification. The authors lay out the eight critical steps in implementing TQM. These are: deciding to implement TQM; formation of a quality council; training the quality council and key managers; establishing/evaluating the firm's mission and vision; selecting the pilot process; forming the pilot team; evaluating the pilot team; and selecting additional processes and teams. The pilot processes selected by Robinson & Wetmore were insurance certification compliance and rent escalation billings. The pilot team included representatives of each major step of the process to be improved. The process improvement process itself as outlined by the authors consists of eight critical steps. These include: establishing a team mission and vision; conducting customer surveys; flowcharting an existing process; developing performance measures; data collection and analysis; formulating the improvement proposal; implementing the improvement proposal; and monitoring and improving the process. The company learned to break processes down into sub-processes with a manageable scope. They learned to look for general rules in analyzing a process rather than focusing on all variations. The company learned the value of establishing a clearinghouse for their TQM activities so teams would not duplicate efforts. Another practical lesson was the need to develop reusable templates in order to ensure consistency and to save time. Another lesson was to document every step.

SIC 7011: Hotels and motels

Banks, Dana
"The Ritz-Carlton Hotel Company: Reducing Service Variability with Human Resources Systems." In *Managing Quality in America's Most Admired Companies* (San Francisco: Berrett-Koehler Publishers; Norcross, GA: Industrial Engineering and Management Press, 1993), 269–273.

The Ritz-Carlton Hotel Company was a 1992 Baldrige Award winner. The hotel chain caters to prestigious travel consumers, corporate travelers, and meeting planners. In analyzing these three market groups, Ritz-Carlton found one commonality. All three groups expected highly personalized service delivered from responsive and caring employees. Consequently, Ritz-

Carlton concluded that the selection of the right employee is critical. Ritz-Carlton studied successful employees and identified behavioral traits exhibited by these employees. This information was used in the selection process for new employees. As a result of this selection process, the employee turnover rate was reduced to 45 percent from 80 percent.

Buzanis, Christin H.
"Hyatt Hotels and Resorts: Achieving Quality Through Employee and Guest Feedback Mechanisms." In *Managing Quality in America's Most Admired Companies* (San Francisco: Berrett-Koehler Publishers; Norcross, GA: Industrial Engineering and Management Press, 1993), 251–259.

Buzanis describes Hyatt's "In Touch" initiative. As part of this initiative, Hyatt holds an "In Touch Day." The purpose is for management to get back in touch with employees. Another development is Hyatt's "In Touch 100" quality assurance program. "In Touch 100" consists of seven components: quality standards; the use of advanced technology; training; measurement methods (such as guest surveys, confidential employee opinion surveys, focus groups, comment cards, and a secret shopper program); employee recognition for exceptional customer service; communication tools (such as In Touch Day, video newsletters, employee focus groups, quality circles, bulletin boards, and a suggestion box); and continuous improvement. Hyatt's strategy for obtaining employee feedback has led to lower employee turnover. Hyatt's turnover rate is below 40 percent, in an industry where turnover averages between 100 and 150 percent.

Cannon, Debra Franklin, and William E. Kent
"What Every Hospitality Educator Should Know About Benchmarking." *Hospitality & Tourism Educator* 6, no.4 (Fall 1994): 61–64.

The authors provide an excellent introduction to benchmarking. Xerox introduced this concept to the United States in the 1970s. Following this overview is a discussion of the five stages of the benchmarking process. These major stages are: identifying core issues; identifying companies to benchmark; collection of data; analysis of data; and implementation. Although Xerox has used benchmarking for more than twenty years, it is a recent concept for the hospitality industry. One hospitality company at the forefront of benchmarking is the Ritz-Carlton Hotel Company. Cannon and Kent provide a relatively detailed discussion of Ritz-Carlton's benchmarking process. Ritz-Carlton not only benchmarks hospitality companies but it benchmarks leading companies in a variety of settings, including manufacturing. Ritz-Carlton is also benchmarked by other companies since it has received the 1992 Malcolm Baldrige National Quality Award. Ritz-Carlton is the benchmark used by Mobile and Triple A (two hospitality service rating organizations). The authors, both hospitality educators, urge other educators to not only include benchmarking in the curriculum but to use benchmarking as a tool for improving teaching techniques and overall programs.

Galagan, Patricia A.

"Putting on the Ritz." *Training & Development* 47 (December 1993): 40–45.

Ritz-Carlton Hotels is the only hospitality organization to win the Malcolm Baldrige National Quality Award. However, the thirty-hotel chain is not resting on its laurels. By 1996, Horst A. Schulze, the president and chief operating officer of Ritz-Carlton Hotels, wants to decrease deficits in eighteen key processes involving customers, to just four deficits for every one million encounters. Other goals include 50 percent reduction in cycle time for certain pro-cesses and a 100 percent customer retention rate. Training has been the key to Ritz-Carlton's success. Each employee receives at least 100 hours of training annually, making them among the best and most intensively trained staff in the hospitality industry.

Moyer, James A.

"Marriott Corporation: Improved Customer Satisfaction Through Real Time Complaint Feedback and Resolution." In *Managing Quality in America's Most Admired Companies* (San Francisco: Berrett-Koehler Publishers; Norcross, GA: Industrial Engineering and Management Press, 1993), 261–268.

This article describes the new customer strategy developed by Marriott Hotels and Resorts in 1990. Three division-wide initiatives were developed: a customer rapid response system to support guest issues at Marriott properties; uniform on-property customer service provided by a guest relations manager; and a customer survey system executed by mail after a customer's visit. These three initiatives were tested in a group of seven hotels in the Washington DC area and all three received positive feedback from pilot participants.

Partlow, Charles G.

"How Ritz-Carlton Applies TQM." *The Cornell Hotel & Restaurant Administration Quarterly* 34 (August 1993): 16–24.

This cover story focuses on the Ritz-Carlton Hotel Company, a winner of the 1992 Malcolm Baldrige National Quality Award. The company's commitment to superior service is imbedded in its "Gold Standards" which include a credo, three steps of service, and twenty "Ritz-Carlton Basics" which put the needs of the customers first. This list of the basics of customer service includes policies such as instant guest pacification, escorting guests to another area of the hotel (rather than pointing out directions), proper telephone etiquette, and the use of guest-incident action forms to document every incident of guest dissatisfaction. Each hotel (the privately owned company operates almost 30 hotels and resorts) has a designated quality leader. Individual employees have the authority to identify and solve customer service problems. In fact, Ritz-Carlton permits employees to spend up to $2,000 to satisfy a guest. What can other companies in the hospitality industry learn from the Ritz-Carlton experience? Some important lessons are that a customer orientation must be integrated into management processes and supported through systematic data collection, total employee involvement, and training for all levels of staff.

Rowe, Megan

"Hyatt Does a Reality Check." *Lodging Hospitality* 50, no.9 (September 1994): 30–34.

Hyatt, a leader in the first-class segment of the lodging industry, reengineered the entire company, from housekeeping to management. The process, directed by Hyatt's executive vice president, involved outside consultants, a steering committee, task forces of top corporate and field managers, and various process review teams. A more streamlined operation has emerged. Purchasing, previously done at the property level, has been centralized to increase efficiency and cost effectiveness. Sales representatives are now assigned to specific properties since clients complained about having several salespeople call on them about an individual property. The sales and marketing department has also been divided into teams focusing on four segments of travelers: groups; individual business; leisure; and international. In addition, cross-training has become common at limited-service properties. Food and beverage operations have also been redesigned. For example, menus have been standardized to contain costs and provide a consistent product.

SIC 7300: Sales and selling

Cortada, James W.
TQM for Sales and Marketing Management. New York: McGraw-Hill, 1993.

This is one of the few existing books on the application of TQM to sales and marketing. It is directed to sales and marketing managers. Cortada has many years of experience in marketing and sales, having worked for IBM for almost twenty years. Beginning chapters discuss the evolution of TQM and its principal components. Cortada then discusses a corporate-wide marketing strategy for quality improvement. He explains how TQM can be implemented in the sales force, sales districts, and branch offices. The book provides specific suggestions for creating a quality-oriented, market-driven sales environment. Three useful appendices are provided: a brief introduction to the Baldrige Award; instructions on how to do benchmarking; and advice on how to learn more about quality.

Miranda, Elizabeth, ed.
Reinventing the Sales Organization. New York: The Conference Board, 1995.

This report summarizes the findings of a one-day conference sponsored by The Conference Board in June 1994. This conference brought together executives from sales organizations including The Alexander Group, Inc., 3M, Times Mirror, Merck & Company, Inc., and IBM. The executives attending addressed quality related issues such as the development of a customer orientation, strategies that can be used to deliver

real value to customers, the trend toward a team approach, and the use of activity tracking.

Oakland, John S.
"Total Quality Management (TQM)." In *Companion Encyclopedia of Marketing.* London: Routledge, 1995; pp. 953–978.

The author, who is affiliated with the European Centre for TQM, explains how TQM applies to marketing. In fact, Oakland's contention is that the marketing function of an organization should take the lead in determining the needs and requirements of customers and should establish systems for monitoring customer feedback on a continuous basis. Quality standards are no longer confined to the manufacturing sector. Oakland describes the Marketing Quality Assurance's (a third party certification organization) specification for marketing, sales, and customer service activities. This specification, called Quality Assurance Specification, has fifty-eight requirements which relate to the ISO 9000 series. The Exxon Chemical International Marketing B.V. was the first company to achieve registration to Marketing Quality Assurance.

Peeler, George H.
Selling in the Quality Era. Cambridge, MA: Blackwell Business, 1996.

Peeler has had extensive experience in sales and sales management. He has won numerous sales awards and gained recognition as IBM's top National New Account Sales Representative. He has also worked as an IBM sales training instructor and has taught marketing management. He is currently Executive Vice President of Product Development for BioChem Tech and an independent sales consultant. His book, which is designed for salespersons, sales managers, and business students, applies the concepts of quality to the selling process and sales management. However, what distinguishes this title from similar books, is Peeler's discussion of ethics and values as necessities in a quality-driven market. He begins with a historical perspective on key market principles. The second chapter looks at the new sales arena, the global marketplace. Subsequent chapters explore insights into the art and science of selling. He also looks at selling from the customer's point of view. Personal selling is perceived as a process that can be measured and improved. Peeler emphasizes the need to focus on value as perceived by customers, building relationships for long-term profitability, and how the sales group can bring customer concerns to design and production teams in order to improve the development of products.

Petrone, Joe
Building the High Performance Sales Force. New York: AMACOM, 1994.

In the 1990s, many companies are downsizing their sales force in an effort to reduce costs. Petrone's book shows salespeople and sales managers how to increase productivity, maximize sales performance, win and retain customers, and gain a competitive edge through total quality selling (TQS). The author cites a study conducted by Learning International that found that less than 10 percent of companies have incorporated the concept of quality in the area of sales. TQM has probably not been widely implemented in sales because in contrast to manufacturing, the sales process is more difficult to control since it is variable and occurs throughout a territory or region (rather than in one site). However, Petrone's contention is that quality can easily be applied to sales when quality is reduced to its most basic definition (that is, meeting and exceeding customer expectations). Quality can be achieved in sales by monitoring and controlling processes, by making small continuous improvements, by focusing on the customer on a continuous basis, by monitoring salespeople and giving them frequent feedback, through process improvement tools, and by rewarding salespeople for their efforts toward achieving quality.

Reddy, Allan C.
Total Quality Marketing: The Key to Regaining Market Shares. Westport, CT: Quorum Books, 1994.

Reddy's premise is that American companies can regain market shares by using total quality marketing (TQM). Although many firms have embraced TQM, Reddy insists that improving product quality alone is not sufficient. Since most of the quality gurus such as Deming and Juran have focused on product quality, marketing quality has been ignored. He uses the American automobile industry as an example. Although car manufacturers have significantly improved the quality of their products, many Americans still perceive imported cars to be higher in quality. The premise of TQM is that product quality by itself does not sell product. Companies need to not only produce but market products that consumers perceive as good quality and value. TQM is concerned with the production, promotion, pricing, and distribution of products.

SIC 7372: Computer software

Arthur, Lowell Jay
Improving Software Quality: An Insider's Guide to TQM. New York: Wiley, 1993.

This practical guide is part of the *Wiley Series in Software Engineering Practice.* Arthur is the author of several popular books on software engineering. He has more than twenty years of practical experience, including his work as a consultant to well-known companies such as Motorola and Kodak. This well-written book clearly explains how TQM can be applied to software development and how software managers can benchmark their firm against the best in the world.

Brinkworth, John W. O.
Software Quality Management: A Pro-Active Approach. New York; London: Prentice Hall, 1992.

This title is part of the BCS Practitioner Series. It has been designed as a practical guide for professionals involved in software development or software procurement. Each stage of the development process is covered in a separate chapter. Chapters can be read consecutively or can be read on a stand-alone basis. Although this book is not intended as a college textbook, chapters conclude with a list of questions to stimulate thought and discussion.

Card, David N., and Robert L. Glass
Measuring Software Design Quality. Englewood Cliffs, NJ: Prentice Hall, 1990.

This text, written by two practitioners, has been designed as a practical guide to software metrics. It demonstrates how software measurement can be used to support engineering design and to improve quality control. Software development managers, lead software engineers, and software product assurance professionals will find this manual useful.

Cho, Chin-Kuei
Quality Programming: Developing and Testing Software with Statistical Quality Control. New York: Wiley, 1987.

This book builds upon Cho's earlier work, *An Introduction to Software Quality Control*, published by Wiley in 1980. Cho's book demonstrates how statistical quality control can be used in the software industry. This book can serve not only as a textbook for undergraduate and graduate level courses in software engineering and software methodology, but it can serve as a handbook for practicing professionals, including software developers and software users.

Deutsch, Michael S., and Ronald R. Willis
Software Quality Engineering: A Total Technical and Management Approach. Englewood Cliffs, NJ: Prentice Hall, 1988.

This textbook on software quality is part of the Prentice Hall series in software engineering. It has been designed as a basic text for software engineers, software managers, system engineers, and procuring agencies. Part I provides an overview of software quality. Part II focuses on understanding software quality, specifying software quality specifications, and achieving software quality specifications. Part III examines the topic of verification and validation to review defects and test out errors. The final part of the book looks at management aspects, such as the economics of software quality.

Dobbins, James H.
Software Quality Assurance and Evaluation. Milwaukee, WI: ASQC Quality Press, 1990.

This practical manual on integrating software quality assurance into the software production process will be useful to any professional involved in the production or procurement of software products. The author has more than twenty years of industrial experience. His book covers issues relating to quality measurement, computer-aided software quality assurance, and software quality assurance management. He demonstrates how software quality assurance can save millions of dollars in developmental costs.

Dunn, Robert H.
Software Quality: Concepts and Plans. Englewood Cliffs, NJ: Prentice Hall, 1990.

This book has been designed for software managers, system engineers, software quality engineers, and programmers. Part 1 provides background information. Part 2 examines the nature of programming work and programmers. Part 3 focuses on quality construction, while Part 4 examines quality management. The final section focuses on quality planning.

Dunn, Robert H., and Richard S. Ullman
TQM for Computer Software. 2nd edn. New York: McGraw-Hill, 1994.

This is the revised edition of the 1982 classic *Quality Assurance for Computer Software*. It provides step-by-step instructions for applying TQM to software. This basic manual will no doubt become a bestseller – all software professionals will want to have it on their shelves.

Ebenau, Robert G., and Susan H. Strauss
Software Inspection Process. New York: McGraw-Hill, 1994.

This book shows software engineers how to use inspection techniques to identify and correct problems in the early phases of the design and development process. It explains how inspections can be integrated into existing software development procedures. The authors provide useful information such as sample inspection forms and checklists, sample procedures, a sample inspection implementation plan, a sample inspection procedures guide, and a sample description of the Lotus Inspection Data System (LIDS). In addition, there is an annotated bibliography on the topic of software inspections.

Gilb, Tom, and Dorothy Graham
Software Inspection. Wokingham (England): Addison-Wesley, 1993.

Gilb is a leading consultant in the area of software engineering and process improvement. Graham is a recognized international authority on software testing and quality techniques. Both authors work as consultants and both have taught many training seminars world-wide. The authors outline inspection techniques that can result in lower defects, increased productivity, better project tracking, and improved documentation.

They show how these techniques have been successfully used by companies such as AT & T and Douglas Aircraft. The case studies which are included are based on the real-world experiences of companies such as IBM, Thorn EMI, Cray Research, Racal Redac, Applicon, and the Soma Group.

Gillies, Alan C.
Software Quality: Theory and Management.
London: Chapman & Hall Computing, 1992,

This book, part of the Chapman & Hall Computing series, focuses on the theory of quality management and its application to software development. The book is divided into three parts. The first part covers the concept of quality and describes techniques used in software quality assurance. The second part focuses on the management of quality, including a discussion of the ISO 9000 series of standards. The final section of the book looks at future challenges.

Glass, Robert L.
Building Quality Software, Englewood Cliffs, NJ: Prentice-Hall, 1992.

Robert Glass, an experienced practitioner, is a noted authority on software quality. This book explores several issues including the importance of software quality in the 1990s, a life-cycle approach to quality, an attribute approach to quality, quality automation advances, quality metrics, and the management of quality. The case study section is particularly interesting since it demonstrates what corporations and government agencies have done in order to build quality software. The companies featured in the case studies section include IBM, GTE, TRW, Monsanto, Hallmark, and Boeing.

Hoecherl, Larry J.
"Novell, Inc. Customer Driven and Loving It!"
In *Managing Quality in America's Most Admired Companies* (San Francisco: Berrett-Koehler Publishers; Norcross, GA: Industrial Engineering and Management Press, 1993), 161–192.

Novell, Inc., an operating system software company, also develops network computing products. In this article Hoecherl describes what customer-responsive actions have worked at Novell, what actions have not worked, and what Novell would do differently as a result. He

discusses sixteen major events at Novell and the customer actions that Novell took to demonstrate its commitment to customer service. Hoecherl lets the reader know how customers felt at the time of the event and how customers perceived the action that Novell took. Hoecherl is Vice President, Quality and Customer Satisfaction.

Huff, Sid L.
"Six-Sigma Systems." *Business Quarterly* 57 (Summer 1992): 49–53.

TQM can result in fewer errors and higher programmer productivity when applied to the computer software development process. The major obstacle to TQM is the individualistic and creative approach that is found in most firms. However, as a result of this approach there are many redundant efforts by programmers. According to the author, the area of application development and maintenance could benefit from TQM. Application system quality could be improved by reusing tested error-free software modules. This could reduce the development time for new systems and provide a more consistent set of designs and interfaces for all application systems.

Ince, Darrel, ed.
Software Quality and Reliability. London: Chapman & Hall, 1991.

This book is part of the UNICOM Applied Information Technology Reports series of books based upon a seminar organized by UNICOM Seminars Ltd. Ince brings together chapters on concepts and issues in quality assurance, reliability, and testing. The contributors are leading experts in software engineering.

Ince, Darrel
An Introduction to Software Quality Assurance and its Implementation. London: McGraw-Hill, 1994.

This title is part of the McGraw-Hill International Software Quality Assurance Series. The author is frequently asked by the British press to comment on computing issues. He is a prolific author and holds a chair in computing at the Open University. This book provides an introduction to software quality. It is particularly useful for firms seeking ISO 9001 certification, since it devotes an entire chapter to ISO 9001, describing what these standards mean for the software industry.

Ince, Darrel
ISO 9001 and Software Quality Assurance. London: McGraw-Hill, 1994.

This title is part of the McGraw-Hill International Software Quality Assurance Series. It focuses on the ISO 9001 quality standard and its application to software development. More than 130 countries have adopted the ISO 9000 series of standards and the number of software developers who are adopting the standards has increased dramatically in the last five years. Since the ISO 9001 series standard is not industry-specific, Ince discusses the standards that are relevant to the software industry. In the UK, the ISO 9000 series of standards is known as BS 5750. The requirements are organized into twenty broad categories, including design control, purchasing, process control, inspection and testing, management responsibility, contract review, corrective action, document control, internal quality audits, training, and statistical techniques. Each chapter of Ince's book corresponds to one of these twenty categories. This book will be indispensable to any software firm seeking ISO 9001 certification.

Kane, Edward F.
"Implementing TQM at Dun & Bradstreet Software." *National Productivity Review* 11 (Summer 1992): 405–416.

Kane chronicles the history of TQM at Dun & Bradstreet Software (D & B Software). In 1991, D & B Software was awarded the Information Technology Association of America's Total Quality Award. The award recognized D & B Software's improvements in several areas. In addition to improving overall customer satisfaction, the company reduced error rates, cycle times, and costs by 50 percent or more. D & B Software's success is largely due to the company's ability to build a shared vision. Their holistic approach, integrating quality values and continuous improvement, has become part of the fabric of the organization.

Kaplan, Craig, Ralph Clark, and Victor Tang
Secrets of Software Quality: 40 Innovations from IBM. New York: McGraw-Hill, 1995.

The fresh approach of this book on software quality sets it apart from competing titles. The authors use forty proven techniques developed by IBM to demonstrate how the Baldrige Award

criteria can be used to improve software quality. These real-world examples are enhanced by the book's hands-on-approach. A disk, based on the Baldrige Award template, is enclosed. Readers can use it to perform a Baldrige-style assessment of their organization. This highly practical and engaging text will benefit professionals who develop or manage software as well as computer engineering students.

Kelly, Mike, ed.
Management and Measurement of Software Quality. Aldershot (England): Avebury Technical, 1993.

This collection of papers is part of UNICOM's *Applied Information Technology Series.* Contributors include noted authorities such as Dorothy R. Graham, Ernest Wallmüller, and Darrel Ince. Among the topics covered are software testing, metrics, planning for quality, and the management of the software development process. This compilation is a good representation of British, German, and French views on the need for quality in software engineering.

Keyes, Jessica
Solving the Productivity Paradox: TQM for Computer Professionals. New York: McGraw-Hill, 1995.

This book, designed for managers, programmers, and developers in the information technology industry, explores the use of TQM methods and techniques to solve or eliminate employee productivity problems. Keyes shows how TQM methodologies can solve problems ranging from information illiteracy to misleading press reports. She includes anecdotes and case studies from Fortune 500 firms in the information technology industry. This provocative book should be required reading for any professional concerned with quality and productivity issues. Keyes is president of Technisider/New Art Inc., a technology consultancy and research firm. She is perhaps better known as a columnist (having written more than 150 articles in major trade publications such as *Software Magazine, Computerworld, AI Expert,* and *Datamation*) and the author of several books, including the acclaimed *Infotrends: The Competitive Use of Information* (which *Library Journal* recognized as one of the best business books of 1992).

Ross, M., C. A. Brebbia, G. Staples, and J. Stapleton, eds
Software Quality Management II. Southampton (England): Computational Mechanics Publications, 1994.

This two-volume set consists of the edited proceedings of the second International Conference on Software Quality Management. The conference was held in Edinburgh in July 1994. The proceedings present a good balance of theory and practical advice. About one-half of the papers were presented by academicians and the rest were presented by individuals working in industry. Volume 1 is entitled *Managing Quality Systems.* Papers are presented in nine topical areas: establishing and monitoring a quality management system; process improvement; SEI capability maturity model; quality metrics; quality of engineering software; human factors in quality management; education for quality; financial and management aspects; and software quality management in other parts of the world (that is, North America and Western Europe). The second volume is entitled *Building Quality into Software.* Papers are organized under the following categories: approaches to quality; approaches to systems development; testing and validation; object oriented systems development; formal methods; software tools; expert systems; and software maintenance and reuse.

Schulmeyer, G. Gordon, and James I. McManus, eds
Handbook of Software Quality Assurance. 2nd edn. New York: Van Nostrand Reinhold, 1992.

This handbook brings together chapters written by noted experts in the field of software quality assurance, including internationally recognized experts Chin Kuei Cho and James H. Dobbins. Virtually all of the contributors are experienced practitioners. The first half of the handbook provides an overview of software assurance. The second half focuses on applications and techniques.

Schulmeyer, G. Gordon, and James I. McManus
Total Quality Management for Software. New York: Van Nostrand Reinhold, 1992.

This advanced computing book is the first book to focus on the application of TQM in software development. Chapters are written by noted experts in the area of software quality. Numerous examples of practical applications help to explain theoretical ideas. Part I provides an introduction to TQM while Part II discusses software directions. Part III examines methods of TQM implementation in software. Part IV focuses on achieving TQM in software. Among the topics covered in this practical text are zero defect software, Department of Defense requirements for software development, cleanroom engineering, AT & T's unique method of statistical process control, software reuse in quality improvement, Japanese software TQM methods, software testing methods, software quality evaluation methodology, and software metrics. This book will be useful to software managers, software developers, and software engineering students.

Wallmüller, Ernest
Software Quality Assurance: A Practical Approach. Hemel Hempstead (England): Prentice-Hall, 1994.

This book is a translation of *Software-Qualitätssicherung in der Praxis.* The original German work was published by Carl Hanser Verlag in 1990. Prentice-Hall has published this title as part of its BCS Practitioner Series, a series of books designed for practicing computer professionals. Wallmüller's book assumes a basic knowledge of software engineering. It can be used as a text in software engineering courses examining quality assurance issues or as a guide for computer professionals who have to consider quality assurance when developing software products.

SIC 7374: Computer processing and data preparation and processing services

Beckley, Glen B.
"TQM: Finding the Red Flags Hiding in Existing Systems." *Datamation* 40 (September 1, 1994): 63–64.

Information systems professionals can take the lead in a company's quality effort by designing an information system that can extract useful data from existing purchasing, inventory, and accounting systems. The cost to pull data from these traditional systems is minimal. For example, software packages can be designed to attach a "reason code" such as pricing error, quantity error, or wrong item shipped to a credit memory, making it easy to produce reports on credit memo frequency by week or month, broken down by the reason that credit had to be given. These reports can be used by TQM teams to identify problem areas.

Fuld, Leonard M.
"Achieving Total Quality Through Intelligence." *Long Range Planning* 25 (February 1992): 109–115.

Information that should be shared and used throughout a firm can help a company's quality efforts. However, designing a computer-based intelligence system can be complex, especially since managers need intelligence, not simply mounds of raw data. The Information Exchange, Corning Incorporated's computer-based intelligence system, is used as the model of a well-designed intelligence system.

Ward, James A.
"Meeting Customer Requirements First Time, Every Time." *Information Systems Management* 11 (Summer 1994): 75–78.

The information systems organization that is interested in applying TQM to its operations must focus on three critical factors. The first is the identification of internal and external customers. Next, an organization must define customer requirements and expectations. Finally, an organization must deliver information products or services that meet or exceed these requirements. Ward cautions that development of a prototype, a trend that is popular among information systems professionals, must not be a substitute for analyzing the environment in which a system will be used, analyzing existing systems, or interviewing users and customers.

SIC 7379: Computer related services, not elsewhere classified

---

Shrednick, Harvey R., Richard J. Shutt, and Madeline Weiss
"Empowerment: Key to IS World-Class Quality." *MIS Quarterly* 16, no.4 (December 1992): 491–505.

Corning Incorporated instituted a company-wide quality program in 1983. This case study is about the total quality management approach in place in Corning Incorporated's Information Services Division (ISD). The ISD high performance work system is characterized by self-managing teams that have empowered workers, improved customer satisfaction, delivered world-class service, and reduced costs. Ninety percent of ISD employees belong to cross-functional teams. The authors analyze eight factors that were critical to the success of this strategy in an information services organization. These key factors included the following: starting with a vision and clear goals; management commitment and willingness to take risks; paying particular attention to middle managers and supervisors who resisted empowered work systems; involvement of staff in all phases of the project; communication within teams, across ISD, with senior ISD managers, and customers; staying focused on the business; educating everyone involved; and development of a reward system.

Terplan, Kornel
Benchmarking for Effective Network Management. New York: McGraw-Hill, 1995.

This handbook shows computer network managers how to benchmark. Since benchmarking is an integral part of TQM and ISO 9000 certification, more network managers will be required to understand the practice of examining "best practices." The first chapter defines typical targets that can be used as comparisons with the best practice. The second chapter outlines the phases of benchmarking. Chapter 3 looks at the critical success factors of network management. Chapter 4 covers questionnaires and generic indicators. The fifth chapter explains data collection techniques for benchmarking indicators. Chapter 6 covers data interpretation. Chapter 7 explains gap analysis. Chapter 8 focuses on outsourcing network management. Chapter 9 provides advice on preparing the benchmarking report. The final chapter looks at the future of network management benchmarking.

SIC 8011: Offices and clinics of doctors of medicine

Headrick, Linda A., Duncan Neuhauser, Paul Schwab, and David P. Stevens
"Continuous Quality Improvement and the Education of the Generalist Physician." *Academic Medicine* 70, no.1, Supplement (January 1995): S104-S109.

Generalist physicians can use CQI to improve health care. For example, pediatricians at a health maintenance organization in Phoenix (Arizona) used CQI to improve the care of patients with asthma. However, these physicians need new knowledge and skills for continuous quality improvement. CQI is slowly being introduced into the medical school curriculum. Efforts to teach medical students and residents about CQI have demonstrated that CQI skills training should focus on the basics and should be taught in the context of clinical care.

Kibbe, David C., Eleanor Bentz, and Curtis P. McLaughlin
"Continuous Quality Improvement for Continuity of Care." *The Journal of Family Practice* 36, no.3 (March 1993): 304–308.

There is a relatively large body of literature on TQM in hospitals. However, there are few published works on TQM in family medicine. This article describes how TQM can be successfully implemented in primary care settings. It reports the results of a project in which CQI was implemented in the Family Practice Center at the University of North Carolina School of Medicine. A CQI team was formed to study the process of continuity of care after patients complained about not being able to see their regular physician when they wanted. One year after the implementation of selected process improvements, the level of continuity of care improved by 64 percent.

Perry, Kristie
"Where Salaried Practice Feels Like Private Practice." *Medical Economics* 71, no.17 (September 12, 1994): 64–75.

Mullikin Medical Centers is one of the largest multispecialty groups (i.e. group medical practices) in the Los Angeles area. It has facilities spread over 36 towns and cities in southern California. It has recruited physicians who feel that they've been pushed out of private practice by managed care. Mullikin has implemented TQM as a way to improve patient care. TQM has helped to shorten hospital stays, eliminate unnecessary testing, and decrease the use of medications and supplies. As a result of TQM, Mullikin physicians reduced the surgery rate for ectopic pregnancies by 85 percent.

SIC 8021: Offices and clinics of dentists

"Developments of Standards of Care – the U.S. Experience." *British Dental Journal* 170, no.6 (March 23, 1991): 228–230.

This article advocates continuous quality improvement as a goal for the dental profession world-wide. The American Association of Oral and Maxillofacial Surgeons (AAOMS) has developed standards of care for the major areas of oral and maxillofacial surgery, published in the AAOM's *Standards of Care*. The article urges that these published standards be used as the baseline for assessing improvements in dental care.

SIC 8051: Skilled nursing care facilities

Gustafson, David H.
"Lessons Learned from an Early Attempt to Implement CQI Principles in a Regulatory System." *Quality Review Bulletin* 18, no.10 (October 1992): 333–339.

This article describes the Quality Assurance Project, a demonstration project carried out between 1978 and 1982 by a Wisconsin research team. The purpose of the project was to implement and evaluate new methods for carrying out the regulatory roles of facility and resident assessment in Wisconsin nursing homes. This project presents an early case study of CQI implementation in a regulatory agency. The demonstration project focused on measuring the quality of nursing home care and the detection of nursing home problems. The lessons learned from this early project can be useful to regulatory organizations interested in integrating CQI into their external review process. For example, the QAP highlighted the importance of adequate training and the importance of management leadership.

Miller, Douglas K., *et al.*
Total Quality Management in Geriatric Care.
New York: Springer, 1995.

The book examines the application of TQM to care settings for the elderly. Case presentations demonstrate how quality improvement processes can be applied to nursing homes, acute care facilities, home care, and medical office practices. The authors identify ways for the professional geriatric community to promote quality improvement in geriatric care and medicine. Some recommended strategies include establishing interdisciplinary councils, developing consensus on appropriate outcomes for common geriatric conditions and problems, conducting controlled tests of quality improvement approaches, and expanding quality improvement training to all health professionals.

SIC 8062: General medical and surgical hospitals

Abramowitz, Paul W., *et al.*
"Evolving to Provide Pharmaceutical Care Without Additional Resources in a University Hospital." *Topics in Hospital Pharmacy Management* 12, no.3 (October 1992): 28–46.

The authors describe the changes that occurred within the Department of Pharmaceutical Services at the University of Minnesota Hospital and clinics over a seven-year period in order to improve the delivery of pharmaceutical services. The drug-distribution system was centralized for greater efficiency and pharmacists were decentralized so they could become involved in the drug therapy of hospital patients. Eventually, these decentralized positions were converted to full-time clinical pharmacist positions. In this evolution toward patient-oriented pharmaceutical services, other changes are planned. Future enhancements will include further automation of the drug-distribution system, further expansion in ambulatory services, development of an automated patient-care system with direct physician order entry, and an analysis of the role of pharmacy technicians.

Alba, Timothy, James Souders, and Gloria McGhee
"How Hospitals Can Use Internal Benchmark Data to Create Effective Managed Care Arrangements." *Topics in Health Care Financing* 21, no.1 (Fall 1994): 51–64.

Typically, hospitals have used in-patient price and length of stay (sometimes calculating price per day) as the primary measures of hospital performance. However, hospital benchmarking can use other measures including mortality, complications, comorbidity, functional status, nosocomial infection, readmissions within thirty days, patient satisfaction, unplanned surgery, and appropriateness of admission. Benchmark data enables hospitals to show payers (that is, employers) what their costs will be. However, few hospitals are using this benchmark data to influence managed care contracting.

Allen, Mel L.
"Using Quality Focus Teams in the Diagnostic Imaging Department." *Radiology Management* 15, no.3 (Summer 1993): 31–34.

Allen provides an introduction to the use of quality focus teams (QFTs) to address ways of continually improving service or care. These teams play a key role in any CQI or TQM strategy and accreditation agencies, such as the Joint Commission on Accreditation of Healthcare Organizations (JCAHO) stress the value of this team approach to problem-solving. The author describes how QFTs have been used in the diagnostic imaging department at the University of Kansas Medical Center. Teams have addressed issues such as the installation of a second MRI scanner.

Anderson, Craig A., and Robin D. Daigh
"Quality Mind-Set Overcomes Barriers to Success." *Healthcare Financial Management* 45 (February 1991): 20–24.

American hospitals have to balance rising costs and declining revenues. The authors propose TQM as a solution, since it can result in reduced costs, increased employee motivation, and improved operations. Health care organizations that want to move from traditional management to quality management need an understanding of these ten basic principles underlying TQM: development of a workable definition of quality; a customer orientation; effective supplier partnerships; a work process focus; establishment of preventive systems to prevent recurring errors; error-free goals; employee involvement; management by fact rather than intuition; quality as the responsibility of the total organization not just the quality assurance department; and continuous improvement rather than an acceptable level of quality as a goal. Each of these elements is defined and illustrated with an example from a health care setting.

Anderson, Howard J.
"The New Finance Department: CQI Triggers Big Changes in Role." *Hospitals* 66, no.19 (October 5, 1992): 40–43.

The role of hospital finance departments is evolving as more hospitals begin to implement TQM. At Morton Plant Hospital in Clearwater, Florida, members of the finance department have worked with managers of other units to develop systems to track progress toward these defined continuous quality improvement goals: a 10 percent reduction of patient billing complaints; a 10 percent reduction of the cost of supplies in cardiology; and the delivery of more prompt service. For example, in order to measure the latter, nurses in an express care unit of the emergency department track how long patients must wait before receiving treatment. Finance experts can develop systems that measure the cost of providing a service. The Medical Center Hospital of Vermont has used a cost accounting-oriented information system to identify lab tests that have been over used by physicians and to reduce the overall length of stay for cardiac care patients by cutting the length of time between a cardiac test and heart surgery. As more hospitals move toward the patient-centered care model of management, finance experts will play an increasingly important role in training other departments to track costs. The patient-centered care concept assumes that the tracking of costs is no longer the sole responsibility of traditional departments such as finance, but the responsibility of various departments and patient care units. As cost tracking becomes decentralized, the staff of finance departments will serve as coaches for members of management teams throughout a hospital.

Andrews, Heather A., *et al.*
Organizational Transformation in Health Care: A Work in Progress. San Francisco: Jossey-Bass, 1994.

The authors look at the delivery and quality of health care in the Canadian health care organization, a national health care system that is undergoing profound change. The University of Alberta Hospital in Edmonton is used as a model of a hospital that has effectively used total quality management to transform health care. Part I introduces readers to the Canadian health care system. Part II covers the principles of TQM in detail. Part III reflects on future challenges and opportunities for the entire health care system, not just Canadian health care organizations.

Ballinger, Walter F., and James O. Hepner
"Total Quality Management and Continuous Quality Improvement: An Introduction for Surgeons." *Surgery* 113, no.3 (March 1993): 250–254.

Surgeons have been interested in measuring quality since the 1930s, when outcome statistics were developed to measure standards of care. However, quality concerns more than the measurement of variables such as the rate of infections, complications, and deaths. It also includes variables that are more difficult to measure, such as the skills of a surgeon. According to the Joint Commission on Accreditation of Health Care Organizations, the measurement of quality involves the assessment of the following: accessibility of care; appropriateness of care; continuity of care; effectiveness of care; efficacy of care; efficiency of care; patient perspective issues; safety of the care environment; and timeliness of care. The Joint Commission has adopted TQM as a model and has made its application to health care a leading goal. Ballinger and Hepner outline four essential steps in a TQM program. The first is the ability to distinguish internally caused problems from externally caused problems. The second step is data collection and analysis. During this phase extrasystemic problems can be identified and remedied. Step 3 uses data to identify new systemic problems. The final step involves continuous evaluation. The authors do acknowledge that there are two problems associated with TQM. The first is a concern among surgeons that the approach interferes with their independence. The second concern is that CQI requires a considerable time commitment. However, the authors urge surgeons to become involved in TQM since they feel that with this approach, improvement in quality rather than cost containment drives the delivery of health care.

Basmajian, Darlene
"Seeking Cost-Effectiveness and Improved Outcomes, Kaiser Permanente Cuts Variation In Clinical Care Through The TQM Process." *Strategies for Healthcare Excellence* 6, no.3 (March 1993): 7–12.
Kaiser Permanente based in Oakland, California, decided to implement TQM in 1990. The corporation, operating in twelve geographic regions, operates 29 medical centers, almost 8,000 hospital beds, 200 outpatient medical and dental offices. It has a staff of 9,000 physicians and more than 75,000 non-physician employees. Kaiser Permanente decided to launch its "Quality Agenda" in order to regain its competitive edge in an increasingly competitive managed care environment. The Quality Agenda calls for efforts to improve patient care and reduce the variation in clinical practice to produce the best possible outcomes. Kaiser's outcomes-based guidelines for clinical decision-making are being developed with the assistance of Dr. David Eddy, a national expert on outcomes-based guidelines. Eddy projects that as a result of this change in clinical practice, costs could be reduced by about 30 percent without negatively impacting quality. As of the beginning of 1993, 350 to 400 quality improvement projects were underway at Kaiser Permanente.

Bechtel, Gregory A., Janet L. Vertrees, and Barbara Swartzberg
"A Continuous Quality Improvement Approach to Medication Administration." *Journal of Nursing Care Quality* 7, no.3 (1993): 28–34.
The authors describe how a continuous quality improvement process was used in a 64-bed multi-specialty unit to track and reduce the incidence of medication errors. Flowcharting was used to visualize the medication administration process. A tracking tool was developed to sort data by event. The tracking sheet was used to code the nature, cause, and effect of the errors. Through the use of group consensus and variations, causes

for variation from the norms were established. This approach to problem-solving, which focused on the process itself rather than on penalizing individuals, decreased the incidence of medication errors.

Bender, A. Douglas, and Carla J. Krasnick
"Implementing Total Quality Management in the Medical Practice: Managing the Transition." *Health Care Supervisor* 12, no.1 (September 1993): 61–69.
The implementation of TQM in health care facilities has been critical since many employer health care plans select preferred medical care providers and hospitals based on quality and cost rankings. TQM can benefit medical practices by resulting in increased levels of patient satisfaction, reduced costs, and improved quality of work life by the fostering of teamwork, and increased productivity. Bender and Krasnick explore five aspects relating to the implementation of TQM in medical practices: patient satisfaction; billing and reimbursement; compliance with regulations and guidelines; improved documentation of patient care; and the monitoring of vendors and suppliers. The authors conclude that the successful implementation of TQM into medical practices requires the collecting and sharing of relevant information, a sense of teamwork and empowerment, and the development of problem-solving and decision-making skills.

Berwick, Donald M.
"Continuous Improvement as an Ideal in Health Care." *New England Journal of Medicine* 320, no.1 (1989): 53–56.
Donald Berwick is considered to be the "father" of the quality improvement movement in health care. This 1989 article is an important milestone. In this article, Berwick promotes the use of industrial quality techniques in health care.

Berwick, Donald M., A. Blanton Godfrey, and Jane Roessner
Curing Health Care, New Strategies for Quality Improvement: A Report on the National Demonstration Project on Quality Improvement in Health Care. San Francisco: Jossey-Bass, 1990.
The authors describe the results of the National Demonstration Project on Quality Improvement

in Health Care, an eight-month experiment directed by Dr. Donald Berwick, CEO of Boston's Institute for Health Care Improvement and A. Blanton Godfrey, chairman and CEO of the Juran Institute. They recruited 21 U.S. hospitals to use TQM to solve problems ranging from nursing/staff turnover to reducing hospital admission waiting times. The study demonstrated that quality improvement tools that have worked in other industries can work in health care. The authors drew ten major conclusions: quality improvement tools are applicable to health care; cross-functional teams are valuable in health care settings; abundant data already exists in health care organizations that quality improvement teams can use; health care staff are often receptive to learning how to use quality improvement tools; the cost of poor quality is as high in health care as in other industries; involving doctors is a challenge; training needs to be done early on; most projects chosen by quality improvement teams tend to be on nonclinical processes; health care organizations need a broader definition of quality; and successful quality improvement efforts depend on leadership.

Blunt, Mary Lucas
"Continuous Quality Improvement in Radiology." *Administrative Radiology* 11, no.11 (November 1992): 34, 39–41.

Blunt describes the continuous quality improvement process initiated by the Department of Radiology at Sentara Norfolk General Hospital in Virginia Beach, Virginia. The radiology department processed more than 135,000 examinations a year and the performance of this department directly impacted on the hospital's quality of care. Before the CQI process was in place, it took an average of 72.5 hours for physicians to get radiology test results. The CQI process, which reengineered the way work was performed, reduced this time to 11.3 hours. As a result of this dramatic improvement, the radiology department received the 1992 Quality Cup from the Rochester Institute of Technology and *USA Today*.

Bridging the Gap Between Theory + Practice: Exploring Outcomes Management. Chicago: Hospital Research and Educational Trust, 1994.

This volume contains the major papers presented at the third National Quality of Care Forum. This April 1994 symposium, held in Denver, brought together health care providers and health services researchers. This symposium examined outcomes management as a strategy to improve the quality of health care.

Burda, David
"The Two (Quality) Faces of HCHP." *Modern Healthcare* 21, no.11 (March 18, 1991): 28–29, 31.

Harvard Community Health Plan (HCHP), a health maintenance organization based in Brookline, Massachusetts, is recognized as a leader in the area of total quality management. HCHP's success was largely due to the quality improvement projects initiated by Dr. Donald Berwick, the former vice president of HCHP's quality-of-care measurement department. Dr. Berwick was awarded a grant from the John A. Hartford Foundation to test the application of TQM in health care. This and subsequent grants funded the National Demonstration Project on Quality Improvement in Health Care. Although HCHP implemented a $500,000 total quality management program, the National Demonstration Project generated almost $2 million in additional revenue for HCHP.

Bushy, Angeline
"Considerations on Implementing CQI in Rural Hospitals." *Journal of Nursing Care Quality* 7, no.2 (January 1993): 63–73.

This article focuses on the challenges involved in implementing continuous quality improvement in small, rural hospitals. Small and rural hospitals often have limited resources (in terms of time, money, and staff), making the collection and analysis of quality assurance data problematic. They also frequently lack the funds to purchase information systems to store, tabulate, and retrieve data. Only a small percentage of the budget can be allocated to continuing education, and training costs are high because of the need to travel out-of-state or great distances in order to attend seminars and conferences. A scarcity of professionals means that most professionals have multiple responsibilities, making the implementation of a continuous quality improvement program problematic because of time constraints and the potential for professional conflicts. In rural and small hospitals, maintaining confidentiality and anonymity can be more difficult, and rumors can result in misinformation about the purpose of a quality assurance program and the public perception that a hospital is providing poor service. The author offers several suggestions to help rural and small hospitals address these challenges including collaboration among several rural hospitals within a region.

Buterbaugh, Laura

"The Quality-Care Revolution." *Medical World News* 33, no.6 (June 1992): 17–21.

Strong Memorial Hospital in Rochester, New York is featured in this cover story on TQM in health care. Strong Memorial is one of more than 100 hospitals across the United States using TQM to revamp everything from the flow of preoperative tests to procedures in place for premature infant care. The author provides a selective listing (including telephone numbers) of other hospitals using TQM and describes TQM projects undertaken by other hospitals. Buterbaugh's article provides a nice summary of TQM in health care as well as a brief general history of the movement.

Cesta, Tony G.

"The Link Between Continuous Quality Improvement and Case Management." *Journal of Nursing Administration* 23, no.6 (June 1993): 55–61.

Traditionally, quality assurance in health care focuses on indicators of quality within the hospital. Some examples of global indicators include medication errors, falls, infections, deaths, and returns to the operating room. Quality assurance focuses on the measurement of these indicators. In contrast, CQI focuses on improving the conditions under which these errors occur. Cesta outlines each step in the CQI process.

Chaufournier, Roger L., and Christine St. Andre

"Total Quality Management in an Academic Health Center." *Quality Progress* 26, no.4 (April 1993): 63–66.

The George Washington University Medical Center (GWUMC) initiated a TQM program in 1989. GWUMC consists of a School of Medicine and Health Sciences, a 501 bed-licensed tertiary-care hospital, a 250-member group practice, and a health plan with 50,000 prepaid subscribers. Because management initiatives had failed in the past, GWUMC established a quality council led by the chief executive officer and executive dean of GWUMC. The council formulated the quality policy, prioritized improvement projects, supervised and supported intradepartmental and cross-functional teams, and developed strategies for identifying customer needs and expectations. GWUMC chose to follow a process improvement model developed by the Hospital Corporation of America. This model, called FOCUS-PDCA, consists of the following steps: finding a process to improve; organizing a team to improve the process; clarifying understanding of the process; understanding the source of variation; selecting interventions; planning the improvement and data collection; doing the improvement, data collection, and data analysis; checking data for process improvement, customer outcome, and lessons learned; and acting to hold, gain, and continue improvement. The model uses typical quality tools such as flowcharts, Pareto charts, and Ishikawa diagrams. Although the quality results are just becoming evident, several benefits have been noted. The accounts receivable turnaround has been reduced by twenty days over five months (the lowest recorded level in eight years). $75,000 has been saved annually in lower expenditures. Waiting time in the preadmission surgical-screening service has been decreased from several hours to an average of 50 minutes. Written complaints to the hospital have steadily decreased.

Cook, Lynn

"On the Road to TQM: A New Compensation Model." *Leadership in Health Services* 2, no.3 (May/June 1993): 26–28.

The University of Alberta Hospitals recently implemented a TQM program. In fact, it was one of the first major Canadian health care facilities to adopt TQM. This article describes how it approached the issue of management compensation. A management consulting firm worked with the hospital to develop a "competency modeling" approach. This approach describes the behavior needed for each managerial position and evaluates employee performance according to this specified set of behaviors.

Corbett, Carolyn, and Barbara Pennypacker
"Using a Quality Improvement Team to Reduce Patient Falls." *Journal for Healthcare Quality* 14, no.5 (September/October 1992): 38–41, 44–54.

These two veteran nurses describe how the nursing staff at the Robert Packer Hospital (located in Sayre, Pennsylvania) applied the principles of TQM to the problem of patient falls. A quality improvement team was established to address this serious problem (falls and complications from falls are a leading cause of death in older patients). The team (which involved nurses, nursing managers, and internal quality consultants) used a cause-and-effect diagram and a structure tree diagram to identify root causes for falls. The team targeted specific corrective actions, including the development of a fall prevention process. The fall prevention process was implemented and data indicates that it has been effective in reducing the number of falls.

Counte, Michael A., Gerald L. Glandon, Denise M. Oleske, and James P. Hill
"Total Quality Management in a Health Care Organization: How Are Employees Affected? *Hospital & Health Services Administration* 37, no.4 (Winter 1992): 503–518.

The authors studied the impact of a large-scale TQM program on employees. The site selected was an academic medical center that had introduced a large-scale TQM program two years earlier. Three types of employee outcomes were assessed: levels of job satisfaction; perceptions of organizational climate; and additional employee opinions about the organization and their specific work environment. The authors used a survey to compare the responses of TQM program participants to nonparticipants. They found that participation in the TQM program was related to a higher level of job satisfaction, more favorable perceptions of the organizational climate, more positive opinions about the organization, and a stronger endorsement of the basic principles of TQM. These findings support the general contention of TQM proponents that the implementation of a TQM program results in favorable employee outcomes.

Cox, Diane S.
"TQM: A Primer." *Association for Healthcare Philanthropy Journal* (Spring 1993): 21–24.

This article discusses how TQM can be applied to a hospital's development efforts (i.e. philanthropy). Development professionals should make donors and prospective donors feel like valued customers. Donors should be segmented (this can be done by age, sex, income level, specific interest, etc.) and development professionals should find out how to meet their individual needs. Although hospitals often survey customers about their satisfaction with care, hospitals seldom ask donors for feedback on the service they receive from the hospital's development department. Quality improvement can be just as important to the development department as it is to clinical departments.

Crawford, Frances J.
"Managing Quality and Reducing Risks in Ambulatory Surgery." *Seminars in Perioperative Nursing* 1, no.3 (July 1992): 153–166.

The Gumenick Ambulatory Care Center, an ambulatory surgery facility affiliated with Miami Beach's Mt. Sinai Medical Center, developed a ten-step quality assurance/continuous quality improvement (QA/CQI) plan in 1992 to monitor and evaluate patient care. The first step is assigning responsibility. The Gumenick Care Center's medical directors are responsible overall for the QA/CQI program. However, the nurse managers, quality assurance representatives, nursing administrator, and nursing staff are all responsible for specific tasks. For example, all of the nursing staff collect data. Step 2 is a delineation of scope of care including a description of services, staffing, and hours of service. The third step identifies "aspects of care", areas of care that frequently subject patients to risk. Step 4 identifies quality indicators related to these aspects of care. The fifth step establishes thresholds for these quality indicators. Step 6 involves the collection of data. The next step is to evaluate care when thresholds are reached. The eighth step is to take corrective action to improve care. Step 9 requires that these interventions be evaluated for effectiveness and that improvement be documented in monthly and quarterly meetings and reports. The final step requires that relevant information be reported to the hospital-wide quality assurance program.

Creps, Linda Boyle, Richard J. Coffey, Patricia A. Warren, and Kenneth D. McClatchey "Integrating Total Quality Management and Quality Assurance at the University of Michigan Medical Center." *Quality Review Bulletin* 18, no.8 (August 1992): 250–258.

In 1990, the University of Michigan Medical Center (UMMC) received the third annual Commitment to Quality Award, the only national quality award in the United States that is conferred to health care organizations. This article describes how UMMC integrated its quality assurance program with TQM. As a result, the definition of quality was expanded from improving the quality of patient care to improving the quality of all services and products for all customers (patients, physicians, suppliers, payers, etc.) While UMMC's quality assurance approach was outcome-oriented, TQM has required UMMC to focus on the improvement of processes. The quality assurance program required limited involvement by staff. In contrast, TQM required total institutional involvement. While TQM has replaced some of the weaknesses of the quality assurance program, UMMC has retained the strengths of its quality assurance program, such as its mechanism for data collection. Both of these quality approaches are regarded as compatible.

Dasbach, Erik J., and David H. Gustafson "Impacting Quality in Health Care: The Role of the Health Systems Engineer." *Journal of the Society for Health Systems* 1, no.1 (May 1989): 75–84.

This article describes the role of the health systems engineer in a hospital's TQM program. The health systems engineer can be more than a cost-cutter. A health systems engineer can support quality improvement by serving as technical facilitator, measurer, and modeler.

Decker, Michael D. "The Application of Continuous Quality Improvement to Healthcare." *Infection Control and Hospital Epidemiology* 13, no.4 (April 1992): 226–229.

The author explains how the principles of continuous quality improvement (CQI) or TQM can be applied to health care. CQI can be an effective strategy for those health care organizations that want to gain a competitive edge, reduce costs, and improve employee satisfaction. However, there is one compelling reason for adopting TQM: the Joint Commission for the Accreditation of Healthcare Organizations (JCAHO) will incorporate new standards (effective with the 1994 *Accreditation Manual for Hospitals* (AMH) that address quality improvements in several areas. Consequently, it is crucial that health care professionals familiarize themselves with the theory and practice of total quality management.

Downs, Kathleen, and Willard D. McKinney "Providing Justification for Training: An Application of Total Quality Management Tools." *Biomedical Instrumentation & Technology* 27, no.2 (March/April 1993): 109–115.

The authors describe the quality management program (QMP) implemented at the University of California, San Diego Medical Center. Clinical Engineering Services (CES) was the first department to receive training in the QMP process. All thirteen members of CES participated in a team. The article describes the team's training. Training covered five major areas: administrative training; electronic training; mechanical training; new equipment training; and interdepartment training. The time spent on training averaged 56 hours (over four months) per employee.

Dressman, Kathleen L. "Lessons Learned From an Early TQM Effort: Surgical Prophylaxis." *Journal of Nursing Care Quality* 7, no.4 (July 1993): 73–81.

Dressman, a Nursing Quality Improvement Coordinator at Cincinnati's Bethesda North Hospital, describes how TQM can be used to improve the timeliness of administration of preoperative prophylactic antibiotics for surgical patients. The hospital's parent company, Bethesda Hospital Inc., initiated a five-year organization-wide TQM implementation plan in 1989. Bethesda Hospital, Inc. is a not-for-profit hospital system in Cincinatti, Ohio that operates two acute care hospitals, a home health agency, a durable equipment company, and a senior services division. A team decided to study the process of preoperative prophylactic antibiotic administration. Five different processes were flowcharted. During the study period, a total of 345 antibiotics were administered and data indicated that 49 percent of the antibiotics were administered too early or too late. Histograms helped the team identify the root causes of the problem.

Dunne, Patrick K.
"Total Quality Management: The Results of Quality Improvement Teams." *Topics in Hospital Pharmacy Management* 12, no.4 (January 1993): 43–57.

Dunne describes the accomplishments of the quality improvement teams within the pharmacy department at The Toledo Hospital in Toledo, Ohio. There are four quality improvement program (QIP) teams – one lead team and three functional teams. The lead team monitors the QIP of the entire pharmacy department, provides motivation for the other teams, and ensures that the department provides resources for QIP teams. The RXEllence functional team was established to develop a system to decrease the number of unnecessary phone calls to the unit dose area of the pharmacy department. The Med Masters functional team focused on theophylline usage and monitoring. The Pills and Thrills functional team looked at the prescription-filling process for take-home prescriptions for patients being discharged from the hospital.

Dwore, Richard B.
"Managing Hospital Quality Performance in Two Related Areas: Patient Care and Customer Service." *Hospital Topics* 71, no.2 (Spring 1993): 29–34.

Customer service and patient care are complementary aspects of quality. While patient care is the core product, customer service augments it by adding value and giving hospitals an advantage over their competitors. This article differentiates patient care from customer service, discusses issues that hospital administrators need to consider before including customer service as an element of quality improvement, and identifies interventions necessary in order for hospitals to change.

Eastman, C. J.
"Total Quality Management: The Challenge for Hospitals in the 1990s." *Medical Journal of Australia* 157, no.4 (August 17, 1992): 219–220.

Although traditional quality assurance methods and programs have been extensively applied at all levels of the Australian health care system, few Australian hospitals or large health care institutions have implemented TQM. In this editorial, Eastman contends that the application of TQM to the delivery of health care in Australia will require a dramatic change in the way health care organizations think about quality. Eastman's theory is that Australian health care providers have been reluctant to embrace TQM because they think they are already practicing TQM.

Eubanks, Paula
"Work Redesign Calls for New Pay and Performance Plans." *Hospitals* 66, no.19 (October 5, 1992): 56, 58, 60.

TQM/CQI initiatives in health care are forcing hospitals to change employee payment and performance systems. Traditional compensation systems tend to reward individual achievement and competition rather than teamwork and collaboration. Pay and performance systems have to be redesigned to address hospitals' growing use of self-directed teams, cross-functional workers, and multi-skilled employees.

Evaluating the Performance of the Hospital CEO in a Total Quality Management Environment. Chicago, IL: American College of Healthcare Executives; American Hospital Association, 1993.

This monograph, published jointly by the American College of Healthcare Executives and the American Hospital Association, addresses several issues related to CEO evaluation in a TQM environment. For example, who should evaluate the CEO? How frequently should evaluation be performed? This book flowcharts the process for evaluating CEO performance.

Flanel, Deborah Ford, and Michele M. Fairchild
"Continuous Quality Improvement in Inpatient Clinical Nutrition Services." *Journal of the American Dietetic Association* 95, no.1 (January 1995): 65–74.

The Yale–New Haven Hospital Department of Food and Nutrition has had quality programs in place since 1984. This article describes how the Department applied Joint Commission on Accreditation of Healthcare Organizations (JCAHO) quality improvement initiatives to their existing nutrition practice guidelines. This case study can serve as a model for other dietetics departments that are developing a CQI program or building upon an existing quality program.

Flower, Joe

"Benchmarking: Tales From the Front." *Healthcare Forum* 36, no.1 (January/February 1993): 37–51.

Flower discusses why health care organizations should benchmark. Two reasons for benchmarking are that it allows organizations to identify gaps in performance and to select processes to improve, and secondly, it accelerates change in an organization. The benchmarking experiences of several organizations are profiled. Although most are hospitals and health care organizations, Flower includes other types of organizations that have led the way in benchmarking. This excellent article concludes with a descriptive listing of benchmarking resources in health care and an annotated bibliography of books on benchmarking.

Fried, Robert A.

"TQM in the Medical School: A Report From the Field." *Annual Quality Congress Transactions* 45 (1991): 113–118.

The Department of Family Medicine at the University of Colorado School of Medicine operates a clinical practice, the Family Medicine Center (FMC). During the 1987–88 academic year, the staff of the FMC concluded that quality of service had to improve, or the patient base might erode. Several quality improvement projects were undertaken during the next few years. The author describes both the successful and not so successful quality improvement initiatives. Projects have addressed issues ranging from nurse preparation of patients for physicians to patient flow.

Friedman, Candace, *et al.*

"Use of the Total Quality Process in an Infection Control Program: A Surprising Customer-Needs Assessment." *American Journal of Infection Control* 21, no.3 (June 1993): 155–159.

The University of Michigan Hospitals (UMH) began a quality improvement initiative in 1987 under the name Total Quality Process (TQP). The Infection Control Services (ICS) department (which consists of six staff members) became a functional quality improvement team in 1989.

The team used TQP to develop a mission statement, identify their customers, and collect data regarding customers' needs and expectations. A telephone survey was used to gather information about customers needs and their suggestions for improvement. Customers were defined to include physicians, nurses, ancillary and support staff, patients, the patient's family, visitors, regulatory agencies, other infection control departments, and the public. The survey revealed differences between perceived customer requirements (that is, what the team thought customers needed) and actual requirements for customers. As a result of these differences, several improvements were outlined and implemented within six months of the survey. For example, customers indicated that they wanted ICS staff to be more accessible. In order to improve this situation, the department made paging system changes and added a phone message system.

Frist, Thomas, Jr.

"TQM at HCA." *Health Systems Review* 25, no.3 (May/June 1992): 15–18.

Health Corporation of America (HCA) has been a pioneer in the quality improvement movement. Although HCA's corporate overhead was reduced from $100 million to $24 million between 1987 and 1990, the company increased its commitment to HCA's quality resource group. This feature article includes an interview with HCA's chief executive officer. HCA's commitment to quality has led to some impressive results. For example, at one HCA hospital, the Caesarean section rate decreased from 21 percent to 15 percent. Another hospital saved up to two days of hospital stay for patients undergoing total joint replacement, by changing the pain management process.

Gann, Margery, J., and Joseph D. Restuccia

"Total Quality Management in Health Care: A View of Current and Potential Research." *Medical Care Review* 51, no.4 (Winter 1994): 467–500.

The literature on TQM in health care has exploded since the publication of a seminal article on continuous improvement by Donald M. Berwick in the January 1989 issue of *The New England Journal of Medicine*. Gann and Restuccia break down the health care literature on TQM into five broad categories: literature discussing the philosophy of TQM; literature discussing theoretical implementation models; literature that provides anecdotal accounts of implementation; literature produced by consultants for largely publicity purposes; and technical papers demonstrating how to adapt CQI/TQM to health care. This review article is indispensable, given the sheer volume of articles on continuous improvement in health care. More importantly, the authors identify basic criteria for reliability and validity in research and judge twenty-five published studies about TQM in health care against these criterion. For example, their review of the literature indicates that there is a need for reliable and validated studies on the effectiveness of TQM in four critical areas: the efficiency of the health care process; improving patient outcome; cost controls; and perceived quality of health care by customers. Research also needs to be conducted in order to determine what a health care organization means by TQM/CQI, the value of TQM to the organization, and which components of TQM have the greatest impact on operational, financial, and clinical success.

Gaucher, Ellen J., and Richard J. Coffey

Total Quality in Healthcare: From Theory to Practice. San Francisco: Jossey-Bass, 1993.

This is an account of the development of total quality management at the University of Michigan's Medical Center (UMMC). UMMC has been involved in TQM since 1987, when it participated in the National Demonstration Project on Quality Improvement in Health Care. Pilot teams were established in 1988. In 1990, UMMC was awarded the Healthcare Forum/Witt Award for its commitment to quality. This chronicle is divided into four parts. Part One sets the stage, discussing UMMC's reason for implementing TQM. Part Two shows how UMMC created a TQM culture. Part Three examines quality improvement methods. In the final section, the authors give some advice for organizations considering TQM. This well-written practical guide has been designed as a "how to" book for health care professionals.

Geber, Beverly

"Can TQM Cure Health Care?" *Training* 29, no.8 (August 1992): 25–34.

This cover story traces the history of the quality improvement movement in the health care industry. Hospitals were relatively late to implement TQM. The health care industry did not realize TQM's potential for lowering costs and improving care until the late 1980s. Most hospitals began to implement TQM with small team-based process improvement efforts involving support services (e.g., improving patient meals), direct medical care – such as lowering the Caesarean section rate, or the medical infrastructure – such as revamping the scheduling of operating rooms.

Gelinas, Lillie Smith, and Marie Manthey

"Improving Patient Outcomes Through System Change: A Focus on the Changing Roles of Healthcare Organization Executives." *Journal of Nursing Administration* 25, no.5 (May 1995): 55–63.

VHA, Inc., is a national network of more than 1,100 health care organizations. The authors conducted thirty-six in-depth interviews with executives from thirteen VHA health care organizations that have undergone work redesign. The motivations for redesign ranged from a need to reassess operations because of funding shortages, to concern that inefficiencies of operations and work redundancies would impair the organization's ability to move into the future. The specific change process used these elements: visioning; interdisciplinary team building; work process analysis; interactive planning; and extensive training of managers and staff. There were three major types of changes: delivery of patient care; administrative/management changes; and consortium development. When asked how their role changed, CEOs commented on the kinds of skills and attributes required for success. Some traits included creativity, an ability to cope with ambiguity, and a willingness to give up control. Several suggested techniques for enlisting physician support including the use of well-respected "champion" physicians to carry the message and achieving tangible benefits before involving physicians. Although the authors' observations are based on a limited number of responses, their research does indicate that those organizations that have successfully managed change have been led by managers who are committed to work redesign and who are willing to take risks.

Graham, Nancy O., ed.
Quality in Health Care: Theory, Application, and Evolution. Gaithersburg, MD: Aspen, 1995.

This is a revised edition of Graham's earlier book *Quality Assurance in Hospitals*, which was first published in 1982 and updated in 1990. This version brings together reprints of significant works on quality in health care as well as some important general works on quality such as Peter Senge's 1992 article "Building Learning Organizations." The books is organized in three parts: "Yesterday," "Today," and "Tomorrow." Several valuable appendices are included: a case study of TQM in a community hospital; an article about the Health Care Quality Improvement Initiative, the Health Care Financing Administration's new approach to quality assurance in Medicare; the Joint Commission on Accreditation of Healthcare Organizations' clinical performance standards; and a glossary of terms. This compilation of essential articles on quality in health care will be invaluable to students in health care, health care managers, health planners, quality improvement professionals, health care practitioners, and other professionals.

Grayson, Mary A.
"Benchmark TQM Survey Tracks a New Management Era in Administration." *Hospitals* 66 (June 5, 1992): 26–27.

A March 1992 survey conducted by *Hospitals* magazine and the ServiceMaster Company found that almost 60 percent of 781 responding hospital CEOs indicated that they have a TQM/CQI program in place. Seventy-five percent of those without a program indicated that they planned to start one within the next fiscal year. Data indicated that large urban hospitals are more likely to have a TQM program up and running. Most TQM programs are relatively new – survey data indicated that the average program was only 1.4 years old. The survey also looked at CEO support, consultant support, TQM budgets, return on investment, and leadership. Survey data revealed that CEOs spend an average of about 17 percent of their time directing or reviewing TQM activities. Their level of commitment to TQM (on a scale of one to five, five being most committed) averaged 4.6. Most CEOs (61.2 percent) have not hired a TQM consultant. Ninty-four percent of CEOS indicated that the expense of their TQM program would not threaten its continuation, while 94.1 percent of CEOs expect a financial return in terms of improved operational efficiency. Only 77 percent of CEOs indicated that they regretted implementing TQM.

Hamilton, Jim
"Toppling the Power of the Pyramid: Team-Based Restructuring for TQM, Patient-Centered Care." *Hospitals* 67, no.1 (January 5, 1993): 38–41.

The success of TQM in the health care industry depends upon changing the organizational structure of hospitals and other health care organizations. The traditional functional-hierarchical organization must be replaced with a team-based structure. In this new model, different teams would focus on major care processes involved in delivery and supporting patient care. While some teams would be ongoing, others would be short-term special project teams. In this team-based structure, team leaders and facilitators replace layers of management. Authority and decision-making are the responsibility of each team member. Each team communicates directly to customers, suppliers, and other teams. Reward systems acknowledge team contributions.

Hard, Rob
"Hospitals Look into Hospitality Service Firms to Meet TQM Goals." *Hospitals* 66 (May 20, 1992): 56, 58.

Hospitals that hire contract management firms to manage their foodservice, housekeeping, and laundry services are expecting these contract management firms to help meet their TQM goals. Peter Drucker has argued that contracting out production-type service work may be the only way for an organization to obtain productivity gains. A 1992 survey of 1,090 hospital CEOs found a high degree of satisfaction with contract service firms. Approximately 44 percent of the 495 hospitals responding to this survey indicated that their service contracts included quality improvement specifications.

Headrick, Linda, Duncan Neuhauser, and Joy Melnikow
"Asthma Health Status: Ongoing Measurement in the Context of Continuous Quality Improvement." *Medical Care* 31, no.3, Supplement (March 1993): MS97-MS105.

Since 1989, medical students enrolled in the primary care core clerkships at Case Western Reserve University's School of Medicine have used CQI methods to collect data about the health status of asthma patients in the Cleveland area. This task was part of a project to introduce them to CQI techniques. However, students found that CQI techniques could be used to understand and reduce variation in health status.

Headrick, Linda, William Katcher, Duncan Neuhauser, and Edward McEachern
"Continuous Quality Improvement and Knowledge for Improvement Applied to Asthma Care." *The Joint Commission Journal on Quality Improvement* 20, no.10 (October 1994): 562–568.

This article explores the relationship between professional knowledge and knowledge for improvement and the "bad apple" theory to explain variation in outcomes. These theories are applied to data from the Cleveland Asthma Project, an ongoing project at Case Western Reserve University in which medical students observe and report on the cost and outcomes of care for asthma patients in the Cleveland area. The authors found that most of the causes of variation in asthma care are not due to professional knowledge (that is, pathophysiology and therapeutics). The most frequent cause of variation was disease severity. Since only one site classified as a bad apple (a site where average costs fell outside the upper boundary of expected costs), eliminating bad apples will have little impact on overall improvement. The authors concluded that improving asthma care will require combining professional knowledge with knowledge for improvement.

Horine, Patrick D., Eric D. Pohjala, and Randall W. Luecke
"Healthcare Financial Managers and CQI." *Healthcare Financial Management* 47, no.9 (September 1993): 34, 36–37.

This article discusses the role health care financial managers can play in the CQI process. In addition to supporting a hospital's CQI process, financial managers can provide teams with data, answer questions on reimbursement matters, and perform financial modeling to assess the impact of recommendations made by teams. The authors provide financial managers with a brief overview of five commonly used quality tools: brainstorming, checklists, flowcharts, cause-and-effect diagrams, and Pareto diagrams. They also provide some examples of practical applications of CQI in hospitals. For example, CQI can be used to improve the accuracy of patient information, reduce waiting time, reduce the number of forms that need to be completed, improve operating room turnaround time, reduce supply costs, reduce and eliminate rebilling, and improve billing accuracy.

Hughes, Jay M.
"Total Quality Management in a 300-Bed Community Hospital: The Quality Improvement Process Translated to Health Care." *Quality Review Bulletin* 18, no.9 (September 1992): 293–300.

The Winter Park Memorial Hospital (WPMH), located in Winter Park, Florida, is a 300-bed nonprofit community hospital that includes an ambulatory care center, a cancer care center, a women's health center, an outpatient diagnostic clinic, and a psychiatric pavillion. In 1987, WPMH began to implement TQM. TQM guru Philip Crosby serves on the hospital board of trustees and his consulting firm, Philip Crosby Associates, is headquartered there. Although Crosby had a vast amount of experience with industrial quality management, few hospitals had much experience with TQM in 1987. However, through the help of Crosby Associates, the hospital successfully implemented TQM, saving thousands of dollars. This article describes the TQM implementation process at WPMH.

The International Quality Study: Best Practices Report – An Analysis of Management Practices that Impact Performance. Cleveland, OH: Ernst & Young; New York: American Quality Foundation, 1992.

The International Quality Study (IQS) was a study of the best management practices across four industries (health care, banking, automotive, and computer) within four industrialized countries (Canada, Germany, Japan, and the United States).

This study was a joint project of Ernst & Young (one of the world's leading consulting firms) and the American Quality Foundation (an independent, nonprofit research organization established by the American Society of Quality Control). The results of the IQS has international significance since the findings serve as a benchmark for quality progress. The IQS was conducted using a self-administered questionnaire. The survey grouped questions into five major categories: business organization; product/service development; delivery process and customer satisfaction; quality and strategic positioning; and culture. The IQS study found that these four industries have many common practices contributing to world class quality and service delivery. The IQS also demonstrated that industries can learn from unrelated industries. The IQS has analyzed more than 900 management practices in more than 500 organizations. Analysts found that some practices take longer to impact performance. The *Best Practices Report* identifies which management practices work. Earlier IQS reports included *The Top-Line Findings*, a report focusing on the ways businesses across all these industries and companies are managing the improvement process, and the four IQS industry reports detailing the specific findings for the health care, automotive, banking, and computer industries. All these reports may be obtained through the American Society of Quality Control.

Jablonski, Robert
"Customer Focus: The Cornerstone of Quality Management." *Healthcare Financial Management* 46, no.11 (November 1992): 17–18.

Identifying customers is more difficult for health care organizations because of the unique nature of the industry. Most service industries define customers as the party receiving service and the party from whom revenue is received. However, in the case of health care, revenue is collected from many third parties (such as insurance companies and government agencies) that are not even present when a service is performed. Health care organizations must define customers to include not only patients but other internal customers and external customers (that is, individuals or groups outside the organization) who receive services and/or provide revenue. Examples of internal customers are physicians, nurses, technicians, administrators, and other professionals who provide services. Some examples of external customers include referring physicians, regulatory agencies, patients' families, and third party payers.

Kaluzny, Arnold D., Curtis P. McLaughlin, and B. Jon Jaeger
"TQM as Managerial Innovation: Research Issues and Implications." *Health Services Management Research* 6, no.2 (May 1993): 78–88.

The authors analyze TQM as an innovation. Innovation theory is associated with two perspectives: variance and process. Variance theory is concerned with outcomes that are measured quantitatively. Process theory is concerned with the particular steps or events in the overall adoption process. The authors discuss the managerial implications for each perspective.

Katz, Jacqueline, and Eleanor Green
Managing Quality: A Guide to Monitoring and Evaluating Nursing Services. St. Louis, MO: Mosby, 1992.

The purpose of this book is to help nursing professionals make the transition from quality assurance to total quality management/continuous quality improvement. Part One provides an overview of quality management. The second part outlines a step-by-step plan for using the Joint Commission on Accreditation of Health Care Organization's ten-step process for monitoring and evaluating quality. This "blueprint for quality management" consists of the following steps: assigning responsibility; delineating the scope of care and service; defining important aspects of care and service; identifying indicators; establishing thresholds for evaluation; collecting and organizing data; evaluating variations; taking action; assessing the actions and documenting improvement; and communicating relevant information to the organization-wide quality assurance program. The final section of the book focuses on the management of quality in a quality management program.

Kerley, Frank R., and Brent E. Nissly
"Total Quality Management and Statistical Quality Control: Practical Applications to Waste Stream Management." *Hospital Material Management Quarterly* 14, no.2 (November 1992): 40–59.

The authors use a hypothetical scenario involving a 400-bed hospital to demonstrate how TQM can be applied to medical waste stream management. The application of TQM requires quality improvement teams to apply statistical process control techniques to reduce medical waste. Among the techniques for studying and analyzing the flow of medical waste are histograms, control charts, check sheets, Pareto charts, cause-and-effect diagrams, and scattergrams. Each technique is defined and illustrated with great clarity, making this case study useful to managers in general, not just hospital administrators.

Kerr, Bernard J., Jr.
"The TQM Critic: A Rational Revolutionary?" *Healthcare Financial Management* 47, no.9 (September 1993): 76–81.

Kerr's contention is that employees should be able to offer constructive criticism on the TQM process itself. In fact, their criticism can be conducive to TQM. Enlisting criticism is consistent with one of TQM's basic principles – a willingness to accept risk.

Koch, Marylane Wade, and Terryl Macline Fairly
Integrated Quality Management: The Key to Improving Nursing Care Quality. St. Louis, MO: Mosby, 1993.

The authors outline a model for integrating quality management into continuous quality improvement for improved patient care outcomes. The first chapter provides an introduction to quality management and discusses the implications for nursing. Chapter 2 discusses the processes of quality management. Chapter 3 reviews the history of quality management in business and health care. Chapter 4 describes regulations that impact quality management. Chapters 5 through 8 describe specific processes in integrated quality management. Chapter 9 explains Neuman's Systems Model, a conceptual framework for the integrated quality management model. Chapter 10 shows how improved patient outcomes can result from interdisciplinary quality improvement teams. Chapters 11 through 14 provide examples of integrated quality management in diverse health care settings including acute care, home care, long-term care, and ambulatory care. The final chapter explores future issues and trends.

Koska, Mary T.
"Case Study: Quality Improvement in a Diversified Health Center." *Hospitals* 64 (December 5, 1990): 38–39.

In 1987, Chicago's Rush-Presbyterian-St. Luke's Medical Center became the Minnesota Mining and Manufacturing (3M) Company's alpha site for testing TQM in health care. The Rush health system includes an urban 983-bed facility, two suburban hospitals, a health sciences university, an HMO (health maintenance organization) with sixteen sites, a preferred provider organization, an independent practice association, a home health nursing service, six occupational health clinics, and a for-profit subsidiary that markets health care products to corporations and other health care settings. The entire system was scheduled to be using the TQM process in some form by late 1995. Within three years of implementing TQM, Rush has seen a return on its investment in the form of a decrease in the X-ray repeat rate, a reduction in laboratory result turnaround time, a reduction in the number of checks manually typed by the accounts payable department, and an improvement in patient transport.

Koska, Mary T.
"Using CQI Methods to Lower Postsurgical Wound Infection Rate." *Hospitals* 66, no.9 (May 5, 1992): 62–64.

One Salt Lake City (Utah) hospital has significantly lowered the rate of postsurgical wound infection thanks to continuous quality improvement techniques. Researchers at the Intermountain Health Care's (IHC) LDS Hospital found that antibiotics administered to patients within two hours of surgery dramatically reduced post surgical wound infections. LDS researchers tracked infection rates in almost 3,000 elective surgeries conducted at the hospital between 1985 and 1986. As a result of clinical research, the hospital changed its antibiotics protocols, reducing the postsurgical wound infection rate from 1.8 percent to 0.4 percent over a six-year period.

Koska, Mary T.
"CEOs Say Hospitals Must Learn From Each Other for TQM Success." *Hospitals* 66 (June 20, 1992): 42, 46, 48, 50.

These interviews with hospital CEOs who were three to five years into their TQM/CQI programs offer hospital administrators many practical tips on implementing TQM. The CEO of Atlanta's West Paces Ferry Hospital (one of the first hospitals to implement TQM) stressed the importance of physicians buying into TQM and concluded that this can be more easily achieved by appealing to physicians' scientific backgrounds and by avoiding the use of TQM jargon. The CEO of Cincinnati's Bethesda Hospital, Inc., stressed the value of having a physician champion to introduce staff to TQM. Bethesda hired a physician with an MBA to introduce TQM to hospital staff. Most of the CEOs interviewed believed that a focus on the patient yields the best results.

Koska, Mary T.
"Surveying Customer Needs, Not Satisfaction, is Crucial to CQI." *Hospitals* 66, no.21 (November 5, 1992): 50–54.

Hospitals have to expand their definition of customers to include patients, third-party payers, government regulators, employees, physicians, and other internal customers. Survey instruments and other data collection tools must focus on determining customers' specific needs in order to chart process improvement plans. The article uses a customer satisfaction survey designed by the University of Wisconsin Hospital (UWH) in Madison, Wisconsin as an example. When UWH surveyed breast cancer patients, the questionnaire asked questions such as "How well did we help you understand what it would be like when you woke up after surgery?", instead of a general question such as "How do you like our doctors?". The survey results indicated that breast cancer patients needed quick access to information about the disease and that they wanted to be able to communicate with other breast patients privately. UWH established a service giving patients diagnosed with breast cancer the opportunity to take home a computer allowing them to access a library of articles, consult a list of frequently asked questions about breast cancer, and write letters to other breast cancer patients.

Kravolec, O. John, Carol A. Huttner, and Mark D. Dixon
"The Application of Total Quality Management Concepts in a Service-Line Cardiovascular Program." *Nursing Administration Quarterly* 15, no.2 (Winter 1991): 1–8.

In 1989, Abbott Northwestern Hospital in Minneapolis applied the principles of TQM/CQI to its cardiovascular program, which is the largest product line of the hospital and the largest cardiovascular program in the region. In 1989, the unit performed 5,000 cardiovascular laboratory procedures, 1,168 open heart surgeries, and 972 percutaneous coronary angioplasty procedures. Within a two-year period, the continuous quality improvement process yielded a 6 percent saving and the construction of a new 22-bed telemetry unit was deferred by reducing the overall length of stay in the cardiovascular program.

Kritchevsky, Stephen B., and Bryan P. Simmons
"Continuous Quality Improvement: Concepts and Applications for Physician Care." *JAMA* 266, no.13 (October 2, 1991): 1817–1823.

After presenting an overview of CQI, the authors provide examples of how these concepts can be applied to improve the quality of physician care. They break down CQI into four tasks. The first is the separation of externally caused problems from systemic problems. The second task is to monitor the system to make sure no new external causes are introduced. The third step is studying the system to identify how problems arise within the system. The final step is evaluating the efficacy of changes to the system.

Larsen, Gail
"Improving Outpatient Registration with TQM." *Healthcare Financial Management* 47, no.8 (August 1993): 75, 77, 79–81.

Larsen describes how TQM can be applied in outpatient services. She provides an example of using TQM to improve the performance of a hospital's outpatient registration department. Quality improvement can easily be measured by using quantifiable benchmarks already existing in most hospital information systems, such as average waiting time in registration, number of patient complaints, and the number of rejected outpatient bills due to registration errors. Improvements in the registration department can result in improved customer satisfaction, increased revenue, and enhanced hospital–physician relationships.

Leebov, Wendy, and Gail Scott
Service Quality Improvement: The Customer Satisfaction Strategy for Health Care. Chicago, IL: American Hospital Publishing, 1994.

The authors have assisted numerous hospitals, ambulatory care centers, and nursing homes in the implementation of quality improvement strategies, They firmly believe that a successful quality improvement program begins with recognition of the importance of a customer focus. This practical handbook introduces readers to service quality improvement and discusses the "ten pillars" of continuous improvement: management vision and commitment; accountability; measurement and feedback; problem-solving and process improvement; communication; staff development and training; physician involvement; reward and recognition; employee involvement and empowerment; and reminders and refreshers. They also outline operational strategies for achieving service quality in health care.

Lengnick-Hall, Cynthia A.
"The Patient as the Pivot Point for Quality in Health Care Delivery." *Hospital & Health Services Administration* 40, no.1 (Spring 1995): 25–39.

The author presents a patient-centered model of quality. This conceptual model focuses on the four diverse roles that patients play in health care systems. These multiple roles include the patient as supplier, the patient as product, the patient as participant, and the patient as recipient. This article represents an important contribution to the health care literature since this multidimensional role is generally ignored. Most of the literature on health care quality simply views patients as service recipients. Lengnick-Hall outlines strategies for enhancing quality through patient/suppliers, through patient/participants, through patient products, and through patient/recipients.

Le Tort, Nancy R., and Jane Boudreaux
"Incorporation of Continuous Quality Improvement in a Hospital Dietary Department's Quality Management Program." *Journal of the American Dietetic Association* 94, no.12 (December 1994): 1404–1408.

The authors outline how hospital dietary departments can make the transition from quality assurance to continuous quality improvement.

Their transition strategy consists of the following steps: educating managers and other involved staff about CQI; identifying customers' needs and expectations through oral and/or written surveys; and using the FOCUS-PDCA method to implement a CQI program. The FOCUS-PDCA technique was developed by the Quality Resource Group at Hospital Corporation of America (Nashville Tennessee). The acronym stands for the following sequential steps: finding a process to improve; organizing a team; clarifying current knowledge of the process; understanding the cause of process variation; selecting the process improvement; planning; doing; checking; and acting.

Lewis, Al
"Too Many Managers: Major Threat to CQI in Hospitals." *Quality Review Bulletin* 19, no.3 (March 1993): 95–101.

In order for CQI to work, the author contends that the number of middle managers must be decreased and employees must be empowered. However, most hospitals have failed to do this because of their failure to understand the concept of "span of control" and their fear that staff reductions would jeopardize the implementation of CQI. Lewis provides case studies of both effective and ineffective management of CQI in health care organizations.

Lewis, Al, and Joanne Lamprey
"Averting CQI Failure: Five Early Warning Signs." *Health Care Strategic Management* 10, no.7 (July 1992): 9–10.

This article identifies five signals that may be warnings to hospital administrators that their TQM/CQI program is in danger of failing. The first sign is lack of employee interest. The second warning signal is when hospitals opt for an activity-oriented CQI program rather than a results-oriented program. The third problem is mistaken priorities. Warning sign number four is physician indifference. The fifth red flag is a failure to define quality. For each warning sign, the authors propose a solution.

Lumsdon, Kevin
"TQM Shifts Hospital – Vendor Focus to Total Value, Productivity." *Hospitals* 66, no.13 (July 5, 1992): 114–117.

Hospitals are working with suppliers and vendors to cut costs. It is estimated that 75 percent of a hospital's supply costs involve the logistics of moving supplies and the expense of completing the paperwork involved with the distribution and delivery of products. This article describes several successful partnerships between hospitals and vendors that have resulted in savings. The Baton Rouge (Louisiana) General Medical Center is pilot testing a vendor certification program which involves collecting data on the accuracy of shipments from suppliers and eventually, the implementation of an electronic payment system in order to eliminate billing paperwork. The Atlantic City (New Jersey) Medical Center has formed an alliance with four vendors. This system has been modeled after 3M Health Care, the 3M Corporation's alliance with Abbott Laboratories, General Medical Corporation, and Standard Register. Many hospitals have learned that vendors can offer insight about what works in quality improvement, since they have been involved in TQM much longer than most hospitals.

Lumsdon, Kevin, and Rob Hard
"Medical Imaging." *Hospitals* 66 (November 5, 1992): 56–62.

Medical imaging departments may be perfect candidates for TQM because of their linkages to other areas and functions of the hospital, the amount of money spent on the purchase and maintenance of expensive equipment, the health risks posed by unnecessary testing, and radiology's important links to physician and patient satisfaction. In recent years, hospitals have paid more attention to two important issues in radiology: the management of equipment maintenance costs and investments in image storage and transfer systems (also known as PACS, or picture archiving and communications systems). Radiology departments are turning to TQM to tackle problems such as missing film, patient waiting time, delayed test report results, and escalating equipment repair costs.

McEachern, J. Edward, Lorraine Schiff, and Oscar Cogan
"How to Start a Direct Patient Care Team." *Quality Review Bulletin* 18, no.6 (June 1992): 191–200.

HCA West Paces Ferry Hospital, a hospital located in suburban Atlanta (Georgia) has seventeen direct patient care teams. The authors outline the subtle differences between direct patient care teams and administrative cross-functional teams. They believe that direct patient care teams will become more prevalent in hospitals. Two case studies from HCA West Paces Ferry Hospital are used to illustrate factors that can enhance as well as hinder the success of direct patient care teams. One case study involves an HIV team. The other case study involves a chest pain team.

McLaughlin, Curtis P., and Arnold D. Kaluzny
"Total Quality Management in Health: Making it Work." *Health Care Management Review* 15, no.3 (Summer 1990): 7–14.

The authors view TQM as a total paradigm shift in health care management. They identify potential conflicts between TQM and traditional health care management. Some potential conflict areas include TQM's emphasis on collective responsibility versus individual responsibility, accountability versus autonomy, participation versus administrative and professional authority, and benchmarking versus responding to complaints. McLaughlin and Kaluzny suggest eleven action guidelines for the successful implementation of TQM, ranging from redefining the role of the professional to making the TQM program a model for organization-wide continuous improvement.

Mannello, Tim
A CQI System for Healthcare: How the Williamsport Hospital Brings Quality to Life. New York: Quality Resources, 1995.

This entire book is the study of continuous quality improvement in one hospital, the Williamsport Hospital & Medical Center, located in Williamsport, Pennsylvania. In 1993, the hospital received Healthcare Forum's "Commitment to Quality Award." This well written account provides a wealth of practical information that can be useful to any hospital involved in implementing a quality improvement program.

McLaughlin, Curtis P., and Arnold D. Kaluzny
Continuous Quality Improvement in Health Care: Theory, Implementation, and Applications. Gaithersburg, MD: Aspen, 1994.

This book has been designed primarily as a text for graduate students in health services management. It consists of writings reprinted or adapted from previously published books and articles as well as original material. The book is divided into five parts. Part I brings together chapters that introduce readers to the principles of TQM/CQI and the application of TQM/CQI to health care organizations. The second part focuses on the basics of TQM/CQI: the outcome model of quality, measurement and statistical analysis, measuring customer satisfaction, the role of teams, and the economic context of TQM. Part III looks at the implementation of TQM, including a chapter on involving clinicians. Part IV includes chapters dealing with the application of TQM/CQI in various settings including primary care, laboratories, public health organizations, and academic health centers. Part V includes five case studies of the development of TQM/CQI in various settings.

"Medical Imaging: Hospitals Give Renewed Attention to Service, Costs, Flow of Images." *Hospitals* 66 (November 5, 1992): 56–62.

This special report on medical imaging concludes that hospital imaging departments could benefit from the implementation of a TQM program. Radiology departments across the United States are coping with a growth in the volume of patients and procedures. Yet most radiology departments are unable to track costs such as a missing or lost film, or the expenses incurred in maintaining expensive equipment. This report focuses on two areas of improvement: controlling equipment repair costs and the development of picture archiving and communications systems (i.e. image storage and transfer systems).

Melum, Mara Minerva
"Total Quality Management: Steps to Success." *Hospitals* 64 (December 5, 1990): 42, 44.

This brief introduction to TQM for health care professionals identifies seven critical success factors. These include the following: a vision of quality; an understanding of the TQM process; a motivation to change; management leadership; physician commitment; teamwork; and the integration of TQM into the hospital's support system.

Milakovich, Michael E.
"Creating a Total Quality Health Care Environment." *Health Care Management Review* 16 (Spring 1991): 9–20.

Milakovich defines the concept of Total Quality Care (TQC) and illustrates how hospitals and other health care organizations can implement continuous quality improvement. TQC is a combination of the following characteristics: applied modern high technology; access to facilities at reasonable costs; patient-centered care; and low-tech holistic human healing skills. TQC stresses continuous process improvement, the use of statistical tools for decision-making and evaluation, teamwork, and a customer orientation. Milakovich provides guidelines for the implementation of TQC.

Moskowitz, Samuel E., James E. Hosking, and Boyd O. Bower
"Community Leads to Hospital Planning." *Trustee* 46, no.2 (February 1993): 20–22.

The principles of TQM were used by the planning and building committee of the Atlantic General Hospital, a hospital under construction in Berlin, Maryland. This committee was composed of physicians, nurses, trustees, and members of the community. Two basic tenets of TQM are recognizing customer expectations, and improving products or services through the use of teams. The Atlantic General Hospital defined customers as the community-at-large, medical staff, nursing staff, and other professional services personnel from area hospitals. Interdisciplinary teams were established to broaden input on the hospital's design. These working groups made many suggestions that were incorporated into the design. These included: 100 percent private rooms, locating pharmacies on patient floors close to nursing staff, allocating space for mobile technology, and creating a flexible emergency department capable of serving a greater number of emergencies during peak periods such as the tourist season. This case study illustrates the value of including customers in the planning and design stage of capital projects.

Mudie, Sheila
"TQM: Everyone's Business." *Nursing* (London) 4, no.39 (July 25-August 21, 1991): 26–28.

The purpose of this article is to introduce nurses to the topic of TQM. The author interviewed quality experts outside the nursing profession for background information, including managers at Nissan UK and Marks & Spencer. This basic, well-written introduction to TQM will be of value to the nursing profession in general, not just nursing professionals in the United Kingdom

Parsons, Mickey L., and Carolyn L. Murdaugh
Patient-Centered Care: A Model for Restructuring. Gaithersburg, MD: Aspen, 1994.

This book has been designed as a comprehensive how-to guide to patient care restructuring. It provides an in-depth description (this book exceeds 600 pages in length) of the model of patient-centered care developed by the University Medical Center (UMC) at the University of Arizona Health Services Center (Tucson, Arizona). The UMC model consists of three major components: restructured care delivery; interdisciplinary team management; and shared values of excellence in patient care. This is an important book since health care professionals world-wide can learn important lessons from the UMC experience.

"A Quality Cure for Healthcare." *Profiles in Healthcare Marketing* 51 (January/February 1993): 18–31.

Three hospitals are profiled in these quality case studies. The first is the University of Massachusetts Medical Center in Worcester, Massachusetts. The University of Massachusetts initiated a TQM/CQI program simultaneously at its hospital and medical school in 1989. A mini-grant program was established to fund faculty proposals for improvements in patient care and clinical outcomes. Another result was the successful pilot that improved service in the emergency department. The second case study features the West Paces Ferry Hospital, a full-service hospital that is part of the Hospital Corporation of America's for-profit hospital system. This Atlanta hospital began a TQM/CQI program in 1987. As a result, more than $300,000 has been saved through a reduction of inappropriate cardiac admissions and an increase in appropriate admissions to 88 percent from 28 percent. One improvement has been the streamlining of the admissions process, resulting in an increase of preadmission from 17 percent of all cases to 72 percent. Another tangible result has been the assignment of some registered nurses' duties to non-licensed staffers. The Memorial Medical Center in Jacksonville, Florida is the focus of the third case study. This hospital, assisted by the consulting group Ernst & Young, implemented a TQM/CQI program in mid-1989. As a result, waiting time for bed assignments has been reduced from eight minutes to five minutes. With the implementation of a seven-step problem-solving system, meetings have become more efficient and productive. Although quality management is relatively new to health care, all three examples demonstrate that it can result in greater cost efficiency and improved patient care and clinical outcomes.

Reed, James III, *et al.*
"Total Quality Management System: Its Application in a Community Hospital Research Department." *Journal of Medical Systems* 17, no.1 (February 1993): 17–24.

The Lehigh Valley Hospital, an 831-bed regional community hospital in Eastern Pennsylvania, introduced a TQM program in 1990 based on the Crosby model. The hospital has facilities in the center of Allentown and in a suburban location. This article describes the Research Department's use of the Crosby model to identify, define, and chart the processes that a research project moves through from conception to publication. The Research Department, with a staff of six, serves physicians and other professional staff at both of Lehigh Valley Hospital's locations. This charting process helped staff to identify and correct problem areas.

"The Role of Hospital Leadership in the Continuous Improvement of Patient Care Quality." *Journal of Healthcare Quality* 14, no.5 (September/October 1992): 8–14, 22.

This article, prepared by the American Hospital Association Division of Quality Resources, is directed to hospital CEOs, senior managers, medical staff leaders, and trustees. It was written to clarify the relationship of existing quality assurance activities to CQI/TQM. The division believes that quality assurance efforts can be enhanced by CQI/TQM. This technical briefing outlines steps that a hospital's leadership might take in implementing CQI. This article compares three major approaches to quality improvement: Deming's fourteen steps, Juran's ten-step plan, and Crosby's fourteen-step process. There is also a list of recommended readings.

Sandrick, Karen
"Clinical Quandaries: Getting MD's to Buy into CQI Means Making Adjustments." *Hospitals* 67, no.1 (January 5, 1993): 29–30.

Only a few hospitals have involved their medical staff in TQM/CQI programs. Some experts think that physicians find TQM too theoretical and not oriented enough on patient care processes. The Henry Ford Hospital in Detroit has undertaken a number of CQI clinical projects targeted at specific aspects of treatment. A CQI program that standardized procedures on pap smears resulted in a 50 percent decrease in inadequate smears. Methodist Health Systems has focused its clinical CQI efforts on medical problems such as surgical procedures. A CQI project involving joint replacement resulted in a reduction of the average length of stay from 10.7 days to 6.7 days. Both of these hospitals have also restricted the number of clinical CQI projects that they are involved in. According to both hospitals, the key to getting physicians to buy into CQI is to concentrate on clinical projects that make a visible difference in patient care.

Schroeder, Patricia
Improving Quality and Performance: Concepts, Programs, and Techniques. St. Louis, MO: Mosby, 1994.

This book provides an excellent introduction to quality improvement in health care settings. The author makes good use of real-world examples, resulting in a text that carefully blends theory and practical experience. The first section provides an overview of quality improvement principles, programs, tools, and techniques. The second section uses examples to show how quality improvement can be applied to hospitals and other health care settings.

Shortell, Stephen M., Daniel Z. Levin, James L. O'Brien, and Edward F. X. Hughes
"Assessing the Evidence on CQI: Is the Glass Half Empty or Half Full?" *Hospital and Health Services Administration* 40, no.1 (Spring 1995): 4–24.

The authors (all of whom are affiliated with Northwestern University) review the research literature on TQM/CQI in both health and non-health care settings. The research studies included in their review were published in health services and business journals directed to managers and academicians. Most of the articles were published between 1991 and 1993. They drew several conclusions about TQM in non-health care settings based on their review of the literature. First, their review indicated that broad-based, large-scale surveys generally indicated dissatisfaction with CQI. More empowered work approaches seem to have more impact than less-empowered approaches. Finally, the literature reveals a gap between management theory and practice. Although corporate America understands the concepts underlying CQI, implementation has not always been successful. Their review indicated one major difference between CQI/TQM applications in health care and CQI/TQM applications in other fields. While applications outside of health care have been directed at the core processes of the company in areas of greatest strategic priority, most of the TQM applications in health care have been in functions providing administrative support to patient care activities, not clinical processes themselves. There are several obstacles to TQM in health care organizations. The authors have grouped these barriers into cultural, technical, strategic, and structural categories. They conclude that they do not know whether the CQI glass is half empty or half full. They advocate more research on TQM/CQI efforts, since most of the existing studies are based on single or small sample case studies. This important article is essential to all health care organizations involved in quality improvement. The overview provided is also helpful to managers and researcher in non-health care settings.

Smith, Jackie A., Debra L. Scammon, and Susan L. Beck
"Using Patient Focus Groups for New Patient Services." *The Joint Commission Journal on Quality Improvement* 21, no.1 (January 1995): 22–31.

This article demonstrates how focus group discussions can be used to obtain patient input for strategic planning. It describes the University Hospital's "Program to Improve Patient Care" at the University of Utah (Salt Lake City). Focus group data were used in planning, developing, and implementing new patient services. This is an important case study, since large health care organizations often neglect to include patients in the strategic planning process.

Solovy, Alden T.
"Champions of Change." *Hospitals* 67, no.5 (March 5, 1993): 14–19.

This cover story examines how three management movements (total quality management, patient-centered care, and critical paths) are changing the roles of hospital chief financial officers (CFOs), the role of hospital financial staff, and methods of operational and capital budgeting. TQM in particular has changed the way in which budgets are presented to hospital boards. For example, one CFO described how TQM prompted him to use control charts and other graphic devices when presenting financial reports. TQM has also influenced how capital expenditure decisions are made and who has the power to spend money. Some hospitals now use a capital expenditure committee (composed of a variety of representatives) to review and recommend capital investments. In addition, some hospitals have proposed that quality improvement teams be authorized to expend funds. TQM, patient-centered care, and critical paths have radically changed the budgeting process, since they require that both clinical outcomes and financial effects be understood by both clinical and financial managers. As a result, a CFO has to be knowledgeable about more than bills, payroll, budgets, and financial reports.

Suver, James D., Bruce R. Neumann, and Keith E. Boles
"Accounting for the Costs of Quality." *Healthcare Financial Management* 46, no.9 (September 1992): 29–37.

The authors have adapted this article from the third edition of their book *Management Accounting for Healthcare Organizations*, which was published by HFMA and Pluribus Press in 1992. The emphasis on TQM in the health care industry will dramatically change accounting practices since financial managers will need to calculate the direct and indirect costs of quality. Some examples of direct or apparent costs of quality in health care facilities include unnecessary diagnostic tests, an inordinate amount of overtime, and insurance billing errors. Indirect or concealed costs of quality in health care can include overdue receivables, inaccurate or incomplete insurance information, and lack of teamwork among physicians, nurses, technicians, and other staff. The authors separate the costs of quality into three major categories: prevention costs; appraisal costs; and failure costs. Prevention costs are those incurred in the effort to prevent errors and include costs associated with employee training and the development of quality monitoring and reporting systems. Appraisal costs are those incurred with the evaluation of services or processes and can include quality audits; accreditation and state surveys; and licensure and certification reviews. Failure costs are those incurred with correcting or replacing defective processes or services as well as waste of any kind. Some examples of failure costs include defective tests and other errors; the unnecessary repetition of tasks; and the use of unnecessary supplies. The authors include a sample of a worksheet that can be used to calculate prevention, appraisal, and failure costs. This example of the calculated costs of quality will be extremely useful to financial managers since quality costs are often not collected by health care organizations.

"Total Quality Management: Measuring Costs of Quality." *Hospital Cost Management and Accounting* 5, no.5 (August 1993): 1–6.

Although increasing quality is associated with higher costs, this article notes that lowering the quality of care also has costs to a health care organization. These costs may be a declining reputation, or an increase in the number of malpractice cases. In order to measure how much cost is incurred because of a lack of quality control, a quality cost accounting and reporting system needs to be established. One individual, such as a Director of Quality Assurance, should be responsible for the system. Through an analysis of monthly and annual reports, important patterns or trends can be discerned and failures can be corrected. TQM is perceived by many health care managers to be more than a fad. Many believe that it will have significant implications for cost accounting throughout the 1990s and beyond.

Williams, Timothy P., and Rufus S. Howe
Applying Total Quality Management: A Nursing Guide. Chicago, IL: Precept Press; Deerfield, IL: National Association of Quality Assurance Professionals, 1991.

This practical text with a workbook format has been designed to introduce nursing students, staff nurses, nurse managers, and directors of nursing to total quality management. Not only does it provide a theoretical background but it shows how TQM concepts can be applied to real-world nursing situations. The first section provides an introduction to TQM as a management concept. The second section focuses on the application of TQM in nursing. The final section consists of a series of practical exercises. A helpful glossary rounds out the book.

Young, Mary J., Steven Rallison, and Philip Eckman
"Patients, Physicians, and Professional Knowledge: Implications for CQI." *Hospitals & Health Services Administration* 40, no.1 (Spring 1995): 40–49.

The spring 1995 issue of *Hospital & Health Services Administration* focuses on CQI. This article describes how physicians can move from the traditional medical model emphasizing the hierarchical role of physicians, to the partnership model inherent in CQI. It also examines the implications for the individual patient–doctor relationship.

SIC 8071: Medical laboratories

Bartlett, Raymond C.
"Trends in Quality Management." *Archives of Pathology and Laboratory Medicine* 114, no.11 (November 1990): 1126–1130.

This article traces the history of quality control in the clinical laboratory. Control charts were used in the clinical laboratory as early as 1950. The author views CQI as an opportunity for the reduction of costs and improvement of quality in an atmosphere of increasing competition and cost containment.

Bluth, Edward I., *et al.*
"Improvement in 'Stat' Laboratory Turnaround Time." *Archives of Internal Medicine* 152, no.4 (April 1992): 837–840.

This article describes a model project undertaken by a tertiary-care multispecialty group practice. The model project chosen by the ten-member team was to determine if turnaround time could be improved from "Stat" laboratory examinations performed in a large outpatient facility. The team consisted of all those individuals involved in the process of laboratory testing, including physicians, a clinical pathologist, clinic nurses, a clinic administrator, an operations systems analyzer, a laboratory technologist, and a member of the laboratory front desk reception area. Each team member was empowered to evaluate the current process and make appropriate changes. The introduction of these changes through this pilot CQI project led to impressive results. The institution saved $225,000 on a one-time basis and between $40,000 and $50,000 on a recurring basis. Waiting time for patients was reduced by an average of 62 percent.

Engebretson, Mara J., and George S. Cembrowski
"Achieving the Health Care Financing Administration Limits by Quality Improvement and Quality Control: A Real-World Example." *Archives of Pathology and Laboratory Medicine* 116, no.7 (July 1992): 781–787.

As a result of the enactment of the Clinical Laboratory Improvement Amendments of 1988 (CLIA 88), the federal government uses proficiency testing as the primary indicator of laboratory quality. Laboratories with proficiency test failures face harsh consequences, including large fines and suspension of operations. The Park Nicollet Medical Center (PNMC) Laboratory in Minneapolis, Minnesota initiated a continuous quality improvement program in their general chemistry laboratory in conjunction with the use of a survey-validated quality control product in order to minimize the risk of failed proficiency testing. Despite this initiative, significant analytical errors still existed in analytes measured by the laboratory's chemistry analyzer. However, the errors are present in almost the same analytes measured by other chemistry analyzers, indicating the need for improvement in their design and manufacture. This valuable CQI case study reveals that much of the responsibility for error reduction in these analytes resides with an instrument's manufacturer, not the individual laboratory.

Inhorn, Stanley L., John E. Shalkham, and
Daniel F. I. Kurtycz
"Total Quality Management in Cytology." *Acta
Cytologica* 37, no.3 (May/June 1993): 261–266.

This is a case study of TQM in a cytology
laboratory. The Cytology Department at the
Wisconsin State Laboratory of Hygiene initiated
a quality improvement program in January 1991
in an effort to identify inefficiencies in laboratory practices and improve the laboratory
operation. The Cytology Department has an
annual work load of approximately 100,000
cytology cases and in late 1990, the backlog had
grown to an unacceptable level of 12,000 to
14,000 cases with a 70 to 80-day turnaround time.
Public officials, Planned Parenthood of
Wisconsin, and state-supported family planning
clinics demanded prompt action. As a result of
TQM, marked improvements were achieved
within four months.

SIC 8093: Specialty outpatient facilities, not elsewhere classified

Gibbs, W. N., and A. F. H. Britten
*Guidelines for the Organization of a Blood
Transfusion Service.* Geneva: World Health
Organization, 1992.

This manual has been designed for any organization responsible for the operation of a blood
transfusion service. All blood transfusion
services, from the very simple to the most sophis-
ticated, must be concerned with many quality
assurance issues. This guide covers all aspects of
the operation of a transfusion service, including
a chapter on quality assurance. The principles of
quality assurance outlined in this chapter can be
applied to all transfusion services in developed
and developing countries.

*Guidelines for Quality Assurance Programmes
for Blood Transfusion Services.* Geneva: World
Health Organization, 1993.

These guidelines have been designed for
professionals who work in hospital blood banks
and blood transfusion services. The manual
provides step-by-step instructions for establishing
quality assurance measures. Among the topics
covered are donor selection, blood collection,
testing, storing and transporting, blood and blood
components, documentation, audits, and the role
of management in quality assurance. This guide
will be useful to all blood transfusion services
and blood banks, regardless of their size.

Smit Sibinga, C. Th., P. C. Das, and H. J.
Heiniger, eds
*Good Manufacturing Practice in Transfusion
Medicine.* Dordrecht (the Netherlands): Kluwer
Academic, 1994.

This volume consists of the edited proceedings
of the Eighteenth International Symposium on
Blood Transfusion, a 1993 conference organized
by the Red Cross Blood Bank Groningen-Drenthe
(the Netherlands). The concepts of Good Manufacturing Practice (GMP), Total Quality Management (TQM), and Quality Assurance (QA) will
dramatically impact the field of transfusion medicine. The quality movement will affect blood
banks, physicians, manufacturers of products orig-
inating from human blood, and regulatory agencies (such as the Food and Drug Administration
in the United States and the EC Commission in
Europe) involved in blood transfusion. Contributors include more than twenty authors from
North America and Europe with hospital, laboratory, pharmaceutical, and industrial experience.

SIC 8099: Health and allied services, not elsewhere classified

Fountain, Douglas L.
"Avoiding the Quality Assurance Boondoggle in
Drug Treatment Programs Through Total Quality
Management." *Journal of Substance Abuse
Treatment* 9, no.4 (Fall 1992): 355–364.

Fountain describes how TQM can be used to
improve the quality of substance abuse treatment
programs. This is an important contribution to the
scant literature on this particular application of
TQM. Managers of drug abuse treatment
programs will become increasingly interested in
this managerial tool as accrediting bodies, private
payers, and state and local governments call for
greater accessibility. In addition, accrediting
bodies such as the Joint Commission on the
Accreditation of Healthcare Organizations
(JCAHO) and the Commission on the Accreditation of Rehabilitation Facilities (CARF) require
written plans for quality improvement from
programs seeking accreditation.

Parry, Glenys

"Improving Psychotherapy Services: Applications of Research, Audit and Evaluation." *British Journal of Clinical Psychology* 31, no.1 (February 1992): 3–19.

The author reviews several approaches to evaluating and improving the delivery of psychotherapy services within the United Kingdom Health Services. One methodology is TQM. This method is compared with other management tools, including service evaluation, operational research, professional audit, service audit, and quality assurance. Parry recommends that six criteria, previously identified by R. J. Maxwell, be used to evaluate psychotherapy services: appropriateness, equity, accessibility, acceptability, effectiveness, and efficiency.

SIC 8111: Legal services

Goldberg, Stephanie B.

"The Quest for TQM." *ABA Journal* 79 (November 1993): 52–58.

In the 1990s, many law firms are exploring TQM. Some are experimenting with it because of external pressure. A 1992 survey of the legal departments of the Fortune 500 companies, indicated that 47 percent of in-house law departments had implemented TQM and 80 percent planned to have a TQM program in place by 1994. A 1993 Gallup poll of 400 lawyers indicated that almost half of the profession (49 percent) had some knowledge about TQM. However, this same poll revealed that most firms believe they already provide quality service. Overall, the legal profession has been slow (and often loath) to embrace TQM. Corporate legal departments are more likely to adopt TQM principles and tools than law firms. Some law firms reject TQM on the basis that TQM training is too costly and too time-consuming. Other lawyers dismiss TQM because they are uncomfortable about having clients surveyed, the teamwork aspect of TQM is anathema, or they are unfamiliar with the discipline of business management. However, the American Bar Association's Law Practice Management Section is sponsoring a TQM demonstration project. Ten law firms, ranging in size from two to 260 lawyers, are participating. Some projects these firms are addressing through

TQM include the following: tracking incoming and outgoing phone calls; tracking client costs for faxes, photocopies, and express mail services; and using flowcharts to analyze banking procedures in order to create forms for routine motions in a bankruptcy department. This article includes a listing of TQM resources for lawyers which includes books, articles, videotapes, and audiotapes.

Smith, Duncan C.

"Total Quality Leadership: Building Your Team, Keeping Your Clients." *Law Practice Management* 19, no.2 (March 1993): 34–45.

This journal is published by the American Bar Association's Section on Law Practice Management. Smith believes that TQM can be applied to law offices and that good leadership is a critical success factor. She breaks "total quality leadership" into six steps: practicing good leadership; focusing on clients; planning and analyzing; building a team and maintaining team spirit; producing and delivering services; and getting client feedback.

SIC 8211: Elementary and secondary schools

Baldwin, Fred

"A Community Commits to Quality." *Appalachia* 27, no.3 (Summer 1994): 12–17.

Erie, Pennsylvania has applied TQM across a wide range of community institutions. Local manufacturers and businesses, a nonprofit hospital, and the school district are involved in this unique approach. The Erie Chamber of Commerce initiated the program in the late 1980s, forming the Erie Excellence Council (EEC), a new division of the Chamber. The EEC brought national quality leaders to Erie (including Deming) and created the Erie Quality Award, an award modeled after the Malcolm Baldrige National Quality Award. In 1992, the Total Quality Management Institute was formed to offer affordable training to organizations in Erie and other northwestern Pennsylvania communities. Erie views TQM as part of a long-term economic development plan. As a result of TQM, the Perry Mills Supply Company increased sales by 20 percent over two years without increasing personnel. Erie's Shriner's Hospital reduced staff turnover to less than 4 percent (the rate was 15 to 20 percent before the implementation of TQM). The school district found that over a five-year period, the district average on a national test of basic skills increased from the 50th to the 70th national percentile.

Bayne-Jardine, Colin, and Peter Holly, eds
Developing Quality Schools. London: Falmer Press, 1994.

This book focuses on changes in the educational system in England and Wales. Local power is being decentralized to schools, which are becoming semiautonomous. However, at the same time, central government is becoming more aggressive about demanding change in the schools. Some schools, influenced by the total quality management movement, are developing a service orientation, with the goal of developing quality schools.

Bradley, Leo
Total Quality Management for Schools. Lancaster, PA: Technomic Publishing Co., 1993.

This book will be useful to school administrators, teachers, and school boards. The author, prior to becoming a university professor, spent three decades in the Ohio Public School System as teacher, principal, assistant superintendent, and superintendent. In addition, he worked in quality control for the Magnavox Corporation. Chapters cover a variety of issues including a brief history of quality control, quality systems in industry, client satisfaction, continuous improvement, measuring progress in schools, and the reallocation of resources.

Brooks, Susan Hardy
"The Quest for Quality: Francis Tuttle Vo-Tech Employees Don't Just Teach TQM – They Live It." *Vocational Education Journal* 68, no.6 (September 1993): 42–44.

This vo-tech school in Oklahoma city began to implement TQM in 1989. During the first year, employees completed a questionnaire asking for their input about changes they would like to see made in the organization. Employees responded candidly, indicating that they felt Francis Tuttle was too bureaucratic and that there was a need for employees to be more informed about

top-level decisions. As a result of this employee survey, the entire organization was reorganized. Titles such as assistant superintendent, director, and coordinator were dropped and some managers were no longer in a supervisory role. Instead, employees were organized into teams with department chairs. In 1990, the school hired outside experts to assist in-house trainers. Employees were led through a series of workshops on implementing change, teamwork, leadership, and customer service. The meeting structure was dramatically altered. Team meetings replaced faculty meetings, and quarterly staff recognition meetings and semi-monthly management team meetings were established. A cross-functional team developed a set of thirteen quality foundation principles, creating a climate which fosters innovation, quality work, and self-improvement. In the third year, Francis Tuttle hired an outside consultant to help the school with the actual implementation of TQM. The next step planned for Francis Tuttle is the full integration of TQM into all aspects of the school's operation. TQM has already resulted in benefits such as reduced bureaucracy, ongoing teacher evaluation, and collective decision-making.

Colonna, Frank A.
Total *Quality Education: Creating Excellence in Education Using the Secrets of Japanese Quality Management*. Melbourne, FL: Educational Publishing Inc., 1992.

This is a sound introduction to total quality management in education. Theoretical concepts are conveyed through clear text, excellent graphics, and interesting real-world examples. The book is structured around twelve imperatives that Colonna has identified for the transformation of education to total quality education.

Crawford, Donna K., Richard J. Bodine, and Robert G. Hoglund
The School for Quality Learning: Managing the School and Classroom the Deming Way. Champaign, IL: Research Press, 1993.

This book is influenced by the writings of W. Edwards Deming and Dr. William Glasser. The first part of the book provides an overview of the philosophies of Deming and Glasser. Part Two focuses on managing the school for quality learning. The authors outline the roles of principals and teachers. The principal's role is to be a noncoercive lead manager who can serve as a model for teachers since the teacher's role is to be a noncoercive lead manager in the classroom. Since the relationship between principal and teacher is so critical to quality learning, the authors stress that any barriers to this relationship (such as middle management positions) must be removed. The final section of the book focuses on managing the classroom for quality learning. The student learner is viewed as the worker and the teacher is viewed as the manager of the learning environment. In addition to being an effective teacher, the lead-manager teacher needs to have the following attitudes and behaviors: an understanding of quality, a need for power, an ability to collaborate with numerous colleagues, needs to hold himself or herself accountable for outcomes, needs to have highly developed questioning skills, accepts that each learner is unique, is consistent in his or her behavior, understands conflict resolution strategies, avoids adversarial confrontations with learners, is people-oriented, uses open-ended classroom discussions and meetings, facilitates learning, is a risk-taker, has vision, and demonstrates trust in each learner.

Freeston, Kenneth R.

"Getting Started with TQM." *Educational Leadership* 50, no.3 (November 1992): 10–13.

The public school system in Newtown, Connecticut used the principles of TQM to develop the "Newtown Success-Oriented School Model." This model incorporates both Deming's and Glasser's approaches to quality. The stated mission of the Newtown schools is that "all children can and will learn well." Five quality outcomes have been identified for children: self-directed learning; cognitive achievement and mastery of curriculum; the acquisition of decision making, problem-solving and critical thinking skills; development of a concern for others; and self-esteem. As a result of this model, the school system has changed its orientation for new teachers; the superintendent teaches a 12-hour course on quality to parents, community members, and staff; and quality core groups address curriculum changes. This school system is committed to a long term approach to quality.

Glasser, William

The Quality School: Managing Students Without Coercion. 2nd edn. New York: HarperPerennial, 1992.

Glasser's model of transforming schools is based on Deming's quality management principles. Glasser's view is that lead management is the key to educational reform. Both Deming and Glasser argue that lead management should replace boss management. Lead management removes obstacles to motivation, recognizes group achievement, and establishes well-defined procedures. Glasser's contention is that boss management does not work because it fails to understand that motivation comes from within. Glasser's understanding of motivation is based on control theory, the theory that only individuals choose and have control over their behavior and actions. Glasser believes that teachers can use reality therapy (a noncoercive method of communication) to help students learn to be in control of their behavior.

Glasser, William

The Quality School Teacher. New York: HarperCollins, 1993.

Glasser has been instrumental in explaining how Deming's theories can be applied to schools. His 1990 book, *The Quality School*, was immensely successful – so successful that it was revised and expanded in 1992. In this book, Glasser shows teachers how they can implement the lead-management ideas of the quality school in their classrooms. He outlines specific teaching practices that will help teachers lead-manage.

Horine, Julie E., William A. Hailey, and Laura Rubach

"Transforming Schools." *Quality Progress* 26, no.10 (October 1993): 31–38.

One hundred and five public and private school districts in the United States responded to this survey of quality management efforts in American schools conducted by *Quality Progress*. Most districts were in the early phases of TQM. Almost 80 percent indicated that they had been using TQM for less than two years. Reported levels of employee participation were relatively low (more than half reported employee participation levels of 25 percent or less). Almost two-thirds of districts reported that their TQM efforts were district-wide. More than two-thirds of the districts have formed partnerships with other educational institutions, state agencies, and community groups. A particularly valuable feature is the listing of districts that have implemented TQM.

Kohn, Alfie
"Turning Learning into a Business: Concerns About Total Quality." *Educational Leadership* 51, no.1 (September 1993): 58–61.

Kohn raises concerns about the application of TQM to education. Although the author embraces TQM in a business context, he worries about a "marketplace model in the classroom." His fear is that TQM in schools is not only inappropriate, but possibly detrimental since it may emphasize performance on grades and tests over creative thinking and conceptual learning.

McLeod, Willis B., Brenda A. Spencer, and Leon T. Hairston
"Toward a System of Total Quality Management: Applying the Deming Approach to the Education Setting." *ERS Spectrum* 10, no.2 (Spring 1992): 34–41.

The Petersburg, Virginia public schools (with an enrollment of approximately 60,000 students) moved from a highly centralized organizational structure to a system emphasizing shared decision-making and school-based management practices. This organizational change was a direct result of applying Deming's philosophy of management. Deming's fourteen points were translated to action statements. Within two and a half years, test scores improved significantly and the drop-out rate decreased by more than 50 percent.

Moore, Donald R.
"Chicago School Reform Meets TQM." *Journal for Quality and Participation* 16, no.1 (January/February 1993): 6–11.

The Chicago public school system is being restructured as a result of a 1989 change in state law mandating decentralization. Authority is being transferred from a central bureaucracy to principals, teachers, and parents. Moore describes one Chicago school's experiment with TQM. The Lovett Elementary School, an African American school on the West Side, with assistance from Participation Associates (a consulting group), is applying the principles of TQM in an effort to improve the quality of education. The strategy being used is known as the "Z process." This process, created by John Simmons and Terry Mazany, consists of three phases: readiness; redesign; and implement and improve. The Z process has been used in more than one hundred schools.

Murgatroyd, Stephen
"A New Frame for Managing Schools: Total Quality Management." *School Organisation* 12, no.2 (1992): 175–200.

Murgatroyd provides a model for the implementation of TQM in elementary and secondary schools. Schools in Canada and the United States are experimenting with many of his suggestions. His model includes the following key elements: developing a strong sense of school vision; encouraging all employees to focus on personal learning and personal development; focusing strategy on customer-driven values; using hoshin planning to develop challenging goals; working effectively through teams; and improving the quality of daily management within the school.

Murgatroyd, Stephen
"Implementing Total Quality Management in the School: Challenges and Opportunity." *School Organisation* 13, no.3 (1993): 269–281.

Murgatroyd is affiliated with Canada's Athabasca University. He has previously published several articles on school-wide quality improvement in elementary and secondary education. This article focuses on why schools have failed at applying TQM principles. Murgatroyd's insights into this problem are based not only on his own experiences, but from information he has gathered through interviews with TQM consultants and practitioners. According to the author, TQM initiatives sometimes fail from the beginning due to lack of commitment by leaders, poor data, poor deployment plans, and lack of managerial skills. Murgatroyd also identifies five other problems that are common after TQM programs have been launched: the formation of too many teams; the measurement of too many activities and processes; a focusing on outcomes rather than a rethinking process; perceiving TQM as a quick fix; and a loss of momentum. The author suggests that in order to avoid these start-up and post-launch problems, schools should focus on leadership and training for TQM.

Rappaport, Lewis A.
"A School-Based Quality Improvement Program." *NASSP Bulletin* 77 (September 1993): 16–20.

The author is the principal of George Westinghouse Vocational and Technical High School in Brooklyn, New York. This inner-city high school has received much media attention because of its success in applying the concepts of TQM. Rappaport discusses the key elements to Westinghouse's successful quality improvement program. They include the following factors: an immersion into the writings of Deming, Juran, Feigenbaum, and other theorists; committed leadership; a clearly defined mission and vision; ongoing training of personnel involved in quality improvement; the use of quality tools such as flowcharts and the Deming Cycle (or Shewhart Cycle) of Plan-Do-Check-Act; voluntary and goal-oriented teamwork; and an understanding that TQM is not a quick fix.

Sabo, Sandra R.
"Getting it Right." *The American School Board Journal* 181, no.4 (April 1994): 35–37.

This article describes the use of TQM as a tool for the school design process. It can be used by school districts that are building or renovating a school. The TQM approach to school design is used by the architectural firm of Steed Hammond Paul Architects. This Cincinnati firm calls its approach "The Schoolhouse of Quality". The process begins with a series of ten-person focus groups. Phone or mail surveys supplement these focus group findings. The results are analyzed by a computer model. This process helps Steed Hammond Paul Architects identify and weight the values of their customers and helps the firm translate them into design concepts. The firm designed a $6.25 million elementary school in Lebanon, Ohio. Their process indicated that the community placed a high value on environmental consciousness. The firm integrated this value into the school's design through the inclusion of a recycling center to handle the school's waste.

Schmoker, Michael J., and Richard B. Wilson
Total Quality Education: Profiles of Schools that Demonstrate the Power of Deming's Management Principles. Bloomington, IN: Phi Delta Kappa, 1993.

The authors profile five schools or districts that have successfully applied Deming's principles to improve their productivity and effectiveness. These include the Johnson City School District (Broome County, New York); the Daniel Webster Elementary School (San Francisco); Central Park East Secondary School (New York City); the Clovis Schools (near Fresno, California); and the Mt. Edgecumbe High School (Sitka, Alaska). The appendix briefly describes three school programs that use Deming's principles: the Comer School Development Program (a program developed in 1968 by Dr. James P. Comer, a child psychiatrist at Yale University's Child Study Center); Northview Elementary School's program (a school in Manhattan, Kansas that serves lower-middle class students); and the George Westinghouse Vocational and Technical High School's program (an urban high school in Brooklyn, New York).

Scholtes, Peter R.
The Team Handbook for Educators: How to Use Teams to Improve Quality. Madison, WI: Joiner Associates, 1994.

Joiner Associates is a consulting firm specializing in quality management. This practical book is designed to help quality improvement teams working in educational settings. The first two chapters provide an overview of quality, quality tools, and the role of teams and teamwork. Subsequent chapters explain how to select a project, how to establish a team, how to have effective meetings, how to employ strategies that can solve problems or improve processes, and how to build and maintain team support. The final chapter provides excellent team-building activities and exercises.

Siegel, Peggy, and Sandra Byrne
Using Quality to Redesign School Systems: The Cutting Edge of Common Sense. San Francisco: Jossey-Bass; Milwaukee, WI: ASQC Quality Press, 1994.

This practical guide shows education and business leaders how they can form a partnership to improve school systems. The book is based on more than 200 interviews in eleven education sites that have used quality tools and processes to improve their school systems. These sites are the Rappahannock County Public Schools (Sperryville, Virginia), the Prince William County Public Schools (Manassas, Virginia), the Parkview School District (Orfordville, Wisconsin), the Pecatonica School District (Pecatonica, Wisconsin), the Vermont Department of Education (Montpelier, Vermont), the George Westinghouse Vocational and Technical High School (Brooklyn, New York), the Mt. Edgecumbe High School (Sitka, Alaska), the School District of Beloit Turner (Beloit, Wisconsin), the Brodhead School District (Brodhead, Wisconsin), the Oregon School District (Oregon, Wisconsin), and the Millcreek Township School District (Erie, Pennsylvania). In addition, the authors visited four companies that have won the coveted Malcolm Baldrige Award (Xerox, Motorola, Globe Metallurgical, and Federal Express) and seven educational organizations practicing TQM. The authors reached four major conclusions after these extensive on-site visits and interviews. First, quality principles are applicable to an educational setting. The second finding was that TQM is not a quick fix. Third, schools will need to utilize industry experience and gain political support for quality education. Finally, a bridge needs to be built between business and education leaders in order to make business–education collaboration possible.

"Total Quality Management: Now, It's a Class Act." *Business Week* (October 31, 1994): 72, 76.

Vocational schools such as Brooklyn's George Westinghouse Vocational and Technical High School are using TQM principles to improve students' work, attendance, and parental involvement. This Brooklyn school has received help from several companies, including Xerox, Ricoh, IBM, and Peart. The school introduced TQM in 1990, and results have been impressive. The dropout rate has decreased from 12.9 percent to 2.1 percent. In 1994, the American Society for Quality Control estimated that 127 public school districts were using TQM. The federal government is developing a Baldrige Quality Award for educators that will be delivered for the first time in 1996.

SIC 8221: Colleges, universities, and professional schools

Assar, Kathleen E.
"Phoenix: Quantum Quality at Maricopa: TQM on Campus, Case Study Number Two." *Change* 25, no.3 (May/June 1993): 32–35.

The Maricopa County Community College District of greater Phoenix is one of the largest community college districts in the United States. It was also ranked as one of the best in a 1992 report in *U.S. News & World Report*. Maricopa has initiated Quantum Quality, a TQM initiative. Quantum Quality is a major undertaking since the Maricopa District consists of ten colleges serving 180,000 students annually across a 10,000 square mile area. Although the program is in its early stages, it has two ingredients that are critical for success. The first is strong and visible administrative support (the Chancellor leads the initiative). The second is thorough training. While other community colleges have implemented TQM, Maricopa is unique for several reasons. For example, other colleges train faculty in one group and staff in another. Training is typically done by function and level. Maricopa trains faculty and staff from different divisions and levels of responsibility together. Many colleges have adopted TQM with the goal of improving functional areas such as mail delivery. However, Maricopa is using TQM to improve teaching and learning.

Bemoski, Karen
"Restoring the Pillars of Higher Education." *Quality Progress* 24, no.10 (October 1991): 37–42.

American colleges and universities may face reduced enrollments due to three trends. These include increasing costs and reduced funding, competition from colleges and universities in Europe, Japan, and other countries, and a corporate movement toward educating executives internally. Although these developments may not motivate most colleges and universities to change, some institutions of higher education are applying the principles of TQM to improve how they carry out their teaching and research missions. Bemoski summarizes the findings of a 1991 survey conducted by Robert Kaplan, a professor in

Harvard University's Graduate School of Business. Kaplan surveyed the top U.S. business schools to determine the extent of TQM in the business school curriculum. He found that most of the nineteen responding schools devoted only 12 percent of introductory operations management courses to TQM. However, there were some exceptions, notably the University of Chicago, which spent 35 percent of class time on quality issues. Also, twelve out of the nineteen schools had at least one elective in quality management. Bemoski found that other schools have integrated TQM into the curriculum. For example, Columbia University is redesigning the business school curricula and quality is one of the five themes being integrated into the curriculum (the remaining themes being globalization, ethics, teamwork, and change). Columbia University has also established the Deming Center for Quality Management. The University of Miami's School of Business Administration has integrated TQM into its curriculum through TQM education modules, courses on TQM, and a TQM master's degree program. Colleges and universities interested in implementing TQM can also learn from the experiences of Oregon State University, the North Dakota University System, and Wisconsin's Fox Valley Technical College.

Burton, Jennus L.
"Hopping Out of the Swamp: Management of Change in a Downsizing Environment." *Business Officer* 26, no.8 (February 1993): 42–45.

Burton describes Total Quality Service (TQS), Arizona State University's variation of TQM. The principal components of TQS are a customer focus, continuous quality improvement, competitive services, benchmarking, leadership, decision-making, and innovation by substitution. TQS also involves environmental scanning, clarification of administrative unit functions, unit self-examination, the establishment of institutional priorities, the creation of an infrastructure to manage change, communication across the organization, implementation of decisions, and an established appeals procedure.

Chaffee, Ellen·Earle, and Daniel Seymour
"Quality Improvement With Trustee Commitment." *AGB Reports* 33, no.6 (November/December 1991): 14–18.

The authors conclude that trustee commitment and leadership are central to the success of TQM in college and university settings. However, trustees who want to foster TQM at their campuses have several obligations. These important responsibilities include the following: gaining an understanding of the needs of students, parents, faculty, staff, and funders through surveys or focus groups; using data to solve problems; eliminating unnecessary complexity in rules and regulations; viewing problems as symptoms of organizational processes that need improvement; providing funds to implement a comprehensive human resources development plan that includes training in teamwork, problem solving, participative management, and other skills relating to TQM; ensuring that the board agenda includes reports on quality improvement initiatives, adopt a long-term view; and learning about TQM through reading, discussion, and campus training opportunities.

Chaffee, Ellen Earle, and Lawrence A. Sherr
Quality: Transforming Postsecondary Education. ASHE-ERIC Higher Education Report no.3. Washington, DC: The George Washington University, School of Education and Human Development, 1992.

This is an excellent introduction to TQM in general and the application of TQM to colleges and universities. Chaffee and Sherr summarize the principal concepts of total quality management and explain how colleges and universities can apply these principles to both academic and administrative areas. The clarity of text, use of abundant real-world examples, and wealth of practical advice makes this an exceptional work on TQM in higher education.

Chizmar, John F.
"Total Quality Management (TQM) of Teaching and Learning." *Journal of Economic Education* 25, no.2 (Spring 1994): 179–190.

Chizmar is a professor of economics at Illinois State University. He proposes that the principles of TQM be applied to undergraduate education in order to empower both students and teachers, satisfy customers (in this case, students), and foster an atmosphere for innovation and continuous organization-wide improvement. In addition, a TQM teaching/learning model can help students develop important skills such as the ability to make decisions and to work successfully in teams.

Clayton, Marlene

"Towards Total Quality Management in Higher Education at Aston University – A Case Study." *Higher Education* 25 (1993): 363–371.

Aston University (Birmingham, England) used the principles and methods of quality management to progress toward its strategic goal of becoming a leading technological university. In the 1970s and early 1980s, Aston University, like other technological universities in the United Kingdom, suffered severe funding cutbacks. Aston University has used various quality management tools and techniques since the 1980s. For example, a variety of quality circles have been established to address issues ranging from the establishment of an on-site laundry to campus security. Recently, a Quality Council was established to identify and prioritize improvement projects. One faculty member, the Head of the Department of Vision Sciences, has experimented with Quality Function Deployment (QFD), and its usefulness as a tool for evaluating existing degree programs.

Coate, L. Edwin

"TQM on Campus: Implementing Total Quality Management in a University Setting." *Business Officer* 24, no.5 (November 1990): 26–35.

Coate describes Oregon State University's total quality management implementation model. The model includes the following nine phases: exploration of TQM by top administrators (the president and his cabinet); formation of a pilot study team (the University initiated a TQM study team in the Physical Plant Department); identification and prioritization of customer needs; development of a vision statement; identification of priority breakthrough items and development of a preliminary five-year plan by the president's cabinet; breakthrough planning and five-year planning by divisions and colleges; establishment of daily management teams to solve process problems; initiation of cross-functional pilot teams; development of a system of rewards and recognition; and establishment of cross-functional management teams. Coate concludes that, based on his experiences at Oregon State University (where he is vice-president for finance and administration), the successful implementation of TQM depends on six key variables. These central principles are a strong commitment to TQM from the university's president or chief operating officer; an allocation of resources; a willingness to act (practical experience is more important than exhaustive research); well-trained teams; breakthrough planning; and initially implementing TQM with a service unit rather than an academic unit.

Coate, L. Edwin

"TQM at Oregon State University." *Journal for Quality and Participation* (December 1990): 90–101.

In 1989, the president of Oregon State University (OSU) made a commitment to implement TQM throughout the university by 1994. This article describes the implementation process in detail. The implementation of TQM has moved through the following nine phases: exploration of the TQM concept; formation of a pilot team; the definition of customer needs through quality function deployment, the use of top management breakthrough planning; breakthrough planning by divisions and colleges; the formation of daily management teams; the establishment of cross-functional pilot projects; the use of cross-functional management; and the introduction of monthly reports and the establishment of a rewards and recognition system.

Coate, Edwin

"The Introduction of Total Quality Management at Oregon State University." *Higher Education* 25, no.3 (April 1993): 303–320.

Oregon State University (OSU) was one of the first American research universities to implement TQM. OSU introduced TQM in 1989 in response to downsizing. The first areas where TQM was applied were finance and administration. Over the next four years, TQM was expanded to all administrative areas. It has also been used in curriculum development, research proposal development, and to improve teaching. More than 85 process improvement teams are now in place and OSU has received wide recognition for its pioneering efforts in both administrative and academic units. Faculty members in the colleges of business, engineering, and liberal arts have also integrated TQM into the curriculum. TQM concepts and techniques are taught in a wide range of courses such as speech communication, public administration, management, management science, logistics, project planning, statistics, industrial and manufacturing engineering, and mechanical engineering.

Cornesky, Robert A.

The Quality Professor: Implementing TQM in the Classroom. Madison, WI: Magna Publications, 1993.

The purpose of this book is to guide faculty in applying TQM processes and tools to instruction. Cornesky demonstrates how to implement TQM and continuously improve classroom effectiveness. The book is organized like a class syllabus, discussing the basic requirements of change, providing historical background, and using case studies to demonstrate the use of specific quality tools. Among the quality tools and techniques covered are flowcharts, nominal group processes, cause-and-effect diagrams, affinity diagrams, force field analysis, relations diagrams, Pareto diagrams, histograms, run charts, control charts, scatter diagrams, quality function deployment, and systematic diagrams. Many of the charts and graphs can be photocopied and adapted by the reader for use in his or her classroom. The final chapter provides the "quality index profile for teaching," a self-assessment checklist. Other Magna publications related to quality in higher education include *Using Deming to Improve Quality in Colleges and Universities, Implementing Total Quality Management in Higher Education,* and *Total Quality Improvement Guide for Institutions of Higher Education.*

Cornesky, Robert A., *et al.*

W. Edwards Deming: Improving Quality in Colleges and Universities. Madison, WI: Magna Publications, 1990.

The purpose of the book is to show that Deming's principles can be applied to higher education. Each chapter illustrates one of Deming's fourteen points and translates theory into practical terms. The authors, all academic administrators, provide concrete examples of applying Deming's points to colleges and universities. Deming's fourth point is developing long-term relationships. In terms of higher education, this can be translated into working closely

with school districts and community colleges. One interesting feature of this book is the inclusion of case studies of situations that could have been averted if Deming's principles had been applied.

Cowles, Deborah

"Total Quality Management at Virginia Commonwealth University: An Urban University Struggles with the Realities of TQM." *Higher Education* 25, no.3 (April 1993): 281–302.

Virginia Commonwealth University (VCU), a large urban university in Richmond, Virginia implemented several pilot programs using a TQM approach. These TQM pilots have included improvement of the University's Personnel Action Form (the document used to process all VCU personnel and payroll transactions), creation of a tracking system to monitor service requests made to the academic computing center, and the development of an advancement records database. Members of these three TQM teams were asked to assess the merits of TQM, their experience with the TQM process, and the climate for quality improvement at VCU. One team suggested that key leaders be more involved in quality planning and implementation. This same team suggested that experts outside the university be used to guide senior management through the initial phase of a university-wide TQM program. However, Cowles indicated that TQM has been put on hold at VCU due to other competing priorities.

CQI 101: A First Reader for Higher Education. Washington, DC: American Association for Higher Education, 1994.

This volume brings together reprints, excerpts, and adaptations of some of the best (and now classic) articles and books on quality in general, quality improvement in higher eduction, and the quality movement in other sectors. The works selected for inclusion are essentially the core literature on the topic of quality improvement. Among the books excerpted are *The Race Without A Finish Line,* Warren Schmidt and Jerome Finnigan's history of the continuous quality improvement program; *Organizational Architecture: Designs for Changing Organizations,* Jeffrey Heilpern and David A. Nadler's book on organizational change; and *Kidgets: And Other Insightful Stories about Quality in Education,* stories about quality in industry and education written by Maury Cotter and Daniel Seymour. Among the journal articles included are those written by prominent authorities such as Peter Senge, Curtis McLaughlin, Arnold Kaluzny, and L. Edwin Coate.

Doherty, Geoffrey D.

"Towards Total Quality Management in Higher Education: A Case Study of the University of Wolverhampton." *Higher Education* 25, no.3 (April 1993): 321–339.

This article describes the quality initiatives undertaken by the University of Wolverhampton. This British university, formerly named Wolverhampton Polytechnic, began to explore TQM in 1989. Several factors led to the decision to implement TQM and BS 5750 (the British standard equivalent to ISO 9000) initiatives. One factor was an institutional desire to improve an existing quality assurance system. Another reason was market pressure from the newly established Training and Enterprise Councils (TECs). TECs have implied that they will only do business with companies that are BS 5750 accredited. The university spent one and a half years planning for the implementation of TQM and the development of a quality assurance system that would conform to BS 5750/ISO 9000. During this first phase, the university reviewed the literature on TQM and BS 5750, arrived at an agreement on the definition of quality, developed written "codes of practice," conducted a quality survey, and hired consultants. Doherty estimates that the visible costs of phase one was approximately £14,500. This does not include hidden costs such as staff time and the photocopying and distribution of documents. The university decided to use Crosby's model, adapting it to higher education. The second phase involved the steps taken to implement TQM, including the development of quality circles and quality implementation teams. During this second stage, there was training on quality circle methods, TQM tools, client awareness, and BS 5750/ISO 9000 auditing, procedure writing, and monitoring. The costs incurred in phase two were greater than those in phase one. Overall, Doherty estimates that the university spent approximately £160,000 over a two-year period in direct and indirect costs (excluding opportunity costs). When assessing the university's experiences with TQM, Doherty acknowledges that there have been successes and failures. Although TQM is not a cheap quick fix approach, the university remains committed to TQM's philosophy as it strives to receive BS 5750 accreditation and its stated mission of becoming "the best university for mass higher education in the UK."

Doherty, Geoffrey D.

Developing Quality Systems in Education. London: Routledge, 1994.

Doherty, Pro Vice Chancellor (Quality Assurance) and Dean of the Faculty of Education at the University of Wolverhampton, has brought together nineteen thoughtful chapters, contributed by both British and American practitioners, on the problems, pitfalls, and challenges of implementing quality standards in education. The contributors offer case studies of both successes and failures. While some chapters examine theoretical issues (such as the relationship between the customer and academic culture), most have a practical orientation. The first seven chapters explore some general and theoretical issues. Chapters 8 through 11 focus on TQM in higher education while Chapters 12 through 15 cover the topics of TQM in continuing education, quality systems in vocational education, and total quality in the Avon Training and Enterprise Council. The final chapters of the book present articles about quality improvement across the education sector, and specific case studies including the application of quality management at Mt. Edgecumbe High School (located in Sitka, Alaska), the Buckpool (UK) experience with quality systems, and the Dudley Local Education Authority's (UK) strategy for quality improvement.

Dooris, Michael

"A Planner Studies Physics." *Planning for Higher Education* 21, no.4 (Summer 1993): 1–8.

The author, a research and planning associate in the Pennsylvania State University's (Penn State) Office of Planning and Analysis, sat in on Physics 201, an introductory physics course, as part of an institution-wide continuous quality improvement (CQI) effort. He was part of a ten-member CQI team that was appointed in 1992 to improve the quality of instruction in introductory physics, especially for undergraduate engineering students. The team also included physics professors, engineering professors, students, and other staff members. Dooris found that most of the learning in introductory physics occurs outside class and that lectures merely reinforce concepts introduced in the textbook. Although the author concluded that good math skills (preferably algebra or trigonometry) are essential, he maintains that introductory physics should focus on how physics affects the real physical world. He felt that Physics 201 was designed for mathematically well prepared and highly motivated students who are self-directed learners. As a result, he recommended that Penn State redesign the course to accommodate those students who are not as well prepared and those students with different learning styles. Based on his experience in the course, Dooris also recommended that more frequent quizzes and graded homework be added to provide incentives for students to increase their out-of-class study time. The CQI team also recommended a grading policy for homework to encourage more out-of-class study. The team concurred that good mathematical skills are a crucial prerequisite for this course and has correlated scores on a math pre-test with Physics 201 grades. The team will also investigate the possibility of using this pre-test to place students into optional one-credit sections that emphasize necessary mathematical and analytical skills. In addition to these changes, the physics department plans to offer sections of four small classes per week as an alternative to the existing course structure of two large lectures and two small recitations. Although the physics department has a learning resource center in place (offering personal tutoring by teaching assistants), a survey indicated that students make little use of the help. The CQI team is exploring the use of programmed instruction, that is, computerized assistance. Dooris concludes that his team's experience demonstrates that CQI principles can be applied to teaching.

Entin, David H.
"Boston: Less than Meets the Eye: TQM on Campus, Case Study Number One." *Change* 25, no.3 (May/June 1993): 28–31.

Entin's purpose is to objectively analyze the implementation of TQM in ten colleges and universities in the Boston area. The institutions selected for study are: Babson College, Bentley College, Boston College, Boston University, Lesley College, Massachusetts Institute of Technology, Tufts University, University of Massachusetts at Boston, Wentworth Institute of Technology, and Worcester Polytechnic Institute. Seven of the ten institutions began to investigate TQM in the 1990–91 academic year. College presidents played an important role in the implementation of TQM on campuses. College presidents were involved in TQM in six of the ten campuses. In all six of these institutions, senior management received initial TQM training. The college president was a key leader on three of the campuses. Only one college institutionalized TQM with the creation of a funded and staffed Office of Quality. Although Entin found genuine support for TQM on campuses, he noted a degree of skepticism from core academic units. He concluded that the success of TQM is dependent upon two factors: the support of the college president and the support of faculty and senior academic affairs administrators.

Entner, Donald
"DCCC Takes the TQM Plunge ... And Tells How." *Educational Record* 74, no.2 (Spring 1993): 28–34.

The Delaware County Community College in Pennsylvania was one of the first colleges in the United States to adopt TQM. In 1986, the College decided to apply TQM to its own management, to develop TQM training for local businesses, and to integrate the concepts and techniques of TQM into the classroom. A ten-year implementation plan was developed in order to achieve these three goals by 1996. Some of these goals were completed ahead of schedule. TQM was integrated in all administrative units by 1992. The college has provided TQM training to business and industry since 1993. As of 1993, fifteen out of 120 full-time faculty had used TQM principles and tools to improve their teaching. Two factors appear to be critical to the college's success: a comprehensive training program and a system of rewards and recognition for staff who have successfully completed quality improvement projects.

Feigenbaum, Armand V.
"We Can't Improve American Quality If We Aren't Teaching It." *National Productivity Review* 12 (Spring 1993): 139–141.

Feigenbaum is regarded as the father of total quality control. In this commentary, Feigenbaum takes the American educational system to task. According to Feigenbaum, American colleges and universities treat quality as a narrow specialty, an amorphous factor, or something that can be taught by simply inserting the study of statistics or organizational behavior into existing courses. In order for the United States to effectively compete with other nations in the global marketplace, Feigenbaum argues that education in quality must be integrated throughout America's educational infrastructure (from the lower grades to university level) and must involve efforts by education, business, and government. Feigenbaum proposes that educators and policymakers undertake five initiatives in order to develop a strong quality education process. The first is to integrate quality education throughout the educational system. His second recommendation is that quality be taught as a fundamental element of the fields of economics, engineering, technology, business, and management. The third suggestion is that quality be taught as a body of knowledge throughout many dimensions of education. The next recommendation is that research in quality be expanded at American universities. His fifth proposal is that universities take the lead in developing quality education.

Fisher, James L.
"TQM: A Warning for Higher Education." *Educational Record* 74, no.2 (Spring 1993): 15–19.

Fisher, an author and consultant in higher education, raises doubts about the success of TQM in higher education. He questions whether TQM can solve academia's problems, noting that TQM has been abandoned by some of the corporations that once advocated its implementation in industry. Some of these companies have criticized TQM as being too costly and time-consuming. Fisher concludes that TQM can only work in colleges and universities that have inspirational leadership, a long-range plan, and emphases on individual accountability and cost reduction.

Fried, Sheryl, and Emily Richardson
"Total Quality Management: Should Hospitality Programs Teach It?" *Hospitality & Tourism Educator* 6, no.1 (Winter 1994): 57–61.

Fried and Richardson are both faculty members in the School of Hotel and Restaurant Management at Widener University. They conducted a survey to determine the extent to which universities with hospitality programs teach TQM. The questionnaire was sent to 140 colleges and universities in the United States offering four-year programs or a master's level program in hotel and restaurant management. Sixty-nine institutions responded. Although only five schools offered a course in TQM, 90 percent of the respondents indicated that they were teaching TQM concepts in other courses. The authors also surveyed the attendees at the 1991 American Hotel and Motel Association (AH & MA) Quality Assurance Conference in order to determine what the hotel industry expects from graduates in regard to their knowledge of TQM. Eighty-three of the 150 attendees responded to the questionnaire. Overall, industry professionals ranked the following as the most important concepts for graduates to learn: a general conceptual knowledge of TQM; team problem-solving; action planning; strategic planning; and group dynamics. Fried and Richardson concluded that based on these two separate surveys, there is a gap between what universities are teaching and what the hospitality industry expects of graduates. They recommend that universities teach a specific course on TQM, and provide a model for teaching TQM within a hospitality program. Their excellent model could easily be used for students in other management programs.

Froiland, Paul
"TQM Invades Business Schools." *Training* 30 (July 1993): 52–56.

The business school at the University of Tennessee has adopted TQM as an approach in order to remedy shortcomings identified by a commissioned task force on management education and representatives of three major firms (Xerox, Procter & Gamble, and Texas Instruments). A 1992 survey conducted by the Total Quality Forum found that 40 percent of 515 business and engineering schools responding to the survey had incorporated TQM principles into as many as six to ten courses; 45 percent had applied TQM to administrative areas; and 21 percent had applied TQM to teaching and research. Industry has pushed colleges and universities to include TQM in the curriculum. Some companies have offered threats as well as rewards. While Procter & Gamble announced to business schools that they wouldn't hire their graduates unless they begin to teach TQM, IBM established nine $1 million grants in 1992 to be awarded to schools teaching TQM. Some schools have formed a partnership with industry. For example, Kansas Newman College in Wichita developed a TQM major and offers some of its classes at Boeing facilities.

Geddes, Tommy
"The Total Quality Initiative at South Bank University." *Higher Education* 25, no.3 (April 1993): 341–361.

South Bank, a university in inner city South London, was a polytechnic until 1992. It has an annual budget of around £60 million and employs 1400 people. In 1992, it launched a TQM program to improve the efficiency of support departments and to improve the quality of teaching and learning. Thirty-two customer/supplier working groups were charged with the task of establishing quality service agreements between the academic units and support units, and between the school and its students. Since TQM is still in its early stage of development at South Bank University, it is impossible to assess the effectiveness of this initiative. However, student reactions have been favorable.

"Getting Started in TQM – A Tennessee Experience." *Journal of Career Planning and Employment* 53, no.3 (March 1993): 36–44.

This article was a collaborative effort by members of the University of Tennessee's Project Fill Schedule team, a project carried out by the department of career services. The goal of this narrowly defined project was to fill interview spaces in the university's recruiting schedule in order to maximize employment opportunities for students. The team used TQM techniques such as flowcharting and diagramming to find out why interview schedules didn't fill up. Major improvements in the interview sign-up process were made as a result of the TQM project. These changes have allowed the university to do a better job at filling interview schedules.

Gilbert, James P., Kay L. Keck, and Ronald D. Simpson
"Improving the Process of Education: Total Quality Management for the College Classroom." *Innovative Higher Education* 18, no.1 (Fall 1993): 65–85.

TQM has been used in the classroom at several colleges and universities. Some examples of TQM efforts in the classroom are those experiments taking place at the University of Chicago, the University of Wisconsin, the University of Michigan, Columbia University, and the University of Tennessee. The authors outline a six-step strategy for continuous classroom improvement that is based on a self-assessment guide developed by the U.S. Department of Defense. These-steps are: establishing a TQM environment for classroom improvement; defining general objectives for the course and defining specific objectives for each module or section of the course; setting performance improvement opportunities, goals, and priorities; selecting teaching methods that keep students focused and participating; frequent evaluation during and at the end of the course; and frequent review with revision when necessary.

Grace, Richard E., and Thomas J. Templin
"QSS: Quality Student Services." *NASPA Journal* 32, no.1 (Fall 1994): 74–80.

Purdue University (West Lafayette, Indiana) instituted a year long project within twelve student services departments to improve services for students and other customers. The participating departments ranged from the bursar's office to the student health center. The goals of the project were fourfold: to identify customers and their needs; to get customer feedback; to identify methods of monitoring and measuring quality; and to identify changes that would result in improved services for customers. The scope of the project involved more than 400 staff members and thousands of customers, ranging from college students to outside agencies. The project was conducted on three levels: staff initiatives; departmental initiatives; and customer initiatives. As a result, several problems have been remedied and TQM is viewed as a strategy worth implementing throughout the university.

Greenbaum, Stuart I.
"TQM at Kellogg." *Journal for Quality and Participation* 16, no.1 (January/February 1993): 88–92.

The J. L. Kellogg Graduate School of Management at Northwestern University offers a course in TQM in its degree program and is considering additional course offerings in this area. In addition, many Kellogg faculties integrate TQM in their courses. There is also a week-long TQM course for executives (an offering developed in partnership with Motorola). The principles of TQM have also guided other initiatives such as new faculty orientation and the faculty mentor program. Proposed TQM initiatives involve curricular reform; redesign of the grading system; and hiring of an instructional specialist to help faculty improve their teaching.

Hansen, W. Lee
"Bringing Total Quality Improvement into the College Classroom." *Higher Education* 25, no.3 (April 1993): 259–279.

The author describes his application of Total Quality Improvement (TQI) into an upper level economics course at the University of Wisconsin-Madison. This integration of TQI into the classroom involved three major components: a customer orientation; student involvement; and continuous improvement. A customer focus was achieved by identifying almost twenty specific proficiencies for the undergraduate economics major. For example, Hansen determined that graduating economics majors should be able to do the following: locate published information in economics and related disciplines; understand how economic data are derived; summarize a current controversy in economics; explain a current economic policy issue; write a short statement on current economic conditions; summarize the major ideas of a prominent living economist; read and interpret a theoretical or quantitative analysis from a research journal in economics; write a proposal for a research project; and conduct a research project. The second element, student involvement, was accomplished through team-oriented research projects. Continuous improvement was achieved through ongoing course and instructor evaluations. Students were graded on their individual and team performances. Hansen found that students were pleased with their improvement in these proficiencies. They were also positive about team projects even though they noted negatives such as the difficulty of scheduling team meetings or an unfair workload on the part of some team members. Students also liked the idea of ongoing evaluation.

Heverly, Mary Ann, and Robert A. Cornesky
"Total Quality Management: Increasing Productivity and Decreasing Costs." *New Directions for Institutional Research* 75 (Fall 1992): 103–114.

The authors explore TQM as a long-term technique that colleges and universities can use to increase productivity and decrease costs. The basic tenet of TQM is that continuous quality improvement leads to improved productivity and lower costs. Although many colleges and universities were in the early phases of a TQM program at the time this chapter was written, they use data on productivity and cost reductions from the few available studies. Among the institutions profiled in these studies are the Fox Valley Technical College, Oregon State University, Delaware County Community College, and Edinboro University of Pennsylvania.

Horine, Julie E., William A. Hailey, and Laura Rubach
"Shaping America's Future." *Quality Progress* 26, no.10 (October 1993): 41–60.

Some 139 universities and forty-six community colleges responded to this survey of quality management efforts in higher education conducted by *Quality Progress*. Seventy-eight percent of the institutions responding indicated that they are in the early phases of TQM (with most reporting that they have been using TQM for two years or less). About half of the institutions have quality councils, offices, or centers to coordinate TQM efforts. The greatest percentage of quality improvement projects are in administrative areas. Many institutions have formed partnerships with industry. The "Quality in Education Listing" appended to the article provides contact names and phone numbers for each institution. Another useful feature is the comparative table on colleges and universities offering courses relating to quality improvement.

Hunt, C. Steven
"Group Support Systems: A New Frontier for Amplifying Creativity and Collaborative Learning", *Business Education Forum* 48, no.3 (February 1994): 31–34.

The author discusses Group Support Systems – software packages that can help total quality management teams in elementary, secondary, and postsecondary schools brainstorm, assess ideas, and formulate policies. He reviews groupware packages that have been used by many schools. Among the packages that have been selected for review are CoNexus Teamware, EIES2, Group System V, Lotus Notes, OptionFinder, SAMM, and VisionQuest.

"Implementing TQM at the University of Bradford Management Centre." In *Cases in Total Quality Management* (Oxford (England): Butterworth-Heinemann, 1994), 253–268.

This case study examines the implementation of TQM at one of Europe's oldest and largest business schools. The University of Bradford Management Centre launched a TQM program in 1991. The Centre's goals are to achieve a University Funding Council research rating of 5, to be the leading business school in the UK in terms of services and products offered to targeted markets, and to empower employees to make continuous improvements to meet customers' requirements. Although the Centre's program is still in its early stages, the Centre has achieved its goal of a research rating of 5.

Ivancevich, Daniel M., and Susan H. Ivancevich
"TQM in the Classroom." *Management Accounting* 74 (October 1992): 14–15.

The University of Michigan and Oregon State University have proceeded to implement TQM organization-wide. Some universities have implemented TQM or other quality techniques into their business curricula. These schools include the University of Chicago, Carnegie-Mellon University, Duke University, University of North Carolina, Northwestern University, New York University, University of California-Berkeley, University of Virginia, University of Pennsylvania, Yale University, University of Tennessee, and Fordham University. TQM can easily be implemented into managerial accounting classes. For example, TQM can be used to develop a more informative method for tracking costs. In addition, accounting faculties should apply TQM to their customers (that is, their students). Businesses that routinely hire accounting graduates should also be surveyed to determine their perceptions and suggestions for improvement in the accounting curriculum. Faculty members should be encouraged to attend TQM forums and seminars.

Lewis, Ralph G., and Douglas H. Smith
Total Quality in Higher Education. Delray Beach, FL: St. Lucie Press, 1994.

This title is part of the St. Lucie Press Total Quality Series. It introduces readers to the topic of total quality management in higher education. The first chapter discusses why TQM should be implemented in colleges and universities and presents some caveats for those attempting to implement total quality organization-wide or in part of a college or university. The second chapter provides an overview of the history of the total quality movement. The third chapter describes The House of Quality, a metaphor for total quality. Chapters 4 through 7 discuss the four cornerstones of total quality: strategy management; process management; project and team management; and individual and task management. Chapter 8 provides guidelines for initiating a quality improvement program and describes various implementation models. The last chapter focuses on ISO 9000 issues.

Macchia, Peter, Jr.
"Assessing Educational Processes Using Total-Quality-Management Measurement Tools." *Educational Technology* 33, no.5 (May 1993); 48–54.

The author introduces educators to the following quality tools: cause-and-effect diagrams; Pareto diagrams; control charts; histograms; check sheets; scatter diagrams; and flowcharts. Although there are many books on quality tools, most are oriented to manufacturing processes. This well-written article does an exceptional job of explaining each technique and how it can be applied to the educational setting. Macchia's article should be required reading for all nonstatisticians attempting to understand these measurement techniques.

McDaniel, Thomas R.
"College Classrooms of the Future: Megatrends to Paradigm Shifts." *College Teaching* 42, no.1 (Winter 1994): 27–31.

McDaniel discusses the megatrends that he sees in college teaching. These trends include total quality management, a move to capitalize on intrinsic motivation to make learning more satisfying and teaching more rewarding, service learning (integrating community service into the curriculum), and authentic assessment (evaluation which focuses on measurable outcomes). He believes that TQM is a megatrend that will result in a paradigm shift. McDaniel believes that this new paradigm will dramatically alter the way professors teach. For example, TQM means that professors will coach and counsel more than teach or lecture, adjust teaching strategies to foster cooperation and teamwork, and reduce or eliminate formal teaching in favor of monitoring for continuous improvement.

Marchese, Ted
"TQM: A Time for Ideas." *Change* 25, no.3 (May/June 1993): 10–13.

A few campuses began implementing TQM in the 1980s. Since 1990, there has been great interest on the part of colleges and universities. Marchese outlines six important components of TQM: a customer focus; continuous improvement; management by fact; benchmarking; an emphasis on employee training and teamwork; and collaboration across the organization.

Melan, Eugene H.
"Quality Improvement in Higher Education: TQM in Administrative Functions." *CUPA Journal* 44, no.3 (Fall 1993): 7–8, 10, 12, 14–18.

This article focuses on the application of TQM in administrative areas of higher education. These include the following functional areas: admissions; finance; food services; grounds; human resources; information systems; mail distribution; physical plant; purchasing; registration; security; and student services. The authors then outline the process of implementing TQM. Case studies are used to demonstrate types of problems universities can tackle with TQM. A quality team at the University of Pennsylvania found ways to lower the cost of mailing, saving the university nearly $100,000 a year. Another team at the University of Pennsylvania found that by removing waste papers on a demand basis rather than on a regular schedule they could save $175,000 a year.

Melissaratos, Aris, and Carl Arendt
"TQM Can Address Higher Ed's Ills: Westinghouse Executive Offers Advice." *Business Officer* 25, no.10 (April 1992): 32–35.

Westinghouse is viewed as one of the "founding fathers" of American TQM. In 1980, it established a Productivity and Quality Center in its Pittsburgh headquarters. It won the first Baldrige Award in 1988. The authors explain how colleges and universities can implement TQM in higher education. Their discussion draws upon Westinghouse's three-year involvement with the University of Maryland at College Park. Westinghouse has worked with the University of Maryland on several cycle time reduction projects. For example, the time for obtaining emergency financial approvals has been reduced from 24 hours to 20 minutes, and the athletic services unit has reduced waiting times for season ticket holders.

Miller, Henry D. R.
The Management of Change in Universities: Universities, State and Economy in Australia, Canada and the United Kingdom. Buckingham (England): The Society for Research into Higher Education & Open University Press, 1995.

Miller interviewed approximately 100 academic and senior administrators in twenty universities across Australia, Canada, and the United Kingdom to find out what developments have significantly impacted these institutions during the past five years. Based on these interviews, he explores how managerialism and market forces have impacted the governance and culture of universities. Chapter 5, a case study featuring Aston University (located in Birmingham), is particularly valuable to researchers and university administrators looking at the application of TQM in a British university. In fact, the recent changes that have occurred in this university are probably more profound than in any other institution in the UK university system.

Muller, Dave, and Patty Funnell
"An Exploration of the Concept of Quality in Vocational Education and Training." *Educational and Training Technology International* 29, no.3 (August 1992): 257–261.

The authors, both on the faculty at Suffolk College (Ipswich, UK) review the quality movement in vocational education in the United Kingdom. Quality has been promoted in vocational education and training since the late 1980s. However, Muller and Funnell found no consensus among vocational educators about the definition of quality. They contend that the centrality of the learner in the learning process is the critical element when applying the concept of quality to vocational education and training.

Nagy, Joanne et al.
"Madison: How TQM Helped Change an Admissions Process, TQM on Campus, Case Study Number Three." *Change* 25, no.3 (May/June 1993): 36–40.

The University of Wisconsin-Madison Graduate School used the tools of total quality management to revamp the admissions process. The Graduate School spent an average of 26 days processing an application, and overall the average time from application to admission was 99 days. Many departments felt that they were losing top-quality graduate students to other schools because of Madison's lengthy and complicated admissions procedures. As a result of implementing TQM, the Graduate School reduced Graduate School processing time and reduced the overall time from application to admissions decision. A five-day admissions procedure is now in place for the Graduate School and overall, the average time to admission has gone from 99 days to 60 days.

Neves, João S., and Benham Nakhai
"The Baldrige Award Framework for Teaching Total Quality Management." *Journal of Education for Business* 69, no.2 (November/December 1993): 121–125.

Colleges and universities have been slow in integrating the Baldrige Award criteria into coursework and only recently have some textbooks included brief sections on the Award. However, it can be argued that the Baldrige Award represents the American model of TQM. The authors explore how the Baldrige Award guidelines can be effectively used for teaching TQM concepts in both undergraduate and graduate level courses. Their article outlines the ten-point program they developed using the Baldrige Award as a framework for teaching TQM. These ten core concepts are customer-driven quality, leadership, continuous improvement, employee participation and development, fast response, design quality and prevention, long-range outlook, management by fact, partnership development, and corporate responsibility and citizenship.

Nightingale, Peggy, and Mike O'Neil
Achieving Quality Learning in Higher Education. London: Kogan Page, 1994.

Nightingale is Director of the Professional Development Centre at the University of New South Wales. O'Neil is principal lecturer in higher education at Nottingham Trent University. Their book focuses on achieving quality teaching and quality learning in higher education. They provide numerous examples of "good practice" in the text and include case studies written by experienced practitioners from the United Kingdom and Australia.

"An Open Letter: TQM on the Campus." *Harvard Business Review* 69 (November/December 1991): 94–95.

The publication of this letter from the chairmen of six major corporations (American Express, Ford, IBM, Motorola, Procter & Gamble, and Xerox) marked an important development in the evolution of TQM in higher education. These six companies sponsored the 1991 Total Quality Forum, an annual meeting of academic leaders. At the conclusion of the 1991 forum, academic and industry leaders agreed to work together to increase higher education's awareness of TQM. In this letter, these corporate leaders call for closer cooperation between universities and companies to promote TQM. Specifically, they ask companies to invite faculty and students to their facilities to study TQM practices, ask that they make their TQM leaders available to local colleges and universities for seminars and lectures, and integrate TQM into the recruiting process by establishing guidelines for hiring that include a minimum level of TQM coursework. They ask colleges and universities to learn what companies are teaching employees about TQM, to establish a research agenda in TQM, and to take an inventory of quality-related course content in the curriculum.

Plice, Samuel J.
"Changing the Culture: Implementing TQM in an IT Organization." *Cause and Effect* 15, no.2 (Summer 1992): 20–25.

Plice describes the implementation of TQM at the University of Michigan's Information Technology Division (ITD). TQM was perceived as a strategy for improving service to customers. ITD began six pilot quality improvement teams. Although this article was written before any of these teams completed their projects, progress has been made. For example, customers have commented on instances where service has exceeded their expectations. In addition, ITD training for TQM has been so successful that it has served as the model for a campus-wide training program. Finally, meetings are conducted using TQM concepts. ITD's experiment indicates that TQM can help centralized computing departments respond to the changing needs of their clients.

"Quality Improvement in Health Management Education." *The Journal of Health Administration Education* 13, no.1 (Winter 1995): 3–196.

This entire issue of *The Journal of Health Administration Education* explores the integration of TQM into health management education. Part I of this special issue contains articles addressing the question of why TQM should be taught. John P. Evans writes about TQM success stories in the manufacturing sector. The article by Joel Shalowitz looks at Motorola's blueprint for success. Part II brings together articles addressing the questions of what should be taught about TQM. Vinod Sahney, Lisa Higgins, and Gail Warden identify TQM core concepts that should be integrated into health management education. James L. Reinertsen's article addresses the need for health administrators to change the way they think. James Hart, M. Michelle Coady, and George Halvorson look at TQM in a managed care organization. Part III assembles articles focusing on health administration's responses to TQM. The article by Paul B. Batalden and others presents a conceptual framework for learning and teaching about the continual improvement of health care. The next article, by Sherril B.

Gelmon and G. Ross Baker, provides guidelines for incorporating TQM in the health administration curriculum. Sherril Gelmon, Marie E. Sinioris, and Kevin Najafi discuss the use of the Baldrige criteria to improve a health administration program. Paul Schwab looks at TQM in the public sector. Susan Osborn and Stephen Shortell identify topics in the area of quality improvement in health care organizations that need further research and exploration. Robert C. Bradbury and Bernardo Ramirez Minvielle's unique article examines the evolution of continuous quality improvement in Latin American health systems. Wayne Lerner's article summarizes the activities of the Task Force on Quality Improvement. The final article, by Bright Dornblaser, summarizes the findings from a 1991 symposium on managing TQM sponsored by the University of Minnesota.

Reynolds, Gary L.
"Total Quality Management for Campus Facilities." *Facilities Manager* 8, no.3 (Summer 1992): 14–20.

Reynolds examines six basic principles of TQM in relation to the management of college and university facilities: customer-centered orientation; leadership; improved communication; continuous improvement; accountability; and quality of worklife. Facilities managers can become customer-oriented through meetings with administrators, faculty, and students. Participative management and leadership at all levels can help a support services unit create a vision for the future. The formation of cross-functional teams including physical plant, purchasing, and accounting can enhance problem-solving. Continuous improvement can occur through small incremental changes or large fundamental changes. Managers will be held accountable for continuous change. A work environment that empowers employees is a prerequisite to continuous improvement.

Richards, John D., and Marc G. Cloutier
"TQM, Healthcare Education and Customer Satisfaction." *Journal for Quality and Participation* 16, no.1 (January/February 1993): 94–96.

The U.S. Army Medical Department (AMEDD) Center and School is the largest school of allied health services in the world. It offers more than 200 courses which train 35,000 students annually. It also trains 14,000 Reserve and National Guard students annually. In addition, 35,000 students are enrolled in courses offered through the extension services department and correspondence courses. This article describes how the AMEDD Center and School assesses external customer satisfaction. One measurement technique is to send teams of evaluators to various hospitals and installations to interview graduates and their supervisors. Another technique is to send teams to Combat Training Centers to observe graduates providing medical support in a simulated combat environment. Information from both types of visits is reported to senior educators at the AMEDD Center and School. Faculty provide written comments on the issues raised by evaluators and develop action plans to address problem areas. The authors conclude that this model could be adopted by other educational institutions.

Ruben, Brent D., ed.
Quality in Higher Education. New Brunswick, NJ: Transaction, 1995.

Ruben has done an exceptional job of bringing together a collection of readings on quality in general, quality in business and industry, and quality in higher education. Some chapters are reprints of classic articles (including articles by leading authorities such as Peter F. Drucker, Karl Albrecht, Ron Zemke, J. M. Juran, and Ted Marchese). Other chapters are first-time publications. The chapter by A. Blanton Godfrey explores ten trends for quality management over the next decade. The final chapter includes an extensive bibliography on quality management and a selective listing of other resources (including associations, organizations, educational resources and consultants, periodicals, Baldrige and Baldrige-based assessments for higher education, and Internet sources). This outstanding volume is essential to any administrator, instructor, consultant, or trainer involved in the implementation of TQM on a college campus.

Seymour, Daniel T.
"TQM on Campus: What the Pioneers are Finding." *AAHE Bulletin* 44, no.3 (November 1991): 10–13, 18.

Seymour reports the results of a 1991 analysis of quality initiatives at twenty-two colleges and

universities. The full research report, *Quality Management in Higher Education* (which Seymour coauthored with Casey Collett) is available from GOAL/QPC in Methuen, Massachusetts. Faculty, staff, and administrators actively involved with TQM efforts were surveyed regarding their beliefs about the key benefits of TQM and the major problems inherent in implementing TQM. Eighty-three responses were analyzed. Among the benefits identified were empowerment, a customer orientation, an elimination of redundancies, increased efficiency, improved morale, a breaking down of campus barriers, improved communication across departments and units, a renewed focus on the institution's mission, and improved cost effectiveness. Some of the problems identified included an enormous commitment of time, lack of leadership from the top, resistance to change (particularly organizational change), and the difficulty of developing effective teamwork.

Seymour, Daniel T.
On Q: Causing Quality in Higher Education. New York: American Council on Education; Macmillan Pub. Co., 1992.

Seymour, a prominent authority on quality in higher education, examines the importance of quality in three types of organizations: a university, a hospital, and an automobile manufacturer. He chronicles the history of the quality improvement movement from the pre-1930s through the 1990s. Seymour shows how elements of a quality improvement program (e.g., teamwork, customer satisfaction, corporate culture) can work in an academic setting, using examples from several colleges and universities that have implemented quality improvement. His research is based on interviews with administrators at many institutions. He found that many colleges and universities share the quality improvement philosophy even though they may not have a formal quality improvement program in place.

Seymour, Daniel
"Quality on Campus: Three Institutions, Three Beginnings." *Change* 25, no.3 (May/June 1993): 14–27.

Seymour, a leading authority on TQM in higher education, describes three university quality improvement programs. The universities featured in these case studies are the Georgia Institute of Technology, the Pennsylvania State University, and the University of Maryland at College Park. Seymour visited each of these campuses which were among the nine U.S. colleges and universities awarded cash and equipment in 1992 by the IBM Corporation as part of IBM's Total Quality Management University Competition. He describes what is being done at each of these institutions. Georgia Tech is using CQI techniques to attract and retain more minorities and women. Penn State has seventy quality teams in place. Among them are the team whose goal is to improve the teaching of basic physics to engineering undergraduates and a team whose purpose is to improve the process and reduce the cycle time in the procurement of scientific equipment. The University Health Center at the University of Maryland has improved the quality of care and reduced waiting time by revamping its telephone procedures, triage system, and medical excuse policy. Seymour provides many more examples of quality initiatives at these institutions.

Seymour, Daniel
Total Quality Management in Higher Education: Clearing the Hurdles. Methuen, MA: GOAL/QPC, 1993.

Seymour surveyed thirty colleges and universities that have implemented quality management organization-wide or in selective areas. Twenty-one institutions responded to the survey (with a total of seventy-three surveys completed). Seymour's survey focused on barriers to the implementation of quality management and strategies for overcoming these obstacles. Respondents from all types of colleges and universities reported that time constraint is the major hurdle to the successful implementation of quality management. Some approaches identified by respondents for overcoming this primary hurdle included these four strategies: arguing that quality management is a long-term investment that will improve productivity and the quality of work life; selecting improvement projects that have shorter completion times in order to demonstrate results; making quality management practices part of everyday work life; and being honest about TQM. This *GOAL/QPC Application Report* is a sequel to a 1991 *GOAL/QPC*

Application Report authored by Daniel Seymour and Casey Collett. This 1991 report, entitled *Total Quality Management in Higher Education: A Critical Assessment*, surveyed twenty-two colleges and universities that were implementing TQM. The survey asked basic questions such as "What areas of your university are using TQM?", "What factors motivated your institution to consider TQM?", "What process improvement efforts have been initiated?", and "What TQM tools have been useful?"

Seymour, Daniel
Once Upon a Campus: Lessons for Improving Quality and Productivity in Higher Education. Phoenix, AZ: American Council on Education; Oryx, 1995.

Seymour proposes a "Performance Improvement Framework" in *Once Upon a Time*. This framework can be used as an audit or planning tool by college and university administrators committed to continuous quality improvement. The framework has five components: direction-setting; process design and management; feedback; enablers; and personal involvement. This framework serves as an organizing scheme for a series of stories. Each story is based upon an actual event that a campus practitioner shared with Seymour. These stories provide a series of lessons on continuous improvement. There are fourteen lessons in total. Four lessons relate to process design and management, one lesson relates to feedback, six relate to the enablers component of the framework, one lesson relates to personal involvement, and two lessons relate to direction-setting.

Seymour, Daniel, and Ellen E. Chaffee
"TQM For Student Outcomes Assessment" *AGB Reports* 34, no.1 (January/February 1992): 26–30.

Seymour and Chaffee discuss how TQM can be used in student outcomes assessment, that is, measuring what students have learned. When this assessment is part of a larger quality improvement effort, colleges and universities can use data derived from the assessment to improve institutional processes. The purpose of assessment shifts from accountability to quality improvement. The authors outline how student outcomes have effected change in several institutions, including Alabama's Samford University, the University of

Montevallo in Alabama, the Alabama State University, the University of Wisconsin-Madison, and the United States Air Force Academy in Colorado.

Shaw, Kenneth A.
"Sunflower Seeds at Syracuse." *Educational Record* 74, no.2 (Spring 1993): 20–27.

The intriguing title of this article refers to the problem that piles of sunflower seed hulls created for custodians at Syracuse University. Sunflower seeds, a popular snack among Syracuse students, tended to jam up cleaning equipment, causing delays in the classroom-cleaning schedule. This snack problem was studied by one of Syracuse's first quality improvement pilot teams. The solution was to stock only hulled sunflower seeds in vending machines. Syracuse has applied TQM to problems more complex than sunflower seed residue. For example, as part of its new focus on the customer, Syracuse designed a food court according to students' requests. Another quality improvement team found that students had problems accessing information about their financial status. As a result, a computer terminal dedicated to providing students' information about their bursar accounts was installed in the main library. Although Syracuse has just experimented with TQM through pilot projects, it is likely that this focused collaborative approach will become the norm.

Sherr, Lawrence A., and Deborah J. Teeter, eds
Total Quality Management in Higher Education, New Directions for Institutional Research no.71. San Francisco: Jossey-Bass, 1991.

This entire volume examines the topic of total quality management in colleges and universities. There are seven papers in total. The first introduces the principles of TQM and discusses the benefits of TQM to higher education. The second paper is a case study of TQM in a community college (Delaware County Community College) and the third article is a case study of TQM at Oregon State University. Chapter 4 discusses assessment and TQM. The fifth paper analyzes barriers to TQM and discusses how colleges and universities can overcome these obstacles. The sixth paper examines the development of a leadership team at Virginia Tech University. The final chapter outlines the role that institutional

researchers and planners can play in the implementation of TQM. Three valuable appendices are included. The first describes basic TQM tools. The second appendix is a listing of suggestions for further reading. Appendix C lists twenty-five U.S. colleges and universities involved in TQM. This listing (although not comprehensive) includes four-year institutions, two-year institutions, and a university system.

Stern, Bruce L., and Douglas P. Tseng
"U.S. Business Schools' Reaction to the Total Quality Management Movement." *Journal of Education for Business* 69, no.1 (September/October 1993): 44–48.

The authors conducted a mail survey of U.S. business school deans in spring 1992 to determine what organizational, faculty development, and curricular changes business schools have made as a result of the total quality management movement. Responses were received from 117 deans, 34.4 percent of the sample. Although several schools implemented TQM almost a decade ago, most schools are in a wait-and-see, exploratory, or experimental mode. Approximately 27 percent of the deans reported that they used TQM in their operations. Schools having graduate business programs as well as those feeling pressure from the outside to adopt TQM were more likely to use TQM in their operations. Schools in which TQM was used in their operations have faculty who were perceived to be more aware of TQM. Less than 25 percent of deans noted that their school had initiated faculty development programs relating to TQM. However, deans who sensed pressure from the business community to adopt TQM were almost twice as likely to implement faculty development programs. Almost seven out of ten deans reported that their school had made some curricular efforts in the area of TQM. Approximately 27 percent of these schools developed a TQM class. Another 24 percent were considering a TQM-based curriculum, and 21 percent were incorporating TQM into existing core courses. Almost 5 percent had TQM continuing education courses and about 3 percent offered TQM concentrations, minors, or certificates. Among the impediments noted were lack of awareness and understanding, lack of funding, faculty perception of TQM as a fad, resistance to change, and inertia. The authors recommend that faculty be educated about TQM through reading, workshops, seminars, faculty internships, and interactions with business. In addition, influence from the business community can increase the interest of business schools in TQM.

Wasson, Dale
"Quality Control in the Application Process." *College & University* 68, no.2 (Spring/Summer 1993): 108–111.

The admissions office at Georgia Southern University implemented TQM to control the quality of the application process. The application process was divided into three primary processes: coding and data entry; transcript evaluation; and notification and file maintenance. Two types of information are audited: information that affects the office's ability to communicate with a student, and information which affects the decision to admit or deny a student. The auditing process involves a simple paper checklist for each employee. For example, the checklist for the coding and data entry process includes checking for the accuracy of items such as name, address, phone, intended degree/major, social security number, etc. The audits can also help gauge the need for training for new employees. Every month, employees with a perfect audit receive special recognition. This is an interesting case study since it illustrates that TQM does not have to be implemented on an institution-wide basis in order to be effective.

SIC 8231: Libraries

Barnard, Susan B.
"Implementing Total Quality Management: A Model for Research Libraries." *Journal of Library Administration* 18, no.1/2 (1993): 57–70.

The author, Head of Periodical Information and Access Services at the Kent State University Libraries, points out that TQM can be easily implemented in research libraries since many of the essential elements of TQM (e.g., participative management, staff training and development, a service philosophy) are already in place. Barnard presents an implementation process for research libraries in four phases and ten steps. These stages and steps are not meant to be mandatory or

sequential, but are descriptive of the activities that comprise a total quality approach. Phase One involves first-steps. Step One is the exploration phase and Step Two is the decision to implement TQM. The second phase is organizing or preparing for quality. During this phase, organizations should address leadership planning. This third-step involves the following three activities: organizational assessment; understanding customers; and development of a vision and guiding principles. Phase Three is a start-up and includes steps four through eight: identifying products, services, and customers; assessing customer needs; identifying critical processes; pilot projects; and skill development. The final phase is evaluation and expansion. During this fourth phase, senior management creates a three- to five-year TQM strategic plan and divisional and departmental planning takes place.

"Benchmarking, Total Quality Management and The Learning Organization: New Management Paradigms for the Information Environment." *Special Libraries* 84, no.3 (Summer 1993): 120–157.

This entire issue of *Special Libraries* is devoted to the concepts of total quality management, benchmarking, and the learning organization in the information environment. There are eight articles in total. Contributors include Guy St. Clair, Ferne C. Allan, Miriam A. Drake, Crit Stuart, Elizabeth Duffek, Warren Harding, Ann Lawes, and Christine M. Pearson. Among the topics covered are the role of benchmarking, TQM in research libraries, TQM applications in the military, the benefits from quality improvement programs, the learning organization, and management and measurement techniques for library and information services.

Berry, John
"Austin Public Library." *Library Journal* 118, no.11 (June 15, 1993): 30–33.

The Austin (Texas) Public Library was awarded the *Library Journal* 1993 Library of the Year Award. This article looks at the library's outreach program, volunteer program, partnership with local government, and use of total quality management. Austin's city manager brought the concept of TQM to Austin government. The Austin Public Library established a Quality Resource Center at one of its branches to support the city's quality initiative. The library also adopted the process and tools of TQM to its operation.

Brockman, John R.
"Just Another Management Tool?: The Implications of TQM for Library and Information Services." *Aslib Proceedings* 44, nos.7–8 (July/August 1992): 283–288.

Using case studies from the United Kingdom and North America, the author presents an overview of the development of quality management in library and information services. He traces the evolution of the quality movement from quality control to total quality management. The author concludes that library and information services professionals need to be knowledgeable about TQM and how their organization could benefit from its implementation.

Butcher, Karyle S.
"Total Quality Management: The Oregon State University Library's Experience." *Journal of Library Administration* 18, nos.1–2 (1993): 45–56.

Total quality management had been introduced to Oregon State University in 1989. The library was the first academic unit to explore TQM. This article describes the pilot projects carried out by two library teams. Both pilot projects involved the public services sector of the library. One pilot examined the reshelving process in the library while the other pilot analyzed the flow of government publications from the time they arrived in the library to the time they were available on the shelves to the public. Both teams have made recommendations for improvement that are being implemented. For example, the team analyzing the flow of government publications found that signage was a problem. As a result of this discovery, larger and easier-to-read signs were created. The other pilot team made several recommendations that are being considered, including reorganizing library materials to make a more logical stacks arrangement and providing better training of shelvers so they can provide accurate information to users in the stacks.

Gapen, D. Kaye, Queen Hampton, and Sharon Schmitt
"TQM: The Director's Perspective." *Journal of Library Administration* 18, nos.1–2 (1993): 15–28.

What are the merits of TQM as a management approach for large academic and research libraries? The authors' response is that TQM challenges libraries to do the following: identify customers; identify what customers want; identify what libraries need to do to meet users' expectations; decide on how to measure services; and evaluate services to determine what processes should be continued or changed. The University Libraries at Case Western Reserve University (CWRU) in Cleveland, Ohio provide an interesting case study of TQM applied to academic libraries. The library used TQM techniques to plan for the construction of the Kelvin Smith Library, a new library facility on the CWRU campus that will take advantage of future information technologies. As part of this approach, the library conducted an extensive user survey to collect data on the information-gathering behaviors of the campus community. This information is being used to create a library that will serve 21st century users.

Jurow, Susan
"Tools for Measuring and Improving Performance." *Journal of Library Administration* 18, nos.1–2 (1993): 113–126.

Jurow, Director of the Association of Research Libraries' Office of Management Services, introduces library administrators and managers to five quality tools. She uses library-based examples (such as tracking the acquisitions process, factors in patron search success, and reason for lack of patron success) to explain the Shewhart Cycle (also known as Plan-Do-Check-Act), flowcharts, cause-and-effect diagrams, Pareto charts, and control charts. There is also an excellent introduction to the topic of benchmarking.

Jurow, Susan, and Susan B. Barnard, eds
Integrating Total Quality Management in a Library Setting. New York: Haworth Press, 1993.

The articles in this volume have also been published in *The Journal of Library Administration* (18, nos.1/2 1993). This compilation in book form will be useful to libraries that do not subscribe to *The Journal of Library Administration* or to those libraries that want this convenient compendium for their circulating collection. These articles provide a good overview of TQM in libraries. Some of the articles describe the application of TQM in specific libraries (such as Harvard and Oregon State) while others discuss the application of TQM in higher education and in the public sector (specifically, the federal government). The remaining articles focus on the tools and techniques of TQM and issues such as training and the use of teams.

Loney, Tim, and Arnie Bellefontaine
"TQM Training: The Library Service Challenge." *Journal of Library Administration* 18, nos.1–2 (1993): 85–95.

Th authors identify the training and skill development required for each of the phases of TQM implementation in libraries. These phases include exploration and commitment, organizing for quality, start-up, and expansion and integration. Although training will overlap from one phase to another, each phase has specific training requirements. For example, an orientation to quality customer service is one of the training requirements for phase one. Benchmarking is one of the skills needed for phase two. Teamwork and client survey techniques are required for the third phase. The fourth stage requires a knowledge of customer focus tools and techniques, client relations training, and instruction on conducting service audits.

Miller, Rush G., and Beverly Stearns
"Quality Management for Today's Academic Library." *College & Research Libraries* News 55, no.7 (July/August 1994): 406–408, 409. 422.

In this basic introduction to TQM, the authors outline barriers to quality management. TQM has failed in some academic settings for the following reasons: some middle managers feel threatened by a perceived loss of power in a flattened organizational structure; some academicians, including librarians, are unfamiliar with the terminology associated with TQM; some managers perceive TQM as being extraordinarily time-consuming; some managers feel that TQM means capitulating to the whims of customers; and some managers view it as just another management fad. The authors, however, identify six benefits of quality management: continuous improvement; development of leadership skills; increased staff participation results in the feeling of "ownership" of decisions; improved training results in

increased skills; improved communication within the organization; and improved services to users in a time of fiscal constraint. Miller and Stearns describe the experience of Bowling Green State University (BGSU) Libraries in implementing team management. Miller is Dean of Libraries and Stearns is an assistant to the Dean. Teams have been established in the BGSU Libraries to identify problems and solutions relating to the following areas: collection development; preservation; access services; technical services; physical facilities; human relations; and professional development and training.

O'Neill, Rosanna M.
Total Quality Management in Libraries: A Sourcebook. Englewood, CO: Libraries Unlimited, 1994.

This book consists primarily of reprinted articles written by academic and special librarians on TQM in libraries. Most of the essays were originally published between the early 1980s and 1994. A selective annotated bibliography leads readers to other writings on TQM in libraries. Several appendices are included, such as the one suggesting quality-related titles for a library's in-house and circulating collections.

Riggs, Donald E.
"Managing Academic Libraries With Fewer Resources." *Journal for Higher Education Management* 8, no.1 (Summer/Fall 1992): 27–34.

Restricted budgets will force libraries to dramatically alter how work is currently being done in libraries in order to contain costs, maximize staff productivity, and deliver more efficient service. Many current practices are exceedingly labor intensive. For example, the cost of ordering and cataloging a book typically exceeds the cost of the book itself. Because TQM requires institutions to identify and eliminate unnecessary processes, Riggs argues that academic libraries should implement TQM. Although TQM can be time-consuming, in the long run it can reduce costs, improve efficiency, and result in better service to library users.

Shaughnessy, Thomas W.
"Benchmarking, Total Quality Management, and Libraries." *Library Administration & Management* 7, no.1 (Winter 1993): 7–12.

Some academic libraries have begun to apply TQM concepts. Shaughnessy, the university librarian at the University of Minnesota, provides an introduction to TQM applications in higher education and in academic libraries. He focuses on the methods for measuring quality: benchmarking; performance measures; and the use of quality tools such as flowcharts, check sheets, Pareto charts; fishbone diagrams, run charts, histograms, and scatter diagrams. He provides a good example of a benchmarking exercise within a library's circulation service. For example, the exercise indicates that the following functions might be benchmarked: unit costs; billing errors; name/address errors; service requests rejected; queue waiting time; system performance; percentage of satisfied users; and book availability. This example demonstrates the usefulness of benchmarking in a library setting.

Siggins, Jack, and Maureen Sullivan, compilers
Quality Improvement Programs in ARL Libraries. SPEC Kit 196. Washington, DC: Association of Research Libraries, Office of Management Studies, 1993.

The SPEC Kit series, published by the Association of Research Libraries (ARL), provides timely information about ARL member libraries. The SPEC kits frequently summarize survey results. This kit summarizes the results of an April 1993 survey conducted by ARL to determine the existence of quality improvement programs and/or the use of quality improvement processes in research libraries. Ninty-one libraries responded to the survey, resulting in a response rate of 76 percent. Fifteen libraries responded that they have a formal quality improvement program in place. However, more than one-third (36 percent) of the institutions whose libraries responded to the survey have a quality improvement program in one or more departments, including computer science, finance, accounting, physical plant, hospitals, human services, and purchase. The SPEC kit does not explain why seventy-six out of the ninety-one responding libraries do not have a quality improvement program. However, the fifteen libraries with quality programs have focused their improvement efforts on a wide range of departments and functions. TQM is library-wide in six of the fifteen libraries. The other nine libraries have focused on serials, administration, cataloging, circulation, acquisitions, interlibrary loan, automation, personnel, processing, preservation, and collection development. None of these nine libraries has expanded TQM to reference services or branch libraries. The most frequent TQM strategies implemented by all fifteen libraries include team building, a customer orientation, continuous improvement, and statistical process control. Training is a critical element in fourteen out of fifteen programs. In most of the fifteen libraries, the percentage of staff involved in TQM is 50 percent or less. Although a minority of ARL libraries have an established TQM program, ARL predicts that more ARL libraries will apply quality improvement techniques in the 1990s.

Total Quality Management in Academic Libraries: Initial Implementation Efforts. Proceedings From the 1st International Conference on TQM and Academic Libraries. Washington, DC: Association of Research Libraries, Office of Management Services, 1995.

This conference on total quality management in academic libraries was held in Washington DC in April 1994. Daniel T. Seymour was the keynote speaker at the opening session. Presenters were affiliated with a wide range of institutions, including the Pennsylvania State University, Duke University, the University of Wisconsin System, Oregon State University, Wayne State University, Mankato State University, Centenary College, University of the West Indies, University of Minnesota, University of Connecticut, University of California-Berkeley, Kent State University, Indiana University, University of Michigan, University of Illinois at Chicago, Illinois Institute of Technology, Texas A & M University, University of Arizona, and Samford University. Some of the presenters were affiliated with library vendors. Among the topics covered were qualitative and quantitative research techniques, reorganization, benchmarking, teamwork, customer satisfaction, performance appraisal, and partnering.

SIC 8307: Performing arts

Welch, Samuel
"Total Quality Management in the Performing Arts." *Quality Progress* 26, no.1 (January 1993): 31–36.

This unique article explores the idea of implementing TQM in a performing arts organization. In the United States, private support for the performing arts is becoming increasingly important as public subsidies have eroded. The author proposes TQM as an alternative to the traditional arts management model since it would enable a not-for-profit arts organization to increase community loyalty, involvement, and financial support.

SIC 8711: Engineering services

Hayden, William M.
"Management's Fatal Flaw: TQM Obstacle." *Journal of Management in Engineering* 8, no.2 (April 1992): 122–129.

Many architectural, engineering, and construction (AEC) firms are exploring TQM only because of pressure from their clients. Hayden identifies denial by management as the single biggest obstacle to TQM. Managers who deny that problems exist in their firm continue to do business as usual. However, Hayden claims that companies that have not implemented TQM will be noncompetitive in the next five to ten years. Hayden stresses the importance of TQM leadership. Managers must establish the firm's TQM vision for the future and personally communicate it to employees. Hayden concludes that more information and case studies are needed on TQM applications in the design and construction industries.

Higgins, Ronald C., and Michael L. Johnson
"Total Quality Enhances Education of U.S. Army Engineers." *National Productivity Review* 11 (Winter 1991/92): 41–49.

The Department of Engineering in the School of Engineering and Logistics (SEL) trains engineers in specialty areas including quality/product assurance. SEL is a federal government organization employing civilian Army engineers.

Students with a college degree in engineering are hired as civilian employees and are sent to SEL for a year of training. This is followed by six months of additional training at Texas A & M University. Graduates are assigned to commands, agencies, and activities of the Army Material Command (AMC) and have worked on projects such as the Patriot Missile, Apache Helicopter, and the MI Abrams Battle Tank. TQM principles are practiced in the daily operations of SEL. This is accomplished through fostering job ownership, encouraging creativity, promoting teamwork, using communication for continuous improvement, and building trust and confidence.

Jones, Thomas E., and James J. Wolf
"New Application in TQM: Executing Development Contracts 'The Missing Link'." *Annual Quality Congress Transactions* 45 (1991): 264–269.

Harris Corporation produces communication and information processing equipment. One of its divisions, the Electronic Systems Sector, includes the Aerospace Systems Division. Aerospace Systems develops and manufactures systems for communication, intelligence, advanced avionics, and space applications. In 1988 Aerospace Systems adopted a program team organization structure, a structure where the work of the division is organized around self-managing teams. These multidisciplinary teams meet regularly to analyze problems and solutions and to change processes and strategies. One program where teams were implemented has shown cost savings and an improvement in delivery time.

Kasser, Joe
Applying Total Quality Management to Systems Engineering. Boston: Artech House, 1995.

Kasser discusses how systems engineering, systems engineers, and project management relate in a cost-effective engineering environment. He assumes that readers have some knowledge of systems engineering, software development, hardware development, and management techniques. After describing theoretical concepts, he describes a scenario in which principles may or may not have been applied. The scenarios, most of which are in fictitious settings, are analyzed for lessons learned. Kasser has a wealth of practical experience, having spent two decades applying TQM to systems engineering in the aerospace industry. In addition to discussing the application of TQM to systems engineering, Kasser describes one way to use the ISO 9001 standard to make the systems engineering process more cost effective. At present, the ISO 9000 series do not apply to systems engineering. However, this discussion is extremely relevant since Kasser predicts that ISO 9000 or an equivalent standard will probably apply to systems engineering in the future.

Kazmierski, Thomas J.
Statistical Problem Solving in Engineering. New York: McGraw-Hill, 1995.

This practical guide shows engineers how statistical techniques can solve productivity, cost, and quality problems in design and manufacturing. The organization of the book follows many process improvement efforts. Chapters cover the seven stages of quality evolution, the costs of poor quality, common obstacles to the successful implementation of process improvement, Pareto analysis, brainstorming techniques, variation and statistics, measurement systems analysis, Shewhart control charts, capability, variables control charts, multivariate charting, precontrol charts, attribute control charts, check sheets, scatter plots, and design of experiment. Several quality engineering case studies are included.

Kohnen, James B.
"Design Engineering & TQM – A Powerful Union." *Annual Quality Congress Transactions* 47 (1993): 119–125.

Traditionally, design engineers have worked alone at drafting tables or computer work stations to develop new products. Kohnen describes how the design engineering process can be redefined through the addition of teamwork and the notion of a customer orientation. He uses two case studies to illustrate how this approach can lead to innovative solutions to design problems.

Lacy, James A.
Systems Engineering Management: Achieving Total Quality. New York: McGraw-Hill, 1992.

Systems engineering can help companies design and produce products effectively and efficiently. This text blends theory with real-world

examples to show systems engineers and production managers how to translate customer needs into "design to" and "build to" requirements, how to establish planning and control to save time and money, how to integrate specialty engineering tasks with the requirements, and how to use quality tools for design engineering. A variety of American and Japanese techniques are covered, including Quality Function Deployment, Taguichi methods, Pugh convergence, and Joint Application Design.

Lauritsen, Gary L.
"A Method for Total Quality Management in Consulting Engineering Firms." *Proceedings of the Project Management Institute Annual Seminar Symposium* (1991): 737–743.

Although this article is directed to engineering and architectural consultants, it is applicable to other professionals in the building/environmental design industry. The author describes how Coffman Engineers, Inc. (CEI), a Seattle-based consulting engineering firm implemented TQM. He examines four aspects of CEI's TQM program: corporate attitude, procedural considerations in managing quality during the design process, tools for achieving a quality design product, and procedures for improving quality during the construction and start-up stages of the project. Although CEI was still in the early stages of implementing TQM in 1991 (when this article was written), the firm believes that a TQM program will allow the firm to attract clients who will be willing to pay higher fees for a better product.

Menon, H. G.
TQM in New Product Manufacturing. New York: McGraw-Hill, 1992.

This practical guide shows industrial practitioners (engineers, technicians, and managers) how to use mathematical and statistical tools to systematize the manufacturing process, minimize variation in manufactured products, and reduce the costs of manufacturing new products. It walks readers through the planning and implementation of a TQM system step-by-step, using the production of a new camshaft design as a manufacturing case example. Readers learn how to develop a quality manufacturing plan, establish machine and gauge acceptance criteria, conduct failure modes and effects analysis, use statistical process control systems, design statistically valid experiments, quantify the quality and consistency of supplier parts and products, select appropriate computer hardware and software, and measure levels of customer satisfaction.

Noori, Hamrid, and Russell Radford
Production and Operations Management: Total Quality and Responsiveness. New York: McGraw-Hill, 1995.

This textbook on production management is part of the McGraw-Hill Series in management. However, unlike most texts in this area, this one focuses on total quality and responding to customer needs and expectations. The underlying premise is that the leading-edge firm (referred to as "the fast-response organization", or "FRO") is organized around six competitive factors: product quality; total service support for products and for suppliers and customers; product and process flexibility; the strategic use of time (especially as a value-added concept); costs (particularly in a customer-oriented, not value sense); and dependability in honoring commitments in the marketplace. The authors conclude that the qualities that distinguish FROs today will become essential to companies in the future. Quality will be a basic function, not a differentiator. Chapter material is reinforced through chapter summaries, discussion questions, problems, and group exercises. A separate combined workbook and study guide has been designed for use with this text as well as a graphic-based software package. Contact McGraw-Hill for additional information.

Peterson, Winfield A., and Paul D. Weisman
"Survival in the 90s: TQM." *Water Environment and Technology* 4, no.7 (July 1992): 20, 22.

Woodard & Curran, an environmental engineering firm, initiated TQM in 1989. The firm was still committed to TQM three years later (when this article was written) and predicted that TQM would result in a complete transformation of the firm. The authors describe the evolution of TQM at Woodard & Curran. The firm has four major TQM initiatives: focusing on client needs; definition of production systems; project management; and service quality. In 1992, Woodard & Curran won its first national engineering excellence award from the American Consulting Engineers Council for a stormwater treatment system design. Woodard & Curran believes that this recognition was due in part to its TQM commitment.

Sweeney, Patrick J., ed.
TQM for Engineering: Applying Quality Principles to Product Design and Development. White Plains, NY: Quality Resources, 1993.

TQM for Engineering has been written for design engineers, research scientists, and production managers. It shows how TQM can be integrated into the technical environment from the shop floor to the research and development department. Chapter contributors include scientists, engineers, and scholars from industry, government, and academia. Although there are many books on the management of manufacturing and on production processes, this is one of the few to focus on the application of quality concepts to the research and development, and the product and process design functions.

Traver, Robert W.
Manufacturing Solutions for Consistent Quality & Reliability: The Nine-Step Problem-Solving Process. New York: Amacom, 1995.

Traver stresses problem-solving as a system for continuous improvement, emphasizing the use of graphical analysis in problem-solving rather than complex statistical tools. Graphical analysis is part of key variable isolation, the systematic approach Traver uses to analyze and understand variation. Key variable isolation using multi-vari can help nontechnical people solve complex problems quickly. Traver outlines a nine-step process for using key variable isolation to reduce variability. The Traver process includes the following sequential steps: determining the importance of the problem; seeing what is really going on; quantifying the output; running multivariable studies; designing experiments; proving you have the answer; running tests with proven variables; installing process controls on key variables; and measuring before-and-after results. Traver also includes case studies in reliability engineering and quality control.

Wesner, John W., Jeffrey M. Hiatt, and David C. Trimble
Winning With Quality: Applying Quality Principles in Product Development. Reading, MA: Addison-Wesley, 1995.

This title is part of Addison-Wesley's Engineering Process Improvement series, a series of books that looks at major processes and the end-to-end process for new product development. The goal of the series is to enable engineers at all levels of experience to increase product quality and become more productive. *Winning With Quality* is a practical book that has been written by experienced engineers at AT & T Bell Laboratories. All three authors have worked in the area of product development and by focusing on processes and people, have shortened development intervals and improved product quality while lowering costs. Many examples and figures are used throughout the book to illustrate quality, concepts and principles. *Winning With Quality*, which can be read from cover to cover, or used on a section-by-section basis, is arranged in five parts. The first part provides an overview and introduction. The second part covers quality concepts, principles, methods, and tools. Part III focuses on implementing a comprehensive quality program. Part IV discusses how readers can learn from their experience. The final section of the book provides a summary, an appendix, a glossary, and a list of references.

Zairi, Mohamed
Total Quality Management for Engineers. Houston, TX: Gulf Publishing Co., 1993.

This book, first published in the United Kingdom in 1991 by Woodhead Publishing Ltd., has been designed as a basic guide to TQM for engineers. Zairi assumes that the reader has no or only limited knowledge of TQM. Although many of the TQM books directed to engineers tend to focus on tools and techniques, Zairi's book is unique because of its broad approach. Chapters cover the link between TQM and engineering, the role of the engineer in a TQM environment, the philosophies of TQM pioneers (specifically, Deming, Juran, Crosby, Feigenbaum, Conway, Ishikawa, Taguchi, Shingo, and Ouchi), the principle concepts of TQM, the meaning of quality systems, the ISO 9000 series of standards, British Standards BS 5750/ISO

9000, TQM tools and techniques, total preventive maintenance for TQM, total safety systems for TQM, leadership, customer–supplier chains, continuous improvement, implementation issues, quality costing, and quality measurement.

SIC 8712: Architectural services

Stasiowski, Frank A., and David Burnstein
Total Quality Project Management for the Design Firm: How to Improve Quality, Increase Sales, and Reduce Costs. New York: Wiley, 1994.

This is one of the few books on quality assurance and quality control techniques for design and construction projects. Professionals in architectural firms and engineering firms need an understanding of quality control techniques, since it is estimated that an average design project can require 30 to 50 percent of its budget to detect and correct errors. In addition, more clients are refusing to accept these higher costs and are demanding higher quality. Total Quality Project Management (TQPM) allows design firms to prevent problems while reducing costs. The authors are design professionals who have had actual experience with TQPM in design firms.

SIC 8721: Accounting, auditing, and bookkeeping services

Armstrong, Rod
"TQM in the Office." *Australian Accountant* 62, no.11 (December 1992): 10–11.

This case study demonstrates how TQM can be successfully applied to accounting procedures. In 1990, the accounting department of Alcoa of Australia launched a "Month End Closing" project as a critical activity for the TQM process. The accounting department reports to management on a monthly cycle through the production of a board report. Typically, this board report was not completed until the ninth or tenth working day of the following month. The goal of the "Month End Closing" project was to have this financial report completed by the second working day of the month (final project results would be available by the first working day of the month). The project is progressing toward this goal and achievements have exceeded Alcoa's expectations. The author is the project coordinator for the Month End project.

Banks, Brian
"The Rites of Service." *CA Magazine* 125, no.7 (July 1992): 20–28.

Companies no longer choose accounting firms for life. Several studies indicate that poor service prompts clients to trade one accounting firm for another. In addition, many companies that have embraced TQM seek out accounting firms that have TQM programs in place. This emphasis on quality, combined with fierce competition for fewer clients, has forced Canadian accounting firms to develop quality improvement programs. While these programs differ, most share two characteristics. The first commonality is the use of formal client surveys to find out what clients want. The second standard element is a re-evaluation of each staff member's roles and responsibilities.

Finkler, Steven A.
Essentials of Cost Accounting for Health Care Organizations. Gaithersburg, MD: Aspen, 1994.

Cost accounting has become an integral part of the quality movement. Although there are several general books on cost accounting, most focus on manufacturing accounting. This is one of the few textbooks to focus on cost accounting from a health care perspective. Chapter 18 covers TQM exclusively, explaining the relationship between TQM and accounting. This book will be useful to health care administrators and both undergraduate and graduate level students in the field of health administration.

Jeffords, Raymond, and Greg M. Thibadoux
"TQM and CPA Firms." *Journal of Accountancy* 175, no.7 (July 1993): 59–63.

The authors propose that CPA firms use TQM to gain a competitive advantage. The first step is to identify customers and their specific requirements. The second step is to use customer requirements to improve the work process. The third step is to regularly measure work activity against customer requirements. Each of these steps is illustrated with an example from auditing and accounting.

Levine, Constance
"How TQM Worked for One Firm." *Journal of Accountancy* 176, no.3 (September 1993): 73–79.

MacDonald, Levine, Jenkins & Co., a twenty-person Boston CPA firm, turned to TQM in 1990 in an effort to improve the firm's competitiveness and client service. The first step was to introduce staff to TQM concepts. Everyone in the firm participated in this training. One of the directors went to a 3M "train the trainer" session so he could become an in-house facilitator. A full-time non-CPA was hired to direct the firm's TQM efforts and to train new employees. The firm spent more time listening to clients and used client surveys to gather data on clients' satisfaction and interest in other firm services. Although the firm came up with more than fifty potential quality improvement projects at a brainstorming session, the company decided to take on the top five projects. These projects include the following: networking office computers; developing a strategic account process for managing client relationships; improving the time and billing process; improving the firm's image; and managing the overall TQM process itself. The out-of-pocket costs for training and implementation were slightly more than $13,000 (the total cost over a five-month period). This does not include the nonbillable time that firm members devoted to the process. Levine believes that TQM has forced the firm to improve performance and profitability and that TQM may have given the company a competitive edge.

Lynch, David
Quality in the Finance Function. London: Kogan Page, 1994.

This practical guide for UK accountants is part of Kogan Page's Financial Skills series. Lynch introduces finance professionals to the concept of quality (making a good case for integrating quality into finance) and explains how quality can be implemented in finance functions in manufacturing, the public sector, and service industries. The author also cautions against common pitfalls to implementing quality. All accountants in the UK will want this highly readable manual on their bookshelf.

Peters, Bruce J.
"The Quality Revolution." *The Internal Auditor* 49 (April 1992): 20–24.

According to Peters, TQM offers four important benefits to auditors: a new philosophy; enhanced methodology; the concept of audit, itself, as a quality system; and the potential for expanded services. In the long run, TQM can result in reduced costs, improved productivity, greater effectiveness, competitive advantage, and improved job prospects. The author outlines how internal auditing can develop quality in other audit processes.

Raaum, Ronell B.
"Measuring and Reporting Performance in Government." *Government Accountants Journal* 41, no. 3 (Fall 1992): 19–25.

This article is directed to public sector accountants. Because of the influence of TQM, many government agencies in the United States are preparing or auditing measures of program and service performance. Accountants will be asked to prepare information about the costs, outputs, outcomes, efficiency, and financial condition of governmental programs and services. Raaum outlines the seven key steps involved in measuring and reporting on performance: affirming the program or service mission and purpose; identifying the internal users and uses; identifying what performance aspects to measure; developing the measures; choosing a comparative benchmark or benchmarks, providing explanatory information; and using graphs, charts, and other visual aids to display the indicators.

Riahi-Belkaoui, Ahmed
Quality and Control: An Accounting Perspective. Westport, CT: Quorum Books, 1993.

This book has been written for accounting students, accountants, quality managers, and researchers in the area of management accounting. After introducing readers to the concept of quality, the author shows how quality can be achieved through a process of accounting and control – that is, accounting for quality costs and controlling direct costs, overhead costs, and mix and yield factors.

Wilcox, Kirkland, and Richard Discenza
"The TQM Advantage." *CA Magazine* 127 (May 1994): 37–41.

TQM can be successfully applied to auditing since there are several points in an audit where the process can break down. These primary sources of quality problems are: procedures, staffing, conduct of the audit, and independence. All four of these problems are described in detail. TQM concepts can help auditing firms increase the quality of the audit process in order to decrease the risk of loss from litigation while reducing costs and increasing profits.

Woods, Michael D.
"How We Changed Our Accounting." *Management Accounting* 70 (February 1989): 42–45.

This article describes how six U.S. Naval Aviation Depots changed the cost accounting practices as part of a TQM initiative. A typical cost accounting system assigns costs to products using direct labor as an allocation base. This model pays little attention to the cost of internal services. By changing the cost accounting procedures, naval depots are now able to assign costs by process and track cost accumulations as products move through manufacturing processes. One of the six depots, the Naval Aviation Depot at Cherry Point, North Carolina was awarded the IIE (Institute of Industrial Engineers) Award for Excellence in Productivity Management and was selected by the Office of Management and Budget as a productivity/quality improvement prototype in the Federal Productivity Improvement Program.

Woods, Michael D.
Total Quality Accounting. New York: Wiley, 1994.

This is a good introduction to total quality accounting, a new approach to cost accounting. It has been designed for both general managers and accountants with the goal of showing both groups how the total quality process can be used to create total quality accounting. Part 1 introduces the reader to TQM. This exceptionally well written introduction to the topic would benefit any novice to TQM. Part 2 explains the general principles of cost accounting, explaining how they can be applied to TQM. Part 3 shows how TQM and cost accounting can be integrated to serve both internal and external customers. The final chapter in the book discusses why TQM fails in an effort to prevent companies from making some common mistakes (such as a lack of a long-term commitment, viewing TQM as a quick fix, establishing too many teams, etc.).

SIC 8731: Commercial physical and biological research

Edwards, John, and Alan Hodgson
"Amersham International PLC: Stimulating Participation in Quality Improvement." In *Achieving Quality Performance: Lessons From British Industry* (London: Cassell, 1994), 3–24.

Amersham International PLC is a major health science company that has helped advance break-throughs in the diagnosis and treatment of disease, in the development of new drugs; and in our understanding of the role of genetics in disease. The company is also working to develop products and services to detect environmental pollutants and microbial contaminants in food and water. Amersham International has nineteen subsidiary companies, customers in 150 countries, and manufacturing facilities in Europe and the United States. It has three major manufacturing sites in the United Kingdom: Amersham, Cardiff, and Gloucester. Edwards and Hodgson chronicle the development and progress of Amersham's quality improvement program. The company launched its quality improvement initiative in April 1988 at its Cardiff Laboratories facility and achieved ISO 9002 certification in March 1993. A four-phase approach was used to implement TQM. The first phase was providing a vision for the future. Phase 2 focused on management actions. Quality improvement began with and included managers. In this phase, managers addressed their "vital few" problems. During this early phase, a training program was developed, a quality council concept was adopted, and an individual was designated as "the quality champion". During Phase 3, participation was increased and a system of recognition and rewards was developed. During Phase 4, quality efforts were linked to overall business goals through department purpose analysis, bench-marking, and ISO 9002 certification. Overall, there have been more than 200 quality circles and

quality improvement team projects. Seventy percent of the employees at Cardiff Laboratories have participated in at least one project. These projects have resulted in savings of more than £600,000. In addition, the company estimates that the cost of poor quality was reduced by more than £3 million for major projects. Lead times for both the preparation and testing of one product have fallen by 80 percent.

Montana, Anthony J.
"If It Isn't Perfect, Make It Better." *Research Technology Management* 35 (July/August 1992): 38–41.

The author describes how quality improvement can be integrated into the research and development (R & D) function. Montana's observation is that R & D is typically the last area of a company to be involved in the implementation of a TQM initiative. However, TQM can be beneficial to R & D in many ways. It can help an R & D unit reduce errors, improve efficiency, increase productivity, and speed up the entry of new products into the marketplace. Montana provides suggestions on how to incorporate quality within R & D and presents examples of measurement criteria to monitor the success of the quality process. His criterion consists of four major categories: quantity (such as number of repeat tests/equipment failures, number of customer complaints, number of patents/patent applications); timeliness (such as time to perform test, downtime due to equipment failures, time in training); cost (such as cost savings/value added, return on R & D investment/payback); and quality (such as customer satisfaction index, peer review of quality, employee turnover/attendance).

SIC 9199: General government, not elsewhere classified

Bates, Jonathan G.
Managing Value for Money in the Public Sector. London: Chapman & Hall, 1993.

This book focuses on the need to reform public sector management in Great Britain. It describes changes that have already been implemented to reduce waste and inefficiency. However, the primary purpose of the book is to describe in detail the tools of managerial reform, providing examples of how these techniques can be applied to produce high-quality public services. This text should be essential reading for all public administrators in the United Kingdom, especially since there are few books on quality in the UK public sector.

Bowman, James S., and Barbara J. French
"Quality Improvement in a State Agency Revisited." *Public Productivity & Management Review* 16, no.1 (Fall 1992): 53–64.

The Florida Department of Transportation (DOT) launched a quality improvement initiative in 1984 modeled after Florida Power & Light's TQM program (Florida Power & Light was the recipient of Japan's Deming Prize and widely regarded as the most efficient electric utility in the United States in the 1980s). The Florida DOT quality initiative is an important case study in the area of TQM since it is one of the earliest and most comprehensive public sector TQM programs in the United States. In 1988, Bowman reported on the Florida DOT project in an article published (and coauthored by J. Steele) in *Public Productivity Review* (see vol. 11, no.4, pp. 11–31). This 1992 article reviews the agency's quality improvement process, provides an update about the status of quality improvement at Florida DOT, and assesses the program's strengths and weaknesses.

Brough, Regina Kay
"Total Quality Management in State Government: The Eight Rules for Producing Results." *The Journal of State Government* 65 (January/March 1992): 4–8.

The author provides a brief introduction to the quality movement in general and to the application of TQM to the public sector. She then outlines her eight rules for applying TQM to public service. Rule 1 is that quality is everyone's job. Rule 2 is that quality comes from prevention. The third rule is that quality means meeting the needs of customers (anyone who receives or uses government services). Rule 4 is that quality is dependent upon teamwork. Rule 5 is that quality requires continuous teamwork. Rule 6 is that quality involves strategic planning. The seventh rule is that products and services should be continually reviewed to ensure that they meet customers' needs. Rule 8 is that quality is measurable.

Carr, David K., and Ian D. Littman
Excellence in Government: Total Quality Management in the 1990s. 2nd edn. Arlington, VA: Coopers & Lybrand, 1993.

This is the second edition of a classic work on total quality management. The first edition of *Excellence in Government*, published by Coopers & Lybrand in 1990, sold more than 20,000 copies. Since the publication of the first edition, the number of government organizations practicing TQM has grown dramatically. While TQM was a relatively new concept to government organizations in 1990, by 1993 most federal agencies, more than a dozen states, and almost 200 local governments were involved with quality management. The second edition is divided into three parts. Part I introduces the reader to TQM, explaining why and how governments use it. Part II focuses on TQM's objectives, tools, and procedures for improving processes. Part III explains how government organizations can implement TQM. Two helpful appendices are included. Appendix A lists resources and Appendix B summarizes the results of four surveys of quality in government: the Coopers & Lybrand 1989 survey; the Florida 1991 survey; the American Society for Quality Control 1992 survey; and the U.S. General Accounting Office 1992 survey. Coopers & Lybrand has published other titles relating to quality management, including *BreakPoint Business Process Redesign* (1992), *Process Improvement: A Guide for Teams* (1993), and *Measuring Quality: Linking Customer Satisfaction to Process Improvement* (1993).

Cohen, Steven, and Ronald Brand
Total Quality Management in Government: A Practical Guide for the Real World. San Francisco: Jossey-Bass, 1993.

This book has been designed as both a TQM primer and a "how-to-do-it" book on TQM. Both authors have successfully applied TQM in their own work settings, Cohen at a dean's office at Columbia University and Brand at the U.S. Environmental Protection Agency's (EPA) underground tank office. The first chapter establishes the rationale for applying TQM to public organizations. The second chapter explains the basic concepts of TQM. The third chapter focuses on organizational change and the following chapter explains why organizations have a tendency to resist change. Chapter 5 focuses on getting started and introduces some basic quality tools such as fishbone diagrams, Pareto charts, flowcharts, run charts, and control charts. Chapter 6 looks at the role of managers in implementing TQM. Chapter 7 presents a case study, Brand's experiences in implementing TQM in his office at the EPA. Chapter 8 provides some examples of TQM success stories. Chapter 9, the final chapter, provides a synthesis and identifies critical success factors for making TQM work in public agencies.

Cohen, Steven, and William Eimicke
"Project-Focused Total Quality Management in the New York City Department of Parks and Recreation." *Public Administration Review* 54 (September/October 1994): 450–456.

The New York City Department of Parks and Recreation has experienced severe cutbacks over the past several years. The Department has responded to these cuts with TQM. TQM training involved faculty from Columbia University's Public Administration program. The authors have analyzed the costs and benefits of the Department's first twenty-four improvement projects. They estimate that the annual recurring savings approximate $1.7 million. In addition, several hundred employees are now conditioned to think about customers, suppliers, and work processes.

Davies, Ken, and Peter Hinton
"Managing Quality in Local Government and the Health Services." *Public Money & Management* 13, no.1 (January-March 1993): 51–54.

This article reports the results of a study conducted by Liverpool Business School regarding the extent of TQM implementation in local government and health service authorities in north west England and north Wales. Twelve organizations were selected for in-depth study. The study focused on these broad topics: general awareness of quality management; type of quality policies; management arrangements; methods and techniques; training; and budgets for quality. Overall, there was a good awareness of quality approaches. Organizations created a range of structures for managing quality, including quality councils, quality task groups, quality improvement teams, quality circles, quality coordinators,

and quality facilitators. No single management model emerged. Most organizations emphasized formal training, often in the form of two- or three-day courses. Most training covered typical problem-solving methods and techniques such as brainstorming, flowcharting, fishbone diagrams, action planning, and Pareto analysis. No organization had a separate budget for its quality program.

Dilulio, John J., Jr., Gerald Garvey, and Donald F. Kettl
Improving Government Performance: An Owner's Manual. Washington, DC: The Brookings Institution, 1993.

This book presents a historical and theoretical overview of efforts to reform the federal bureaucracy in the United States. The authors contend that this reform is more likely to be gradual and that this effort to improve government is an "evolution" rather than a "reinvention", a concept popularized by David Osborne's and Ted Gaebler's best-selling book *Reinventing Government: How the Entrepreneurial Spirit is Transforming the Public Sector*, published by Addison-Wesley in 1992.

Durant, Robert F., and Laura A. Wilson
"Public Management, TQM, and Quality Improvement: Toward A Contingency Strategy." *American Review of Public Administration* 23, no.3 (September 1993): 215–245.

This lengthy review article documents the chain of research on TQM applications in the public sector. Some of the empirical studies that are summarized were published in books and journals in the fields of public policy, organizational behavior, and bureaucratic politics. This scholarly article should be required reading for public administrators needing a theoretical background on TQM interventions in government agencies.

Frank, Robyn C.
"Total Quality Management: The Federal Government Experience." *Journal of Library Administration* 18, nos.1–2 (1993): 171–182.

Frank chronicles the implementation of TQM in the federal government, citing TQM's benefits as well as obstacles to its implementation. The article provides a nice introduction to the origins of TQM in the federal government. The quality movement in government can be traced back to the Department of Defense's program of productivity improvement in the mid-1970s. Frank, a librarian at the National Agricultural Library, outlines strategies for locating additional information on TQM in the federal sector. For example, the Federal Quality Institute (FQI) is a primary source of information. The FQI maintains both a database of information (articles, essays, handbooks, etc.) about TQM applications and an electronic bulletin board service. It also maintains a list of certified private sector contractors who are qualified to assist federal agencies in implementing TQM.

From Red Tape to Results: Creating a Government That Works Better & Costs Less: Report of the National Performance Review. Washington, DC: U.S. Government Printing Office, 1993.

The National Performance Review began in March 1993 when President Clinton announced a six-month review of the federal government. *From Red Tape to Results* is the report of the National Performance Review, prepared by Vice President Al Gore. It was unveiled as a blueprint for reinventing government at a presidential press conference in 1993. The title suggests the need to move from red tape to results to create a government that is more efficient and more cost effective. The report includes hundreds of recommendations, that if enacted would produce estimated savings of $108 billion over five years. There are four major sets of recommendations. The first are designed to cut red tape, streamline the budget, simplify procurement, decentralize personnel policy, and streamline regulation. The second focus on giving the public a voice in government. The third set of recommendations focus on transforming the culture of employees. The fourth category of recommendations focus on cutting costs through several methods: the elimination or reduction of facilities, programs, and subsidies; increased user fees; and reengineering.

Garrity, Rudolph B.

"Total Quality Management: An Opportunity for High Performance in Federal Organizations." *Public Administration Quarterly* 16, no.4 (Winter 1993): 430–459.

Garrity, an advocate of TQM, begins his essay by differentiating TQM from other improvement strategies. He summarizes key writings about TQM in both the private and public sectors. He then reviews the ideas of major theorists in the areas of individual development, group development, and organizational behavior. Garrity's premise is that TQM is the logical outgrowth of these theories.

Gold, Richard, and Warren De Luca

"TQM in P & R." *Parks & Recreation* 28, no.9 (September 1993): 86–91.

Total quality management has helped the New York City Department of Parks and Recreation maintain properties and facilities, and manage programs. The Department maintains properties totaling 26,000 acres. Due to budget cuts and chronic underfunding, the Department is allocated less than one half of one percent of the city's operating budget. The Department's level of staffing has reached the lowest point in half a century. Since 1991, the Department has trained more than 400 employees in TQM. Although some of the early teams were unsuccessful (because they pursued problems that were too vague or too big to solve, such as neighborhood decline), a number of teams have been successful. For example, by tracking a mobile crew team in Brooklyn, slack time equaling $27,000 in annual personnel costs was eliminated. More importantly, throughout the organization, employees are showing an interest in improving how things are done. The authors have found that activity has replaced inertia. This is an important article since there are few case studies on integrating TQM into park and recreation management.

Hyde, Albert C.

"The Proverbs of Total Quality Management: Recharting the Path to Quality Improvement in the Public Sector." *Public Productivity & Management Review* 16, no.1 (Fall 1992): 25–37.

Hyde's premise is that TQM must be carefully modified to work in public sector agencies. TQM has to address the following six critical issues. First, basic quality measurement systems have to be developed and used for decision making at all levels. Second, employees must participate in the initial design of these systems. There must be negotiation and consultation with union leaders.

Major modifications must be made in applying customer feedback on quality for recipients of public sector services and products. TQM has to address budgeting and resource allocation issues. Finally, TQM and human resource management systems must be refocused.

Keehley, Pat
"TQM for Local Governments: The Principles and Prospects." *Public Management* 74 (August 1992): 10–16.

This article is a good introduction to the topic of quality management in local government. It provides examples of TQM applications that have resulted in savings and improved services to citizens. Some local governments in the United States that have adopted TQM include those in the following communities: Austin, Texas; Madison, Wisconsin; Palm Beach County, Florida; Volusia County, Florida; Erie, Pennsylvania; Brighton, Colorado; and Wilmington, North Carolina. These governments have used TQM to solve problems ranging from mosquito control to the simplification of zoning permit applications.

Kettl, Donald, and John J. Dilulio, Jr., eds
Inside the Reinvention Machine: Appraising Governmental Reform. Washington, DC: The Brookings Institution, 1995.

This book looks at the successes and failures of the first full year of the Clinton Administration's National Performance Review (NPR), the Administration's blueprint for streamlining regulations, reducing bureaucracy, and improving civil service personnel practices and federal procurement processes. Overall, the authors who have contributed to this book are optimistic and believe that the NPR can produce real change. However, most caution that a number of issues must be addressed in order for the NPR to succeed, such as the need for a long-term leadership commitment to organizational change.

Kline, James F.
"State Governments' Growing Gains from TQM." *National Productivity Review* 12, no.2 (Spring 1993): 259–271.

State governments can benefit from the implementation of TQM. Some benefits include increased productivity, reduced bureaucracy, and lower costs. Kline's article provides an excellent overview of the quality movement in both the public and private sectors. He highlights quality initiatives undertaken by state agencies in Arkansas, Colorado, Florida, Minnesota, Missouri, and Wisconsin. Kline concludes that the adoption of TQM can help states protect their economic base, gain public support, increase efficiency, and receive in-kind support from the private sector.

Kline, James J.
"Total Quality Management in Local Government." *Government Finance Review* 8, no.4 (August 1992): 7–11.

Kline provides examples of four municipalities that have implemented TQM: Madison, Wisconsin; Phoenix, Arizona; Fort Collins, Colorado; and Fort Lauderdale, Florida. Madison began a quality improvement process in 1983. A 1990 analysis of fifty-six improvement projects showed that these activities resulted in positive cost savings of between $1,100,000 and $1,140,000. TQM has been implemented into five departments: police; Madison Metro; public health; data processing; streets; and community services. In addition to the cost savings, other benefits were noted such as a decrease in grievances, improvement in staff morale, a greater sensitivity to customer needs; a faster turnaround time; improved customer service, and improved intra-agency and inter-agency cooperation and teamwork. Phoenix began its total quality process in 1989. The chief elements in Phoenix's TQ process are: customer satisfaction; continuous improvement; quality results; employee empowerment; leadership; reduced cycle time; information management; and quality planning. Fort Collins began its quality efforts in 1987 and hired Florida Power & Light's consulting branch to conduct TQM training. In 1992 there were fifty teams looking at problems ranging from the use of safety equipment in city vehicles to reducing the mortality rate of newly planted trees. In 1984, Fort Lauderdale declared a ten-year "Decade of Excellence," with the goal of making Fort Lauderdale the best city of its size by 1994. The city adopted the quality improvement process used by Florida Power & Light. Teams have solved problems ranging from clogged sump pumps to reducing the city's cost for paper, printing, and postage through simplifying procedures and forms.

Kline, James L.
"Quality Tools Are Applicable to Local Government." *Government Finance Review* 9 (August 1993): 15–19.

Kline explains three types of quality tools (flow charts, control charts, and cause-and-effect diagrams) and how they can be used in government applications. He assesses the strengths and weaknesses of each tool. His clarity of explanation and use of interesting examples makes this article required reading for all public administrators. Readers can use his excellent brief bibliography to identify other key articles and books on quality tools and statistical process control techniques.

Kravchuk, Robert S., and Robert Leighton
"Implementing Total Quality Management in the United States." *Public Productivity & Management Review* 17 (Fall 1993): 71–82.

This article examines factors that are critical to the successful implementation of TQM in state government. According to Kravchuk and Leighton, the two most important factors are strong managerial leadership and a hospitable administrative culture. These conclusions are based on their 1992 survey regarding the implementation of TQM in state government. A survey was mailed to all fifty states and the District of Columbia. Thirty-one states, reported that some TQM interventions were underway. Arkansas took the lead, having begun to implement TQM in 1989 under the direction of former governor Bill Clinton. Only fourteen states reported no TQM activity. What factors motivated states to implement TQM? The factors most frequently cited were the opportunity to improve, gubernatorial mandate, and financial/fiscal distress. Most states reported that they used a "hybrid" approach in implementing TQM, that is, a methodology drawing from many models. Implementation is decentralized in most states, with TQM being implemented on a piecemeal basis (generally in those agencies that express an interest in TQM). Agency head interest appears to be a critical factor, with fifteen states responding that agency heads exerted TQM leadership. Twenty-three states responded that the organizational culture would pose a serious challenge to the successful implementation of TQM in their state. Finally, the authors found that it was still too early for states to evaluate their overall success with TQM, since many of the states (twenty-one in total) reported that TQM initiatives were only in the beginning or early phases.

Milakovich, Michael E.
"Total Quality Management in the Public Sector." *National Productivity Review* 10 (Spring 1991): 195–213.

Milakovich describes how the principles and concepts of TQM can be applied to public administration. He also suggests strategies that public managers can use to overcome barriers to TQM (obstacles such as distrust, inadequate knowledge, concerns about job security, etc.). Finally, he presents an overview of TQM in the federal government. In the United States, the federal government's formal quality program began when Executive Order 12637, "Productivity Improvement Program for the Federal Government" was issued on April 27, 1988. This is a critical article for those readers needing background information on the evolution of TQM in the federal government.

Osborne, David, and Ted Gaebler
Reinventing Government: How the Entrepreneurial Spirit is Transforming the Public Sector. Reading, MA: Addison-Wesley, 1992.

The authors believe that government has the potential to solve societal problems. Their contention is that the governmental system, not government employees, is responsible for inefficient and ineffective government. In this bestseller, they outline the principles for reinventing government. These include the following: "steering rather than rowing"; "empowering rather than serving"; "injecting competition into service delivery"; moving from a rule-driven organization to a mission-driven organization; becoming results-oriented; focusing on the needs of the customer; becoming enterprising by "earning rather than spending"; becoming anticipatory by focusing on "prevention rather than cure"; moving from a hierarchical structure to one emphasizing participation and teamwork; and becoming market-oriented.

Raisbeck, Ian
"Making Customer Satisfaction a Business Priority." In *German Perspectives on Total Quality* (New York: The Conference Board, 1993), 27–30.

This is the edited transcript of an address given at the "Quality Management Forum", a 1993 symposium hosted by The Conference Board's European Council on Quality. Raisbeck is Director of Quality for Britain's Royal Mail. The Royal Mail employs about 170,000 workers and has a revenue exceeding £4 billion. In 1988, the Royal Mail began to plan a quality initiative using the model established by the European Foundation for Quality Management. This model puts equal emphasis on the "enablers" of total quality (leadership, people management, policy and strategy, and resources) and on the "results" (customer satisfaction, people satisfaction, business results, and impact on society). Improving performance and increasing customer satisfaction is critical for the Royal Mail since the British government is exploring privatization of the service.

Reynolds, Larry
"The Feds Join the Quality Movement." *Management Review* 81 (April 1992): 39–40.

Reynolds describes the Federal Quality Institute (FQI), a federal agency created by former president Ronald Reagan. The FQI's charge is to improve the quality, timeliness, and efficiency of services provided by the federal government. The FQI, with a staff of 35 and an annual budget of only $1 million dollars offers quality seminars and in-house consulting services. More than thirty federal agencies have used FQI's services.

Swiss, James E.
"Adapting Total Quality Management (TQM) to Government." *Public Administration Review* 52, no.4 (August 1992): 356–362.

Swiss's view is that TQM cannot be applied to the management of government agencies unless it is substantially modified to adapt to the unique characteristics of public sector agencies. According to Swiss, a business-oriented TQM approach will not work in public administration because it stresses products and routine processes. He proposes a revised version of TQM for the public sector that would emphasize client feedback, performance tracking, continuous improvement, and worker participation.

Total Quality Management: Strategies for Local Government. Washington, DC: The ICMA Training Institute, 1993.

This handbook has been designed to give local government managers and employees practical and tested guidelines for implementing a quality improvement program. It explains basic quality concepts such as customer focus, teamwork, process improvement, data-based decision-making, and continuous improvement. The handbook can be used as a self-guided study or as part of a group training course. It has been produced in two volumes. Volume 1 is the *Participant's Handbook* and Volume 2 is the *Leader's Guide.* This is an important contribution since the establishment of formal quality improvement programs is relatively new in the public sector and there are few in-depth and practical texts to guide local governments through this process.

Wargo, Michael J.
"The Impact of the President's Reinvention Plan on Evaluation." *Evaluation Practice* 15, no.1 (February 1994): 63–72.

Wargo summarizes President Clinton's plan for reinventing the federal government and considers its impact on the practice and profession of evaluation. The author has more than thirty years of experience evaluating federal programs. He believes that the plan will reduce midlevel management evaluation and change the roles of federal, state, and local evaluators. However, Wargo predicts that overall, the plan will improve the efficiency and effectiveness of the federal government and make all levels of government more responsive to the public's needs.

Wholey, Joseph P., and Harry P. Hatry
"The Case for Performance Monitoring." *Public Administration Review* 52, no.6 (November/December 1992): 604–610.

A number of federal, state, and local governments have begun to use performance monitoring to provide information on the quality of service delivery and on program outcomes. Performance monitoring is used frequently in the private sector. The authors argue that performance monitoring can help public administrators improve public programs and that elected officials and citizens are entitled to regular reports on the performance of public programs and services. They urge that performance monitoring be used by more agencies at all levels of government.

Wood, Patricia B.

"How Quality Government is Being Achieved." *National Productivity Review* 11 (Spring 1992): 257–264.

Wood looks at several government agencies that have won federal quality awards. Among them is the Aeronautical Systems Division (ASD) of the Air Force Systems Command at Wright-Patterson Air Force base in Dayton, Ohio. ASD was one of the federal agencies selected as Quality Improvement Prototype Award winners in 1992. The author describes four basic steps to implementing TQM, drawing upon ASD's experiences with TQM. The first-step is becoming knowledgeable about quality management. Step 2 is developing a vision. Step 3 is organization-wide training. Step 4 is to continuously seek TQM improvements.

SIC 9221: Police protection

Cole, Allen W.

"Better Customer Focus: TQM & Law Enforcement." *The Police Chief* 60 (December 1993): 23–26.

The Lawrence (Massachusetts) Police Department used a survey in order to determine how well the department was meeting the needs of its customers, in this case, citizens. An affinity diagram was used to clarify customer needs. The affinity diagram revealed that most of all, citizens wanted to feel safe in neighborhoods free of disorder. The department had assumed that citizens would be most concerned with the apprehension of criminals. A matrix diagram was then used to provide a better picture of what the department should be doing. This process indicated that random patrols would have the greatest impact on meeting customer needs. TQM's emphasis on problem-solving and its use of analytical tools helped the Lawrence Police Department determine and meet customer needs.

Galloway, Robert A.

"Quality Improvement and Heightened Self-Esteem: The Brighton Police Story." *National Productivity Review* 11 (Autumn 1992): 453–461.

In the 1980s, the Brighton, Colorado police department was plagued with a 45 percent turnover rate, vacant supervisory positions, low morale, poor facilities, and antiquated equipment. Complaints about poor police service were routine. In 1985, a new chief of police turned the situation around. A Total Quality Service (TQS) program was developed with the assistance of an organizational development consultant. The police department changed its motto to "We are here to serve you." Annual performance evaluations for employees considered service quality. Those employees who were not service-oriented were terminated. The department made a deliberate effort to hire service-oriented recruits. By 1991, the department was so proud of its service that it offered a guarantee for its service. This guarantee states that police will respond to requests for help as quickly as possible and in a caring manner, that citizens will be treated with respect and compassion, and that employees will be held accountable for meeting minimum performance standards. The department even used techniques from the private sector to get feedback. A survey is mailed monthly to those who have received noncriminal police services. Over the past four years, these surveys have indicated an overall satisfaction rate of 97 percent. The Brighton Police Department provides an interesting case study, demonstrating that TQM concepts can be successfully applied to any public service-oriented organization.

Simonsen, Clifford E., and Douglas Arnold

"TQM: Is It Right for Law Enforcement?" *The Police Chief* 60 (December 1993): 20–22.

The authors make a case for the implementation of TQM in law enforcement. Four of Deming's "fourteen points" can be readily applied to law enforcement: client identification and feedback; tracking performance with statistically valid methods; continuous improvement; and employee participation. Although the concept of "customer" might seem inapplicable to this field, the authors argue that law enforcement has many customers. Law enforcements clients and customers include prosecuting attorneys, the courts, taxpayers, witnesses, victims, jailers, state and local elected officials, other police agencies, and the media. Four factors are critical to the success of TQM in law enforcement: a commitment from all members of the management team (including the police chief or sheriff) and their full participation; an identification of the strategic processes that are necessary for improved customer satisfaction; incremental implementation of TQM, beginning with demonstration pilots; and continuous training of workers at all levels.

SIC 9223: Correctional institutions

James, Richard W.
"Total Quality Management: Can It Work in Federal Probation? *Federal Probation* 57 (December 1993): 28–33.

The author, a supervising United States probation officer in the Southern District of Florida, explores whether TQM can be successfully implemented in a federal probation office. He concludes that TQM can work if the following recommendations are considered. First, TQM should be slowly implemented and supported by top management. Teams must be created with specific goals. Performance must be measured and comparison must be made to the best in the field. Training must be ongoing. The focus must be on internal and external customers. Work processes should be streamlined. Finally, middle managers in particular must accept the concept of self-directed teams and resist the tendency to resist change.

SIC 9311: Public finance, taxation, and monetary policy

Ferrero, Matthew J.
"Self-Directed Work Teams Untax the IRS: Customer Service and Employee Involvement Have Improved Since the Agency Generated a Total Quality Organization." *Personnel Journal* 73 (July 1994): 66–71.

The Internal Revenue Service (IRS) operates sixty-three district offices and ten service centers, employing 115,000 workers in total. Since 1987, the agency has developed more than 400 cross-functional teams nationwide. Improvements have resulted in $27 million in savings, while $100 million has been generated in additional tax revenue. In addition, customer service has improved. The IRS uses material from the Juran Institute to train team members.

SIC 9431: Administration of public health programs

Brooks, Tessa
"Total Quality Management in the NHS." *Health Services Management* 88, no.2 (April 1992): 17–19.

In 1989, the Department of Health (United Kingdom) introduced the concept of total quality management to the UK public health sector. In 1990, twenty-three sites were included in the TQM pilots. Brooks concludes that if TQM was initiated NHS-wide, it would require substantial investments in time and money. She estimates that an NHS-wide commitment to TQM would cost approximately £500,000 over a three-year period. Although TQM is not a cheap or quick fix, she maintains that over time, it can substantially reduce costs.

De Geyndt, Willy
Managing the Quality of Health Care in Developing Countries. Washington, DC: The World Bank, 1995.

How can developing countries measure and improve the quality of health care? This paper provides several definitions of quality and presents various models and approaches that can be used to measure, assure, and improve quality. TQM is one of the approaches described. The author includes a review of quality of health care studies that have been conducted in developing countries between 1981 and 1993. In addition, there is an excellent bibliography on health care quality and quality in general.

Dingwall, Robert, and Paul Fenn
Quality and Regulation in Health Care: International Experiences. London: Routledge, 1992.

The origin of this book is papers presented in a session of the 1989 meeting of the Law and Society Association in Madison, Wisconsin. Contributors to this volume include scholars from the United Kingdom and the United States. Health care systems throughout Western Europe and the United States are trying to assure quality while containing costs. Governments and insurers are trying to control escalating health care costs. At the same time, patients and consumer groups are insisting that patients are not denied access to treatment. All of these parties are looking at systems of regulation as a mechanism for monitoring quality, while being sensitive to costs and consumer demands. These essays explore the relationship between regulation and quality in the area of health care.

Kaluzny, Arnold D., Curtis P. McLaughlin, and Kit Simpson
"Applying Total Quality Management Concepts to Public Health Organizations." *Public Health Reports* 107, no.3 (May/June 1992): 257–264.

While TQM has been implemented by many hospitals, health maintenance organizations (HMOs), and other health care organizations in the private sector, it has not been widely adopted in public health organizations. The authors urge American public health administrators to introduce TQM as a method to achieve and exceed national performance standards for community health agencies. The successful application of TQM in public health agencies requires organizations to take specific actions. These steps include: redefining the role of management; defining a common corporate culture; redefining the role of citizen oversight functions; establishment of a series of objectives; empowering staff to address problems; benchmarking with local hospitals, private clinics, and other human service organizations; and seeking realistic estimates of time required to implement TQM.

Kirkman-Liff, Bradford, and Eugene Schneller
"The Resource Management Initiative in the English National Health Service." *Health Care Management Review* 17, no.2 (Spring 1992): 59–70.

The authors describe the development and implementation of the Resource Management Initiative (RMI) in the United Kingdom. This policy was designed to more effectively utilize the resources of the United Kingdom's National Health Service by this three-prong approach: integrating physicians, nurses, and other clinicians

into management; by establishing a closer external audit of the medical profession; and by implementing information systems. The RMI is also relevant to health care practitioners outside of the United Kingdom, since RMI and TQM/CQI have many of the same components.

Parberry, A. C., and A. K. Banerjee
"Quality Assurance and Quality Management in the National Health Service." *Journal of the Royal Society of Health* 115, no.2 (April 1995): 109–112.

The authors define quality management, provide a brief history of quality in the National Health Service, and explore factors which have acted as forces for and against the development of quality management in the health services. These factors are grouped into the categories of political forces, economic forces, and social forces. They also discuss the possible impact of health service reforms on quality management.

SIC 9441: Administration of social, human resource, and income maintenance programs

Martin, Lawrence L.
Total Quality Management in Human Service Organizations. Newbury Park, CA: Sage, 1993.

This title is part of the Sage Human Services Guides series. Although there is a growing body of literature on TQM in public administration, there is little mention of TQM in the human services and social work literature. Consequently, Martin's book fills an important gap. After introducing the concepts of TQM, Martin explores the application of TQM in human services organizations. He shows how teamwork, brainstorming, cause-and-effect diagrams, check sheets, and Pareto analysis can be used to improve processes. He uses actual examples from the fields of public administration, public health, gerontology, and management of nonprofit organizations.

Muffolett, Joseph R., and Craig S. Rogers
"Implementing Total Quality Management in the Government." *Annual Quality Congress Transactions* 45 (1991): 310–315.

The authors describe in detail the implementation of TQM in the Office of Disability and

International Operations (ODIO), a unit within the U.S. Social Security Administration (SSA). The ODIO processes thousands of claims daily. Like other federal agencies, it has experienced substantial staff reductions. In 1990, ODIO began training modules on quality awareness and established pilots with problem-solving teams and self-managing teams. Although this article was written during the first phases of ODIO's TQM initiative, there was already evidence that this effort would succeed. Teams have been enthusiastic, motivated, and productive.

SIC 9511: Air and water resource and solid waste management

Lillian, Daniel
"Making a Difference in Environmental Cleanup –Applying TQM in DOE." *Annual Quality Congress Transactions* 46 (1992): 821–827.

The Department of Energy's (DOE's) Laboratory Management Branch (LMB) is charged with providing the environmental data needed by the DOE site environmental cleanup program. The LMB has applied the principles of TQM to its environmental data operations in order to ensure that the data collection process is cost effective as well as credible. Since the cost of obtaining reliable environmental data to support this cleanup effort is estimated to be somewhere between 15 and 45 billion dollars, this TQM initiative has the potential to produce substantial cost savings.

SIC 9711: National security

"Benchmark Matrix and Guide: Part I. Headquarters Air Force Logistics Command, Wright Patterson Air Force Base, OH." *Journal of Quality Assurance* 13, no.5 (September/October 1991): 14–19.
"Benchmark Matrix and Guide: Part II." *Journal of Quality Assurance* 13, no.6 (November/December 1991): 10–15.
"Benchmark Matrix and Guide: Part III." *Journal for Healthcare Quality* 14, no.1 (January/February 1992): 8–13.

In 1991, Headquarters Air Force Logistics Command at Wright-Patterson Air Force Base was awarded the President's Award for Quality and Productivity Improvement. This award, equivalent to the Malcolm Baldrige Award, is the highest recognition of improvement in quality and productivity in the federal government.. This three-part series, authored by a special working group within Headquarters Air Force Logistics Command, describes the benchmarking system that was developed to measure progress in implementing total quality management. This benchmark matrix has five horizontal levels delineating progress in TQM: business as usual; initiation; implementation; expansion; and integration. There are six vertical categories that represent factors that are critical to the success of TQM: leadership; structure; training; recognition; process improvement; and customer focus.

McCarthy, Kimberly M., and Ahmad K. Eishennawy
"Implementing Total Quality Management at the U.S. Department of Defense." *Computers & Industrial Engineering* 21, nos.1–4 (1991): 153–157.

The authors outline the Department of Defense's (DOD) plan for implementing TQM. In 1989, the DOD established a policy to serve as a guideline in the implementation process. This policy was published by the Government Printing Office in 1989 as the *Total Quality Management Guide*. The DOD's implementation policy consists of ten basic elements: pursuing new strategic thinking; knowing your customers; establishing true customer requirements; concentrating on prevention instead of correction; reducing chronic waste; pursuing a continuous improvement strategy; using structured methodology for process improvement; reducing variation; using a balanced approach; and applying TQM to all functions. The DOD's model can be completed in seven steps: establishing the management and cultural environment; defining the mission; setting performance improvement goals; establishing improvement projects and action plans; implementing projects with performance tools and methodology; evaluation; and review and recycle. The DOD has identified seventeen quality management tools to be used in the implementation process, including benchmarking, quality function deployment, statistical process control, design of experiments, cost of quality, team-building, and work flow analysis. The authors conclude that the most serious obstacle to the successful implementation of TQM in the DOD is the uncertainty of the defense budget.

III

Focus on Specific Aspects of Quality Management

I Teams

Buchholz, Steve, and Thomas Roth
Creating the High Performance Team. New York: Wiley, 1987.

The authors are affiliated with Wilson Learning Corporation, a training group that has worked with a number of Fortune 100 companies. This book is designed to give managers the skills to create high-performance teams. The Wilson Learning Corporation has identified eight attributes of high-performance teams. These characteristics are: participative leadership; shared responsibility; a sense of common purpose; high communication; future-focused; focused on task; creative talents; and rapid response.

Butman, John
FlyingFox: A Business Adventure in Teams and Teamwork. New York: Amacom, 1993.

Butman uses the form of a business novel to create a story about a fictional company that uses cross-functional teams. The hero of the novel is Ron Delaney. Ron's mission is to direct a cross-functional team charged with bringing a new product to market. This high-tech product is named FlyingFox. This anecdote illustrates the conflicts and pressures that arise in work groups.

Cox, Allan
Straight Talk for Monday Morning: Creating Values, Vision, and Vitality at Work. New York: Wiley, 1990.

This bestseller consists of 100 short essays about leadership, empowerment, and team effectiveness. Cox effectively blends group relations theory with practical examples for empowering teams. Among the topics covered are building a foundation for teams, recognizing values, managing conflict, and getting the most out of your team.

Douglass, Merrill E., and Donna N. Douglass
Time Management for Teams. New York: American Management Association, 1992.

The authors are time management experts. They are also the authors of another book on time management: *Manage Your Time, Manage Your Work, Manage Yourself.* This latest time management book focuses on managing the use of a group's time to make teamwork more effective. *Time Management for Teams* is a practical guide that will help team leaders maximize team performance. This is a critical issue since team members who waste time can interrupt the team's work flow and cause costly delays.

Frangoes, Stephen J., with Steven J. Bennett
Team Zebra. Essex Junction, VT: Oliver Wight Publications, 1993.

Frangoes is a manager of Eastman Kodak's black and white film-making division. This is an account of the turnaround of this unit (an operation employing 1,500 workers). The division was reorganized into high-performance teams that saved the division from business failure. As a result of Team Zebra (Frangoes' name for this team-based structure), this division became one of Kodak's most efficient and productive units.

Gordon, William I., et al.
The Team Trainer: Winning Tools and Tactics for Successful Workouts. Alexandria, VA: American Society for Training and Development; Chicago, IL: Irwin Professional Pub., 1996.

This is a practical handbook for team members and team leaders. Its purpose is to help transform work groups into high-performance teams. The first part of the book establishes a foundation. It describes the do's and don'ts of team-based organizations, guidelines for team-shared leadership, and problems that teams typically encounter. The second part of the book includes more than twenty activities. The third part of the book summarizes research on work groups that has been conducted from the 1920s to the present.

Katzenbach, Jon R., and Douglas K. Smith
The *Wisdom of Teams: Creating the High Performance Organization.* Boston, MA: Harvard Business School Press, 1993.

The authors studied teams in more than forty organizations to find out how successful teams are created and sustained. Some of the teams researched for the book included those at Citibank, Conrail, Desert Storm, Dun & Bradstreet, Eli Lilly, General Electric, the Girl Scouts, Hewlett-Packard, Knight-Ridder, Kodak, Motorola, Pfizer, Prudential, and schools featured in the PBS program "Schools in America." The book is organized into three parts: understanding teams, becoming a team, and exploiting the potential. Katzenbach and Smith found that teams respond to performance challenges. Companies committed to strong performance standards have the greatest success with teams. The most successful team leaders are those that believe in the team's purpose and in the people on the team.

Kelly, Mark
The Adventures of a Self-Managing Team. Raleigh, NC: Mark Kelly Books, 1992.

Mark Kelly & Associates is a consulting and training firm. This is a unique book on teamwork since it presents teamwork from the view of the members of a self-managing team. Kelly's book is based on his experience in helping the James River Kendallville Plant convert to a self-managing team environment.

Lipnack, Jessica, and Jeffrey Stamps
The TeamNet Factor: Bringing the Power of Boundary Crossing into the Heart of Your Business. Essex Junction, VT: Oliver Wight Publications, 1993.

The authors are consultants who advocate the use of teams made up of individuals from various functions and levels of an organization to achieve a common goal. These teams are called teamnets. Teamnets can range in size from small, cross-functional teams to regional or industrial groups. *The TeamNet Factor* shows how teamnets have been used around the world in organizations ranging from McDonnell Douglas to Habitat for Humanity. Tom Peters described this book as "brilliant" and concluded that it is "one of the most important management books in recent times."

Quick, Thomas L.
Successful Team Building. New York: Amacom, 1992.

This is part of Amacom's WorkSmart Series of do-it-yourself guides to skill building. Quick heads a consulting firm that specializes in training practice, performance management, group building, and persuasive skills. *Successful Team Building* shows readers how to build team commitment, handle team conflict, use creativity in team problem-solving and decision-making, and how to evaluate and reward team players.

Robbins, Harvey, and Michael Finley
Why Teams Don't Work: What Went Wrong and How to Make It Right. Princeton, NJ: Peterson's/PacesetterBooks, 1995.

This provocative book acknowledges that things can go wrong in the team process. One reviewer concluded that *Why Teams Don't Work* is "one of the best business books of 1995." Teams are prone to many problems. For example, some team members don't accept their roles, some teams have a difficult time making decisions, and some teams become confused about their goals. There are many barriers to team success. Some common obstacles are people problems, leadership failure, and the lack of compensation, rewards, and recognition for teams. However, the authors strongly believe in the value of teamwork and suggest ways to remove these obstacles.

Rosen, Ned
Teamwork and the Bottom Line: Groups Make A Difference, Hillsdale, NJ: Lawrence Erlbaum Associates, 1989.

Teamwork and the Bottom Line is part of Erlbaum's series in Applied Psychology. It focuses on the theories behind group interaction. Managers interested in teamwork will benefit from this discussion of the behavioral aspects of teambuilding.

Scholtes, Peter R.
The Team Handbook: How to Use Teams to Improve Quality. Madison, WI: Joiner, 1988.

This comprehensive and easy-to-read handbook has become the standard reference work on work groups. It has been designed as a practical guide to working in or with teams. The detailed instructions and illustrations are excellent. Team leaders, in particular, will appreciate the inclusion of well-designed worksheets. Scholtes has also written a handbook for educators entitled *The Team Handbook for Educators: How to Use Teams to Improve Quality*.

Shonk, James H.
Team-Based Organizations: Developing a Successful Team Environment. Homewood, IL: Business One Irwin, 1992.

The author is a consultant who has helped many companies make the transition to a team-based organization. This book is directed to managers who want to establish effective organization-wide teamwork. The first chapter provides an overview, discussing the origin of team-based organization and its impact on American business. Chapter 2 outlines the process that managers need to go through to determine whether a team-based organization is appropriate for them. The following chapter reviews the different types of teams. Subsequent chapters look at the startup phase, evolution and redesign (two approached to change), creating a design team to redesign the organization around teams, training, the role of a team leader, and the keys to success.

Staff of Goodmeasure, Inc.
Solving Quality and Productivity Problems: Goodmeasure's Guide to Corrective Action. Milwaukee, WI: ASQC Quality Press, 1988.

Goodmeasure, Inc. is a management consulting firm that specializes in quality improvement and the management of change. This is a practical guide to techniques that can be used to solve quality and productivity problems. Since teams are used to solve both problems, there is an extensive discussion on the creation and management of teams.

Tjosvold, Dean, and Mary M. Tjosvold
Leading the Team Organization: How to Create an Enduring Competitive Advantage. New York: Lexington, 1991.

The authors create a model for achieving teamwork. Their model addresses the issue of how to get people with different backgrounds and personalities to work together to improve an organization. They outline techniques that can be used to foster cooperation.

Townsend, Patrick L., with Joan E. Gebhardt
Commit to Quality. New York: Wiley, 1990.

This book is based on Townsend's experience with organizing quality teams at the Paul Revere Insurance Company. Townsend developed a technique called "Quality Has Value" (QHV). QHV emphasizes the creation of teams involving everyone in the company. This model has received much national attention, particularly since the Paul Revere Insurance Company was one of the two service companies considered for the first Malcolm Baldrige Award.

Wellins, Richard S., William C. Byham, and George R. Dixon
Inside Teams: How 20 World-Class Organizations are Winning Through Teamwork. San Francisco: Jossey-Bass, 1994.

This is a behind the scenes look at teams in twenty of the best team-based organizations worldwide. The organizations profiled range from the Cape Coral Hospital in Florida to K Shoes Ltd in the UK. The authors asked each firm the same series of questions. Among the subjects covered in each profile are why teams were chosen, how teams were started, how work was organized, training provided, the problems encountered, the lessons learned, and the impact of teams on the company's bottom line. In the final section of the book, the authors identify the "best practices" that are common to all twenty teams.

Zenger, John H., et al.
Leading Teams: Mastering the New Role.
Homewood, IL: Business One Irwin, 1994.

Leading Teams shows how the quality of team leadership can make or break a team. Chapter 1 provides background on organizational change. Chapter 2 examines the role of the team leader. Chapters 3 through 10 look at the skills required to succeed as a team leader. The second part of the book uses case studies from work groups in North America so readers can learn from the experiences of real-world team leaders. These team leaders are affiliated with a wide range of organizations including Amex Life Assurance, Levi Strauss & Co., Raychem Corporation, Subaru-Isuzu Automotive, Inc., Boeing, Spectra Physics, Allied Signal Aerospace, and the University of Alberta Hospitals.

Zoglio, Suzanne Willis
Teams at Work: 7 Keys to Success. Doylestown, PA: Town Hill Press, 1993.

Zoglio is an organizational consultant who has created many work teams. Her book is organized around seven key elements of effective teams, which she calls the "7 keys to success". These are: commitment, contribution, communication, cooperation, conflict management, change management, and connections. This guide includes many practical suggestions as well as structured activities and individual exercises. *A Leader's Guide for Teams at Work* is also available from Town Hill Press.

2 Customers

Albrecht, Karl
The Only Thing That Matters: Bringing the Power of the Customer into the Center of Your Business. New York: HarperBusiness, 1992.

Albrecht is the author of the bestseller *Service America!* and the coauthor of *The Service Advantage: How to Identify and Fulfill Customer Needs. The Only Thing That Matters* is based on his eight-year study of the practices of outstanding service-providers. According to Albrecht, the only thing that matters is the customer's experience and organizations need to move toward customer value, a new view of customer service. Albrecht defines customer value as a combination of tangibles and intangibles that create a total customer perception of value received. Organizations must advance into what Albrecht refers to as "the fifth dimension of Total Quality Service," where service is an artform.

Anderson, Kristin, and Ron Zemke
Delivering Knock Your Socks Off Service. New York: Amacom, 1991.

Zemke is one of the best known authorities on service quality in the United States. This easy to comprehend guide for front-line service providers has been written for any employee who has contact with customers, from sales clerks to CEOs. Zemke has authored and coauthored many other bestsellers, including *Managing Knock Your Socks Off Service* and *Sustaining Knock Your Socks Off Service*, sequels to *Delivering Knock Your Socks Off Service*.

Babich, Pete
"Customer Satisfaction: How Good is Good Enough?" *Quality Progress* 25, no.12 (December 1992): 65–67.

Many companies are conducting surveys to measure customer satisfaction levels. Babich has constructed a customer satisfaction model to provide an analytical approach to customer retention. The first step in this modeling process is to define customer satisfaction. The model assumes that satisfied customers continue to purchase products from the same company, while dissatisfied customers will buy them from another company. Babich developed an algorithm to determine how dissatisfied customers select their next supplier. Babich's model assumes that dissatisfied customers from one supplier will be distributed to the other suppliers based on their current market shares. His model predicts a final value of market share based on fixed satisfaction levels. Babich's model is intriguing because it measures not only customer satisfaction level but the satisfaction level of competitors.

Band, William A.
Creating Value for Customers: Designing and Implementing a Total Corporate Strategy. New York: Wiley, 1991.

Creating value for customers means that customers must not only receive quality but they must feel that they have received value for their money. Band describes value creation as the "ultimate customer strategy" since it integrates quality, service, and customer satisfaction tools. A firm with a value creation orientation asks "What do our customers want from us?", rather than "Why don't customers buy what we make."

Barsky, Jonathan D.
World-Class Customer Satisfaction. Burr Ridge, IL: Irwin Professional, 1995.

Barsky has studied companies around the world that are renowned for their customer service. *World-Class Customer Service* is based on research involving 250 organizations noted for their innovative approaches to customer satisfaction. Barsky focuses on the techniques that these world-class companies use to satisfy customers. Each chapter defines a problem (such as listening to customers and employees) and uses cases from a variety of industries to illustrate the steps for building customer satisfaction.

Bell, Chip R.
Customers as Partners: Building Relationships That Last. San Francisco: Berrett-Koehler, 1994.

Bell is the coauthor (with Ron Zemke) of *Managing Knock Your Socks Off Service.* In *Customers as Partners* Bell explains the qualities that form the core of lasting customer relationships. According to Bell, these relationships are based on attributes such as honesty, trust, and faith. By establishing lifelong partnerships with customers, companies benefit because customers will supply feedback, recommend your company to others, and overlook mistakes.

Blanding, Warren
Customer Service Operations: The Complete Guide. New York: Amacom, 1991.

This book is an extension of *Practical Handbook of Distribution Customer Service,* Blanding's earlier book on customer service. Blanding has worked with thousands of customer service managers from all types and sizes of American, Canadian, and Japanese firms. *Customer Service Operations* has been designed as a practical guide to developing and managing a customer-oriented, profit-oriented customer service department. Blanding writes from the point of view of line managers in customer service.

Brothers, Theresa, and Kathleen Carson, eds
Creating a Customer-Focused Organization. New York: Conference Board, 1993.

This Conference Board report brings together nine speeches presented by manufacturing and service executives at the 1992 Board conference "Creating and Maintaining Customer-Focused Organizations." The speakers were affiliated with a wide range of organizations including John Hancock Financial Services, Johnson & Johnson Hospital Services, Inc., Weyerhaeuser Paper Company, Corning Incorporated, General Motors, Federal Express, and the Canadian Imperial Bank of Commerce. Three themes emerged from the conference: creating a customer-focused organization requires a radical change in corporate culture; everyone should be treated as a customer; and empowering employees and soliciting customer feedback are critical to achieving customer satisfaction.

Cannie, Joan Koob, with Donald Caplin
Keeping Customers for Life. New York: American Management Association, 1991.

This book on customer-driven management successfully blends theory and practice. The authors provide numerous real-world examples of companies that have moved from cost-driven to customer-driven management. *Keeping Customers for Life* outlines a twelve-step strategy for building customer loyalty. These steps are: top management commitment; internal evaluation; determining customer requirements; goals and performance measures; customer-driven management; becoming a customer-champion; employee motivation and self-esteem; empowerment and training; empowering employees to solve and prevent problems; communicating feedback; recognition, rewards, and celebrations; and a continuous improvement network. An entire chapter is devoted to each step.

Carr, Clay
Front-Line Customer Service: 15 Keys to Customer Satisfaction. New York: Wiley, 1990.

This book is structured around Carr's fifteen keys of successful customer satisfaction. The fifteen keys are: from the point of view of your customers, your only reason for being in business is to satisfy them; you sell value; customers define value in their own terms; if anything happens after the sale to prevent the customer from getting the value he or she expected, you've created a dissatisfied customer; dissatisfied customers are opportunities; if you keep satisfying very demanding customers, you're in business for life; when dealing with dissatisfied customers, focus on saving the customer, not the sale; customer satisfaction and loyalty are primary; frontline employees won't treat customers any better than managers treat front-line employees; when customers respond with honest comments, they are doing you a favor; to satisfy a dissatisfied customer, add extra value; never treat a customer as though you will never see him or her again; give a dissatisfied customer a positive reason for interacting with you again; the process by which a firm creates and delivers a product or service must support the creation of customer satisfaction and loyalty; and every organization has customers. Carr provides a series of checklists that can be used to help organizations apply these fifteen keys in order to become customer-focused.

Cottle, David W.

Client-Centered Service: How to Keep Them Coming Back For More. New York: Wiley, 1990.

Cottle begins by noting that a dissatisfied customer typically tells nine to ten other people about his or her bad experience. The leading reason for losing clients to competitors is poor quality in service. Cottle outlines how firms can find out what their clients value in terms of quality and use client-centered service to retain clients.

Davidow, William H., and Bro Uttal

Total Customer Service: The Ultimate Weapon. New York: Harper & Row, 1989.

The authors major premise is that customer service is a powerful competitive weapon in every area of business, not just the service industries. After numerous interviews with managers and a review of the literature on service, Davidow and Uttal identified six categories of principles for improving customer service. An entire chapter is devoted to each category. These categories are: developing a service strategy; leadership; a recognition of the importance of front-line employees; designing core services or products with customer service in mind; creating infrastructures to support customer service; and measuring service performance or quality.

D'Egidio, Franco

The Service Era: Leadership in a Global Environment. Cambridge, MA: Productivity Press, 1990.

This is a unique source, since it includes both American and European strategies for achieving quality customer service. Both the manufacturing and service industries are analyzed. Scandinavian Air Systems, Ford, IBM, and British Airways are among the companies used in examples.

Desatnick, Robert L.

"Inside the Baldrige Award Guidelines–Category 7: Customer Focus and Satisfaction." *Quality Progress* 25, no.12 (1992): 69–74.

Many companies use the Baldrige Award criteria for self-assessment. Category 7 of the Award criteria focuses on customer satisfaction. This category is weighted more heavily than any of the other examination categories. Desatnick summarizes the criteria against which companies are judged in the area of customer focus and satisfaction and shows how companies can use Category 7 as a learning tool.

Donnelly, James H., Jr.

Close to the Customer: 25 Tips From the Other Side of the Counter. Homewood, IL: Business One Irwin, 1992.

Donnelly has created twenty-five lessons from the customer's point of view about customer service, customer satisfaction, managing people, and leadership. Each of these lessons is in the form of an essay. The essays are arranged in three parts: what customers know about customer satisfaction; what customers know about managing people; and what customers know about leadership. At the conclusion of each part, Donnelly provides a checklist that summarizes the major parts of these individual lessons.

Flanagan, Theresa A., and Joan O. Fredericks

"Improving Company Performance Through Customer-Satisfaction Measurement and Management." *National Productivity Review* 12, no.2 (Spring 1993): 239–258.

Flanagan and Fredericks are both experts on customer-satisfaction research. This article outlines a customer-satisfaction measurement and management process. The model consists of six phases: the development of realistic and concrete objectives; discovering internal needs and customer issues; conducting a careful assessment of critical needs; action planning; improving products, services, and the organization; and measuring and monitoring results. Why should companies invest in customer-satisfaction research? Customer-satisfaction research can help companies prioritize their quality improvement activities according to customer needs, can reveal unmet or unforeseen needs, can suggest ideas for new products or services, and can create an internal climate that cultivates employee commitment to customer service.

Gale, Bradley T., with Robert Chapman Wood
Managing Customer Value: Creating Quality and Service That Customers Can See. New York: Free Press, 1994.

According to Gale, few companies have attempted to track "market-perceived quality," which Gale defines as "the customer's opinion of your products (or services) compared to those of your competition." However, a few leading-edge companies have focused on market-perceived quality. Gale uses Milliken Company, AT & T, United Van Lines, and Gillette as examples. Based on his research at these companies, he outlines methods for defining, measuring, and improving market-perceived quality.

Goldzimer, Linda Silverman, with Gregory L. Beckman
"I'm First": Your Customer's Message to You. New York: Rawson Associates; Macmillan, 1989.

"I'm First" is an acronym for Goldzimer's seven principles of customer service: integration; mission; feedback; interviewing; reward; support; and training. This is a practical handbook that can be used in any work setting. One helpful feature is the inclusion of sample surveys, – in particular, the employee feedback survey and the customer feedback survey.

Guaspari, John
The Customer Connection: Quality for the Rest of Us. New York: Amacom, 1988.

John Guaspari is a noted authority on quality and customer focus. He is the author of several other bestselling books on quality issues including *I Know It When I See It, Theory Why: In Which the Boss Solves the Riddle of Quality*, and *It's About Time: A Fable About the Next Dimension of Quality*. The Customer Connection focuses on the connection between quality and customer satisfaction.

Hanan, Mack, and Peter Karp
Customer Satisfaction: How to Maximize, Measure, and Market Your Company's "Ultimate Product". New York: American Management Association, 1989.

This book on customer satisfaction has been written for every manager. The five chapters comprising the book cover the topics of maximizing customer satisfaction, managing customer satisfaction, measuring customer satisfaction, marketing customer satisfaction, and self-satisfaction and customer satisfaction. According to the authors, the 1990s require a new definition of customer satisfaction, one that integrates the concept of added customer value, since "a satisfied customer is one who receives significant added value from a supplier."

Harris, R. Lee
The Customer is King! Milwaukee, WI: ASQC Quality Press, 1991.

This easy to read motivational guide to quality service outlines a step-by-step approach to customer service. Harris's advice is applicable to service and manufacturing sectors. He includes examples from the Xerox Corporation, H. J. Heinz, Delta Air Lines, American Express, and Marriott Hotels and Resorts.

LeBoeuf, Michael
How To Win Customers and Keep Them For Life. New York: Berkely Books, 1989.

This motivational book has become a classic. It builds upon the lessons of LeBoeuf's earlier bestseller, *GMP: The Greatest Management Principle in the World. How to Win Customers and Keep Them For Life* outlines ten action plans that will transform people into customers, and customers into lifetime partners.

Liswood, Laura A.
Serving them Right: Innovative and Powerful Customer Retention Strategies. New York: HarperBusiness, 1990.

Liswood identifies practical ways to keep customers. Some of her advice is based on the practices of the Ford Motor Company, L. L. Bean, Disney Productions, Corning Glass Works, Federal Express, McDonald's, and other companies that have developed a reputation for excellent customer service. She also proposes some innovative ideas, such as the development of a new type of corporate executive, the Chief Service Officer.

Morgan, Rebecca L.
Calming Upset Customers. Los Altos, CA: Crisp Publications, 1989.

This inexpensive manual is part of Crisp's "Fifty-Minute" series, a series of short, self-study books that combine practical advice with cases, exercises, and hands-on-activities. Morgan shows readers how to distinguish between a disturbed and an upset customer, and identifies effective strategies for dealing with both. For example, techniques to diffuse anger include learning to listen, being attentive to body language and voice tone, and careful word choice. Other customer service titles in the "Fifty-Minute" series include *Telephone Courtesy & Customer Service*, *Measuring Customer Satisfaction*, and *Quality Customer Service*. Crisp has published other hands-on books relating to customer service. Among the best is Scott Dru's *Customer Satisfaction: The Second Half of Your Job*, a book that shows readers how to improve customer relations inside their organization.

Morris, Ted
"Customer Relationship Management." *CMA Magazine* 68, no.7 (September 1994): 22–25.

Morris provides a good introduction to the topics of customer value and long-term customer relationships. Although he notes that Peter Drucker wrote about the importance of customers forty years ago, many companies did not pay attention to customer retention until the 1980s, when companies like Xerox, AT & T, and General Electric introduced the concept of market-driven quality. However, customer loyalty is critical, since retaining customers is cheaper

than attracting customers. Morris outlines some strategies for managing customer relationships and describes performance measures for evaluating quality and customer satisfaction activities.

Myers, Ken, and Jim Buckman
"Beyond the Smile: Improving Service Quality at the Grass Roots." *Quality Progress* 25, no.12 (December 1992): 55–59.

The author presents the concept of breakthrough action teams (BAT) as a new tool to improve service quality for internal and external customers. BATs are groups of five to eight employees, supervisors, and managers who select small improvement projects, called breakthrough projects. The purpose of the team is to help an organization break through to new levels of performance.

Rust, Roland T., and Richard L. Oliver, eds
Service Quality: New Directions in Theory and Practice. Thousand Oaks, CA: Sage, 1994.

According to the editors, the first wave of research on service quality occurred in the 1980s. Many of these pioneering researchers are now household names in the field of customer satisfaction. A second wave of research is occurring in the 1990s by a new generation of researchers. Many of these researchers have backgrounds in psychology, sociology, anthropology, and quantitative methods. *Service Quality* brings together articles by these second-wave researchers, as well as some recent papers by first-wave researchers.

Smith, Ian
Meeting Customer Needs. Oxford (England): Butterworth-Heinemann, 1994.

This book was published in association with the Institute of Management, the leading management institute in the UK. The author is Royal Mail Lecturer in Marketing at the Open Business School and has developed the course "Managing Customer and Client Relations." *Meeting Customer Needs* is designed to help managers achieve quality customer service. The first part of the book focuses on customers: who they are, how to identify them, how to understand them, and how to listen to them. The second part of the book focuses on interactions with customers. The remainder of the book concentrates on managing the processes. Smith makes heavy use of real-world examples and case studies to illustrate concepts.

Sviokla, John J., and Benson P. Shapiro, eds
Keeping Customers. Boston: Harvard Business School Press, 1993.

This volume is a collection of articles on customer service and customer satisfaction that were originally published in the *Harvard Business Review* between the years 1968 and 1992. The articles in *Keeping Customers* focus on developing profitable, long-term relationships with customers. *Seeking Customers*, a companion volume also edited by Sviokla and Shapiro, reprints *Harvard Business Review* articles that focus on competitive customer acquisition.

Tschohl, John, with Steve Franzmeier
Achieving Excellence Through Customer Service. Englewood Cliffs, NJ: Prentice-Hall, 1991.

This step-by-step guide to developing a quality service program has been designed for managers. It includes many practical ideas and strategies that can be applied immediately. However, the clarity of writing and rich use of case studies and real-world examples makes this an ideal text for students enrolled in courses with a customer service component.

3 Analytical and statistical tools

Amsden, Robert T., Howard E. Butler, and Davida M. Amsden
SPC Simplified: Practical Steps to Quality. White Plains, NY: Quality Resources, 1989.

This straightforward practical book on statistical process control has been written for the nonstatistician – no mathematical background is required. *SPC Simplified* is organized around seven modules. Module 1 presents the basic principles behind statistical quality control methods. Module 2 covers frequency histograms. The third module focuses on variable control charts. Module 4 discusses attribute control charts. Machine and process capability is covered in Module 5. Module 6 covers the following problem-solving tools: brainstorming, cause-and-effect diagrams, and Pareto analysis. Module 7 describes the elements of a quality control system.

Most of the modules include practice problems that give readers the chance to use these statistical techniques. A companion workbook, *SPC Simplified Workbook*, is also available from Quality Resources.

Badiru, Adedeji B., and Babatunde J. Ayeni
Practitioner's Guide to Quality and Process Improvement. London: Chapman & Hall, 1993.

This book has been designed as a practical guide to statistical techniques for improving quality, increasing productivity, and reducing product development costs. These techniques can be applied in manufacturing or service organizations. This guide will be useful to a wide range of practitioners, including industrial and systems engineers, manufacturing engineers, process engineers, quality engineers, R & D managers, plant managers, production supervisors, quality consultants, and corporate and business planners. The authors begin with an exceptionally well written introduction to the quality movement. The following chapter presents the fundamental components of quality improvement. Chapter 3 covers the basics of process improvement. Subsequent chapters focus on the project management approach to quality and process improvement, process management and control, and statistical tools for quality improvement.

Balm, Gerald J.
Benchmarking: A Practitioner's Guide for Becoming and Staying Best of the Best. Schaumburg, IL: QPMA Press, 1992.

Balm describes the benchmarking process and shows how it can be applied to industry, education, government, health care, the military, and other settings. Much of his book is based on the benchmarking process at IBM Rochester. IBM Rochester is a former Baldrige Award winner. Balm presents benchmarking as an affordable and practical tool that any organization can use in an effort to improve their processes, products, and services. Several helpful appendices are provided, including a benchmarking checklist.

Barker, Thomas B.
Quality by Experimental Design. 2nd edn. New York: Marcel Dekker, 1994.

Barker is a noted authority on experimental design and the use of Taguchi methods. Although he is currently on the faculty at Rochester Institute of Technology's College of Engineering, he has more than two decades of industry experience. *Quality by Experimental Design* is a practical guide that is intended as an introduction to the methods of experimental design. Although there are many books on statistically designed experiments, this one is directed to nonstatisticians.

Bechtell, Michele L.
The Management Compass: Steering the Corporation Using Hoshin Planning. New York: American Management Association, 1995.

This AMA Management Briefing provides an introduction to hoshin planning. Bechtell's book is an important contribution since there are only a few texts and a handful of book chapters and articles on this methodology. Although this technique was relatively unknown only a few years ago, it is becoming increasingly popular.

Belavendram, N.
Quality by Design. London: Prentice-Hall, 1995.

The author is an expert on Taguchi techniques, having completed a doctoral dissertation entitled *Taguchi Methods for Manufacturing System Design.* His current research topic is advanced quality by design. *Quality by Design* can be used as an undergraduate or graduate level text on Taguchi methods for students enrolled in quality engineering courses. While there are many books on Taguchi methods, most are written by statisticians and assume an extensive background in statistics and mathematics. Belavendram is an engineer by training and his intention is to simplify these statistical concepts for nonstatisticians. The ten chapters introduce readers to the theoretical and practical aspects of quality by design, the roles of quality assurance and the quality loss function, orthogonal arrays and matrix experiments, objective functions in robust design, basic analysis of variance, modifying orthogonal arrays, computer-aided parameter design, computer-aided tolerance design, managing the design of experiments, and conducting an experiment.

Benchmarking: Focus on World-Class Practices. Indianapolis, IN: AT & T's Customer Information Center, 1992.

This title is part of the AT & T Quality Library series. *Benchmarking* was developed by the AT

& T Benchmarking Team, a consortium of internal AT & T benchmarking service-providers. The team developed a benchmarking process that serves as the basis for this book. *Benchmarking* outlines a nine-step process for identifying and using world-class practices to achieve process improvement and competitive advantage. The benchmarking process includes the following steps: project conception; planning; preliminary data collection; best-in-class selection; best-in-class data collection; assessment; implementation planning; implementation; and recalibration. The AT & T Quality Library includes many other titles relating to improving business performance. Among them are: *Process Quality Management & Improvement Guide*; *Analyzing Business Process Data: The Looking Glass*; *Policy Deployment: Setting the Direction for Change*; and *Using ISO 9000 to Improve Business Processes.*

Bendell, A., J. Disney, and W. A. Pridmore, eds
Taguchi Methods: Applications in World Industry. Kempston, Bedford (England): IFS; Berlin: Springer, 1989.

This volume brings together twenty-three papers covering general aspects of Taguchi's methods, application of Taguchi's methods in specific industries, and future developments. The following industries have been selected for inclusion: electronics; information technology; process; automotive; and plastics. The case studies include companies from around the world. This is an important contribution, since many case studies on Taguchi's methods have been available in Japanese only or have been very difficult to obtain. Four of the case studies have been translated into English (the original languages being Japanese and French).

Besterfield, Dale H.
Quality Control. 4th edn. Englewood Cliffs, NJ: Prentice-Hall, 1994.

This practical textbook provides a basic introduction to quality control concepts. It has been written for a wide audience: undergraduate students, graduate students, students in technical institutes and community colleges, and industry practitioners. Chapters cover control chart methods for variables and attributes, acceptance sampling and standard sampling plans, quality costs, product liability, reliability, and computers in quality control.

Bhote, Keki R.

World Class Quality: Design of Experiments Made Easier, More Cost Effective Than S.P.C. New York: AMA Membership Publications Division, American Management Association, 1988.

The purpose of this AMA Management Briefing is to describe statistical process control (SPC) techniques in nonmathematical terms. This practical guide is directed to employees at all levels, from line workers to managers. Part I provides an introduction to elementary statistical process control tools. Part II focuses on design of experiments. Part III discusses SPC as a maintenance tool (rather than a problem-solving tool) and the role of SPC in reducing variation.

Brassard, Michael

The Memory Jogger Plus+: Featuring the Seven Management and Planning Tools. Methuen, MA: Goal/QPC, 1989.

This bestseller has become the standard work on the seven management and planning tools for both novices and experienced users. These tools include the following: affinity diagram; interrelationship digraph; tree diagram; prioritization matrices; matrix diagram; PDPC (process decision program chart); and affinity network diagram. GOAL/QPC has also released Windows-based software that automates these seven tools.

Brown, Mark Graham

Baldrige Award Winning Quality: How to Interpret the Malcolm Baldrige Award Criteria. 5th edn. New York: Quality Resources, 1995.

This title has been a bestseller since the first edition was released in 1991. It is probably the most heavily used book on the Baldrige Award. Since it is updated routinely, it provides the most current information on the award criteria. Brown's book is an excellent companion to the Baldrige Award guidelines. In addition to providing background information, he shows companies how to prepare an application, how to interpret the criteria, how to audit their organization against the Baldrige Award criteria, and

how to use the Baldrige assessment as a strategic planning tool. Brown has also prepared *The Pocket Guide to Baldrige Award Criteria*, a pocket guide that summarizes the Baldrige Award criteria. The *Pocket Guide* was published by Quality Resources in 1995.

Buch, Kim, and Dave Wetzel

"The Evolution of SPC in Manufacturing." *Journal for Quality and Participation* 16, no.6 (October/November 1993): 34–37.

In the United States, widespread adoption of SPC by manufacturers began in the 1980s. Many manufacturing firms expanded SPC beyond quality control departments. Buch and Wetzel's article focuses on this shift, which they refer to as the evolution from "strictly technical SPC to socio-technical SPC." The authors view SPC as a living decision-making technique in a manufacturing setting. This view is called the "open systems model." The open systems model identifies the subsystems in an organization that are impacted by SPC and shows how the extent of this impact determines the success or failure of an SPC process.

Camp, Robert C.

Benchmarking: The Search for Industry Best Practices that Lead to Superior Performance. Milwaukee: ASQC Quality Press, 1989.

This is the first book to have been published on the topic of benchmarking. It remains a bestseller – in fact, it is now in its tenth printing. Camp defines benchmarking, outlines the benchmarking process, and uses detailed case studies to demonstrate the benchmarking process from beginning to end. Camp builds upon *Benchmarking* in his newest book, *Business Process Benchmarking: Finding and Implementing Best Practices* which was released in 1995 by Quality Resources. *Business Process Benchmarking* updates Camp's benchmarking process by including strategies on the leadership and management of benchmarking. Camp uses case studies of benchmarking projects undertaken by Baldrige Award winning companies. Camp's newest book will no doubt become another bestseller.

Campanella, Jack
Principles of Quality Costs. 2nd edn. Milwaukee, WI: American Society for Quality Control, 1990.

The first edition of this book sold 10,000 copies and became a bestseller for the American Society for Quality Control. This second edition serves as a valuable reference work on quality costs. It provides a good introduction to the concept of quality costs. This practical guide will be useful to managers in both manufacturing and nonmanufacturing settings.

Carter, Charles W.
"How Quality Costs Drive TQM." *Annual Quality Congress Transactions* 45 (1991): 482–487.

Carter briefly defines quality costs, then relates four major difficulties in obtaining quality costs: problems with getting the right data from accounting department's reports, problems with the perception of dollar values assigned to quality, inconsistency in data due to reporting differences over time, and the amount of clerical effort needed to gather data. The author suggests ways to overcome these difficulties and then discusses the importance of quality costs in a TQM program. Quality costs function as ongoing controls, assist in the development of improvement goals, and provide executive direction. Graphical summaries of the relationship between the cost of goods sold and quality cost categories (prevention, appraisal, internal failure, and external failure) are presented.

Dale, Barrie G., and James J. Plunkett
Quality Costing. London: Chapman & Hall, 1991.

Dale and Plunkett's book was one of the first English language texts to be published on the topic of quality costing. The authors begin by establishing the background of quality costing. Subsequent chapters cover the definitions of quality costs, collection of quality costs, analysis and reporting of quality costs, and the uses of quality costs. The text is illustrated with examples from both manufacturing and service operations. Case studies are provided. The case studies show how different companies from the mechanical and electronic industries collect, analyze, and report quality costs. A second edition was scheduled for release in 1995.

Ealey, Lance A.
Quality by Design: Taguchi Methods and US Industry. 2nd edn. Burr Ridge, IL: ASI Press, Irwin Professional Publishing, 1994.

The first half of this book provides a historical overview of Dr. Taguchi's methodology, explaining why his approach was different from the American approach to quality and productivity. This section also uses case studies to illustrate Taguchi techniques. It also includes an interview with Dr. Taguchi. The other half of the book consists of five appendices that provide more detail about the basic aspects of Taguchi's methods. The appendices provide a technical explanation of parameter design, the quality loss function, the signal-to-noise ratio, on-line quality control, and quality engineering for technology development.

Eureka, William E., and Nancy E. Ryan, eds
Quality Up, Costs Down: A Manager's Guide to Taguchi Methods and QFD. Dearborn, MI: ASI Press; Burr Ridge, IL: Irwin Professional Pub., 1995.

This is the revised edition of *Taguchi Methods and QFD: How's and Why's for Management* which was published by the ASI Press in 1988. Ten papers are included in this revised edition. Several were presented previously at recent conferences on Taguchi's methods and QFD. Three of the papers have been retained from the first edition. The remaining two papers are excerpts from books published by the ASI Press: *Quality by Design: Taguchi Methods and US Industry* and *The Customer-Driven Company: Managerial Perspectives on QFD*. Both books were originally published in the late 1980s and have recently been reissued by ASI Press and Irwin Professional Publishing. *Quality Up, Costs Down* shows managers how Taguchi methods and QFD can help companies improve product quality and gain market share while reducing costs and product development times.

Feigenbaum, A. V.
Total Quality Control. 3rd rev. edn. New York: McGraw-Hill, 1991.

Feigenbaum is credited with introducing the concept of total quality control. This book is the fortieth anniversary edition of his classic *Total Quality Control* which was first published in

1951. Feigenbaum's book was revolutionary because it advocated the prevention rather than correction of quality problems. In addition, Feigenbaum's ideas were radical because he proposed that quality control be extended to all areas of production.

Garvin, David A.
"How the Baldrige Award Really Works." *Harvard Business Review* 69, no.6 (November-December 1991): 80–95.

This is an excellent account of the Baldrige Award judging process. It is based on in-depth interviews with Baldrige Award judges and senior examiners. The author is personally familiar with the Baldrige process, having served as a member of the Board of Overseers of the Malcolm Baldrige National Quality Award.

Grunewald, William J.
"Cost of Quality as a Baseline for Total Quality Management (TQM) Implementation." *IEEE Proceedings of the National Aerospace and Electronics Conference* 4 (1989): 1611–1613.

In implementing TQM, cost of quality is presented as an efficient means of identifying opportunities for improvement in a logical manner. Cost of quality is relevant to the work performed in most organizations and involves identifying and classifying work in terms of why it occurred and whether the cost of that work and the output were productive or non-productive in the pursuit of the organization's objectives. Cost of quality data functions as a baseline and can be used to rank areas which contribute most to non-value added costs. This insures that the investment of an organization's time and money in TQM will then be spent on those areas most likely to offer a return on such investment. Grunewald summarizes construction of a baseline, gives examples of costs that figure in determining cost of quality, and argues for the ongoing value of baseline data as TQM brings processes under control.

Hansen, Bertrand L., and Prabhakar M. Ghare
Quality Control and Application. Englewood Cliffs, NJ: Prentice-Hall, 1987.

This text (which is a revision of Hansen's *Quality Control: Theory and Applications*) will be useful to both students and practitioners. The

first part of the book introduces the basic concepts of quality control. The second part describes techniques for monitoring and maintaining quality during processing and production operations. Part III discusses acceptance control procedures. The final section of the book, Part IV, looks at the management of quality and product liability.

Harrington, H. J.
Business Process Improvement: The Breakthrough Strategy for Total Quality, Productivity, and Competitiveness. New York: McGraw-Hill, 1991.

Harrington is the international quality advisor for Ernst & Young. He has served as president and chairman of the board of the American Society for Quality Control. He is regarded as an international authority on quality improvement. *Business Process Improvement* presents strategies for improving business processes. Harrington defines business process as "all service processes and processes that support production processes." The goal of business process improvement (BPI) is to make effective and efficient use of all resources – facilities, equipment, inventory, capital, time, and people. BPI's goals are to make processes effective, make processes efficient, and make processes adaptable to changing customer and business needs. Harrington includes a discussion of flowcharting, benchmarking, and measurement and feedback systems.

Heinrich, George
"Integrating TQM with Statistical and Other Quantitative Techniques." *National Productivity Review* 13 (Spring 1994): 287–295.

TQM requires the integration of quantitative and qualitative techniques. Some examples of quantitative techniques are sampling, statistical process control, and design of experiments. Qualitative techniques include development of an integrated mission statement/goals, employee participation, employee empowerment, teams, and continuous improvement. Heinrich's contention is that this integration can be achieved through the use of team tools such as nominal group techniques, multi-voting, brainstorming, rank ordering, flowcharts, cause-and-effect diagrams, quality function deployment, Pareto charts, run charts, scatter diagrams, affinity charts, relations diagrams, systematic diagrams, matrix diagrams, process decisions charts, and arrow diagrams.

Ishikawa, Kaoru
Introduction to Quality Control. London: Chapman & Hall, 1990.

The late Dr. Kaoru Ishikawa was a leading Japanese quality expert. This is an English translation of his classic work *Dai-3-pan Hinshitsu*, which was first published in 1954. In the past four decades, his book has been revised and reprinted many times. It remains a classic in the area of quality control. Ishikawa is credited with developing the concept of quality circles and with introducing simple and practical quality tools such as the fishbone diagram, often referred to as the Ishikawa diagram. Ishikawa believed that all employees should be involved in a company-wide quality effort.

Johnson, Perry L.
Keeping Score: Strategies and Tactics for Winning the Quality War. New York: Harper & Row, 1989.

Johnson is president of Perry Johnson, Inc., a well-known consulting firm. *Keeping Score* is organized in three parts. Part I discusses the role of quality. Part II looks at the issue of a quality work force. Part III focuses on quality tools and techniques. Among the techniques covered are statistical process control, the quality/productivity index, and design of experiments.

Juran, J. M.
Juran's Quality Control Handbook. 4th edn. New York: McGraw-Hill, 1988.

Juran is one of the leading quality gurus in the quality management movement. He is a world authority on quality control. His basic premise is that more than 80 percent of quality defects are caused by a few factors. His approach to quality emphasizes problem-solving and teamwork. Juran is credited with the development of the Pareto chart. *Juran's Quality Control Handbook* is regarded worldwide as the standard reference book on quality control. It has been translated into many languages. Juran is the author of many books on quality management and management in general. His list of publications includes the following books: *Juran on Leadership for*

Quality; *Juran on Planning for Quality*, *Juran on Quality by Design*, *Quality Planning and Analysis* (with F. M. Gryna); *Managerial Breakthrough*, and *The Corporate Director*.

Kelly, Michael R.
Everyone's Problem Solving Handbook: Step-By-Step Solutions for Quality Improvement. White Plains, NY: Quality Resources, 1992.

Kelly served as a quality specialist for Florida Power & Light. This clear, concise, and easy-to-use training manual shows readers how to use bar charts, brainstorming, cause-and-effect diagrams, checksheets, flowcharts, histograms, interviews, the Barrier & Aids analysis and planning technique, line graphs, list reductions, matrices, Pareto charts, pie charts, and surveys in conjunction with problem-solving steps to improve quality. Kelly uses five case studies to demonstrate how these tools work. He also includes the "QI story," a description of problem-solving activities. This handbook will be a valuable training tool for employees working in manufacturing and service industries.

King, Robert E.
"Hoshin Planning: The Foundation of Total Quality Management." *Annual Quality Congress Transactions* 43 (1989): 476–480.

This brief article provides a clear introduction to the fundamentals of hoshin planning, a methodology that is largely unknown in the United States. One reason for this unfamiliarity is that most of the sources about it (such as key books) have not been translated into English. Yet this concept is gaining popularity in the United States. Florida Power & Light, Mead Imaging, Omark, 3M Floppy Disc, and Weyerhaeuser are among the companies that have experimented with hoshin planning.

Kolarik, William J.
Creating Quality: Concepts, Systems, Strategies, and Tools. New York: McGraw-Hill, 1995.

This comprehensive text (the book exceeds 900 pages in length) introduces the concept of quality, quality philosophies, and strategies and approaches to achieving quality. There are several sections relating to statistical and analytical tools. Among the tools covered are the seven new Japanese tools, benchmarking, strategic thinking, the seven basic tools, process flow diagrams, quality function planning and deployment, failure mode and effects analysis, logic tree analysis, design review and value analysis, variables control charts, attributes control charts, and quality-designed experiments. Cases, examples, and exercises are used extensively to reinforce the text.

Liebfried, Kathleen H. J., and C. J. McNair
Benchmarking: A Tool for Continuous Improvement. New York: HarperBusiness, 1992.

Liebfried is a manager with the consulting firm of Coopers & Lybrand. She has designed and implemented dozens of benchmarking systems. Liebfried's wealth of experience is reflected in this book, which she coauthored with McNair, an accounting professor. Along with providing an excellent introduction to benchmarking, the authors provide numerous examples of diverse companies that have conducted benchmarking studies. These benchmarking projects are discussed in detail.

Lochner, Robert H., and Joseph E. Matar
Designing for Quality: An Introduction to the Best of Taguchi and Western Methods of Statistical Experimental Design. New York: Quality Resources; Milwaukee, WI: ASQC Quality Press, 1990.

This manual has been designed for engineers and engineering students who need to know more about Taguchi methods and design of experiments. It does not assume extensive knowledge of experimental design. However, a prerequisite is a grounding in basic statistics and an understanding of the concept of random variation.

Lock, Dennis, ed.
Gower Handbook of Quality Management. 2nd edn. Aldershot (England): Gower, 1994.

This handbook was first published in 1987 under the title *Project Management Handbook.* The second edition of this comprehensive work is the product of more than twenty contributors, most of whom have extensive experience with quality improvement efforts in the manufacturing and service sectors. The handbook is divided into nine parts that relate to quality concepts and principles, quality-related costs and benefits, legislation and standards, quality organization and

administration, quality in design and engineering, purchasing and materials handling, statistical process control, quality functions in manufacturing, and participative quality improvement. Although all aspects of quality management are covered in this encyclopedic work, the chapters relating to statistical techniques are particularly useful.

McNeese, William H., and Robert A. Klein
Statistical Methods for the Process Industries. Milwaukee, WI: ASQC Quality Press; New York: Marcel Dekker, 1991.

This title is part of the *Quality and Reliability* series, a series of books on quality, statistical applications, quality and reliability engineering, and management that are designed for professionals in manufacturing, engineering, management, and marketing. *Statistical Methods for the Process Industries* has been written to help organizations in the process industries implement the use of statistical techniques. It is organized around a seven-step problem-solving model. This model involves the following steps: defining the problem; analyzing the process; determining causes; identifying solutions and selecting the best solution; implementing the solution; evaluating action; and changing the system. *Statistical Methods for the Process Industries* can serve as a basic text on quality tools, a reference book on the quantitative tools of process improvement, or can be used as a framework for a short course on process improvement.

Melnyk, Steven A., and Ram Narasimhan
Computer Integrated Manufacturing: Guidelines and Applications From Industrial Leaders. Homewood, IL: Business One Irwin, 1992.

This is a good introduction to computer integrated manufacturing (CIM). The first half of the book provides an overview, history, and grounding in the basic concepts of CIM. The second half of the book presents five detailed case studies of companies that have used CIM. Several useful appendices are provided including a glossary of CIM terms and a bibliography of books and articles relating to CIM.

Menke, Michael M.
"Improving R & D Decisions and Execution."
Research-Technology Management 37, no.5
(September/October 1994): 25–32.

Management of research and development
(R & D) activities includes identifying the
projects that have the greatest potential to create
value for the organization while balancing them
against factors such as time, cost, and difficulty.
Application of quality management tools to R &
D activities within an organization can improve
the quality of R & D project evaluation, project
management, project execution, project decisions,
and resource allocation. Five project evaluation
tools are discussed which can assist organizations
in both "doing the right R & D, and doing the
R & D right". The tools are: strategy tables used
to clarify a team's vision of a new product; influence diagrams which can identify sources of
commercial value for a new product or define and
quantify the probability of a successful new
product introduction; sensitivity analysis which
indicates risks and opportunities associated with
a product; decision trees used to improve project
decisions under different scenarios; and expected
value calculation which measures the return on
investment for projects. The authors also discuss
strategic management of R & D through use of
a portfolio grid which assists in evaluating the
balance of R & D projects, use of an R & D
productivity curve in improving the efficient use
of R & D resources, portfolio segment return
analysis and a new product revenue forecast.

Mittag, H. J., and H. Rinne
Statistical Methods of Quality Assurance.
London: Chapman & Hall, 1993.

This textbook is based on a German correspondence course which was developed by the
authors in the late 1980s. The text has been well
received. This English translation corresponds to
the third German edition and the text has been
translated into Russian. As well as being a textbook for students in engineering, computer
science, economics, and other programs
concerned with quality assurance, the book can
be used as a self-instructional introduction to
statistical quality assurance. The book particularly
lends itself to self-study given the heavy use of
problems to reinforce learning. There are more
than 100 exercises and worked examples.

Mizuno, Shigeru, ed.
*Management for Quality Improvement: The Seven
New QC Tools.* Cambridge, MA: Productivity
Press, 1988.

The "seven new QC tools" were developed by
the Society for QC Technique Development in
conjunction with the Union of Japanese Scientists
and Engineers (JUSE). These tools are: the relations diagram; the KJ method (often referred to
as the affinity diagram); the systematic diagram;
the matrix diagram; matrix data analysis; the
process decision program chart (PDPC); and the
arrow diagram. The first part of the book provides
an overview of the seven new tools and describes
the background and rationale behind the tools.
The second half of the book describes each tool
in detail and provides examples of how these
tools can be applied. These tools can be used for
planning, goal-setting, problem-solving, and
strategic planning.

Mori, Teruo
*The New Experimental Design: Taguchi's
Approach to Quality Engineering.* Dearborn, MI:
ASI Press, 1990.

This book (which has been translated from
Japanese) is essentially a revision of *Case Studies
in Experimental Design*, an earlier book written
by Mori. The first three chapters compare and
contrast traditional experimental design with
experimental design today. Chapters 4 and 5
introduce an experimental design application
manual that includes orthogonal array assignment
and procedures for data analysis. Chapters 6
through 9 consist of case studies that follow the
manual. The final chapter describes some useful
programs for personal computers.

Ozeki, Kazuo, ed.
*Handbook of Quality Tools: The Japanese
Approach.* Cambridge, MA: Productivity Press,
1990.

This handbook, translated from Japanese, has
been designed as a practical guide to statistical
tools for supervisors who are implementing
quality improvements. Part I provides background
on the philosophy underlying quality improvement with a discussion of the management
aspects of quality improvement, leadership, small
group improvement activities, process control,
quality function deployment, and operating

standards. Part II illustrates the "twelve quality tools": graphs, Pareto diagrams, cause-and-effect diagrams, check sheets, histograms, control charts, scatter diagrams, affinity diagrams, relations diagrams, systematic diagrams, matrix diagrams, and arrow diagrams. The step-by-step approach is particularly effective, especially for readers unfamiliar with statistical techniques for assessing quality.

Ranky, Paul G.
Total Quality Control and JIT Management in CIM. Guildford (England): CIMware Limited, 1990.

This text has been designed as an introduction to CIM (computer integrated manufacturing). Among the topics covered are: CIM strategy, total quality management concepts, quality assurance standards, machine vision systems, quality control equipment and technology, statistical quality control methods, and total quality methods and tools. Ranky also includes industrial case studies. The author has been involved in the design and implementation of advanced manufacturing systems for almost two decades.

Ritter, Diane
"A Tool for Improvement Using the Baldrige Criteria." *National Productivity Review* 12 (Spring 1993): 167–182.

The author shows how companies can use Baldrige Award criteria to improve their operations. She describes the seven categories of criteria against which companies are judged: leadership; informational analysis; strategic quality planning; human resource development and management; management of process quality; quality and operational results; and customer focus and satisfaction. Ritter includes a self-assessment that was developed by GOAL/QPC.

Rolstadas, Asbjorn, ed.
Benchmarking: Theory and Practice. London: Chapman & Hall, 1995.

This volume brings together more than forty papers presented at the IFIP workshop, "Benchmarking–Theory and Practice", held in Trondheim, Norway in 1994. Presenters included both academicians and experienced industrial benchmarkers. The book is organized around five themes: management issues; applications; modeling; tools and techniques; and performance measurements. There is also a section including reports from group work sessions that were conducted at the workshop. These sessions focused on three topics: implementing benchmarking; modeling for benchmarking; and performance indicators. This is one of the few research-oriented books on benchmarking. Industrial engineers, managers, quality consultants, and other professionals involved with benchmarking will find this a useful source on trends within the field of benchmarking.

Roy, Ranjit
A *Primer on the Taguchi Method*. New York: Van Nostrand Reinhold, 1990.

This title is part of the *VNR Competitive Manufacturing Series*. It has been designed for managers and engineers who need a basic understanding of Taguchi concepts and methodologies. Roy uses application examples and case studies to illustrate these statistical concepts.

Shunta, Joseph P.
Achieving World Class Manufacturing Through Process Control. Englewood Cliffs, NJ: Prentice-Hall, 1995.

Shunta demonstrates how process control can help manufacturing plants achieve world-class performance. His text is practical rather than theoretical. He shows some practical ways in which automatic process controls can be applied to reduce variability. By reducing variability, companies can reduce costs and increase quality. Engineers, managers, quality experts, and applied statisticians will find Shunta's book useful.

Spendolini, Michael
The Benchmarking Book. New York: Amacom, 1992.

This practical guide to benchmarking is particularly useful to novices. However, more experienced benchmarkers can use it as a type of self-audit. The benchmarking model that Spendolini outlines can be used in any industry. Each chapter outlines one of the stages in his five-step process. This highly readable book belongs on the shelves of all managers involved in a benchmarking study.

Watson, Gregory H.

The Benchmarking Workbook: Adapting Best Practices for Performance Improvement. Cambridge, MA: Productivity Press, 1992.

Advance praise for this book called it "the benchmarking bible of the '90s." Watson's practical guide, which brings together tools to support and facilitate benchmarking, will be particularly helpful to organizations starting a benchmarking study. The first chapter provides an introduction to process benchmarking and presents the six stages of a benchmarking study. Chapters 2 through 7 cover each of these six steps. The final chapter looks at benchmarking as a process within a company and discusses the type of support it requires. The author is a leading authority on benchmarking. His list of publications includes the following books: *Business Systems Engineering: Managing Breakthrough Changes for Productivity and Profit* and *Strategic Benchmarking: How to Rate Your Company's Performance Against the World's Best.*

Wilkerson, David, and Jeffrey Kellogg

"Quantifying the Soft Stuff: How to Select the Assessment Tool You Need." *Employment Relations Today* 19 (Winter 1992/93): 413–424.

This easy to understand article can help managers select the right assessment tools for a cultural (i.e, organizational culture) assessment survey, a benchmarking system, and total quality management. Both authors are affiliated with the consulting firm of Coopers & Lybrand and have extensive experience developing cultural assessment surveys. However, the types of survey and assessment tools described can be used with or without the help of a consultant.

Young, S. Mark

"A Framework for Successful Adoption and Performance of Japanese Manufacturing Practices in the United States." *Academy of Management Review* 17, no.4 (October 1992): 677–700.

Young's contention is that American firms are having only moderate success with Japanese manufacturing methods such as total quality control, Kaizen, and Just-in-Time (JIT) production. His review of the literature indicated that three general strategies are being used to integrate Japanese manufacturing practices into the United States. The first strategy is to maintain these practices as they are employed in Japan and to modify features of the American manufacturing environment. The second strategy is to modify some or all of Japanese manufacturing practices but to maintain the features of the American manufacturing environment. The third strategy, and the one Young believes to be the most successful, is to modify some or all of the Japanese practices and to modify features of the U.S. manufacturing environment.

4 Corporate culture

Block, Peter

The Empowered Manager: Positive Political Skills at Work. San Francisco: Jossey-Bass, 1987.

Block's premise is that organizations will have to become more entrepreneurial in the future, and less bureaucratic, in order to prosper and survive. He compares and contrasts the attributes of the two organizational forms. Bureaucratic organizations have top-down management and individuals are rewarded on the basis of their own performance. An entrepreneurial organization is based more on a participative model and individuals generally feel that they are stakeholders in the organization. Block's conclusion is that managers in an entrepreneurial organization are empowered and more capable of contributing successfully.

Connor, Patrick E., and Linda K. Lake

Managing Organizational Change. 2nd edn. Westport, CT: Praeger, 1994.

The authors are concerned with helping managers make changes in organizations in ways that are beneficial to the organization and to the people within the organization. They present a model of managed change. Understanding the origin of factors creating a need for change sheds light on the question of where and how managed change should be effected. Connor and Lake identify four major strategies that managers can use in conducting organizational change: facilitative (share power and use the abilities and resources of people who are part of a change); informational (educate people about change and defuse resistance); attitudinal (persuade and convert people); and political (giving, withholding, competing, and bargaining to accomplish objectives). The authors discuss criteria that impact the success or failure of such strategies and the implications of their use. In the final chapters Connor and Lake provide sample diagnostics that can assist in managing change and talk about ethical issues in managing change. An appendix containing ethical guidelines for "change managers and their agents" is included.

Deal, Terrence E., and Allan A. Kennedy
Corporate Cultures: The Rites and Rituals of Corporate Life. Reading, MA: Addison-Wesley, 1982.

This book is a classic in examining the impact of corporate culture on corporate success. Deal and Kennedy conclude that companies that are successful have strong positive cultures with well-articulated values. Such organizations also have their corporate heroes who exemplify the culture of the corporation, and formalized rites and rituals that reinforce the values of the corporation. The authors discuss the ways in which communication contributes to corporate culture; the way language is used can unify members of the organization and communicate organizational beliefs and values as well.

Eccles, Tony
Succeeding with Change: Implementing Action-Driven Strategies. London: McGraw-Hill, 1994.

This book is designed to persuade managers that big shifts in the way an organization runs are often practical and to help managers see opportunities for implementation of strategic changes. Eccles discusses several misconceptions regarding change, then looks at six contexts of change (takeovers, an outsider brought in as a top manager, succession from below, reorganization, new partners, and consultants brought in). Following this, Eccles spends considerable time on fourteen factors of change and relates them to managers' experiences in implementing change. The last chapter deals with eight elements necessary for change to occur and specifies the likely reaction if that particular element is missing. The elements are: pressure for change, shared vision, trust, will and power to act, capable people and sufficient resources, rewards and accountability, clear starting point, and the capacity to learn and adapt.

Farrow, Brad W.
"Coaching: From Theory To Results. The 'How To' Of TQM Implementation." *Annual Quality Congress Transactions* 47 (1993): 335–341.

Farrow contends that traditional TQM training gives an organization various tools that can be used to change processes, but that not enough attention has been paid to development of the skills needed to transform an organization's culture. The author believes that the benefits of TQM are not fully realized until TQM is part of the day-to-day culture, as opposed to being thought of as a "project." Utilizing a full-time TQM professional in the role of a coach is presented as a mechanism for a more effective implementation of TQM. Farrow discusses some of the difficulties organizations have with coaching, discusses the selection of a coach and summarizes the primary tasks of a TQM coach within an organization. Those tasks are to provide direction, establish accountability, promote involvement, and to work closely with managers to ensure that their leadership skills are developing concurrently with their skills in the technical aspects of TQM.

Friesen, Michael E., and James A. Johnson
The Success Paradigm: Creating Organizational Effectiveness Through Quality and Strategy. Westport, CT: Quorum Books, 1995.

The "success paradigm" described by the authors is based upon "critical success factors," a concept developed by Jack Rockart in 1979. Friesen and Johnson outline a multistep process that enables a management team to work toward a shared purpose. Different units of an organization can work toward a shared purpose if a common vision has been defined. Successful organizations also focus their attention on a few key elements or critical success factors. Friesen and Johnson's success paradigm model emphasizes these four basic elements: an articulated vision, a focus, quality improvement, and learning. The second half of the book provides several real-world examples of organizations that have attempted to create an organizational success paradigm. Among those included are Fortune 500 manufacturing and service firms, nonprofit organizations, health care organizations, and public education.

Gouillart, Francis J., and James N. Kelly
Transforming the Organization: Reframing Corporate Issues, Restructuring the Company, Revitalizing the Spirit of Enterprise, Renewing People. New York: McGraw-Hill, 1995.

This book is intended to be used as a practical guide to organizational restructuring and renewal. The authors discuss the corporation as a living organism with a body, mind, and spirit. The authors present the concept of organizational transformation as an attempt to make use of the best of the old and the new in management thinking. The four parts of the book deal with reframing an organization's self-concept, restructuring the corporate body to make it more competitive, spurring growth in existing business and actively pursuing new kinds of business, and renewing the individual, the organization, and the community. The key to an organization's ability to adapt and grow is a shared pursuit of common goals. This is achieved by making sure a number of structures are working in tandem (for example, technology, "work architecture," and rewards). Numerous case histories are provided. The authors advocate the creation of "natural work teams" (small groups of people with diverse skills who have been empowered to take action as needed). Rewards within an organization should be linked to an employee's skills and participation in "individual learning," with emphasis placed on encouraging employees to make full use of their expanding opportunities.

Green, Richard Tabor
"Organizational Change Approaches for Implementing Quality." In *Global Quality: A Synthesis of the World's Best Management Methods* (Milwaukee, WI: ASQC Quality Press; Homewood, IL: Business One Irwin, 1993), 608–621.

Starting with the premiss that any quality approach used by an organization must be treated as an organizational change, Green presents a variety of approaches to changing organizations. He begins by listing thirteen principles of organizational change in general (along the lines of "obtain buy-in by informal leaders" and "balance bold change with easily doable change"), and follows with a list of twenty-three fundamental quality principles (place customers first, distinguish variation in work processes from variation caused by worker effects, strive to prevent defects

instead of "handling" them, etc.). Green then discusses sixteen basic approaches to organization change and suggests that they be combined as an organization deems appropriate. Some of the models are the: parallel organization model, training and quality college model, top-down leadership model, open systems customer linking model, systems redesign model, and the educative workplace model. Models of parallel organization are discussed in the greatest detail. Green concludes by offering six principles for using parallel organizations to implement quality.

Groocock, John M.
"Organizing for Quality – Including a Study of Corporate-Level Quality Management in Large U.K.-Owned Companies." *Quality Management Journal* 1, no.2 (January 1994): 25–35.

Groocock gathered data from thirty-eight large companies detailing the way they deal with quality at the corporate level. Two factors appear to determine the way a company organizes for quality: its size and complexity, and its quality philosophy (quality assurance versus quality improvement). Smaller businesses with a quality assurance philosophy do best when they have a strong quality assurance department that performs all testing and inspection. ISO 9000 is essentially a quality assurance system, thus the organization of quality in many firms is highly influenced by what customers demand of suppliers. Smaller companies with a quality improvement philosophy should have testing and inspection performed by the manufacturing department. Quality departments in such organizations should be responsible for obtaining, analyzing, and publishing quality data. Most large firms follow a quality improvement philosophy. These organizations need to take care to ensure that quality managers at all levels apply a consistent company quality philosophy.

Guillen, Mauro F.
"The Age of Eclecticism: Current Organizational Trends and the Evolution of Managerial Models." *Sloan Management Review* 36 (Fall 1994): 75–86.

This article examines the three basic management models (scientific management, human relations, and structural analysis) from a historical perspective and discusses the circumstances which prompted the development of each. Guillen provides a table comparing the features and techniques of the three models (for example, how workers are managed under each: close supervision vs. gaining confidence of workers, and leading vs. decentralization which develops initiative and responsibility). Guillen also examines the role that religion has historically played in affecting the adoption of a particular management model. Eastern religious beliefs appear to encourage definition of the firm as a community, while the Christian ethic emphasizes individual effort and is more consistent with the principles of the scientific management model. Guillen looks at the evidence for cyclical patterns in managerial practices and discusses the tension between individualism and communalism. He believes the evidence does not support cyclical patterns so much as it indicates the adoption of "eclectic models." This approach demonstrates that current managerial trends like lean production and total quality management are hybrid models incorporating aspects of each of the three basic models. Guillen argues that instead of continually trying to define the best organizational model or "best practice" there should be more emphasis on understanding the cultural and institutional circumstances that have an impact on how people prefer to organize.

Hampden-Turner, Charles
Creating Corporate Culture: From Discord to Harmony. Reading, MA: Addison-Wesley, 1992.

This book takes a look at what corporate culture is and describes some basic models. Hampden-Turner then discusses issues that have an affect on the economic cultures of different nations (class relationships and manager worker tensions; hierarchy or equality in communications; rational or intuitive thinking styles; and individualism vs. cooperativism). Subsequent chapters present eight case studies of corporate cultures which demonstrate how particular organizations have managed to change their culture, and in some cases have had to learn to deal with dilemmas posed by national culture. The final chapter discusses methods for altering corporate culture which are related back to the case studies. Key points are to first find the taboos, bring conflicts into the open, discuss conflicts and widen the discussion to include other related factors, reinterpret corporate myths, look at the way cultural values get reinforced, and create new learning systems to support the desired change.

Heilpern, Jeffrey, and David Nadler
"Implementing Total Quality Management: A Process of Cultural Change." In *Organizational Architecture: Designs for Changing Organizations* (San Francisco: Jossey-Bass, 1992), 137–154.

In this chapter the authors focus on the questions of what quality really is, why it matters, how TQM relates to organizational change, and how to implement TQM. Their basic premise is that success in implementing TQM and receiving a return on that investment depends on understanding, positioning, and managing TQM as large-scale organizational change that involves fundamental aspects of an organization's corporate culture. Heilpern and Nadler make the point that quality management is not a solution for all organizational problems, nor is it a substitute for effective organizational design. TQM does impact almost all of an organization's components (the work it does, the people that perform the work, the formal structures and processes that are created to get work done, and the informal operating style, culture, and values that develop over time).

Organizations need transition strategies in moving toward TQM. They need: tools for analyzing problems and enhancing team effectiveness, training, information, technical support, leadership from management, transition management structures, reward and recognition, and effective communication. The authors discuss some of their insights in helping companies manage the change TQM requires (expect some pain and crisis, be consistent across the organization and over time, don't neglect the importance of learning, etc.). The responsibility for managing large-scale change is clearly a senior management job and should not be undertaken unless management is willing to make the needed investments over time and it is important to the success or survival of the business.

Huber, George P., and William H. Glick, eds
Organizational Change and Redesign: Ideas and Insights for Improving Performance. New York: Oxford University Press, 1993.

This book is a collection of articles about different dimensions of organizational change. Two chapters are particularly useful. The first chapter "Sources and Forms of Organizational Change" provides a summary of the fundamental causes of the environmental changes faced by organizations (information technology and transportation technology), the changes in organizational processes that follow from environmental changes, the way top managers influence organizational change (four roles include being sources of change, constraints on change, interpreters, and manipulators). The last chapter "What Was Learned About Organizational Change and Redesign" deals with ways organizations can be changed and redesigned to be more effective. The most important lessons for managers appear to be that: even change is changing (appears to be nonlinear and unpredictable); organizational success and survival depend on continuous and discontinuous improvements; increased information processing and analysis are the norm for successful organizations; and teamwork and shared values are critical for managing change and enhancing organizational performance.

Hurst, David K.

Crisis & Renewal: Meeting the Challenge of Organizational Change. Boston, MA: Harvard Business School Press, 1995.

The author discusses the role that crisis plays in organizational renewal. Hurst contends that oftentimes "organizations advance strategically by accident, economically by windfall, and politically by disaster." He believes that the ability of management to remain in control of organizations is overplayed and that as organizations grow they develop vulnerabilities that leave them ready for renewal. The aim of the book is to assist managers in understanding this process because they have power to shape outcomes. Hurst presents three models of management action: rational action, constrained action, and emergent action. Managers need to learn when and under what circumstances these models help them understand what to do. Hurst investigates: whether bureaucracies can be changed back into entrepreneurial organizations; whether successful mature organizations develop vulnerabilities to catastrophe (an organizational "ecocycle" model derived from ecology); and whether managers of mature organizations ought to deliberately create crises if they want to preserve their organizations from destruc-

tion (positing that crisis can lead to innovation). Hurst is careful to point out that the third point sounds similar to reengineering, but is profoundly different. Reengineering is a rational management practice built around the idea that a leader knows what he "wants", while Hurst's "renewal cycle" is a creative process leading to learning and answers to the question of "What do we want?".

Imai, Masaaki

Kaizen: The Key to Japan's Competitive Success. New York: Random House Business Division, 1986.

Kaizen is the Japanese word for the concept of continuing improvement in all spheres of life. In the workplace the term stands for ongoing improvement involving everyone. Imai contends that the internalization of this concept in Japan is the key to Japanese competitive success. Imai reviews the way Kaizen is exemplified in Japanese business and follows with a comparison of eastern and western approaches to progress and improvement. Generally speaking, the west has most valued innovation, while the east has favored gradual changes. Japanese management has focused more on processes, while the west has focused on results. Imai discusses total quality control in the context of achieving Kaizen. The primary characteristics of Kaizen are that it: is continuous and incremental, involves everyone in an organization, can be used by individuals or teams, requires little investment but great effort to maintain, is process oriented, is concerned with the development of a quality workforce, and works well in a slow growth economy. Imai also discusses the changes in western corporate culture that must be effected if Kaizen is a goal. Some tools for achieving change are suggested along with questions for management aimed at determining if they have the level of commitment needed to make the changes Kaizen entails.

Joiner, Brian L.

Fourth Generation Management: the New Business Consciousness. New York: McGraw-Hill, 1994.

Fourth generation management is based on an understanding that quality is defined by the customer, learning to manage the organization as a system, and treating all stakeholders in an organization with respect. Joiner provides numerous examples of the way this management style can be used to foster improvement and organizational change.

Kline, Peter, and Bernard Saunders
Ten Steps to a Learning Organization. Arlington, VA: Great Ocean Publishers, 1993.

Using integrative learning tools, the authors propose a ten-step process to building a learning organization capable of continuous improvement and maximum use of its resources. The process is designed to create organizational change through involvement of everyone in the organization. The steps are to 1) assess the strengths and weaknesses of the current corporate culture, 2) learn to think positively about the organization, 3) make the workplace "safe for thinking", 4) reward risk-taking, 5) help people become resources for each other, 6) implement effective training that helps people at all levels learn, 7) learn to work effectively in groups, 8) create models for adjusting the way things are normally done, 9) implement systems thinking, and 10) internalize what has been learned and put it into action.

Mawhinney, Thomas C.
"Total Quality Management and Organizational Behavior Management: An Integration for Continual Improvement." *Journal of Applied Behavior Analysis* 25, no.3 (Fall 1992): 525–543.

This article begins with a discussion of quality problems with American goods and services. The author reviews Deming's TQM approach to quality problems as well as the contributions organizational behavior management has made to performance management. Mawhinney then looks at areas of agreement and disagreement between TQM and organizational behavior management with the goal of identifying contributions organizational behavior management (OBM) can make to the TQM movement. Areas of agreement between TQM and OBM include a reliance on data and standards, but a major difference lies in the area of consequences. A typical OBM model for making a change consists of specifying the change desired, agreeing on how the accomplishment of the change will be documented or measured, and dealing with "consequences" (arranging reinforcers which are contingent upon observance of the desired outcome). Deming's

TQM approach identifies what is wrong with behavior in many American corporations, but the author believes TQM fails to deal with the issue of progressively reinforcing the new behavior desired. Mawhinney examines the difficulties of changing executive behavior and continually relates the OBM model for change to Deming's fourteen points. The author concludes that interventions which combine OBM, statistical process control, and the Deming philosophy of TQM will be more effective than using any of these techniques alone.

Mohr-Jackson, Iris
"Quality-Starter Versus Quality Advancer Organizations." *Quality Management Journal* 1, no.2 (January 1994): 47–56.

This article examines the differences between companies that are just starting quality improvement efforts (quality starters) and companies that are well advanced in their TQM implementation (quality advancers). Information was gathered from interviews with fifty-four corporate quality executives from a variety of manufacturing and service organizations. Three criteria were used to separate quality starters from quality advancers. Areas covered in the interviews were definitions of quality, leadership, strategic quality planning, human resource utilization, quality assurance, quality results, and customer satisfaction. Results indicate that quality starters and advancers are quite different on several dimensions lending support to the idea that a quality effort has the potential to transform an organization. Examples: leadership of quality starter firms tends to be more authoritarian, individual-oriented, and numbers-driven than quality advancer firms (where the corresponding attributes are participative, team-oriented, and quality-driven). Similarly, the management of process quality is based more on inspection, traditional practices, and quick fixes at quality starter firms; and oriented toward prevention, best-quality practices, and continuous improvement at quality advancers.

Nadler, David, Robert Shaw, and Elise Walton
Discontinuous Change: Leading Organizational Transformation. San Francisco: Jossey-Bass, 1994.

The authors argue that the long-term success of any organization is dependent upon its ability to adapt to a changing environment and its ability to retain an edge instead of becoming complacent. Widespread performance improvement is a necessity and this book contends that the senior leadership of an organization should be held accountable for achieving such change; management of change is a basic competency. They provide a model for the change they advocate which involves improvisational skills. In the past, the authors believe managers dealt mostly with incremental change. Managers in the 1990s have to deal with dramatic discontinuous change. The book presents a strategy for managing discontinuous change. The authors have included chapters on designing organizational architecture, transforming organizational culture, reengineering business processes, and executives as change agents. Examples of effective change are presented in the book.

Peak, Martha H.
"Managing for Radical Change." *Management Review* 82 (February 1993): 22–26.

This article is based on the "Third Annual Global Conference on Management Innovation" sponsored by the American Management Association/International in association with the Japan Management Association. The consensus appears to be that a major paradigm shift on the part of management will be needed to successfully compete in the future. In the global economy, people and infrastructure are the two commodities that do not travel well and can make a competitive difference. Executives at the conference also agreed that companies must hold themselves to the same ethical standards and manufacturing standards in all countries they operate in. There should be no conflict between doing well and doing right. The organization of a global corporation may take many forms (no "right" way), but ethics and human resources may ultimately define success.

Peters, Tom
Liberation Management: Necessary Disorganization for the Nanosecond Nineties. New York: Alfred A. Knopf, 1992.

Although somewhat disjointed in style, Peters has written a book detailing some of the changes organizations will have to make in order to survive. His basic message is that large compa-

nies will have to learn to decentralize and become more entrepreneurial. Companies that are best able to respond to the constantly changing business environment will have a competitive economic advantage. Organizations will have to be more flexible, and are going to have to place more emphasis on product design and innovation to succeed. They will also have to cut the time needed to get new products out and must be aggressive in seeking new markets. Additionally, the trend toward employee empowerment will increase. Middle management is on its way out as organizations become increasingly less hierarchical. Information technology is viewed as the driver of changes in the way products are manufactured and services are delivered. Peters bolsters his arguments with a multitude of examples.

Pinchot, Gifford, and Elizabeth Pinchot
The End of Bureaucracy & the Rise of the Intelligent Organization. San Francisco: Berrett-Koehler, 1994.

This book advances the argument that we should give up on attempts to make bureaucracies work better within organizations. Instead, bureaucracies should be replaced altogether and adoption of the "intelligent organization" model should follow. Decentralized teams are the forerunner of this organization that will capitalize on the intelligence of all of its employees and use the creativity of people at all levels, not just those at the top. The intelligent organization will consist of small, "intrapreneurial" teams that function like independent businesses. These teams will compete within the organization for markets and will have control over the revenue they generate. Employees of these organizations will be "free-holders" with freedom to choose their own projects and team members, full access to the information they need, and all the learning opportunities they deem necessary. Responsibility and the creation of community spirit will be encouraged. In jettisoning the hierarchical structure of the bureaucracy and focusing on customer satisfaction, the intelligent organization will be able to respond much more effectively to customers, partners, and competitors.

Rieley, James B.
"How to Make TQM and CI Programs Work."
Quality Progress 25, no.10 (October 1992): 92–99.

Organizations that are involved with TQM are in one of three places: looking for a starting point, organizing a plan, or proceeding to implement their strategic plan. Commitment to making the quality journey is the prerequisite for a successful quality effort. The planning process is crucial to the success of TQM. An effective planning process deals with the implementation of a vision (policy deployment). Rieley briefly summarizes the principles of policy deployment, then discusses seven management planning tools that can be used to develop the plan. Rieley provides examples of an affinity diagram and an interrelationship diagram which demonstrate the interrelatedness of objectives and the organizational culture. Rieley also advises organizations to begin with small programs or pilot projects instead of trying to overachieve.

Ritvo, Roger A., Anne H. Litwin, and Lee Butler, eds
Managing in the Age of Change. Burr Ridge, IL: Irwin Professional Publishing, 1995.

The first part of this book is concerned with how to manage effectively in times of change. Topics covered in the sixteen chapters include: dealing with intergroup competition and conflict, employee appraisals, career development, the effective use of consultants, developing high-performance teams, and resistance to change. The second part of the book revolves around the issue of managing diversity effectively. Chapters in this section include: "Meeting the Challenge of Cultural Diversity", which discusses the kinds of skills needed to manage a multicultural workforce (and also recruiting and employee appraisal issues); "The Clonal Effect in Organizations" (describes the tendency of people to hire people like themselves and discusses ways to adapt to a changing workforce); "Issues for Women Managers" (discusses issues such as balancing work and family, the undervalued management style of many women, career patterns, sexist language, etc. This chapter suggests working from a systems perspective to manage more effectively instead of concen-trating on individual competence). Chapters on Asian-American, Hispanic,

and African-American diversity issues in the workplace are also present, as is an article on workers with disabilities.

Schaffer, Robert H., and Harvey A. Thomson
"Successful Change Programs Begin With Results." *Harvard Business Review* 70, no.1 (January/February 1992): 80–89.

The authors state that too many companies equate ends with means and processes with outcomes. Managers believe that if they benchmark, assess customers' expectations and go through training then their sales will increase and quality will improve. The pursuit of activity-centered programs should be replaced by results-driven improvement processes. This tactic leads companies to introduce only those changes in management methods and business processes that can actually help achieve specific goals. Shaffer discusses six reasons why activity-centered programs generally fail: they're not tied to specific results; they're too large-scale and diffuse; people are afraid to talk about results because that implies they're only interested in short-term gains; too much reliance on measurement and "quality processes" and not enough emphasis on genuine improvement; too much delegation to consultants or reliance on staff-driven programs; and a failure to modify approaches based on what is learned about techniques that just don't work in a particular organizational setting. The author believes that results-driven programs are much more likely to transform an organization over time and require minimal investment. Examples are provided. Empirical testing will reveal what has worked and frequent reinforcement provided by successful changes will energize the improvement process. It is the job of management to identify the performance improvements that are most needed, but they should take care to pair short-term improvement projects with long-term strategic objectives.

Senge, Peter M.
The Fifth Discipline: The Art and Practice of the Learning Organization. New York: Doubleday, 1990.

Senge discusses the need to build "learning organizations" as the ability for organizations to learn quickly may eventually be the primary competitive tool. Organizations need to be able to make full use of their human capital. The learning organization is one in which five learning "disciplines" are at work. The five are: personal mastery (focusing energies, developing patience, being objective); mental models (subjecting our internal pictures of the world to scrutiny and thinking about alternatives); building shared vision (holding a shared picture of the future the organization wants to create); team learning (the ability to think together instead of being defensive); and systems thinking (the "fifth discipline" – an awareness of patterns and interrelated actions that result in an intuitive view of the world). The fifth discipline ties the other four disciplines together. Learning-disabled organizations are those not capable of thinking systematically. Senge describes the changes that occur in organizations as they practice the disciplines and continually relates the importance of systems thinking to the change process.

Senge, Peter M.

The Fifth Discipline Fieldbook: Strategies and Tools for Building a Learning Organization. New York: Currency/Doubleday, 1994.

This is a companion volume to Senge's earlier book *The Fifth Discipline* (see previous entry). It is intended as a guide to the practical applications of his theory of the learning organization. There are examples of how organizations have dealt with "learning disabilities" and have managed to evolve into highly successful entities. Cross references included in the book are designed to facilitate its use a practical working tool.

Westbrook, Jerry D.

"Organizational Culture and Its Relationship to TQM." *Industrial Management* 35, no.1 (January/February 1993): 1–3.

This article makes the point that if an organization wants to adopt TQM as a guiding principle, then an effort by management to create a supportive culture must be the first step. The author believes that most people have only a hazy idea of what corporate culture is; the emphasis is usually on the paradigm shift required by TQM (like the need to empower people) and not on what culture is and how to effect a shift. Westbrook examines five attributes of corporate culture: language, artifacts and symbols, patterns of behavior, basic underlying assumptions, and subcultures. He

examines each attribute and discusses the ways a culture reveals itself. By understanding the existing culture prior to implementing TQM, the factors which might complicate or foster resistance to TQM can be identified and neutralized. Westbrook looks at the role played by jargon, metaphors, myths, heroes, and celebrations. He also makes interesting points about symbols such as timeclocks and keys (the presence or absence of which continuously reinforces a particular type of culture). Thus, choosing the symbols that best represent a desired culture can be a viable option for change. Rituals, behavioral norms, and values are similarly discussed. The author recommends replacing negative cultural components with positive ones that are positively reinforced.

Wheatley, Margaret J and Myron Kellner Rogers

"Breathing Life Into Organizations." *Journal for Quality and Participation* 18, no.4 (July/August 1995): 6–9.

The authors discuss the emerging changes in how people think about work and organizations. They contend that a shift is being made from a mechanistic view of the world (organizations as machines) to a living systems model. Important features of this model are that: living systems learn constantly and adapt by tinkering; living systems are self-organizing with innate capacities to respond to change; life seeks supportive systems; life is attracted to order but there isn't a linear road to order; organizations are living systems; most people are intelligent, creative, adaptive, and self-organizing and we need to learn how to capitalize on this. The authors challenge people to think about how quality efforts would differ in a living system (as opposed to a mechanistic system). They surmise that less effort would be spent on training programs and motivational efforts; more time would be spent in engaging the talents of people in figuring out resolutions to quality problems; better resources for supporting the inquiry process would be provided; and there would be less emphasis on finding the "perfect" improvement program – parallel efforts might be made.

Whiteside, John

The Phoenix Agenda: Power to Transform Your Workplace. Essex Junction, VT: OMNEO/Oliver Wight Publications, 1994.

This book presents a twelve-step approach for

"effectively renewing companies in the face of turbulent change." The book is aimed at threatened businesses as well as individuals trying to survive such transformations. Topics covered by the author include: management skills appropriate for use with empowered employees; action skills that help teams get organized quickly and achieve results; extensive information on coaching skills; and tools necessary for creating a shared vision, sense of focus, and commitment to change across organizational boundaries. Three fundamental actions can transform an organization: change in culture and attitudes at the individual and corporate level; change in an organization's way of communicating; and individual courage to create change.

Williams, Allan, Paul Dobson, and Mike Walters
Changing Culture: New Organisational Approaches. 2nd edn. London: Institute of Personnel Management, 1993.

This is the second edition of a work first published in 1989. The authors have re-examined the conclusions of their earlier research. Among the factors they expected to have an impact on their original findings were global economic changes, structural changes occurring in businesses, and the push toward privatization. The authors conclude that organizational culture and the need to manage change effectively are increasingly important to the long-term success of organizations. In fact, managing change has been mainstreamed and is assumed to be inevitable. The book focuses on the role of human resources in effecting a change in culture. Case studies of challenges faced by a range of businesses are provided to illustrate the author's points.

---

5 Leadership

Aubrey, Charles A.
"Should the Board of Directors Be Involved in TQM?" *National Productivity Review* 12 (Summer 1993): 317–323.

Increasingly, change in the management of American corporations has been at the behest of the board of directors and disgruntled shareholders. Boards are becoming more assertive and are changing the traditional management/board of directors relationship. A survey by the American Society for Quality Control and the Gallup organization attempted to determine if this changing environment has had any effects on the determination of companies' strategic quality directions. Results indicate that most executives clearly believe that management has total responsibility for developing a quality policy. Most outside directors also agreed with this position. Aubrey says this indicates that executives are not getting guidance on quality direction from their bosses (the board), and without this guidance or a critical element of long-term strategy they can't be held accountable. Both executives and boards split on the question of whether this role may change in the future. If one of the roles of the board is to define what success means for a company, then that necessarily means discussing quality. Aubrey doesn't advocate having the board manage quality, but suggests they provide oversight, request pertinent reports, and provide management with a basis for accountability. It is in management's best interests to pursue this arrangement. They could make a start by providing the board with better quality information and educating them on quality issues.

Barclay, Charles A.
"Quality Strategy and TQM Policies: Empirical Evidence." *Management International Review* 33 (First Quarter 1993): 87–98.

Barclay surveyed a sample of large service and manufacturing organizations. His findings indicate that most executives see quality as a very important strategic objective as well as a very important strategic advantage. However, most executives fail to communicate this well to employees. A surprising majority of firms in the sample did not have company-wide quality definitions. Most did not have quality characteristic measures or defective product definitions. The author states that a common "quality vocabulary" is essential to TQM implementation. Executives somewhat supported cross-functional teams, but most employees were not even involved in such basic things as setting work schedules or taking responsibility for quality. Thus, executives are not implementing their strategic intentions through appropriate policy implementation. The author concludes that there is a strong strategic intent to promote quality as a strategic advantage using a

TQM process. However, there is a clear lack of effective implementation of TQM. Effective communication channels are not being used.

Bednarczyk, Betty L., David P. Negus, and John Persico
"The Role of the Union, Management, and Consultant in a Total Quality Transformation Effort." *Annual Quality Congress Transactions* 43 (1989): 41–59.

This article by a union leader, employee relations manager, and total quality control consultant outlines the steps necessary to achieve a successful total quality effort in a unionized setting. Companies that attempt to implement total quality control in a unionized work-setting may find that they face difficulties. Too often, labor-management relations in these companies are adversarial. The authors state that labor and management must both take steps to change before progress can be made. They recommend use of a neutral third party or outside consultant to facilitate this process. In working with unions, the job of the consultant is to help the union with such things as learning about total quality control; arranging training; defining a leadership role for the union leadership in the total quality implementation process; helping the union work with management on job security issues; and assisting the union in working with management on problem areas between total quality control programs and collective bargaining agreements. The consultant's role in working with management is quite similar (for example, helping management understand union concerns about the changes total quality brings to the workplace; helping management learn to treat unions as equal partners in the total quality process; and helping management understand how labor relations laws may impact the implementation of their total quality program).

Bennis, Warren
An Invented Life: Reflections on Leadership and Change. Reading, MA: Addison-Wesley, 1993.

Essays in this book deal with the subject of facilitating leadership and managing change, and the ethics of organizational life. The concept of invention is important to Bennis. He believes that the process of discovering energies and desires and then acting on that understanding is the way individuals discover their potential and thus

"invent" their lives. Among the concepts addressed by Bennis is the "Wallenda Factor." This refers to the ability of some leaders to accomplish extraordinary things; primarily by taking risks without dwelling on failure, and viewing mistakes in terms of growth. Bennis also includes his 1966 essay on "The Coming Death of Bureaucracy" which proved to be prescient in many ways and a 1984 essay on the four competencies of leadership which lead to empowerment: management of attention (ability to attract people); management of meaning (ability to communicate a vision); management of trust (standing for certain known quantities); and management of self (knowing one's skills and using them effectively). One other key essay, "On the Leading Edge of Change", makes the point that leaders of the future will need to be increasingly concerned with generating intellectual power. Effective leaders will have to learn to orchestrate ideas and make full use of the collective brain power of their organizations.

Cocheu, Ted
"Building a Leadership Foundation for Quality." *Training and Development* 47 (September 1993): 51–58.

Cocheu states that leadership for quality improvement has to come from executives, but too many leaders don't provide this leadership. Many executives have inappropriately delegated quality efforts to subordinates or have hoped for a quick fixes. Cocheu paraphrases Juran in maintaining that senior managers may be reluctant to accept insiders and subordinates as teachers. Human resources practitioners can assist quality efforts with the process of gaining senior manager's commitment. This may be best accomplished by hiring an outside consultant to educate senior managers about quality. Cocheu warns that one should be sure that the consultant fits with the organization's culture and will be perceived as a peer by senior executives. The author proposes a model for a process that will help executives learn, and thus build a foundation of leadership for improvement. Points are to: develop a vision for improvement through active methods (competitive analysis, cost of non-conformance); build a shared vision and philosophy for improvement; use criteria of awards to build a unique quality management system; and assess the differences between reality and an organization's goals.

Cound, Dana M.

A Leader's Journey to Quality. Milwaukee, WI: ASQC Quality Press; New York: Marcel Dekker, 1992.

Cound is a past president of the American Society for Quality Control. Cound has structured a book that intersperses the inner thoughts of a fictitious executive with conventional text that explains the key concepts of quality (economics of quality, statistical thinking, statistical process control, culture change, etc.). The model presented by Cound for achieving continuous improvement within an organization parallels the executive's growth as a quality leader.

Crosby, Philip B.

Leading: The Art of Becoming an Executive. New York: McGraw-Hill, 1990.

Crosby firmly believes that leadership is a skill that can be learned. This informal book relays his thinking on the subject of what constitutes an effective leader. Characteristics such as a willingness to learn, ethical behavior, personal availability, tenacity, and reliability are discussed. Leaders must focus their attention on three areas: finance, quality, and relationships. Cosby provides anecdotes and cases demonstrating how leaders have learned to deal with these issues.

Deal, Terrence and Lee G. Bolman

Reframing Organizations: Artistry, Choice, and Leadership. San Francisco: Jossey-Bass, 1991.

This book is concerned with the need for both good management and effective leadership and presents practical ideas for achieving both. The authors believe we need leaders who are capable of reflecting on experiences and seeing new issues and possibilities as well as managers capable of finding order. In emphasizing the concept of "reframing," the authors attempt to continually show how the same situation in an organization can be viewed in four different ways: from structural, human resource, political, and symbolic perspectives (or frames). The book deals with the important relationship between reframing and effective management and leadership. The authors explain the basic factors that complicate organizational life through use of an example of

a disaster in which everyday theories for action led to catastrophe (the Korean Airlines jet shot down by the Soviet Air Force). Areas discussed in the book include: designing structural forms for an organization (and the problems which can arise from inappropriate structures); the relationship between organizations and human resources (including conflicts); political dynamics in organizational decision-making, the power of symbol and culture in organizations, and methods of improving leadership practice (which are linked back to the use of different frames and achieving a meld). The book includes examples from a wide range of organizations representing many nations and cultures (in both the public and private sector).

Deal, Terrence E. and William A. Jenkins

Managing the Hidden Organization: Strategies for Empowering Your Behind-the-Scenes Employees. New York: Warner Books, 1994.

Deal and Jenkins use the theater as a metaphor for making their points about the "hidden" support staff that make an organization successful (just as the backstage workers and technicians make a play successful). Support staff need to be recognized, involved in planning, empowered, etc. Although this may seem commonsensical, it's contrary to practice in many organizations. Managers need to learn how to capitalize on the expertise and skills of their "backstage" employees to get full value for the organization. Examples of companies that have made strides in recognizing the contributions of behind-the-scenes employees are included; as are discussions of the practices that have made them successful.

Drummond, Helga

"Measuring Management Effectiveness." *Personnel Management* 25, no.3 (March 1993): 38–41.

TQM has put a renewed emphasis on the performance of management. With TQM, managers should be active in designing and operating a quality improvement system. However, many managers urge employees to work around problems instead of solving them, delegate inappropriately, and demand results without adequate investigation. A major difficulty with managing the performance of managers is that it's hard to quantify. The author explains an approach to performance analysis for managers that is consistent with TQM philosophy. With this "task-based" performance management, the key is to define expectations. This requires more effort than traditional target-setting, but ensures that specific steps will be taken to ensure that projects are completed as agreed upon. Communicating proactively avoids later misunderstandings. Managers should expect to be held accountable for certain agreed-upon expectations.

Feigenbaum, Armand
"Creating the Quality Mindset Among Senior Managers." *National Productivity Review* 12 (Summer 1993): 313–315.

Feigenbaum advises managers to take a competitive stance with regard to quality. He states that the "quality mindset" has become a key issue in competitive leadership. Senior managers must have: a clear sense of what consumers and companies are buying and how they're buying in international markets; complete understanding of a total quality strategy that provides a base for satisfying these customers; and management skills for creating an environment in which quality will thrive. Most managers have not taken a competitive stance when it comes to quality. Instead, they have been reacting to customer quality requirements rather than leading the requirements. Evaluating products against customer and market-oriented productivity measurements will lead to competitive quality leadership.

Gibson, Thomas C.
"Helping Leaders Accept Leadership of Total Quality Management." *Quality Progress* 23, no.11 (November 1990): 45–47.

Gibson believes that the question facing quality professionals is: what (besides a crisis) can get leaders to see value in truly leading a quality effort? Too many leaders don't appear to be committed to quality. Gibson says this is because 1) looking for chronic problems and trouble areas runs counter to the way leaders have approached management in the past (they have been trained to accent the positive); 2) leaders think they're already managing costs effectively; and 3) leaders resist radical change. Gibson says that the ways quality professionals can help leaders are to: 1) educate leaders on cost of quality and help target areas for improvement (this emphasizes a poten-

tially positive outcome); 2) suggest changes that can be made in small increments and help leaders implement quality projects in areas where improvement is most needed (then expand from that base); and help leaders be successful with visible improvements.

Harris, Philip R.
High Performance Leadership: HRD Strategies for the New Work Culture. Amherst, MA: Human Resources Development, 1994.

This is a revised edition of a book first published in 1989. It is aimed at supervisors and managers with human resource development responsibilities. The book is primarily concerned with triggering change, energizing people, and helping people develop through learning. Each chapter has a similar structure, with an introduction (laying out the objectives of the chapter); a section on input (inventory of the management theories applicable to the chapter topic); interaction (examples of processes for sharing information); and instrumentation (surveys and questionnaires). Chapter topics include: increasing quality of performance, improving communication skills, team relations, and meeting effectiveness. There is also a chapter on cultural diversity and the influence of culture on work habits, behavior in the workplace, and learning styles.

Heller, Robert
"Putting the Total Into Total Quality." *Management Today* (August 1994): 56–60.

This article reports on the results of a survey of directors and managers of large UK firms. Seventy percent of those interviewed said they had a great or fair familiarity with what's involved in quality improvement, and two-thirds of the respondents said their companies have a quality improvement program. More than half said quality improvement made a significant contribution to achieving business goals. Previous research has generally indicated that senior managers are not sufficiently committed to quality programs – and that such programs lack effectiveness as a result. This survey generally appeared to find positive attitudes on the part of management toward quality initiatives, but the same lack of commitment could be discerned. There appeared to be a rather limited understanding of what quality really means; and a lack of interest in receiving training was voiced. Heller concludes that the real story behind the survey results is that British management is failing to keep up with the revolutionary change affecting business practice. Managers may be doing well in improving products, and are working on process, but are not paying similar attention to the other "pillars" of TQM (organization, leadership, and commitment). Perhaps this is because the last three pillars require changes in the behavior of leaders and organizational objectives (which may be unwelcome on the part of managers).

Johnson, Richard S.

TQM: Leadership for the Quality Transformation. Milwaukee, WI: ASQC Quality Press, 1993.

Johnson's book is generally concerned with how organizations can increase their competitiveness in the world market. Several of the chapters discuss leadership issues. Johnson states that leadership style is important in the TQM process. Johnson believes that some styles are more appropriate than others at times and that leadership style is a learned skill. Democratic and autocratic are the two poles of leadership theories – each with attendant styles. The theory of situational leadership is based on the idea that leadership style varies along the democratic/autocratic continuum, depending upon different situational influences; which have to do with whether supportive or directive action seems called for. Leaders become successful by directing and supporting their employees as appropriate for each situation. Johnson is concerned with four leadership styles that can be derived from a supporting/directing matrix. A high-direction, low-support style works best in some training situations where close supervision is necessary. Coaching works well with a high-direction, high-support style; delegating to an employee requires a low-direction, low-support style; and participatory leadership works best with a low-direction, high-support style. These leadership styles can also be applied to work with teams (in a continuum tied to the team's level of experience.) Delegating is viewed as the style producing the greatest performance potential, thus leaders should work effectively toward this goal. Delegating receives additional treatment in Johnson's book, along with a guide to determin-

ing when a leader should delegate more. Empowerment is also discussed at length. Johnson reviews the importance of empowerment; excuses leaders use for not empowering employees and the underlying reasons; and reasons subordinates resist empowerment at times. Johnson stresses planning for empowerment.

Kouzes, James M., and Barry Z. Posner

The Leadership Challenge: How to Get Extraordinary Things Done in Organizations. San Francisco: Jossey-Bass, 1987.

The authors begin by describing five practices of exemplary leadership (challenge the process, inspire a shared vision, enable others to act, model the way, encourage) and ten ways to implement those practices. They also examine the traits followers admire. Successive chapters explore the five practices in greater detail and provide examples of successful leadership experiences drawn from a variety of organizations. The final chapter poses the question "How do you learn to lead?" The authors provide a variety of practical suggestions as well as advice from a selection of leaders. They also include two appendices: a "personal best questionnaire" designed to be used in assessing leadership skills; and a report on development of the "Leadership Practices Inventory" which validates the importance of the five leadership practices described by the authors.

McDermott, Lynda C.

"Jump Starting Managers on Quality." *Training and Development* 47, no.9 (September 1993): 37–40.

To make a quality effort succeed, many organizations are finding that they need to pay more attention to the role of middle managers. While senior management need to be the champions of the quality cause, middle managers are often the ones who actually lead the quality effort. They have to know how to translate quality strategies into organizational values and practices, how to empower employees, and coach teams. Middle managers have to internalize total quality and see it as part of their daily routine. Many total quality programs orient the senior management, then skip middle managers and begin training the rank-and-file employees. Or, if middle managers are trained, what they get are only basic skills. They don't learn skills on working with employees to implement change. Middle managers too often operate as order-takers and order-givers – they don't see themselves as leaders. Middle managers should be encouraged by senior management to help set quality goals as well as assist in designing strategies for achieving quality goals. Middle managers should be held accountable for quality, customer service results, and customer satisfaction. They need to be given the development resources they need. Middle managers should integrate quality objectives with accountability and the reward structure for their employees.

McFarland, Lynne Joy, Larry E. Senn, and John R. Childress

21st Century Leadership: Dialogues With 100 Top Leaders. New York: Leadership Press, 1994.

The authors look at several themes within the topic of successful leadership strategies. They present the ideas of a cross-section of America's leaders (in business, government, education, non-profit organizations, etc.) as they relate to such themes as: the model of leadership by empowerment; the demise of hierarchy; shaping a healthy culture; achieving diversity; implementing, perfecting, and evaluating the quality/service imperative; the role of corporate America in education; and global interconnectedness. The book culminates in a model for effective leadership in the twenty-first century.

Nutt, Paul C., and Robert W. Backoff

"Transforming Public Organizations With Strategic Management and Strategic Leadership." *Journal of Management* 19 (Summer 1993): 299–347.

Nutt and Backoff begin by summarizing factors in public organizations that create unique differences (in comparison to private sector firms) in how such organizations deal with change. Private firms make strategic changes with the goal of producing a profit, while public sector organizations need to employ different strategic methods in some cases because their goals are different. Some contemporary problems faced by public sector firms are pressure to downsize, fiscal stress, media scrutiny, and a civil service that needs to be revamped. The authors review some strategic management approaches with their associated procedures, primary uses and limitations. They state that the strategy created depends on the strategic approach selected and that to create a successful transformation, strategic management processes should be tailored to meet the special needs of public sector organizations. Before an organization can decide its future route, the organization should explore its history. Uncovering important directions will help create productive change. Nutt and Backoff also state that public organizations tend to be "threat driven" and that they need to find new opportunities to create successful transformations.

A discussion of approaches to strategic leadership is also provided. After contrasting the theories, the authors explain the role of vision and varying kinds of guidance that might be needed. Last, use of total quality in the public sector is described. Nutt and Backoff believe that public organizations need to clearly specify the beneficiaries of a total quality effort before using a quality program. Total quality programs provide a way to link strategic management, strategic leadership, and empowerment which ultimately effects a transformational change.

Oakley, Ed, and Doug Krug

Enlightened Leadership: Getting to the Heart of Change. New York: Simon and Schuster, 1993.

The authors believe that the ongoing transformation of the workplace requires a new kind of leadership. The primary job of leaders will be to empower people so that they can bring the benefit of their intelligence and creativity to organizational problems. This book provides insight about issues involved in dealing with resistance to change, tools for generating a willingness to change in an organization, an approach to implementing a culture of continuous improvement, and leadership skills in continuously improving organizations.

"Open Learners." *Training & Development* 48 (May 1994): 14–19.

This article reports on a survey conducted by Cook Associates. The consulting firm interviewed twenty-five quality leaders from twenty Fortune 500 firms that have pursued TQM. The firm says its research indicates that leaders who effectively apply TQM principles combine effective leadership characteristics with an "open" approach to learning. Open learners work at personal development, use participatory management techniques, share information, practice systems thinking, and continuously look for new ideas to improve performance. Effective leaders look for ways to help with problem solving and take personal responsibility for the implementation of TQM. Organizations need to establish support systems that make their core values visible. They also need to teach people the skills that quality leaders seem to master intuitively.

Patten, Thomas H.
"Beyond Systems: The Politics of Managing in a TQM Environment." *National Productivity Review* 11 (Winter 91/92): 9–19.

This article begins by looking at some of the dangers resistant individuals pose in organizations trying to implement TQM – especially people who are motivated primarily by self-interest and perceive TQM to be a threat to their way of life. The organizations whose managers and employees are not empowered must engage in extensive skill development before TQM can take hold. Employees won't take actions that they perceive to be threatening to themselves. Thus, management must create a supportive atmosphere through positive reinforcement of desired changes. Patten discusses the skills and new learning required for managing in a TQM environment; several of which require beginning to work in a less bureaucratic style. Among them are: defining internal and external customer requirements; ensuring ongoing quality efforts; development of a life-long learning style; team-building with the goal of ultimately having self-directed teams; understanding diversity and multiculturalism; delegating and coaching; creating employee empowerment; and building continuous improvement into everyday management. The author states that changing an organization's culture takes at least five years and that resistance to change will be around for a significant part of that time.

Pierce, Richard J., ed.
Leadership, Perspective, and Restructuring for Total Quality. Milwaukee, WI: ASQC Quality Press, 1991.

This book has been designed to share successful approaches of leaders with readers involved in total quality efforts. One of the primary themes is that leadership by chief executive officers is paramount in a quality effort.

Only the CEO can commit to and implement the massive changes required. Leaders of quality programs must create a solid foundation for quality by changing attitudes and management styles. Pierce has created a book that explores the approaches used by CEOs to establish foundations for quality tailored to their own organizations. The relationship between these quality foundations and the criteria for total quality (as exemplified by the Baldrige Award, for example) is also discussed. Contributors are drawn from the public and the private sector. Several appendices are included, one of which is a summary of the basic philosophies of W. Edwards Deming, Joseph Juran, Philip Crosby, and William Conway. Another, by Japanese professor Kaoru Ishikawa, summarizes the historical development of thinking about quality in Japan and looks at current quality practices.

Sayles, Leonard R.
The Working Leader: The Triumph of High Performance Over Conventional Management Principles. New York: Free Press, 1993.

Sayles believes that scientific management principles still represent the core values of most managers. Sayles examines basic failures which have resulted from attempts to continue managing scientifically. He contends that his analysis of case data related to the problem reveals some very different management principles which ought to be implemented. In looking at leadership, Sayles states that a systems view lies at the core of successful leadership; along with a willingness to challenge the status quo. Negotiating skills and techniques for empowering employees are also crucial to leadership. Sayles contends that leadership skills coupled with a willingness to take risks, improvise, and look for alternative explanations, would do more to improve competitive position than most current management techniques.

Wheatley, Margaret
Leadership and the New Science, Learning About Organizations from an Orderly Universe. San Francisco: Berrett-Koehler, 1992.

In this award-winning book, Wheatley develops her thesis that leadership has a scientific basis. Wheatley's book is organized around themes developed from her study of the "new science" (branches of which include quantum physics, self-organizing systems, and chaos theory). Wheatley investigates the connections between participative management, self-directed teams, boundaryless organizations, empowerment, whole systems thinking, and visioning and the new science. She does an excellent job of linking new science concepts such as chaos theory, strange attractors, and dissipative structures to the modern organization. Her book does not debunk "scientific management," but helps readers see it in a new light and to reinterpret its history. Wheatley believes that the earlier view of the world as a machine has led to an unnatural style of management. A new model is evolving which has the potential to reintegrate people into well-ordered organizations in new ways.

Zoglio, Suzanne Willis
The Participative Leader. Boston: Irwin Professional Publishing, 1994.

Being a participative leader means communicating an organization's priorities and goals to all employees involved in decision-making – especially in those areas that directly affect such employees. The author points out that this also means letting employees figure out how they can do their jobs better, and then holding management/employee discussions regarding recommendations. This process leads to a continuous improvement effort, which should ultimately be driven by increasing customer satisfaction. Zoglio discusses management of the shift to participation, how to get employee commitment and motivation and how to empower employees. She also discusses the facilitation of teamwork and has suggestions for how to implement and integrate teams in the workplace. Some checklists have been included to help assess progress toward a more participative environment.

---

6 Training, human resource issues, and communication

Antonioni, David
"Improve the Performance Management Process Before Discontinuing Performance Appraisals." *Compensation and Benefits Review* 26 (May/June 1994): 29–37.

The author states that dissatisfaction with performance appraisals has reached a critical level. Antonioni believes that discontinuing appraisals isn't the answer; he believes that the process can be made effective if it can be designed to meet the needs of the organization as a whole, work groups, and the individual. He advocates a structure for performance appraisal based on planning, implementing, reflecting, and compensating. Managers would conduct four sessions per year to address each of these components. The model is based on the idea of employees as customers and the result is a contract of sorts that links individual performance to both company strategies and compensation.

Anfuso, Dawn
"Self-Directed Skills Building Drives Quality." *Personnel Journal* 73 (April 1994): 84–93.

This article examines the Granite Rock Company's "Individual Professional Development Plan" which employees use to set developmental goals for the upcoming year. Granite Rock is a construction materials supplier and manufacturer and won the Baldrige Award in 1992 in the small business category. Use of the plan is voluntary for the company's unionized workers (about two-thirds of the workforce) and mandatory for salaried employees. About 85 percent of the workforce participates. Employees and their supervisors work out a development plan (including personal and professional goals) which is then reviewed at a management roundtable. Managers review their employees' plans and can make suggestions (which may involve suggestions for benchmarking, partnering, or education). One of the strengths of the plan is that goal-setting is backed by training opportunities. Training needs become evident as a result of management roundtable discussions. Training is delivered both on-site and off, by consultants, suppliers, and internal experts. Training efforts have been directly linked to an increase in customer satisfaction.

Bowen, David E., and Edward E. Lawler
"Total Quality-Oriented Human Resources Management." *Organizational Dynamics* 20, no.4 (Spring 1992): 29–41.

Human resources issues are extremely important in creating quality-oriented organizations. Many of Deming's fourteen points relate directly to human resources issues (training, breaking down barriers to build teams, driving out fear, eliminating quotas, creating conditions that foster pride of workmanship, including doing away with annual reviews and merit ratings, and supporting education and life-long learning). Strategic human resources management is proposed by the author of this article. Human resources departments must first practice TQM themselves (doing quality work the first time, focusing on their customers, and taking a strategic approach to improvement). Following this, human resources departments can expand their role in the organization they serve. Areas where human resources should become more involved include: employee selection; development and training; career development; performance management (aligning appraisal more with shared responsibility for quality, involving peers); designing innovative pay systems; taking a hard look at perquisites and status symbols within the organization; improving labor relations in unionized settings; and supporting widespread communication of performance results, objectives, and strategic plans.

Brown, Alan
"TQM: Implications for Training." *Industrial & Commercial Training* 25, no.1 (1993): 20–26.

Introducing a TQM effort requires a significant training effort. Training is needed to educate people about the nature of TQM; to develop new attitudes that will lead to the cultural change TQM requires to succeed; to equip people with the skills and techniques they need for problem-solving and teamwork; and to foster career development. Training should be viewed as a strategy and not as an event. There must be a supportive culture for TQM before any training in tools and techniques occurs. The training process plays an important role in creating a supportive culture. Assessing the current culture and determining what kind of change is necessary should be the first step; training can then be targeted to these needs. The enthusiasm of TQM supporters should be used immediately; resistors should be won over slowly. Training should support the organizational quality improvement strategy, and should be targeted to the differing needs of participants. Use of external trainers

appears to have some advantages over the use of internal trainers.

Carson, Kenneth P., Robert L. Cardy, and Gregory H. Dobbins
"Upgrade the Employee Evaluation Process." *HRMagazine* 37, no.11 (November 1992): 88–92.

Although organizations realize performance appraisals aren't perfect, they continue to use them to: provide feedback on improving performance; help with administrative decisions such as promotion and pay; measure the effectiveness of programs in upgrading employee skills; and document poor performance. The authors discuss the problems with traditional performance appraisals from a TQM standpoint. They recommend a model for developing a more effective performance appraisal system based on TQM principles. The six points made are that: raters need to be trained in evaluating system and personal factors; performance ratings should be collected from multiple perspectives; performance appraisal interviews should focus on potential barriers to individual improvement; ratings should not be a source of alienation among employees; group-based evaluations should be considered in some cases; and performance measures should be tailored to specific needs.

Caudron, Shari
"How HR Drives TQM." *Personnel Journal* 72, no.8 (August 1993): 48B–480.

Caudron makes the point that human resources systems often get in the way of the cultural change that is one of the goals of TQM. Organizations need to align human resource systems with quality goals. The author discusses some of the ways a company should be communicating about quality through their human resources department. She summarizes methods used by companies such as Volkswagen. Communicating information about quality efforts also work best when done in a small group setting where it can be personalized. Training offered should focus on building quality skills with equal attention paid to behavioral skills and quality tools. Many companies have neglected behavioral skills in the past. Caudron explores the need for change in performance-management systems. These systems need to reinforce behaviors necessary for quality initiatives. Other areas highlighted in this article are the role that recognition plays in enhancing quality efforts, and the role human resources should play in hiring new employees.

Caudron, Shari
"Change Keeps TQM Programs Thriving." *Personnel Journal* 72 (October 1993): 104–109.

Human resources departments are finding that they need to undergo changes in order to sustain long-term TQM efforts. Results of a survey of human resources practices in companies that have won the Baldrige Award indicate that human resources must partner with other departments in the organization to support TQM effectively. Options include using human resources representatives as internal consultants to other departments; as members of cross-functional teams; or restructuring the whole department so that individual business units are billed directly for personnel services they use. This last option forces human resources to become competitive in terms of cost and quality. One of the biggest problems organizations encounter is effective communication. Baldrige Award winners appear to consistently communicate both good and bad news. Human resources can take an active role in facilitating communication; particularly in terms of aiding employees in asking questions of management. Human resources also needs to communicate more effectively with its "customers" by monitoring the progress of quality efforts they have implemented (such as employee development, compensation programs, and employee involvement programs). Continuous improvement of the human resources function will result. Examples of successful changes made by companies like IBM, Motorola, Cadillac, and AT&T are provided.

Cocheu, Ted
"Training with Quality." *Training and Development* 46, no.5 (May 1992): 22–29, 31–32.

Training is critical to the successful implementation of TQM, but many organizations are not receiving effective training. This article examines some of the limitations of quality awareness training, employee involvement training, and training in statistical process control. The author believes that development of quality strategy must precede training. Training can then be used

to communicate the strategy. Cocheu presents a six-step quality improvement strategy that incorporates training at each step: preparation, planning, awareness, deployment, implementation, and continuous improvement. The six-phase training approach which parallels the improvement strategy is: building understanding and commitment; training in quality management systems; training in improvement teams; customer service training; training in process control and improvement; and training in quantitative methods. All training must be preceded by development and communication of a quality strategy; and must be designed to facilitate the implementation of that quality strategy.

Cohen-Rosenthal, Edward, and Cynthia Burton
"Improving Organizational Quality By Forging the Best Union–Management Relationship." *National Productivity Review* 13 (Spring 1994): 215–231.

A positive union–management relationship can contribute greatly to organizational improvement. Many organizations underestimate the difficulty of implementing a successful total quality or participative management program in a unionized workplace. This article provides a seven-step model for improving the union–management relationship. The intent is to ultimately broaden involvement in organizational change and create a supportive environment for positive change. The seven steps are: 1) define the best possible union–management relationship; 2) address the current union–management relationship; 3) identify the barriers to moving toward the ideal relationship; 4) identify each party's interests and unilateral actions for improvement; 5) identify joint interests and actions for improvement; 6) establish strategies, structures, and plans for improvement and communication; and 7) review accomplishments, the current relationship, and the description of the ideal relationship.

Dawson, Graydon
"The Critical Elements Missing From Most Total Quality Management Training." *Performance and Instruction* 31, no.9 (October 1992): 15–21.

TQM training that focuses on how to cultivate an effective relationship between managers/supervisors and the people that report to them provides the best foundation for a quality initiative.

Without this basic relationship in place, many programs founder. The kinds of experiences managers need to have during training are those that will bring about a shift in their basic frame of reference. If they don't have an outlook consistent with TQM precepts, they need effective training to address counter-productive habits. There are no quick-fix techniques for this. The author contends that a self-assessment of assumptions concerning human motivation in the workplace is a good starting point. Dawson includes an "empowerment indicator" survey designed to help a manager assess his/her attitude shifts over time toward a more TQM/supportive outlook.

Flannery, Thomas P., David A. Hofrichter, and Paul E. Platten
People, Performance, and Pay: Dynamic Compensation for Changing Organizations. New York: Free Press, 1996.

While TQM and reengineering have radically changed corporations, one element of organizational change that is often overlooked is compensation strategies. Most companies still compensate employees the way they did decades ago. However, these pay strategies no longer work in process and team-based cultures. The authors identify four work cultures (functional, process, time-based, and network) and explain how to align pay strategies with each one. They use examples of organizations such as Lego, Hallmark, and Holiday Inn that have been taking the lead in developing innovative pay policies.

Froiland, Paul
"Reproducing Star Performers." *Training* 30, no.9 (September 1993): 33–37.

This article discusses the idea of teaching average and below-average performers the strategies used by top performers in an effort to increase their productivity. A large number of companies, (like Bell Labs, Dupont, Sprint, and Unigate) have adopted the "mastery-performance" model to improve their workforces. The first step should be to make sure mediocre performance isn't due solely to poor management, poorly defined jobs, or some other organizational problem. If a performance gap does exist, then the star performer must be defined and identified.

Determining the real reasons star performers manage to do what they do is not always easy. Examples are provided for some methods companies have used. Training the average performer follows, and again, examples of how this can be accomplished, are provided.

Hayes, Theodore L., Harper A. Roehm, and Joseph P. Castellano
"Personality Correlates of Success in Total Quality Manufacturing." *Journal of Business & Psychology* 8 (Summer 1994): 397–411.

The authors of this study administered a personality inventory measure to 136 factory workers. The objective of the study was to identify the personality characteristics of individuals who were successful employees in the total quality manufacturing environment, and to identify characteristics of less successful employees. They made use of the "Big Five" factors of normal personality, which are roughly as follows: emotional stability, extraversion, agreeableness, conscientiousness, and openness to experience. Level of success was based on behaviorally based performance measure. Results were somewhat surprising. More successful employees tended to be more reserved, prudent and conscientious, and less interested in intellectual pursuits.

Kroeger, Otto with Janet M. Theusen
Type Talk at Work. New York: Delacorte, 1992.

This book explains the Myers-Briggs Type Indicator, a popular psychological instrument that categorizes normal personality types. Since personality traits affect how we learn, work, and interact with others, the authors recommend that employees benefit from "typewatching." This technique (developed by Kroeger and Theusen) involves understanding more about the preferred working styles of different personality types. The authors offer suggestions for achieving better working relationships.

Larkin, T.J. and Sandar Larkin
Communicating Change: How to Win Employee Support for New Business Directions. New York: McGraw-Hill, 1994.

This book makes the point that an organization must make effective communication with supervisors a priority. When supervisors are well-informed they are in a better position to shape the opinions of employees who report to them. It is important for supervisors to be perceived as knowledgeable and part of the communications loop by their subordinates. The Larkins believe that supervisors are seen as the most credible source of information by front-line workers. The authors suggest three primary rules for communication: 1) communicate directly to supervisors; 2) use face-to-face communication; and 3) make communication relevant to each work group by indicating how a change will affect them. The authors illustrate their points by including actual examples of successful communication as well as communication failures in large multinational corporations.

McDermott, Robin E., Raymond J. Mikulak, and Michael R. Beauregard

Employee-Driven Quality: Releasing the Creative Spirit of Your Organization Through Suggestion Systems. White Plains, NY: Quality Resources, 1993.

The authors of this book present a new model for an employee suggestion system. The model, known as EDIS (Employee-Driven Idea System) is designed to contribute to an organization's total quality program by spurring employee involvement in the quality effort. The authors discuss some of the reasons other employee suggestion systems have failed to work and provide a guide to the implementation and integration of their model. The book also summarizes basic TQM concepts. Case study examples of Employee-Driven Idea Systems within major companies are provided.

Magjuka, Richard J.

"The 10 Dimensions of Employee Involvement." *Training & Development* 47, no.4 (April 1993): 61–67.

A core component of competitive strategies in manufacturing industries has been to create a link between employee-involvement programs and continuous improvement. However, this often does not work well. The historical objectives of employee involvement programs (increasing trust in the organization, provide a forum to discuss beliefs and attitudes about daily operations, etc.) don't relate well to the strategic objectives of a TQM environment (improving manufacturing processes, reducing set-up times, etc.). The author

looks at ten dimensions of employee-involvement processes. He suggests that managers who want to create corporate cultures that combine employee involvement with continuous improvement should explicitly link the design of an employee involvement program to attainment of TQM objectives. The themes that influence effectiveness of such programs are: the range of problems a team is allowed to address; team staffing policies (cross-functional is best); team membership policies (required or voluntary participation); resources allocated to teams; training practices; access to information for team members; financial rewards for team members; links between the employee-involvement program and performance-management systems; goal-setting practices; and supervisors' roles in employee-involvement team leadership.

Miller, John A.

"Training Required to Support Total Quality Management." *CMA Magazine* 66, no.9 (November 1992): 29.

Basic training in TQM can be purchased from many sources, but this generic approach to TQM often ends up being ineffective. Miller makes some suggestions for designing training which fits the specific requirements of an organization and can be taught by in-house personnel: examples and case studies should be based on the organization itself; assess the existing skill level before designing a training package; design the package to fit existing tools and techniques if appropriate (this way they get reinforced); design the training to support management's vision of improvement; and design exercises that contribute to an existing work situation.

Olian, Judy D., and Rynes, Sara L.

"Making Total Quality Work: Aligning Organizational Processes, Performance Measures, and Stakeholders." *Human Resource Management* 30 (Fall 1991): 303–333.

This article examines the organizational factors that are critical in achieving a pervasive total quality culture. The authors look at organizational processes that encourage people to adopt behaviors that support total quality; the outcome measures that track manufacturing and service processes and provide information to be used in continuous improvement; and sources of both support and opposition to changes which lead to a total quality culture. Supportive organizational processes include communicating a quality vision, setting quality goals, training, team-building to enable quality processes, recognizing and rewarding for quality, etc. Outcome measures include quality assurance programs, financial measures that track the cost of quality, and measures of employee contribution. Support for changes required by TQM must be provided by top management. Middle managers are often sources of opposition – they often receive inadequate information and support. Additionally, middle managers' sense of personal security is threatened by the trend toward flatter organizations. Only top management can provide the resources and support middle managers need to become effective supporters of TQM. The authors also examine potential sources of support and resistance to TQM among professional staff and front-line employees.

Quirke, Bill
Communicating Change. London: McGraw-Hill, 1995.

Effective communication enables change in organizations. However, while organizations have changed tremendously over the years and companies have recognized the importance of good communication, employee satisfaction with communication efforts remains low. The author of this book provides some strategies that organizations can use to get a better return on their investment in communication. Better communication will help organizations become more competitive by allowing them to respond to change more quickly. The author argues that communication strategies are often developed in isolation from the business strategy. He looks at the kinds of communication needed at different stages in an organization's development (ranges from informal to structured, with an "orchestrated informality" in highly evolved organizations); how to communicate and build a greater customer orientation within an organization; how to use communication to get teams to work together more effectively; and communication clutter.

Rainbird, Helen and Malcolm Maguire
"When Corporate Need Supersedes Employee Development." *Personnel Management* 25, no.2 (February 1993): 34–37.

The authors of this article look at the question of how effective employers' policies on continuing education will be in the long term. The premise is that employers are focusing on meeting organizational needs and neglecting employees' personal development. The results of a survey in the UK indicate that employees who start out better educated continue to have the greatest access to continuing education and training. The authors looked at the state of training related to quality initiatives, changing corporate culture, organizational development; and employee turnover. The results seem to indicate a certain disjuncture between corporate structure and organization of training, although a number of organizations are successfully integrating training and business strategies. The training most commonly received by employees did not involve acquisition of transferable skills, nor did it contribute to personal and educational development.

Rough, Jim
"Measuring Training From a New Science Perspective." *Journal for Quality and Participation* 17, no.6 (October/November 1994): 12–16.

The author asks how certain competencies should be measured. He contends that measurement can alter and interfere with the process of learning at times, but people responsible for training still need to know how to improve training materials or whether seminars are effective. Rough states that there are two kinds of learning processes: one for the acquisition of hard skills (operation of a machine) and the other which causes a transformational effect (breakthroughs to new levels of understanding). Acquisition of hard skills can be measured in traditional ways, but transformational learning requires different measurement techniques. Such techniques include gathering anecdotal evidence, asking questions which spark discussions, asking people to assess their own level of growth, and assessing progress by comparing the organization to the way it was in the past. In other words, the basic principle in measuring transformational change is self-reference. Individuals need to learn when the use of objective measures is important, and when self-reference should be used as a guide.

Scholtes, Peter R.

"Total Quality or Performance Appraisal: Choose One." *National Productivity Review* 12 (Summer 1993): 349–363.

The author examines the reasons Deming feels performance appraisals should not be conducted. Some of the problems with appraisals are: they undermine teamwork by putting a focus on the individual; they encourage individuals to work the system for personal gain instead of improving it for collective gain; appraisals increase variability in the system; they use a measurement system that is unreliable and not constant; appraisals encourage a system that seeks to place blame; they tend to support the establishment of "safe" goals; they waste human resources; and appraisals are used to determine pay, promotions, feedback, and set goals, (yet they don't do any of these well). Scholtes provides some suggestions for ways to find alternatives to performance appraisals. One is to stop doing them, and the other is to "debundle" them (take the appraisal apart to find new ways of dealing with each component).

Schonberger, Richard J.

"Human Resource Management Lessons From a Decade of Total Quality Management and Reengineering." *California Management Review* 36 (Summer 1994): 109–123.

The author states that conventional human resources management practices conflict with TQM and should be changed. In terms of people and their roles, Schonberger discusses such things as the shift needed to make process improvement part of everyone's job (not just a manager/specialist responsibility); the need for managers to evolve into facilitators; and use of multifunctional teams instead of single-function teams. In looking at employee performance, public and team-oriented recognition should be emphasized (instead of private, boss/subordinate); performance evaluation should be broadened to take more relationships into account (instead of boss/subordinate); and promotion and pay should be based more on acquisition of additional skills. In terms of the human resource department itself, the author believes they should do things such as

letting line people handle most personnel functions; shrink the number of job classifications; focus more on training for everyone; and spend less time on employee relations and wage/classification issues. Specific examples of successful changes made by organizations are provided.

Walley, Paul, and Emil Kowalski

"The Role of Training in Total Quality Implementation." *Journal of European Industrial Training* 16, no.3 (1992): 25–31.

This article takes a look at employees' reasons for participating in total quality initiatives and discusses the implications for the design of total quality training programs. A representative sample of Hewlett-Packard employees in the United Kingdom were surveyed. Employees tended to get involved with total quality because: they recognize a general need for improvement in their work area; they can identify a specific problem that might be solved using total quality techniques; and they know total quality is something that management wants them to be involved in. Few employees were encouraged to participate by colleagues or team leaders. Training was not a motivation either – it was perceived as a means toward an end. The factors that seemed to support long-term involvement in total quality were: increased customer satisfaction, personal benefits, an enhanced company image, factors related to improved corporate culture, attitude of other staff, and the desire to be more involved in decision-making. Implications for training are to make training relevant to employees' individual work situations; to help employees learn to choose appropriate total quality projects; and to use the training to communicate more information about the competitive environment the organization exists within.

Younger, Sandra Millers

"Four by Four: Finding Time for TQM Training." *Training and Development* 47, no.2 (February 1993): 11–15.

This article discusses the difficulties of finding time for TQM training. Four quality experts offered ideas which include: don't waste time on premature or unnecessary training; senior leadership has to change the organization to accommodate training; conduct after-hours training and offer incentives for attendance; use existing communication tools such as employee newsletters; use accelerated training techniques that tie basic concepts to the organization itself; provide a context for the training so that it's value-added for each participant and more relevant; make a long-term commitment to quality so that people are more willing to budget the time for training; and look at training as an investment in saving time.

IV

Quality in the Future – What Role Does ISO 9000 Play?

The relationship between ISO 9000 and the broader theme of quality management is important. ISO 9000 by itself is not a continuous quality improvement program, nor is it concerned with the overall effectiveness or profitability of an organization. The primary tie between ISO 9000 standards and total quality management is the ISO 9000 focus on the process of assuring quality. ISO 9000 is concerned with establishing, documenting, and maintaining a system designed to ensure the quality of a product or service; it can be thought of as the foundation for a more comprehensive quality management program.

The ISO 9000 quality management system standards were created in 1987 by the International Organization for Standardization (ISO) which is based in Geneva, Switzerland. ISO exists to promote the development of international standards, and as such the membership of ISO consists of the standards organizations of about ninety-five member countries (such as the American National Standards Institute and the British Standards Institute). National standards from several countries played a role in the development of the original ISO 9000 series of standards. The standards were revised in 1994, with the majority of changes reflecting needs for clarification.

The roots of the ISO 9000 series of standards can be found in quality standards originally developed by military procurement agencies in both the United States and Great Britain. Promulgation of standards by different government agencies and industries on an international basis followed. In the late 1970s and early 1980s the need for international standardization of quality standards became apparent as countries in the European Community began preparing for a single economic marketplace. In 1979 the International Organization for Standardization formed a Technical Committee (ISO/TC 176) charged with developing a single set of quality system standards. The resulting standards have been adopted by member countries, although each country publishes the series with a unique name and numbering system. Some ISO member countries also maintain nationally recognized quality standards in addition to the ISO series.

ISO 9000 certificates are obtained through registrars (also known as certifiers). Registrars are companies or individuals who have been authorized by the national accreditation boards of ISO member countries to offer certification. Certification means that a company's quality system has been assessed by a qualified third party (the registrar) with the conclusion that the company's quality system meets the criteria of the standard being registered to.

The ISO 9000 series actually consists of five basic subsets; thus companies pursuing ISO 9000 certification must first select the standard (ISO 9001, 9002, or 9003) that best suits their needs. The series is made up of:

- ISO 9000: A guideline for determining which of the series of contractual series an organization should apply.
- ISO 9001: The contractual standard for companies that research, design, ship, install, and service what they manufacture. The most comprehensive of the contractual standards.
- ISO 9002: The contractual standard for companies that manufacture and install products, but are not involved in design.

- ISO 9003: The contractual standard for companies that assemble and test products that have been designed and produced elsewhere (typically includes warehousing and distribution companies).
- ISO 9004: A guidance document for a quality system more comprehensive than those laid out in the contractual standards. Designed to be used as a first-party document by an organization as it designs and implements an internal quality management system.

Each of the contractual standards (ISO 9001, 9002, and 9003) contains what is known as "quality system elements." As mentioned earlier, ISO 9001 is the most comprehensive standard and as such contains twenty separate required elements that must be implemented before an organization can become registered (some elements drop out and are not requirements for ISO 9002 and ISO 9003). The elements are:

1 Management responsibility – defines the role management must play before a company can become registered.
2 Quality system – contains requirements for quality systems. For example, the quality system must be documented and a quality manual must be developed.
3 Contract review – requires a review of the way a company deals with clients contractually. The purpose is to avoid a breach of contract.
4 Design control – ensures that procedures are established and maintained for reviewing the way a company designs and develops products.
5 Document control – requires a company to prove it is doing what it says it is doing through controlling all documents that relate to the requirements defined in the quality manual.
6 Purchasing – requires a system to ensure that all requirements for purchased goods/services impacting quality are specified and communicated to suppliers.
7 Purchaser–supplied product – requires a system to ensure that all products supplied by customers are acceptable before they're used.
8 Product identification and traceability – ensures the ability to identify and trace all products during each stage of the production, delivery, and installation of that product.
9 Process control – companies must specify the processes that directly affect product quality and ensure that such processes are carried out under controlled conditions.
10 Inspection and testing – verification that products conform with specifications, i.e. quality control.
11 Inspection, measuring, and test equipment – the system for calibrating and maintaining all inspection and test equipment that a company uses as part of its quality control efforts.
12 Inspection and test status – requires a system for determining the accuracy of the inspection (quality control) process.
13 Control of nonconforming product – requires a system to deal properly with any products or services that do not meet specifications.
14 Corrective action – requires a process for investigating problems and eliminating their recurrence.
15 Handling, storage, packaging, and delivery – requires a policy aimed at preventing damage after production.
16 Quality records – requires a company to demonstrate that its quality system works through a retention/retrieval mechanism for appropriate records.
17 Internal quality auditing – requires an internal system for conducting audits (throughout an organization) of all quality system elements.
18 Training – deals with the system that identifies needed skills, establishes and conducts training, and keeps appropriate records.
19 Servicing – requires documentation of procedures related to services provided after sale.
20 Statistical Techniques – Companies should be able to demonstrate that they have used appropriate statistical techniques in monitoring quality.

Additionally, the ISO 10000 series includes supporting documents containing guidelines for auditing quality systems (covering the audit process, qualification criteria for auditors, and managing audit programs), guidance in developing quality manuals, a guide to the economic effects of quality, continuing education and training guidelines, and requirements for measuring equipment. Lastly, a series of environmental management standards, ISO 14000, has been drafted by a technical committee (ISO/TC 207). A final version is not expected until some time in 1996.

ISO 9001, ISO 9002, and ISO 9003 were designed to be used as second-party documents between a buyer and a seller. As an alternative to the contractual "third party assessment" which organizations undertake with a registrar in seeking ISO 9000 certification, some companies have elected instead to pursue "compliance" with standards and forgo certification. In this case companies perform their own "first-party assessments" and declare themselves in compliance with standards. A second variation on use of the standards occurs through the use of a "second-party assessment". With this scenario a company's customers or potential customers assess the quality system using the ISO 9000 standards as a basis. These alternatives are no substitute for official certification by a third-party assessor, but in some cases may be sufficient for a company's needs.

In some ways, the perceived need for ISO 9000 certification is currently driving the quality movement. Many organizations have pursued certification as a means to do business in the European Community. While the European Community requires certification for suppliers of regulated products (goods and services that have some direct connection to health and safety), many producers of non-regulated products are also finding that their customers are requesting certification. Another factor in the trend toward certification is the pressure put on suppliers to certified companies to also achieve registration. ISO 9000 certification is also a marketing tool for many companies and confers some degree of advantage as a "preferred supplier" over competitors who are not registered.

The annotations for books and journal articles contained in this chapter will help illuminate the connection between the ISO 9000 series of standards and TQM/continuous quality improvement activities. Some sources have been included to provide comprehensive overviews of ISO 9000, while others address specific aspects of ISO 9000 and the relationship of ISO 9000 to other "quality programs."

Standards can be obtained through an ISO member country's national standards organization, or from ISO itself. A few helpful addresses follow:

International Organization for Standardization
Case Postale 56, CH-1211
Geneve 20, Switzerland
Phone: 22 749 0111
Fax: 22 733 3430

In the United Kingdom:

British Standards Institute
2 Park Street
London, W1A 2BS
England
Phone: 0171 629 9000
Fax: 0171 629 0506

In the United States:

The American National Standards Institute
11 West 42nd Street, 13th Floor
New York, NY 10036
Phone: (212) 642 4900
Fax: (212) 398 0023
Orders Only: (212) 302 1286

The American Society for Quality Control
  Quality Press
611 East Wisconsin Avenue
P.O. Box 3005
Milwaukee, WI 53201-3005
Phone: (414) 272 8575
Fax: (414) 272 1734

In Canada:

Standards Council of Canada
1200 45 O'Connor Street, Suite 1200
Ottawa, Ontario K1P 6N7
Phone: (613) 238 3222
Fax: (613) 995 4564

Canadian Standards Association
178 Rexdale Boulevard
Etobicoke (Toronto), Ontario
M9W 1R3
Phone: (416) 747 4368

I Books on ISO 9000

Brown, Tony
Understanding BS5750 and Other Quality Systems. Aldershot, England: Gower, 1993.

Although BS5750 no longer exists (it was the British counterpart to ISO 9000) and the British version of ISO 9000 is now BS EN ISO 9000, this book still includes some information likely to be useful to companies desiring a basic understanding of ISO 9000 and certification, particularly with regard to the advantages and pitfalls of registration. The book has been written with an eye toward helping the novice determine the relevance of the standards, and explores the relationship between ISO 9000 and differing industries. A substantial list of resources (among them Training and Enterprise Councils in the United Kingdom and a multitude of ideas for gathering additional information) is also provided.

Clements, Richard Barrett
Quality Manager's Complete Guide to ISO 9000. Englewood Cliffs, NJ: Prentice Hall, 1993.

Clements begins by providing an overview of ISO 9000 followed by information about the standards which will assist a company in determining which standard seems to apply best to their circumstances. The main portion of the book is devoted to a detailed evaluation of the twenty elements in ISO 9001. Checklists for each requirement are provided which will enable an organization to gather the detailed information needed to write the required documentation. The author also reviews the types of questions an assessor may ask during the registration audit for each requirement and provides examples of the documents an organization must write to comply with the standard. A section on preparing for assessment includes advice on selection of a registrar, information on what to expect during the assessment, and advice on protocol.

Craig, Robert J.
The No-Nonsense Guide to Achieving ISO 9000 Registration. New York: ASME Press, 1994.

The author provides an implementation guide to be used in developing a quality system that can be certified to meet any of the ISO 9000 series standards. Craig discusses the basic elements of a successful registration effort, the role management commitment plays in pursuing registration, training needed, strategies for developing an ISO 9000 quality manual, methods of documenting a quality system, development of an internal auditing system, and offers advice concerning the actual registration assessment process. In addition, the author provides a concise summary of the relationship between ISO 9000 and the Malcolm Baldrige National Quality Award in which he makes the case that the ISO 9000 standards are not as comprehensive as the Baldrige Award criteria, but are compatible and can be used as the foundation for a system aimed at continually improving a quality management system.

Hoyle, David
ISO 9000 Quality Systems Handbook. 2nd edn. Oxford: Butterworth Heinemann, 1994.

This text functions as a practical guide to the design, implementation, management, and assessment of a quality system based on ISO 9000. The author covers basic concepts used in the ISO standards, reviews the origin and content of the standards, discusses quality system development, assessment, and the use of certification as a step to continuous improvements in quality. The main portion of the book addresses each individual requirement of each clause in ISO 9001, explains the purpose of the requirements, and offers guidance in meeting them, as well as advice to help implement and audit systems. Each chapter dealing with the individual ISO 9001 elements also includes questionnaires to assist with self-assessment, task lists to assist with implementation, and a list of do's and don'ts. An appendix lists the procedures required by ISO 9001 along with an indication of status (required, optional, or implied).

Huyink, David Stevenson, and Craig Westover
ISO 9000: Motivating the People, Mastering the Process, Achieving Registration. Burr Ridge, IL: Irwin Professional Publishing, 1994.

This book consists of four sections in which the authors present ISO 9000 in an organizational context. They discuss the process of getting started in a registration effort, managing compliance of the quality system and meeting the criteria of the appropriate ISO 9000 standard, managing the actual ISO 9000 registration project including information on determination of readiness for assessment, and managing maintenance of a quality system which complies to an ISO 9000 standard. Interspersed in the text are examples drawn from the authors' experiences with NCR (now AT & T Global Information Solutions) and its successful pursuit of registration. Huyink and Westover present a thorough overview of internal assessments conducted to the ISO 9000 standards, documentation of quality systems, and internal audit programs. The amount of practical detail included on preparation for assessment is also quite useful.

Johnson, Perry
ISO 9000: Meeting the New International Standards. New York: McGraw Hill, 1993.

This text functions as a guide to ISO 9000 standards and certification for readers with little prior experience with the ISO 9000 series. Each element in the ISO 9000 series is described in detail. The author has also provided a system for self-assessment and a sample quality manual which readers will find helpful. Johnson includes practical advice and clarifies many misconceptions surrounding ISO 9000.

Kantner, Rob
The ISO 9000 Answer Book. Essex Junction, Vermont: Oliver Wight Publications, 1994.

The author answers 101 questions pertaining to ISO 9000 which basically attempt to explain what ISO 9000 is, where it came from, what it means, why it matters, and how to prepare for it. The book is designed for people who know very little about ISO 9000 and who need to become familiar with basic concepts quickly. Sections of the book include an ISO 9000 overview, the origin of ISO 9000 and what it actually consists of, management and quality systems, developing and documenting quality systems, how product design relates to ISO 9000, ISO 9000 registration, and the future of ISO 9000. Questions are posed in a logical sequence with clearly written explanations.

Peters, Eric D., ed.
ISO 9000 Almanac: 1994–95 Edition. Burr Ridge, IL: Irwin Professional Publishing, 1994.

The *ISO 9000 Almanac* is a guide to ISO 9000 resources and materials. It includes listings for consultants, registrars, seminars, books, videos, and software.

Randall, Richard C.
Randall's Practical Guide to ISO 9000: Implementation, Registration, and Beyond. Reading, MA: Addison-Wesley, 1995.

This book is a discussion of the practical quality concepts and principles necessary to develop and implement a quality system compliant with ISO 9000 standards. It has been designed for use as a handbook in developing the different elements of a quality system. The author has included references in the text to different ISO 9000 guidance documents as appropriate. Each of the twenty specific quality system elements found in the ISO 9000 series is described in a separate section. For each of these twenty requirements Randall provides a description, advice on the kind of material to put in the quality manual, sample quality manual entries covering all points that must be addressed in the manual, advice regarding the procedures that must address every clause, and questions that a registrar may ask during an audit. The chapter on registration includes useful information on selecting a registrar and goes into some detail on areas of concern (such as the lack of international recognition of all registrars, questions regarding accreditation of registrars, negotiating on registration fees, etc.).

Tibor, Tom
ISO 14000: A Guide to the New Environmental Management Standards. Chicago, IL: Irwin Professional Publishing, 1996.

The ISO 14000 series of environmental management standards are currently under development with a release date anticipated sometime in 1996. Tibor presents a review of the proposed ISO 14000 standards and attempts to indicate the probable effect of the standards; that is, what organizations will be affected, and how they are most likely to be affected. The author discusses the history and development of the standards and provides full descriptions of each standard in the series.

Zuckerman, Amy
ISO 9000 Made Easy: A Cost-Saving Guide to Documentation and Registration. New York: American Management Association, 1995.

Zuckerman's book is designed to help an organization make its way through the ISO 9000 certification process cost-effectively. The author is quite blunt in describing problems and excessive costs that can be incurred in pursuing certification. In a section entitled "Sorting Out the Pros and Cons of Registration", Zuckerman provides much helpful advice and clarification of "ISO 9000 misinformation" which will assist organizations in determining if ISO 9000 certification is even necessary or beneficial in their particular circumstances. Similarly, the author provides some very practical advice on selecting a registrar, picking the right ISO 9000 series, and negotiating the best price possible with a registrar. The book includes sections on quality system audits, documentation systems, and use of consultants in working toward registration. Examples drawn from individual companies' experiences are interspersed in the text. The final chapter deals with anticipated changes in ISO 9000 and places it in a global context. Finally, a list of accredited registrars (in the U.S.) and an ISO-compliant quality assurance manual (with a template) have been provided.

2 Articles on ISO 9000

"After ISO 9000." *Electronic Business Buyer* 20, no.10 (October 1994): 48–64.

This special report is a series of articles revolving around the issue of what happens to a company's quest for quality after achieving ISO 9000 registration. A general discussion of the value of ISO 9000 in assuring quality and its relationship to quality improvement is presented. Critics argue that companies with a mediocre level of quality will document their procedures and maintain a mediocre level. Others argue that ISO 9000 is merely a marketing tool and has little to do with continuous improvement in quality. Supporters contend that the process of securing certification leads to quality improvements and that the follow-up audits necessary to maintaining registration lead to a cycle of continuous improvement. The process of using certification

as a screening device with suppliers, and varying motivations for seeking certification, are also discussed.

Many believe that quality improvements come more slowly after certification has been achieved, because the easy improvements have already been made and further improvements are harder to make. A number of companies are focusing on customer satisfaction as the next step in their quality plans; updates on the activates of several companies in this area are presented. Inspections are also discussed, including the methods used by several companies. The impact of ISO 9000 on new product development is also reported on.

"1995 ISO 9000 International Directory." *Chemical Week* 156, no.13 (April 5, 1995): S1-S63.

Chemical Week produces an annual directory of ISO 9000 registrations in the chemicals industry. This is also the source of a complete list of United States ISO 9000 registrars. Selected consultants are also listed.

Askey, J.M. and B.G. Dale
"From ISO 9000 Series Registration to Total Quality Management: An Examination." *Quality Management Journal* 1, no.4 (July 1994): 67–76

The authors report on the experiences of a medium-sized manufacturer of specialty chemicals based in the United Kingdom in implementing the requirements of ISO 9002. The article is based on a three-year research project which examined the advantages and disadvantages of registration and appraised the company's strategies for progressing from registration to total quality management. Askey and Dale conclude that ISO 9000 registration has the potential to be a good foundation for development of a TQM approach. However, if registration is viewed as the ultimate goal (and not pursued in the context of total quality management) then a company may fail to progress beyond the minimum requirements specified by the standard being registered to.

Avery, Susan
"What's Wrong With ISO 9000?" *Purchasing* 116 (March 3, 1994): 49–53.

Avery examines some of the criticism being leveled at the ISO 9000 standards from both a European and an American perspective.

Detractors argue that the standard is too general to be of much use to specific industries (and many industries already have in place more stringent requirements than ISO 9000), adherence to the standards discourages creativity, certification is cost-prohibitive for many small businesses, ISO 9000 is a tremendous income source for consultants, the credibility of the U.S. program is suspect – in some cases leading European buyers to sometimes reject certificates earned by firms in the U.S. On the other hand, supporters of ISO 9000 claim that the standards are often a springboard for real quality improvement and at least indicate the existence of an adequate quality system, certification can help cut time and effort spent on supplier qualification, certification encourages communication and teamwork among employees and encourages consistency, savings accrued when operating as an ISO 9000-certified company outweigh certification costs, and certification opens a company to international markets. Reactions of the U.S. military and the automotive industry to the standards are also discussed, as are some plans underway to improve the standards and the certification process on both sides of the Atlantic.

Barrier, Michael, and Amy Zuckerman
"Quality Standards the World Agrees On." *Nation's Business* 82 (May 1994): 71–73.

A look at what ISO 9000 standards and certification can mean to a small company. The authors present a general discussion of costs likely to be faced by a company in achieving registration and factors to take into consideration in determining if registration will be cost-effective. Ways small companies can deal with costs associated with certification are presented. Among them are negotiating with registrars and ISO 9000 consultants for lower prices, asking customers for subsidies, seeking alternatives to consultants (for example, educators and networking groups), and making a decision about whether a company's goals indicate the company should pursue registration or achieve compliance but forgo the certificate. The authors also examine some of the problems likely to arise in documenting procedures. Lastly, Barrier and Zuckerman report on cost savings and other benefits some smaller companies feel have been achieved as a result of ISO 9000 certification.

Beardsley, Jeff, and Dick Schaefer
"One Company's Journey to ISO 9000 Registration." *Journal for Quality and Participation* 18, no.2 (March 1995): 66–71.

The authors review the reasons Kind & Knox Gelatine, Inc. decided to pursue ISO 9000 registration and summarize the company's experiences during the registration process. Kind & Knox were developing their total quality management and statistical process control programs, and while examining ISO 9000 came to the conclusion that overlaying the ISO 9000 registration process would provide the best framework for actually improving internal control and quality. Maintaining or increasing market share would be an additional incentive. The company learned they had to determine what they "should" be doing in their manufacturing processes before they could follow the ISO 9000 maxim of "Say what you do and do what you say." The company made extensive use of teams in documenting procedures, and involved employees at every level in conducting internal audits. At the end of the registration process the company characterizes itself as focused on TQM as a goal. The company finds that quality goals are clearly defined and understood, communication has improved greatly, pride in work has increased, and many customers have curtailed supplier audits.

Benson, Roger S., and Richard W. Sherman
"ISO 9000: A Practical Step-By-Step Approach." *Quality Progress* 28, no.10 (October 1995): 75–78.

Benson and Sherman summarize the details of one company's registration efforts, Grace Specialty Polymers (GSP). This company had a strong total quality improvement program already in place and thus had solid experience with team activities and training. The company had also achieved automotive quality requirements. The authors discuss the formation of an ISO implementation team and provide information on the various types of training the company undertook. They present the overall plan for the registration process that GSP prepared, the manner in which GSP conducted its own preliminary audit, and discuss the policies and procedures training program the company implemented after developing a quality system document. The company's final assessment went smoothly and GSP saved time and money in the process. They conclude with some brief recommendations from GSP on achieving ISO 9000 certification.

Chauvel, Alain-Michel
"Quality in Europe: Toward the Year 2000." *Quality Management Journal* 1, no.2 (January 1994): 71–77.

Chauvel reports on the trend toward certification of quality systems in Europe and examines data collected in a survey of European professionals involved in the quality movement. Data is presented which shows geographic differences in the prevalence of certification as well as the standard being registered to. Respondents appear to believe that their individual countries have the necessary resources to certify their own companies (with the exception of respondents from Eastern Mediterranean countries). Most respondents did not think that certification of quality systems is a way of improving company performance. The author contends that a rising number of certification procedures and a faster certification process lead to a situation in which firms cannot manage cultural changes needed for quality to contribute to business performance. Chauvel also feels that rising levels of requirements in standards will lead to the development of a bureaucracy, making company structures more inflexible. However, Chauvel envisions an eventual melding of ISO 9000 standards with total quality management – companies will realize that ISO 9000 encourages them to do things right, while total quality management leads them to do the right things. Greater interest and participation of managers in an approach to improving quality will be a necessary precursor to this development.

Corrigan, James P.
"Is ISO 9000 the Path to TQM?" *Quality Progress* 27, no.5 (May 1994): 33–36.

The author views TQM and ISO 9000 registration as complementary. An organization that has successfully embraced TQM should need only minor changes to its quality system to achieve ISO 9000 registration. Similarly, a company that successfully pursues registration will have built a foundation for a more comprehensive commitment to quality (such as implementing TQM). Corrigan cautions organizations to keep expectations regarding the benefits of either TQM or ISO 9000 realistic, and to understand their different aims and focuses. Some fundamental differences are that ISO 9000 is basically a prevention-based quality assurance system. If the system is adhered to, a supplier will always produce and deliver a predictable product or service. ISO 9000 standards do not measure the efficiency of a system or how good a product/service is. TQM, on the other hand, is a philosophy that builds organizations that are focused on total customer satisfaction, striving for continuous improvement in their effectiveness and efficiency and in their processes.

The customer focus supplied by TQM and process for achieving continuous improvement can serve as the means of obtaining ongoing quality and business improvements in an ISO 9000 registered firm. Alternatively, the effective quality assurance system developed as a part of ISO 9000 certification is a basic prerequisite for TQM, but one which is not always in place in companies practicing TQM. Thus, by integrating the processes for TQM and ISO 9000 registration, organizations operating in a variety of contexts will strengthen their positions.

De Meulder, Roland
"Meeting the challenge of ISO." *Internal Auditor* 50 (April 1993): 24–30.

The author provides a list of most ISO member bodies (the ISO member countries' national standards organizations) complete with addresses, telephone, and fax numbers. The primary content of the article is focused on quality system audits. There is a discussion of the differences between external quality system audits (performed when a potential purchaser wants to be assured that the supplier's quality system will provide a product that satisfies specific quality requirements – which can be a "second party audit" or a third party certification) and internal quality system audits (performed by a company itself to prepare either for certification or for mandatory follow-up reviews). The article also examines the effect of both types of audits on an organization's internal audit function and discusses areas of concern if internal auditors' responsibilities are extended to include assessments of an organization's entire quality system.

Dzus, George, and Edward G. Sykes
"How to Survive ISO 9000 Surveillance." *Quality Progress* 26, no.10 (October 1993): 109–112.

This article discusses the routine surveillance audits conducted by most registrars to ensure that registered firms maintain compliance with the ISO 9000 standard to which registration was achieved. The surveillance process is not standardized amongst registrars – differences in the rigor and timing of follow-up audits are common. Some registrars employ periodic reassessment methods while others opt for continuous reassessment. The author discusses the elements of a typical audit and presents a summary for a routine assessment. Audits are viewed by many as a route to continuous improvement.

Emmons, Sidney L.
"ISO 9001 On a Shoestring." *Quality Progress* 27, no.5 (May 1994): 49–50.

Emmons reviews the progress of the Electronics Division at ACME Electric toward ISO 9001 registration. The company failed in its registration efforts the first time around. The division couldn't back up its activities with written procedures. The second registration attempt coincided with the advent of total quality management and Just-in-Time production within the division. This provided a new foundation for the ISO 9001 effort which was ultimately successful. Advice from ACME includes two points: don't think of ISO 9001 as a guarantee that quality products will be produced (it can't substitute for proper internal attitudes), and ongoing efforts are necessary to evaluate the quality of products and compliance with standards.

Ferguson, Kelly
"World Quality Guide: Special Report." *Pulp & Paper* 68 (January 1994): S3-S44.

This special report contains three editorials (applicable to industry in general) presenting information on changes to the ISO 9000 standards, thoughts on areas where more changes are still needed, and ideas relating to directions companies can move in once certification is achieved and a higher level of quality management is desired. Additionally, a list of world-wide certification agencies has been included along with an international listing of supplier companies to the pulp and paper industry

that have achieved or are working toward certification.

Ferguson, Wade
"EC Product and Service Standards." *Journal of Small Business Management* 32 (October 1994): 84–87.

A basic explanation of ISO 9000 is provided along with a definition of registration, a review of the process required to obtain registration, a summary of the benefits of obtaining certification, and an idea of the costs that will be incurred in obtaining and maintaining certification (as well as the amount of time typically spent in achieving certification). The author contends that certification is essentially a new tax on business, and one that is particularly onerous for small businesses. Cost reductions achieved by some manufacturers as a result of certification may be illusionary, as well-managed firms do not reduce operating costs substantially and must attract more customers to offset the costs incurred by pursuing and maintaining registration. Additionally, the problem of certificates awarded in one country but not accepted in another is discussed.

Freese, Jesse D., and Emily Konald
"Teamwork Pays Off for Firm." *Quality Progress* 27, no.5 (May 1994): 53–55.

This article discusses the manner in which a small software firm (Help/Systems, Inc.) used a total quality management framework for process improvement and extensive teamwork to achieve ISO 9001 registration efficiently. Team training addressed "soft" issues (human) as well as "hard" issues (technical). Addressing soft issues helped teams overcome resistance to change. Customer satisfaction and the need for process and product improvement were built into the process-assessment phase of the registration effort. The company made use of the Software Engineering Institute's Capability Maturity Model in working toward registration.

Garver, Roger
"How to Implement ISO 9000." *Transportation & Distribution* 35 (September 1994): 36–42.

Garver reports on the improvements in quality levels, market share, and on-going cost reductions experienced by many companies that implemented ISO 9000. However, the number of failed attempts greatly exceeds the successes. Common reasons for failure include an inability to demonstrate management involvement in the quality system and problems with document and data control. An implementation guide is presented that summarizes key points for each required element.

Hayes, H. Michael
"ISO 9000: The New Strategic Consideration." *Business Horizons* 37 (May/June 1994): 52–59.

The author provides a brief background on ISO 9000, describes trends related to the standards, and discusses implications of the standards with particular emphasis on those for marketing. Marketing's responsibilities for quality are addressed. Hayes contends that marketing managers must become more skilled at determining customer wants and needs in the context of total quality, must measure the satisfaction of customers on an ongoing basis, need to learn and apply quality and productivity improvement processes, and realize that their own activities contribute to perceptions of quality.

Hockman, Kymberly K.
"Taking the mystery out of Quality." *Training & Development* 46 (July 1992): 34–39.

Hockman discusses a training curriculum that can be used as a company works toward certification. During the first phase management receives training aimed at building support and developing a strategic plan to implement and guide the registration effort. During the second phase training should cover implementing the ISO 9000 standards and auditing the quality system. The third phase involves instruction and hands-on experience in the preparation of a quality manual, which then leads to the actual work with a registrar and formal assessment.

Hockman, Kymberly K., Rita Grenville, and Suzan Jackson
"Road Map to ISO 9000 Registration." *Quality Progress* 27, no.5 (May 1994): 39–42.

The authors present a concise summary of the process for implementing ISO 9000. They address some of the benefits DuPont has achieved as a result of investing in ISO 9000 registration, then outline the working guide to quality system registration that DuPont developed. For each of the

nine milestones to ISO 9000 registration that DuPont identified for itself, the internal activities necessary to achieve that milestone and the corresponding consulting and training services needed have been specified. DuPont also developed an 18-month time line as part of the guide. The milestones are 1) securing the management decision and commitment to pursue ISO 9000 registration; 2) establishing and training internal resources; 3) conducting internal audits; 4) creating the quality manual; 5) choosing a registrar; 6) implementing the quality system and conducting a management review; 7) conducting a pre-assessment to identify weaknesses; 8) undergoing the registration assessment; and 9) achieving registration.

Lal, Harbans
"Quality Management Systems: Guidelines for Export Companies." *International Trade Forum* 2 (1993): 10–29.

Discusses the effect of the ISO 9000 standards on exporters in developing countries. Reviews the development of a quality policy, activities of a quality council within a company, responsibility for quality, and documentation of a quality system. Provides an example of the quality records of a manufacturer and discusses the contents of a quality manual.

Marash, Stanley A., and Donald W. Marquardt
"Quality, Standards, and Free Trade." *Quality Progress* 27, no.5 (May 1994): 27–30

The authors discuss international harmonization of standards as it relates to the advancement of free trade. Situations in which standards are used voluntarily (driven by marketplace forces) are differentiated from situations in which standards are mandatory (driven by regulations). Management system standards are contrasted to product technical requirement standards. Marash and Marquardt look at the interplay of standards in Europe in hopes of providing insight into the future of standards and free trade in North America. They discuss the European Community contention that third-party assessments by mutually recognized certification agencies increase free trade (as a company – regardless of nationality – will be able to market its goods anywhere in Europe if in compliance with EC product directives and quality standards). North America must harmonize its certification process with such processes in other parts of the world to facilitate free trade. The authors note that the motivations underlying North American free trade differ from those that led to the formation of the European Community, and contrast goals of the North American Free Trade Agreement to European Community agreements. Marash and Marquardt believe that the United States, Canada, and Mexico must agree on the principles for the accreditation and recognition of certification bodies and harmonize standards to promote free trade across North America.

Merrill, Peter
"ISO 9000: On the Road to Total Quality." CMA – *The Management Accounting Magazine* 69, no.4 (May 1995): 21–29.

The author advises companies to think of ISO 9000 registration as "partial quality," not a total quality improvement process. For companies that have just started a quality initiative, ISO 9000 can be a useful foundation. Companies further along can benefit from the structure and business process analysis that is one of ISO 9000's strengths. Few ISO 9000 requirements address issues like teamwork, communication, and recognition (in comparison to the Baldrige Assessment). The only area in which ISO 9000 is more comprehensive than the Baldrige Assessment is process management. ISO 9000 is highly compatible with TQM; continuous improvement of processes can be worked into an organization through the internal audit, management review, and corrective and preventative action. Working toward ISO 9000 registration can be supported by TQM in several ways: 1) develop a Just-in-Time education plan to give people skills when they need them; 2) create a communication system based on the team briefing concept; 3) institute a recognition system to endorse desired new behaviors; and 4) invest in development of team skills.

Merrill looks at five groups of ISO 9000 standard requirements and specifies ways in which TQM principles can be built in to devise a plan for registration that will truly improve an organization. The history behind the idea of improving an organization's operation with a balance of changes in processes and "soft skills" (like teamwork) is also addressed.

Morrow, Mark
"Who Will Accredit ISO 14000 Registrars? No Easy Answer." *Chemical Week* 157, no.17 (November 8, 1995): 50.

This article reveals some of the difficulties with the registrar accreditation process in the United States. Currently the U.S. Registrar Accreditation Board (RAB) the American National Standards Institute (ANSI) work together to provide ISO 9000 accreditation services. RAB and ANSI, however, have given up on providing a joint ISO 14000 accreditation program. ANSI is the U.S. representative to ISO, and will most likely establish its own ISO 14000 registrar accreditation program. The original goal of having a single ISO 9000 and ISO 14000 registrar accreditation program is further away; registrars in the United States may need to obtain two accreditations (one for quality management and one for environmental management system standards). European-based accreditation bodies able to offer a combined service will attract registrars looking for dual accreditation.

Parisher, James W.
"ISO 9000 Documentation: A TQM Journey in the Making." *National Productivity Review* 14, no.4 (Fall 1995): 77–88.

The author states that most of the gains organizations accrue as a result of subscribing to the ISO 9000 standard are actually part of the total quality management process. Critics of ISO 9000 focus on the documentation aspects of the standard and resulting bureaucracy (i.e. paperwork). Parisher advises organizations to circumvent the problem of bureaucratic paperwork by using documentation and the structure used to create documentation as a positive tool in achieving business and production process improvements.

Four ways to document processes for ISO 9000 are discussed: 1) hiring a consultant to do it; 2) assigning someone in the organization the task; 3) buying ready-made ISO documentation and filling in the blanks; and 4) having process owners document their own processes (best option). Parisher contends that up to 80 percent of the businesses that fail to register to ISO 9000 on their first attempt do so because of problems with the documentation requirement. He recommends using cross-functional teams to document and improve processes and presents a model known as a "documentation hierarchy" for meeting requirements of the standard. Level 1 consists of a quality policy, level 2 consists of procedures for meeting the policy identified in level 1, level 3 consists of standard operating procedures which specify how a process is performed, and level 4 consists of documents that support the procedures and work instructions. Parisher includes a number of useful suggestions regarding what to leave out at level 4 (watch out for duplicative information, too many details, responsibilities of various personnel, etc.). Following this more inclusive process for working toward registration will not only enhance the likelihood of achieving registration, but also sets the stage for further progress toward TQM once registration has occurred.

Russell, John F.
"The Stampede to ISO 9000 (Special Report). *Electronic Business Buyer* 19 (October 1993): 100–134.

Russell presents opinions of supporters and critics of the ISO 9000 standards. The author contends that most companies pursue certification because of customer requests, or to gain access to European markets (or protect such access), or because they believe certification is a marketing tool. He asserts that improved quality is not a driving force for certification. Russell looks at the decline in Baldrige Award applicants and surmises it may be related to the tremendous increase in the number of companies pursuing ISO 9000 certification. The author discusses problems middle managers may have with supporting ISO 9000 certification, and the more general question of when certification actually pays off.

The second part of the special report presents case studies of different companies' certification experiences. Among the topics are the way one company shortened the time involved in becoming certified (paying bonuses to employees), another company's change of heart about the economic value of certification (a skeptic became a believer), and a rush certification effort aimed at preventing a substantial loss of European business. Other sections present advice from an auditor on passing an ISO 9000 audit, and advice on choosing the right ISO 9000 registrar.

Sakofsky, Steven
"Survival After ISO 9000 Registration." *Quality Progress* 27, no.5 (May 1994): 57–59.

This article is concerned with the improvements organizations can make after they become ISO 9000 certified. Registration audits reveal minor deficiencies that should be corrected. The author lays out the development of a corrective-action plan that can be used to make improvements. Sakofsky also advises examining critical processes to identify potential improvements in an organization. The management review required under ISO 9001 and ISO 9002 is intended to determine the overall effectiveness of a quality system; this can also reveal opportunities for improvement. Quality costs should be monitored and internal audits should be treated as improvement tools. The author contends that the ISO 9000 process is not an end in itself, but should be viewed as a foundation for total quality management.

Sissell, Kara, and Rick Mullin
"Fitting in ISO 14000: A Search for Synergies." *Chemical Week* 157, no.17 (November 8, 1995): 39–43.

Companies want to see ISO 14000 integrated as much as possible with ISO 9000. However, managers wonder if a single registrar is capable of an audit covering quality and environmental management, given the specific skills required in both areas. Additionally, there are still uncertainties about whether ISO 14000 will add value to environmental management programs already underway in many organizations. Some companies are worried that they will spend large sums on a management system that doesn't have paybacks, or that they will find they're only pursuing registration to retain access to customers and markets. One of the main areas of concern for companies is what they will do if ISO 14000 auditors discover areas of non-compliance with federal regulations. If a system audit reveals a company is not in compliance with an Environmental Protection Agency rule, the company must report that fact to government authorities which may lead to substantial fines. Many are advocating a system by which companies could audit themselves without being punished. The author reports on the results of a survey by the Arthur D. Little consulting firm of

115 companies with sales of greater than one billion per year; 62 percent said ISO 14000 would be essential to business success.

Stephens, Kenneth E.
"ISO 9000 and Total Quality." *Quality Management Journal* 2, no.1 (Fall 1994): 57–71.

A discussion of what the ISO 9000 series of standards is and what it is not. The author emphasizes that the standards did not invent quality systems, and discusses historical influences in the development of standards for quality systems (beginning with American and British military procurement standards). He also notes the historical absence of Japanese quality concepts and techniques in the ISO 9000 series and questions the merit of continuing to emphasize third party certification and registration of quality systems instead of including techniques introduced by Japan. The author points out that the Japanese showed little interest in the early developments related to ISO 9000 because their quality systems were presumably already superior to quality systems specified by ISO 9000. Japanese adoption of the ISO 9000 standards ultimately had more to do with international harmonization of standards, increased trade opportunities, and cooperation, than with quality systems. Strengths and weaknesses of the current standards as well as positive and negative aspects of certification and accreditation programs (especially in relation to trade barriers) are also examined.

Townsend, Patrick L., and Joan E. Gebhardt
"Do ISO Instead of Applying Baldrige Criteria. . . Not!" *Journal for Quality and Participation* 17, no.1 (January/February 1994): 94–95.

The authors contend that the drive to attain ISO 9000 registration is having a detrimental impact on the progress of the American quality revolution. They believe that managers of too many companies either misunderstand the basic intent and meaning of ISO 9000 certification (especially as it fits into the subject of quality management and more comprehensive programs such as the Malcolm Baldrige National Quality Award) or because companies are acceding to real or perceived customer demands and allocating their limited budgets to ISO registration efforts and postponing Baldrige Award involvement. They contend evidence indicates that the information,

procedures, and material on which ISO 9000 certification requirements focus amounts to only 10 percent of the scope of the Baldrige Award program. Townsend and Gebhardt view ISO 9000 as a minor subset of the Baldrige Award. ISO 9000 established quality minimums through emphasis on current procedure and documentation, while the Baldrige Award provides a way for an organization to reach for maximums through a focus on customers and continuous improvement methodology.

The authors note that a counter-revolution of sorts has occurred. The prescribed checklists and procedures associated with ISO 9000 appeal to many quality control practitioners who had reservations about the TQM movement and the change in organizational culture it encouraged. Townsend and Gebhardt warn that equating ISO 9000 registration with quality is dangerous and that American industry should look to developments in Europe involving national quality awards based on the Baldrige model.

Waring, Jeffrey G., and Peter Mears
"An ISO 9000 Certified Pizza Isn't All That Far-Fetched." *Journal for Quality and Participation* 16, no.6 (October/November 1993): 20–23.

This article presents a common-sense explanation of what the steps to ISO 9000 certification really mean. The authors use a familiar product and a well-known type of company (a pizza-maker) to make their points. They review the purpose of developing a quality policy, what requirements a quality manual has to address and how to write it (with an example provided), what the responsibility of management is in developing a quality system (defining policies, defining specifications on incoming food supplies, preventing use of unspecified food products, ensuring personnel are trained, keeping records pertaining to quality, etc.), how procedures have to be written (an example of a written procedure is provided: determining when to offer a free pizza), and setting expectations for employee responsibility (follow all pizza-making procedures, taking action when a quality problem occurs, etc.).

Weise, Carl E., and Peter G. Stamoolis
"ISO 9000: An Opportunity for Records Management Professionals." *Records Management Quarterly* 27 (October 1993): 3–11.

The authors present a discussion of the need for records management involvement in the ISO 9000 series registration. The standards emphasize documentation and evidence indicates that a substantial number of the companies that fail to achieve registration do so because of inadequate record systems. Job opportunities for records management professionals are forecast. The records management implications for each of the twenty elements within the series are discussed. The kinds of records which relate to each element are specified.

Weston, F.C.
"What Do Managers Really Think of the ISO 9000 Registration Process?" *Quality Progress* 28, no.10 (October 1995): 67–73.

Weston reports on a study which examined forty ISO 9000-registered firms in Colorado. Goals of the study were to discern links between the ISO 9000 registration process, total quality management, and the Malcolm Baldrige National Quality Award. An overwhelming majority (85 percent) of the respondents indicated that their primary reason for seeking ISO 9000 registration was pressure from customers or because their own management believed it would become a customer requirement or because their marketing departments felt certification would achieve product differentiation. Facilitating foreign trade was also a very important factor. In looking at the degree to which a company's quality philosophy extended beyond ISO 9000, the results indicate that 87 percent of the respondents felt their corporate quality philosophy extended beyond ISO 9000 (and included ideas from Deming, Juran, Crosby, the Baldrige Award, and TQM in general). However 40 percent felt that registration was an independent effort not related to continuous improvement efforts such as TQM. Most of the companies (72.5 percent) indicated they had not considered applying for the Baldrige Award.

The study looked at the level of involvement of various groups in the registration effort (top management, customers, suppliers, and information systems). The time and cost involved in registration was also examined. The most common time frame was twelve to eighteen months. Surprisingly, 70 percent of the firms did not track time involved in the registration process, and 58 percent did not keep track of costs. Most of the firms (93 percent) did not attempt to justify the cost of the ISO 9000 registration process. Some obstacles to achieving registration are presented (not understanding the ISO 9000 requirements, having trouble with documentation control, getting resistance from within the company to registration, etc.) as well as some benefits (establishes a framework for a formal quality system, provides a competitive advantage, better understanding of processes, etc.). The authors discuss some lessons respondents felt they learned (for example, importance of teamwork, how to manage a project, importance of cooperation and information sharing) and what companies felt they should have done differently (more training, greater appreciation of time required, more emphasis on top-down commitment, etc.). They conclude with a summary of what companies are focusing on after registration in terms of quality (about half are pursuing continuous improvement).

Williams, Frances
"Survey of International Standards." *The Financial Times* (October 13, 1995): p. III.

Williams examines the growth in the service industries and the percentage of cross-border trade it accounts for (nearly 30 percent). However, standards for services have been slow to emerge. Some of the difficulties in devising global standards for services are detailed. Many argue that standards for many services could be extremely beneficial to consumers by defining a standard service package that could be used as the basis for comparison shopping. Williams uses tourism as an example of an area in which pressure for standards is increasing. An international standard for classifying hotels (so that a three-star rating is consistent globally) is desirable, but faces resistance from those who feel that the necessary benchmarking would result in a general downgrading. Additionally, national tourist authorities are loath to agree to a standard which might force them to give up control. Some work toward developing standards based on the ISO model has occurred; however, the demand for such standards from various industries has been mixed. Switching from "industry codes of practice" (which are perhaps both more comprehensive and more flexible than standards) to a reliance on standards is an enormous cultural shift.

Zaciewski, Robert D.

"ISO 9000 Preparation: The First Crucial Steps." *Quality Progress* 28, no.11 (November 1995): 81–83.

The author contends that even if an organization never seeks ISO 9000 registration, it should still adopt the standards as the basic foundation for its total quality management system. Zaciewski states that the first steps to ISO 9000 certification seem easy, but actually require a disciplined and systematic approach if the results are to be successful. A careful initial approach will prepare an organization for the process of integrating the ISO 9000 standards with its quality system. After reviewing the process for selecting the appropriate ISO 9000 standard, Zaciewski discusses the process a company should use in comparing its quality system to the requirements of the appropriate ISO 9000 standard. He recommends using a "modified house of quality" in identifying gaps between what a company has in place and what the ISO 9000 standard requires. A house of quality is a matrix in which the ISO 9000 standard's requirements are the "whats" and a company's quality system elements are the "hows". An example is provided. The idea is to assess how useful each of the company's internal quality system elements is in fulfilling a particular ISO 9000 requirement. This process should reveal strengths, weaknesses, and redundancies in an organization's quality system in addition to identifying the areas where an organization comes up short in meeting ISO 9000 requirements.

Zuckerman, Amy

"A European View of Quality, ISO 9000 and Trade Barriers." *Journal for Quality and Participation* 18, no.4 (July/August 1995): 102–104.

The author presents results of an interview with Jacques McMillan that covered quality and standards-related issues affecting European and American industry. McMillan is a standards expert and the chief of the European Union's Senior Policy Standard Group for Directorate-General III.

McMillan expresses a high level of concern regarding QS 9000, the U.S. automakers' common quality program. He contends that if ISO 9000 were understood and implemented properly, QS 9000 would not have been developed. McMillan views QS 9000 as a threat to ISO 9000, believes it to be unjustified, and feels it will be a barrier to trade. He has similar opinions regarding Japan's proposed standard JIS Z9901 aimed at software manufacturers. On the subject of European quality efforts, McMillan discussed the European Union goal of promoting the quality process and deemphasizing the certification aspects of ISO 9000. The European quality program being examined by the European Commission emphasizes a Malcolm Baldrige approach. Industry will be encouraged to think of quality first, instead of merely pursuing certification as an end in itself. In McMillan's opinion, many organizations become certified unnecessarily. Manufacturers share some of that blame as they ask suppliers for certificates instead of examining the quality of a supplier's goods; misinformation about the need for certification and the for-profit nature of the business of registration are responsible as well.

Zuckerman, Amy

"ISO 9000: Free Trade Boon, Barrier or Boondoggle?" *Journal for Quality and Participation* 17, no.1 (January/February 1994): 88–90.

The author contends that the question of how to make international trade work well has not received enough attention. The interplay between quality assurance standards and domination of markets has had repercussions which reveal themselves in the form of competing standards and attacks on the credibility of accreditation programs. Regulatory efforts related to ISO are under discussion as are suggested reforms related to conflict of interest problems with registrars, but the issue of using standards to control trade either directly or indirectly will be increasingly important.

V

Resource Materials

I Strategies for locating additional information

i Book publishers and distributors

Many quality related books are published by smaller presses, presses affiliated with associations, and specialized publishers. The following is a selective listing of companies that publish and/or distribute books relating to quality improvement. Most publishers and distributors will provide free catalogs upon request.

Addison-Wesley Publishing Co.
One Jacob Way
Reading, MA 01867
Phone:　(800) 447 2226
　　　　(617) 944 3700

AMACOM (American Management
　Association)
135 W. 50th St.
New York, NY 10020
Phone:　(800) 262 9699
　　　　(212) 903 8315

ASQC Quality Press
611 E. Wisconsin Ave.
P.O. Box 3005
Milwaukee, WI 53201 3005
Phone:　(800) 248 1946

AT & T Quality Library
Subsidiary of AT & T
2855 N. Franklin Rd.
Indianapolis, IN 46219

Phone:　(800) 432 6600
　　　　(317) 352 0011

Berritt Koehler Publishers Inc.
155 Montgomery St.
San Francisco, CA 94194 4109
Phone:　(415) 288 0260

Crisp Publications
1200 Hamilton Court
Menlo Park, CA 94025 9600
Phone:　(800) 442 7477
　　　　(415) 323 6100

Development Dimensions International
1225 Washington Pike
Bridgeville, PA 15017 2838
Phone:　(412) 257 0600

The Free Press
866 Third Ave.
New York, NY 10022
Phone:　(800) 257 5755
　　　　(212) 702 2004

GOAL/QPC
13 Branch St.
Methuen, MA 01844 1953
Phone:　(800) 643 4316
　　　　(508) 685 6370

Gower Publishing
Gower House
Croft Rd.
Aldershot, Hampshire GU11 3HR
England
Phone:　01252 331551

Harvard Business School Press
Harvard Business School
Boston, MA 02163
Phone: (800) 545 7685

Institute of Personnel Management
IPM House
Camp Rd., Wimbledon
London SW19 4UX
Phone: 0181 946 9100

Irwin Professional Publishing
1333 Burr Ridge Pkwy.
Burr Ridge, IL 60521
Phone: (800) 634 3961
               (708) 789 4000

John Wiley & Sons
605 Third Ave.
New York, NY 10158 0012
Phone: (800) 225 5945
               (212) 850 6000

Joint Commission on Accreditation of
   Healthcare Organizations
One Renaissance Blvd.
Oakbrook Terrace, IL 60181
Phone: (708) 916 5800

Jossey-Bass, Inc.
350 Sansome St.
San Francisco, CA 94104
Phone: (415) 433 1767

Juran Institute, Inc.
P.O. Box 811
11 River Rd.
Wilton, CT 06897 0811
Phone: (203) 834 1700

McGraw-Hill
1221 Ave. of the Americas
New York, NY 10020
Phone: (800) 262 4729
               (212) 512 2000

Marcel Dekker, Inc.
270 Madison Ave.
New York, NY 10016
Phone: (800) 228 1160
               (212) 696 9000

Nicholas Brealey Publishing Ltd.
21 Bloomsbury Way
London WC1A 2TH
England
Phone: 0171 430 0224

OMNEO/Oliver Wight Publications Inc.
5 Oliver Dr.
Essex Junction, VT 05452 9985
Phone: (800) 343 0625

Productivity Press
P.O. Box 13390
Portland, OR 97213 0390
Phone: (800) 394 6868
               (503) 235 0600

Quality Resources
902 Broadway
New York, NY 10010
Phone: (800) 247 8519

Sage Publications, Inc.
2455 Teller Rd.
Thousand Oaks, CA 91320
Phone: (805) 499 0721

Sheldon Press
Holy Trinity Church
London NW1 4DV
England
Phone: 0171 387 5282

SPC Press, Inc.
5908 Toole Dr., Ste. C
Knoxville, TN 37919
Phone: (615) 584 5005

St. Lucie Press
100 E. Linton Blvd., Ste. 403B
Delray Beach, FL 33483
Phone: (407) 274 9906

Tower Hill Press
Sky Run Business Center
P.O. Box 1132
Doylestown, PA 18901
Phone: (215) 345 1338

TQM International Ltd.
The Stables
Tarvin Rd.
Frodsham, Cheshire WA6 6XN
England

ii Periodicals

The following is a selective listing of quality-related periodicals and newsletters. While some are general in nature, others are directed to specific audiences such as manufacturers, industrial engineers, health care administrators, and college and university administrators. The listing of a title in this section does not constitute an endorsement of the periodical by the authors or by Routledge.

American Journal of Medical Quality
William & Wilkins
428 E. Preston St.
Baltimore, MD 21202
Phone: (410) 528 4000
Quarterly
$82 (individual subscribers); $103 (institutional subscribers)

AQP Report
Association for Quality and Participation
801-B W. 8th St., Ste. 501
Cincinnati, OH 45203
Phone: (513) 381 1959
Bimonthly
$45

Benchmarking for Quality Management and Technology
MCB University Press Ltd.
60–62 Toller Ln.
Bradford, W. Yorks BD8 9B4
England
Phone: 01274 499821
3 issues/yr
$139.95

Business Change and Re-engineering
John Wiley & Sons Ltd. Journals
Baffins Ln.
Chichester, W. Sussex PO19 1UD
England
Phone: 01243 779777

Quarterly
$225

Continuous Journey: The Magazine for Continuous Improvement
American Productivity & Quality Center
123 N. Post Oak Ln., Ste. 300
Houston, TX 77024 7797
Phone: (713) 681 4020
Bimonthly
$75 (non-members); $50 (members)

Customer Service Newsletter
Alexander Research & Communications Inc.
215 Park Ave., South, Ste. 1301
New York, NY 10003
Phone: (212) 228 0246
Monthly
$122

Customer Service Report
Stovall Communications
310 E. Interstate 30, Ste. M102A
Garland, TX 75043
Phone: (214) 203 1515
Bimonthly
$39

European Quality
European Quality Publications Ltd.
172 North Gower St.
London NW1 2ND
England
Phone: 0171 388 7362
Bimonthly
£72

International Journal for Quality in Health Care
Elsevier Science Ltd.
Pergamon
P.O. Box 800
Kidlington, Oxford OX5 1DX
England
Phone: 01865 843000
4 issues/yr
£115

*International Journal of Quality & Reliability
Management*
MCB University Press Ltd.
60–62 Toller Ln.
Bradford, W. Yorks BD8 9B4
England
Phone: 01274 499821
9 issues/yr
$1,399.95

Journal for Quality and Participation
Association for Quality and Participation
801-B W. 8th St., Ste. 501
Cincinnati, OH 45203
Phone: (513) 381 1959
7 issues/yr
$52

Journal of Organizational Change Management
MCB University Press Ltd.
60–62 Toller Ln.
Bradford, W. Yorks BD8 9B4
England
Phone: 01274 499821
6 issues/yr
$759.95

Journal of Productivity Analysis
Kluwer Academic Publishers Boston
Box 358, Accord Station
Hingham, MA 02018 0358
Phone: (617) 871 6600
Quarterly
$169.50

Journal of Quality Technology
American Society for Quality Control
611 E. Wisconsin Ave.
Box 3005
Milwaukee, WI 53201 3005
Phone: (414) 272 8575
Quarterly
$30

Leadership and Organization Development Journal
MCB University Press Ltd.
60–62 Toller Ln.
Bradford, W. Yorks BD8 9B4
England
Phone: 01274 499821
8 issues/yr
$2269.95

Managing Service Quality
MCB University Press Ltd.
60–62 Toller Ln.
Bradford, W. Yorks BD8 9B4
England
Phone: 01274 499821
6 issues/yr
$349.95

Process Control and Quality
Elsevier Science B.V.
P.O. Box 211
Amsterdam, Netherlands
Phone: 20 5803911
8 issues/yr
$515

*Productivity: Improving Productivity and Quality by
Learning What's Working at Other Companies*
Productivity, Inc.
101 Merritt 7, 5th Fl.
Norwalk, CT 06851
Phone: (203) 846 3777
10 issues/yr
$67

*Productivity Views: Solutions, Tips and Action Ideas
From Service Quality Leaders*
Productivity Development Group, Inc.
Box 488
Westford, MA 01886
Phone: (508) 692 1818
Bimonthly
$295

QC Circle
Union of Japanese Scientists and Engineers
Nihon Kagaku Gijutsu Renmei
5–10–11 Sendagaya
Shibuya-ku, Tokyo 151
Japan
Phone: 03 5379 1227
Monthly
1000 yen

QI-TQM
American Health Consultants, Inc.
Six Piedmont Center, Ste. 400
Atlanta, GA 30305
Phone: (404) 262 7436
Monthly
$269

QRC Advisor: Managing Hospital Quality, Risk, &
   Cost
Aspen Publishers, Inc.
200 Orchard Ridge Dr.
Gaithersburg, MD 20878
Phone: (301) 417 7500
Monthly
$199

Quality and Reliability Engineering International
John Wiley & Sons Ltd.
Journals
Baffins Ln.
Chichester, W. Sussex PO19 1UD
England
Phone: 01243 779777
Bimonthly
$495

Quality & Risk Management in Health Care: An
   Information Service
Aspen Publishers, Inc.
200 Orchard Ridge Dr.
Gaithersburg, MD 20878
Phone: (301) 417 7500
Semi-annual
$260

Quality Assurance Bulletin
Bureau of Business Practice
24 Rope Ferry Rd.
Waterford, CT 06386
Phone: (203) 442 4365
Semi-monthly
$118.80

Quality Assurance: Good Practice, Regulation, and
   Law
Academic Press, Inc.
Journal Division
525 B. St., Ste. 1900
San Diego, CA 92101 4495
Phone: (619) 230 1840
Quarterly
$167

Quality Assurance in Education
MCB University Press Ltd.
60–62 Toller Ln.
Bradford, W. Yorks BD8 9B4
England

Phone: 01274 499821
3 issues/yr
$219.95

Quality Digest
QCI International
Box 882
Red Bluff, CA 96080
Phone: (916) 527 8875
Monthly
$75

Quality Engineering
American Society for Quality Control
Marcel Dekker Journals
270 Madison Ave.
New York, NY 10016
Phone: (212) 696 9000
4 issues/yr
$35 (individual subscription); $200 (institutional
subscription)

Quality-Europe
Hitchcock Publishing
191 S. Gary Ave.
Carol Stream, IL 60188
Phone: (708) 665 1000
Quarterly
Contact publisher for pricing information

Quality in Manufacturing
Huebcore Communications, Inc.
29100 Aurora Rd.
Solon, OH 44139
Phone: (216) 248 1125
Bimonthly
$75

Quality Management Journal
American Society for Quality Control
611 E. Wisconsin Ave.
Box 3005
Milwaukee, WI 53201 3005
Phone: (414) 272 8575
Quarterly
$60 (non-members); $50 (members)

Quality New Zealand
New Zealand Organisation for Quality, Inc.
P.O. Box 622
Palmerston North, New Zealand

Phone: 06 3569099
Semi-annual
$20

Quality Progress
American Society for Quality Control
611 E. Wisconsin Ave.
Box 3005
Milwaukee, WI 53201 3005
Phone: (414) 272 8575
Monthly
$50

Quality: The Magazine of Product Assurance
Hitchcock Publishing
191 S. Gary Ave.
Carol Stream, IL 60188
Phone: (708) 665 1000
Monthly
$65

Quality Today
Nexus Business Communications Ltd.
Warwick House
Azalea Dr.
Swanley, Kent BR8 8HY
England
Phone: 01322 660070
10 issues/yr
£64.75

Quality World: For the Quality Professional
Institute of Quality Assurance
P.O. Box 712
61 Southwark St.
London SE1 1SB
England
Phone: 0171 401 7227
Quarterly
£30

The Service Edge: The Newsletter of Bottom-Line Ideas for Customer-Driven Organizations
Lakewood Publications
50 S. Ninth St.
Minneapolis, MN 55402
Phone: (612) 333 0471
12 issues/yr
$98

Service Quality
American Management Association
135 W. 50th St.
New York, NY 10020
Phone: (212) 903 8075
Monthly
$125

Strategic Insights into Quality
MCB University Press Ltd.
60–62 Toller Ln.
Bradford, W. Yorks BD8 9B4
England
Phone: 01274 499821
4 issues/yr
$529.95

Tapping the Network Journal
Quality and Productivity Management
   Association
300 N. Martingale Rd., Ste. 230
Schaumburg, IL 60173
Phone: (708) 619 2909
Quarterly
$48 (non-members)

Tom Peters on Achieving Excellence
TPG Communications
555 Hamilton Ave.
Palo Alto, CA 94301
Phone: (415) 326 4496
Monthly
$150

Total Quality Management
Carfax Publishing Co.
P.O. Box 25
Abingdon, Oxon OX14 3EU
England
Phone: 01235 555335
5 issues/yr
$138 (individual subscription); $348 (institutional subscription)

Total Quality Newsletter
Lakewood Publications
50 S. Ninth St.
Minneapolis, MN 55402
Phone: (612) 333 0471
Monthly
$128

The TQM Magazine
MCB University Press Ltd.
60–62 Toller Ln.
Bradford, W. Yorks BD8 9B4
England
Phone: 01274 499821
Bimonthly
$349.95

iii Databases

Because articles relating to quality improvement appear in a wide range of periodicals, a great many databases will provide citations to relevant literature. Listed below are the most important databases containing references to total quality management in general, specific aspects of TQM, and the application of TQM in manufacturing and service industries. Although all these databases allow users to search by keyword or phrase, we have provided a listing of relevant descriptors or subject headings in each database to increase the likelihood of finding relevant citations.

ABI Inform

This is one of the largest and oldest business-oriented databases. This is a critical database for any researcher examining the topics of quality management in general, organizational change, change management, teamwork, reengineering, and quality initiatives in specific companies or industries. Some relevant descriptors or subject headings include: benchmarks; business process reengineering; corporate culture; flowcharts; International Standards Organization; organizational change; production planning and control; quality control; total quality; and value added.

Business Periodicals Index

This database indexes popular, trade, and scholarly journals in all fields of business. It provides a good starting point for researchers needing quality-related articles in specialized business periodicals as well as broader business publications. It indexes articles, interviews, biographical sketches, and book reviews that have been published in more than 300 periodicals. Some relevant descriptors or subject headings include: American Association for Quality Control;

benchmarking (business); chemical plants/quality control; continuous improvement process; control charts; corporate culture/evaluation; customer satisfaction; customer satisfaction/measurement; employee empowerment; information systems/ quality control use; industrial purchasing/quality control; ISO 9000 series standards; leadership/ employee training; Malcolm Baldrige National Quality Award; paper industry/quality control; quality circles; quality consultants; quality control; quality control/awards; quality control/ accounting firms; quality control/administrative agencies; quality control/automotive parts industry; quality control/costs; quality control/forecasting; quality control/health care industry; quality control/history; quality control/hospitals; quality control/hotels and motels; quality control/human resource management; quality control/international aspects; quality control/management; quality control/measurement; quality control/ plastics plants; quality control/public administration; quality control/small business; quality control/strategic planning; quality control/study and teaching; quality of products; real estate brokers/quality control; reengineering (business); return on quality; self directed work teams; statistical process control; Taguchi methods (quality control); and team work in industry.

EI Compendex Plus

This database is the electronic version of *The Engineering Index*, the premier index to the literature of engineering and technology. The database covers more than 9,000 journals from around the world, as well as selected books and government reports. This is an essential database for manufacturers and industrial engineers researching quality control and quality improvement. Some relevant descriptors or subject headings include: flowcharting; process engineering; productivity; quality assurance; quality control; statistical process control; and total quality management.

ERIC

This is the most comprehensive database in the area of education. It is a critical database for those researching quality improvement in any level of educational institution.

However, it is very broad in scope and can also be used to retrieve quality related articles that have been published in other social science periodicals, including business and management journals. Some relevant descriptors or subject headings include: Baldrige Award; benchmarking; change strategies; continuous improvement; continuous quality improvement; corporate culture; customer satisfaction; customer services; Deming management method; Deming (W. Edwards); educational quality; empowerment; flowcharts; histograms; ISO 9000; organizational change; organizational culture; Pareto diagrams; process improvement; quality circles; quality control; quality indicators; systemic change; teamwork; and total quality management.

Health Planning and Administration Database

This database is a good choice for researchers needing information about quality improvement in hospitals and other health care facilities. Some relevant descriptors or subject headings include: consumer satisfaction; hospital restructuring–organization and administration–og; institutional management teams; management quality circles; management quality circles–organization and administration–og; organizational culture; organizational innovation; outcome and process assessment (health care); patient satisfaction–statistical and numerical data–sn; process assessment (health care)–organization and administration–og; quality assurance; quality circles; quality of health care; quality of health care–standards–st; total quality management; total quality management–legislation and jurisprudence–lj; total quality management–organization and administration–og; total quality management–standards–st; and total quality management–trends.

Periodical Abstracts

This database indexes and abstracts articles from more than 1,500 general interest periodicals. It is a good beginning point for any quality-related research. Some relevant descriptors or subject headings include: corporate reorganization; quality control; International Organization for Standardization; teamwork; and total quality.

Social Sciences Index

This is a database of citations to articles in the social sciences. It indexes more than 300 periodicals. Some relevant descriptors or subject headings include: Deming, W. Edwards; organizational change; quality circles; quality control; quality of products; reengineering (business); and total quality management.

Trade and Industry Index

This database indexes major trade journals and industry-related periodicals representing all Standard Industrial Classification (i.e. SIC CODES). This is an essential database for any research on quality initiatives in business and industry. Some relevant descriptors or subject headings include: automobile industry–quality control; benchmarks–management; benchmarks–research; corporate culture–analysis; corporate culture–management; corporate culture–research; corporate reorganizations–analysis; corporate reorganizations–cases; corporate reorganizations–technique; customer satisfaction–technique; customer service–management; health maintenance organizations–quality control; hospitality industry–quality control; International Organization for Standardization–standards; Malcolm Baldrige National Quality Award; manufacturing processes–quality control; medical care–quality control; organizational change–analysis; organizational change–management; organizational change–surveys; organizational change–technique; product quality–management; quality control–analysis; quality control–international aspects; quality control–management; quality control–statistics; total quality management–analysis; total quality management–laws, regulations, etc.; total quality management–measurement; total quality management–research; total quality management–surveys; total quality management–technique; total quality management–usage; value analysis (cost control)–management; work groups–evaluation; and work groups–management.

iv Useful Library of Congress subject headings

Search the following subject headings to locate additional quality-related books.

Benchmarking (Management)
Corporate Culture
Corporate Reorganization
Customer Relations
Customer Service
Deming, W. Edwards, William Edwards, 1900–1993
Malcolm Baldrige National Quality Award
Organizational Change
Production Management–Quality Control
Quality Assurance
Quality Assurance–Management
Quality of Products
Quality of Products–Management
Quality Control
Quality Control–Standards
Quality Control–Standards–Europe
Quality Control–Standards–United States
Service Industries–Management
Service Industries–Quality Control
Total Quality Management
Total Quality Management–Awards
Total Quality Management–Case Studies
Total Quality Management–England
Total Quality Management–Evaluation
Total Quality Management–Great Britain
Total Quality Management–Handbooks, Manuals, etc.
Total Quality Management in Government
Total Quality Management–Japan
Total Quality Management–Standards
Total Quality Management–United States
Work Groups

2 Training materials

i Audio-visual and interactive multimedia training resources

The following is a selective listing of videos, audio cassettes, games and activities, computer-based training programs, and interactive multimedia that have received high ratings by training experts. The listing of products in this section does not constitute an endorsement of the product by the authors or by Routledge. In order to facilitate users, the products described below have been grouped into broad categories.

Those interested in identifying additional media relating to quality improvement, customer service, team building, organizational change, ISO 9000 standards, and other quality issues should consult Laura Winig's excellent *Field Guide to Current Training Videos* (Harvard Business School Press, 1995). This handbook is a compendium of reviews of business and training videos. It is also useful to scan the following periodicals for media reviews: *Training Media Review*; *Audiovisual* (UK); *Videography* (which incorporates *Corporate Video Decisions*); *Training*, *HR Focus*; and *Personnel Management*. *Media Review Digest*, a guide to media reviews, is another valuable source.

In addition, the Excellence in Training Corporation (ETC), located in Des Moines (Iowa), is another important resource for corporate trainers and human resource specialists in the United States and Canada. ETC distributes more than 2,000 video titles from more than 100 leading video producers. ETC also produces customized video training programs and produces its own films in several areas, including team-building, quality, and customer relations. For further information, phone ETC at (800) 747 6569. Finally, the producers of the products listed in this section can be contacted directly for further information, catalogs, or brochures.

Change

Title: Discovering the Future series
Producer: ChartHouse International Learning
         Corporation
         221 River Ridge Circle
         Burnsville, MN 55337
         Phone: (612) 890 1800
               (800) 328 3789
         Fax: (612) 890 0505
Format: Video
Date released: 1989, 1990, 1993
Length: 98 minutes (total running time for three videos)
Price: $2,013.75 (series purchase); $540 (series rental); $671.25 (purchase of individual title); $200 (rental of individual title); free preview
Description: This bestselling film series is hosted by futurist Joel Barker. Barker, a consultant, author, and teacher, was named the 1993 International Educator of the Year by Pi Lamda Theta, a professional education association. This series is about change,

organizational vision, and leadership. It consists of the following three videos: *The Business of Paradigms*, *Paradigm Partners*, and *The Power of Vision*.

Title: Leadership and the New Science
Producer: CRM Films
    2215 Faraday Ave.
    Carlsbad, CA 92008 7214
    Phone: (800) 421 0833
    Fax: (619) 931 5792
Format: Video
Date released: 1993
Length: 23 minutes
Price: $745 (purchase); $195 (rental)
Description: This video has been created by Margaret Wheatley, the author of the acclaimed management book with the same title. She uses analogies from quantum physics and evolutionary biology to convey the idea that chaos in organizations is natural. This video should be considered by organizations undergoing significant change. It includes a leader's guide with exercises and a participant's workbook.

Title: Managing at the Speed of Change
Producer: Mentor Media
    1929 Hillhurst Ave.
    Los Angeles, CA 90027
    Phone: (800) 359 1935
    Fax: (213) 667 0029
Format: Video
Date released: 1992
Length: 25 minutes
Price: $895 (purchase); $195 (rental); $49 (preview)
Description: Using interviews, narration, and documentary footage, this video examines how individuals deal with change. It suggests behavior that can help individuals in organizations cope with change. The video, *Resilience: A Change for the Better*, is a sequel.

Title: Mastering Revolutionary Change
Producer: Video Publishing House, Inc.
    Four Woodfield Lake
    930 National Parkway, Ste. 505
    Schaumburg, IL 60173 9921
    Phone: (708) 517 8744
    (800) 824 8889
    Fax: (708) 517 8752

Format: Video
Date released: 1994
Length: 100 minutes (total running time for two videos)
Price: $1,990 (purchase); $375 (rental); $75 (preview)
Description: Video Publishing House, Inc. produced this video on organizational change in conjunction with *Fortune* magazine. It features Noel Tichy, a professor from the University of Michigan's Graduate School of Business Administration and Stratford Sherman, a member of *Fortune* magazine's board of editors. Tichy and Sherman go on location to four corporations that have visionary leadership. They interview the CEOs of General Electric, AlliedSignal, Tenneco, and Ameritech. John F. Welch (General Electric), Lawrence Bassidy (AliedSignal), Michael Walsh (Tenneco), and William Weiss (Ameritech) describe their experiences in bringing about dramatic organizational change. The video has been designed as a complete workshop. It includes exercises, assessment instruments, a facilitator's guide, viewer's guides, a reprint of an article from *Fortune* magazine, and one copy of *Control Your Destiny or Someone Else Will*, a book coauthored by Sherman.

Title: The Path to Change series
Producer: Change Lab International
    Video Publishing House (distributor)
    Four Woodfield Lake
    930 North National Parkway, Ste. 505
    Schaumburg, IL 60173 9921
    Phone: (708) 517 8744
    (800) 824 8889
    Fax: (708) 517 8752
Format: Video
Date released: 1994
Length: 68 minutes (total running time for four videos)
Price: $2,000 (series purchase); $795 (purchase of individual title); $200 (rental); $50 (preview)
Description: In this series, Dr. Gerald Ross reduces organizational change to four levels. The video explores how organizations can move from a product-driven organization to a

molecular, customer-focused organization. The series consists of the following four videos: *The Customer-Focused Organization, Identifying a Market Segment, The Market-Driven Organization,* and *The Molecular Organization.*

Title: A Quality Foundation: 50 Activities for Organizational Change
Producer: Human Resource Development Press
22 Amherst Rd.
Amherst, MA 01002
Phone: (800) 822 2801
Fax: (413) 253 3490
Format: Three-ring binder
Price: $139.95
Description: This collection of activities, developed by Mardy Wheeler and Betsy Kendall, cover the following topics: employee commitment to quality; managing conflict; problem-solving; accepting change; and mind-mapping. Activities include group discussion, case studies, instruments, and action planning. Each activity takes between 20 and 45 minutes.

Title: Resilience: A Change for the Better
Producer: Mentor Media
1929 Hillhurst Ave.
Los Angeles, CA 90027
Phone: (800) 359 1935
Fax: (213) 667 0029
Format: Video
Date released: 1992
Length: 12 minutes
Price: $595 (purchase); $110 (rental); $49 (preview)
Description: This video is a companion to *Managing at the Speed of Change.* It uses narration, interviews, and documentary footage to explore how individuals can respond positively to change. The theme is that change should be viewed as an opportunity rather than a threat. The video is directed to frontline supervisors, middle managers, and senior managers. It could be used as a discussion starter or part of an introduction to TQM team training.

Title: Survival Skills for the Future
Producer: Enterprise Media Inc.
91 Harvey St.
Cambridge, MA 02140
Phone: (617) 354 0017
(800) 423 6021
Fax: (617) 365 1637
Format: Video
Date released: 1993
Length: 22 minutes
Price: $695 (purchase); $225 (rental)
Description: This is another bestselling video hosted by cultural anthropologist Jennifer Jones. Jones is a noted author, columnist, and corporate speaker. The goal of this award-winning video is to help employees understand change, become more receptive to change, and solve old problems with different ways of thinking. A viewer's guide is included.

Title: Windows of Change
Producer: Enterprise Media Inc.
91 Harvey St.
Cambridge, MA 02140
Phone: (617) 354 0017
(800) 423 6021
Fax: (617) 365 1637
Format: Video
Date released: 1993
Length: 25 minutes
Price: $695 (purchase); $225 (rental); $40 (preview)
Description: Jennifer Jones, the cultural anthropologist, hosts this video on the topic of change. Jones identifies four categories of change: incremental; change by exception; pendulum; and paradigm shift. According to Jones, there are four types of employees: visionaries; adapters; followers; and bullfrogs. She explains how each type of individual approaches the eight or nine types of change that she has identified. Jones recommends several strategies for organizations dealing with change, including training, lateral movements, and outplacement services.

Customer service

Title: Alessandra On ... Customer-Driven Service
Producer: Alessandra & Associates
6361 Yarrow Dr., Ste. B
Carlsbad, CA 92009
Phone: (800) 222 4383
Fax: (619) 459 0435
Format: Video

Date released: 1993
Length: 57 minutes
Price: $95 (purchase)
Description: This training video on customer service is directed to line supervisors and new employees. Two audio tapes and a workbook are included.

Title: An Inside Job: Stuck on Quality
Producer: Video Arts
8614 W. Catalpa Ave.
Chicago, IL 60656
Phone: (312) 693 9966
(800) 553 0091
Fax: (312) 693 7030
Format: Video
Date released: 1990
Length: 23 minutes
Price: $870 (purchase); $250 (rental); $50 (preview)
Description: This video focuses on internal customer care. It outlines three steps to meeting the needs of internal customers. The first step is to identify who your internal customers are. The next step is to consult them about their needs. Step 3 is serving internal customers as though they were external customers. The video includes a leader's guide and booklets for participants.

Title: At Your Service: Designing and Delivering Top-Notch Customer-Focused Service
Producer: Quality Resources
One Water St.
White Plains, NY 10601
Phone: (914) 761 9600
(800) 247 8519
Fax: (914) 761 9467
Format: Video-Workbook Training Modules
Price: $395 (Trainer's Kit); $39.95 (Participant Kit)
Description: This training system has been developed by two acclaimed service quality experts, Chip Bell and Ron Zemke. *At Your Service* is an interactive workshop that consists of the following six modules: service feedback; service strategy; service delivery; service recovery; service standards; and service challenges. This training system includes trainer's guides, activities, lesson plans, overhead transparencies, and participant workbooks.

Title: Calming Upset Customers
Producer: Crisp Publications
1200 Hamilton Court
Menlo Park, CA 94025
Phone: (800) 442 7477
Fax: (415) 323 5800
Format: Video
Date released: 1993
Length: 19 minutes
Price: $495 (purchase); $150 (rental); $25 (preview)
Description: This video is based on the Crisp Publications book of the same title. The video uses interviews with real frontline employees, managers, and customers to explain why customers get upset, and presents strategies for winning them over. For example, the video advises employees to listen actively, to be sympathetic to customers, and to watch their nonverbal behavior (as well as the customer's body language). The video includes an extensive leader's guide and a copy of the book.

Title: Candid Camera Goes to Work: Expect the Unexpected
Producer: Video Publishing House, Inc.
Four Woodfield Lake
930 National Parkway, Ste. 505
Schaumburg, IL 60173 9921
Phone: (708) 517 8744
(800) 824 8889
Fax: (708) 517 8752
Format: Video
Date released: 1993
Length: 20 minutes
Price: $595 (purchase); $200 (rental); $50 (preview)
Description: This entertaining video uses the format of the *Candid Camera* television program to reinforce the theme that excellent customer service is important. The underlying message is that customer service employees need to be courteous, flexible, and should expect the unexpected.

Title: Candid Camera Goes to Work: Too Close to the Customer
Producer: Video Publishing House, Inc.
Four Woodfield Lake
930 National Parkway, Ste. 505
Schaumburg, IL 60173 9921

Phone: (708) 517 8744
(800) 824 8889
Fax: (708) 517 8752
Format: Video
Date released: 1993
Length: 20 minutes
Price: $595 (purchase); $200 (rental); $50 (preview)
Description: This humorous video uses the format of the *Candid Camera* television program to convey the challenge of providing excellent customer service. The four segments, which use real-life case studies, show the reactions of both customers and customer service employees.

Title: Customer-Driven Service
Producer: AMA (American Management Association)
Video Customer Service Center
9 Galen St., P.O. Box 9119
Watertown, MA 02272 9939
Phone: (617) 926 4600
(800) 225 3215
Fax: (617) 923 1875
Format: Video
Date released: 1993
Length: 50 minutes total (two 25-minute videos)
Price: $975 (purchase); $895 (purchase price for AMA members); $380 (rental); $360 (rental price for AMA members); $645 (purchase of a single tape); $595 (purchase price of a single tape for AMA members)
Description: This training package includes two videos and a leader's guide. The first video, *Achieving a Customer Focus*, uses real-life examples to show managers how to regain a focus on service excellence. The second video, *Becoming a Customer Champion*, uses the inspirational examples of two companies that have superior customer service. These companies are Network Equipment Technologies and Marriott's Camelback Inn. The first has never lost a customer or had a product returned, and the latter is one of only eight resorts to be awarded both the Mobil Five Star and AAA Five Diamond awards.

Title: Customer Service: Or Else!
Producer: Enterprise Media Inc.
91 Harvey St.
Cambridge, MA 02140
Phone: (617) 354 0017
(800) 423 6021
Fax: (617) 365 1637
Format: Video
Date released: 1994
Length: 59 minutes
Price: $795 (purchase); $225 (rental); $40 (preview)
Description: Author and consultant Peter Glen hosts this motivational video on customer service. The production consists of five sections: the customer; bad service; good service; great service; and you (the employee). The video has been designed to allow for discussion breaks between each part. A viewer's guide, which provides tips for trainers, is included.

Title: 50 Ways to Keep Your Customers
Producer: JWA Video
411 S. Sangamon #2 B
Chicago, IL 60607
Phone: (312) 829 5100
Fax: (312) 829 9074
Format: Video
Date released: 1992
Length: 60 minutes
Price: $99.95 (purchase)
Description: This video uses narration and realistic scenarios to dramatize the importance of good customer service. Along with providing a good introduction to the theory of quality customer service, it offers practical advice and tips. Supplementary training materials include a workbook and an audio cassette tape.

Title: Good Old Days of Quality Service
Producer: American Media Inc.
4900 University Ave.
West Des Moines, IA 50266 6769
Phone: (800) 262 2557
Fax: (515) 224 0256
Format: Video
Date released: 1992
Length: 4 minutes
Price: $350 (purchase); $260 (rental)
Description: This fun and fast-moving video uses music and colorful graphics to contrast

old-time quality service with modern-day quality service. The video emphasizes the value of delivering high-quality service. Its purpose is to motivate front-line employees. It could be used to begin a meeting or to stimulate discussion. A discussion guide is included.

Title: No Complaints?
Producer: Video Arts
8614 W. Catalpa Ave.
Chicago, IL 60656
Phone: (312) 693 9966
(800) 553 0091
Fax: (312) 693 7030
Format: Video
Date released: 1994
Length: 56 minutes (total running time)
Price: $870 (purchase price for each part); $250 (rental price for each part); $50 (preview, both parts)
Description: This video consists of two parts: Part 1: Complaints and the Customer, and Part 2: Complaints and Quality Management. The video uses humorous vignettes to show employees how to deal with customer complaints and how to make the complaint process part of a company's quality process. Excellent supplementary materials are included. Video Arts has also produced a Workshop version and a compact disc interactive version of *No Complaints?* Contact Video Arts for further information.

Title: One Ringy Dingy, You Are the Customer
Producer: Mentor Media
1929 Hillhurst Ave.
Los Angeles, CA 90027
Phone: (800) 359 1935
Fax: (213) 667 0029
Format: Video
Date released: 1993
Length: 18 minutes
Price: $860 (purchase); $195 (rental); $49 (preview); $2,800 (price for series of four videos)
Description: Lily Tomlin stars in this humorous training video on the do's and don'ts of telephone customer service. It is part of "Knock the Socks Off Service" video series developed by Performance Research Associates, Inc., the training and consulting firm headed by service quality guru Ron Zemke. A facilitator's guide and a participant's workbook accompany the video. Tomlin also stars in the other exceptional videos in this series: *What Customers Want*; *Dealing with Disappointed Customers*; and *the Seven Deadly Sins of Customer Service*. Each video runs 18 to 21 minutes and includes a facilitator's guide and a participant's workbook. This video series is based on the following books published by AMACOM: *Delivering Knock Your Socks Off Customer Service, Managing Knock Your Socks Off Customer Service*, and *Sustaining Knock Your Socks Off Customer Service*. In September 1994, *Human Resource Executive Magazine* selected this series as one of the top ten training products of the year.

Title: A Passion for Customers
Producer: Video Publishing House, Inc.
Four Woodfield Lake
930 National Parkway, Ste. 505
Schaumburg, IL 60173 9921
Phone: (708) 517 8744
(800) 824 8889
Fax: (708) 517 8752
Format: Video
Date released: 1987
Length: 67 minutes
Price: $795 (purchase); $200 (rental); $50 (preview); $495 (purchase, short cut version); $175 (rental, short cut version); $25 (preview, short cut version)
Description: Tom Peters goes on location to five customer-driven organizations. The companies he profiles that have gained a competitive edge through exceptional customer service are Federal Express, the Limited, Worthington Industries, University National Bank & Trust, and the Louisville Redbirds. A viewer's guide is included. A Spanish language version is available. A 25-minute short cut version is also available.

Title: Service with Soul
Producer: Video Publishing House, Inc.
Four Woodfield Lake
930 National Parkway, Ste. 505
Schaumburg, IL 60173 9921
Phone: (708) 517 8744
(800) 824 8889
Fax: (708) 517 8752

Format: Video
Date released: 1994
Length: 70 minutes
Price: $895 (purchase); $250 (rental); $50 (preview)
Description: This video, hosted by Tom Peters, is the sequel to *A Passion for Customers*. Peters goes on location to five diverse organizations that have exceeded customer's expectations. These organizations are K. Barchetti Shops (a retail fashion business), DeMar Plumbing, NYPRO (a custom plastics molder), Southwest Airlines, and Chicago's Alternative Policing Strategy. Peters compares and contrasts today's customer service expectations to those from a decade ago. A discussion guide is included.

Title: *Stuck on Quality*
Producer: Video Arts
8614 W. Catalpa Ave.
Chicago, IL 60656
Phone: (312) 693 9966
(800) 553 0091
Fax: (312) 693 7030
Format: Video
Date released: 1991
Length: 25 minutes
Price: $870 (purchase); $250 (rental); $50 (preview)
Description: An angry customer is used to dramatize lessons about quality control and customer service. The theme of this video is that customer satisfaction should be the measure of quality performance and that the key to customer focus is employee empowerment. By empowering employees, employees can use their own discretion to focus on what matters to customers.

Title: *10 Steps to Improved Customer Service*
Producer: Alpha Consulting Group
101 First St., Ste. 362
Los Altos, CA 94022
Phone: (415) 949 2322
Format: Video
Date released: 1992
Length: 22 minutes
Price: $545 (purchase); $150 (rental); free previews
Description: This video, one which is appropriate for all employees, uses narration and dramatization to convey the message that improved customer service is important to any company that wants to stay in business. A leader's guide accompanies the video.

Title: *20 Training Workshops for Customer Service, Volume 1*
Producer: Human Resource Development Press
22 Amherst Rd.
Amherst, MA 01002
Phone: (800) 822 2801
Fax: (413) 253 3490
Format: Three-ring binder
Price: $139.95
Description: These ready-to-use training workshops on customer service have been developed by Terry Gillen. Most of the workshops take between two and four hours. Each workshop includes trainer's notes, detailed instructions, transparency masters, and handouts. All materials are fully reproducible. Among the lessons covered are barriers to good service, the customer's point of view, complaints; telephone service; body language, and managing customer service.

Title: *20 Training Workshops for Customer Service, Volume 2*
Producer: Human Resource Development Press
22 Amherst Rd.
Amherst, MA 01002
Phone: (800) 822 2801
Fax: (413) 253 3490
Format: Three-ring binder
Price: $139.95
Description: These ready-to-use training workshops on customer service skills and customer service policy have been developed by Sarah Cook. Among the workshops included are those relating to communication skills, listening skills, letter-writing, handling complaints, dealing with customers by telephone, teamwork, service mission statements, service action plans, establishing standards of service, measuring customer service, staff training, and the internal customer. Most of the workshops take between two and four hours. All materials are fully reproducible.

ISO 9000

Title: A Guide to ISO 9000: A Video Series
Producer: The Media Group, Inc.
18 Blair Park Rd., Ste. 100
Williston, VT 05495
Phone: (802) 879 5403
(800) 678 1003
Fax: (802) 879 2702
Format: Video
Date released: 1994, 1995
Length: 88 minutes (complete set); individual titles in this series range from 12 to 30 minutes in length
Price: $975 (complete set); each video in this series may also be purchased separately, with prices ranging from $129 to $379 per title
Description: This video training series consists of four titles: *ISO 9000, Making Your Company Competitive: A Management Overview*; *Employee Intro to ISO 9000*; *A Practical Guide to Documenting & Implementing ISO 9000*; and *Internal Auditing for ISO 9000*. Each title has been designed as a stand-alone module. The set can be used as part of a comprehensive training course on ISO 9000. The series was developed in cooperation with several corporations, including the Polaroid Corporation, Bull HN Information Systems, HWI Group-Johnson Filaments, Karl Suss, and Powertex. *Employee Intro to ISO 9000* is also available in Spanish.

Title: ISO 9000: The First Step to the Future
Producer: Du Pont Quality Management & Technology
Louviers, 33 W46, P.O. Box 6090
Newark, DE 19714 6090
Phone: (800) 441 8040
Format: Video
Date released: 1991
Price: $495 (purchase)
Description: This video consists of two modules: "ISO 9000: Fact vs. Fiction" and "ISO 9000: Just the Facts". The first module provides an overview while the second module provides information about requirements, registration, and cost. It has been designed as an introduction to the ISO 9000 standards. The video can be used to train employees at all levels of the organization.

Title: Quality in Practice
Producer: BBC Training Videos
Woodlands, 80 Wood Lane, London W12 0TT
Video Publishing House (distributor)
Four Woodfield Lake
930 North National Parkway, Ste. 505
Schaumburg, IL 60173 9921
Phone: (708) 517 8744
(800) 824 8889
Fax: (708) 517 8752
Format: Video
Date released: 1994
Length: 51 minutes
Price: $595 (series purchase); $395 (purchase of individual title); $200 (rental); $50 (preview)
Description: This series includes two titles: *BS 5750* and *Kaizen*. *BS 5750* is a documentary about introducing the quality standard BS 5750. It presents an honest and balanced portrayal of both the problems and benefits related to implementing BS 5750. It features five companies that have achieved their quality goals through implementing BS 5750. The companies profiled are Avis, Ilford, Rover, Revill Industrial Finishes (a small company supplying the electronics industry), and Homewood (a home for adults with learning disabilities). *Kaizen*, a film about a system of continuous quality improvement, has been designed as a companion video.

Title: Understanding ISO 9000 Video Tutorial
Producer: ASQC (American Society for Quality Control)
611 East Wisconsin Ave.
P.O. Box 3005
Milwaukee, WI 53201 3005
Phone: (414) 272 8575
(800) 248 1946
Fax: (414) 272 1734
Format: Video Tutorial
Date released: 1993
Length: 2 hours, 30 minutes (total running time)
Price: $985
Description: This video tutorial, developed by Micron International, introduces organizations to the ISO 9000 standards. The three-tape series includes interviews with consultants,

registrars, and officials from both the American National Standards Institute and British Standards Institute. In addition to the videos, the tutorial includes a reference manual and a *Demonstration Quality System Manual* containing checklists and worksheets.

Leadership and empowerment

Title: Flight of the Buffalo: Soaring to Excellence, Learning to Let Employees Lead
Producer: corVision Media
Enterprise Media Inc. (distributor)
91 Harvey St.
Cambridge, MA 02140
Phone: (617) 354 0017
(800) 423 6021
Fax: (617) 365 1637
Format: Video
Date released: 1994
Length: 31 minutes
Price: $695 (purchase); $150 (rental); $40 (preview)
Description: This video is based on James A. Belasco and Ralph Stayer's bestselling book of the same title. It shows how organizations like Owens & Minor, the Furon Company, and the U.S. Naval Depot in San Diego have empowered employees to share leadership and organizational vision. A leader's guide is included.

Title: The New Partnership:
Managing for Excellence with Tom Melohn
Producer: Enterprise Media Inc.
91 Harvey St.
Cambridge, MA 02140
Phone: (617) 354 0017
(800) 423 6021
Fax: (617) 365 1637
Format: Video
Date released: 1990
Length: 38 minutes
Price: $695 (purchase); $225 (rental); $40 (preview)
Description: This video shows how North American Tool & Die (NATD) used employee empowerment and teamwork to turn the company around. The video includes on-site visits with two of NATD's customers, Apple Computer and NUMMI (a joint venture of Toyota and General Motors). Employee empowerment and teamwork helped NATD build relationships with their customers. This award-winning video won a Red Ribbon at the American Film & Video Festival and a Finalist Award at the New York International Film Festival. A workbook is included.

Title: The New Workplace
Producer: Quality Media Resources
10929 South East 23rd St.
Bellevue, WA 98004
Phone: (800) 800 5129
Fax: (206) 462 7087
Format: Video
Date released: 1993
Length: 46 minutes total (two videos, 23 minutes each)
Price: $795 (purchase); $250 (rental); $30 (preview); $525 (purchase of a single tape); $150 (rental of a single tape)
Description: This two-part video uses narration and interviews to discuss changes in the workplace, including teamwork, facilitative management, employee empowerment, and the changing role of unions. It has been designed as a training tool for all employees and managers. One of the videos is directed to employees and the other is designed for managers. The latter video is appropriate for all managers, especially supervisors and middle managers, and includes a facilitator's guide. This guide contains helpful handouts, individual and group activities, and a detailed bibliography.

Title: Total Quality Management and Employee Empowerment: The Ritz-Carlton's Success Story
Producer: CHRIE (Council on Hotel, Restaurant, and Institutional Education)
1200 17th St., N.W.
Washington, DC 20036 3097
Phone: (202) 331 5990
Fax: (202) 785 2511
Format: Video
Date released: 1993
Length: 75 minutes
Price: $29 (purchase)
Description: This is a videotape of one of the general sessions of the 1993 annual CHRIE

Conference. The Ritz-Carlton Company was the recipient of the 1990 Malcolm Baldrige Award. In fact, it was the first time that a company in the hospitality industry has received this prestigious award. In this video, three Ritz-Carlton executives share their insights about their firm's quality efforts.

Title: *Zapp! The Lightning of Empowerment*
Producer: Development Dimensions International
Video Publishing House (distributor)
Four Woodfield Lake
930 North National Parkway, Ste. 505
Schaumburg, IL 60173 9921
Phone: (708) 517 8744
(800) 824 8889
Fax: (708) 517 8752
Format: Video
Date released: 1992
Length: 26 minutes
Price: $895 (purchase); $250 (rental); $50 (preview)
Description: This video is based on William C. Byham's bestselling book with the same title. The goal of the video is to help managers understand how empowerment improves quality, productivity, and service. A leader's guide is included.

Quality

Title: *Continuous Quality Improvement: A New Look for Education*
Producer: ASQC (American Society for Quality Control)
611 East Wisconsin Ave.
P.O. Box 3005
Milwaukee, WI 53201 3005
Phone: (414) 272 8575
(800) 248 1946
Fax: (414) 272 1734
Format: Video
Date released: 1992
Length: 23 minutes
Price: $49.95 (purchase)
Description: This video was a joint production of the American Association of School Administrators and ASQC. Using interviews with school officials, it examines quality improvement programs in four school districts

and one vocational-technical school. The programs profiled include those in the Kyrene School District (Phoenix), the Kenmore/Tonawanda School District (New York), the Beloit Turner School District (Wisconsin), the Eden Prairie School District (Minnesota), and the George Westinghouse Vocational-Technical School in Brooklyn.

Title: *The Customer is Always Dwight*
Producer: Video Arts
8614 W. Catalpa Ave.
Chicago, IL 60656
Phone: (312) 693 9966
(800) 553 0091
Fax: (312) 693 7030
Format: Video
Date released: 1989
Length: 21 minutes
Price: $870 (purchase); $250 (rental); $50 (preview)
Description: This video features John Cleese, the cofounder of Video Arts. Video Arts, a twenty-million-dollar a year business, is one of the largest producers of business-training films. Video Arts films are used by more than 100,000 organizations around the world. The major theme of *The Customer is Always Dwight* is that in order to achieve 100 percent quality, companies need to identify their internal and external customers, find out what their needs are, and look at processes and improve the way they work. The video could be used as part of an organization-wide training program on quality or could be used for training sessions on process management, team-building, and internal customer care.

Title: *The Deming Videotapes*
Producer: The Massachusetts Institute of Technology Center for Advanced Engineering Study
Video Publishing House (distributor)
Four Woodfield Lake
930 North National Parkway, Ste. 505
Schaumburg, IL 60173 9921
Phone: (708) 517 8744
(800) 824 8889
Fax: (708) 517 8752

Format: Video

Date released: 1991

Length: 179 minutes (total running time for four videos)

Price: $975 (purchase); $50 (preview)

Description: This series of videos introduces employees in both manufacturing and service organizations to the philosophy of the late Dr. Deming. Tape One covers Deming's early years and outlines his views on the way systems can be improved. Tape Two covers Deming's Fourteen Points for management. The third tape covers the history, purpose, and use of control charts; Deming's perspectives on training and supervision; and Deming's list of obstacles to organizational change. Tape Four looks at the relationship between quality, productivity, and customer input. A program guide is included as well as a copy of Deming's book *Out of the Crisis.*

Title: Implementing TQM in Health Care Videotape Series

Producer: GOAL/QPC
13 Branch St.
Methuen, MA 01844 1953
Phone: (508) 685 6370
(800) 643 4316
Fax: (508) 685 6151

Format: Video

Date released: 1992

Length: 63 minutes (total running time for four videos)

Price: $350 (series purchase); $150 (series preview); $245 (purchase of individual title); $50 (preview of individual title)

Description: This series includes an introductory tape and four case study videotapes. The individual titles include: *SSM Healthcare Systems: The TQM Decision*; *Bethesda Hospital: Customer Focus Through QFD*; *University of Michigan Hospital Teams*; and *Our Lady of Lourdes Medical Center Hoshin Planning.* The package includes one copy of *Putting the "T" in Health Care TQM,* GOAL/QPC's two-year study of TQM in health care, based on the experiences of the University of Michigan Medical Center, Intermountain Health Care, and Park Nicollet Medical Center.

Title: In Search of Excellence

Producer: A Nathan/Tyler Production
Video Arts (distributor)
8614 W. Catalpa Ave.
Chicago, IL 60656
Phone: (312) 693 9966
(800) 553 0091
Fax: (312) 693 7030

Format: Video

Date released: 1986

Length: 90 minutes

Price: $690 (purchase); $270 (rental); $50 (preview)

Description: This award winning video has been used by more than 16,000 companies around the world. It is based on Tom Peters and Bob Waterman's bestselling book, *In Search of Excellence.* It uses case studies of companies committed to quality and customer service. The companies profiled include Disney World, Apple Computers, 3M, the Dana Corporation, North American Tool & Die, McDonald's, and IBM.

Title: In Search of Quality Series

Producer: Enterprise Media Inc.
91 Harvey St.
Cambridge, MA 02140
Phone: (617) 354 0017
(800) 423 6021
Fax: (617) 365 1637

Format: Video

Date released: 1991

Length: 130 minutes (total running time for four videos)

Price: $1,390 (series purchase); $400 (series rental); $40 (series preview); $795 (purchase of individual title); $25 (rental of individual title)

Description: This series, which has received both a Gold Apple Award and a Silver Cindy, is hosted by Robert H. Waterman, Jr., coauthor of *In Search of Excellence.* It uses real-life examples to demonstrate how implementing Malcolm Baldrige Award criteria can lead to quality results. The series consists of the following two parts: *Quality Through People: The Wallace Company* and *Quality through Systems: Motorola and the Goal of Six Sigma. Quality Through People* shows how Baldrige criteria, teamwork, and employee empowerment turned the Wallace company around. *Quality Through Systems* shows how Motorola's five-year quality goal, Six sigma, has resulted in reduced cycle time and non-zero defect quality. Both parts include an action guide and workbook.

Title: *Just Change It!: Creating a Government That Works*
Producer: Video Publishing House, Inc.
Four Woodfield Lake
930 National Parkway, Ste. 505
Schaumburg, IL 60173 9921
Phone: (708) 517 8744
(800) 824 8889
Fax: (708) 517 8752
Format: Video
Date released: 1994
Length: 42 minutes
Price: $695 (purchase); $200 (rental); $50 (preview)
Description: This motivational video featuring Ted Gaebler, the coauthor of *Reinventing Government: How the Entrepreneurial Spirit is Transforming the Public Sector*, encourages government employees to take charge and change government from within. Gaebler encourages a shift from bureaucratic thinking to entrepreneurial government. A discussion guide is included.

Title: *Leading the Nation* series
Producer: Enterprise Media Inc.
91 Harvey St.
Cambridge, MA 02140
Phone: (617) 354 0017
(800) 423 6021
Fax: (617) 365 1637
Format: Video
Date released: 1992
Length: 51 minutes (total running time for two videos)
Price: $990 (series purchase); $450 (series rental); $40 (series preview); $595 (purchase of individual title); $225 (rental of individual title)
Description: This series focuses on quality in the public sector. It consists of the following two videos: *Team-Based Quality* and *Customer-Driven Quality*. *Team-Based Quality* looks at how the Sacramento Air Force

Logistics Center used teamwork to win the Federal Quality Improvement Prototype Award. *Customer-Driven Quality* looks at how the Fresno IRS (Internal Revenue Service) Center shifted its focus to internal and external customer service in order to improve quality. The IRS initiated a nationwide total quality management program in 1985. Both videos include a facilitator's guide.

Title: *Managing Performance for Quality*
Producer: Longman Productions
CRM Films (distributor)
2215 Faraday Ave.
Carlsbad, CA 92008 7214
Phone: (800) 421 0833
Fax: (619) 931 5792
Format: Video
Date released: 1993
Length: 30 minutes
Price: $645 (purchase); $225 (rental); free preview
Description: A scenario involving a research and development quality team at a high-tech manufacturing company is used to convey the message that a product must meet customer's needs.

Title: *A Passion for Excellence*
Producer: Video Publishing House, Inc.
Four Woodfield Lake
930 National Parkway, Ste. 505
Schaumburg, IL 60173 9921
Phone: (708) 517 8744
(800) 824 8889
Fax: (708) 517 8752
Format: Video
Date released: 1985
Length: 63 minutes
Price: $795 (purchase); $200 (rental); $50 (preview); $495 (purchase, short cut version); $175 (rental, short cut version); $25 (preview, short cut version)
Description: This video, hosted by Tom Peters, draws upon his book *In Search of Excellence*. Peters explains how organizations in fast food, travel, retailing, and public service have gained a competitive edge through excellence. A viewer's guide is included. A 25-minute short cut version is also available.

Title: Prescription for Change: Total Quality in Health Care
Producer: Enterprise Media Inc.
  91 Harvey St.
  Cambridge, MA 02140
  Phone: (617) 354 0017
     (800) 423 6021
  Fax: (617) 365 1637
Format: Video
Date released: 1992
Length: 29 minutes
Price: $595 (purchase); $225 (rental); $40 (preview)
Description: The major theme of this video is learning how to control costs and learning how to treat patients as customers while improving quality of care. It uses Baptist Memorial Hospital in Memphis as a case study. This hospital implemented a continuous quality improvement program in 1989, a process that has increased the quality of care in this organization. A facilitator's guide is included.

Title: Quality in the Office
Producer: AMA (American Management Association)
  Video Customer Service Center
  9 Galen St., P.O. Box 9119
  Watertown, MA 02272 9939
  Phone: (617) 926 4600
     (800) 225 3215
  Fax: (617) 923 1875
Format: Video
Date released: 1992
Length: 20 minutes
Price: $695 (purchase); $645 (purchase price for AMA members); $190 (rental); $180 (rental price for AMA members)
Description: This video can be particularly helpful for firms introducing quality efforts into nonmanufacturing areas. Quality expert John Guaspari explains how quality principles can be applied to office functions. He uses the example of Hutchinson Technology, Inc. which shortened a procedure from three weeks to three days. A leader's guide accompanies the video.

Title: Quality Management Report

Producer: ASQC (American Society for Quality Control)
  611 East Wisconsin Ave.
  P.O. Box 3005
  Milwaukee, WI 53201 3005
  Phone: (414) 272 8575
     (800) 248 1946
  Fax: (414) 272 1734
Format: Video Magazine Subscription
Frequency: Six issues per year
Price: $2, 295
Description: This is the first video magazine subscription in the area of quality management. It is a joint venture of the American Society for Quality Control, the Center for Video Education, and the Juran Institute. Each issue presents up-to-date information about quality advances in specific industries, benchmarking, strategic quality planning, and other headline stories. Participant workbooks and a leader's guide accompany each hour-long video. This series has been designed for human resource directors, corporate trainers, quality project team managers, managers, CEOs, and other quality professionals.

Title: Quality Minutes
Producer: Center for Video Education
  Juran Institute, Inc. (distributor)
  P.O. Box 811
  11 River Rd.
  Wilton, CT 06897 0811
  Phone: (203) 834 1700
  Fax: (203) 834 9891
Format: Video Subscription Series
Price: $1,200 (52 issues per year)
Description: This video subscription series was selected as one of the best training products of 1994 by *Human Resource Executive* magazine. Each month, subscribers receive a video containing four or five segments running 90 seconds each. They also receive a quarterly segment running three to four minutes each. The videos use real-life case studies that reinforce key concepts in quality. Besides being excellent discussion starters, the segments can introduce others (such as vendors and suppliers) to the major principles of quality management. This timely series also lets companies find out how others are managing quality.

Title: Reinventing Government
Producer: Video Publishing House, Inc.
Four Woodfield Lake
930 National Parkway, Ste. 505
Schaumburg, IL 60173 9921
Phone: (708) 517 8744
(800) 824 8889
Fax: (708) 517 8752
Format: Video
Length: 60 minutes
Price: $895 (purchase); $375 (rental); $50 (preview)
Description: This video is hosted by David Osborne and Ted Gaebler, authors of the best-selling book *Reinventing Government: How the Entrepreneurial Spirit is Transforming the Public Sector.* The authors go on location to four diverse organizations that have improved services, cut costs, or empowered employees while achieving excellence. The organizations profiled are the Minnesota public schools, the Langley Air Force Base, the city of Indianapolis, and Chicago's Cabrini Green housing. A user's guide is included.

Title: Revitalizing Your Company: Creative Ways to Build Profits
Producer: Community Television Foundation of South Florida (a special edition of PBS's "Nightly Business Report")
Enterprise Media, Inc. (distributor)
91 Harvey St.
Cambridge, MA 02140
Phone: (617) 354 0017
(800) 423 6021
Fax: (617) 365 1637
Format: Video
Date released: 1994
Price: $695 (purchase); $225 (rental); $40 (preview)
Description: This video goes on location to AT & T, Tenneco, and 3M and shows how these companies used reengineering, restructuring, horizontal management, team accountability, and employee empowerment to increase customer satisfaction, encourage entrepreneurship, and reward employees. A viewer's guide is included.

Title: Time: The Next Dimension of Quality
Producer: AMA (American Management Association)
Video Customer Service Center
9 Galen St., P.O. Box 9119
Watertown, MA 02272 9939
Phone: (617) 926 4600
(800) 225 3215
Fax: (617) 923 1875
Format: Video
Date released: 1993
Length: 18 minutes
Price: $745 (purchase); $695 (purchase price for AMA members); $190 (rental); $180 (rental price for AMA members)
Description: This video uses interviews with well-known quality consultants John Guaspari and Edward Hay to explain the concept of value-added time. By eliminating steps that do not add value, companies can save time, serve customers better, and achieve higher levels of quality. A leader's guide accompanies this award-winning video. This video was awarded third place in the U.S. International Film and Video Festival and was a finalist in The New York Festivals.

Title: Total Quality Management in Education Videotape Series
Producer: GOAL/QPC
13 Branch St.
Methuen, MA 01844 1953
Phone: (508) 685 6370
(800) 643 4316
Fax: (508) 685 6151
Format: Video integrated training package
Price: $2,495 (purchase of complete package)
Description: This package includes the following: fourteen videotapes, facilitator guides, participant guides, overhead transparencies, copies of *The Memory Jogger for Education*, a copy of *The Educator's Companion to the Memory Jogger Plus* and "GOAL/QPC Research Reports" related to the topics covered in this workshop. The goal of this workshop is to help educational administrators implement TQM in the K-12 school systems. The package consists of two series: *Awareness*, which introduces educators to the theories and tools of TQM, and *Getting Started*, which guides participants through the

beginning stages of a TQM implementation program. The videotapes included interviews with educators from twenty-five urban, suburban, and rural school districts that have successfully used TQM to improve their schools. Each series may be purchased separately. It is also possible to purchase individual tapes. Contact GOAL/QPC directly for further information.

Title: *Total Quality Management in State and Local Government Videotape*
Producer: GOAL/QPC
13 Branch St.
Methuen, MA 01844 1953
Phone: (508) 685 6370
(800) 643 4316
Fax: (508) 685 6151
Format: Video
Date released: 1993
Length: 27 minutes
Price: $495 (purchase); $50 (preview)
Description: This video features government workers who are using TQM. Government officials and employees talk about process improvement, cross-functional teams, customer orientation, leadership, training, and data-based decision-making. A viewer's guide is included.

Title: *TQM for Small Business*
Producer: ASQC (American Society for Quality Control)
611 East Wisconsin Ave.
P.O. Box 3005
Milwaukee, WI 53201 3005
Phone: (414) 272 8575
(800) 248 1946
Fax: (414) 272 1734
Format: Video workshop
Date released: 1993
Length: 1 hour, 45 minutes
Price: $249
Description: This video workshop on implementing TQM in small business includes one video with five training sessions and one 83-page workbook. The training sessions are to be viewed once per week for five weeks. Weekly exercises are included. These exercises, which range from three to four per session, can be completed by individuals or teams.

Title: *The Total Quality Service Model*
Producer: Karl Albrecht & Associates
4320 La Jolla Village Dr., Ste. 310
San Diego, CA 92122 1204
Phone: (619) 622 4884
Fax: (619) 622 4885
Length: 13 minutes
Price: $295 (purchase); $95 (rental); $45 (preview)
Description: This video focuses on the five steps of total quality service outlined by management consultant Karl Albrecht. It uses interviews with managers, supervisors, and employees to clarify each step. This introductory video to the total quality approach would work well in small groups or as a discussion starter. A leader's guide is included.

Title: *Total Service: The Fizzle Factor*
Producer: Karl Albrecht & Associates
4320 La Jolla Village Dr., Ste. 310
San Diego, CA 92122 1204
Phone: (619) 622 4884
Fax: (619) 622 4885
Format: Video
Date released: 1992
Length: 17 minutes
Price: $295 (purchase); $95 (rental); $45 (preview)
Description: This video, based on the ideas of management consultant Karl Albrecht, outlines six common problems associated with the implementation of a quality service program. It is directed to managers and supervisors. A leader's guide accompanies the video.

Title: *The Trust Factor*
Producer: Quality Learning Services, U.S. Chamber of Commerce
1615 H St., N. W.
Washington, DC 20062 2000
Phone: (800) 835 4730
Format: Video
Date released: 1994
Length: 2 hours
Price: $179 (purchase)
Description: The message in this video is that mistrust is the underlying cause of inefficiency in business. Because of mistrust, companies adopt an extensive number of procedures that double the cost of doing business.

Title: *What America Does Right*
Producer: Enterprise Media Inc.
91 Harvey St.
Cambridge, MA 02140
Phone: (617) 354 0017
(800) 423 6021
Fax: (617) 365 1637
Format: Video
Date released: 1995
Length: 60 minutes total (two videos, 30 minutes each)
Price: $795 (purchase price for each video); $1, 390 (purchase price for series); $225 (rental price for each video); $425 (rental price for series); $40 (preview, series)
Description: This two-part video series is a sequel to *In Search Of Excellence*. It is based on Robert Waterman's recent book, *What America Does Right*. The first part, "Management Turned Upside Down," explores how horizontal management, cross-functional teams, and reengineering can help organizations manage change. It features on-location visits with Sun Microsystems, Raychem Corporation, and The Career Action Center, a nonprofit organization located in Palo Alto, California. Part 2, "Organization is Strategic," shows how organizational arrangements can motivate employees. Two companies are profiled: Merck (the pharmaceutical giant), and AES Corporation (an independent power provider with headquarters in Arlington, Virginia). The series includes a training guide.

Title: *Winning Through Baldrige*
Producer: Video Arts
8614 W. Catalpa Ave.
Chicago, IL 60656
Phone: (312) 693 9966
(800) 553 0091
Fax: (312) 693 7030
Format: Video
Date released: 1992
Length: 45 minutes
Price: $830 (purchase); $230 (rental)
Description: This video shows how the implementation of a quality program helped GTE, AT & T, Avis, Southeastern Freight lines, and Cateraire International to improve customer satisfaction, employee involvement, and corporate leadership.

Reengineering

Title: *The Reengineering Roadmap: A How-To Approach*
Producer: AMA   (American   Management Association)
Video Customer Service Center
9 Galen St., P.O. Box 9119
Watertown, MA 02272 9939
Phone: (617) 926 4600
(800) 225 3215
Fax: (617) 923 1875
Format: Video
Date released: 1994
Length: 60 minutes
Price: $995 (purchase); $895 (rental price for AMA members); $190 (rental); $180 (rental price for AMA members
Description: This video, based on Raymond L. Manganelli and Mark M. Klein's book, *The Reengineering Handbook*, discusses the steps involved in the reengineering process. The reengineering efforts of the Polaroid Corporation, AT & T Capital Leasing Services, and Grace Logistics Services, Inc., a subsidiary of W. R. Grace, are profiled. This practical video can be used to educate employers throughout an organization. A leader's guide is included. The AMA recommends that their companion video, *Reengineering the Future*, be viewed before this video.

Title: *Reengineering the Future*
Producer: AMA   (American   Management Association)
Video Customer Service Center
9 Galen St., P.O. Box 9119
Watertown, MA 02272 9939
Phone: (617) 926 4600
(800) 225 3215
Fax: (617) 923 1875
Format: Video
Date released: 1994
Length: 20 minutes
Price: $695 (purchase); $645 (purchase price for AMA members); $190 (rental); $180 (rental price for AMA members); $50 (preview)
Description: This video introduces the concept of reengineering, explaining how it differs from other management approaches. Raymond L. Manganelli,   a   reengineering   consultant,

outlines both the benefits and problems associated with reengineering efforts. This award winning video was a finalist in The New York Festivals. The AMA recommends this film as a prerequisite for their video *The Reengineering Roadmap: A How-To Approach.*

Team building

Title: The Abilene Paradox
Producer: CRM Films
2215 Faraday Ave.
Carlsbad, CA 92008 7214
Phone: (800) 421 0833
Fax: (619) 931 5792
Format: Video
Date released: 1984
Length: 28 minutes
Price: $745 (purchase); $195 (rental); free preview
Description: This video dealing with group consensus has become a classic. It has been used during team training by a wide range of organizations.

Title: America3: The Power to Create
Producer: Enterprise Media Inc.
91 Harvey St.
Cambridge, MA 02140
Phone: (617) 354 0017
(800) 423 6021
Fax: (617) 365 1637
Format: Video
Date released: 1993
Length: 26 minutes
Price: $795 (purchase); $225 (rental); $440 (preview)
Description: This motivational video uses the example of the victory by *America3* in the 1992 America's Cup to demonstrate the importance of teamwork. It could be used as an effective meeting opener with all levels of employees.

Title: Building Blocks for Team Performance: How to Develop Top Performers
Producer: Audio Video Campus
7825 Fay Ave., Ste. 200
La Jolla, CA 92037
Phone: (800) 235 3288
Fax: (619) 456 5207
Format: Video

Date released: 1992
Length: 25 minutes
Price: $295 (purchase); $120 (rental); $65 (preview)
Description: This video, which is directed to managers and front-line supervisors, focuses on the role of managers in developing high-performing teams. The theme is that managers need to take more responsibility for developing the skills of their employees.

Title: Deming Quality: The Right Medicine
Producer: Coronet/MTI
108 Wilmot Rd.
Deerfield, IL 60015
Phone: (800) 621 2131
Fax: (708) 940 3600
Format: Video
Date released: 1993
Length: 18 minutes
Price: $495 (purchase); $125 (rental); $35 (preview)
Description: This video uses case studies of West Paces Hospital and Hospital Corporation of America to demonstrate how teams can improve processes.

Title: The Facilitator's Toolkit: Tools and Techniques for Generating Ideas and Making Decisions in Groups
Producer: Human Resource Development Press
22 Amherst Rd.
Amherst, MA 01002
Phone: (800) 822 2801
Fax: (413) 253 3490
Format: Three-ring binder
Price: $95
Description: This toolkit, developed by Lynn Kearny, an experienced trainer, includes forty-nine fully reproducible tools and activities for team decision-making. These tools include the following: brainstorming; data dump; force-field analysis; Gantt Chart; idea weaving; manipulative verbs; prioritization matrix; and upward delegation. A user's guide helps you select the most appropriate tools given your group's needs, level of experience, and time constraints.

Title: Faultless Facilitation: A Resource Guide for Group and Team Leaders
Producer: Human Resource Development Press
22 Amherst Rd.
Amherst, MA 01002
Phone: (800) 822 2801
Fax: (413) 253 3490
Format: Three-ring binder
Price: $49.95
Description: This guide, authored by Lois B. Hart, can be used alone as a self-study manual on facilitating groups or together with Hart's companion volume *Faultless Facilitation: An Instructor's Manual for Facilitation Training*. It is particularly useful to new facilitators. Participant materials may be reproduced.

Title: Faultless Facilitation: An Instructor's Manual for Facilitation Training
Producer: Human Resource Development Press
22 Amherst Rd.
Amherst, MA 01002
Phone: (800) 822 2801
Fax: (413) 253 3490
Format: Three-ring binder
Price: $99.95
Description: This manual provides information, activities, and exercises for trainers who are teaching others to facilitate. It has been written by Lois B. Hart, a noted consultant and trainer who studied under Kenneth Blanchard, the coauthor of the bestselling book the *One Minute Manager*. This manual can be used together with Hart's companion volume *Faultless Facilitation: A Resource Guide for Group and Team Players*. All participant materials are fully reproducible.

Title: 50 Activities for Self-Directed Teams
Producer: Human Resource Development Press
22 Amherst Rd.
Amherst, MA 01002
Phone: (800) 822 2801
Fax: (413) 253 3490
Format: Three-ring binder
Price: $139.95
Description: This collection of training activities, developed by consultants Glenn M. Parker and Richard P. Kropp, Jr., cover all aspects of team development. Each activity takes between thirty minutes and three hours. All of the

questionnaires, exercises, and handouts are fully reproducible.

Title: 50 Activities for Team Building, Volume 1
Producer: Human Resource Development Press
22 Amherst Rd.
Amherst, MA 01002
Phone: (800) 822 2801
Fax: (413) 253 3490
Format: Three-ring binder
Price: $139.95
Description: This collection of activities, developed by consultants Glenn Parker and Richard P. Kropp, Jr., covers the following topics: team effectiveness; conflict resolution; problem-solving; decision-making; group skills; team communication; and team leadership. Activities take between thirty minutes and eight hours. All of the exercises are fully reproducible.

Title: 50 Activities for Team Building, Volume 2
Producer: Human Resource Development Press
22 Amherst Rd.
Amherst, MA 01002
Phone: (800) 822 2801
Fax: (413) 253 3490
Format: Three-ring binder
Price: $139.95
Description: This collection of activities, developed by Mike Woodcock, covers the following topics relating to team development: creating balanced team roles; establishing common objectives; improving interpersonal communication; developing support, trust, and cooperation; handling conflict; and developing leadership. Each activity takes between one and four hours. All of the exercises are fully reproducible.

Title: Lessons in Teamwork: Computer-Based Training Modules
Producer: Human Resource Development Press
22 Amherst Rd.
Amherst, MA 01002
Phone: (800) 822 2801
Fax: (413) 253 3490
Format: Computer-based training program
Requirements: IBM-compatible computer, 386 or higher; 640K Ram; DOS 3.1 or higher; hard drive; VGA monitor; mouse is optional.

Price: $95

Description: This software program, developed by Kimberly Mullins, includes more than two and a half hours of self-paced instruction with exercises and interactive feedback. The following eight lessons are included: What is a team?; What makes a team effective?; evaluating and rewarding success; motivation and commitment; team roles; effective communication; conflict resolution; and participative management. A paperback book accompanies the 3½" disk.

Title: *Keeping Teams Together*
Producer: AMA (American Management Association)
Video Customer Service Center
9 Galen St., P.O. Box 9119
Watertown, MA 02272 9939
Phone: (617) 926 4600
(800) 225 3215
Fax: (617) 923 1875
Format: Video
Date released: 1993
Length: 30 minutes
Price: $89.95 (purchase); $80.96 (purchase price for AMA members)
Description: Using the analogy of a jazz quartet, this video demonstrates how teams can maintain their cohesion even when team members disagree. In fact, according to this video, the team can use these differences of opinion to its advantage. This video was awarded a Silver Medal by the Association of Visual Communicators.

Title: *Making TQM Work: The Human Factor*
Producer: Society for Human Resource Management (SHRM)
606 N. Washington St.
Alexandria, VA 22314 1997
Phone: (703) 548 3440
(800) 283 7476
Fax: (703) 836 0367
Format: Video-integrated workbook program
Price: $695 (purchase); $595 (purchase price for SHRM members); $50 (rental); no preview
Description: This video-workbook program shows how TQM has been successfully implemented in both manufacturing and service industries. It looks at the successes of past Malcolm Baldrige winners and organizations such as Saturn, Motorola, and The New England.

Title: *Straight Talk on Teams*
Producer: Coronet/MTI Film & Video
108 Wilmot Rd.
Deerfield, IL 60015
Phone: (800) 621 2131
Fax: (708) 940 3600
Format: Video
Date released: 1992
Length: 85 minutes
Price: $1,495 (purchase of series)
Description: This four-part video series is based on Allan Cox's book *Straight Talk for Monday Morning*. The four parts include: *Building a Foundation for Powerful Teams*; *Recognizing Values*; *Managing Conflict*; and *Getting the Most Out of Your Team*. Each video includes a workbook.

Title: *Team Building Blocks: Practicing Group Collaboration*
Producer: Human Resource Development Press
22 Amherst Rd.
Amherst, MA 01002
Phone: (800) 822 2801
Fax: (413) 253 3490
Format: Game
Price: $139.95 (complete game); $49.95 (additional set of blocks)
Description: This game, developed by Carmine Consalvo, uses a set of fourteen wooden blocks to build team skills such as problem-solving, consensus building, and resolution of differences. The game comes with an activity manual including detailed exercises.

Title: *Team Player*
Producer: American Media Inc.
4900 University Ave.
West Des Moines, IA 50266 6769
Phone: (800) 262 2557
Fax: (515) 224 0256
Format: Video
Date released: 1992
Length: 21 minutes
Price: $650 (purchase); $175 (rental); $40 (preview)
Description: This video uses the realistic example of a problem in a claims processing

department to illustrate the need for teamwork. When the supervisor in this department discusses that there have been repeated problems with callbacks, teamwork is encouraged to solve this problem. The video is accompanied by materials for conducting a workshop on improving teamwork. These supplementary materials include handouts, worksheets, a leader's guide, and a package of building blocks.

Title: *Teams for Excellence*
Producer: Technicomp
    1111 Chester Ave.
    300 Park Plaza
    Cleveland, OH 44114
    Phone: (216) 687 1122
    Fax: (216) 687 0637
Format: Video
Date released: 1991
Length: 270 minutes (total for ten tapes)
Price: $4,377 (purchase); $2,475 (purchase price for five module version); no rental; no preview
Description: This ten tape series uses narration, interviews, and real-life discussions with teams to teach the basics of teamwork. The series has been designed for multi-session team training. The following topics are covered in these ten modules: an introduction to teamwork; the development of a team; roles of team members; conducting effective meetings; types of teams; technical requirements of teams; decision-making; the importance of interpersonal skills; handling problems; and achieving team excellence. Extensive supplementary materials are provided, including guides for instructors, transparencies, exercises, a facilitator's handbook, and a participant's guide.

Title: *Win Teams*
Producer: Video Visions
    4508 Richard Dr.
    Los Angeles, CA 90032
    Phone: (213) 227 1022
Format: Video
Date released: 1994
Length: 23 minutes
Price: $595 (purchase); $140 (rental); $35 (preview)
Description: This video demonstrates how teams and employee involvement turned around

General Electric's mobile-communications plant in Lynchburg, Virginia. The plant had been losing money and General Electric intended to sell or close it. According to the video, more than thirty teams were responsible for ideas and problem-solving solutions that saved the plant more than seven million dollars in the first year that the team structure was adopted.

Title: *Workplace Teams*
Producer: AMA (American Management Association)
    Video Customer Service Center
    9 Galen St., P.O. Box 9119
    Watertown, MA 02272 9939
    Phone: (617) 926 4600
          (800) 225 3215
    Fax: (617) 923 1875
Format: Video
Date released: 1992
Length: 55 minutes total
Price: $975 (purchase); $895 (purchase price for AMA members); $645 purchase price for individual videos); $595 (AMA member purchase price for individual videos); $380 (rental); $360 (rental for AMA members)
Description: This video consists of two videos: *Building Successful Teams* and *Helping Your Team Succeed*. It uses real-life examples from General Electric and Litton Industries. A leader's guide is included. This award-winning video was the recipient of a Gold Medal at the International Film and TV Festival of New York.

Title: *Workteams and the Wizard of Oz*
Producer: CRM Films
    2215 Faraday Ave.
    Carlsbad, CA 92008 7214
    Phone: (800) 421 0833
    Fax: (619) 931 5792
Format: Video
Date released: 1993
Length: 13 minutes
Price: $595 (purchase); $195 (rental); free preview
Description: This video uses clips from the movie *The Wizard of Oz* to illustrate teamwork. The video is accompanied by a leader's guide. Participant workbooks are also available.

Tools for continuous improvement

Title: Basic Tools for Quality & Process Improvement Videotape series
Producer: GOAL/QPC
13 Branch St.
Methuen, MA 01844 1953
Phone: (508) 685 6370
(800) 643 4316
Fax: (508) 685 6151
Format: Video
Date released: 1994
Length: 50 minutes (total running time for four videos)
Price: $1,595 (series Purchase); $150 (series preview); $495 purchase of individual title); $50 (preview of individual title)
Description: This series covers the most commonly used quality control tools. The following titles are included in the series: *Checksheet and Pareto Chart*; *Flowchart Run Chart*, and *Cause & Effect Diagram*. The package includes a facilitator's guide and participant guides.

Title: Integrated Management & Planning Tools: A Company Case Study Videotape
Producer: Amatulli & Associates with Michael Brassard GOAL/QPC (distributor)
13 Branch St.
Methuen, MA 01844 1953
Phone: (508) 685 6370
(800) 643 4316
Fax: (508) 685 6151
Format: Video
Date released: 1994
Length: 45 minutes
Price: $795 (purchase); $50 (preview)
Description: This video features a case study of a fictional uniform rental company using the "Seven Management and Planning Tools." Ten viewer's guides are included. This video could be used in combination with The Memory Jogger+ Videotape series.

Title: The Memory Jogger Plus+ Videotape series
Producer: GOAL/QPC
13 Branch St.
Methuen, MA 01844 1953
Phone: (508) 685 6370
(800) 643 4316
Fax: (508) 685 6151

Format: Video
Date released: 1993
Length: 3½ hours (approximate total running time); individual titles in series range from 19 to 33 minutes
Price: $2,995 (purchase of series); $495 (purchase of individual tapes); $150 (preview, series); $50 (preview, individual tape)
Description: This series includes an introductory videotape and seven individual videotapes designed to teach employees how to use the following management and planning tools: affinity diagram; interrelationship diagraph; activity network diagram; matrix diagram; prioritization matrices; tree diagram; process decision; and program chart. The package includes one facilitator guide, twenty participant guides, and twenty sets of pocket cards.

Title: Tools for Continual Improvement, Video Training Modules, series 1
Producer: Executive Learning, Inc.
7101 Executive Center Dr., Ste. 160
Brentwood, TN 37027
Phone: (615) 373 8483
(800) 929 7890
Fax: (615) 373 8635
Format: Video training modules
Price: $1,675 (purchase of five video set); $395 (price for each video if purchased separately)
Description: This training module covers specific continual improvement tools. This series includes the following five modules: the flowchart; the cause-and-effect diagram; team meeting skills; idea generating tools; and consensus decision-making tools. Each module includes a videotape, trainer's notes, wall charts, pocket reference cards, and flowchart templates. This module can be used for individual tutorials, team training, or in training courses.

Title: Tools for Continual Improvement: Video Training Modules, series 2
Producer: Executive Learning, Inc.
7101 Executive Center Dr., Ste. 160
Brentwood, TN 37027
Phone: (615) 373 8483
(800) 929 7890
Fax: (615) 373 8635
Format: Video training modules

Price: $995 (purchase of three video set); $395 (price for each video if purchased separately)

Description: This training module covers the following skills for continual improvement: Pareto analysis; planning for data collection; and data collection methods. Each module includes a videotape, trainer's notes, wall charts, and pocket reference guides.

Title: *Tools for Quality Improvement*
Producer: AMA (American Management Association)

Video Customer Service Center
9 Galen St., P.O. Box 9119
Watertown, MA 02272 9939
Phone: (617) 926 4600
(800) 225 3215
Fax: (617) 923 1875

Format: Video
Date released: 1994, 1995
Length: 61 minutes (total for four videos)
Price: $1,584 (purchase of series); $1,425.60 (AMA member price for purchase of series); $495 (price for each video when purchased separately); $455 (AMA member price for each video when purchased separately); $190 (rental price for each video); $180 (AMA member rental price for each video).

Description: This series, based on consultant Steve Sarazen's book *Using Quality Improvement Tools to Build Customer Satisfaction*, includes the following four videos: *Team Planning: Relationship Diagram and Prioritization Matrix*; *Team Planning*; *Tree Diagram and Process-Decision-Program Chart*; *Flow diagrams*; and *Idea Generation: Affinity Diagram and Cause and Effect Diagram*. Each video includes a leader's guide with an overview of the topic and group exercises.

Title: *Tools of Total Quality on CD-ROM*
Producer: MicroMentor, Inc.
124 Mt. Auburn St.
Cambridge, MA 02138
Phone: (617) 868 8500
(800) 887 3917
Fax: (617) 497 5716

Format: CD-ROM
Date released: 1994
System requirements: IBM-compatible computer, 386 or higher; VGA 16-color graphics adapter and monitor; a double-speed CD-ROM drive; Windows 3.1 with sound device; minimum 8 MB of RAM

Price: $895
Description: MicroMentor, a Massachusetts-based management education and multimedia software firm, develops customized training projects. MicroMentor's clients have included Fortune 500 companies, the Polaroid Corporation, Ernst & Young, and Holiday Inn. While most of their training programs have been delivered on floppy or hard disks, MicroMentor has recently delivered many of their major training projects on CD-ROM, combining audio and graphics to create inter-active multimedia products. The *Tools of Total Quality* is a CD-ROM that can be used by individuals or teams as an introductory or refresher course or as a highly interactive game. Users learn when and how to use fourteen selected quality tools. These include the following: affinity diagram; brainstorming; cause and effect diagram; control chart, decision matrix; flowchart; force field analysis; histogram; multivoting; Pareto chart; process mapping; run chart; scatter diagram; and the "Three Actual" rule.

Title: *Variation: The Foundation for Run Charts*
Producer: Executive Learning, Inc.
7101 Executive Center Dr., Ste. 160
Brentwood, TN 37027
Phone: (615) 373 8483
(800) 929 7890
Fax: (615) 373 8635

Format: Video training module
Price: $495
Description: This module explains the concept of variation, a concept that is often difficult to understand. However, a basic understanding of variation is critical for any organization involved with improving products or services. The module includes a videotape, participant notes, trainer's notes, pocket reference cards, and a wall chart.

ii Software packages

The following is a selective listing of software packages, many of which have been favorably reviewed in software magazines and other trade publications. Since many of these software packages have more than one application, consult the finding aid at the end of this section. The listing of products in this section does not constitute an endorsement of the product by the authors or by Routledge. Although prices are included, many producers offer discounts for educational institutions as well as site license options and special networking prices. Consequently, it is best to call producers directly for complete pricing information. Those interested in identifying additional software related to quality improvement, quality assurance, and ISO 9000 standards should consult the excellent and comprehensive *Annual QA/QC Software Directory* published by *Quality Progress*. This directory is published in the March issue of this periodical. In addition, a listing of software relating to SPC, SQC, TQM, ISO 9000, design of experiments, multipurpose statistics, and flowcharting is published in the December issue of *Quality* magazine.

Product name: ABC FlowCharter
Producer: Micrografx
1303 Arapaho
Richardson, TX 75081
Phone: (214) 234 1769
(800) 603 0074
Description: FlowCharter 4.0 contains four modules: FlowCharter, DataAnalyzer, Viewer, and Snapgraphics. Two of these modules, FlowCharter and DataAnalyzer, were previously marketed as ABC Toolkit. FlowCharter 4.0 integrates diagramming and analysis tools, including everything from simple templates for basic business charts to analysis tools for business process reengineering. FlowCharter 4.0 also offers OLE 2.0 automation, E-mail, and the ability to integrate with other applications via Visual Basic or Visual C++.
Requirements: IBM computer or compatible, 386 or higher; Windows 3.1 or later; 5 MB RAM; 21 MB hard disk for installation; VGA monitor or better; Windows-compatible mouse.
Price: $495

Product name: allCLEAR III
Producer: CLEAR Software, Inc.
199 Wells Ave.
Newton, MA 02159
Phone: (617) 965 6755
(800) 338 1759
Fax: (617) 965 5310
Description: allCLEAR III is the latest version of a diagramming and flowcharting package that has been used by more than 120,000 customers world-wide. allCLEAR can be used to produce presentation quality flowcharts, process flow diagrams, organizational charts, fishbone diagrams, deployment charts, and other diagrams without drawing. allCLEAR completely automates the flowcharting process. A review appearing in the January 1995 issue of *PC World* concluded that allCLEAR III is "the best flowcharter for Windows."
Requirements: IBM or compatible computer, 386 or higher; 6 MB hard disk space; 4 MB RAM; Windows 3.1 or higher; at least VGA graphics; a mouse.
Price: $299 (standalone); $995 (five-user LAN); $1,790 (ten-user LAN)

Product name: Applied CIM
Producer: Applied Statistics, Inc.
2055 White Bear Ave.
Maplewood, MN 55109
Phone: (612) 481 0202
(800) 207 5631
Fax: (612) 481 0410
Description: From any PC on the factory floor, this Windows-based software product provides access to CAD information, CAM files, distributed numerical control (DNC) capabilities, and statistical process control (SPC) functionality. Applied CIM also allows information to be shared in a networked environment. This software package addresses increased productivity, improved quality, and ISO 9000 certification in real time on the factory floor.
Requirements: IBM-compatible computer, 386 or faster: 5 MB RAM; floppy disk drive; 5 MB RAM for program; VGA monitor; Windows 3.1; network version available.
Price: $895 Applied CIM workstation (concurrent user pricing, one-four users); $2,995 Applied CIM Administrator (file server software). Call Applied Statistics for other

concurrent user pricing and the price of Applied CIM optional modules and accessories.

Product name: Applied Stats
Producer: Applied Statistics, Inc.
2055 White Bear Ave.
Maplewood, MN 55109
Phone: (612) 481 0202
(800) 207 5631
Fax: (612) 481 0410
Description: This Windows-based manufacturing software acquires and analyzes data as parts are being produced. The software warns operators when parts are out of tolerance or approaching out-of-tolerance. This real time software allows manufacturers to prevent problems before they happen and saves time since manufacturers don't need to do as many inspections of the final product.
Requirements: IBM-compatible computer, 386 or faster; 1 MB RAM; floppy disk drive; 1 MB RAM for program; 10K RAM for data; VGA monitor; Windows 3.1.
Price: The following pricing is for quantities of one or two and includes DDE Dynamic Link Library. Call Applied Statistics for pricing for different quantities. $1,1695 (short run or variables); $895 (attributes); $1,995 (variables and short run or variables and attributes); $2,495 (variables, attributes, and short run).

Product name: Applied Stats Analyst
Producer: Applied Stats, Inc.
2055 White Bear Ave.
Maplewood, MN 55109
Phone: (612) 481 0202
(800) 207 5631
Fax: (612) 481 0410
Description: This cost-effective desktop package allows engineers and plant managers to review and analyze production data collected on the factory floor. Although it lacks the comprehensive data collection abilities of Applied Stats, it provides off-line SPC and statistical analysis of any ASCII files. The software includes the following analysis tools: x-bar; R control chart analysis; x-bar, s control chart analysis; x-bar, MR control chart analysis; Pre-Control chart analysis; p, np, c, and u control chart analysis; histograms; ppm

defective; chi-square normality test; Shapiro Wilk normality test; performance indices; capability indices; and scatter plot.
Requirements: This package runs under the Apple Macintosh and Microsoft Windows 3.X operating systems.
Price: $995 (for quantities of one or two). Call Applied Statistics for pricing for other quantities.

Product name: Audit Master
Producer: The Harrington Group, Inc.
3208-C East Colonial Dr., Ste. 253
Orlando, FL 32803
Phone: (407) 898 7101
Fax: (407) 898 5725
Description: This Windows program is designed to make auditing to ISO standards simple. It can be used when auditing a supplier or when performing in-house audits. Features allow users to plan and create audits, track major and minor findings, create a schedule of open and closed audits, track corrective actions, generate reports summarizing the findings for an audit, and document follow-up on the findings.
Requirements: IBM-compatible computer, 386 or higher; Windows 3.1; VGA monitor; minimum 4 MB RAM with a hard disk.
Price: $199

Product name: BenchMarker Plus
Producer: Fleet & Partners, Inc.
P.O. Box 373
Richford, VT 05476
Phone: (905) 855 9095
Fax: (905) 855 9661
E-mail: Internet:
74403.3261@Compuserve.com;
Compuserve: 74403,3261
Description: This process modeling and analysis software can be used to support continuous process improvement, quality management, business process reengineering, and benchmarking. It automatically maps processes, calculates the cost of a process, tracks cycle time improvement, calculates the cost of quality, suggests and models alternatives, and creates presentation quality charts and reports. This inexpensive and easy-to-use deployable tool lets users analyze and improve

existing processes. BenchMarker Plus lets you import data from programs like allCLEAR, ABC FlowCharter, and ABC Toolkit.

Requirements: IBM computer or compatible, 386 or higher; Windows 3.1 or later; DOS 5.0 or later; 7 MB HD; 4 MB RAM; Windows-compatible mouse and display.

Price: $690

Product name: Calibration Manager
Producer: Blue Mountain Software Inc.
208 W. Hamilton Ave.
State College, PA 16801
Phone: (814) 234 2417
Fax: (814) 234 7077

Description: This software helps facilities document and track tool and equipment calibrations. It can generate calibration due dates, produce calibration schedules, and create calibration histories. This record-keeping feature is particularly useful for companies complying with ISO 9000 guidelines as well as the FDA's good manufacturing practices (GMPs) requirements. Calibration Manager has been installed at more than 500 locations in twenty countries, including nine of the top ten Fortune 500 pharmaceutical companies.

Requirements: IBM-compatible computer; DOS 3.0 or higher; 640K RAM; hard disk drive; 1 MB RAM for program; 1.5–2.5 MB RAM for data per 1,000 records.

Price: $1,295

Product name: Calibration Recall System
Producer: The Harrington Group, Inc.
3208-C East Colonial Dr., Ste. 253
Orlando, FL 32803
Phone: (407) 898 7101
Fax: (407) 898 5725

Description: This software is designed to help plant managers control calibrated equipment. It tracks the location and status of calibrated equipment, identifies equipment due and overdue for calibration, maintains a history for each calibrated tool, and identifies equipment found to be out of tolerance.

Requirements: IBM-compatible computer, 386 or higher; Windows 3.1; VGA monitor; minimum 4 MB RAM with a hard disk.

Price: $199

Product name: Corrective Action: Problem Management Software for Windows
Producer: The Harrington Group, Inc.
3208-C East Colonial Dr., Ste. 253
Orlando, FL 32803
Phone: (407) 898 7101
Fax: (407) 898 5725

Description: This problem-solving software helps managers track problems and customer complaints, determine their root causes, and implement corrective action. It provides the following features: a problem filter which allows users to review problems and identify trends; Pareto reports which indicate the major problems in a company, and trend reports which let managers monitor problems, preventive action, and quality improvement over time.

Requirements: IBM-compatible computer, 386 or higher; VGA monitor; Windows 3.1; minimum of 4MB RAM; hard disk.

Price: $299

Product name: Cost of Quality
Producer: The Harrington Group, Inc.
3208-C East Colonial Dr., Ste. 253
Orlando, FL 32803
Phone: (407) 898 7101
Fax: (407) 898 5725

Description: This unique software program allows users to identify and track quality costs in four cost categories: prevention; appraisal; internal failure; and external failure. It has been designed for both the manufacturing and service sectors.

Requirements: IBM PC compatible, 386 or faster; VGA monitor; MS-DOS 3.0 or higher; minimum of 1 MB RAM with a hard disk.

Price: $299

Product name: CPCI
Producer: Cuthbert Productivity Concepts
81 Milton Rd
Kirkcaldy, Fife
Scotland KY1 1TP
Phone: 01592 643571
Fax: 01592 643571

Description: This statistical process control software helps improve productivity by identifying specific causes of variation within a wide range of manufacturing and processing technologies. It provides variables charts, attributes charts, correlation, and a detailed analysis capability.

Requirements: Any PC with a hard disk plus floppy (3½" or 5¼") runnning MS-DOS with VGA graphics capability and at least 640 kbyte of memory. MS-DOS version 5 (upwards) is required for chart printing.

Price: $400

Product name: Database for Quality (DBQ)

Producer: Murphy Software Co.
1000 Town Center, Ste. 1950
Southfield, MI 48075
Phone: (810) 351 0900
Fax: (810) 351 0906

Description: This quality management software product for manufacturers is a multiuser relational database system that automates the quality control process. It coordinates record keeping, data collection, statistical process control, traceability, test certificates, statistical analysis, customized reporting, and Pareto charting.

Requirements: DBQ runs on IBM's AS/400 platform. Ten modules are available.

Price: Pricing ranges from $10,000 to $100,000.

Product name: Design/IDEF

Producer: Meta Software Corporation
125 Cambridge Park Dr.
Cambridge, MA 02140
Phone: (617) 576 6920
Fax: (617) 661 2008

Description: This modeling and simulation tool for reengineering allows users to analyze existing processes and evaluate the impact of proposed changes. It has been used by many corporations involved in reengineering projects, including Bristol-Myers Squibb, Alcatel Network Systems, Reebok, Allergan Inc., Litton Industries, IBM, and Fiat. It has also been used to reengineer processes performed by NASA and the Department of Defense.

Requirements: Versions are available for the following platforms: MS Windows; Macintosh Plus or higher; Sun Solaris under X Window System; and HP 9000 (700/800) under X Window System.

Price: $3,995 (one–four licenses, per license,

includes the first year's maintenance); $600 annual maintenance (per license).

Product name: Document Manager 9000

Producer: Powerway, Inc.
9855 Crosspoint Blvd.
Indianapolis, IN 46256
Phone: (317) 577 8100
(800) 964 9004
Fax: (317) 577 0450

Description: This economical Windows-based software package was one of *Document Management* magazine's 1994 "Product Choice" award winners. Document Manager 9000 helps companies manage the document control requirements of ISO 9000. Document Manager 9000 allows users to index already created documents by topic and item, such as process, machine, part number, etc. Since its Windows format requires no additional technical expertise, it can be used by everyone in a company. Document Manager 9000 lets users create user groups with assigned access to documents and automates the approval routing process.

Requirements: IBM computer or compatible, 386 or better; 4 MB RAM or higher; 11 MB available on hard disk; Windows 3.1 or higher.

Price: $89

Product name: DOE-PC IV

Producer: Quality America Inc.
7650 East Broadway, Ste. 208–210
Tucson, AZ 85710
Phone: (602) 722 6154
(800) 722 6154
Fax: (602) 722 6705

Description: This menu-driven Design of Experiments (DOE) package requires limited knowledge of DOE designs. The system generates designs from a long list of design types including fractional factorials, Taguichi, John's 3/4, Plackett-Burman, Box-Behnken, and central composites. Users can perform various types of analyses and have the results displayed graphically. DOE-PV IV lets users plot experimental results. The software lets users overlap one plot onto another to allow for comparison of results.

Requirements: 386 machine or better; 4 MB RAM; hard or floppy disk drive; 1.59 MB

RAM for program; 512K RAM for data; MS Windows 3.1 or higher, MS Windows NT, IBM OS/2 2.0 or higher; CGA, EGA, or VGA monitor; network version available.
Price: $495

Product name: EasyFlow for Windows
Producer: HavenTree Software Limited
P.O. Box 470
Fineview, NY 13640 0470
Phone: (613) 544 6035
(800) 267 0668
Fax: (613) 544 9632
Headquarters: P.O. Box 2260
Kingston, Ontario
Canada K7L 5J9
Description: This easy-to-use charting and diagramming program can be used to produce presentation quality flowcharts, organizational charts, audit diagrams, flow diagrams, event and causal factor diagrams, and process mapping charts. The program includes comprehensive shape libraries.
Requirements: IBM-compatible computer, 386 or faster; 4 MB or more of RAM; hard disk drive with 3 MB free storage; Windows 3.1 or higher; DOS 3.1 or higher.
Price: $299

Product name: Essentials of SPC Computer-Based Training
Producer: Qualitran Professional Services Inc.
P.O. Box 295
Stroud, Ontario
Canada L0L 2M0
Phone: (705) 722 8550
(800) 461 9902
Fax: (705) 722 0324
Description: This training program, which has been used by Pepsi-Cola, Michelin Tire, Dow Chemical, and the U.S. Navy, uses an interactive approach to teach SPC concepts. It demonstrates how process changes are reflected in control charts. Users learn about variation, process capability, variable and attribute control charts, control plans, and how to construct a histogram.
Requirements: Any IBM PC/XT/AT or 100 percent compatible with 512K; 1 disk drive; CGA, EGA, or VGA monitor.
Price: $955

Product name: FACTORYnet Q/S
Producer: Intercim Corporation
501 East Highway 13
Minneapolis, MN 55337 2877
Phone: (612) 894 9010
(800) 445 7785
Fax: (612) 894 0399
Description: Intercim is a leading supplier of networked factory floor information management systems. FACTORYnet Q/S is designed to collect and analyze manufacturing process data quickly so plant operators can correct problems before they become costly mistakes.
Requirements: FACTORYnet Q/S is available on UNIX and DEC VMS environments.
Price: $23,000 (for FACTORYnet Q/S base software); $1,800 (for each user license)

Product name: FlowChart Express
Producer: Kaetron Software Corp.
25211 Grogans Mill Rd., Ste. 260
The Woodlands, TX 77380
Phone: (713) 298 1500
(800) 938 8900
Fax: (713) 298 2520
Description: This easy-to-use cross-platform flowcharting software can be used to create and modify flowcharts. Quality improvement teams can use it to chart processes. FlowChart Express allows users to exchange files between the Windows and Macintosh platforms. Features include twelve ANSI symbols, color and pattern support, and twelve system defined line paths.
Requirements: Macintosh: System 6.07 or later; a hard disk is recommended. Supports printing on Macintosh-compatible laser printers, dot matrix printers, and plotters. Windows: IBM-compatible computer, 386 20 MHz or faster; Windows 3.1 or higher; VGA monitor; 4 MB RAM, 2 MB hard disk space; mouse or compatible pointing device; compatible plotter, laser, and dot matrix printers.
Price: $149

Product name: Flow Charting 4
Producer: Patton & Patton Software Corporation
485 Cochrane Circle
Morgan Hill, CA 95037
Phone: (800) 525 0082
Fax: (408) 778 9972

Description: This easy-to-use Windows-based flowcharting program produces presentation quality flowcharts, network diagrams, process control charts, data flow diagrams, work flow diagrams, and deployment flowcharts. The software comes with templates containing shapes and users can also create their own templates from the existing shapes. Patton & Patton introduced a DOS-based version of this flowcharting program more than a decade ago.

Requirements: Microsoft Windows 3.1 or later; minimum of 4 MB RAM, one 3½ high density (1.44 MB) disk drive; graphics card and monitor supported by Windows; mouse or compatible pointing device; any printer or plotter supported by Windows.

Price: $199 (single-user package); $795 (five user LAN package).

Product name: GageTalker DataPage III
Producer: GageTalker
13680 NE 16th St.
Bellevue, WA 98005 2376
Phone: (206) 644 4860
(800) 955 7100
Fax: (206) 747 5769

Description: This process analysis and database software lets users import SPC data from GageTalker III workstations, GageTalker Softstations, and other SPC data collection systems. It allows users to import and export data in ASCII, Lotus, and dbase-compatible formats. The software includes tests for normality, control, runs, trends, patterns, capability, and projected percent of defects. It creates customized management reports and performs "what-if" analysis.

Requirements: 640K or more RAM; 2 MB disk storage capacity; PC-DOS or MS-DOS version 3.1 or greater; a video card with EGA or better resolution.

Price: $995

Product name: GageTalker III Plus Real Time
Producer: GageTalker
13680 NE 16th St.
Bellevue, WA 98005 2376
Phone: (206) 644 4860
(800) 955 7100
Fax: (206) 747 5769

Description: This package transforms a personal computer into a complete data collection and analysis workstation. It has been designed for labs, receiving inspection areas, and other plant environments. It provides comprehensive attribute and variables analysis, special SPC charts for short-run data, and traceability information.

Requirements: IBM computer or 100 percent compatible; minimum 640K RAM; 1 MB or more of disk storage space; DOS version 3.1 or later; VGA monitor; IBM-compatible graphics printer.

Price: $995

Product name: The Gauge Program Software
Producer: The Crosby Company
P.O. Box 2433
Glen Ellyn, IL 60138
Phone: (708) 790 1711
Fax: (708) 790 1768

Description: This software, guaranteed to pass any gauge-control audit, can be used for calibration recall, calibration frequency analysis, inventory control, gauge R & R, and calibration history.

Requirements: a 386/16 computer with DOS 3.1 or higher; a hard disk drive; any graphics card.

Price: $599

Product name: Helping an Organization Succeed: Using the Malcolm Baldrige National Quality Award Criteria
Producer: AT & T Technical Education Center
Dept. JS; Room C-116
140 Centennial Ave.
Piscataway, NJ 08854
Phone: (800) 840 1218
Fax: (908) 457 6145

Description: This software, which does not require users to be familiar with the Baldrige Award criteria, lets up to 250 individuals in an organization assess how well their organization is doing when compared against the Baldrige Award criteria. Although this software is not intended as a substitute for a detailed assessment that an organization would complete as part of the Baldrige application process, it can be a good starting point for an organization as it provides managers with employees perceptions of the organization's strengths and weaknesses. Although this package can be used alone, the AT & T Technical Education Center has also produced a 60-minute videotape that is accompanied by a facilitator's guide. The purpose of the videotape, *Helping an Organization Succeed*, is to introduce employees to the Baldrige criteria.

Requirements: This PC-based software (DOS) runs on any version of DOS. It is available on 5¼" and 3½" disks.

Price: $750 (for one set of software which includes ten individual disks, evaluator disk, and user guide); $1,250 (price for introductory package which includes one set of software, one videotape and facilitator's guide, and one participant's resource manual); quantity discounts are available.

Product name: The Idea Generator Plus
Producer: Experience in Software, Inc.
2000 Hearst Ave.
Berkeley, CA 94709
Phone: (510) 644 0694
(800) 678 7008
Fax: (510) 644 3823

Description: This interactive software helps users generate solutions to problems. The program is based on Gerald Nierenberg's book *The Art of Creative Thinking*. A copy of the book is included. Seven idea-generating techniques are outlined, such as finding metaphors for your problem, adopting other perspectives, reversing your goals, and thinking of similar situations.

Requirements: IBM PC, XT, AT, PS/2 or compatible; Dos 2.0 or higher; 256K RAM.
Price: $195.

Product name: Inspiration
Producer: Inspiration Software, Inc.
2920 S. W. Dolph Ct., Ste. 3
Portland, OR 97219
Phone: (503) 245 9011
(800) 877 4292
Fax: (503) 246 4292

Description: This idea-development software lets users turn ideas into outlines or flowchart like diagrams. It enables users to brainstorm visually. Inspiration can be used to create idea maps, flowcharts, tree charts, TQM diagrams, presentation visuals, outlines, and written documents.

Requirements: Windows version: IBM-compatible computer, 386 or higher with 4 MB RAM; Microsoft Windows 3.1 or later; Microsoft mouse or other Windows 3.1 compatible pointing device; VGA, Super VGA, XGA, 8514/A or other Windows 3.1 compatible graphics card and monitor. Macintosh version: System 6.0.4 or higher; minimum 1 MB available RAM; hard disk drive; network version available.
Price: $195

Product name: The Integrated Quality System
Producer: IQS Inc.
20525 Center Ridge Rd., Ste. 400
Cleveland, OH 4416 3453
Phone: (216) 333 1344
(800) 635 5901
Fax: (216) 333 3752

Description: This integrated quality assurance software system consists of thirteen modules: customer management; system documentation; product documentation; process documentation; preventive maintenance; calibration management; employee involvement; data collection; statistical process control; nonconformance reporting and analysis; corrective action; supplier management; and quality costs. The system has been designed to meet and exceed the quality assurance requirements of the automotive, aerospace, defense, nuclear, and health care industries, and the requirements of ISO 9000 certification.

Requirements: IBM-compatible computer, 386 or higher; hard disk; 530K of free RAM; 2 MEG extended memory; DOS 3.1 or higher.
Price: Prices start at $7,500. Some modules can be sold separately. Call IQS for pricing.

Product name: ISOxPERT
Producer: Management Software International, Inc.
38 Montvale Ave.
Stoneham, MA 02180
Phone: (617) 279 1919
(800) ISO-EASY
Fax: (617) 279 2929

Description: This ISO 9000 compliance software can be used by a single user or by multiple users across LANs or across the world since it is based on Lotus Notes. Since it is built upon the Lotus Notes platform it is Windows, Macintosh, UNIX, and Network compatible. ISOxPERT has been designed to help companies complete ISO 9000 certification easily. Electronic Fasteners, Inc., a fastener distributor in Boston, used ISOxPERT to achieve ISO 9000 certification in six months. ISOxPERT includes ready-to-use forms for inspection, audits, corrective actions, calibration records, and other documentation relating to ISO 9000. Users can customize these forms or create their own documents. ISOxPERT's unique feature is its computer-based training system which can eliminate consulting fees and reduce the time and cost of training.

Requirements: IBM computer or compatible, 386 or faster; Windows 3.1, 3.11, or NT; 6 MB RAM; 12 MB HD; Lotus Notes required.

Price: $495

Product name: JMP
Producer: SAS Institute
SAS Campus Dr.
Cary, NC 27513
Phone: (919) 677 8000
Fax: (919) 977 8224

Description: This award winning software, developed initially in 1989 for the Macintosh, integrates statistics with graphics. It provides tools for advanced statistical analysis, statistical process control, and design of experiments. A Windows version has also been released.

Requirements: Macintosh version: Macintosh Plus, Power Macintosh; minimum of System 6.0; 4 MB RAM; hard disk. Windows version: IBM computer or compatible, 386 or faster; Windows 3.1 or later; MS-DOS 5.0 or later; VGA, XGA, SVGA, or IBM 8514 monitor; mouse.

Price: $695

Product name: Juran Quality Improvement Toolkit
Producer: Juran Institute, Inc.
11 River Rd.
P.O. Box 811
Wilton, CT 06897 9858
Phone: (203) 834 1700
(800) 338 7726
Fax: (203) 834 9891

Description: This process improvement software, now available on CD-ROM, provides step-by-step instruction and documentation for teams using the Juran six-step improvement process. The Toolkit recommends which quality improvement tools are best for each of the twenty-three activities in this six-step process. The software includes control charts and other commonly used quality improvement tools such as Pareto analysis, scatter diagrams, cause and effect diagrams, histograms, box plots, and flow diagrams. Toolkit even lets users develop a storyboard to present findings. The CD-ROM version includes two video libraries containing over an hour of video instruction and nine tutorials.

Requirements: IBM computer or compatible, 386 or faster; 486/33 CPU for multimedia version; Windows 3.1 or higher; 5 MB HD; 4 MB RAM; Windows-compatible mouse and display; single speed or higher CD-ROM drive and audio card for multimedia version.

Price: $695 (software only version); $995 (CD-ROM version)

Product name: JUSE-QCAS
Producer: NIMAC Software
500 Marathon Pkwy. N.W.
Lawrenceville, GA 30245
Phone: (404) 339 3983
Fax: (404) 339 4383

Description: This quality control software was developed in Japan by JUSE, The Institute of Japanese Union of Scientists and Engineers, the organization that awards the Deming Prize. JUSE-QCAS is used by manufacturing companies, service companies, educational institutions, government agencies, and health care organizations world-wide. It consists of three compatible modules: QC7 Tools (QCAS I); Design of Experiments (QCAS II); and Regression analysis (QCAS III). The first module, QCAS I, includes the following functions: data analysis; Pareto diagrams; cause and effect diagrams; histograms; control charts; scatter diagrams; and nine types of graphs. The second module, JUSE-QCAS II, is a Design of Experiments package designed for nonstatisticians. It includes the following functions: randomization of the order of experiments; one or two way layout ANOVA; multiple way layout ANOVA; factorial experiments; nested design; split plot; mixed effect; and orthogonal arrays. The third module, JUSE-QCAS III, lets user perform variable transformation, regression analysis, multiple regression analysis, and polynomial regression analysis.

Requirements: IBM PC or compatible; 565 K RAM; DOS 2.11 or higher; hard or floppy disk drive; CGA, EGA, or VGA monitor.

Price: $790 (each module)

Product name: LearnerFirst Benchmarking

Producer: ASQC (American Society for Quality Control)
611 E. Wisconsin Ave.
P.O. Box 3005
Milwaukee, WI 53201 3005
Phone: (414) 272 8575
(800) 248 1946
Fax: (414) 272 1734

Description: This software breaks the benchmarking process into nineteen activities. These simple step-by-step activities will help users identify what to benchmark and how to do it, will improve and streamline an existing benchmarking program, assess a company's internal strengths and weaknesses, and help improve customer satisfaction.

Requirements: An IBM-compatible computer with a 80386 20MHz or higher processor; DOS 5.1 or higher; Microsoft Windows 3.1; Windows-compatible mouse or other pointing device; hard disk with at least 9 MB of free storage; standard VGA monitor, network version available Spring 1995.

Price: $475; $425 (ASCQ members).

Product name: LearnerFirst How to Implement ISO 9000

Producer: ASQC (American Society for Quality Control)
611 East Wisconsin Ave.
P.O. Box 3005
Milwaukee, WI 53201 3005
Phone: (414) 272 8575
(800) 248 1946
Fax: (414) 272 1734

Description: This interactive software, developed by LearnerFirst and ASQC with Dr. Lawrence A. Wilson, has been designed to help companies develop and implement an ISO

9000 program. The revised ANSI/ASQC Q9000 standards are already built into the program. This software breaks the complex registration process into eight simple steps.

Requirements: An IBM-compatible computer, 386 or higher; DOS 5.0 or higher; Microsoft Windows 3.1; Windows-compatible mouse or other pointing device; minimum 4 MB RAM (8 MB RAM recommended); hard disk with at least 10 MB of free storage; standard VGA monitor; $3\frac{1}{2}$" disk drive for installation.

Price: $795; $695 (ASQC members).

Product name: LearnerFirst Process Management

Producer: ASQC (American Society for Quality Control)
611 East Wisconsin Ave.
P.O. Box 3005
Milwaukee, WI 53201 3005
Phone: (414) 272 8575
(800) 248 1946
Fax: (414) 272 1734

Description: This interactive software, developed by LearnerFirst with Tennessee Associates International, is available from ASQC. It uses a twenty-two-step approach to applying process management throughout an organization. The software has been developed to help a company understand its processes, identify which ones to change, and ensures that these changes are made correctly.

Requirements: IBM-compatible computer, 386 or higher; DOS 5.0; Microsoft Windows 3.1; Windows-compatible mouse or other pointing device; standard VGA monitor; minimum 4 MB RAM; hard disk with at least 7 MB of free storage; $3\frac{1}{2}$" disk drive for installation.

Price: $490; $445 (ASQC members).

Product name: Magic Window SPC Software

Producer: The Crosby Company
P.O. Box 2433
Glen Ellyn, IL 60138
Phone: (708) 790 1711
Fax: (708) 790 1768

Description: The Crosby Company has produced SPC software since 1981. Their newest product, Magic Window SPC software, is a Windows-based SPC software with the following capabilities: Average & Range (X

Bar & R); Individual and moving Range; and CuSum. It can produce these SPC charts: Average; Range; Tolerance: Moving Mean; Standard Error; Individual; Moving Range; and CuSum. It lets users select a group of charts, tables, and reports to be included in a "report format."

Requirements: Any computer, printer, plotter, and monitor that can handle Windows 3.1 or higher; a minimum of 3 MB hard disk space and at least 1 MB of free RAM.

Price: $299

Product name: The Memory Jogger Plus+ Software (7 M & P Tools)
Producer: GOAL/QPC
13 Branch St.
Methuen, MA 01844 1953
Phone: (508) 685 3900
(800) 643 4316
Fax: (508) 685 6151

Description: This Windows-based software automates the seven management and planning tools featured in *The Memory Jogger Plus+*, a book first published by GOAL/QPC in 1989. These tools include the following: affinity diagram; interrelationship digraph; tree diagram; prioritization matrix; matrix; PDPC; and activity network diagram. The software produces presentation quality charts and meeting documentation.

Requirements: IBM-compatible computer, 386/16 MHz or higher; Microsoft Windows 3.1 or later; MS DOS 3.1 or later; minimum 1 MB RAM (2 MB or more recommended); hard disk drive with at least 2.5 MB free storage; any Microsoft Windows-compatible printer; VGA monitor recommended.

Price: $695

Product name: The Memory Jogger Software (7 QC Tools)
Producer: GOAL/QPC
13 Branch St.
Methuen, MA 01844 1953
Phone: (508) 685 3900
(800) 643 4316
Fax: (508) 685 6151

Description: This software is based on *The Memory Jogger*, GOAL/QPC's pocket guide to tools for quality improvement. More than four million copies of the pocket guide have been sold since it was first published in 1985. The Memory Jogger Software is an advanced quality control package that lets users create presentation quality flowcharts and cause-and-effect diagrams. It also allows users to collect and analyze data through run charts, histograms, Pareto charts, control charts, and scatter diagrams.

Requirements: IBM-compatible computer, 386/16 MHz or higher; Microsoft Windows 3.1 or later; MS DOS 3.1 or later; minimum 1 MB RAM (2 MB or more recommended); hard drive with at least 2.5 MB free storage); any Microsoft Windows-compatible printer; VGA monitor recommended.

Price: $895

Product name: Minitab Statistical Software
Producer: Minitab Inc.
3081 Enterprise Dr.
State College, PA 16801
Phone: (814) 238 4383
(800) 448 3555
Fax: (814) 238 4383

Description: This leading software package for data analysis and presentation was developed in 1972. It is used by more than 2,000 colleges and universities and by businesses in more than fifty countries. It can perform more than 200 statistical functions, including the following SPC functions: Pareto analysis; fishbone diagram; process capability analysis; probability plots; and variables and attributes control charts.

Requirements: Minitab for Windows: 386 machines and above; DOS 3.3 or later; Windows version 3.1; 4 MB RAM (6 MB RAM recommended); hard disk with 11 MB available space; high density disk drive; VGA or SVGA monitor; mouse required for some capabilities; math coprocessor recommended. Minitab for DOS: 286 machines and above; DOS 3.3 or later; 1 MB RAM (standard worksheet); 4 MB RAM (extended worksheet); hard disk with 6 MB available space; high density disk drive; mouse optional; math coprocessor recommended. Documentation and HELP files also available in French. Minitab for Macintosh: any Macintosh except the 128K, 512K, and 512E; Macintosh system 6.0.1 or higher; 1 MB RAM, hard disk with 3.7 MB available space.

Price: $695 (Minitab for DOS, Minitab for Macintosh); $895 (Minitab for Windows). Call Minitab Inc. for pricing for multiple copies, quantity purchases, network users, and academic discounts.

Product name: Network Monitor
Producer: GageTalker
   13680 NE 16th St.
   Bellevue, WA 98005 2376
   Phone: (206) 644 4860
      (800) 955 7100
   Fax: (206) 747 5769
Description: This real-time production and quality control management tool lets managers monitor up to 512 different processes from a single PC.
Requirements: 640K or more RAM; 2 MB disk storage capacity; PC-DOS or MS-DOS version 3.1 or greater.
Price: $1,795

Product name: Nonconformance Tracking: Reject & Failure Management Software
Producer: The Harrington Group, Inc.
   3208-C East Colonial Dr., Ste. 253
   Orlando, FL 32803
   Phone: (407) 898 7101
   Fax: (407) 898 5725
Description: This software allows users to track and monitor defect levels including quantity and type of nonconformances, disposition, cause determination, corrective action, current status, and cost.
Requirements: IBM-compatible, 386 or higher; VGA monitor; MS-DOS 3.0 or higher; minimum 1 MB RAM with a hard disk.
Price: $149 (special offer)

Product name: Optima!
Producer: AdvanEdge Technologies, Inc.
   10170 S. W. Hedges Ct.
   Tualatin, OR 97062
   Phone: (503) 692 8162
   Fax: (503) 691 2451
Description: This Windows-based process-analysis tool provides process mapping, modeling, a report writer, and "what-if" simulations. It has been designed as a tool for business process reengineering.
Requirements: Microsoft Windows 3.1 or later;

a mouse or compatible printing device; 2 MB of available memory; a high density, $3\frac{1}{2}$" floppy disk drive; a hard disk with at least 3 MB of available space.
Price: $1,500

Product name: Optimum Design of Experiments
Producer: Exact Gestion et Technologies de la Qualité, Inc.
   2750 rue Einstein, Bureau 300
   Parc Technologique du Québec Métropolitain
   Sainte-Foy (Québec)
   Canada G1P 4R1
   Phone: (418) 650 2723
   Fax: (418) 650 5901
Description: This software, designed for scientists and engineers concerned with improving quality and productivity, is based on Taguichi's methods. The software facilitates the design of experimental plans through the construction of fishbone diagrams, selection of interactive scenarios, ANOVA analysis, and the use of confirmation experiments.
Requirements: IBM-compatible computer, 386 or higer; Microsoft Windows 3.1 or later; 1 MB extended memory (2 MB and more are recommended); hard disk space with a minimum of 2 MB; VGA graphic display or higher resolution; mouse.
Price: $750

Product name: Optionist
Producer: HavenTree Software Limited
   P.O. Box 470
   Fineview, NY 13640 0470
   Phone: (613) 544 6035
      (800) 267 0668
   Fax: (613) 544 9632
   Headquarters: P.O. Box 2260 Kingston, Ontario
   Canada K7L 5J9
Description: This decision support software uses HavenTree's unique Seven Step Decision Method to help users analyze the factors involved in making decisions and compares the outcomes of different actions. The seven steps include the following: stating your mission and goals; weighing the factors influencing your decision; rating your options; evaluating the

scores each option receives; verifying your best option and confirming that it meets your objectives and goals; and acting on your decision.

Requirements: An IBM PC, XT, AT, PS/2 or fully compatible personal computer with at least 400K of available RAM and DOS 3.3 or higher; a Microsoft-compatible mouse is supported but not required.

Price: $299

Product name: Prime Factor FFT
Producer: Alligator Technologies
  2900 Bristol St., Ste. E-101
  Costa Mesa, CA 92626 7906
  Phone: (714) 850 9984
  Fax: (714) 850 9987

Description: Alligator Technologies Prime Factor fast Fourier transform (FFT) subroutine library is available as a Windows DDL. It's accessible from a range of Windows programming languages. A DOS version is also available. This product is designed to allow analysis on any data set size and can transform all data arrays. The library also includes Hamming and Hanning windowing functions, and amplitude and phase calculation routines. Package includes example application programs in Basic and C.

Requirements: For Windows DDL version: IMP PC/AT, 386, 486, Pentium or compatible computer; Microsoft Windows 3.0 or higher; DOS 3.0 or higher; math coprocessor for 386 and 486sx-based machines; 4 MBytes of RAM recommended for large data sets. For DOS version: IBM PC/AT 286, 386, 486, Pentium or compatible computer; 512 kbyte DOS memory; DOS 3.0 or higher; math coprocessor for 286, 386, 486sx-based machines; hard disk; high density floppy drive.

Price: $395 (Windows version); $295 (DOS version)

Product name: Process Charter for Windows
Producer: Scitor Corp.
  333 Middlefield Rd.
  Menlo Park, CA 94025
  Phone: (415) 462 4200
  (800) 549 9876
  Fax: (415) 462 4201
  E-mail: info@scitor.com

Description: *PC Week* predicted that this process management software "will be 'must

have' software for managers in 1995." Scitor markets their product as "the flowcharter with brains." It combines flowcharting with process simulation. This versatility lets users create presentation quality flowcharts, simulate real-world situations, and conduct "what-if" scenarios to determine if changing variables can improve a process.

Requirements: IBM-compatible 386 or higher; 4 MB RAM (8 MG recommended); DOS 5.0 or higher; Windows 3.1; VGA or higher resolution monitor; hard drive with 8 MB available; $3\frac{1}{2}$" high density disk drive; Microsoft-compatible mouse input device; printers and plotters supported by Windows 3.1.

Price: $595

Product name: Project Kickstart
Producer: Experience in Software, Inc.
  2000 Hearst Ave.
  Berkeley, CA 94709
  Phone: (510) 644 0694
  (800) 678 7008
  Fax: (510) 644 3823

Description: The purpose of this 30-minute project organizer is to simplify project planning. It lets users outline a project quickly. The menu prompts you to name a project, clarify goals, develop a lists of tasks and assignments, and anticipate obstacles. It can be used as a stand-alone program or as the front end to project management software.

Requirements: IBM PC; 256 K RAM; 360 K on hard disk; DOS 2.0 or higher; enhanced graphics adapter or video graphics array.

Price: $97.50 (This product is also distributed by QSoft Solutions (to order call (800) 669 9701).

Product name: Proquis 9000
Producer: Deans Hill Systems Limited
  The Granary
  Litle Deans Hill Farm
  Brodgar, Sittingbourne
  Kent, England ME9 8BB
  Phone: (01622) 884213
  Fax: (01622) 884714

Description: This software (formerly named Feedback 9000) is designed for companies involved in ISO 9000 implementation and maintenance. It provides extensive reporting and analysis in the following areas: customer care: supplier control; process control; corrective and preventive actions; personnel records; and equipment. More than 500 companies and government agencies world-wide have implemented Proquis 9000 including British Gas North Eastern, Toshiba Medical Systems-Sweden, AT & T Wireless Communication Products Ltd. U.K., the Ministry of Defence (U.K.), Johnson Matthey, Redland, and the Royal Mail. In spring 1995, Dean Hill Systems Limited announced that Santana & Associates (based in Los Angeles) would be their American representative. Santana & Associates can be reached at (818) 503 2515.

Requirements: If running under Windows 386SX25 with 2 MB or RAM, 10 MB of hard drive is required. If running outside Windows as a DOS product 386SX25 with 4 MB of RAM, 10 MB hard drive is required. Currently available under IBM-compatible PCs only and Novell, Lantastics, or similar networking facilities. Alternative platforms expected in 1995: SCO UNIX, Windows. Planned for 1996, AS400 and VAX.

Price: £295 (single user ex-UK); £395 (multi-user network version unlimited users, site license, single server).

Product name: Q9000 Quality Manual Including 26 Operating Procedures on Disk

Producer: The Harrington Group, Inc.
3208-C East Colonial Dr., Ste. 253
Orlando, FL 32803
Phone: (407) 898 7101
Fax: (407) 898 5725

Description: This manual covers Q9000-1, Q9001, Q9002, Q9003, and Q9004-1 requirements. Users can view the contents of each Q9000 standard and corresponding documentation simultaneously.

Requirements: This manual is available in the following format: Wordperfect 5.1 for DOS; Wordperfect 6.0 for Windows; MS DOS 2.0 for Windows; MS Word 6.0 for Windows.

Price: $199

Product name: QC Tools

Producer: Abacus Concepts Inc.
1918 Bonita Ave.
Berkeley, CA 94704

Phone: (510) 540 1949
(800) 666 7828
Fax: (510) 540 0260
E-mail: abacus@applelink.apple.
com

Description: This add-in package to Abacus Concept Inc.'s StatView adds a new set of tools and charts for quality control analyses. These quality control tests include xbar, range, standard deviation, individual measurement, capability, p/np, c/u, and Pareto analysis.

Requirements: Requires StatView 4.0.1. Statview requires the following: Macintosh (LC or better recommended) with at least 2 MB of free RAM for 68K Macs and 4 MB of free RAM for Power Macs; System 7.0 or later; hard disk.

Price: $695 (price when StatView 4.1 and QC Tools are purchased together. StatView 4.1 purchased separately is $595).

Product name: QFD/Capture Software

Producer: International Techne Group, Inc.
GOAL/QPC (distributor)
13 Branch St.
Methuen, MA 01844 1953
Phone: (508) 685 6370
(800) 643 4316
Fax: (508) 685 6151

Description: This software lets users perform quality function deployment (QFD) on a PC. It is the most widely used QFD software package in the world.

Requirements: MS Windows version: IBM or compatible 286 or 386; MS Windows 3.0 or 3.1; 4 MB RAM, 2 MB free; 2 MB hard disk space. DOS version: IBM or compatible 386 or higher; DOS 2.0 or later; minimum 480K RAM; 2 MB hard disk space. Macintosh version: System 7 or later; 4 MB RAM; 2 MB free; 2 MB hard disk space.

Price: $895

Product name: QFD Designer

Producer: Qualisoft Corp.
7395 Bridgeway West
West Bloomfield, MI 48322
Phone: (313) 626 4070
Fax: (313) 851 5547

Description: This easy-to-use software can be used to create and customize quality function deployment charts. It runs as an application of Microsoft Windows and allows users to edit directly on the chart. A German language version is available.

Requirements: IBM or 100 percent compatible computer, AT or better; 1 MB RAM extended; Microsoft Windows 3.0 or later; hard disk; EGA or VGA graphics; mouse.

Price: $975 (This product is also distributed by the American Supplier Institute (to order call (800) 462 4500) and QSoft Solutions (to order call (800) 669 9701).)

Product name: QI Analyst
Producer: SPSS Inc.
　　　　　444 N. Michigan Ave.
　　　　　Chicago, IL 60611 3962
　　　　　Phone: (312) 329 2400
　　　　　　　　　(800) 543 2185
　　　　　Fax: 　 (312) 329 3668

Description: This statistical process control package for Windows provides a set of charts, tests, and statistics to help users improve processes, cut waste, and reduce nonconformance. QI Analyst can be used to perform the following functions: producing control charts, histograms, and Pareto charts; applying Shewhart control tests; running capability tests; testing for normal distributions; and calculating trend lines and statistics.

Requirements: IBM-compatible computer, 386 or faster; minimum of 2 MB of RAM (4 MB or more recommended); disk drive with 2 MB of free storage; Microsoft Windows 3.1 or higher; PC or MS DOS 3.1 or higher; Windows-compatible mouse; VGA monitor.

Price: $695 (corporate price); $495 (academic price)

Product name: QI Analyst for Gage R & R
Producer: SPSS Inc.
　　　　　444 N. Michigan Ave.
　　　　　Chicago, IL 60611 3962
　　　　　Phone: (312) 329 2400
　　　　　　　　　(800) 543 2185
　　　　　Fax: 　 (312) 329 3668

Description: The purpose of this package is to help manufacturers determine the quality of their measurement system. It generates gage performance curves and control charts for repeatability, reproducibility, and accuracy. It is modeled after the *Measurement Systems Analysis Reference Manual* developed by the Automotive Industry Action Group. QI Analyst Gage R & R can be used alone or as an add-on module to QI Analyst.

Requirements: IBM-compatible computer, 386 or faster; minimum of 2 MB of RAM (4 MB or more recommended); hard disk with minimum of 2 MB of storage space; Microsoft Windows 3.1 or higher; PC or MS DOS 3.1 or higher; Windows-compatible mouse; VGA monitor.

Price: $295

Product name: Q-Pulse
Producer: Gael Quality
　　　　　Scottish Enterprise Technology Park
　　　　　East Kilbride, Scotland G75 OQU
　　　　　Phone: 013552 72859
　　　　　Fax: 　 013552 72864

Description: This series of modules is designed to help companies cost effectively manage the paperwork, record keeping, and other administrative tasks involved in achieving and maintaining BS 5750/EN 29000/ISO 9000. It can be used to document the following: training of employees; record of nonconformance; equipment calibration; corrective action; auditing; list of suppliers; and supplier's quality performance.

Requirements: IBM-compatible computer, 386 or faster; 4 MB RAM; Microsoft Windows 3.1; MS DOS 5.0 or higher; 14" color monitor; 2.5 MB hard disk space. Q-Pulse can be accessed on the following networks: Novell, LAN Manager; Workgroup for Windows, and UNIX running NFS.

Price: $750 (standalone version or three user network); $1495 (five user network); $1995 (ten user network)

Product name: Quality Workbench
Producer: IdeaGen Software Limited
　　　　　12 Bank Rd.
　　　　　Matlock, Derbyshire
　　　　　England DE4 3NF
　　　　　Phone: 01629 56600
　　　　　Fax: 　 01629 56060

Description: This Windows application has been designed to simplify documentation and other administrative tasks associated with BS

5750/ISO 9000 compliance. Quality Workbench dramatically reduces the amount of time spent on documentation, freeing managers to focus on quality improvement initiatives. It includes these standard modules: system manager; document control; customers; customer complaints; audits; nonconformance; and personnel. The following modules can be added to the system: vendor assessment, and calibration and test records. Quality Workbench works with standard word processors and spreadsheets. It also works with electronic mail. Quality Workbench's unique "Message Box" feature ensures that users are aware of situations requiring action. Users can respond by simply double-clicking on the message. Everybody on the network has a message box. The messages are automatically generated by the system.

Requirements: IBM or 100 percent compatible PC, 80386SX or higher processor; Microsoft Windows 3.1 or higher; Microsoft DOS 5.0 or higher; 4 MB RAM minimum; Windows-supported VGA monitor; Windows-compatible mouse. The following networks are supported (specified release or higher): Novell Netware version 2.0a; Microsoft LAN Manager version 2.0; 3 Com3+ Share network version 1.5.1; DEC Pathworks version 1.0; Banyan Lines network version 2.1; Microsoft Windows for Workgroups Version 3.1; Microsoft Windows NT version 3.1. Other networks are supported, call IdeaGen Software for details.

Price: £1,995 + VAT for network ready version, additional users £795 + VAT each, five additional user pack £3,200 + VAT; £795 + VAT for Personal Edition; £595 + VAT vendor assessment module.

Product name: Quantum SPC/DC
Producer: Allan-Bradley
DataMyte Division
14960 Minnetonka Industrial Rd.
Minnetonka, MN 55435
Phone: (612) 935 7704
Fax: (612) 935 0018
Description: This Windows-based software allows an IBM PC or compatible computer to be used as a data collector, collecting data directly from gages, barcode readers, or the keyboard.

Requirements: IBM-compatible computer, 286 or higher; minimum of 2 MB RAM; hard disk drive; any monitor compatible with Windows version 3.1; PC DOS or MS DOS version 3.1 or higher; Windows version 3.1.
Price: $1,200

Product name: Quantum SPC/QA
Producer: Allan-Bradley
DataMyte Division
14960 Minnetonka Industrial Rd.
Minnetonka, MN 55435
Phone: (612) 935 7704
Fax: (612) 935 0018
Description: This quality analysis software provides detailed statistical process control analysis and reporting.
Requirements: IBM-compatible computer, 386 or higher; minimum of 8 MB RAM; hard disk drive; any monitor compatible with Windows version 3.1 (a monitor with a resolution of 800 X600 is recommended); PC DOS or MS DOS version 3.1 or higher; Windows version 3.1; a mouse.
Price: $2,500 (In 1995, Allan-Bradley and Intercim Corporation, a Minneapolis-based software company, announced a joint marketing relationship. As a result, the Quantum SPC/QA software is also distributed by Intercim (call (800) 445 7785).)

Product name: Raosoft Survey
Producer: Raosoft, Inc.
6645 NE Windermere Rd.
Seattle, WA 98115 7942
Phone: (206) 525 4025
Fax: (206) 525 4947
E-mail: raosoft@halcyon.com
Description: This versatile software package can be used to create questionnaires, analyze data, and generate reports and graphics. It includes more than twenty ready-to-use survey form templates and there is no limit to the number of questionnaires it can handle (except for system capacity). In 1992, *Human Resource Executive* magazine designated it as one of the "Best New HR Products." Raosoft also offers SurveyFirst, a version which will support up to 1,000 questionnaires.
Requirements: IBM computer or compatible with at least 512K memory; DOS 2.0 or later;

CGA, EGA, VGA, or Hercules graphics card; networkable.

Price: $495 (Raosoft Survey); $195 (Raosoft SurveyFirst)

Product name: The SAS System
Producer: SAS Institute
SAS Campus Dr.
Cary, NC 27513
Phone: (919) 677 8000
Fax: (919) 677 8123
Description: This modular, integrated, hardware-independent system is used by more than three milllion users world-wide to access, manage, analyze, and present data. It can be used for a range of applications including design of experiments, statistical process control, and process capability analysis. It supports quality improvement and reengineering efforts. It is used by companies in almost every type of industry as well as by governmental agencies and educational institutions.
Requirements: The SAS System operates on a wide range of computing platforms, from mainframe to minicomputers to UNIX workstations to Windows and OS/2.
Price: $3,395

Product name: 7MP-PC IV
Producer: Quality America Inc.
7650 East Broadway, Ste. 208 210
Tucson, AZ 85710
Phone: (602) 722 6154
(800) 722 6154
Fax: (602) 722 6705
Description: This Windows-based software package can be used to create the following seven management and planning tools: affinity diagram; interrelationship diagraph; prioritization matrix; matrix diagram; process decision program chart; tree diagram; and activity network diagram. The system gives detailed descriptions of each tool, helps users decide which tool is best for a situation, and guides users through the formation of the chart.
Requirements: 386 machine or better; 4 MB RAM; hard or floppy disk drive; 1.59 MB RAM for program; 512K RAM for data; MS Windows 3.1 or higher, MS Windows NT,

IBM OS/2 2.0 or higher; CGA, EGA, or VGA monitor; network version available.
Price: $695

Product name: SigmaPlot
Producer: Jandel Scientific Software
2591 Kerner Blvd.
San Rafael, CA 94901
Phone: (415) 453 6700
(800) 874 1888
Fax: (415) 453 7769
E-mail: sales@jandel.com
Description: Jandel Scientific develops scientific and engineering software that is used around the world. This graphing software can be used by scientists and engineers to produce publication-quality graphs. It includes a full range of scientific graphing options such as multiple plot types, technical axis scales, error bars, axis breaks, and multiple axes.
Requirements: SigmaPlot for Windows: IBM-compatible, 386 or higher; 4 MB RAM; hard drive with 5 MB free; Windows 3.1; math coprocessor is recommended, SigmaPlot for DOS: IBM-compatible, 386 or higher; 4 MB of RAM with 1.5 MB dedicated as Expanded (EMS) LIM version 4.0 memory; 6 MB of available disk space upon installation and at least VGA or Super VGA card and monitor; DOS 2.0 or greater; math coprocessor is recommended. Will run as a DOS application under Windows. SigmaPlot for Macintosh: MacPlus or higher with 2 MB RAM; hard drive with 5 MB free and System 4.2 or greater; math coprocessor is recommended.
Price: $495

Product name: SPC 9000
Producer: Powerway, Inc.
9855 Crosspoint Blvd.
Indianapolis, IN 46256
Phone: (317) 577 8100
(800) 964 9004
Fax: (317) 577 0450
Description: This real-time statistical process control software lets users collect data manually or electronically and responds to process variation immediately. It can be used to lower defect rates, detect process variation, respond to out-of-control conditions, reduce audit preparation time, and reduce or eliminate final

inspection. It analyzes and graphs collected data into the following charts and reports: X-bar and Range; X-bar and Sigma; individual and moving range; median; P chart; U chart; C chart; nP chart; histograms; Paretos; and pie charts. It can help companies comply with ISO 9000 and other regulatory programs.

Requirements: IBM computer or compatible, 386 or higher; 4 MB RAM or higher; 7 MB available on hard disk; VGA monitor; Windows 3.1 or higher.

Price: $89

Product name: SPC-PC IV Windows
Producer: Quality America Inc.
7650 East Broadway, Ste. 208-210
Tucson, AZ 85710
Phone: (602) 722 6154
(800) 722 6154
Fax: (602) 722 6705

Description: This Windows-based SPC software includes the following charting capabilities: individual x/moving range; x-bar/range; x-bar/sigma; histogram; capability analysis; CuSum; EWMA; auto correlation; scatter diagram; moving average/moving range; moving average/moving sigma; Pareto charts; multivariate control charts; short run analysis; p charts; np charts; c charts; u charts; and checksheets.

Requirements: 386/16 machine or better; 2 megabytes or more RAM; 1.2 MB hard disk space; MS Windows 3.1 or higher, MS Windows NT, IBM OS/2 2.0 or higher; VGA or better monitor; network version available.

Price: $795

Product name: S.P.C. Training Simulator
Producer: Qualitran Professional Services Inc.
P.O. Box 295
Stroud, Ontario
Canada L0L 2M0
Phone: (705) 722 8550
(800) 461 9902
Fax: (705) 722 0324

Description: This SPC training software can be used to demonstrate the following: natural variation; distributions; average, range, and standard deviation; areas under the curve; process capability; process shifts and spread; and process improvements. It generates control charts with simulated results.

Requirements: IBM PC/XT/AT or compatible; 128 K RAM, one drive.

Price: $389

Product name: SPC3D
Producer: SPC3D
30011 Ivy Glenn Dr., Ste. 107
Laguana Niguel, CA 92677
Phone: (714) 249 4210
(800) 89-SPC3D
Fax: (714) 249 1663

Description: SPC3D markets this product as "the next generation of SPC software." It supports seventy different statistics and eighty-nine different types of control charts. SPC3D calculates both Shewhart and Burr charts. It has more types of variable and attribute control charts than any other major SPC software package. SPC3D helps users select the correct control chart. Charts can be displayed in 3D or 2D.

Requirements: SPC3D supports more than 400 terminals, printers, and plotters. It runs on DOS (without Windows), Windows, OS/2, and NT. It will be available soon on Macintosh, Sun, and UNIX platforms.

Price: $895

Product name: SPCI+
Producer: Advanced Systems & Designs, Inc.
1270-F Rankin St.
Troy, MI 48083
Phone: (810) 616 8818
Fax: (810) 585 7408

Description: This statistical process control software performs both attribute (qualitative) and variable (quantitative) data analysis. Control charts include: X and R; X and Standard Deviation; Moving Average and Moving Range; Individuals and Moving Range; Linear X and R charts for variable data; Cumulative Sum; p, np, c, and u charts for attribute data. Statistical analyses include histogram, process capability, cumulative probability, and Pareto charts.

Requirements: IBM PC or compatible; 640K RAM; DOS 3.0 or greater; hard disk; CGA, EGA, or VGA graphics.

Price: $950 (This product is also distributed by the American Supplier Institute (call (800) 462 4500).)

Product name: SPCI+ Professional

Producer: Advanced Systems & Designs, Inc.
1270-F Rankin St.
Troy, MI 48083
Phone: (810) 616 8818
Fax: (810) 585 7408

Description: This package combines the features of SPCI with automated data collection, gaging R & R software, and a DataMyte interface. A multiuser version (SPCI+ Network) is also available.

Requirements: IBM PC or compatible; 640K RAM; DOS 3.0 or greater; hard disk; EGA or VGA graphics.

Price: $1,395 (SPCI+ Professional); $3,500 (SPCI+ Network 10 users). This product is also distributed by the American Supplier Institute (call (800) 462 4500).

Product name: SPC/PI+ Advanced SPC Software

Producer: Qualitran Professional Services Inc.
P.O. Box 295
Stroud, Ontario
Canada L0L 2M0
Phone: (705) 722 8550
(800) 461 9902 (in U.S. only)
Fax: (705) 722 0324

Description: This Windows-based SPC software includes the following features: statistical analysis; process capability; basic control charts; cummulative sum control charts; control charts for non-normal data; exponentially weighted moving average (EWMA) charts; and the correlogram and the EWMA Predict chart.

Requirements: IBM-compatible computer, 386 or higher; 640K RAM plus 2 MB RAM (4 MB RAM recommended); Windows 3.0 or 3.1; 3 MB hard disk space required; network version available.

Price: $995

Product name: SPSS 6.1 for Windows

Producer: SPSS Inc.
444 N. Michigan Ave.
Chicago, IL 60611 3962
Phone: (312) 329 2400
(800) 543 2185
Fax: (312) 329 3668

Description: SPSS has been a leader in the area of statistical software for more than two decades. An earlier version of this software, SPSS 5.0 for Windows, won the *PC Magazine* Editor's Choice award in 1993. SPSS for Windows can be used for survey research, quality improvement, and other research projects.

Description: IBM-compatible computer, 386 or faster; 8 MB RAM; hard disk with at least 20 MB of storage space with an additional 10 MB for a swap file; Microsoft Windows 3.1 or higher; PC or MS DoS 3.1 or higher; Windows-compatible mouse; VGA monitor or better.

Price: $695

Product name: SQCpack for Windows

Producer: PQ Systems (Productivity-Quality Systems Inc.)
10468 Miamisburg-Springboro Rd.
Miamisburg, OH 45342
Phone: (513) 885 2255
(800) 777 3020
Fax: (513) 885 2252
E-mail: sales@pqsys-hq.mhs.
compuserve.com (Internet)
mhs:sales@pqsys-hq
(CompuServe)

Description: The first version of this easy-to-use statistical process control software was developed in 1981. This version combines statistical process control techniques with the flexibility of the Windows platform. SQCpack software provides the following charting capabilities: x-bar; individuals (x); moving range (MR); range; sigma; median; run chart; out-of-control test; histograms; capability indices; and p, np, c, and u charts. It includes the SQC Quality Advisor, which provides online real-time SPC assistance and advice.

Requirements: IBM PC or compatible; 4 MB RAM; Windows 3.1; network version available.

Price: $595

Product name: SQCpack/PLUS

Producer: PQ Systems (Productivity-Quality Systems Inc.)
10468 Miamisburg-Springboro Rd.
Miamisburg, OH 45342
Phone: (513) 885 2255

(800) 777 3020
Fax: (513) 885 2252
E-mail: sales@pqsys-hq.mhs.
compuserve.com (Internet)
mhs:sales@pqsys-hq
(CompuServe)

Description: SQCpack/PLUS is one of the best-selling statistical process control software programs for DOS. It combines control charting with problem-solving tools. SQCpack/PLUS has the following charting capabilities: variables; histogram; capability analysis; descriptive statistics; attributes; Pareto; and cause and effect.

Requirements: IBM PC or compatible with MS-DOS 3.1 or higher; minimum 512K memory; a hard disk; network version available.

Price: $995

Product name: SQCsignals

Producer: PQ Systems (Productivity-Quality Systems Inc.)
10468 Miamisburg-Springboro Rd.
Miamisburg, OH 45342
Phone: (513) 885 2255
(800) 777 3020
Fax: (513) 885 2252
E-mail: s a l e s @ p q s y s - h q . m h s .
compuserve.com (Internet)
mhs:sales@pqsys-hq
(CompuServe)

Description: This online, real-time process monitoring software provides instant process feedback and information. Operators can respond to processes by following the signals that the software provides. SQCsignals produces charts and reports quickly and the online SPC Quality Advisor provides SPC assistance and advice. In addition, SQCsignals can be set to create an audit trail of critical information. This record keeping function is helpful to firms complying with ISO 9000 standards. DOS, Windows, and network versions are available.

Requirements: DOS version: IBM PC or compatible, 386 or higher; MS-DOS 3.3 or higher; 4 MB memory; a hard disk. Windows version: IBM PC or compatible; Windows 3.1 or higher; 4 MB memory.

Price: $495

Product name: Statistica/w

Producer: StatSoft
2825 E. 18th St.
Tulsa, OK 74104
Phone: (918) 583 4149
Fax: (918) 583 4376

Description: StatSoft, with headquarters in Oklahoma, has sales offices in Germany and the United Kingdom. The company was formed in 1984 by a group of professors and scientists. Statistica is a fully integrated statistics, graphics, and analytic data management system. The first version of Statistica, the DOS version, was released in 1991. The complete Windows version, Statistica/w, was released in 1994. Statistica/w has received high ratings from major software periodicals including *Byte*, *Windows Magazine*, *Insight*, *Government Computer News Technology Report*, *Medical Software Reviews*, *MacWelt* (the German edition of MacWorld), and *C'T Magazin* (a German equivalent of *Byte*). In February, 1995 *Windows Magazine* named Statistica one of the "Top 100 Software Products."

Requirements: 386 machine or better; 4 MB RAM; hard or floppy disk drive; 10.4 MB RAM for program; Windows 3.1 or higher; CGA, EGA, or VGA monitor, network version available.

Price: $995

Product name: STATnet/2

Producer: Intercim Corporation
501 East Highway 13
Minneapolis, MN 55337 2877
Phone: (612) 894 9010
(800) 445 7785
Fax: (612) 894 0399

Description: This network-based information management system provides real-time, plant-wide quality data collection, analysis, and management. Its purpose is to improve the quality and productivity of manufacturing processes. STATnet/2 provides a real-time view of all manufacturing processes and gives plant manufacturers immediate feedback on process performance.

Requirements: This DOS-based information system operates on PC workstations that use a local area network to manage the flow of information among production workers, supervisors, engineers, and managers.

Price: $13,500 (STATnet/2 base software); $1,000 (each user license)

Product name: Statselect
Producer: Objectives Management
8415 Granville St., #2
Vancouver, British Columbia
Canada V6P 4X9
Phone: (604) 880 2230
Fax: (604) 880 2230
E-mail: OMG@MINDLINK.BC.
CA

Description: The DOS version of this SQC software tool for non-statisticians was developed in 1992. A Windows version was developed in 1994. Statselect is a multiuser spreadsheet with SPC charting, data collection, and forecasting tools that can be used in labs, offices, and production areas. It can be used to perform the following functions: histograms; Pareto analysis; frequency distributions; quality analysis and CpL, CpU, and CpK; trend, individual, X & R, and X & S charts; EWMA; multiple regression; polynomial regression; and c, u, and NP charts.

Requirements: DOS version: IBM or compatible computer, 286 or higher; 365K RAM; PC DOS or MS DOS. Windows version: IBM or compatible computer, 386 or higher; 4 MB RAM; 2 MB of free hard disk space; MS Windows 3.1; a VGA monitor; a mouse.

Price: $695

Product name: StatView
Producer: Abacus Concepts Inc.
1918 Bonita Ave.
Berkeley, CA 94704
Phone: (510) 540 1949
(800) 666 7828
Fax: (510) 540 0260
E-mail: abacus@applelink.apple.
com

Description: This award-winning integrated data analysis and presentation package performs complex statistical analysis and creates publication quality reports with easy-to-read charts and graphs. It is a six time *MacWorld* World Class winnner and a *MacUser* Eddy winner.

Requirements: Macintosh (LC or better recommended) with at least 2 MB of free RAM for 68K Macs and 4 MB of free RAM for Power Macs; System 7.0 or later; hard disk. Abacus plans to introduce a Windows version of StatView in the fall of 1995.

Price: $595 (purchased separately); $695 (price when StatView and QC Tools are purchased together)

Product name: Supplier Quality 9000
Producer: Powerway, Inc.
9855 Crosspoint Blvd.
Indianapolis, IN 46256
Phone: (317) 577 8100
(800) 964 9004
Fax: (317) 577 0450

Description: Supplier quality 9000 lets users configure, schedule, complete, and review supplier evaluations. Although it is useful to anyone working with vendors, it has been especially designed for companies seeking ISO 9000 registration. It is not necessary to re-enter supplier data since the software accepts data from other applications.

Requirements: IBM computer or compatible, 386 or higher; 4 MB RAM or higher; 11 MB available on hard disk; Windows 3.1 or higher.

Price: $89

Product name: The Survey Manager
Producer: Insync Corporation
1420 Spring Hill, Rd., Ste. 600
McLean, VA 22102
Phone: (703) 847 1497
Fax: (703) 847 9803

Description: The Survey Manager is Insync's base software system. This easy-to-use software helps users design, administer, and analyze surveys. Insync also markets four other PC-based software systems that are extensions of the Survey Manager program. These include "Assess-TQM," "The Customer Manager," "The Organization Manager," and "Task." The programs come with resident survey questionnaires that have been developed by recognized experts in their respective fields. Contact Insync about further information about these software systems. In 1991, *Human Resource Executive* magazine recognized "Assess-TQM" as a "Best New HR Product."

Requirements: IBM PC or compatible; 640K RAM; hard or floppy disk drive; 400 K RAM for program; monochrome, CGA, EGA, or VGA monitor; PC DOS or MS DOS.
Price: $645

Product name: Survey Pro
Producer: Apian Software
P.O. Box 1224
Menlo Park, CA 94026 1224
Phone: (415) 694 2900
(800) 237 4565
Fax: (415) 694 2904
Description: This economical and easy-to-use software designs questionnaires, tabulates responses, and generates cross-tabulations, graphs, and reports. The first version, Survey Pro for DOS, was introduced in 1991 and received *PC Week* magazine's "Analyst's Choice" award. A Windows version has been introduced for frequent or large surveys. Many companies have used Survey Pro to measure customer satisfaction, an integral element of a TQM program.
Requirements: DOS version: IBM PC or 100 percent compatible; DOS 2.0+; 520 kb minimum available base RAM; dual or single floppy disk; hard disk recommended; any display type; mouse optional; Hewlett-Packard Laser Jet II/III/IV, DeskJet 500, or 100 percent PCL compatible. Windows version: IBM computer or compatible, 386 or faster; Windows 3.1; 4 MB RAM; mouse.
Price: $249 (DOS version); $695 (Windows version)

Product name: TeamFlow
Producer: CFM Inc.
60 The Great Rd.
P.O. Box 353
Bedford, MA 01730
Phone: (617) 275 5258
(800) 647 1708
Fax: (617) 275 7008
E-mail: teamflow@world.std.com
Description: This software can be used to create flowcharts that document team based work processes. In addition to mapping processes, it links tasks to agendas, minutes, guidelines, spreadsheets, drawings, reports, and other documents that may be viewed online. This easy-to-use workflow software lets team members visualize what is to be done, who is involved, and when and how tasks are to be completed. Both Macintosh and Windows versions are available. TeamFlow is also available in network versions. TeamFlow is used by more than 1,000 companies world-wide, including 3M, American Standard, Apple Computer, Bechtel Corporation, Boeing, General Motors, Hewlett Packard, Host Marriott Hotels, and Texas Instruments. In the fall of 1994, CFM released TeamFlow Charter, a trimmed down version of TeamFlow priced at $95. It is aimed at companies involved in TQM. Like TeamFlow, it can be used to create graphic presentation of the workflow for any TQM project.
Requirements: Windows version: Intel 386 class computer with 4 MB RAM; 2 MB of free disk space; Windows 3.1 or greater. Macintosh version: Mac SE or later with 2 MB RAM; 1 MB of free disk space; Mac System 7.0 or greater.
Price: $295

Product name: Top Down Flowcharter
Producer: Kaetron Software Corp.
25211 Grogans Mill Rd., Ste. 260
The Woodlands, TX 77380
Phone: (713) 298 1500
(800) 938 8900
Fax: (713) 298 2520
Description: This cross-platform flowcharting program allows flowcharting files to be shared in Macintosh and Windows. It can be used to produce flowcharts, organizational charts, process flow diagrams, dataflow diagrams, work flows, project flows, functional diagrams, matrix diagrams, brainstorming diagrams, and other flowcharts, diagrams, and charts.
Requirements: Macintosh version: System 6.07 or later; a hard disk is recommended; supports printing on Macintosh-compatible laser printers, dot matrix printers, and plotters. Windows version: IBM-compatible computer with a 20 MHz 80386 or higher processor; Windows 3.1 or higher; VGA monitor; mouse or compatible pointing device; 6 MB RAM; 4 MB hard disk space; compatible plotter, laser, and dot matrix printers.
Price: $345

Product name: TQM Toolkit

Producer: Kaetron Software Corp.
25211 Grogans Mill Rd., Ste. 260
The Woodlands, TX 77380
Phone: (713) 298 1500
(800) 938 8900
Fax: (713) 298 2520

Description: This TQM implementation package for Windows and Macintosh includes the following components: a practical TQM implementation guide; a glossary of TQM terms; definitions of the symbols used in flow-charting; TopDown Flowcharter software; examples of TQM charts created using TopDown Flowcharter; templates; and custom charting symbols for TQM.

Requirements: Macintosh version: System 6.07 or later; a hard disk is recommended but not required; supports printing on Macintosh compatible laser printers, dot matrix printers, and plotters. Windows version: IBM-compatible computer with a 386 20MHz or higher processor; Windows 3.1 or higher; VGA monitor; mouse or compatible pointing device; 4 MB RAM; 3 MB hard disk space; compatible plotter; laser, and dot matrix printers.

Price: $399

Product name: Visual Assessor

Producer: American Information Systems, Inc.
P.O. Box 387, Charleston Rd.
Wellsboro, PA 16901
Phone: (717) 724 1588
(800) 903 4000
Fax: (717) 724 2554

Description: This easy-to-use PC-based software helps companies collect and maintain data relating to their internal assessment, client assessment, and supplier assessment. It instantly converts these results into graphic displays. The software comes bundled with the Malcolm Baldrige Award guidelines and ISO 9000 criteria. The software can also be bundled with Quality Air Force criteria or other customized assessment criteria.

Requirements: Runs on networked 386 and 486 microcomputers; requires at least a 386 computer with 4 MB of RAM; Windows 3.1 or higher; a color monitor.

Price: $595 (This product is also distributed by QSoft Solutions (call (800) 669 9701).)

Product name: Winflow

Producer: Quality America Inc.
7650 East Broadway, Ste. 208 210
Tucson, AZ 85710
Phone: (602) 722 6154
(800) 722 6154
Fax: (602) 722 6705

Description: This Windows-based software creates presentation quality flowcharts, cause-and-effect diagrams, and organization charts. Users can use one of two options for chart formation: the simple "drag and drop" symbol placement, or the text-based system which translates typed words into diagrams.

Requirements: 368/16 machine or better; 2 MB or more RAM, 12 MB hard disk space; MS Windows 3.1 or higher, MS Windows NT, IBM OS/2 2.0 or higher; VGA or better monitor recommended.

Price: $200; $100 (as an add-on to SPC-PC IV or 7 MP-PC IV)

Product name: Workflow Analyzer

Producer: Meta Software Corporation
125 Cambridge Park Dr.
Cambridge, MA 02140
Phone: (617) 576 6920
Fax: (617) 661 2008

Description: This business reengineering tool lets users model business problems and perform "what if" analyses of possible solutions. It can be used to study any workflow-oriented process such as the movement of checks through a bank. In fact, Workflow Analyzer has been used by Chemical Bank, First Fidelity Bank (based in Newark, NJ), and Centerbank (a savings bank based in Waterbury, CT) in several process improvement efforts, including check encoding, reengineering of the teller function at branch banks, and in consumer lending operations.

Requirements: Runs on Macintosh (MacIIfx, Centris, Quadra), Sun (Sparc, Solaris), or HP (9000/700, PA-RISC) workstations; a minimum of 32 MB RAM; hard disk drive with 36 MB free storage; CGA, EGA, or VGA monitor.

Price: $34,995 (per license, includes the first year's maintenance); $29,995 (two to four licenses, per license, includes the first year's maintenance); $5,000 annual maintenance (per license)

iii Software finding aid

Consult the categories of applications listed below to locate software useful for your needs. Profiles of each product can be found above in alphabetical order.

Audits

Audit Master
ISOxPERT
Proquis 9000
Q-Pulse
Quality Workbench
SQCsignals

Baldrige Award

Helping an Organization Succeed: Using the Malcolm Baldrige National Quality Award Criteria
Visual Assessor

Benchmarking

BenchMarker Plus
LearnerFirst Benchmarking

Calibration management

Calibration Manager
Calibration Recall System
The Gauge Program Software
The Integrated Quality System
ISOxPERT
Proquis 9000
Q-Pulse
Quality Workbench

Decision analysis

Optionist
The SAS System

Design of experiments

DOE-PC IV
JMP
JUSE-QCAS
Optimum Design of Experiments
The SAS System

Flowcharting/diagramming

ABC FlowCharter 4.0
allCLEAR III
Design/IDEF
EasyFlow for Windows
FlowChart Express
Flow Charting 4
Process Charter for Windows
TeamFlow
TopDown Flowcharter
Winflow
Workflow Analyzer

Gauge repeatability and reproducibility (gauge R & R)

CPCI
Database for Quality (DBQ)
FACTORYnet Q/S
GageTalker III Plus Real Time
GageTalker DataPage III
The Gauge Program Sofware
ISOxPERT
QI Analyst Gage R & R
STATnet/2

Generating ideas

The Idea Generator Plus
Inspiration

ISO 9000 Implementation/documentation

Applied CIM
Audit Master
Calibration Manager
Corrective Action: Problem Management Software for Windows
Cost of Quality
Document Manager 9000
The Integrated Quality System
ISOxPERT
LearnerFirst How to Implement ISO 9000
Nonconformance Tracking: Reject & Failure Management Software
Proquis 9000
Q9000 Quality Manual Including 26 Operating Procedures on Disk
Q-Pulse
Quality Workbench

SPC 9000
SQCsignals
Supplier Quality 9000
Visual Assessor

QC Tools
The SAS System
7 MP-PC IV
TQM Toolkit

Manufacturing process data collection and analysis

Applied CIM
Applied Stats
Applied Stats Analyst
FACTORYnet Q/S
Gagetalker III Plus Real Time
Gagetalker Datapage III
The Integrated Quality System
ISOxPERT
JUSE-QCAS
Network Monitor
Nonconformance Tracking: Reject & Failure Management Software
Prime Factor FFT
QI Analyst Gage R & R
Quantum SPC/DC
SPC 9000
SQCsignals
STATnet/2

Process modeling

BenchMarker Plus
Design/IDEF
LearnerFirst Process Management
Optima!
Worklfow Analyzer

Project planning

Project Kickstart

Quality function deployment (QFD)

QFD/Capture Software
QFD Designer

Quality tools

Juran Quality Improvement Toolkit
JUSE-QCAS
The Memory Jogger Plus+ Software (7 M & P Tools)
The Memory Jogger Software (7 QC Tools)

Reengineering

ABC FlowCharter 4.0
allClear III
Benchmarker Plus
Design/IDEF
Optima!
The SAS System
Workflow Analyzer

Scientific graphing

SigmaPlot

Simulation

Design/IDEF
JMP
Optima!
Process Charter for Windows
The SAS System
S.P.C. Training Simulator
Workflow Analyzer

Statistical methods

JMP
Minitab Statistical Software
The SAS System
SigmaPlot
SPSS 6.1 for Windows
Statistica/w
StatView

Statistical process control (SPC)

Applied CIM
Applied Stats Analyst
Corrective Action: Problem Management Software for Windows
Cost of Quality
CPCI
Database for Quality (DBQ)
Essentials of SPC Computer-Based Training
FACTORYnet Q/S
GageTalker III Plus Real Time

GageTalker DataPage III
The Integrated Quality System
JMP
JUSE-QCAS
Magic Window SPC Software
Network Monitor
Nonconformance Tracking: Reject & Failure
    Management Software
Prime Factor FFT
QI Analyst
Quantum SPC/QA
Quantum SPC/DC
The SAS System
SPC 9000
SPC3D
SPC-PC IV Windows
SPC Training Simulator
SPCI+
SPCI+ Professional
SPC/PI+ Advanced SPC Software
SQCpack for Windows
SQCpack/PLUS
SQCsignals
STATnet/2
Statselect

Supplier/vendor quality assurance

Audit Master
Cost of Quality
GageTalker III Plus Real Time
GageTalker DataPage III
The Integrated Quality System
Proquis 9000
Q-Pulse
Quality Workbench
Supplier Quality 9000

Survey tools

Raosoft Survey
The Survey Manager
Survey Pro

3 Executive development programs

The following is a selective listing of executive
development programs sponsored by universities
and nonprofit institutes world-wide that include
components relating to quality improvement,
change management, team building, customer
service, and other quality issues. Those interested
in identifying additional programs or locating in-
depth information about the programs below
should consult *Bricker's International Directory*.
This annual directory, published by Peterson's, is
the definitive guide to university-based executive
development programs. Users may also contact
the sponsors of the programs for further information. The listing of programs in this section
does not constitute an endorsement of the
program by the authors or by Routledge. Finally,
users should keep in mind that professional development programs, seminars, and courses are also
offered by consultants, associations, and other
organizations.

Change management

Program: Accelerated Development Programme
Sponsor: London Business School
              Sussex Place, Regent's Park
              London NW1 4SA
              United Kingdom
              Phone 0171 262 5050
              Fax: 0171 724 6051

Program: Advanced Human Resource Execu-
              tive Program
Sponsor: University of Michigan
              Michigan Business School
              Room E2540 Executive Education
              Center
              700 East University Ave.
              Ann Arbor, MI 48109 1234
              Phone (313) 763 3154
              Fax: (313) 763 9467

Program: Advantage Program
Sponsor: University of Minnesota
              Curtis L. Carlson School of
              Management
              Room 280 Humphrey Institute
              271 19th Ave. South
              Minneapolis, MN 55455
              Phone (612) 624 2545
              Fax: (612) 626 9264

Program: The Change Program
Sponsor: International Institute for Management Development
23 chemin de Bellerive
CH-1007 Lausanne
Switzerland
Phone 21 618 0342
Fax: 21 618 0715

Program: Continuous General Management Programme
Sponsor: Henley Management College
Greenlands, Henley-on-Thames
Oxfordshire RG9 3AU
United Kingdom
Phone 01491 571454
Fax: 01491 571635

Program: Cooperative Approaches in the Workplace
Sponsor: Queen's University
Industrial Relations Center
Kingston, ON K7L 3N6
Canada
Phone (613) 545 6628
Fax: (613) 545 2560

Program: Core Human Resources Executive Development Program
Sponsor: Cornell University
School of Industrial and Labor Relations
222 ILR Conference Center
Ithaca, NY 14853 3901
Phone (607) 255 1540
Fax: (607) 255 3274

Program: Effecting Change
Sponsor: Center for Creative Leadership
One Leadership Place P.O. Box 26300
Greensboro, NC 27438 6300
Phone (910) 545 2810
Fax: (910) 282 3284

Program: The Effective Chief Executive
Sponsor: Irish Management Institute
Sandyford Rd.
Dublin 16
Ireland
Phone: 1 295 6911
Fax: 1 295 5150

Program: Executive Program for Mid-Sized Companies
Sponsor: Cornell University
Johnson Graduate School of Management
Statler, Ste. 509
Ithaca, NY 14853 6901
Phone: (607) 255 4251
Fax: (607) 255 0018

Program: Executive Program in Business Administration: Managing the Enterprise
Sponsor: Columbia University
Columbia Business School
Armstrong Hall-4th Floor, Executive Education
2880 Broadway
New York, NY 10025
Phone: (212) 854 6015
Fax: (212) 316 1473

Program: Executive Program in Organization Change
Sponsor: Stanford University
Graduate School of Business
Stanford, CA 94305 5015
Phone: (415) 723 3342
Fax: (415) 723 3950

Program: General Management for Mid-Sized Companies
Sponsor: Duke University
Fuqua School of Business
R. David Thomas Center
One Science Dr.
Durham, NC 27708 0116
Phone: (919) 660 8011
Fax: (919) 681 7761

Program: Human Resource Management Program
Sponsor: Pennsylvania State University
The Smeal College of Business Administration
310 Business Administration Bldg.
University Park, PA 16802 3003
Phone: (814) 865 3435
Fax: (814) 865 3372

Program: International Managers Programme
Sponsor: Ashridge Management College
Berkhamsted, Hertfordshire HP4
1NS
United Kingdom
Phone: 01442 843491
Fax: 01442 841209

Program: Leading and Managing People
Sponsor: Columbia University
Columbia Business School
Armstrong Hall 4th Floor,
Executive Education
2880 Broadway
New York, NY 10025
Phone: (212) 854 3395
Fax: (212) 316 1473

Program: Leading the Human Resource
Function
Sponsor: University of Minnesota
Curtis L. Carlson School of
Management
Room 280 Humphrey Institute
271 19th Ave. South
Minneapolis, MN 55455
Phone: (612) 624 2545
Fax: (612) 626 9264

Program: Making Change Work
Sponsor: Ashridge Management College
Berkhamsted, Hertfordshire HP4
1NS
United Kingdom
Phone: 01442 843491
Fax: 01442 841209

Program: Management Development Program
Sponsor: University of Tennessee
College of Business Administration
Management Development Center
708 Stokely Management Center
Knoxville, TN 37996 0570
Phone: (615) 974 50001
Fax: (615) 974 4842

Program: Management Development Programme
Sponsor: Ashridge Management College
Berkhamsted, Hertfordshire HP4
1NS

United Kingdom
Phone: 01442 843491
Fax: 01442 841209

Program: Management Development Seminar
Sponsor: University of Chicago
Center for Continuing Studies
Judd Hall, Room 207
5835 Kimbark Ave.
Chicago, IL 60637
Phone: (312) 702 1730
Fax: (312) 702 6814

Program: Management of Managers: A
Leadership Renewal Program
Sponsor: Southern Methodist University
Edwin L. Cox School of Business
Dallas, TX 75275 0333
Phone: (214) 768 3335
Fax: (214) 768 2987

Program: Managing Change
Sponsor: University of Washington
School of Business Administration
Executive Programs, Lewis Annex
III, DJ-10
Seattle, WA 98195
Phone: (206) 543 8560
Fax: (206) 685 9236

Program: Managing Individual and
Organizational Change
Sponsor: University of Virginia
The Darden Graduate School of
Business Administration
Darden Executive Education
P.O. Box 6550
Charlottesville, VA 22906 6550
Phone: (804) 924 3000
Fax: (804) 982 2833

Program: Managing Multinational Enterprise:
The Renewal Challenge
Sponsor: INSEAD
Boulevard de Constance
77305 Fontainebleau cedex
France
Phone: 1 60 72 42 90
Fax: 1 60 72 42 42

Program: Managing Organizational Change
Sponsor: University of Pennsylvania
Wharton Executive Education
255 South 38th St.
Philadelphia, PA 19104 6359
Phone: (215) 898 1776
(800) 255 3932
Fax: (215) 386 4304

Program: Managing Strategic Innovation and
Change
Sponsor: Columbia University
Columbia Business School
Armstrong Hall-4th Floor,
Executive Education
2880 Broadway
New York, NY 10025
Phone: (212) 854 3395
Fax: (212) 316 1473

Program: Managing Strategic Change
Sponsor: Cranfield University
Cranfield School of Management
Cranfield, Bedford MK43 0AL
United Kingdom
Phone: 01234 751122
Fax: 01234 750835

Program: Mastering Change
Sponsor Harvard University
Graduate School of Business
Administration
Glass Hall, Executive Education
Soldiers Field
Boston, MA 02163
Phone: (617) 495 6555
Fax: (617) 495 6999

Program: McGill University
Sponsor: McGill Executive Program
1001 Sherbrooke St., West
Montreal, PQ H3A 1G5
Canada
Phone: (514) 398 3970
Fax: (514) 398 7443

Program: Modular General Management
Programme
Sponsor: Henley Management College
Greenlands, Henley-on-Thames
Oxfordshire RG9 3AU
United Kingdom
Phone: 01491 571454
Fax: 01491 571635

Program: Nonprofit Management Institute
Sponsor: Carnegie Mellon University
H. John Heinz III School of Public
Policy and Management
Pittsburgh, PA 15213 3890
Phone: (412) 268 6082
Fax: (412) 268 7036

Program: Organizational Change Skills for
General Managers
Sponsor: Cornell University
222 ILR Conference Center
Ithaca, NY 15853 3901
Phone: (607) 255 1540
Fax: (607) 255 3274

Program: Organizational Change Skills for
Human Resource Managers
Sponsor: Cornell University
222 ILR Conference Center
Ithaca, NY 15853 3901
Phone: (607) 255 1540
Fax: (607) 255 3274

Program: Organizational Transformation:
Critical Success Factors
Sponsor: Cornell University
222 ILR Conference Center
Ithaca, NY 15853 3901
Phone: (607) 255 1540
Fax: (607) 255 3274

Program: Program for Manager Development
Sponsor: University of North Carolina
Kenan-Flagler Business School
Campus Box 3445, Kenan Center
Chapel Hill, NC 27599 3445
Phone: (800) 862 3932
Fax: (919) 962 1667

Program: Restructuring Canadian Business:
  Strategies for Success
Sponsor: University of Western Ontario
  Western Business School
  London, ON N6A 3K7
  Canada
  Phone: (519) 661 3295
  Fax: (519) 661 3485

Program: Senior Executives Program
Sponsor: Massachusetts Institute of
  Technology
  Sloan School of Management
  50 Memorial Dr., Ste. E52 126
  Cambridge, MA 02142 1347
  Phone: (617) 253 7168
  Fax: (617) 258 6002

Program: Senior Managers' Programme
Sponsor: Cranfield University
  Cranfield School of Management
  Cranfield, Bedford MK43 0AL
  United Kingdom
  Phone: 01234 751122
  Fax: 01234 751806

Program: Strategic Management in the
  Service Sector
Sponsor: Cranfield University
  Cranfield School of Management
  Cranfield, Bedford MK43 0AL
  United Kingdom
  Phone: 01234 751122
  Fax: 01234 751806

Program: Strategic Management Programme
Sponsor: Ashridge Management College
  Berkhamsted, Hertfordshire HP4
  1NS
  United Kingdom
  Phone: 01442 843491
  Fax: 01442 841209

Program: Strategy and Strategic Management
Sponsor: Cranfield University
  Cranfield School of Management
  Cranfield, Bedford MK43 0AL
  United Kingdom
  Phone: 01234 751122
  Fax: 01234 751806

Program: The USC Executive Program
Sponsor: University of Southern California
  School of Business Administration
  Office of Executive Education
  Davidson Conference Center 107
  Los Angeles, CA 90089 0871
  Phone: (213) 740 7075
  Fax: (213) 749 3689

Program: Windsor Program
Sponsor: Mt. Eliza Australian Management
  College
  Kunyung Rd.
  Mt. Eliza, Victoria 3930
  Australia
  Phone: 03 215 1139
  Fax: 03 787 5139

Customer service

Program: Advanced Executive Program
Sponsor: University of California, Los
  Angeles
  John E. Anderson Graduate School
  of Management
  Office of Executive Education
  405 Hilgard Ave., Ste. 2381
  Los Angeles, CA 90024 1464
  Phone: (310) 825 2001
  Fax: (310) 825 3340

Program: Advanced Management Program
Sponsor: Duke University
  Fuqua School of Business
  R. David Thomas Center
  One Science Dr.
  Durham, NC 27708 0116
  Phone: (919) 660 8011
  Fax: (919) 681 7761

Program: Becoming Customer Driven
Sponsor: Duke University
  Fuqua School of Business
  R. David Thomas Center
  One Science Dr.
  Durham, NC 27708 0116
  Phone: (919) 660 8011
  Fax: (919) 681 7761

Program: Building Customer Value for the
'90s
Sponsor: University of Tennessee
College of Business Administration
Management Development Center
708 Stokely Management Center
Knoxville, TN 37996 0570
Phone: (615) 974 50001
Fax: (615) 974 4842

Program: Creating the Customer-Oriented
Firm
Sponsor: Columbia University
Columbia Business School
Armstrong Hall 4th Floor,
Executive Education
2880 Broadway
New York, NY 10025
Phone: (212) 854 3395
Fax: (212) 316 1473

Program: Customer Satisfaction: Management
Strategies and Tactics
Sponsor: University of Chicago
Center for Continuing Studies
5835 Kimbark Ave.
Chicago, IL 60637
Phone: (312) 702 1723
Fax: (312) 702 6814

Program: Customer Service: Building,
Maintaining, and Enhancing a
Customer-Centered Organization
Sponsor: University of Texas at Austin
Executive Education, Graduate
School of Business
P.O. Box 7337
Austin, TX 78713
Phone: (512) 471 5893
Fax: (512) 471 0853

Program: Delivering Excellent Customer
Service
Sponsor: Northwestern University
Kellogg Graduate School of
Management
Executive Programs
Evanston, IL 60208 2800
Phone: (708) 467 7000
Fax: (708) 491 4323

Program: Information Technology
Management
Sponsor: MacQuarie University
MacQuarie Graduate School of
Management Proprietary
Limited
Sydney, New South Wales 2109
Australia
Phone: 02 850 9006
Fax: 02 850 8630

Program: Logistics Management Programme
Sponsor: Cranfield University
Cranfield School of Management
Cranfield, Bedford MK43 0AL
United Kingdom
Phone: 01234 751122
Fax: 01234 751806

Program: Managing Service: Reengineering
for Customer Satisfaction
Sponsor: University of Pennsylvania
Wharton Executive Education,
Unisys Corporation
255 South 38th St.
Philadelphia, PA 19104 6359
Phone: (215) 898 1776
(800) 255 3932
Fax: (215) 386 4304

Program: Measuring Customer Satisfaction
Sponsor: Vanderbilt University
Owen Graduate School of
Management
401 21st Ave. South
Nashville, TN 37203
Phone: (615) 322 2513
Fax: (615) 343 2293

Program: Michigan-IESE Global Program for
Managing Development
Sponsor: University of Michigan
Michigan Business School
International Graduate School of
Management (IESE)
Room E2540 Executive Education
Center
Ann Arbor, MI 48109 1234
Phone: (313) 763 3154
Fax: (313) 763 9467

Program: Strategic Marketing
Sponsor: University of Minnesota
Curtis L. Carlson School of
Management
Room 280 Humphrey Institute
271 19th Ave. south
Minneapolis, MN 55455
Phone: (612) 624 2545
Fax: (612) 626 9264

Program: Using Customer Satisfaction to
Improve Organizational
Performance
Sponsor: University of Michigan
Michigan Business School
Room E2540 Executive Education
Center
700 East University Ave.
Ann Arbor, MI 48109 1234
Phone: (313) 763 4229
Fax: (313) 763 9467

ISO 9000

Program: Using ISO 9000 to Design and
Implement Your Quality
Management System
Sponsor: Louisiana State University
College of Business
LSU Executive Education
P.O. Box 25054
Baton Rouge, LA 70894
Phone: (504) 388 8544
Fax: (504) 388 6983

Leadership and empowerment

Program: Accelerated Development Program
Sponsor: University of New South Wales
Australian Graduate School of
Management
P.O. Box 1
Kensington, New South Wales 2033
Australia
Phone: 02 931 9334
Fax: 02 662 8862

Program: Building the Learning Organization
Sponsor: University of Virginia
The Darden Graduate School of
Business Administration
Darden Executive Education
P.O. Box 6550
Charlottesville, VA 22906 6550
Phone: (804) 924 3000
Fax: (804) 982 2833

Program: Contemporary Executive
Development
Sponsor: George Washington University
School of Business and Public
Management
Office of Professional Development
2020 K St., NW, Ste. 230
Washington, DC 20052
Phone: (202) 994 5200
Fax: (202) 994 5225

Program: Creating the Future: The Challenge
of Transformational Leadership
Sponsor: University of Virginia
The Darden Graduate School of
Business Administration
Darden Executive Education
P.O. Box 6550
Charlottesville, VA 22906 6550
Phone: (804) 924 3000
Fax: (804) 982 2833

Program: Creating the High-Performance
Workplace
Sponsor: University of Virginia
The Darden Graduate School of
Business Administration
Darden Executive Education
P.O. Box 6550
Charlottesville, VA 22906 6550
Phone: (804) 924 3000
Fax: (804) 982 2833

Program: Effective Leadership
Sponsor: Cornell University
222 ILR Conference Center
Ithaca, NY 15853 3901
Phone: (607) 255 1540
Fax: (607) 255 3274

Program: Engineering and Management
 Program
Sponsor: University of California, Los
 Angeles
 UCLA Extension
 Department of Engineering,
 Information Systems and
 Technical Management
 10995 Le Conte Ave., Room 542
 Los Angeles, CA 90024 2883
 Phone: (310) 825 3858
 Fax: (310) 206 2815

Program: Executive Development Program
Sponsor: University of Tennessee
 College of Business Administration
 Management Development Center
 708 Stokely Management Center
 Knoxville, TN 37996 0570
 Phone: (615) 974 5001
 Fax: (615) 974 4842

Program: General Management Program
Sponsor: University of Toronto
 Faculty of Management
 Executive Programs
 130 Bloor St. West, Ste. 902
 Toronto, ON M5S 1N5
 Canada
 Phone: (416) 978 4094
 Fax: (416) 978 5549

Program: Indiana Executive Program
Sponsor: Indiana University
 School of Business
 Executive Education
 10th and Fee Lane
 Bloomington, IN 47405
 Phone: (812) 855 0229
 Fax: (812) 855 6216

Program: Leadership Across Frontiers
Sponsor: Ashridge Management College
 Berkhamsted, Hertfordshire HP4
 1NS
 United Kingdom
 Phone: 01442 843491
 Fax: 01442 841209

Program: Leadership and Change
Sponsor: University of Toronto
 Faculty of Management
 Executive Programs
 130 Bloor St. West, Ste. 902
 Toronto, ON M5S 1N5
 Canada
 Phone: (416) 978 4094
 Fax: (416) 978 5549

Program: Leadership Competences Program
Sponsor: International Institute for
 Management Development (IMD)
 Center for Technology and
 Management, ETH Zurich
 Zeltweg 48
 8032 Zurich
 Switzerland
 Phone: 41 1632 5929
 Fax: 41 1252 3307

Program: Leadership for Extraordinary
 Performance
Sponsor: University of Virginia
 The Darden Graduate School of
 Business Administration
 Darden Executive Education
 P.O. Box 6550
 Charlottesville, VA 22906 6550
 Phone: (804) 924 3000
 Fax: (804) 982 2833

Program: Leadership for the Year 2000:
 Beyond Team Building
Sponsor: University of Texas at Austin
 Executive Education, Graduate
 School of Business
 P.O. Box 7337
 Austin, TX 78713
 Phone: (512) 471 5893
 Fax: (512) 471 0853

Program: Leading Continuous Improvement
Sponsor: University of Washington
 School of Business Administration
 Executive Programs, Lewis Annex
 III, DJ-10
 Seattle, WA 98195
 Phone: (206) 543 8560
 Fax: (206) 685 9236

Program: Management Development Program
Sponsor: University of Richmond
Management Institute
E. Claiborne Robins School of
Business
Richmond, VA 23173
Phone: (804) 289 8015
Fax: (804) 289 8872

Program: Management Development Program:
Developing Leadership Potential
Sponsor: Georgia State University
Center for Executive Education
University Plaza
Atlanta, GA 30303 3087
Phone: (404) 651 2815
Fax: (404) 651 2757

Program: Managing Innovation
Sponsor: Stanford University
Alumni Association
Bowman Alumni House
Stanford, CA 94305 4005
Phone: (415) 725 0690
Fax: (415) 723 3145

Program: Managing Managers Institute
Sponsor: Texas Christian University
Charles Tandy American Enterprise
Center
M.J. Neeley School of Business
P.O. Box 32896
Fort Worth, TX 76129
Phone: (817) 921 7115
Fax: (817) 921 7227

Program: Managing People: Effectiveness
Through Individual and Group
Dynamics
Sponsor: University of Pennsylvania
Wharton Executive Education
255 South 38th St.
Philadelphia, PA 19104 6359
Phone: (215) 898 1776
(800) 255 3932
Fax: (215) 386 4304

Program: "... On Leadership"
Sponsor: Levinson Institute
404 Wyman St., Ste, 400
Waltham, MA 02154
Phone: (617) 895 1000
Fax: (617) 895 1644

Program: Power and Leadership
Sponsor: University of Virginia
The Darden Graduate School of
Business Administration
Darden Executive Education
P.O. Box 6550
Charlottesville, VA 22906 6550
Phone: (804) 924 3000
Fax: (804) 982 2833

Program: Program for Strategic Leadership
Sponsor: Pennsylvania State University
The Smeal College of Business
Administration
310 Business Administration Bldg.
University Park, PA 16802 3003
Phone: (814) 865 3435
Fax: (814) 865 3372

Program: UCLA Programs at OJAI
Sponsor: UCLA Extension, Anderson
Graduate School of Management
Department. of Engineering,
Information Systems and
Technical Management
10995 Le Conte Ave., Room 542
Los Angeles, CA 90024 2883
Phone: (310) 825 3858
Fax: (310) 206 2815

Program: Women as Leaders: Pursuing the
Challenge
Sponsor: University of Calgary
Faculty of Management
Scurfield Hall
2500 University Dr., NW
Calgary, AB T2N 1N4
Canada
Phone: (403) 220 8576
Fax: (403) 282 0266

Quality improvement tools, methods, and techniques, including benchmarking

Program: Achieving International Excellence in Manufacturing
Sponsor: Cranfield University
Cranfield School of Management
Cranfield, Bedford MK43 0AL
United Kingdom
Phone: 01234 751122
Fax: 01234 751806

Program: Achieving the Sustainable Turnaround
Sponsor: Columbia University
Columbia Business School
Armstrong Hall 4th Floor,
Executive Education
2880 Broadway
New York, NY 10025
Phone: (212) 854 3395
Fax: (212) 316 1473

Program: Benchmarking
Sponsor: California Institute of Technology
Industrial Relations Center
Industrial Relations Center, I-90
Pasadena, CA 91125
Phone: (818) 395 3746
Fax: (818) 795 7174

Program: Creating World-Class Quality: A Strategic Evaluation
Sponsor: Northwestern University
Kellogg Graduate School of
Management, Motorola Inc.
Executive Programs
Evanston, IL 60208 2800
Phone: (708) 467 7000
Fax: (708) 491 4323

Program: Executive Development Consortium
Sponsor: Emory University
Goizueta Business School of Emory
University
Office of Executive Programs
3399 Peachtree Rd., NE, Ste. 850
Atlanta, GA 30326
Phone: (404) 848 0500
Fax: (404) 848 0510

Program: Human Resource Management
Sponsor: Queen's University
Industrial Relations Center
Kingston, ON K7L 3N6
Canada
Phone: (613) 545 6628
Fax: (613) 545 2560

Program: Implementing Total Quality Management
Sponsor: University of Wisconsin-Madison
School of Business: Management
Institute
975 University Ave.
Madison, WI 53706 1323
Phone: (800) 292 8964
Fax: (608) 262 4617

Program: Institute for Productivity Through Quality
Sponsor: University of Tennessee
College of Business Administration
Management Development Center
708 Stokely Management Center
Knoxville, TN 37996 0570
Phone: (615) 974 5001
Fax: (615) 974 4842

Program: Making Quality Happen
Sponsor: Vanderbilt University
Owen Graduate School of
Management
401 21st Ave. South
Nashville, TN 37203
Phone: (615) 322 2513
Fax: (615) 343 2293

Program: Manufacturing Executive Program
Sponsor: Cornell University
Johnson Graduate School of
Management
Statler, Ste. 509
Ithaca, NY 14853 6901
Phone: (607) 255 4251
Fax: (607) 255 0018

Program: Return on Quality
Sponsor: Vanderbilt University
Owen Graduate School of
Management
401 21st Ave. South
Nashville, TN 37203
Phone: (615) 322 2513
Fax: (615) 343 2293

Program: Senior Executive Institute for
Productivity Through Quality
Sponsor: University of Tennessee
College of Business Administration
Management Development Center
708 Stokely Management Center
Knoxville, TN 37996 0570
Phone: (615) 974 5001
Fax: (615) 974 4842

Program: Statistical Process Control
Sponsor: California Institute of Technology
Industrial Relations Center
Industrial Relations Center, I-90
Pasadena, CA 91125
Phone: (818) 395 3746
Fax: (818) 795 7174

Program: Supplier Management
Sponsor: California Institute of Technology
Industrial Relations Center
Industrial Relations Center, I-90
Pasadena, CA 91125
Phone: (818) 395 3746
Fax: (818) 795 7174

Quality management/process improvement

Program: Advanced Management Program
Sponsor: Miami University
Richard T. Farmer School of
Business Administration
Center for Management
Development
114-P Laws Hall
Oxford, OH 45056 1675
Phone: (513) 529 2132
Fax: (513) 529 6992

Program: Advanced Management Program
Sponsor: University of Hawaii
College of Business Administration
2404 Maile Way, B-101
Honolulu, HI 96822
Phone: (808) 956 8135
Fax: (808) 956 3766

Program: Annual Fall Industrial Relations
Seminar
Sponsor: Queen's University
Industrial Relations Center
Kingston, ON K7L 3N6
Canada
Phone: (613) 545 6628
Fax: (613) 545 2560

Program: Basic Management Program
Sponsor: University of New Mexico
Anderson Schools of Management
Albuquerque, NM 87131 1221
Phone: (505) 277 2525
Fax: (505) 277 0345

Program: Creating World-Class Capabilities
Sponsor: University of Pennsylvania
Wharton Executive Education
255 South 38th St.
Philadelphia, PA 19104 6359
Phone: (215) 898 1776
(800) 255 3932
Fax: (215) 386 4304

Program: Development Program for Managers
Sponsor: University of New South Wales
Australian Graduate School of
Management
P.O. Box 1
Kensington, New South Wales 2033
Australia
Phone: 02 931 9339
Fax: 02 662 8862

Program: Executive Development Program
Sponsor: University of New South Wales
Institute of Administration
P.O. Box 1
Kensington, New South Wales 2033
Australia
Phone: 02 661 4144
Fax: 02 694 1752

Program: Global Strategy and Operations
Management Program
Sponsor: International Marketing Institute
Boston College Graduate School of
Management
314 Hammond St.
Chestnut Hill, MA 02167
Phone: (617) 552 8690
Fax: (617) 552 2590

Program: International Manufacturing
Programme
Sponsor: INSEAD
Boulevard de Constance
77305 Fontainebleau cedex
France
Phone: 1 60 72 42 90
Fax: 1 60 72 42 42

Program: Management Development Program
Sponsor: Emory University
Goizueta Business School of Emory
University
Executive Center
3399 Peachtree Rd., NE, Ste. 850
Atlanta, GA 30326
Phone: (404) 848 0500
Fax: (404) 848 0510

Program: Managing Professional and
Organizational Growth
Sponsor: University of Pittsburgh
Joseph M. Katz Graduate School of
Business
Center for Executive Education
Pittsburgh, PA 15260
Phone: (412) 648 1600
Fax: (412) 648 1787

Program: Managing the Closely Held
Company in Changing Times:
The Owner-Manager's Program
Sponsor: Northwestern University
Kellogg Graduate School of
Management
Executive Programs
Evanston, IL 60208 2800
Phone: (708) 467 7000
Fax: (708) 491 4323

Program: Minority Executive Program
Sponsor: University of Miami
School of Business Administration,
Management Dept.
P.O. Box 248505
Coral Gables, FL 33124 6524
Phone: (305) 284 6657
Fax: (305) 284 5905

Program: Program for Management
Development: Managing Critical
Issues
Sponsor: University of Michigan
Michigan Business School
Room E2540 Executive Education
Center
700 East University Ave.
Ann Arbor, MI 48109 1234
Phone: (313) 764 1379
Fax: (313) 763 9467

Program: Quality Management and Innovative
Practices in Business
Sponsor: Brookings Institution
Center for Public Policy Education
1775 Massachusetts Ave., NW
Washington, DC 20036
Phone: (202) 797 6172
Fax: (202) 797 6133

Program: Rutgers Organizational Management
Program
Sponsor: Rutgers University
Center for Management
Development
Janice H. Levin Bldg., Ste. 215
P.O. Box 5062
New Brunswick, NJ 08903 5062
Phone: (908) 932 5639
Fax: (908) 932 5665

Program: Strategic Quality Management
Program
Sponsor: University of Michigan
Michigan Business School
Room E2540 Executive Education
Center
700 East University Ave.
Ann Arbor, MI 48109 1234
Phone: (313) 763 4229
Fax: (313) 763 9467

Program: Transportation Program
Sponsor: McGill University
1001 Sherbrooke St., West
Montreal, PQ H3A 1G5
Canada
Phone: (514) 398 3970
Fax: (514) 398 7443

Reengineering

Program: Beyond TQM
Sponsor: MacQuarie University
MacQuarie Graduate School of
Management Proprietary
Limited
Sydney, New South Wales 2109
Australia
Phone: 02 850 9006
Fax: 02 850 8630

Program: Business Process Innovation
Sponsor: California Institute of Technology
Industrial Relations Center
Industrial Relations Center, I-90
Pasadena, CA 91125
Phone: (818) 395 3746
Fax: (818) 795 7174

Program: Business Process Redesign
Sponsor: Cranfield University
Cranfield School of Management
Cranfield, Bedford MK43 0AL
United Kingdom
Phone: 01234 751122
Fax: 01234 751806

Program: Business Process Redesign
Sponsor: University of Texas at Austin
Executive Education, Graduate
School of Business
P.O. Box 7337
Austin, TX 78713
Phone: (512) 471 5893
Fax: (512) 471 0853

Program: Business Process Reengineering
Sponsor: University of Wisconsin-Madison
School of Business: Management
Institute
975 University Ave.
Madison, WI 53706 1323
Phone: (800) 292 8964
Fax: (608) 262 4617

Program: Logistics Management
Sponsor: MacQuarie University
MacQuarie Graduate School of
Management Proprietary
Limited
Sydney, New South Wales 2109
Australia
Phone: 02 850 9006
Fax: 02 850 8630

Team building/team leadership

Program: Advanced Project Management:
Beyond the Techniques
Sponsor: University of Tennessee
College of Business Administration
Management Development Center
708 Stokely Management Center
Knoxville, TN 37996 0570
Phone: (615) 974 5001
Fax: (615) 974 4842

Program: Building Self-Managed Teams and
Team Leadership Skills
Sponsor: Vanderbilt University Owen
Graduate School of Management
401 21st Ave. South
Nashville, TN 37203
Phone: (615) 322 2513
Fax: (615) 343 2293

Program: Building Teams
Sponsor: Columbia University
Columbia Business School
Armstrong Hall 4th Floor,
Executive Education
2880 Broadway
New York, NY 10025
Phone: (212) 854 3390
Fax: (212) 316 1473

Program: Competing in a Changing World
Sponsor: University of Houston
Center for Executive Development
Houston, TX 77204 6283
Phone: (713) 743 4800
Fax: (713) 743 4807

Program: Creating and Managing High
Performance Teams
Sponsor: Cornell University
Johnson Graduate School of
Management
Statler, Ste. 509
Ithaca, NY 14853 6901
Phone: (607) 255 4251
Fax: (607) 255 0018

Program: Creating the High Performance
Workplace
Sponsor: Queen's University
School of Business
Kingston, ON K7L 3N6
Canada
Phone: (613) 545 2371
Fax: (613) 545 6585

Program: Delegation and the Team Effort:
People and Performance
Sponsor: University of Michigan
Michigan Business School
Room E2540 Executive Education
Center
700 East University Ave.
Ann Arbor, MI 48109 1234
Phone: (313) 764 1379
Fax: (313) 763 9467

Program: Executive Decisions for Self-
Managed/Directed Work Teams
Sponsor: Hillsdale College
Dow Leadership Development
Center
22 East Galloway Dr.
Hillsdale, MI 49242
Phone: (517) 437 3311
Fax: (517) 437 3240

Program: Executive Development *Program:*
The Transition From Functional
to General Management
Sponsor: University of Pennsylvania
Wharton Executive Education
255 South 38th St.
Philadelphia, PA 19104 6359
Phone: (215) 898 1776
(800) 255 3932
Fax: (215) 386 4304

Program: Executive Program
Sponsor: Mt. Eliza Australian Management
College
Kunyung Rd.
Mt. Eliza, Victoria 3930
Australia
Phone: 03 215 1139
Fax: 03 787 5139

Program: Executive Program in International
Management: Managing for
Global Success
Sponsor: Columbia University
Columbia Business School
Armstrong Hall-4th Floor,
Executive Education
2880 Broadway
New York, NY 10025
Phone: (212) 854 6015
Fax: (212) 316 1473

Program: How to Manage Teams Effectively
Sponsor: University of Wisconsin-Madison
School of Business: Management
Institute
975 University Ave.
Madison, WI 53706 1323
Phone: (800) 292 8964
Fax: (608) 262 4617

Program: Human Resource Management:
Effecting Change Beyond the
1990s
Sponsor: Columbia University
Columbia Business School
Armstrong Hall 4th Floor, Executive
Education
2880 Broadway
New York, NY 10025
Phone: (212) 854 3395
Fax: (212) 316 1473

Program: Interpersonal Skills for Senior
Managers
Sponsor: London Business School
Sussex Place, Regent's Park
London NW1 4SA
United Kingdom
Phone: 0171 262 5050
Fax: 0171 724 6051

Program: Introduction to Management
Sponsor: Ashridge Management College
Berkhamsted, Hertfordshire
HP4 1NS
United Kingdom
Phone: 01442 843491
Fax: 01442 841209

Program: The Job of Managing
Sponsor: Cornell University
216 ILR Conference Center
Ithaca, NY 15853 3901
Phone: (607) 255 9212
Fax: (607) 255 3274

Program: Leadership and Decision Making in
Organizations
Sponsor: Yale University
Yale School of Organization and
Management
Box 208200
New Haven, CT 06520 8200
Phone: (203) 432 6038
Fax: (203) 432 5092

Program: Leadership and Teamwork
Sponsor: Center for Creative Leadership
One Leadership Place P.O. Box
26300
Greensboro, NC 27438 6300
Phone: (910) 545 2810
Fax: (910) 282 3284

Program: Leadership and Teamwork
Sponsor: Eckerd College
Management Development Institute
4200 54th Ave. South
St. Petersburg, FL 33711
Phone: (813) 864 8213
Fax: (813) 864 8996

Program: Leadership Development
Programme
Sponsor: Ashridge Management College
Berkhamsted, Hertfordshire
HP4 1NS
United Kingdom
Phone: 01442 843491
Fax: 01442 841209

Program: Leadership in Senior Management
Sponsor: Macquarie University
Macquarie Graduate School of
Management Proprietary
Limited
Sydney, New South Wales 2109
Australia
Phone: 02 850 9006
Fax: 02 850 8630

Program: Management Development Program
Sponsor: University of South Carolina
College of Business Administration
Daniel Management Center
Columbia, SC 29208
Phone: (803) 777 2231
Fax: (803) 777 4447

Program: Management Development
Programme
Sponsor: Irish Management Institute
Sandyford Rd.
Dublin 16
Ireland
Phone: 1 295 6911
Fax: 1 295 5150

Program: Management Effectiveness
       Workshop
Sponsor: University of North Carolina
       Kenan-Flagler Business School
       Campus Box 3445, Kenan Center
       Chapel Hill, NC 27599 3445
       Phone: (800) 862 3932
       Fax: (919) 962 1667

Program: Management II: A Management
       Development Program for
       Mid-Level Managers
Sponsor: Louisiana State University
       College of Business
       LSU Executive Education
       P.O. Box 25054
       Baton Rouge, LA 70894
       Phone: (504) 388 8545
       Fax: (504) 388 6983

Program: Managing People Effectively
Sponsor: Cranfield University
       Cranfield School of Management
       Cranfield, Bedford MK43 0AL
       United Kingdom
       Phone: 01234 751122
       Fax: 01234 751806

Program: Manufacturing Management
       Program
Sponsor: University of Virginia
       The Darden Graduate School of
       Business Administration
       Darden Executive Education
       P.O. Box 6550
       Charlottesville, VA 22906 6550
       Phone: (804) 924 3000
       Fax: (804) 982 2833

Program: Open MBA Master Class
Sponsor: Ashridge Management College
       Berkhamsted, Hertfordshire HP4
       1NS
       United Kingdom
       Phone: 01442 841014
       Fax: 01442 841144

Program: Organizational Excellence
Sponsor: Clemson University
       College of Commerce and Industry
       P.O. Drawer 912
       Clemson, SC 29633
       Phone: (803) 656 2200
       Fax: (803) 656 3997

Program: The Oxford Strategic Leadership
       Programme
Sponsor: Templeton College
       Senior Executive Programmes
       Kennington Rd.
       Kennington, Oxford OX1 5NY
       United Kingdom
       Phone: 01865 735422
       Fax: 01865 36374

Program: Performance Through People
Sponsor: Ashridge Management College
       Berkhamsted, Hertfordshire
       HP4 1NS
       United Kingdom
       Phone: 01442 843491
       Fax: 01442 841209

Program: The Planning Process: Using
       Teamwork to Develop an
       Effective Strategic Plan
Sponsor: Vanderbilt University
       Owen Graduate School of
       Management
       401 21st Ave. South
       Nashville, TN 37203
       Phone: (615) 322 2513
       Fax: (615) 343 2293

Program: Root Cause Analysis
Sponsor: Hillsdale College
       Dow Leadership Development
       Center
       22 East Galloway Dr.
       Hillsdale, MI 49242
       Phone: (517) 437 3311
       Fax: (517) 437 3240

Program: Teams and Beyond . . .
Sponsor: Levinson Institute
404 Wyman St., Ste, 400
Waltham, MA 02154
Phone: (617) 895 1000
Fax: (617) 895 1644

Program: Transformational Teamwork
Sponsor: University of New Hampshire
UNH Kellogg Program Office
11 Brook Way
Durham, NH 03824
Phone: (603) 862 1900
Fax: (603) 862 0245

Program: Young Managers Program
Sponsor: Mt. Eliza Australian Management
College
Kunyung Rd.
Mt. Eliza, Victoria 3930
Australia
Phone: 03 215 1139
Fax: 03 787 5139

4 Quality management consultants survey

The following is a selective listing of consulting firms offering services related to various aspects of quality management. Firms thought to be actively consulting on quality-related topics were identified and asked to complete a questionnaire on the scope of their firm's activities. The listing of consultants in this section does not constitute an endorsement of the consulting firm by the authors or by Routledge.

Those interested in identifying additional firms should consult the annual *QA/QC Services Directory* published by *Quality Progress*. The directory is published in the August issue of this periodical. A source for locating additional consultants with specializations in the quality arena in the United Kingdom is *The Directory of Management Consultants in the UK*, published by AP Information Services. Lastly, some associations maintain personnel listings (for example, The American Society for Quality Control) or provide assistance in securing the services of a consultant (the Association of Quality Management Consultants can be contacted for

assistance in securing a quality assurance consultant in the United Kingdom).

Action Management Associates, Inc.
12201 Merit Drive, Suite 710
Dallas, TX 75251
Phone: (214) 386 5611
Fax: (214) 386 5620
Contact: James M. Dennis, Man. Dir.
Description: Vendors of training programs focusing on the development of the critical thinking assets of organizations. "Problem Solving and Decision Making" program links advanced critical thinking training with total quality.
Seminars/workshops: two-day, three-day, or half-day modular "Problem Solving and Decision Making" programs.

Advanced Management Catalyst Inc.
Churchill Street
Wiscasset, ME 04578
Phone: (207) 882 8093
Fax: (207) 882 8093
Contact: Daniel Thompson
Michael T. Kelly, Ph.D.
Description: Specialize in facilitated and computer assisted team-building. Offer computer software which tracks the facilitated meeting process and yields a working report ready for use at the end of the session.
Seminars/workshops: Offered four times per year.
Publications: AMCat software package

Advanced Quality Engineering
5460 Norwood Lane N.
Plymouth, MN 55442
Phone: (612) 553 9064
Fax: (612) 545 6227
Contact: Dale K. Mize
Description: Training and consulting in quality management and engineering. Assessment, surveys, planning, and coaching for quality improvement. Specializations in manufacturing, government and health care, banking, insurance, and related services.
Seminars/workshops: Seminars in quality management, problem-solving tools, statistical process control, and understanding process variation.

Publications: *An Ounce of Prevention*, personal workbook for production workers.

Advent Management International, Ltd.
P.O. Box 1717
West Chester, PA 19380
Phone: (610) 431 2196
Fax: (610) 431 2641
Contact: John J. Reddish, Pres.
Description: Provide consulting services in the areas of continuous improvement, productivity improvements, process reengineering, new product development, strategic planning, and assistance with ISO 9000 certification to firms in most industries. Also involved in a networking approach to preparation for ISO certification aimed at smaller companies. This approach groups companies together for training leading to individual company ISO 9000 registration.
Seminars/workshops: In-house programs offered in addition to those developed for clients.
Publications: Offer "Software Expert QMS", a software expert approach to ISO 9000 certification.

Argyle Associates, Inc.
79 Locust Avenue
New Canaan, CT 06840
Phone: (203) 966 7015
Fax: (203) 966 7399
Contact: Roger G. Langevin
Description: Management consulting firm specializing in total quality improvement and quality improvement processes for manufacturing companies, process industries, and service organizations. Clients include "Fortune 500" corporations as well as medium-sized and smaller companies world-wide.
Seminars/workshops: Offered to clients on a variety of topics.

Asset Development Group
607 North Easton Road, Building D-1
Willow Grove, PA 19090
Phone: (215) 657 0610
Fax: (215) 657 2440
Contact: Bob Doyle
Description: Total quality and management consulting firm specializing in strategy and TQM for a range of businesses.

Seminars/workshops: Offered in all phases of TQM and leadership.
Publications: *Breakthrough Quality Improvement for Leaders Who Want Results* (ISBN 0873892135)

Aubuchon & Associates
492 Dean Drive
Kennett Square, PA 19348
Phone: (610) 444 5440
Contact: Norbert Aubuchon
Description: Firm is composed of retired DuPont Company executives. Specialize in training people to organize and present information in a logical, persuasive manner. Provide assistance in helping clients gain acceptance for TQM programs and influence the change process. Serve clients in government, agriculture and industry.
Seminars/workshops: Offer a two-day seminar developing persuasion skills. Available at location of client's choosing and customized to client's industry and/or professional requirements.

Avatar International, Inc.
3080 Northwoods Circle, Suite 110
Norcross, GA 30071
Phone: (404) 416 6175
Fax: (404) 416 6177
Contact: Michael Everett, C.E.O.
Dan Johnson
Description: Provide consulting services in continuous quality improvement and training services in areas such as facilitation skills, team development, cultural change, and measurement and statistics. Also provide continuous quality improvement surveys, computer software for team tracking and statistical process control, education and reference materials, speeches and presentations, and assistance with clinical practice improvement in the area of health care. Industries served include health care, aerospace, utilities, finance, and government.
Seminars/workshops: Several workshops of varying lengths available.
Publications: Educational materials licensed for internal use or customized training materials are available.

Basler/Maltz Associates
49 Wright Street
Westport, CT 06880
Phone: (203) 227 3550
Fax: (203) 847 9131
Contact: Frank Basler
Marc Maltz
Description: Strategic and organization development consulting group that specializes in change strategy, work redesign, self-managed teams, and TQM implementation. Among the industries served are chemicals, pharmaceuticals, personal products, as well as state and municipal government.
Seminars/workshops: Offer workshops on managing resistance to change aimed at implementing successful change in organizations.

The Batten Group
2413 Grand Avenue
Des Moines, IA 50312
Phone: (515) 244 3176
Fax: (515) 244 3178
Contact: Joe Batten
Description: Focus on helping organizations create total quality cultures. Provide consulting services and training in areas such as team building, change instrumentation, total quality management, and performance appraisal systems.
Seminars/workshops: Offered world-wide.
Publications: (Books) *Total Quality Leadership*, *Tough-Minded Leadership*, *Tough-Minded Management*, *Building a Total Quality Culture*, as well as audio cassettes and videos on related topics.

Bauer & Associates
210 East Huron
Ann Arbor, MI 48104
Phone: (313) 668 1303
Fax: (313) 668 6789
Contact: Sandra S. Bauer
Description: Providers of cost-effective survey services to organizations of all types and sizes. Survey services designed to assist organizations with TQM, customer service improvement, benchmarking, training needs assessment, etc. Provide survey design, data processing, analysis, feedback, and assist with use of survey results in achieving organizational improvement.

Seminars: Offered to clients.
Publications: Catalog of publications available. Items available include questionnaires for varying assessment purposes, survey design and survey administration books and manuals, as well as training workbooks and videos related to the work climate improvement process.

Raymond Bedwell Associates
18615 West Burleigh Road
Brookfield, WI 53045 2524
Phone: (414) 781 3198
Contact: Raymond T. Bedwell
Description: Provide consulting services to hospitals, health care agencies, clinics, schools, professional associations, and community organizations. Specialize in organizational effectiveness, manager performance, and productivity of human resources. Services in the area of TQM include basic training, development of TQM strategy and design, implementation, and assessment of effectiveness.
Seminars/workshops: Offered to clients on a range of TQM and other management topics.

Berryessa Materials Management Control
869 Dorel Drive
San Jose, CA 95132 3105
Phone: (408) 923 6496
Fax: (408) 923 6496
Contact: Andru Peters, Pres.
Description: Consulting services in the areas of materials management, management information systems, manufacturing operations, warehousing, transportation, physical distribution, and logistics management.
Seminars/workshops: one to three day seminars in "Purchasing in a TQM/ISO 9000 Environment," one day seminars on such topics as "TQM/ISO 9000 Overview" and "TQM/Supplier Certification Guidelines."

R. Breakiron and Associates
5113 West Sanna Street
Glendale, AZ 85302
Phone: (602) 435 1448
Fax: (602) 435 1448
Contact: Robert Breakiron
Description: Management consulting firm offering management advisory services,

productivity improvement in manufacturing systems, turnaround management for distressed businesses, TQM, asset management, partnering in both the public and private sector, acquisition/merger review, human resource management, and arbitration.

Seminars/workshops: Workshops offered.

The Business Center
531 Hickory Woods Road
Knoxville, TN 37922
Phone: (615) 675 2275
Fax: (615) 675 2275
Contact: Don Barkman, Pres.

Description: Provide consulting services in team system design and training services. Areas of consulting expertise include new plant start-ups, change management, team systems, group leadership. Training specialties include needs analysis, leadership styles, interpersonal communications, conflict resolution, business education for hourly employees, problem solving, and performance appraisal. Concentrate on the manufacturing industries.

Seminars/workshops: Offered on topics such as self-directed workforces, personal involvement and cost control, statistical techniques for problem solving, training trainers, and effective team discipline.

Publications: Designing Skill-Based Pay and *Start-Up! A Guide to Getting Off on the Right Foot.*

Business Improvement Professionals
P.O. Box 772
Troy, OH 45373
Phone: (513) 339 5620
Fax: (513) 339 5620
Contact: Paul E. Shiptenko, Pres.

Description: Specialize in strategic planning, organizational development, continuous quality improvement, and human resource services. Among the TQM activities are assistance with ISO 9000, statistical process controls, organizational/quality surveys and audits, quality cost analysis, supplier improvement/partnership and productivity improvement/concurrent engineering.

Seminars/workshops: Offered on TQM-related topics.

Canatech
2434 Bolen Bay
Regina, Saskatchewan S4V OV6
Phone: (306) 789 5091
Fax: (306) 789 5091
Contact: Shannon E. Goldsmith, Pres.

Description: Consulting and training firm offering services in quality needs assessments, design, implementation and evaluation of quality programs, statistical process control training and implementation, quality audits, training in teamwork and problem-solving techniques, preparation for ISO 9000 quality system registration, and preparation of quality assurance manuals.

Seminars/workshops: One- to three-day seminars are offered in areas such as TQM basics, teamwork and problem solving, statistical process control, principles of industrial experimentation, experimental design, ISO 9000 introduction, ISO 9000 documentation, and internal auditing for ISO 9000.

Carson Research Center
2957 Flamingo Drive
Miami Beach, FL 33140
Phone: (800) 541 8846
Fax: (305) 534 8846
Contact: Dr. Gayle Carson, Pres.
　　　　　Sherrin Ann Smith, Nat. Coordinator

Description: Offer training seminars and consulting services aimed at developing learning systems for increased productivity, greater team performance, effective customer satisfaction, and performance excellence.

Seminars/workshops: Programs on topics such as customer service, increasing profits through excellence, and successful business characteristics are available in a variety of formats and lengths.

Publications: Catalog of books, videos and audio tapes is available.

C.L. Carter, Jr. & Assoc. Inc.
ISO 9000, TQM, & Training Consultants
1211 Glen Cove Drive
P.O. Box 5001
Richardson, TX 75080
Phone: (214) 234 3296
Fax: (214) 234 3296
Contact: Dr. Chuck Carter

Description: ISO 9000 and TQM systems from start-up to implementation and/or ISO World-wide Registration. Professional assistance with policies, procedures, work instructions, training and development of management, auditors, and workforce.

Seminars/wokshops: One-, two-, and three-day seminars on topics related to TQM and ISO 9000.

Publications: Quality Assurance, Workmanship Standards & Training Manual (ISBN 1 879519 11 9) and *Quality Assurance, Quality Control & Inspection Handbook* (ISBN 1 879519 09 7).

Center for Breakthrough Thinking, Inc.
P.O. Box 18A12
Los Angeles, CA 90018
Phone: (213) 740 6415
Fax: (213) 740 1120
E-mail: nadler@mizar.usc.edu
Branches: Tokyo, Japan; Tel Aviv, Israel; Palm Desert, California
Contact: Robert J. Leo, Ph.D.
Gerald Nadler, Ph.D.
Description: Specialize in integrating "Breakthrough Thinking" with tools, technology, values, and goals of TQM to achieve more results-oriented practices.
Seminars/workshops: Offered to both the general public and in-house for specific companies.
Publications: Breakthrough Thinking in Total Quality Management (ISBN 0 13 090820 7) and *Breakthrough Thinking, the Seven Principles of Creative Problem Solving.*

Center for Management Assistance
600 Broadway, Suite 170
Kansas City, MO 64105
Phone: (816) 283 3000
Fax: (816) 283 3005
E-mail: cmas@aol.com
Contact: Larry Guillot
Roger Hille
Description: Provide management assistance to nonprofit organizations, primarily in the Greater Kansas City area. Areas of expertise include needs assessments, quality improvement, inter-organizational collaboration, leadership development, fund development, financial management systems, and cost benefit analysis.
Seminars/workshops: Offer a variety of public workshops for nonprofit staffs and board members.

Cheshire Ltd.
1601 Shadowbrook Drive
Acworth, GA 30101
Phone: (404) 928 2700
Fax: (404) 516 9924
Branch office: 2344 Greenview Road, Northbrook, IL 60062
Phone: (708) 272 2243
Fax: (708) 272 1394
Contact: M.C. Meyer, Pres.
Sally Macnamara, V.P.
Description: Offer business process consulting and training services through a network of independent consultants selected to work with Cheshire Ltd. based on their particular areas of experience and expertise. Services include organization analysis, consulting on self-directed/high-involvement work teams, attitude surveys, job task analysis, curriculum planning and development, evaluation of training return-on-investment, training program development and redevelopment, and quality assurance programs. Organizations served in a wide range of industries world-wide.
Seminars/workshops: Offer training and development programs to suit a range of industries and organizational functions on topics such as measuring performance, leadership skills, employment practices, customer satisfaction, conflict management, work teams, TQM, and the management of change.

Colarelli, Meyer & Associates, Inc.
7751 Carondelet Avenue, Suite 302
St. Louis, MO 63105
Phone: (314) 721 1860
Fax: (314) 721 1992
Contact: Nick J. Colarelli, Ph.D., Pres.
Description: Management consultants specializing in organizational planning and strategy, organizational development, and human resource development. Offer customized TQM programs for client firms.
Seminars/workshops: Offered to clients if indicated in organizational development projects.

Columbia Quality, Inc.
P.O. Box 506
Orefield, PA 18069
Phone: (610) 391 9496
Fax: (610) 391 9497
Contact: J.P. Russell, Pres.
Description: Specialize in ISO 9000 quality system assessments, planning, program facilitation, and quality auditor training for ISO 9000 implementation. Also offer services related to implementation of quality management systems and consulting on audit preparation and quality systems improvement. Primary industries served are manufacturing and chemicals.
Seminars/workshops: Public and in-house classes are taught on topics such as internal audit training, performance standard training focusing on the requirements of the ISO 9000 series contractual standards, as well as quality systems and ISO 9000 standards.
Publications: ISO 9000 Data and ISO Audit Program Data (ISO 10011) checklists on disks are available.

Concept III International, Inc.
Meidinger Tower
462 South Fourth Avenue, Suite 714
Louisville, KY 40202 3443
Phone: (502) 584 1447
Fax: (502) 584 3430
Contact: Debbie Tross, Corporate Development Director
Description: Offer consulting services in total quality and continuous improvement to clients in manufacturing and service industries as well as education and government. Areas of expertise include visioning and planning processes, organizational auditing and analysis, organizational redesign, team-based operating systems, and quality systems. Also offer programs to the public and work to develop total quality communities through state and local associations.
Seminars/workshops: Offered throughout the year on approximately twenty topics.

The Consultancy, Inc.
1616 17th Street, Suite 362
Denver, CO 80202
Phone: (303) 628 5502
Fax: (303) 628 5503
Contact: Laurie A. Fitzgerald
Description: Offer assistance in the design and transformation of large, complex systems. Clients served in a range of industries in the United States, Canada, Europe, and the South Pacific.
Seminars/workshops: Offered to clients.
Publications: Designing World-Class Organizations.

Continuous Improvement Technology
113 McHenry Road, Suite 211
Buffalo Grove, IL 60089
Phone: (708) 459 3880
Fax: (708) 459 3881
Contact: Kam Gupta
Description: Provide small and medium-sized companies with support in achieving quality improvement success. Services include guidance in achieving ISO 9000 registration, customized training and seminars to establish quality and a customer focus, evaluating and preparing companies for the implementation of a quality program such as TQM, and evaluation of quality systems. Serve clients in manufacturing, health care, and service industries, as well as education initiatives.
Seminars/workshops: Offered, customized to fit client's needs.

Cooperative Edge
5665 N. Scottsdale Road, F-135
Scottsdale, AZ 85250
Phone: (602) 970 1188
Fax: (602) 970 4383
Contact: Sylvia Bushell, Pres.
Description: Training for team management to small business (under 500 employees). Workshops on managing in a team environment, team leadership and team support structures. Assessments performed using the Malcolm Baldrige criteria.
Seminars/workshops: Offered, focus on leadership, teamwork, problem-solving.

Corporate Management Developers. Inc.
200 South Park Road, Suite 330
Hollywood, FL 33021
Phone: (305) 961 1663
Fax: (305) 961 3440

Health Management Consultants, Inc.
1985 B Villa Ridge Drive
Reston, VA 22091
(affiliate)
Phone: (703) 620 0090
Fax: (703) 620 0091
Contact: Dr. Jacalyn Sherriton, Pres.
            James Stern, V. P.
Description: Management consulting firm
providing organization development and
management, and executive development
services. Areas of expertise include building
high-performance teams, customer service,
restructuring organizations, changes in organizational culture related to quality issues, and
change management. Serve clients in manufacturing, health care, government and
not-for-profit organizations.
Seminars/workshops: Offered on topics such as
team-building, conflict resolution, leadership,
coaching, and managing change.

The Coxe Group, Inc.
Seattle Tower, Suite 1700
1218 Third Avenue
Seattle, WA 98101 3021
Phone: (206) 467 4040
Fax: (206) 467 4038
Branch offices: (U.S.): Pennsylvania;
Massachusetts; Connecticut; California;
Florida; New Jersey; Virginia
Branch offices: (Asia): Hong Kong
Contact: Hugh Hochberg, Pres.
Description: Marketing and management
consultants to the design profession. Among
the services offered to architects, engineers,
and interior designers are TQM, organization
strategies and planning, management retreats
and internal communication, market research
and image studies, marketing plans and tactics,
profitability analysis and financial management, personnel development, motivation, and
incentive compensation, project partnering, and
in-house seminars and training.
Seminars/workshops: Offered.

Publications: *Managing People (Including
Yourself) for Project Success* (ISBN 0 442
00952 6).

CS Consulting Group
3150 Sandrock Road
San Diego, CA 92123
Phone: (619) 279 6849
Fax: (619) 279 6849
Contact: Joseph H. Cady
Description: Firm comprising of management
specialists with expertise in the areas of strategy,
structure, management, and human resources.
Services offered include strategic planning,
developing organizational structure, restructuring, management of emerging businesses, customer service quality, TQM, managing change,
productivity, training, team building, and surveys. Clients served in a range of industries.
Seminars/workshops: Offered.

CSP, Communication Structure
  Perfectionnement
66 rue la Fayette
75009 Paris, France
Phone: 1 42 46 89 99
Fax: 1 40 22 08 83
Contact: Edgard Hamalian, Pres.
Description: Provide training services in TQM,
management and leadership, human resource
development, and marketing. Classes are available on a wide range of topics in varying
lengths and are suitable for personnel representing most industries.
Seminars/workshops: Calendar and brochure on
classes available. Classes held at CSP or location of client's choice.
Publications: Textbooks and videos accompany
some classes.

Dannemiller Tyson Associates, Inc.
303 Detroit Street, Suite 203
Ann Arbor, MI 48104
Phone: (313) 662 1330
Fax: (313) 662 2301
Branch offices: Cleveland, Ohio; Houston,
                   Texas
Contact: Kathleen Dannemiller
            Randall Albert
Description: Consulting firm specializing in
large-scale organizational change and the

implementation of total quality systems. Operate on an international basis serving a range of industries including manufacturing, the public sector, information services, health care, energy, finance, and hospitality.

Seminars/workshops: Offered on topics such as real-time strategic change and skills for internal and external consultants involved in supporting change efforts. Also host on-line conferences. Specialize in large-scale meetings and simultaneous training of large numbers of a client's employees.

Publications: Real Time Strategic Change (ISBN 1881052451), "Large-scale Organizational Change" (audiotape).

Dartmouth Research Company
15 Dartmouth Place
Boston, MA 02116
Phone: (617) 536 8862
Fax: (617) 536 8875
Branch: Avenue Louise 65 Boite 11
1050 Brussels, Belgium
Phone: 2 535 78 77
Fax: 2 535 77 00
Contact: J. Kevin Fisher
Description: International management consulting firm. Practice focuses on organization, information, and infrastructure. Services include reengineering business processes, operations improvement and productivity enhancement, implementation of business and marketing strategies, information technology assessment and implementation, and business research and development.
Seminars/workshops: Offered to clients

Paul DeBaylo Associates, Inc.
P.O. Box 3767
Princeton, NJ 08543
Phone: (609) 497 1992
Fax: (609) 497 2160
Contact: Kathy Debow, V.P.
Description: Management consulting firm specializing in TQM strategy and implementation. Areas of expertise include methodology and application of the Malcolm Baldrige National Quality Award criteria, process management and improvement, ISO 9000 instruction, application, and assessment, customer feedback systems, business process

reengineering, and benchmarking. Assist clients in the private and public sectors, in a range of manufacturing and service industries.
Seminars/workshops: Offered to clients in a variety of areas including TQM awareness, TQM self assessment, visioning, development of a strategic quality plan, leadership that supports TQM implementation, management process improvement, benchmarking strategies, facilitator training, team-building, statistical process control, and customer feedback. Workshops range in length from a half day to five days.

Decision Group
2007 Fromby Court
P.O. Box 15005
Charlotte, NC 28211
Phone: (704) 552 4770
Fax: (704) 364 4619
Contact: Will Kaydos, Pres.
Description: Hands-on assistance and training in TQM, performance measurement, statistical process control, problem-solving and team management. Emphasize practicality, frugality, and focusing on results in order to provide the earliest return on investment.
Seminars/workshops: Offered on topics such as quality improvement and measuring performance.
Publications: Measuring, Managing, and Maximizing Performance (ISBN 0 915299 98 4).

Delta Systems
5621 Somerset Drive
Brooklyn, MI 49230
Phone: (517) 592 5463
Fax: (517) 592 5463
Contact: Renee R. Merchant
Description: Management consulting firm offering TQM training and consulting services. Programs offered in areas such as team building, creative problem-solving, conflict management, design and implementation of self-directed work teams, total quality leadership, process improvement, and business process reengineering. Services are provided to public sector service organizations as well as private sector manufacturing firms.
Seminars/workshops: Offered.

Denehy Group
P.O. Box 537
Gorham, ME 04038
Phone: (207) 839 6940
Fax: (207) 839 6940
Contact: Joseph M. Denehy
Description: Provide consulting services and training in the field of TQM to both manufacturing and service organizations. Areas of practice include TQM, statistical process control, supplier certification, quality cost control, team development, quality problem solving, and quality systems development.
Seminars/workshops: Offered on various aspects of TQM.

Mark M. DoMowne
110 Brooklyn Avenue, Suite 1-X
Freeport, NY 11520 2901
Phone: (516) 868 1128
Contact: Mark M. Domowne
Sylvia F. Domowne
Description: Management consulting firm offering services in the area of corporate planning, marketing studies, organizational structure, quality control implementation, benchmarking, and TQM. Serve clients in a range of industries in both the public and private sector.
Seminars/workshops: In-house workshops offered to suit clients' needs.

Donnell Associates
6971 West Hancock St.
Muskogee, OK 74401 9759
Phone: (918) 683 3986
Fax: (918) 683 2001
Contact: Donald D. McMillan
Description: Offer workshops in a variety of areas related to TQM. Included are topics such as facilitator training, benchmarking, communications and group dynamics, data collection and display, and Malcolm Baldrige overview. Also offer facilitating and mediation as well as coaching and other consulting services.
Seminars/workshops: Offered, range from half-day to 4½ days.

Kevin Drayton Associates
190 Fox Road
Dalton, MA 01226
Phone: (413) 684 4648
(800) 538 3338
Fax: (413) 684 4648
E-mail: Compuserve 70401, 2432
Contact: Kevin Drayton
Description: Provide education, training, and consulting services in all aspects of TQM and ISO 9000. Areas of practice include ISO 9000 certification, total quality performance, reengineering, organizational development for quality, and development of custom-designed training programs.
Seminars/workshops: Workshops offered on topics such as preparing and managing ISO 9000 documentation, quality auditing, managing conflict, facilitation skills, and TQM basics.

Dupont Quality Management and Technology
1007 Market Street
Nemours Building 6502
Wilmington, DE 19898
Phone: (800) 601 3733
Fax: (302) 774 2458
Description: Provide training and consulting services in all aspects of continuous improvement. Primary area of expertise is design of experiments for the chemical and process industries. Serve clients in industries ranging from pharmaceuticals to refining. Operate on an international basis.
Seminars/workshops: Offer a variety of seminars dealing with experimental design. Topics include planning and analyzing efficient experiments, experimental designs for mixtures, and applications for developing quality products. Seminars dealing with statistical process control, using data effectively, and also more general quality improvement topics are available.

Edu-Tech Industries
151 Kalmus Drive, Suite K-2
Costa Mesa, CA 92626
Phone: (714) 540 7660
Fax: (714) 540 8345
Contact: Jocelyn Kamph
Description: Edu-Tech designs, develops and implements strategic quality systems. Services

include TQM, ISO 9000 and Baldrige implementation, continuous improvement programs, custom development of training systems, programs and materials, and market analysis of internal and external customers. Among the industries served are electronics, mining, chemicals, petroleum, and light manufacturing, as well as service industries and government agencies.

Seminars: Offered to clients.

Excalibur Consulting
348 Park Street, South 107
North Reading, MA 01864
Phone: (508) 664 0862
Fax: (508) 664 9826
Contact: Thomas P. Stratigakis, Pres.
Description: Management and organizational consulting company dedicated to helping management more effectively manage change and instill continuous improvement within their organizations. Specialize in leadership development, organizational analysis and change, team-building, operational improvement, training and development programs, and total quality management. Serve both private industry and government agencies.
Seminars/workshops: Offered on topics such as decision-making, managing change, team-building, and customer service.

Excel Partnership, Inc.
75 Glen Road
Sandy Hook, CT 06482 1170
Phone: (203) 426 3281
Fax: (203) 426 7811
Branch offices: United Kingdom; Brazil; Mexico; Hong Kong; Thailand
Contact: David N. Middleton, Pres.
   Dana Pavese, Dir. of Customer
   Relations
Description: Strategic consulting and training firm specializing in ISO 9000 and quality management systems for a wide variety of manufacturing and service industries worldwide. Courses in ISO 9000 ranging from an executive overview to implementation and registration requirements to internal auditor training are offered. Additionally, courses in cycle-time reduction, continuous process improvement in the service industry, and

professional development are offered. Consulting services complement the training courses and focus on successful implementation of an integrated quality management system.
Seminars/workshops: Offered to clients worldwide.

Executive Learning, Inc.
7101 Executive Center Drive, Suite 160
Brentwood, TN 37027
Phone: (615) 373 8483
Fax: (615) 373 8635
Description: Provide consulting and training resources to help organizations create and deploy customer-driven strategies. Resources are also available to assist in applying improvement methods, including process improvement and system reengineering, to accomplish the strategies. Areas of expertise include system reengineering, cost improvement, organizational assessment, and linking improvement work with strategic plans. The firm works with manufacturing, health care, financial, and educational organizations. A variety of video training modules are also offered.
Seminars/workshops: A range of courses are offered. Topics include continual improvement principles, tools for continual improvement, leading and facilitation skills, team development, and continual improvement trainer certification. Additional video training modules and training materials are available.
Publications: Catalog of videos and training materials is available.

FMI
5151 Glenwood Avenue
Raleigh, NC 27612
Phone: (919) 787 8400
Fax: (919) 782 1139
Branch offices: Denver, CO; Tampa, FL;
   Bloomington, MN
Description: Specialize in management consulting and education for the construction industry. Services include quality and productivity improvement, corporate planning and evaluations, marketing services, educational services, educational products, and public programs. Geographic market includes the

United States, Canada, Europe, Pacific Rim, and Latin America. Clients are primarily contractors, manufacturers and distributors of building material products and construction equipment, trade associations, providers of professional services to the construction industry, and government agencies.

Seminars/workshops: sponsor public seminars as well as workshops for clients. Also provide audio and video products.

Publications: Catalog of educational products is available.

H.W. Fahrlander & Associates
640 Downing Drive
Richardson, TX 75080 6117
Phone: (214) 783 1216
Fax: (214) 783 6043
Contact: H.W. Fahrlander, Jr.
Description: Provide hands-on consulting to management in the areas of total quality management, statistical process control, and ISO 9000 quality systems. Areas of expertise include cost improvement programs for service companies and high-technology manufacturers.
Seminars/workshops: Offered on a range of topics including statistical process control, TQM, ISO 9000, supplier quality management, and inspection.

Food Agri International (North America), LLC
5660 Greenwood Plaza Blvd.
Suite 230
Englewood, CO 80111
Phone: (303) 770 0838
Fax: (303) 770 1353
Branch offices: (Australia) Sydney, Adelaide, Brisbane; (England) London
Description: Consulting firm serving the food and agriculture industries. Areas of expertise include quality management, strategic planning, program and project management, organizational assessments, application of technology, computer systems design, information engineering management, ISO 9000 support, customer/supplier audits, and industry and market research.
Seminars/workshops: Offer a continuing program of education in the form of classes,

workshops, seminars, and conferences. Course work can be designed and delivered to any location world-wide.

HJ Ford Associates Inc.
1111 Jeff Davis Highway, Suite 808
Arlington, VA 22202
Phone: (703) 416 6500
Fax: (703) 416 6501
E-mail: p00573@psilink.com
Branch: 2940 Presidential Drive, Suite 320, Fairborn, OH 45324
Phone: (513) 427 1300
Contact: Jorge Alducin, Pres.
Description: Professional services organization. Areas of practice include development and integration of information and telecommunication systems, acquisition management and support, a wide range of engineering activities, logistics planning, document management systems, and training and education programs. All areas of practice are linked to TQM.
Seminars/workshops: Offered.
Publications: "WinScenario" line of commercial software products.

Richard Fudge Associates
4 Lowlyn Road
Westport, CT 06880
Phone: (203) 454 0701
Contact: Richard E. Fudge
Description: Consulting firm focusing on the area of organizational effectiveness and innovation, including provision of services in total quality management and managing diversity. Areas of expertise include education, strategic planning, new business development, organization development and diversity consulting. All industries served.
Seminars/workshops: Offered to clients.

Gelb Consulting Group Inc.
3701 Kirby Drive, Suite 830
Houston, TX 77098
Phone: (713) 526 5711
Fax: (713) 526 4842
E-mail: gelb@aol.com
Contact: Gabriel M. Gelb, Pres.
John B. Elmer, Exec. V.P.
Description: Specialize in construction and implementation of customer satisfaction

measurements, construction and implementation of employee satisfaction and related productivity surveys, and action plans designed to increase customer and/or employee satisfaction. Experience with for-profit as well as not-for-profit organizations in a variety of industry segments.

Gelman & Associates, Inc.
P.O. Box 9175
Englewood, CO 80111
Phone: (303) 691 2080
Fax: (303) 757 0906
Contact: Steve Gelman
Description: Provide consulting and training services in the areas of team facilitation and team-building.
Seminars/workshops: Offered to clients.

GGI
Kings Highway
Landing, NJ 07850
Phone: (201) 770 4700
Fax: (201) 770 4786
Branch offices: Chicago, IL; Dallas, TX; Los Angeles, CA; New York, NY; Palm Beach, FL; Washington, DC; Montreal, Canada; Rome, Italy
Contact: Frank S. Berger
Description: Consulting firm with a specialty in continuous quality improvement and reengineering systems. Processes used are pragmatic and results-oriented, customer-focused, and customized to each organization with continuous implementation support. Serve companies ranging in size from Fortune 500 to smaller firms. Customers drawn from approximately sixty industries including consumer products, high-tech, service, government, and health care.
Seminars/workshops: Offered to clients.

GlennCo Services, Inc.
509 Northeast Third Ave.
Fort Lauderdale, FL 33301 3263
Phone: (305) 764 7291
E-mail: z900526a@bcfreenet.seflin.lib.fl.us
Contact: Donald T. Glenn, Jr.
Description: General management consulting firm offering clients assistance in the areas of general management, management of human resources, financial control, compensation, manufacturing, physical distribution, administration, and information and control systems.
Clients in a variety of industry segments including banking, health care, construction, manufacturing, and government.

Goldman–Nelson Group
20531 Paisley Lane
Huntington Beach, CA 92646 6012
Phone: (714) 962 8029
Fax: (714) 962 8029
Contact: Henry H. Goldman, Ph.D.
Description: Offer executive development and hands-on problem solving. Practice: includes a productivity cycle management (PCM) unit to handle TQM/TQS related programs. Regularly teach TQM/TQS on the university level and offer world-wide support for quality topics.
Seminars/workshops: Offered, usually as in-house programs.

Greenbridge Management, Inc.
Sheridan Corporate Centre
2155 Leanne Blvd., Suite 242
Mississauga, Ontario L5K 2K8
Phone: (905) 855 0975
Fax: (905) 855 0977
Contact: Phil Green, Pres.
Description: Consulting firm specializing in the application of the principles of continuous improvement to environmental performance, quality, productivity, and safety. The combination of quality and environmental management techniques has allowed clients to apply continuous improvement to environmental problems and develop management techniques aimed at pollution prevention and environmental risk reduction. Services include environmental risk assessments, development of improvement plans, and on-site training and consulting. Offer programs in environment training and continuous improvement. Serve companies in most industries.
Seminars/workshops: Training programs include an introduction to continuous improvement in environmental performance, environmental measurement and problem solving, statistical methods for process improvement, and an introduction to lean production.

Haddonfield Group, Inc.
401 White Horse Pike
Haddon Heights, NJ 08035
Phone: (609) 547 6030
Fax: (609) 546 6880
Contact: James McGrane, Pres.
Description: Consulting firm specializing in continuous improvement through activities such as organization development, management skills development, market development, information process improvement, and work process improvement. Industries served include food processing, manufacturing, construction, transportation, and wholesale/retail trade.

Harber and Associates
4646 Poplar, Suite 425
Memphis, TN 38117
Phone: (901) 761 9953
Contact: Jerry L. Harber
Description: Consulting firm with a focus on TQM for service organizations Services include total quality implementation, development of effective customer service, leadership development, development of communication skills, stress management, facilitation of strategic planning, team building, and conflict management skill development.
Seminars/workshops: Offered to clients.

Heller, Hunt and Cunningham
P.O. Box 1567
Brookline, MA 02146
Phone: (617) 734 7604
Fax: (617) 734 9320
Description: A total quality consulting, educating, and training company. Services include developing and implementing total quality strategies, auditing current structures, management practices, leadership styles, and communication systems, education and training, teaching and using analytic problem-solving methods, developing customer service strategies, developing vendor partnerships, coaching and supporting effective team leadership and teamwork, and designing human resource systems. Serve clients of varying sizes in industries ranging from health care to banking, as well as educational institutions and public agencies.

Seminars/workshops: Offered on a wide range of topics to clients.

The Paul Hertz Group
7990 S.W. 117th Avenue, Suite 100
Miami, FL 33183
Phone: (305) 598 2601
Fax: (305) 270 0627
Description: Consulting firm specializing in the creation of regenerated organizations through a proprietary methodology for organizational transformation built on the philosophy of Dr. W. Edward Deming. Components of the "Renewal" process include leadership development, process improvement through empowerment of individuals, optimizing team performance, achieving process improvement through teams, management alignment, and environmental feedback. Training and consulting services offered revolve around this process. Clients include North American and international organizations ranging in size from small entrepreneurial firms to large conglomerates. A wide range of industries are served in addition to government agencies and service organizations.
Seminars/workshops: Offered on a range of topics related to the "Renewal" methodology.

HESTER Associates, Inc.
P.O. Box 669
Chatham, MA 02633
Phone: (508) 945 4860
Fax: (508) 945 4862
Contact: William F. Hester, Pres.
Description: Management consulting in the area of business process assessments, strategic planning, TQM implementations, reengineering, statistical process control and team training. Also assist with ISO 9000 implementation.
Seminars/workshops: Offered, on topics such as facilitator and team training, ISO 9000, Quality awareness, statistical process control, and customer satisfaction.
Publications: *The Quality Newsletter* and the *Statistical Problem Solving Handbook* (resource for teams involved in improving quality).

William L. Holcomb Associates, Inc.
1965 Sheridan Drive
Buffalo, NY 14223 1204
Phone: (716) 873 2882
Fax: (716) 873 2806
Contact: William L. Holcomb, Pres.
Description: Consultants in management labor relations and personnel services. Services include employee benefits design, wage/salary programs, employee communications/handbooks, management/supervisory training, human resources policies and procedures, and safety and health compliance. Serve clients in business, education, government, and service organizations.

Howard-Lancaster & Associates, Inc.
2906B West Long Circle
Littleton, CO 80120
Phone: (303) 795 8036
Contact: Linda L. Lancaster, Pres.
Description: Offer TQM training (covering philosophy of TQM, methodology, statistical techniques, relationship and leadership skills), guide quality management evolution in organizations, work with documentation of policies and procedures, work simplification, methods improvement, and work measurement.
Seminars/workshops: Half-day to two-day workshops offered.

Howick Associates
2828 Marshall Court, Suite 100
Madison, WI 53705
Phone: (608) 233 3377
Fax: (608) 233 1194
Contact: Mary Kessens
Description: Provide education and training in the areas of quality improvement, communication, management/leadership, teams, and career systems. Provide "off the shelf" as well as custom designed programs. Serve clients in industries such as telecommunications, health care, insurance, utilities, manufacturing, and education.
Seminars/workshops: Offered to clients.

HUMA Group, Inc.
P.O. Box 527
107 South Main St.
Harrisonburg, VA 22801
Phone: (703) 434 1151
Fax: (703) 432 9745
Branch offices: Garden City, South Carolina; Cincinnati, Ohio
Contact: William J. Russell, P.E.
Description: Work with companies of all sizes (in North America as well as Europe, Mid-East and Latin America) to enhance profits and assure competitiveness. Technical and organizational capabilities are focused in three practice areas: operations enhancement, operating strategies, and market reconnaissance. The HUMA Group's "Concurrent Management Process" embodies their approach to TQM and represents a process of cultural change, technology application, analytical skill development, and open communications.
Seminars/workshops: Offer client-sponsored as well as focused workshops.
Publications: *CMP – A Step Beyond TQM* and *NAFTA – A Positive Step Forward.*

Human Dynamics
4713 High Point Road, Suite 3
P.O. Box 7241
Greensboro, NC 27417
Phone: (910) 854 0120
(800) 258 1170
Fax: (910) 299 2326
Contact: Raymond P. Cienek, Pres.
Description: Management consulting firm specializing in training and organizational development work for a variety of organizations, primarily in the areas of research, higher education, the military, finance, and federal government. A wide range of TQM services are offered, including training programs, quality surveys, initial implementation and model development, and related consulting services.
Seminars/workshops: Offered on such topics as fundamentals of TQM, facilitator training, team leadership, and statistical tools for TQM.

Incos, Inc. (Innovative Consulting Services, Inc.)
10024 South Shore Drive
Plymouth, MN 55441
Phone: (612) 546 0206
Fax: (612) 546 8686
Contact: Dr. Hana Tomasek, Pres.
Description: Incos assists top management in implementing total quality management. Services offered include training in leadership skills, communication, statistical process control, and training for in-house trainers.
Seminars/workshops: Offered to clients.

Interaction Research Institute, Inc.
4428 Rockcrest Drive
Fairfax, VA 22032
Phone: (703) 978 0313
Fax: (703) 978 1776
Contact: Thomas D. Affourtit
      Barba B. Affourtit
Description: Provide services in quality management, decision/information support systems, consumer research, systems design, motivational assessment, and organizational development. Provide software for statistical process control techniques and graphics management. Serve clients in health care, government, defense industries, hospitality, and manufacturing.
Seminars/workshops: Offered in the area of organizational process management. Programmed workbook, instructors manual, and viewgraphs also available.
Publications: "STATMAN" (statistical management software), "G-MAN" (graphics management software).

International Management Technologies, Inc.
2004 Great Oaks Drive, Suite 100
Burnsville, MN 55337
Phone: (612) 432 6000
Fax: (612) 953 6928
Contact: Mr. Robin Lawton, Pres.
Description: Consulting firm which provides service quality and productivity management systems training. Areas of expertise include customer satisfaction, time-based competition, innovation, measurement and survey research. Serve clients in industries such as manufacturing, electronics, health care and government.
Seminars/workshops: Workshops provided for clients on topics such as strategic planning for organizational transformation, applying quality function deployment to service and knowledge work, creating fast cycle business processes, the dynamics of winning teams, and customer-centered team projects.
Publications: *Creating a Customer-Centered Culture: Leadership in Quality, Innovation, and Speed* (book) and *Customer-Centered Improvement Tools for Teams* (handbook).

International Systems Services Corporation
300 First Stamford Place
Stamford, CT 06902 6748
Phone: (203) 975 0000
Fax: (203) 975 0002
Branch offices: Cambridge, MA; San Francisco, CA; Washington, DC
Contact: O. Bruce Gupton, Pres.
Description: Management consulting firm specializing in revenue enhancement, cost reduction, cycle time reduction, quality improvement, and increased customer satisfaction. Results are obtained through a partnership with clients in implementing significant business and information technology improvements, and assisting in the integration of change. Areas of expertise include business process reengineering, benchmarking, continuous improvement, information technology and planning, technology architecture, reengineering of information technology processes, management of change, and acceleration of results. Serve clients in the financial services industry, consumer products, professional services, publishing, and computers and communications, in addition to public sector and nonprofit organizations. Geographic areas served include North America, South America, Europe, the Middle East, Asia, and the Pacific Basin.
Seminars/workshops: Offered to clients.

Ken Irish Associates
P.O. Box 1159
101 Far Horizon Drive
Cheshire, CT 06410
Phone: (203) 272 6338
Fax: (203) 272 6338
Contact: Kenneth G. Irish, Pres.
      Tim Pacileo

Description: Human resource management consultants specializing in employee/labor relations, training and development, TQM and reengineering, safety, and compensation and employee benefits.
Seminars/workshops: Offered to clients.

JCM-TECH, Inc.
4900 Blazer Parkway
Dublin, OH 43017
Phone: (614) 766 3670
Fax: (614) 792 1607
E-mail: mook@well.sf.ca.us
Contact: Jane Campanizzi, Ph.D.
William H. Mook
Description: Specialize in quality and productivity improvement for service firms, manufacturers, and government agencies. Areas of practice include technical services, management services, and training services. Among the management consulting and training services related to TQM are total quality programs, audits and reviews, team facilitation, customer surveys, statistical process control, and quality costs.
Seminars/workshops: Offered on a variety of quality, productivity, and management topics and ranging in length from one to four days.
Publications: Measuring Quality Costs: An Activity-Based Approach, Process Reengineering: New Way to Compete, and *Total Quality: Making Your Organization More Effective.*

Jewell Consulting Network, Inc.
6595 Roswell Road, Suite 691
Atlanta , GA 30328
Phone: (404) 395 9907
Fax: (404) 395 9908
Contact: Dr. Sandra F. Jewell
Dr. Donald O. Jewell
Description: Consulting firm with a focus on reengineering and empowerment designed to create customer-focused, total quality organizations. Industries served include paper, utilities, finance and banking, textiles, fiber glass, rubber, beverages, flooring, computers, and chemicals.

JLA Consultants, Inc.
3341 SW 15th Street
Pompano Beach, FL 33069
Phone: (305) 971 7595
Fax: (305) 979 0009
Branch office: Cleve Laird, Drial Consultants, Inc., Simi Valley, CA
Contact: Jack Aronowitz
Description: Specialize in biomedical consultation to the international biotechnology community. Areas of expertise include biomedical chemistry, instrumentation, reagent development/production, quality control (evaluation of existing quality programs, development and implementation of programs, and development of testing and sampling protocols), clinical trials, regulatory affairs, management services, and marketing.

The Johnson–Layton Company
8811 Alden Drive, Suite 7
Los Angeles, CA 90048
Phone: (310) 859 2321
Fax: (310) 274 3044
E-mail: johnsone@netcom.com
Branch: St. Petersburg, FL
Contact: Eric Johnson
Description: Provide a broad range of management consulting services in the areas of new business and strategic planning, financial planning, organizational assessment, operational improvement, and TQM programs. Offer training and education in TQM basics, team-building and process improvement implementation, benchmarking, and performance measurement.
Seminars/workshops: Offered in TQM basics, TQM tools, and benchmarking.

Joiner Associates
3800 Regent Street
P.O. Box 5445
Madison, WI 53705 0445
Phone: (608) 238 8134
Fax: (608) 238 2908
Contact: Brian L. Joiner
Description: Management consulting firm specializing in quality management principles and techniques. Provide an array of resources and training materials that help organizations introduce and implement quality improvement. Serve organizations in a range of industries.

Seminars/workshops: Offer a range of public seminars on topics such as design of experiments, statistical tools, teamwork. Also offer video training seminars on management topics.

Juran Institute, Inc.
11 River Road
Wilton, CT 06897 0811
Phone: (203) 834 1700
Fax: (203) 834 9891
Branch offices:
   Juran Institute (Australia)
   118 Mount Street
   P.O. Box 1321
   North Sydney 2059 NSW
   Phone: 2 957 3525
   Fax: 2 959 3461
   Juran Institute (Canada)
   60 Bedford Road
   Toronto, Ontario M5R 2K2
   Phone: (416) 928 1619
   Fax: (416) 928 1304
   Juran Institute B.V.
   Koninginnegracht 60
   1514 AE The Hague
   The Netherlands
   Phone: 70 362 1767
   Fax: 70 392 4628
   Juran Institute Espana, S.A.
   Reina Mercedes, 17, 1
   28020 Madrid
   Spain
   Phone: 1 534 0950
   Fax: 1 534 1549
Description: Offer consulting services, public and on-site workshops, international quality conferences, customized training programs, and software to clients world-wide. Industries served include health care, financial services, manufacturing, aerospace, government, construction, transportation, and small business. Areas of expertise include activity-based costing, benchmarking, business process reengineering, cultural assessment, ISO 9000 preparation and registration, Malcolm Baldrige National Quality Award self-assessment, quality technology systems review, strategic quality planning and design, and total quality system design and implementation.
Seminars/workshops: Catalog of seminars and workshops is available. Offerings cover a wide range of topics including benchmarking, facilitating and leading teams, leadership, quality planning tools, reengineering processes, ISO 9000 quality systems, strategic quality planning, and teaching quality improvement tools. `
Publications: Offer quality improvement software ("Juran Quality Improvement Toolkit"), videos, books, and training packages. Catalog of quality training and education resources is available upon request.

KAIZEN Institute of America
108 El Reno Cove
Austin, TX 78734
Phone: (512) 261 4900
Fax: (512) 261 5107
Branch offices:
   KAIZEN Institute of Japan, Inc.
   2 11 15 Akasaka
   Minato-Ku, Toyko 107, Japan
   Phone: (81) 3 5563 9391
   KAIZEN Support Services
   4 Tavistock Place
   London WC1H 9RA,
   United Kingdom
   Phone: 0171 713 0407
   KAIZEN Institute of Europe Germany
   Niederlassung Deutschland
   Konigsberger Strasse 2
   60487 Frankfurt/Main,
   Germany
   Phone: 69 953012 0
   KAIZEN Institute of Europe Netherlands
   v.d. Boenhoffstraat 1
   6525 BZ Nigmegen, Netherlands
   Phone: 80 232472
   L'Institute de Kaizen France
   19 Avenue de Messine
   Paris 75008, France
   Phone: (33) 1 40 76 64 53
Contact: Kim Kaddatz, Man. Dir.
            Stuart Chalmers, Exec. Dir.
Description: Provide consulting services aimed at improving quality, cost, delivery, and safety by eliminating waste in every process through gradual continual improvement. Offer in-house seminars, development of customized training processes, public and private workshops with leading quality management experts from the U.S. and Japan, public seminars, and tours of

leading Japanese companies in a wide range of industries.

Seminars/workshops: Offer in-house and public seminars covering basics of Kaizen, quality function deployment, and Kaizen and Just-in-Time. Additionally, offer in-house seminars on utilizing Kaizen systems and tools (total quality control, suggestion systems, quality function deployment, policy deployment), leadership workshops, policy deployment and cross-functional management, training for internal consultants, design of experiments, total productive maintenance and statistical process control.

Publications: Catalog of seminars is available, also reprints of newsletter *KAIZEN Communique*, and *KAIZEN: The Key to Japan's Competitive Success* (book).

A.T. Kearney, Inc.
222 West Adams Street
Chicago, IL 60606
Phone: (312) 648 0111
Fax: (312) 223 6200
Branch offices: North America: Atlanta; Cleveland; Dallas; Denver; Houston; Los Angeles; Miami; Minneapolis; New York; Phoenix; San Francisco; Stamford; Toronto; Washington, DC.

South America: Mexico City; São Paulo

Europe: Amsterdam; Barcelona; Berlin; Brussels; Copenhagen; Dusseldorf; Helsinki; London; Madrid; Milan; Moscow; Munich; Oslo; Paris; Prague; Stockholm; Stuttgart.

Asia and Pacific: Hong Kong, Melbourne, Singapore, Syndey, Tokyo.

Contact: Hank Conn
Brian Harrison

Description: International management consulting firm specializing in benchmarking and best practices analysis, business and marketing strategy, business process reengineering, customer satisfaction, environment, health and safety, global business policy, global sourcing, information technology, logistics and supply chain management, manufacturing and operations improvement, marketing and sales, organizational effectiveness, stages of excellence diagnostics, technology assessment and management, time-based management, total quality management, and transfer pricing.

Clients include industry, service organizations, financial institutions, government agencies, and health care institutions.

Seminars/workshops: Offered to clients.

Publications: *Workplace 2000* (book), "Creating the Environment for Total Quality Management" (white paper), "Total Quality Management: A Business Process Perspective" (white paper), and "Transforming the Enterprise" (white paper).

Key Management Strategies
7906 Montgomery Avenue
Elkins Park, PA 19027
Phone: (215) 635 6170
Fax: (215) 635 1044
Contact: Dr. Steven Krupp
Dr. Martin Klein

Description: Management consulting firm specializing in executive and management counseling, strategic planning, restructuring and change management, quality/service improvement, leadership assessment and development, team-building, goal setting and pay-for-performance, customer service, sales and technical training, management advisory services, and conflict resolution. Serve most industries in both the for profit and nonprofit sectors.

Seminars/workshops: Offered to clients.

Klemm & Associates
2400 Cripple Creek Drive
St. Louis, MO 63129 5039
Phone: (314) 846 2440
Fax: (314) 846 2158
Contact: Andy Klemm

Description: Provide consulting services in areas such as change management, productivity improvement, teamwork, workflow, strategy, gainsharing, compensation, and surveys of organizational culture, customer attitudes, and employee opinions. Serve clients in manufacturing, financial services, transportation, telecommunications, education, health care, government, computer services, and not-for-profit organizations.

Seminars/workshops: Offered to clients.

Paul D. Krensky Associates, Inc.
Adams Building
9 Meriam Street
Lexington, MA 02173
Phone: (617) 862 3003
Fax: (617) 862 3004
Contact: Paul D. Krensky
Description: Specialize in the management, engineering, and training aspects of total quality management and customer satisfaction. Areas of specialization include TQM, customer satisfaction improvement, quality cost reduction and error prevention, quality surveys and audits, quality training, supplier quality improvement, statistical process control, ISO 9000, product liability prevention, and personnel recruiting and placement.
Seminars/workshops: Offered to clients.

Landes Communications
1722 Nicholson Place
St. Louis, MO 63104
Phone: (314) 776 2666
Fax: (314) 776 2379
Contact: Les Landes
Description: Assist clients in integrating systematic improvement processes into existing operations. Training and development work focuses on individual readiness and effectiveness, and on problem-solving and communication skills. Offer seminars on transforming quality programs into quality work.
Seminars/workshops: Offered.
Publications: "Total Quality in Communications: Principles and Opportunities" (videotape).

Landis & Associates
200 Mill Pond Road
Sanford, NC 27330
Phone: (919) 776 1302
Fax: (919) 776 1302
Description: Consulting firm offering services in the areas of total quality management (including start-up and training), management team development, team-based compensation, and pay-for-knowledge. Serve clients in the manufacturing and service sectors.

Latzko Associates
215 79th Street
North Bergen, NJ 07057 5727
Phone: (201) 868 5338
Fax: (201) 868 5338
E-mail: latzko@mary.fordham.edu
Contact: W.J. Latzko
Description: Assist clients in a broad range of services in developing quality throughout their organization. Areas of expertise include working with management to develop an understanding of the Deming method, planning for quality (including development and implementation of a quality program), statistical process control, continuous and never ending improvement, on-site consulting, and training courses. Work with clients in service industries, manufacturing, academe, and government.
Seminars/workshops: Offered to clients.
Publications: (books) *Four Days with Dr. Deming: A Strategy for Modern Methods of Management, Quality and Productivity for Bankers and Financial Managers, MICR Quality Control Handbook, Implementing TQM,* and *The Deming Approach in the Service Industry.*

The La Valle Group
P.O. Box 424
Hopatcong, NJ 07843
Phone: (201) 770 0314
Fax: (201) 770 0314
Contacts: John La Valle
　　　　　Kathleen La Valle
Description: Offer consulting and training and development services. Areas of consulting expertise include improving organizational effectiveness (through process consultation, meeting management, team-building and development, group dynamics) and personal coaching. Training and development specialties include customer service, basic management skills, team leadership training, managing for performance, selection interviewing, managing managers, interpersonal skills, staff leadership training, and sales training. Work with industry and service organizations.
Seminars/workshops: Offered in-house and publicly on a range of topics.

Leads–Rivers Group
230 North Elm Street, Suite 1550
Greensboro, NC 27401
Phone: (800) 315 3237
Fax: (910) 275 9952
Branch offices: Orlando, FL; Washington, DC
Contact: J. Michael Crouch, Pres.
Description: Provide consulting and training in the areas of implementing quality improvement, planning strategically, facilitating organizational change, and reengineering critical processes. Quality improvement services include workshops, facilitation, and consulting on topics such as costs of quality, quality function deployment, team facilitation, benchmarking, and advanced planning tools. Industries served include financial services, manufacturing, transportation, defense, government, high technology, as well as public and private service organizations.
Publications: *An Ounce of Application* (ISBN 1 55623 850 9).

Leemak, Inc.
920 Hillview Court, Suite 135
Milpitas, CA 95035
Phone: (408) 945 8666
Fax: (408) 945 8951
E-mail: leemak@aol.com
Contact: Alan J. Leeds, Pres.
Lawrence J. Makal, V.P.
Description: Consulting firm which provides comprehensive systems for continuous process improvement, including custom training programs, hands-on consulting services, and advanced management tools. Provide the tools, techniques, and services necessary to obtain measurable, sustainable results and improve a client's competitive position. Areas of expertise include ISO 9000, audits, quality function deployment, statistical process control, design of experiments, customer-supplier partnerships, concurrent product development, business process reengineering, and empowerment and self-managed teams. Serve clients in the banking, semiconductor, space, medical, defense, utility, food, equipment manufacturing, technical instruments, and electronics industries.
Seminars/workshops: Offered to clients.

Levins & Associates
624 Alton Woods Drive
P.O. Box 442
Concord, NH 03302
Phone: (603) 224 3198
Fax: (603) 226 1831
Contact: John R. Levins, C.M.C.
Description: Management consultant and investment advisor specializing in profit enhancement and cost containment linked to TQM concepts. Areas of practice include cash management, financial analysis, risk management to improve operations, policy and procedures, financial planning, accounting, and team-building. Service provided to a number of industry segments.
Seminars/workshops: Offered.

R.J. Levulis & Associates
601 Sequoia Trail
Roselle, IL 60172
Phone: (708) 924 9494
Fax: (708) 924 9494
Contact: Raymond J. Levulis
Description: Assist clients in becoming more competitive in the world-wide economy. Specialize in operations improvement, strategic planning, logistics/distribution, facilities planning, materials management/purchasing, quality management, industrial engineering, and warehousing.

Brian P. Little & Associates
4018 West 65th Street, Suite 14
Edina, MN 55435
Phone: (612) 922 2411
Branch office: Philadelphia, PA
Contact: Brian Little
Description: Offer quality and productivity consulting for service and manufacturing firms. Areas of practice include TQM, ISO 9000, reengineering, gainsharing, facilities planning, supplier evaluation, and productivity/quality studies.

Long & Vickers, Inc.
1800 Carmel Ridge Road
Charlotte, NC 28226
Phone: (704) 345 5538
Fax: (704) 366 4512
Branch office: Long & Vickers, Inc., 161 W. 15th Street #6J, New York, NY 10011, (212) 627 1254
Contacts: Mary Vickers Koch
Carl Long
Description: Management consulting firm with a specialty in the development and integration of leadership competencies with continuous improvement practices. Provide assistance to clients in building quality processes that are linked to business goals. Serve clients in financial, service, and manufacturing industries.

Luftig & Associates, Inc.
32255 Northwestern Highway, Suite 120
Farmington Hills, MI 48334
Phone: (810) 855 9455
Fax: (810) 855 6240
Contact: Dr. Jeffrey Luftig
Description: Provide training and on-site consulting services in the quality sciences throughout North, South and Central America; Europe; and Australia. Services include policy deployment, daily management, statistical quality assurance (statistical process control, gauge capability analysis, statistical methods for marketing and procurement, experimental design, team problem-solving, quality function deployment and customer quality assurance, advanced statistical techniques, and industrial research. Serve clients in a range of manufacturing industries.
Seminars/workshops: Catalog of seminars is available. Topics include TQM, strategic planning and policy deployment, experimental design, customer and supplier quality assurance, statistical methods, and measurement and gauging.
Publications: Catalog of publications, coursework, and seminars is available; included are technical aids for quality practitioners.

McNair Associates
2193 Northlake Parkway
Building 12, Suite 107
Tucker, GA 30084
Phone: (404) 270 1516
Fax: (404) 270 0942
Contact: Nimrod McNair
Description: Provide project consulting services in areas such as business plans, policy and procedures manuals, code of ethics installation, values audits/values training, and quality improvement programs. Also facilitate strategic planning conferences, hold team building workshops and ethics workshops, and consult in the areas of organization development, franchising/new business start-ups, decision making and problem analysis, and quality education. Serve companies of varying sizes in a range of industries.
Seminars/workshops: Offered to clients.

McNeil & Associates
15601 Brockton Lane
Dayton, MN 55327
Phone: (612) 428 4068
Fax: (612) 428 8484
Contact: Pat McNeil
Description: Offer consulting services in the areas of business development, productivity improvement, service management, service parts and logistics, total quality transformation, computer facility services, training, and multinational operations. Specific quality related areas of expertise include TQM process training, team-building, quality system compliance, process capability analysis, statistical process control techniques, service quality measurement, and service management planning. Clients include independent service organizations, manufacturers, distributors, value added resellers, and utility companies.
Seminars/workshops: Offered to clients.

Macro International, Inc.
11785 Beltsville Drive
Calverton, MD 20705
Phone: (301) 572 0200
Fax: (301) 572 0999
Branches (United States): Atlanta, GA; New York, NY; Burlington, VT

Branches (Europe): Budapest, Hungary; Gyor, Hungary; Moscow, Russia; Warsaw, Poland
Contact: Brad Dude
Description: Professional services company providing research, management consulting, information systems, and training services. In the area of TQM offer services which include TQM workshops for managers, a total quality assessment measuring an organization's performance, quality planning, market research, improvement strategies, training and team building, and a PC-based analysis package.
Seminars/workshops: Offered on a range of topics that can be tailored to meet customer needs.

Management Methods, Inc.
P.O. Box 1484
207 Johnston Street, S.E., Suite 208
Decatur, AL 35602
Phone: (205) 355 3896
Fax: (205) 353 3140
Contacts: Davis M. Woodruff
Felix M. Phillips
Description: Management and manufacturing consultants specializing in three areas: professional speaking, consulting, and customized training. Training and consulting services include quality management, statistical process control, team problem-solving, failure mode effects analysis, assistance with ISO 9000 certification, operator certification, and implementation support.
Seminars/workshops: Programs offered in leadership and management as well as quality and technical topics.
Publications: Articles and reports on quality-related topics available upon request.

Manufacturing & Development Technology
P.O. Box 1746
Soquel, CA 95073
Phone: (408) 475 9357
Fax: (408) 688 5180
Contact: Don Hoernschemeyer
Description: Assist high-technology manufacturing companies in achieving highly effective operations. Produce continuous or focused improvements which lead to successful new product entry, reliable manufacturing operations, high product quality, smooth research

and development to manufacturing transitions, high first pass yields, and meeting ISO 9000 standards.

Marilyn Manning
945 Mountain View Avenue
Mountain View, CA 94040
Phone: (415) 965 3663
Fax: (415) 965 3668
Contact: Marilyn Manning
Description: Offer training and consulting services to clients in government agencies, financial institutions, educational institutions, and non profit organizations, as well as the health care, transportation, and electronics industries. Areas of expertise include team-building for total quality management, facilitation for meetings and retreats, staff training, conflict and change management, strategic planning, customer service, leadership, and organizational development and assessment.
Seminars/workshops: Offered to clients.

Mathews & Company
6 Landmark Square
Stamford, CT 06901 2792
Phone: (203) 325 8419
Fax: (203) 325 0125
Contact: Richard Mathews
Janelle B. Hill
Description: Specialize in customer satisfaction measurement, improvement, and benchmarking for information systems organizations. Areas of expertise include analyzing customer perceptions, establishing a baseline for measuring performance improvement, benchmarking survey results, setting improvement goals, training staff, monitoring performance, development of overall customer satisfaction programs. Serve information systems organizations in all industries.
Seminars/workshops: Offered to clients.

Mauch & Associates
1032 South LaGrange Road
LaGrange, IL 60525
Phone: (708) 352 4301
(800) 956 2824
Fax: (708) 352 4304
Contacts: Peter D. Mauch
Nancy A. Doran

Description: Specialize in quality control training services with courses in TQM basics, team-building, statistical techniques, and ISO 9000 standards which can be tailored to client specifications. Also perform quality audits using ISO 9000 standards, develop ISO 9000 quality systems, offer administrative services such as policy manual development, and provide general quality control consulting. Quality system development services for small business also available.

Seminars/workshops: Catalog of courses available. Certificate programs in quality control also offered through Northern Illinois University.

Millet Group, Inc.
5012 Cliff Point Circle West
Colorado Springs, CO 80919
Phone: (719) 531 0669
Fax: (719) 592 9081
Contact: Ralph G. Rosenberg
Description: Consulting firm specializing in the graphic arts industry. Areas of expertise include Deming quality transformations, return on investment analysis, workflow analysis, strategic planning, and growth plans.
Seminars/workshops: Offered.
Publications: Graphic Arts Profitability: A Money Making Formula (book).

J.J. Moran & Associates
725 Ninth Street, Suite 4
Santa Monica, CA 90402
Phone: (310) 394 5388
Fax: (310) 394 5327
Contact: John Moran
Description: Specialize in the acquisition of market information and the application of the quality process to assist clients in their customer satisfaction, new product development, and marketing needs.
Seminars/workshops: Offered.
Publications: Managing the Development of New Products: Achieving Speed and Quality Simultaneously Through Multifunctional Teamwork (book).

Myers, Marits and Associates
1150 South Washington, Suite 220
Alexandria, VA 22314
Phone: (703) 519 7903
Fax: (703) 519 7906
E-mail: edm748@aol.com
Contact: E. Johnson Marits, Ph.D.
Description: Provide consulting services in total quality research and evaluation. Areas of expertise include program evaluation, customized training, leadership and executive development, total quality management. Work with clients in the public and private sector. Industries served include health care, government agencies, government related industries, and educational institutions.
Seminars/workshops: Offer seminars in areas such as total quality culture, conflict management for team development, and program and project evaluation.

Nelson & Company
1100 Circle 75 Parkway, Suite 800
Atlanta, GA 30339
Phone: (404) 951 4859
Fax: (404) 256 4014
Contact: Robert E. Nelson
Description: General management consulting firm focusing on TQM, continuous operations improvement, and process reengineering. Areas of expertise include development of a total quality strategy, TQM training, development of quality teams, quality techniques, process reengineering, and feedback mechanisms. Serve clients in a wide range of industries.
Seminars/workshops: Offered to clients.

Philip E. Nickerson
314 Haviland Road
Stamford, CT 06903
Phone: (203) 322 5912
Fax: (203) 322 5912
Contact: Philip E. Nickerson
Description: Provide management and technical consulting. Manufacturing services include strategic planning and implementation techniques for pre-production and production methods emphasizing quality assurance and quality control, TQM techniques, process validation studies, quality/productivity improvement techniques, conducting quality surveys/audits,

vendor quality assurance, and statistical process control. Also advise on facility design, assist in developing, implementing, and complying with design control requirements as currently proposed by both the FDA and ISO organizations. Serve clients in industries manufacturing health care products and consumer products, as well as the industrial, aerospace, and defense markets.

Nordli, Wilson Associates
2000 West Park Drive
P.O. Box 5000
Westborough, MA 01581 5000
Phone: (508) 366 0440
Fax: (508) 366 0893
Branch office: 110 Whitney Avenue, New Haven CT 06510
Phone: (203) 777 1199
Contact: Lester L. Tobias, Ph.D.
James E. Dowding, Ph.D.
Description: Management and consulting psychologists. Developers of the Total Quality Opinion Survey (TQOS). Provide consulting services to organizations on change management, change readiness, attitude assessment, and organizational development.

NUTEK, Inc.
30600 Telegraph Road, Suite 2230
Birmingham, MI 48025
Phone: (810) 642 4560
Fax: (810) 642 4609
Contact: Dr. Ranjit K. Roy
Description: Quality engineering specialists offering training seminars, software, and consulting services. Training seminars are aimed at practicing engineers and scientists and focus on use of the Taguchi experimental design technique. The Qualitek-4 software offered automates Taguchi experiment layout, analyzes results, and makes recommendations for product and process design improvements. Serve clients in manufacturing industries.
Seminars/workshops: Offer a three day seminar on design of experiments using the Taguchi approach.
Publications: "Qualitek-4" (software for automatic design and analysis of Taguchi experiments), and *A Primer on the Taguchi Method* (textbook).

Organization Counselors
10 West Broadway
P.O. Box 987
Salt Lake City, UT 84110
Phone: (801) 363 2900
Fax: (801) 363 2942
Contact: John E. Panos
Description: Human resource management and organization improvement consulting firm. Primary focus is on high performance organization development. Offer services in the area of total quality management and customer satisfaction.
Seminars/workshops: Offered to clients.

Organizational Designs in Communication, Inc.
P.O. Box 60609
Santa Barbara, CA 93160
Phone: (805) 968 1666
Fax: (805) 987 5097
Contact: Dr. Frederick Elias
Description: Management consulting firm specializing in provision of training and supporting quality improvement programs aimed at optimizing communication and performance. Areas of expertise include team-building, total quality management, strategic planning, managing organizational change, transition management, organizational behavior and development, productivity/quality improvement, supervisory/management skills, leadership development, conflict resolution, and reengineering. Serve organizations in both the public and private sectors.
Seminars/workshops: Offer team-building workshops.

Orr & Boss
292 South Main Street
Plymouth, MI 48170
Phone: (313) 453 3033
Fax: (313) 453 4320
Branches: 1323 Exmouth St., Suite 202, Sarnia, Ontario N7S 3Y1
Phone: (519) 542 1415
62 St. Martin's Lane, London WC2N 4JS, England
Phone: 0171 240 2644
Untermuhleweg 7, CH 6302 Zug, Switzerland
Phone: 42 310131

Description: Specialize in continuous improvement for companies in manufacturing. Provide consulting and training services in the areas of product design, process development, process control, problem solving, customer satisfaction, service, and ISO 9000 registration.
Seminars/workshops: Offer courses and workshops tailored to the needs of companies or groups.
Publications: Articles and literature available upon request.

The Pacer Group
360 South Patterson Blvd., Suite B
Dayton, OH 45402 2845
Phone: (513) 461 9001
Fax: (513) 461 9004
E-mail: 73651.174@compuserve.com
Contact: Fred Westfall, Ph.D.
Description: Specialize in offering consulting services to health care organizations in the areas of continuous quality improvement, patient-focused care, and strategic planning. Also offer quality and satisfaction measurement tools. Areas of expertise include strategic planning to attain improvement in cost, patient satisfaction, quality, and vertical integration, assistance in developing health care networks, health care process innovation utilizing the best of continuous quality improvement and reengineering, and patient-focused care to improve quality and patient satisfaction. Developers of the proprietary "Quality Measurement Index".
Seminars/workshops: Offered to clients.
Publications: *Pursue* (benchmarking tools for high performance).

Panitz and Associates, Inc.
3981 Wedgewood Southwest
Wyoming, MI 49509
Phone: (616) 534 1017
Contact: Eric Panitz, Ph.D.
Description: Offer services in the areas of market research, marketing and sales training, and TQM. Provide training in total quality management and program development for services organizations. Industries served include health care, retail trade, professional services, manufacturing, and government agencies.
Seminars/workshops: Offered to clients, including a workshop on concepts of quality management.

Paracom Partners International
758 D Street
Petaluma, CA 94952
Phone: (707) 765 6840
Fax: (707) 765 1109
Branch offices: Calgary, Alberta; Los Angeles, CA
Contact: Jim Selman
Description: Offer management consulting and education. Focus on culture change and employee development as related to communication and relationship competencies.
Seminars/workshops: Offered to clients. Also available is a videocourse entitled "Coaching: Beyond Management."
Publications: "Coaching: Beyond Management" (videocourse with workbook).

Patton Consultants, Inc.
4 Covington Place
Hilton Head, SC 29928 7665
Phone: (803) 686 6650
Fax: (803) 585 6651
E-mail: CompuServ 73411,2405
Branch office: Dallas, TX
Contact: Joseph D. Patton, Pres.
Description: Provide assistance to management in customer service, equipment maintenance, logistics, marketing, quality, and support systems. Also provide educational programs, support systems, and textbooks. A range of industries in both the public and private sector are served.
Seminars/workshops: Offered in varying lengths on topics such as service management, selling service, and product reliability, availability, quality and serviceability (PRAQS).
Publications: (Textbooks) *Service Management: Principles and Practices* (ISBN 0 87664 941 X), *Service Parts Management* (ISBN 0 87664 881 1), *Maintainability and Maintenance Management* (ISBN 0 87664 466 3), *Preventive Maintenance* (ISBN 0 87664 639 9), and *Logistics Technology and Management: The New Approach* (ISBN 0 934623 04 X).

Peak International
4500 Campus Drive, Suite 628 E
Newport Beach, CA 92660
Phone: (714) 693 9045
Contact: Ignacio A. Munoz

Description: Provide consulting services in the areas of product development, process development, statistical process control, and continuous improvement. Also offer seminars and supplier support services. Some seminars are offered in Spanish as well as English. Clients include national and international firms in a range of industries including electronics, health care products, food products, and manufacturing.

Seminars/workshops: Offered in-house on topics such as continuous process improvement, statistical process control, quality assurance for medical devices, and ISO 9000.

P-E International
Park House, Wick Road
Egham, Surrey TW20 OHW
Phone: 01784 434411
Fax: 01784 476452
Branch offices: List of world-wide offices available from HQ
Contact: Glyn Read
Description: International management consultancy specializing in TQM projects within a broad range of capabilities. Serve a wide variety of industries within both the public and private sector. World-wide offices.

Daniel Penn Associates
151 New Park Avenue
Hartford, CT 06106
Phone: (203) 232 8577
Fax: (203) 586 7121
Branch Office: 1016 Bridgeton Hill Road, Upper Black Eddy, PA 18972
Phone: (215) 982 5599
Contact: Antonio R. Rodriguez
Michael J. Garofalo
Description: Provide services that help businesses make effective use of resources to continuously improve productivity, quality, customer service, and reduce the cost of operations. Employ a continuous improvement process and process reengineering methodology combined with a systematic approach to managing change. Areas of expertise include continuous process improvement, business process reengineering, production cycle improvement, training/organization development, material/inventory management,

management information systems, shop floor controls, fleet maintenance, production scheduling, cost reduction strategy, and resource modeling. Serve clients in manufacturing, banking and finance, utilities, insurance, and government.

Seminars/workshops: Offer programs in team leadership/facilitation skills, total quality management, managing change, coaching, process mapping and problem-solving, managing a diverse work force, and additional topics.

Perelmuth & Associates
124 East 40th Street
New York, NY 10016
Phone: (212) 986 4180
Fax: (212) 697 6459
Contact: Joel Perelmuth
Description: Marketing and management consulting firm specializing in customer satisfaction and quality management issues.
Seminars/workshops: Offered.

Performance Consulting Group
8535 3 Baymeadows Road, Suite 143
Jacksonville, FL 32256
Phone: (904) 287 1345
Fax: (904) 448 5455
E-mail: PNNNNOB@delphi.com
Contact: Patrick J. O'Brien
James P. Dixon, Jr.
Description: Specialize in instructional design and organizational systems. Areas of expertise include design, development, and implementation of technical, sales, service, and leadership training. Also provide services related to teams and team-building, implementation of quality improvement systems, and strategy development. Work with public and private sector clients in a range of industries including, utilities, defense, health care, finance, and consumer products.
Seminars/workshops: Offered to clients.

Performex
101 The Embarcadero, Suite 206
San Francisco, CA 94105
Phone: (415) 788 7900
Fax: (415) 788 7976
Branch offices: 110 Newport Center Drive, Suite 140, Newport Beach, CA 92660
Phone: (714) 759 1928
78 E. Putnam Ave., Suite 152, Greenwich, CT 06830
Phone: (203) 629 2995
Contact: Ralph Bettman, CEO, Tom Markham, Client Relations
Description: Consulting firm partners with client personnel to plan and implement quality systems. Areas of practice include assistance with basic management processes, interpersonal processes, strategic planning, participative management, productivity management, quality management, and customer orientation. Also specialize in assisting with ISO 9000 registration and Baldrige Award competition.
Seminars/workshops: Offered.

Perry Johnson, Inc.
3000 Town Center, Suite 2960
Southfield, MI 48075
Phone: (810) 356 4410
Fax: (810) 356 4230
Branch offices: Rosemont, IL; El Segundo, CA; Burlington, MA
Description: Provide TQM and ISO 9000 consulting, training, and implementation services to clients world-wide in all industries, as well as QS-9000 audits for the automotive industry. PJI has developed workbooks, overhead transparency presentations, videotapes, software, and a wide range of seminars to assist in understanding, integrating, and implementing ISO and QS-9000 requirements and preparing for ISO/QS-9000 registration. Consulting services include assessment, quality manual review and/or preparation, quality program design, on-site training, ISO 9000/QS-9000 consultation, quality function deployment, failure mode effects analysis, vendor standards, and development of leadership skills.
Seminars/workshops: Catalog of training programs/locations and training materials is available. Included are ISO 9000 and QS-9000 seminars, TQM seminars, overhead presenta-

tions, software and videotapes.

The Pierce Group
P.O. Box 33337
San Antonio, TX 78265
Phone: (210) 829 1911
Fax: (210) 829 1850
E-mail: Piercet@cowboytown.win.net
Contact: Thomas J. Pierce
Description: Human resources management consultants specializing in analysis of organizational effectiveness, building organizational effectiveness, promoting effective labor relations, increasing individual effectiveness, and improving human resources effectiveness. Specific services include employee and customer surveys, assessment measures aimed at organization improvement, team-building, and strategic business planning. Serve clients in a range of industries including electronics, health care, professional associations, foods, and manufacturing.

Plan-Test Associates
3443 North Central Ave., Suite 903
Phoenix, AZ 85012
Phone: (602) 956 0180
Contact: Mike Johnson, P.E., Pres.
Description: Offer workshops and consulting on total quality assurance, statistical process control, statistical design of experiments, and productivity methods. Make use of computer simulations and hands-on use of computers in data analysis during training.
Seminars/workshops: Offered to the public as well as in-house for clients.

P.O.W.E.R., Inc.
9 Pickering Way
Salem, MA 01970
Phone: (800) 633 9003
Fax: (508) 745 9998
Contact: Jacquelyn Bridge
Steve Gaudreau
Description: Provide training programs, consulting services, and educational products to the building cleaning industry. Specialize in total quality management for custodial operations.
Seminars/workshops: Offered to clients in the building cleaning industry.

Publications: Total Quality Management for Custodial Operations.

PQ Systems, Inc.
10468 Miamisburg–Springboro Road
Miamisburg, OH 45342
Phone: (513) 885 2255
(800) 777 3020
Fax: (513) 885 2252
E-mail: Sales@pqsys-hq.mhs.compuserve.com
Branch offices:
PQ Systems Europe Ltd.
73 Ormskirk Business Park
New Court Way
Ormskirk, Lancashire L39 2YT
England
Phone: 01695 570902
Fax: 01695 570916
PQ Systems Pty. Ltd.
Level 5, Peninsula Centre
435–437 Nepean Highway
Frankston, Victoria 3199
Australia
Phone: 03 770 1960
Fax: 03 770 1995
Contact: Michael J. Cleary, Pres.
Description: Full-service firm offering a comprehensive network of products and services designed to improve quality, productivity, and competitive position for all types of industries. Provide consulting services, seminars, statistical application software, a step-by-step training system and support manuals, and quality-related films and books to support quality improvement efforts. Serve clients in a wide range of areas including manufacturing, the service sector, government, and education.
Seminars/workshops: Provide seminars related to software products offered, continuous improvement, and seminars customized to clients' needs.
Publications: Listing of numerous software programs and training materials is available.

Practical Management, Inc.
23801 Calabasas Rd.
Calabasas, CA 91372 8789
Phone: (800) 444 9101
Fax: (818) 223 9112
Branch offices:
Practical Management, Inc.
P.O. Box 792
Charleston, IL 61920
Phone: (217) 345 7307
Practical Management of Canada
P.O. Box 698
Streetsville, ON Canada L5M 2C2
Phone: (905) 542 1570
Fax: (905) 542 9422
Contact: Richard Wigley (California)
Tom Maruna (Illinois)
Gary Peterson (Canada)
Description: Training and consulting firm offering a comprehensive series of courses in TQM. Public seminars and workshops offered as well as in-company programs and consulting services. Clients include companies in manufacturing as well as service sectors.
Seminars/workshops: A range of one to two day seminars offered on topics such as "Managing in a TQM Environment", "Creating a Team Environment", and "Process Improvement".
Publications: Why TQM Fails (audiotape), *Effective Team Building* (audiotape).

PROACTION Management Consultants
5940 Grey Rock Road
Agoura Hills, CA 91301
Phone: (818) 706 2200
Fax: (818) 706 2271
Contact: George J. Miller
Description: Offer manufacturing management consulting and education. Focus on business process reengineering employing total quality management principles. Serve discrete manufacturing industries such as electronics, also transportation, aerospace, defense and foods.
Seminars/workshops: Offered to clients.
Publications: Reengineering the Business System and *Reengineering: 40 Useful Hints.*

Problem Solvers for Industry
P.O. Box 193
Chalfont, PA 18914
Phone: (215) 822 9695
Fax: (215) 822 8086
Contact: Benjamin F. Gerding
Description: Offers classes in statistical process control, TQM, and Just-in-Time concepts and practices for small business companies. Assists in the elimination of scrap, rework and inspection, aids in the development of management personnel.
Publications: Quality Assurance Bulletin.

Process Management International
7801 East Bush Lake Road, Suite 360
Minneapolis, MN 55439
Phone: (612) 893 0313
Fax: (612) 893 0502
Branch offices: (International):
  PMI Ltd.
  Barclay Venture Centre
  Sir William Lyons Road
  Coventry CV47EZ,
  United Kingdom
  Phone: 01 203 419089
  Process Management International
  155 Kent Street
  London, Ontario
  Canada N6A5N7
  Phone: (519) 434 0050
Branch offices (U.S.):
  183 Indian Bend Drive
  LaGrange, GA 30240
  Phone: (706) 884 0933
  15455 Vaughn Road
  Decatur, AR 72722 9710
  Phone: (501) 795 2809
  8505 Cherokee Place
  Leawood, KS 66206 1446
  Phone: (913) 642 3750
  705 Mulberry Court
  Naperville, IL 60540
  Phone: (708) 355 3444
  871 Lakefield Drive
  Galloway, OH 43119
  Phone: (614) 851 9141

Affiliates (U.S. & international):
  ARG, Inc.
  1725 Jefferson Davis Highway, Suite 203
  Arlington, VA 22202
  Phone: (703) 415 1011
  Inter-American Management Consultants
  10544 NW 26th Street, Suite 104
  Miami, FL 33172
  Phone: (305) 471 9887
  Bertoni & Asociados/PMI SA
    Suipacha 1067 4to
  (1008) Buenos Aires, Argentina
  Phone: 541 312 1941
  Hispania Market Research
  Calle Fernando Calder,
  #463 2nd Floor
  Hato Rey, Puerto Rico 00918
  Phone: (809) 753 8370
  Euro-Management Consultants
  P. dela Castellana
  114-ESC.4-7-OFIC 7
  28046 Madrid, Spain
  Phone: 341 5645240
  Lehmann Vogel & Partner Management
  Gerschwister-Scholl-Strabe 40
  14471 Potsdam, Germany
  Phone: 0331 964852
  NOVO Quality Services
  No. 1 Science Park Drive,
  #01-43 SISIR Bldg.
  Singapore 0511, Republic of Singapore
  Phone: 65 777 1855
  P.V.A. Consultores
  Carrera 8 a no. 9661
  Bogota 8 DC, Colombia
  Phone: 571 618 0346
  Pina Ybarra Consultores, C.A.
  Calle Los Mangos, Edf. Escalamo
  Sabana Grande
  Caracas, Venezuela
  Phone: 582 761 4810
  Robere & Associates
  46048 Sukhumvit Sol 8
  CD House
  Bangkok-10110, Thailand
  Sismecon Cia. Ltda.
  P.O. Box 09013575
  Guayaquil, Ecuador
  Phone: 593 4 887 742
Contact: Riva Kupritz, Marketing Man.
     Louis E. Schultz, CEO

Description: World-wide consulting and training firm with a focus on improving performance and driving innovation within organizations. Portfolio of products and services includes consulting, quality training and deployment, reengineering, strategy management, ISO preparation, and information technology. Serve a range of industries in both the public and private sectors.

Seminars/workshops: Offered to clients.

Publications: *Achieving ISO 9000 Registration* (guide to ISO 9000 registration), and *Profiles in Quality Learning from the Masters* (ISBN 0 527 76238 5).

Product Integrity Company

115 Elm Street P.O. Box 255
Enfield, CT 06082
Phone: (203) 745 5225
Fax: (203) 745 7218
Contact: C.W. Carter, Pres.

Description: Offer consulting services in total quality systems and assistance in helping companies meet quality systems standards such as ISO 9000. Areas of expertise include quality cost analysis, quality audits, customer surveys, quality systems reviews, inspection standards, quality engineering, statistical process control, process audits, vendor controls and ratings, product liability prevention, quality manuals, quality cost reduction, design of experiments, Taguchi methods, and product improvement. Also provide software programs for use in quality control programs. Serve clients in all industries.

Seminars/workshops: Total quality management programs offered.

Publications: Descriptions of software programs offered are available.

Productivity Development Group, Inc.

P.O. Box 488
Westford, MA 01886
Phone: (508) 692 1818
Fax: (508) 692 5080
E-mail: martins999@aol.com
Contact: Dr. Martin F. Stankard

Description: Offer training in process improvement and quality assessments.

Publications: *Productivity Views*, a newsletter dealing with service quality and white-collar productivity published 6 times yearly. Also publish a series of management reports (list available upon request).

Productivity Management Consultants

849 Harbor Island
Clearwater, FL 34630
Phone: (813) 447 6409
Contact: Dr. Peter Hunt

Description: Provide training and consulting services to industry and government in the areas of statistical process control, total quality management, ISO 9000, and team-building. Also provide TQM-related training, organizational effectiveness questionnaires, quality system audits, software programs, and management textbooks. Primarily work with clients in manufacturing industries.

Seminars/workshops: Offer training seminars on topics such as implementing statistical process control, TQM and ISO 9000, application of advanced statistical techniques, team problem-solving, increasing productivity through employee development, corporate vision and values, and developing a corporate quality policy.

Publications: Offer statistics software and statistical publications. Titles include: *Statistical Process Control*, *Total Quality Management*, *Statistics for Managers: A Manual for Decision-makers*, and *Completed Lecture Guides and Problem Solutions* (to accompany *Statistics for Managers*).

Productivity Network

P.O. Box 1933
Largo, FL 34649
Phone: (813) 596 3822
Fax: (813) 596 3822
Contact: Wingate Sikes, Pres.

Description: Offer seminars, workshops, and consulting services in the areas of business process reengineering, self-directed teams, leadership of quality improvement teams, and the changing role of management.

Seminars/workshops: Offered.

Publications: Offer manuals, slides, and videos related to seminar and workshop topics.

Productivity Sciences, Inc.
Hayburne Office Center, Suite 300
55 Federal Street
Greenfield, MA 01301
Phone: (413) 774 4424
Fax: (413) 774 5157
E-mail: DEMING@ECS.UMASS.EDU
Contact: Dr. Frank Kaminsky
Dr. Richard J. Burke
Description: Assist industrial and service organizations with their effort in transforming an existing style of management to one that is based on quality and continual improvement. Offer training programs in statistical process control, software products, and consulting services. Areas of expertise include Taguchi methods and experimental design, management data analysis, quality management and process improvement, simulation, forecasting, planning and control of production and inventories, facilities layout and design, and human factors and ergonomics. Serve clients in manufacturing, health care, public service groups, military organizations, electronics, and petrochemicals.
Seminars/workshops: Offer programs in continuous quality improvement and statistical process control.
Publications: Software packages for statistical process control, organizing cost of quality data, and data management systems for quality information are available. List of articles and internal publications available, copies may be requested.

Programs on Change Consulting Services
784 Columbus Avenue, Suite 1C
New York, NY 10025
Phone: (212) 222 4606
Contact: Dr. Dorri Jacobs
Description: Offer human resource consulting, training seminars, and instructional materials to increase organizational effectiveness. Areas of expertise include managing organizational change, morale and downsizing, quality, building better teams, achieving results, and accepting technology. Work with major corporations, government, private and nonprofit agencies, professional associations, and educational organizations.
Seminars/workshops: Offer a range of seminars on topics which include managing change,

team-building, preparing people for a quality process, and achieving results.
Publications: Provide instructional materials (books and audiotapes) for managing organizational change.

Q.A.I. Limited
Belasis Business Centre
Coxwold Way
Belasis Hall Technology Park
Billingham, Cleveland TS23 4EA
Phone: 01642 343452
Fax: 01642 343453
Branch offices: Weymouth, Dorset; Newcastle upon Tyne
Contact: Robert Billam, Technical Dir.
Description: Quality management consultants specializing in system development, personnel training, audits and assessments, and third party certification of quality systems against BS5750/ISO9000 requirements. Approved distributors of British Standard publications. Large and small organizations in a range of manufacturing and service industries as well as professional areas are served internationally.
Seminars/workshops: Offered, range from a basic introduction to BS5750 to internal auditing methods.
Publications: *Quality Management for Food Processing Companies* and *The Rule of Quality in the Organization and the Benefits to Be Enjoyed.*

QCI International
1350 Vista Way
P.O. Box 1503
Red Bluff, CA 96080
Phone: (916) 527 6970
Fax: (916) 527 6983
Branch offices: Chicago; San Francisco. Representatives available in Caracas, Helsinki, Istanbul, London, Melbourne, Paris, Stockholm, Sydney.
Contacts: Joyce McClelland, Executive Dir.
Donald L. Dewar, Pres.
Description: Full-service consulting, training, and publishing firm offering TQM implementation services. Work with organizations in a range of industries including manufacturing, medical, government agencies, armed services, educational, service industries, and financial institutions on an international basis. Offer

public workshops, in-house workshops, a variety of books, manuals, videotapes, and computer programs on quality-related topics, and custom tailoring of products and services.

Seminars/workshops: Offer workshops to the public on topics such as facilitator skills, TQM, and statistical process control. In-house workshop topics include self-managing work teams, ISO 9000, quality function deployment, customer satisfaction, benchmarking, leadership training, and team-building.

Publications: Catalog listing workbooks, manuals, books, videos, and software available from QCI. Also publish *Quality Digest* monthly.

Quality Alert Institute
257 Park Avenue South, 12th Fl.
New York, NY 10010
Phone: (212) 353 4420
Fax: (212) 353 4526
Contact: R.V. Shannon, Pres.
Description: Provide consulting services and training in total quality management and statistical process control. Areas of expertise include designing and implementing quality improvement programs, customer satisfaction surveys, failure mode and effect analysis, implementation of the ISO 9000/Q90 series of quality standards, documentation for quality standards, internal audits, supplier certification, team-building, and use of self-managing teams. Serve clients in a range of manufacturing industries, health care, government agencies, defense, travel, financial services, and consumer products. Provide services to clients in the U.S., Canada, Central and South America, Europe, and the Pacific Rim.
Seminars/workshops: Offer a range of seminars on topics which include benchmarking, ISO 9000, application of quality improvement principles in various industries, writing documentation, internal auditing, statistical process control, and building empowered teams.

Quality America Inc.
7650 East Broadway, Suite 208
Tucson, AZ 85731 8896
Phone: (800) 722 6154
Fax: (602) 722 6705
Contact: Ken Hightower, Marketing Asst.
Description: Provide software and training for quality improvement. Software with applications in a wide variety of industries but focusing on statistical process control, flow-charting, and design and analysis of experiments is the company's focus. Workshops, training, and consulting built around use of the software is available.

Quality for American Communities
600 Promenade Tower, Suite 955
Richardson, TX 75080
Phone: (214) 669 9588
Fax: (214) 669 9478
Contact: Jim Carras
Description: Provide services aimed at small to medium-sized companies designed to make ISO 9000 registration successful. Client companies involved in the training process are encouraged to form an alliance (consisting of a small group of companies) to exchange information and experiences. Serve clients in health care, industry, government, and education.
Seminars/workshops: ISO 9000 training package includes workshops on topics such as management team training, quality manuals, lead assessor training, audit team training, compliance assessment, and registrar compliance.

Quality & Performance Systems, Inc.
4303 Deerfield Circle
West Peabody, MA 01960
Phone: (508) 535 0387
Fax: (508) 535 3767
E-mail: ethera@aol.com
Contact: Nina Fishman Attridge
Description: Offer consulting services in the areas of organizational change, process improvement, communication, team-building, human resource development/training systems, and instructional design. Develop customized solutions using appropriate quality, training, and performance technologies. Serve clients in a variety of industries including telecommunications, utilities, and financial services.
Seminars/workshops: Offered to clients.

Quality Control Institute (Div. of PEL, Inc.)
2644 South Sherwood Forest Blvd., Suite 110
Baton Rouge, LA 70816
Phone: (504) 293 3463
Fax: (504) 293 2160

Contact: Glenda Worm

Description: Consulting firm specializing in statistical analysis and documentation and training. Areas of expertise include all aspects of work with surveys (including design, data collection, and statistical analysis) for large and small databases, as well as presentations. Documentation and training expertise includes work with ISO 9000 documentation, OSHA compliance, and quality systems design, development, and implementation. Also document specialized procedures (including writing compliance reports, safety standards, and administrative procedures), train staff, and develop training materials in a range of areas. Work with clients in both the public and private sectors in a range of industries.

Seminars/workshops: Offered on topics such as quality philosophy, quality systems, ISO 9000, statistical process control, team-building, and quality tools for clients.

Quality Groups

5850 Thille Street, Suite 107

Ventura, CA 93003

Phone: (805) 642 6691

Fax: (805) 642 3815

Contact: Susan Bianchi

Dr. David Richey

Description: Offer consulting services focused on improving quality, productivity, management, and teamwork. Serve both public and private organizations in a range of industries.

Seminars/workshops: Offered on topics such as TQM, coaching skills, building high-performance teams, and supervisory methods.

Quality International Limited

2716 Orthodox Street

Philadelphia, PA 19137 1604

Phone: (215) 533 1060

Fax: (215) 533 1061

Description: Specialize in statistical process control and quality management for manufacturing companies. Provide consulting services and training in the design, development, integration, and installation of statistical process control and quality data management systems.

Quality Way, Inc.

145 East 27th Street, Suite 9C

New York, NY 10016 9034

Phone: (212) 683 5442

Fax: (717) 646 0553

Contact: Carol Hannah, Pres.

Description: Provide consulting services and training in quality improvement. Areas of expertise include customer surveys and customer service planning, TQM, team development, TQM program development and implementation, and development of quality training programs.

Seminars/workshops: Offer a three day course in process management, courses for team members on different aspects of TQM, a team leader course, and additional training on topics such as quality planning, quality function deployment, quality awareness, and communications and interpersonal skills.

Publications: Publish *Q. . . ditions*, a newsletter on total quality management.

Qualtec Quality Services, Inc.

11760 U.S. Highway One, Suite 500

North Palm Beach, FL 33408

Phone: (407) 775 8300

Fax: (407) 775 8301

E-mail: marketing@qualtec.com

Branch offices: Australia; Spain

Contact: Don G. Stidham

Bob Ricker

Description: Offer consulting and training services in the areas of total quality management, change management, and reengineering.

Seminars/workshops: Offered to clients.

RPM Systems, Inc.

938 Chapel Street

New Haven, CT 06518

Phone: (203) 776 2358

Fax: (203) 495 6740

E-mail: RPMSYSTEMS@APPLELINK. APPLE.COM

Branch: 11 Newton House, Newton St. Cyres, Exeter EX5 5BL, U.K.

Phone: 01392 851649

Contact: Howard Brown, Pres.

Jim Dray, V.P.

Description: Environmental consulting company specializing in the integration of environmental concerns with TQM. Areas of practice include industrial management and engineering, environmental engineering, water and energy management, organizational change, information systems, economic development and policy, employee education and training, and planning and systems analysis. Clients include local, state and national government agencies as well as corporations and nonprofit institutions.

Seminars/workshops: Offered.

Rath & Strong, Inc.
92 Hayden Avenue
Lexington, MA 02173
Phone: (617) 861 1700
            (800) 622 2025
Fax: (617) 861 1424
Branch: Bremen, Germany
Contact: Dan Ciampa, C.E.O.
Description: Management consulting firm which began as an industrial engineering firm and now includes practice areas such as process redesign and improvement, TQM, cycle time reduction, and climate/culture change. Focus is on helping organizations address the challenges of managing relationships with customers, suppliers, employees, and business partners with the goal of creating more value for customers.
Seminars/workshops: Offered to clients as part of consulting services. Also give corporate presentations on a variety of topics related to TQM.
Publications: *Touchstones* and *Total Quality* (books), and *The Force of Value* (video).

Charles Reach Associates
599 Riverside Avenue
Westport, CT 06880
Phone: (203) 226 1310
Fax: (203) 226 3225
Contact: Charles Reach, Pres.
Description: Management and supervisory training firm. Services include complete programs/seminars, as well as new program design assistance. Specialize in the use of computer-based simulations in managerial and organizational skill development. Areas of expertise include interpersonal communication skills, planning, problem-solving and decision-

making, leadership, total quality management, and team development.
Seminars/workshops: TQM seminars offered.
Publications: Offer *Quality Communications*, video/workbook modules covering interpersonal communications, team development skills, and team leadership.

Reddy, Traver & Woods, Inc.
Twin Lions on Crooked Lake
Averill Park, NY 12018 9563
Phone: (518) 674 2130
Fax: (518) 674 8086
Contact: Robert W. Traver
Description: Offer management consulting in the quality field. Provide seminars, training, assistance with implementation of quality programs, and consulting on difficulties with existing programs. Serve all manufacturing industries.
Seminars/workshops: Offered to clients.

Reifler Associates, Inc.
8121 Manchester Ave., Suite 255
Playa del Rey, CA 90293
Phone: (310) 823 1882
Fax: (310) 823 1790
Contact: Ron Reifler
Description: Offer consulting services on design and implementation of total quality management programs. Areas of expertise include motivation, productivity, employee empowerment, leadership, and team development. Serve both private industry and government agencies in a range of industries including entertainment, food, and petroleum products.
Seminars/workshops: Offered on topics such as facilitator training, team development, leadership, and TQM.

Resource Management Consultants, Inc.
5098 Vernon Springs Drive
Atlanta, GA 30338
Phone: (404) 392 9174
Fax: (404) 395 6876
Contact: Bernard D. Marino, Pres.
Description: Specialize in the areas of strategic management, quality management, financial management, human resource development, and management education. Offer consulting as well as training and development services.

Seminars/workshops: Workshops offered.

Publications: *Handbook of Capital Expenditure Management.*

Roberts, Curry & Company

8 Williams Street

Greenville, SC 29601

Phone: (803) 233 4321

Fax: (803) 235 4902

Contacts: J. Charles Curry, Jr.

William F. Roberts

John L. Hallman

Description: Management consulting firm specializing in the textile and apparel industries. Practice covers all facets of textile and hosiery operations, with emphasis on total quality systems, management systems, technology assessments, productivity improvements and human resource development.

Seminars/workshops: Offer TQM workshops as well as a variety of workshops dealing with different aspects of ISO 9000 registration.

Roberts & Roberts Associates

3400 Dartmouth

Plano, TX 75075

Phone: (214) 596 2956

Fax: (214) 596 2956

Contact: Lon Roberts, Ph.D.

Description: Provide products, training, and consultation related to quality improvement teams, problem-solving, crisis management, change management, process management, statistical process control, and process reengineering.

Seminars/workshops: Offered in a variety of lengths on topics such as "Putting Quality Improvement Teams to Work", "Statistical Process Control for Users" and "A Systems Approach to Process Reengineering."

Publications: *Selling to Today's Savvy Woman, Process Reengineering, Statistical Process Control for Intuitive Thinkers, Tracking and Controlling Costs in the Project Environment, Managing Multiple Projects and Priorities, Applying SPC in a Service Environment* (books). Briefings on various quality topics also available.

DeAnne Rosenberg, Inc.

28 Fifer Lane

Lexington, MA 02173

Phone: (617) 862 6117

Fax: (617) 863 8613

Contact: DeAnne Rosenberg, Pres.

Description: Provide custom-designed training programs to business and industry for management personnel. Offer consulting services on performance feedback systems, management education, supervisory development, motivational technology, and employee selection.

Seminars/workshops: Topics offered include building effective work groups, facilitating team empowerment, team-building, encouraging creative performance, listening and communication, conflict management, and reengineering the manager's role.

Safatech

31 Nuffield Road,

Poole, Dorset

BH17 7RA

England

Phone: (01202) 668668

Fax: (01202) 685750

Contact: Stephen Feltham

Description: Provide consulting services in the areas of TQM, standards (ISO 9000 and BS 5750), documentation, auditing, statistical process control, as well as services related to reliability and product liability. Training needs analysis and training courses are also offered. Industries served include aerospace, communications, contract cleaning, electronics, education, engineering, medical equipment, and professional practices.

Robert H. Schaffer & Assoc.

401 Rockrimmon Road

Stamford, CT 06903

Phone: (203) 322 1604

Fax: (203) 322 3599

Branch office: 67 Yonge Street, Suite 1400, Toronto, Ontario, M5E 1J8

Phone: (416) 864 9488

Contact: Robert H. Schaffer

Description: Provide consulting services focused on helping management teams accelerate progress toward business goals, developing their skill in managing performance improvement, and using initial successes as building blocks for a comprehensive improvement process. Also provide training and support to internal staff consultants. Industries served include insurance, banking, electronics, utilities, chemicals, pharmaceuticals, food, and building materials in North America.

Publications: Article reprints available upon request.

Service Excellence, Inc.
61 Bennington Drive
East Windsor, NJ 08520
Phone: (609) 443 2843
Fax: (609) 443 5620
Contact: Susan George, Pres.
Description: Consulting firm specializing in work with the service industry. Offer assessment and training aimed at improving the quality of service delivery systems.
Seminars/workshops: Topics include implementing total quality management, reinventing customer service, and a basic introduction to TQM.
Publications: *Achieving Service Excellence.*

Clive Shearer
10655 N.E. 4th Street, Suite 400
Bellevue, WA 98004 5082
Phone: (206) 643 1233
Fax: (206) 746 5912
Contact: Clive Shearer
Description: Management consultant working with the professional services industry. Offers introductory TQM training, continuous improvement consulting, and process improvement team/facilitator coaching.
Seminars/workshops: Offered.
Publications: Practical Continuous Improvement for Professional Services (ISBN 0 87389 281-X).

Shilay Associates, Inc.
1419 Wantagh Avenue
Wantagh, NY 11793
Phone: (516) 783 7600
Fax: (516) 785 5742
Branch offices: Rochester, NY; Scranton, PA
Contact: W. Granger Toper
Description: Firm concentrates on productivity and quality improvement issues and custom

designs programs to fit client's needs. Also provides consulting services to clients seeking ISO 9000 registration. Industries served include a wide variety of manufacturers as well as banking, health care, mining, and utilities.
Seminars/workshops: Offered.

Sirota & Alper Associates, Inc.
1675 3rd Avenue
New York, NY 10128
Phone: (212) 722 8054
Fax: (212) 534 3269
Branch office: Washington, DC
Contact: David Sirota, Ph.D., Chairman
S. William Alper, Ph.D., Pres.
Description: Specialize in conducting opinion surveys of all key corporate constituencies; including employees, customers, suppliers, investors, and communities. Serve private industry as well as government agencies.

Frank E. Smith & Associates
P.O. Box 4191
Glendale, CA 91222 0191
Phone: (818) 244 2311
Contact: Frank E. Smith
Description: Management consultants offering services in the areas of managerial and supervisory responsibilities, functional and supervisory audits, policy and administrative manuals, in-plant training programs, operational-manufacturing systems, total quality management, plant layout and design, work measurement and work output, cost reduction planning and control, quality assurance, and statistical quality control training and implementation. Services offered to a range of industries.
Seminars/workshops: Offer programs entitled "TQM Approach to Work Measurement" and "TQM Approach to Physical Progress Reviews."

M.F. Smith & Associates, Inc.
1201 Mt. Kemble Avenue
Morristown, NJ 07960 6628
Phone: (201) 425 1400
Fax: (201) 425 0800
Contact: Michael F. Smith, Pres.
Joseph P. Kosakowski
Description: Full-service consulting firm with a

practice that embraces all quality paradigms (TQM, ISO 9000, Baldrige Award, etc.) while addressing cultural change initiatives, team-building, organizational design/development, and training within the quality arena. Areas of expertise include customer needs analyses and satisfaction measurements, methods and procedures, ISO 9000, quality deployment programs, vendor certification programs, business process reengineering, information systems planning, and a variety of training solutions. Industries served include telecommunications, information services, manufacturing, data processing, consumer products, pharmaceuticals, chemicals, health care, banking, finance, and transportation.

Seminars/workshops: Offer programs in a variety of quality-related areas to clients.

Publications: Publish a series of "Excellence Briefs."

Software Engineering Consultants, Inc.
10219 Briarwood Drive
Los Angeles, CA 90077
Phone: (310) 278 7241
Fax: (310) 550 1992
Contact: Emanuel R. Baker
Description: Provider of consulting and training in software engineering. Areas of expertise include helping clients define and establish practices to be used for developing and maintaining software, performing software process assessments of clients' software development and maintenance processes to assess capability to produce quality software, developing policies and standards in areas such as quality assurance, and evaluating client software quality assurance and software configuration management capabilities.

Seminars/workshops: Offer three day seminar emphasizing the application of TQM principles to software development and maintenance. Also conduct public seminars and offer in-house training on topics such as software quality management, software process improvement, TQM, and software engineering and development management.

Solution Finders Inc.
112 Cabot Crescent
Lower Sackville, Nova Scotia
Canada B4C 3L3
Phone: (902) 864 2660
Fax: (902) 864 5447
Branch offices: Miami, FL; Detroit, MI; Vancouver, BC; Toronto, ON
Contact: David Quinlivan-Hall
Description: Firm specializes in helping organizations to become more competitive through the use of teams in making changes. Areas of expertise include training for teams in facilitation skills, management, and team-building, quality improvement, work reengineering, strategic planning processes, and application of TQM to marketing. Industries served include manufacturing, hospitality, food processing, and high technology, as well as government and educational organizations in the public sector. Workshops are offered on a range of team and facilitation skills.

Publications: *In Search of Solutions: 60 Ways to Guide a Problem-Solving Group* (book).

Southwest Resource Development
121 Interpark, Suite 103
San Antonio, TX 78216
Phone: (210) 491 6906
Fax: (210) 491 6909
Contact: Joyce M. Hipp
Description: Broad-based consulting firm serving small business, the defense industry, and government agencies. Among services offered are TQM-related assistance to small and disadvantaged minority and women-owned businesses. Many of these clients are contractors to government departments and agencies. Areas of expertise include writing TQM plans, policies, and procedures for government contractors, and training in TQM.

Miles Southworth
3100 Bronson Hill Road
Livonia, NY 14487
Phone: (716) 346 2776
Fax: (716) 346 2276
Contact: Miles Southworth
Description: Offer consulting services to the graphic arts industry and publishers. Areas of expertise include color reproduction, quality

control applications, and total quality management.

Publications: *Quality and Productivity in the Graphic Arts* and *How to Implement TQM* (books), as well as a newsletter entitled *The Quality Control Scanner.*

Spechler Associates

1629 Riverview Road, Suite 321
Deerfield Beach, FL 33441
Phone: (305) 480 2876
Fax: (305) 480 2876
Contact: Dr. Jay W. Spechler
Description: Offer strategic planning and management consulting in implementing total quality management in service organizations. Also provide quality performance assessments using the Malcolm Baldrige criteria and real-time training in reengineering business processes.
Seminars/workshops: Offer certification workshops in the Malcolm Baldrige criteria, as well as TQM and benchmarking workshops.
Publications: *Managing Quality in America's Most Admired Companies* (ISBN 0 89806 118 0) and *When America Does it Right: Case Studies in Service Quality* (ISBN 0 89806 100 8).

STAT-A-MATRIX

2124 Oak Tree Road
Edison, NJ 08820
Phone: (908) 548 0600
Fax: (908) 548 0409
Branch offices (*North America*): Detroit; Ottawa; Washington, DC
Branch offices (*International*): Brussels; Budapest; Dhahran; London; Mexico City; São Paulo; Tokyo
Contact: Alan Marash (Edison) (908) 548 0600
Fred Love (Detroit) (313) 344 9596
Ira Epstein (Washington, DC) (703) 415 2591
Description: Educational and consulting firm devoted solely to quality. Offer training and consulting services in the areas of TQM, quality system development (ISO 9000, the Baldrige Award, and compliance systems for FDA-regulated industries), and preparation of training materials and quality systems documentation. Nonprofit education institute offers over 100 courses each quarter.

Seminars/workshops: Catalog of seminars available. Topics include European Union directives, ISO 9000 quality systems, ISO 9000 as it relates to a variety of industries, TQM courses, and statistical process control. Seminars offered in a variety of languages (depending on site of seminar).

H.J. Steudel & Associates, Inc.

6410 Enterprise Lane, #200
Madison, WI 53719
Phone: (608) 271 3121
Fax: (608) 271 4755
Contact: Sherry Soehnlein
Harry Steudel
Description: Offer consulting services and training in the area of quality and productivity improvement. Specialize in TQM and ISO 9000, including implementation of ISO standards, documentation development, auditing quality systems, and statistical process control.
Seminars/workshops: Offered.
Publications: *Malcolm Baldrige Quality Audit: Assessment Tool and Scoring Guidelines* (book).

Strategic Planning Guild

374 Flores Rosa Street
P.O. Box 8546
Yona, Guam 96914
Phone: (671) 789 2086
Fax: (671) 789 0051
E-mail: EricFreed@Kuentos.Guam.Net
Branch offices: San Francisco; San Diego; Tampa-Orlando; Washington DC
Contact: Eric R. Freed
Langdon Morris
Description: Offer consulting services and seminars designed to facilitate accelerated change in organizations. Use a variety of participative consulting approaches including TQM. Serve clients in a variety of industries including defense, government departments and agencies, educational institutions, service providers, and nonprofit organizations.
Seminars/workshops: Offer "collaborative design workshops" based on a customer needs analysis. Focus on topics such as reengineering, strategic planning, improving quality, developing new products, and business plans.

The Synapse Group
P.O. Box 9715 267
Portland, ME 04104
Phone: (207) 761 4221
Fax: (207) 874 0456
Branch offices: Boston; Atlanta; San Francisco
Contact: Bernard J. Mohr, Pres.
Description: Provide counsel, education, customized tools and facilitation in the areas of business process reengineering, transition and change management, strategic planning and organization design, assessment and transformation of organization culture, leadership and team development, and designing and implementing high performance work systems. Serve clients in all industries as well as government agencies and educational institutions.
Seminars/workshops: Offered to clients.
Publications: *Reading Book in Human Relations Training* (book) and *Obstacles to Participative Management and How to Overcome Them* (Synapse technical monograph).

Systems Theory Management
6 Fayette Street
Boston, MA 02116
Phone: (617) 482 3035
Fax: (617) 482 6911
Branch office: Philadelphia, PA
Contact: Robin Blank, V.P.
Description: Offer education in total quality and organizational systems. Specialize in the implementation of organizational change through the application of tools and techniques of total quality in a hands-on "learn through experience" approach. Business strategy planning and management development are part of the process. Focus on process improvement, employee involvement, total quality, statistical methodologies, policy deployment, process simplification, and strategic linkage. Serve clients in manufacturing, service, and health care industries as well as municipal government and education.
Seminars/workshops: Offered to clients in the areas such as facilitation and facilitative leadership, process improvement problem-solving tools, benchmarking. business planning for cost-center teams, focused market segmentation, and strategic selling.

Take Charge Consultants, Inc.
103 Garris Road
P.O. Box 99
Downingtown, PA 19335
Phone: (610) 269 9590
Fax: (610) 269 2772
E-mail: Compuserve 756 26, 2651 (Daniel Kanouse)
Contact: Filomena D. Warihay, Ph.D., Pres.
Daniel N. Kanouse, Ph.D.
Description: Management and organizational development firm specializing in custom-designed programs in total quality, self-directed teams, mentoring, team-building, and related areas.
Publications: *The Tool-Kit: Tools and Techniques to Unlock the Potential of Your Team* (guidebook), *Process Improvement Simulations*, *The Reinvention Profile*, and *Total Quality Practices in Service Organizations*.

Tomlinson Research
29350 Southfield Road, Suite 121
Southfield, MI 48076
Phone: (810) 557 0104
Fax: (810) 557 0104
Contact: Gene Tomlinson
Description: Provide consulting services to the aerospace, defense, and automotive industries. Areas of expertise include product quality planning, statistical process control, and failure mode and effect analysis.
Seminars/workshops: Offered in the areas of statistical process control, product quality planning, and failure mode and effect analysis.
Publications: *Advanced Product Quality Planning Manual.*

Total Research Corporation
5 Independence Way, CN 5305
Princeton, NJ 08543 5305
Phone: (609) 520 9100
Fax: (609) 987 8839
Branch offices: Chicago, IL; Tampa, FL; Poughkeepsie, NY; Buenos Aires, Argentina; London, England
Contact: Terri Flanagan, V.P., Quality Management
Jim Salter, V.P., The Delphi Group
Description: Market research and consulting firm that provides custom research services,

advanced research technologies, tracking programs, and quality management programs throughout the United States and world-wide. Clients include major companies in markets such as business-to-business, consumer package goods and durables, energy, financial services, health care, information technologies, telecommunications, and transportation as well as work with government agencies. Total Research/Quality Management specializes in measuring and managing quality to improve customer satisfaction. Within Total Research Corporation, the Delphi Group operates as a quality consulting, implementation and training division.

Seminars/workshops: Seminars offered quarterly.

Publications: Publishers of the newsletter *A Total Quality View*. Back issues can be ordered.

Total Quality Manufacturing

Management Consultants
934 Rodney Drive
San Leandro, CA 94577
Phone: (510) 895 5834
Fax: (510) 895 1087
Contact: R. Michael Kirchner
Description: Provide consulting, education, and training in the areas of TQM, ISO 9000 certification, statistical process control, and the Baldrige National Quality Award. Serve manufacturing industries operating in both the commercial and government environment.

Seminars/workshops: Courses of varying lengths are offered on topics such as an ISO 9000 overview, ISO 9000 documentation and procedures writing, TQM overview, TQM planning and implementation, TQM teamwork, and basic and advanced statistical process control techniques.

Total Quality Systems

465 West Eagle Lake Drive
Maple Grove, MN 55369
Phone: (612) 424 2260
Fax: (612) 424 2995
Contact: Robert A. Schwarz, Pres.
Description: Provide total quality management support with a focus on the use of teams, suggestion systems, customer input and supplier inputs to provide the ideas to improve

product, process, and support strategies or goals. Developer of software which supports the process of managing suggestions, teams, and customer ideas.

Seminars/workshops: Offer workshops several times per year in addition to client sponsored seminars.

Publications: "Simplified Idea Management – Super SIM" (software), *Recovering Prosperity Through Quality* (book), and *The Suggestion System, A Total Quality Process* (book).

Triad Performance Technologies. Inc.

30101 Northwestern Highway, Suite 330
Farmington Hills, MI 48334
Phone: (810) 737 3300
Fax: (810) 737 0333
Contact: Ted Apking, Ph.D.
Description: Offer training services which focus on the areas of curriculum design, needs analysis, program design and media selection, development of job aids and documentation, development of performance-based instruction, and training evaluation. Consulting services support quality initiatives through quality performance assessment, quality planning, quality awareness and training, and team implementation.

Seminars/workshops: Offered.

Tri-Tech Services, Inc.

55 Old Clairton Road
Pittsburgh, PA 15236
Phone: (412) 655 8970
Fax: (412) 655 8973
Branch office: 2301 W. Meadowview Road, Suite 101, Greensboro, NC 27407
Phone: (910) 294 9833
Fax: (910) 294 9683
Description: Consulting firm specializing in the development and implementation of quality systems. Provide training, auditing services, and quality systems consulting. Areas of expertise include quality systems design, project management, complete ISO 9000 preparation, calibration programs, reliability-centered maintenance, and statistical process control implementation.

Seminars/workshops: Offered on topics such as TQM, statistical process control, and training for internal auditors.

K.W. Tunnell Company, Inc.
900 East Eighth Avenue, Suite 106
King of Prussia, PA 19406 1324
Phone: (610) 337 0820
Fax: (610) 337 1884
Contact: Pat Heaney, Pres.
Description: Provide a range of technical and consulting services primarily to manufacturing and distribution companies. Areas of practice include TQM, work reengineering, business strategy, materials management, and supporting services such as education and training, industrial and mechanical engineering, statistics and quality control technology, organizational development, and information systems technology.
Seminars/workshops: Offer both in-house and public seminars.
Publications: Publish the newsletter entitled *Perspective.*

Unique Solutions, Inc.
P.O. Box 1711
Royal Oak, MI 48068 1711
Phone: (810) 435 5307
Fax: (810) 435 6349
Contact: Vera-Anne V. Corwin, Ph.D.
John M. Corwin
Description: Offer services which help companies produce better products at lower cost. Provide training and consulting in TQM, team-building, and statistical tools. Also assist in developing methods and document needed for ISO 9000 certification.
Seminars/workshops: Offer workshops ranging in length from one to five days.

Vragel & Associates
8950 Gross Point Road
Skokie, IL 60077
Phone: (708) 470 2531
Fax: (708) 470 3507
Contact: Paul Vragel, Pres.
Description: Offer services in the areas of strategic process management, improving customer service, product improvement, achieving ISO 9000 certification, performance improvement, and use of the Baldrige criteria in day-to-day business. Serve clients in the United States, Europe, and the Far East in all business areas.

Seminars/workshops: Offered on topics such as practical approaches to sustainable high performance, practical approaches to ISO 9000 for small-to-midsized organizations, the Baldrige guidelines, and evaluating strategic alliances.

Warwick Daisley International
51 Castle Street
High Wycombe
Buckinghamshire HP13 6RN
U.K.
Phone: 01494 446895
Fax: 01494 462594
Branch offices (England): Leicester; Newcastle-upon-Tyne; Manchester
Contact: Paul Daisley
Mike Fredericks
Description: Consulting firm offering services in the area of ISO 9000 registration, TQM, development of quality assurance systems, internal auditor training, and temporary or part-time quality management staff. Industries served range from manufacturing to the service sector (including local and national government) and include both large and small organizations in both the United Kingdom and Europe.
Seminars/workshops: Offered in areas such as assessor training, failure mode and effect analysis, and statistical process control.
Publications: *The Role of the Modern Quality Manager* (ISBN 0946655731) and *Implementing TQM in Small and Medium Sized Companies* (ISBN 0946655596).

M.J. Weeks Seminars
3505 Spencer Boulevard
Sioux Falls, SD 57103
Phone: (605) 331 2580
Fax: (605) 331 2580
Contact: M.J. Weeks
Description: International training organization, providing on-site TQM workshops in the United States, Canada, Mexico, and South America. Programs include "Superior Customer Service," "TQM Team Building," and "Patient-Guest Relations."
Seminars/workshops: Offered on-site for clients or conferences
Publications: *Listening to Your Customer* (video) and *Taking Control with Time Management* (book).

Young Systems
1004 Chestnut Street
Boscobel, WI 53805 1418
Phone: (608) 375 5035
Fax: (608) 375 5765
Contact: Gary Young
Description: Specialize in developing and delivering custom training packages that support total quality initiatives and issues. A proprietary specialty is the Quality Systems Productivity Assessment, a TQM-oriented alternative to performance appraisal. Provide services to small companies and nonprofit organizations.
Seminars/workshops: Offer a range of programs in areas such as continuous quality improvement and interpersonal skills, management and leadership fundamentals, resolving conflict, an introduction to TQM philosophy, teamwork, and organizational productivity.

5 TQM associations

The following is a listing of associations involved in advancing various aspects of quality management. Associations were asked to complete a questionnaire describing their role in quality-related activities.

The American Society for Quality Control
611 East Wisconsin Avenue
P.O. Box 3005
Milwaukee, WI 53201 1734
Phone: (414) 272 8575
Fax: (414) 272 1734
Description: Organization focused on quality concepts and technologies and the advancement of quality management. Offer certification in a range of areas within the broader area of quality management and control. Publish *Quality Progress* on a monthly basis, as well as additional journals, books and reports. Offer conferences, seminars, and courses on quality topics, as well as a personnel listing service. Also sponsor several quality awards.

The Association for Quality and Participation
801-B West Eighth Street, Suite 501
Cincinnati, OH 45202
Phone: (513) 381 1959
Fax: (513) 381 0070
Description: Promote quality and participation in the workplace. Offer courses, in-house training, publications, training materials, and sponsor conferences. Publish the *Journal for Quality and Participation*. Formerly known as the International Association of Quality Circles.

Association of British Certification Bodies
398 Chiswick High Road
London W6 4AJ
Phone: 0171 629 9000
Description: Concerned with improving product quality in British industry. Works with members, British industry, and government to foster improvements in quality.

Association of Quality Management Consultants
4 Beyne Road
Olivers Battery
Winchester
Hampshire SO22 4JW
Phone: 01962 864394
Fax: 01962 866969
Description: Professional group whose members meet requirements establishing professional competence in consulting activities related to quality management. Maintain a listing of quality assurance consultants in the United Kingdom.

The British Quality Association
P.O. Box 712
61 Southwark Street
London SE1 1SB
Phone: 0171 401 2844
Description: Serves industrial, commercial, and professional organizations with the goal of promoting understanding of quality issues in commerce and industry. Fosters the development of industry groups concerned with quality improvement techniques.

British Quality Foundation
213 Vauxhall Bridge Road
London SW1V 1EN
Phone: 0171 963 8000
Description: Organization concerned with the

quality improvement of British products and services. Promotes a self-assessment route to quality improvement and sponsors the "UK Quality Award."

British Standards Institution
2 Park Street
London W1A 2BS
Phone: 0171 629 9000
Fax: 0171 629 0506
Description: The British Standards Institution is responsible for the preparation of British Standards and representation of British industry in international standards discussions. The Institution is also closely involved in the development of criteria for quality assessment and certification when international agreement/alignment of standards is the goal. Conducts testing and quality assessment programs as well as research. Publications include the *BSI Standards Catalogue* as well as *Quality in Action* (quarterly magazine) and *BSI News* (monthly newsletter).

European Foundation for Quality Management
Avenue des Pléiades 19
1200 Brussels
Belgium
Phone: 32 2 775 35 11
Fax: 32 2 775 35 35
Description: Supports European organizations with a commitment to quality management and quality improvement that are involved in advancing European industry in the world market. Provides educational opportunities to affiliates. Sponsor of the European Quality Award.

European Organization for Quality
Postfach 5032
CH-3001 Bern, Switzerland
Phone: 31 3206166
Fax: 31 3206828
Description: Organization which facilitates the exchange of information and advances work in the area of quality theory and practice with the goal of enhancing European competitiveness in the international marketplace. Publish the journal *European Quality* as well as proceedings of an annual congress.

The Institute of Quality Assurance
P.O. Box 712
61 Southwark Street
London SE1 1SB
Phone: 0171 401 7227
Fax: 0171 401 2725
Description: Professional association concerned with the advancement of quality management practices. Provides services to management and supervisory personnel involved with quality assurance. Offers courses, seminars, and conferences related to all aspects of quality for a wide range of industries. Publishes *Quality World* monthly, a *Register of Qualified Quality Management System Assessors*, and books on quality management and assurance.

National Institute of Standards and Technology
Route 270 and Quince Orchard Road
Bldg. 101, #A1134
Gaithersburg, MD 20899
Phone: 301 975 2300
Fax: 301 869 8972
Description: The NIST Quality Program assists U.S. businesses and nonprofit organizations with continuous quality improvement efforts. Sponsor of the Malcolm Baldridge National Quality Award.

National Quality Information Centre
P.O. Box 712
61 Southwark Street
London SE1 1SB
Phone: 0171 401 7227
Description: Source of quality improvement information for commerce and industry.

National Society for Quality Through Teamwork
2 Castle Street
Salisbury SP1 1BB
Phone: 01722 326667
Fax: 01722 331313
Description: Concerned with promoting teamwork, continuous improvement, and customer service in all sectors of British industry. Offer training services, courses, and sponsor conferences. Publishes *Circle Magazine* six times yearly.

QFD Institute
1140 Morehead Court
Ann Arbor, MI 48103
Phone: (313) 995 0847
Fax: (313) 995 3810
E-mail: gmazur@engin.umich.edu
Description: Nonprofit organization dedicated to the advancement of quality function deployment in North America. Sponsors quarterly forums on quality function deployment, programs, an annual quality function deployment symposium, and research. Publishes *Forum Hardcopy* quarterly.

Quality Assurance Institute
7575 Dr. Phillips Boulevard
Orlando, FL 32819 7273
Phone: (407) 363 1111
Fax: (407) 363 1112
Description: International association dedicated to promoting and improving quality and productivity within the information systems industry. Majority of members affiliated with organizations such as software companies, banks, insurance companies, and government agencies. Assists members in assessing against and meeting industry models and standards (such as ISO 9000 and the Malcolm Baldrige National Quality Award), and identifies and disseminates best practices based on experiences of member corporations. Teaches and supports best practices in areas such as quality management, reviews and inspections, building controls into processes, acceptance testing, and customer surveys. Offers seminars and sponsor conferences. Publishes the *Journal of the Quality Assurance Institute* quarterly.

Rhode Island Area Coalition for Excellence
P.O. Box 6766
Providence, RI 02940
Phone: (401) 454 3030
Description: Established to promote quality in business, education, and government. Provides quality awareness education and training, networking opportunities, self-assessment and benchmarking services, and sponsors the Rhode Island Quality Awards.

United Kingdom Accreditation Service
Audley House
13 Palace Street
London SW1E 5HS
Phone: 0171 233 7111
Fax: 0171 233 5115
Description: Organization licensed by the Dept. of Trade and Industry as the sole national accreditation body in specified fields. Responsible for assessing and accrediting certification bodies, testing and calibration laboratories. These bodies and laboratories are then authorized to issue formal certificates and reports.

6 Malcolm Baldrige National Quality Award

The Malcolm Baldrige National Quality Award was established by the United States Congress in 1987 to recognize quality achievements of American companies. The Baldrige Award is not for specific products or services. The award is named after the late Secretary of Commerce, Malcolm Baldrige. The award is managed by the U.S. Commerce Department's National Institute of Standards and Technology.

A maximum of two awards may be given annually in each of three categories: small business, manufacturing, and service. Any business located in the United States may apply. Seven broad categories make up the Baldrige Award criteria: leadership; information and analysis; strategic planning; human resource development and management; process management; business results; and customer focus and satisfaction. Applicants must provide evidence of quality achievement and quality improvement in each category.

Winning companies are selected by a board of examiners composed of private and public sector quality experts. This board conducts rigorous on-site visits of those applicants passing an initial screening. Although only a few companies have won this coveted award, many corporations have used the Malcolm Baldrige Award criteria for improving their business performance.

A list of the Malcolm Baldrige National Quality Award winners from 1988 to 1994 follows. Those interested in obtaining profiles of winners as well as additional information about the award should contact the following agency:

Malcolm Baldrige National Quality Award Office
A537 Administration Building
National Institute of Standards and Technology
Gaithersburg, MD 20899 0001
Phone: (301) 975 2036
E-mail: oqp@micf.nist.gov (Internet)

1988

Motorola Inc.
Schaumburg, IL (manufacturing)

Commercial   Nuclear   Fuel   Division   of   Westinghouse Electric Corp.
Pittsburgh, PA (manufacturing)

Glove Metallurgical Inc.
Beverly, OH (small business)

1989

Milliken & Company
Spartanburg, SC (manufacturing)

Xerox Corp.
Business Products and Systems
Rochester, NY (manufacturing)

1990

Cadillac Motor Car Division
Detroit, MI (manufacturing)

IBM Rochester
Rochester, MN (manufacturing)

Federal Express Corp.
Memphis, TN (service)

Wallace Co. Inc.
Houston, TX (small business)

1991

Solectron Corp.
Milpitas, CA (manufacturing)

Zytec Corp.
Eden Prairie, MN (manufacturing)

Marlow Industries
Dallas, TX (small business)

1992

AT & T Network Systems Group/Transmission
   Systems Business Unit
Morristown, NJ (manufacturing)

Texas Instruments Inc.
Defense Systems & Electronics Group
Dallas, TX (manufacturing)

AT & T Universal Card Services
Jacksonville, FL (service)

The Ritz-Carlton Hotel Co.
Atlanta, GA (service)

Granite Rock Co,
Watsonville, CA (small business)

1993

Eastman Chemical Co.
Kingsport, TN (manufacturing)

Ames Rubber Corp.
Hamburg, NJ (small business)

1994

AT & T Consumer Communications Services
Basking Ridge, NJ (service)

GTE Directories Corp.
Dallas/Ft. Worth, TX (service)

Wainwright Industries, Inc.
St. Peters, MO (small business)

1995

Building Products Division of Armstrong World
   Industries
Lancaster, PA (manufacturing)

Corning Telecommunications Products Division
Corning, NY (manufacturing)

Glossary

85/15 Rule

Deming's belief that 85 percent of the problems are due to a system error, rather than an individual error.

80/20 Rule

80 percent of the trouble comes from 20 percent of the problems. Also known as the Pareto principle.

Affinity diagram

A tool used in a group setting to identify patterns and categories in broad or complex issues.

Attribute data

Data that come from nonmeasurable characteristics that can be counted.

Attribute chart

A type of chart in which characteristics are not measured in numbers but are considered acceptable or not acceptable. One example of an attribute chart is the p-chart.

Audit

An assessment to determine the extent to which certain standards or goals have been met.

Benchmarking

Evaluating and comparing how key functions and processes are performed within one's own company and at other companies that are industry leaders.

Best practices

The highest levels of performance in specific categories (such as customer service).

Brainstorming

A tool used in groups for generating ideas and making team decisions.

Business process reengineering

Reorganizing a company around essential business processes.

Capability

A statistical measure of the inherent process variability for a given characteristic. Also known as process capability.

Capability index

The number that expresses the capability of a process or machine.

Cause-and-effect diagram

A graphical tool that illustrates the relationships between causes and problems. Also known as the fishbone or Ishikawa diagram.

Change management

The process of restructuring or reinventing a corporation's culture, organizational structure, or business strategy.

Check sheet

A sheet which tallies the occurrences of selected observations.

Conformance

An indication that a product or service has met the requirements relating to specifications. Conformance to specifications is often defined as an absence of defects.

Continuous improvement

A system in which individuals continually look for ways to do things better.

Control chart

A graphic tool which detects change in a process and monitors the performance of the process over time.

Cost of quality

The costs (rework, scrap, corrections, returns, complaints, and other problems) incurred due to bad quality within a process. This concept was developed by Joseph Juran in the 1950s.

Crosby, Phillip B.

A quality expert who became prominent after the publication of his book *Quality is Free* in 1979. Crosby identified several hidden costs of poor quality, ranging from increased labor costs to delivery delays, and advocated the use of continuous process improvement to achieve zero defects, the ultimate goal in quality management.

Cultural change

The shift from traditional management to total quality management.

Customer

Any individual or organization that receives your work. Customers may be internal (inside the system) or external (outside the system).

Defect

An imperfection that makes a unit of product or output nonconforming.

Deming, W. Edwards

A statistician who is regarded as the founder of TQM. Deming advocated building quality into a product in order to lower costs, improve productivity, and increase customer satisfaction. Deming's approach to quality improvement is summarized in his "fourteen points."

Deming Prize

An annual quality award established in 1951 by the Japanese Union of Scientists and Engineers in honor of W. Edwards Deming. Deming is credited with rescuing Japan's economy after World War II.

Design of experiments

A systematic approach to varying the controllable input factors in a process and analyzing the effect that these factors have on the output. Designed experiments are used to isolate the sources of variability in a process.

Empowerment

Giving employees the authority to make decisions and take actions to satisfy customers and improve processes.

Feedback

Information from customers about how well products and services meet their needs.

Feigenbaum, Armand V.

Introduced the concept of total quality control with the publication of his book *Total Quality Control* in 1951. Feigenbaum suggested that more effort be directed to preventing rather than correcting quality problems.

Flowchart

A graphical tool that diagrams the steps in a process.

Focus group

A form of qualitative research that brings together a small group of people for a focused discussion. A focus group generally consists of eight to twelve participants from a target group who participate in a structured discussion led by a trained moderator.

Force field analysis

A method for identifying the driving and restraining forces that affect process performance.

Histogram

A bar chart used to demonstrate frequency distribution.

Ishikawa, Kaoru

Credited with developing the concept of quality circles and the cause-and-effect diagram (which is often referred to as the Ishikawa diagram).

ISO 9000

A series of quality standards created in 1987 by the International Organization for Standardization (ISO). ISO 9000 is concerned with establishing, documenting, and maintaining a system designed to ensure the quality of a product or service.

Juran, Dr. Joseph M.

A leading authority on quality control. Juran's *Quality Control Handbook* (which was first published in 1951), is the standard reference work on quality control. Like Deming, he was a consultant to Japanese industry after World War II. He separates quality into three processes: quality planning, quality control, and quality management.

Kaizen

The Japanese term for quality improvement. Kaizen is process-oriented, consists of small incremental improvements, does not require additional resources, and can be performed by individuals or teams.

Leadership

Leaders communicating a clear purpose and vision.

Malcolm Baldrige National Quality Award

A prestigious award established by the United States Congress in 1987 to recognize quality achievements of American companies. The award is managed by the U.S. Commerce Department's National Institute of Standards and Technology. The award is named after the late Secretary of Commerce Malcolm Baldrige.

Nominal group process

A structured decision-making process used to arrive at a group consensus.

Organizational architecture

A term popularized by David Nadler. It examines corporate organization from the perspective of how work, people, and formal and informal structures fit together.

Pareto chart

A bar graph that identifies the most frequent causes of problems and where to focus improvement efforts. The tool was developed by Juran and named after the nineteenth century economist Wilfredo Pareto. Pareto is credited with discovering that wealth is not evenly distributed.

PDCA cycle

This acronym stands for Plan-Do-Check-Act, the steps in a model for planning and problem-solving. Also known as the Deming or Shewhart cycle.

Process

A series of ordered steps completed to reach an outcome. The improvement of a process is central to total quality management.

Quality

A product or service that consistently meets or exceeds customer expectations.

Quality assurance

The quantitative and qualitative measurement of the quality of existing processes and systems.

Quality function deployment

A system that identifies the needs of the customer and gets that information to the people in the organization that can effect change.

Reengineering

A fundamental redesign of core processes to make them more efficient and sensitive to customer needs.

Root cause

The underlying reason for not meeting requirements within a process.

Run chart

A graph that plots data over time. It allows users to identify trends.

Scatter diagram

A graph that shows the relationship between two variables.

Seven basic tools of total quality management

These tools are: the Pareto chart; the cause-and-effect diagram; the histogram; the run chart; the top-down chart; the control chart; and brainstorming.

Six sigma

An approach introduced by Motorola. It allows for no more than 3.4 defects per million parts in manufactured goods, or 3.4 mistakes per million activities in a service operation.

Statistical process control

The application of statistical techniques to the control of processes.

Supplier

The source of material for a process.

Taguchi, Genichi

Taguchi's philosophy of quality improvement assumes that there is some level of loss associated with a product, based on whether it falls within or outside specifications. In contrast, the American approach to quality control assumes that if an item falls within specifications, there is no need for improvement.

Team-building

Bringing together a cross-section of people who have some relationship to a particular process.

Teams

A small number of people with complementary skills who work together toward a common purpose.

Top-down flowchart

A chart which lists the major steps in a process along the top. Associated substeps are listed below.

Total quality management

A management style in which processes are examined and refined with the goal of improving the performance of an organization. Total quality management assumes that processes need to be changed, focuses on the customer, advocates the empowerment of employees, relies on a team structure, requires the consistent use of a sequence of steps that are designed to bring processes under control, and requires a long-term commitment from an organization.

Tree diagram

A tool used to break down problems or goals into manageable tasks.

Variable chart

A type of chart on which characteristics are plotted that are measured in numbers. One example of a variable chart is the average and range chart.

Variable data

Data that are derived from things that can be measured.

Vision

Evaluating the focus and activities of an organization and outlining its mission and values.

Work groups

An approach where people get together in teams to work on problems or improve quality. Also known as quality improvement teams, quality action teams, and quality circles.

Name index

Abramowitz, Paul W. et al 57
Alba, Timothy et al 57
Albrecht, Karl 98, 126, 203
Aleo Jr., Joseph P. 34
Allan, Ferne C. 101
Allen, Mel L. 57
Amsden, Robert T. *et al.* 131
Anderson, Craig A. and Daigh, Robin D. 57
Anderson, Doug N. 30
Anderson, Howard J. 58
Anderson, Kristin and Zemke, Ron 126
Andrews, Heather A. *et al.* 58
Anfuso, Dawn 40, 156
Antonioni, David 156
Arendt, Carl 25
Armstrong, Rod 108
Arthur, Lowell Jay 50
Artzt, Edwin L. 23
Askey, J.M., and Dale, B.G. 170; and Turner, F.R. 20
Assar, Kathleen E. 85
Aubrey, Charles A. 149
Avery, Susan 170

Babich, Pete 126
Badiru, Adedeji B. and Ayeni, Babatunde J. 131
Baker, G. Ross 97
Baldwin, Fred 80
Ballinger, Walter F. and Hepner, James O. 58
Balm, Gerald J. 131
Band, William A. 126
Banks, Brian 109
Banks, Dana 47
Barclay, Charles A. 149
Barker, Joel 189
Barker, Thomas B. 131
Barnard, Susan B. 101
Barrier, Michael and Zuckerman, Amy 171
Barsky, Jonathan D. 127
Bartlett, Raymond C. 78
Bartley, Robert E. 28
Basmajian, Darlene 59
Bassidy, Lawrence 190
Batalden, Paul B. 97
Batalden, Paul B. *et al.* 97

Bates, Jonathan G. 111
Bauer, Roy 26
Bayne-Jardine, Colin and Holly, Peter 81
Beardsley, Jeff and Schaefer, Dick 171
Bechtel, Gregory *et al.* 59
Bechtell, Michele L. 132
Becker, Selwyn W. *et al.* 10
Beckley, Glen B. 54
Bednarczyk, Betty L. *et al.* 150
Belasco, James A. and Stayer, Ralph 197
Belavendram, N. 132
Bell, Chip R. 127, 192
Bemoski, Karen 85
Bendell, A. *et al.* 132
Bender, A. Douglas and Krasnick, Carla J. 59
Bennis, Warren 150
Benson, Roger S. and Sherman, Richard W. 171
Berger, Warren 46
Berry, John 101
Berwick, Donald M. 59, 60, 65; *et al.* 59
Besterfield, Dale H. 132
Bhote, Keki R. 133
Bishop-Gains, Lynn 10
Blanding, Warren 127
Block, Peter 140
Blunt, Mary Lucas 60
Bluth, Edward I. *et al.* 78
Boaden, R.J. and Dale, B.G. 41
Bowen, David E. and Lawler, Edward E. 157
Bowman, James S. and French, Barbara J. 112
Bradbury, Robert C. 97
Bradbury, Robert C. and Minvielle, Ramirez 97
Bradley, Leo 81
Brassard, Michael 133
Breckman, John R. 102
Brinkworth, W.O. 50
Brooks, Susan Hardy 81
Brooks, Tessa 119
Brothers, Theresa and Carson, Kathleen 127
Brough, Regina Kay 112
Brown, Alan 157
Brown, Mark Graham 133; *et al.* 3
Brown, Tony 168
Buch, Kim and Wetzel, Dave 133
Buchholz, Steve and Roth, Thomas 123

Burda, David 60
Burton, Jennus L. 86
Busch, Adolfus 17
Bushy, Angeline 60
Butcher, Karyle S. 102
Buterbaugh, Laura 61
Butman, John 123
Buzanis, Christin H. 47
Byham, William C. 198

Camp, Robert C. 133
Campanella, Jack 134
Cannie, Joan Koob and Caplin, Donald 127
Cannon, Debra Franklin and Kent, William E. 47
Card, David N. and Glass, Robert L. 50
Carr, Clay 127
Carr, David K. and Littman, Ian D. 112
Carson, Kenneth P. *et al.* 157
Carter, Charles W. 134
Caudron, Shari 157–8
Cesta, Tony G. 61
Chaffee, Ellen Earle, and Seymour, Daniel 86; and
    Sherr, Lawrence A. 86
Chalk, Mary Beth 46
Chaufournier, Roger L. and St Andre, Christine 61
Chauvel, Alain-Michel 172
Chizmar, John F. 86
Cho, Chin-Kuei 51, 54
Clausen, Jim 3
Clayton, Marlene 87
Cleese, John 198
Clements, Richard Barrett 168
Coady, M. Michell 97
Coate, Edwin 87, 89
Cocheu, Ted 150, 158
Cohen, Steven, and Brand, Ronald 112; and Eimicke,
    William 113
Cohen-Rosenthal, Edward and Burton, Cynthia 158
Colacecchi, Mary Beth 40
Cole, Allen W. 118
Cole, Robert E. 4
Cole, William E. and Mogab, John W. 4
Colonna, Frank A. 81
Comer, James P. 84
Connor, Patrick E. and Lake, Linda K. 140
Consalvo, Carmine 207
Conway, 108
Cook, Lynn 61
Cook, Sarah 195
Cooney, John F. 34
Corbett, Carolyn and Pennypacker, Barbara 62
Cornesky, Robert A. 88; *et al.* 88
Corrigan, James P. 172
Cortada, James W. 49
Cotter, Maury and Seymour, Daniel 89
Cottle, David W. 128
Cound, Dana M. 4, 152
Counte, Michael A. *et al.* 62
Cowles, Deborah 88
Cox, Allan 123, 207
Cox, Diane S. 62
Craig, Robert J. 31, 168

Crawford, Donna K. *et al.* 81
Crawford, Frances J. 62
Creps, Linda Boyle *et al.* 63
Crosby, Philip B. 2, 4, 68, 108, 152, 178, 298

Dale, Barrie G. 5; and Plunkett, James J. 134
D'Angelo, Elizabeth B. *et al.* 22
D'Arbeloff, Alexander 33
Dasbach, Erik J. and Gustafson, David H. 63
Davenport, Thomas H. 11
Davidow, William H. and Uttal, Bro 128
Davies, Ken and Hinton, Peter 113
Davis, Rob 42
Dawson, Graydon 159
De Feo, Joseph A. 21–2
De Geyndt, Willy 119
De Meulder, Roland 172
Deal, Terrence E., and Bolman, Lee G. 152; and
    Jenkins, William A. 152; and Kennedy,
    Allan A. 141
Decker, Michael D. 63
D'Egidio, Franco 128
Deming, W. Edwards 1, 2, 5, 7, 13, 14, 81, 82, 88,
    108, 178, 188, 199, 298
Desatnick, Robert L. 128
Deutsch, Michael S. and Willis, Ronald R. 51
DiIulio Jr., John J. *et al.* 113
Dingwall, Robert and Fenn, Paul 119
Dobbins, James H. 51, 54
Dobyns, Lloyd and Crawford-Mason, Clare 5
Dodson, Robert L. 11
Doherty, Geoffrey D. 89
Dooris, Michael 89
Dornblaser, Bright 97
Doss, Henry 40
Douglass, Merrill E. and Douglass, Donna N. 123
Downs, Kathleen and McKinney, Willard D. 63
Drake, Miriam A. 101
Dressman, Kathleen L. 63
Drucker, Peter F. 67, 98
Drummond, Helga 152
Duffek, Elizabeth 101
Dunne, Patrick K. 64
Dunne, Robert H. 51; and Ullman, Richard S. 51
Durant, Robert F. and Wilson, Laura A. 113
Dusharme, Dirk 3
Dwore, Richard B. 64
Dzus, George and Sykes, Edward G. 173

Ealey, Lance A. 134
Eastman, C.J. 64
Ebel, Kenneth E. 5
Ebenau, Robert G. and Strauss, Susan H. 51
Eccles, Tony 141
Edwards, John and Hodgson, Alan 111
Emmons, Sidney L. 173
Endy, Sam 28
Engebretson, Mara J. and Cembrowski, George S. 78
Entin, David H. 90
Entner, Donald 90
Eubanks, Paula 64

Eureka, William E. and Ryan, Nancy E. 134
Evans, John P. 97

Farrow, Brad W. 141
Feigenbaum, Armand V. 1, 2, 91, 108, 134, 152, 298
Ferguson, Kelly 173
Ferguson, Wade 173
Ferrero, Matthew J. 119
Finkler, Steven A. 109
Fisher, James L. 91
Flanagan, Theresa A. and Fredericks, Joan O. 128
Flanel, Deborah Ford and Fairchild, Michele M. 64
Flannery, Thomas P. et al.. 159
Flower, Joe 65
Foster, Oscar 40
Fountain, Douglas L. 79
Frangoes, Stephen J. and Bennett, Steven J. 123
Frank, Robyn C. 113
Freese, Jesse D. and Konald, Emily 173
Freeston, Kenneth R. 82
Fried, Robert A. 65
Fried, Sheryl and Richardson, Emily 91
Friedman, Candace et al. 65
Friesen, Michael E. and Johnson, James A. 141
Frist Jr., Thomas 65
Froiland, Paul 91, 159
Fry, Darryl 43

Gaebler, Ted 200
Galagan, Patricia A. 48
Gale, Bradley T. and Wood, Robert Chapman 129
Galloway, Robart A. 118
Gan, Gin T. 34
Gann, Margery J. and Restuccia, Joseph D. 65
Gannon, Wynne 44
Gapen, D. Kaye et al. 102
Garrity, Rudolph B. 114
Garver, Roger 173
Garvin, David A. 135
Gaucher, Ellen J. and Coffey, Richard J. 66
Geber, Beverly 66
Geddes, Tommy 92
Gelinas, Lillie Smith and Manthey, Marie 66
Gelmon, Sherril B. 97; and Baker, G. Ross 97; et al. 97
Gennett, Michael 39
Gershon, M. 23
Gibb, Tom and Graham, Dorothy 51
Gibbs, W.N. and Britten, A.F.H. 79
Gibson, Thomas C. 152
Gilb, Tom and Graham, Dorothy 51
Gilbert, James D. 11
Gilbert, James P. et al. 92
Gillen, Terry 195
Gillies, Alan C. 52
Glass, Robert L. 52
Glasser, William 81, 82
Godfrey, A. Blanton 60, 98
Goff, Heidi R. 42
Gold, Richard and De Luca, Warren 114
Goldberg, Stephen B. 80

Goldzimer, Linda Silverman and Beckman, Gregory L. 129
Golomski, William A. 18
Goodman, John A. et al. 12
Gordon, Jack 12
Gordon, William I. et al. 124
Gore, Al 114
Gouillart, Francis J. and Kelly, James N. 142
Grace, Richard E. and Templin, Thomas J. 92
Graham, Dorothy R. 53
Graham, Nancy O. 67
Grayson, Mary A. 67
Green, Richard Tabor 142
Greenbaum, Stuart I. 93
Greising, David 12
Groff, Mary K. 46
Groocock, John M. 142
Grunewald, William J. 135
Guaspari, John 129, 201, 202
Guillen, Mauro F. 142
Gustafson, David H. 56

Haefner, Joseph L. 42
Hall, Phil 45
Hallmark, Clayton 29
Hamilton, Jim 67
Hammer, Michael and Champy, James 6
Hampden-Turner, Charles 143
Hanan, Mack and Karp, Peter 129
Hansen, Bertrand L. and Ghare, Prabhakar M. 135
Hansen, W. Lee 93
Harari, Oren 12
Hard, Rob 67
Harding, Warren 101
Harmening, Thomas E. et al.. 38
Harrington, H. James 6, 135
Harris, Philip R. 152
Harris, R. Lee 129
Hart, James 97
Hart, Louis B. 206
Hay, Edward 202
Hayden, William M. 105
Hayes, H. Michael 174
Hayes, Theodore L. et al.. 159
Headrick, Linda et al.. 56, 68
Hege-Kleiser, Carmen 42
Heilpern, Jeffrey and Nadler, David 88, 143
Heinrich, George 135
Heller, Robert 26, 152
Heverly, Mary Ann and Cornesky, Robert A. 93
Hicks, Jennifer 20
Higgins, Lisa 97
Higgins, Ronald C. and Johnson, Michael L. 105
Hockman, Kymverly K. 174; et al.. 174
Hodgetts, Richard M. 6
Hoecherl, Larry J. 52
Hohner, Gregory 33
Holmes, Jerry D. and McCloskey, David J. 21
Holpp, Lawrence 13
Horine, Julie E. et al. 82, 93
Horine, Patrick D. et al. 68
Howley, Peter A. 28–9

Hoyle, David 168
Huber, George P. and Glick, William H. 143
Hudiburg, John J. 37
Huff, Sid L. 52
Hughes, Jay M. 68
Hultz, J.A. 37
Hunt, C. Steven 94
Hunt, V. Daniel 6
Hurst, David K. 144
Huyink, David Stevenson and Westover, Craig 168
Hyde, Albert C. 114

Idstein, James R. 36
Imai, Masaaki 144
Ince, Darrel 52, 53
Ingman, Lars C. 19
Ingold, Tony and Worthington, Trevor 31
Inhorn, Stanley L. *et al.* 79
Ishikawa, Kaoru 108, 136, 299
Ivancevich, Daniel M. and Ivancevich, Susan H. 94

Jablonski, Joseph R. 6
Jablonski, Robert 69
Jacobson, Gary and Hillkirk, John 34
James, Richard W. 119
Jeffords, Raymond and Thibadoux, Greg M. 109
Johns, Nick and Chesterton, John 26
Johnson, Patrice 39
Johnson, Perry L. 136, 169
Johnson, Richard S. 153
Joiner, Brian L. 144
Jones, Jennifer 191
Jones, Thomas E. and Wolf, James J. 105
Juran, Joseph M. 1, 2, 7, 13, 98, 108, 136, 178, 299
Jurow, Susan 102; and Barnard, Susan B. 102

Kaluzny, Arnold 89; *et al.* 69, 120
Kane, Edward F. 53
Kantner, Rob 169
Kaplan, Craig *et al.* 53
Kasser, Joe 105
Katz, Jacqueline and Green, Eleanor 69
Katzenbach, Jon R. and Smith, Douglas K. 124
Kaydos, Will 7
Kazmierski, Thomas J. 106
Kearns, David T. and Nadler, David A. 35
Kearny, Lynn 205
Keehley, Pat 115
Keiningham, Timothy *et al.* 13
Keiser, Thomas C. and Douglas, A. Smith 18
Kelly, Janet 21
Kelly, Mark 124
Kelly, Michael R. 53, 136
Kendall, Betty 191
Kerley, Frank R. and Nissly, Brent E. 69
Kern, Jill Phelps 27
Kerr Jr., Bernard J. 70
Kettl, Donald and DiIulio Jr., John J. 115
Keyes, Jessica 53
Kibbe, David *et al.* 56
King, Robert E. 136

Kirkman-Liff, Bradford and Schneller, Eugene 120
Kline, James F. 115
Kline, James K. 115
Kline, James L. 116
Kline, Peter and Saunders, Bernard 145
Koch, Marylane Wade and Fairly, Terryl Macline 70
Koenig, Daniel T. 35
Kohn, Alfie 83
Kohnen, James B. 106
Kolarik, William J. 136
Kolesar, Peter J. 14
Koska, Mary T. 70, 71
Köster, Albrecht 31
Kouzes, James M. and Posner, Barry Z. 153
Kravchuk, Robert S. and Leighton, Robert 116
Kravolec, O. *et al.* 71
Kreinbrook, Tom 22
Kritchevsky, Stephen B. and Simmons, Bryan P. 71
Kroeger, Otto and Theusen, Janet M. 159
Kropp Jr., Richard P. 206
Kubal, Michael T. 17
Kumar, Sanjoy and Gupta, Yash P. 30

Lacy, James A. 106
Lal, Harbans 174
Larkin, T.J. and Larkin, Sandar 160
Larsen, Gail 71
Lauritsen, Gary L. 106
Lawes, Ann 101
Le Tort, Nancy R. and Boudreaux, Jane 72
LeBoeuf, Michael 129
Lee, Sang M. *et al.* 28
Lee, Sonja 24
Leebov, Wendy and Scott, Gail 72
Lenckus, Dave 45
Lengnick-Hall, Cynthia A. 72
Lerner, Wayne 97
Levine, Constance 109
Levit, Steve 7
Lewis, Al 72; and Lamprey, Jo Anne 72
Lewis, Ralph G. and Smith, Douglas H. 94
Liebfried, Kathleen H. and Mcnair, J. & C.J. 137
Lillian, Daniel 121
Lipnack, Jessica and Stamps, Jeffrey 124
Liswood, Laura A. 130
Lochner, Robert H. and Matar, Joseph E. 137
Lock, Dennis 137
Loney, Tim and Bellefontaine, Arnie 103
Lumsdon, Kevin 72; and Hard, Rob 73
Lunt, Penny 40
Lynch, David 109

McCamus, David R. 35
McCarthy, Kimberly M. and Eishennawy, Ahmad K. 121
Macchia Jr., Peter 94
McDaniel, Thomas R. 95
McDermott, Lynda C. 153
McDermott, Robert F. 45
McDermott, Robin *et al.* 160
McEarchern, J. Edward *et al.* 73
McFarland, Lynne Joy *et al.* 154

McIntyre, Barry 24
McLaughlin, Curtis P. 89
McLaughlin, Curtis P. and Kaluzny, Arnold D. 73
McLeod, Willis B. *et al..* 83
McMillan, Jacques 179
McNeese, William H. and Klein, Robert A. 137
Magjuka, Richard J. 160
Main, Jeremy 3, 7
Majumdar, Amit *et al..* 24
Manganelli, Raymond L. and Klein, Mark M. 204
Mannello, Tim 73
Marash, Stanley A. and Marquardt, Donald W. 174
Marchese, Ted 95, 98
Marion, Larry 33
Martin, Lawrence L. 120
Mawhinney, Thomas C. 145
Maxwell, R.J. 80
Maya, Victor F. and Carpenter, Charles D. 19
Mazany, Terry 83
Melan, Eugene H. 95
Melissaratos, Aris and Arendt, Carl 95
Melnyk, Steven A. and Narasimhan, Ram 137
Melum, Mara Minerva 74
Menke, Michael M. 138
Menon, H.G. 106
Merrill, Peter 175
Messenger, Sally and Tanner, Stephen 44
Milakovich, Michael E. 74, 116
Miller, David E. 29
Miller, Douglas K. *et al..* 57
Miller, Henry D.R. 95
Miller, John A. 160
Miller, Rush G. and Stearns, Beverly 103
Miller, Thomas O. 27
Minvielle, Bernardo Ramirez 97
Miranda, Elizabeth 49
Mitchell, Donald L. 27
Mittag, H.J. and Rinne, H. 138
Mizuno, Shigeru 138
Mohr-Jackson, Iris 145
Montana, Anthony J. 111
Moore, Beth Ann 29
Moore, Donald R. 83
Morgan, Chris 14
Morgan, Rebecca L. 130
Mori, Teruo 138
Morris, Ted 130
Morrow, Mark 175
Moskowitz, Samuel E. *et al..* 74
Moyer, James A. 48
Mudie, Sheila 74
Muffolett, Joseph R. and Rogers, Craig S. 120
Müller, al.brecht 23
Muller, Dave and Funnell, Patty 96
Murgatroyd, Stephen 83
Myers, Ken and Buckman, Jim 130

Nadler, David *et al..* 145
Nagy, Joanne *et al..* 96
Najafi, Kevin 97
Neves, Joao S. and Nakhai, Benham 96
Nierenberg, Gerald 217

Nightingale, Peggy and O'Neil, Mike 96
Noori, Hamrid and Radford, Russell 107
Nutt, Paul C. and Backoff, Robert W. 154

Oakland, John S. 49; and Porter, Leslie J. 8
Oakley, Ed and Krug, Doug 154
Olian, Judy D. and Rynes, Sara L. 160
O'Neill, Rosanna M. 103
Osborn, Susan 97
Osborn, Susan and Shortell, Stephen 97
Osborne, David and Gaebler, Ted 113, 116, 202
Ozeki, Kazuo 138

Parberry, A.C. and Banerjee, A.K. 120
Parisher, James W. 175
Parker, Glenn M. 206
Parry, Glenys 80
Parsons, Mickey L. and Murdaugh, Carolyn L. 75
Partlow, Charles G. 48; and Wencel, Fred E. 39
Patten, Thomas H. 155
Pattison, Diane D. *et al..* 27
Peak, Martha H. 146
Pearson, Christine M. 101
Peeler, George H. 49
Perry, Kristie 56
Peters, Bruce J. 110
Peters, Eric D. 169
Peters, Tom 146, 194, 200; and Waterman, Robert 199
Petersen, Donald E. and Hillkirk, John 32
Peterson, Winfield A. and Weisman, Paul D. 107
Petrone, Joe 50
Pierce, Richard J. 155
Pinchot, Gifford and Pinchot, Elizabeth 146
Plice, Samuel J. 97
Price, Michael J. and Chen, E. Eva 27
Proske, Robert J. 18

Quirke, Bill 161

Raaum, Ronell B. 110
Raffio, Thomas 44
Rainbird, Helen and Maguire, Malcolm 161
Raisbeck, Ian 117
Rammes, William L. and Waltemade, Lee J. 17
Randall, Richard C. 169
Ranky, Paul G. 139
Rappaport, Lewis A. 84
Reddy, al.lan C. 50
Reed, James III *et al..* 75
Reinerstein, James L. 97
Reinertsen, James L. 97
Reynolds, Gary L. 97
Reynolds, Larry 117
Riahi-Belkaoui, Ahmed 110
Richards, John D. and Cloutier, Marc G. 97
Rieley, James B. 147
Riggs, Donald E. 103
Ritter, Diane 139
Ritvo, Roger A. *et al..* 147
Robbins, Harvey and Finley, Michael 124
Roberts, Joseph M. and Tretter, Daniel W. 35

Roberts, Lon 8
Rolstadas, Asbjorn 139
Rosen, Ned 125
Ross, Gerald 190
Ross, M. *et al.*. 54
Roth, Jill 20
Rough, Jim 161
Rowe, Megan 48
Roy, Ranjit 139
Ruben, Brent D. 98
Rushwin, S.T. 32
Russell, John F. 176
Rust, Roland T. and Oliver, Richard L. 130
Rutherford, John 39
Rutledge, Robert W. 38

Sabo, Sandra R. 84
Sahney, Vinod 97; *et al.* 97
St Clair, Guy 101
Sakofsky, Steven 176
Sandrick, Karen 76
Sayles, Leonard R. 155
Schaffer, Robert H. and Thomson, Harvey A. 147
Schmidt, Warren H. and Finnegan, Jerome P. 8, 88
Scholtes, Peter R. 84, 125, 162
Schonberger, Richard J. 162
Schroeder, Patricia 76
Schulmeyer, G. Gordon and Mcmanus, James I. 54
Schulze, Horst A. 48
Schwab, Paul 97
Seemer, Robert H. 30, 38
Semple, Jack 32
Senge, Peter M. 67, 89, 147–8
Seymour, Daniel T. 98–9, 104; and Chaffee, Ellen 99
Shalowitz, Joel 97
Shaughnessy, Thomas W. 104
Shaw, Kenneth A. 100
Shecter, Edwin S. 8
Shere, Franz 35
Sherman, Stratford 190
Sherr, Lawrence A. and Teeter, Deborah J. 100
Shewhart, Walter A. 1, 14
Shonk, James H. 125
Shortell, Stephen M. 97; *et al.* 76
Shrednick, Harvey R. *et al.* 55
Shunta, Joseph P. 139
Siegel, Peggy and Byrne, Sandra 84
Siggins, Jack and Sullivan, Maureen 104
Simmons, John 83
Simonsen, Clifford E. and Arnold, Douglas 118
Sinioris, Marie E. 97
Sissell, Kara 14
Sissell, Kara and Mullin, Rick 176
Smit Sibinga, C. Th. *et al.* 79
Smith, Anthony W. and Sibler, Jeremy M. 46
Smith, Duncan C. 80
Smith, Frederick W. 36–7
Smith, Ian 130
Smith, Jackie A. *et al.* 76
Smith, Valerie J. 33
Solovy, Alden T. 77
Soper, Alan 37

Spagnola, Robert G. and Spagnola, Cynthia M. 41
Spechler, Jay W. 9
Spendolini, Michael 139
Stasiowski, Frank A. and Burnstein, David 108
Stephens, Kenneth E. 177
Stern, Bruce L. and Tseng, Douglas P. 100
Stuart, Crit 101
Suver, James D. *et al.* 77
Svenson, Ray *et al.* 9
Sviokla, John J. and Shapiro, Benson P. 131
Swart, Philip J. 33
Sweeney, Patrick J. 107
Swiss, James E. 117

Taguchi, 108, 132, 134
Talley, Dorsey 9
Terplan, Kornel 55
Thomas, Michael 14
Thompson, Fred L. 22
Tibor, Tom 169
Tichy, Noel 190
Tjosvold, Dean and Tjosvold, Mary M. 125
Tomlin, Lily 194
Townsend, Patrick L. and Gebhardt, Joan E. 9, 125, 177
Traver, Robert W. 107
Tschohl, John and Franzmeier, Steve 131

Walker, Terry 15
Walklet, R.H. 32
Walley, Paul and Kowalski, Emil 162
Wallmüller, Ernest 53, 54
Walsh, Michael 190
Walton, Wayne and Melton, Steve 18
Ward, James A. 55
Warden, Gail 97
Wargo, Michael J. 117
Waring, Jeffrey G. and Mears, Peter 177
Wasson, Dale 101
Waterman, Robert H. 10, 199, 204
Watson, Gregory H. 140
Weber, Carol A. 19
Weise, Carl E. and Stamoolis, Peter G. 178
Weiss, Daniela 45
Weiss, William 190
Welch, James F. 43
Welch, John F. 190
Welch, Samuel 105
Wellins, Richard S. *et al.* 125
Wesner, John W. *et al.* 108
Westbrook, Jerry D. 148
Weston, F.C. 178
Wett, Ted 22
Wheatley, Margaret J. 156, 190; and Kellner-Rogers, Myron 148
Wheeler, Mardy 191
White, M.L. 41
Whiteside, John 149
Wholey, Joseph P. and Hatry, Harry P. 117
Wilcox, Kirkland and Discenza, Richard 110
Wilkerson, David and Kellogg, Jeffrey 140
William, Frances 178

Williams, Allan *et al.* 149
Williams, Timothy P. and Howe, Rufus S. 78
Wilson, Lawrence A. 219
Winig, Laura 189
Wolak, Jerry 32
Wolf, Nick de 33
Wood, Lindsey V. and McCamey, David A.
  23
Wood, Patricia B. 118
Woodcock, Mike 206
Woods, Michael D. 110
Woods, Robert 19
Worth, Maurice W. 36

Yavas, Burhan F. 15
Young, Mary J. *et al.* 78
Young, S. Mark 140
Younger, Sandra Millers 162
Yovovich, B.G. 30

Zaciewski, Robert D. 179
Zairi, Mohamed 108
Zemke, Ron 98, 192, 194
Zenger, John H. *et al.* 126
Zetie, John Sparrow *et al.* 24
Zoglio, Suzanne Willis 126, 156
Zuckerman, Amy 170, 179

Title index

AAHE Bulletin 98
ABA Banking Journal 40
ABA Journal 80
ABC FlowCharter (software package) 211
The Abilene Paradox (video) 205
Academic Medicine 56
Academy of Management Review 10, 140
Accelerated Development Program (exec.dev.prog) 241
Accelerated Development Programme (exec.dev.prog) 235
Accountancy 21
Achieving Excellence in Business (Ebel) 5
Achieving International Excellence in Manufacturing (exec.dev.prog) 244
Achieving Quality Learning in Higher Education (Nightingale & O'Neil) 96
Achieving Quality Performance: Lessons from British Industry (Cassell Pub.) 24, 26–7, 31, 44, 111
Achieving the Sustainable Turnaround (exec.dev.prog) 244
Achieving World Class Manufacturing Through Process Control (Shunta) 139
Administrative Radiology 60
Advanced Executive Program (exec.dev.prog) 239
Advanced Human Resource Executive Program (exec.dev.prog) 235
Advanced Management Program (exec.dev.prog) 239, 245
Advanced Project Management: Beyond the Techniques (exec.dev.prog) 247
Advantage Program (exec.dev.prog) 235
The Adventures of a Self-Managing Team (Kelly) 124
AGB Reports 86, 99
AI Expert 53
Alessandra On . . . Customer-Driven Service (video) 191
allCLEAR III (software package) 211
America3: The Power to Create (video) 205
American Journal of Infection Control 65
American Journal of Medical Quality 183
American Printer 20
American Review of Public Administration (Durant) 113

The American School Board Journal 84
Analyzing Business Process Data: The Looking Glass (AT & T Quality Library) 132
Annual Fall Industrial Relations (exec.dev.prog) 245
Annual Quality Congress Transactions 10, 19, 21, 65, 105, 106, 120—1, 134, 136, 141, 150
Appalachia 80
Applied CIM (software package) 211
Applied Stats (software package) 212
Applied Stats Analyst (software package) 212
Applying Total Quality Management: A Nursing Guide (Williams & Howe) 78
Applying Total Quality Management to Systems Engineering (Kasser) 105
AQP Report 183
Archives of Internal Medicine 78
Archives of Pathology and Laboratory Medicine 78
Association for Healthcare Philanthropy Journal 62
At Your Service: Designing and Delivering Top-Notch Customer-Focused Service (video-workbook) 192
Audit Master (software package) 212
Australian Accountant 108

Baldrige Award Winning Quality (Brown) 133
Basic Management Program (exec.dev.prog) 245
Basic Tools for Quality & Process Improvement Videotape series (video) 209
Becoming Customer Driven (exec.dev.prog) 239
BenchMarker Plus (software package) 212
Benchmarking (exec.dev.prog) 244
Benchmarking: A Practitioner's Guide (Balm) 131
Benchmarking: A Tool for Continuous Improvement (Liebfried & McNair) 137
The Benchmarking Book (Spendolini) 139
Benchmarking: Focus on World-Class Practices (AT & T Quality Library) 132
Benchmarking for Effective Network Management (Terplan) 55
Benchmarking for Quality Management and Technology 183
Benchmarking: The Search for Industry Best Practices (Camp) 133
Benchmarking: Theory and Practice (Rolstadas) 139

The Benchmarking Workbook: Adapting Best Practices for Performance Improvement (Watson) 140

A Better Idea: Redefining the Way Americans Work (Petersen & Hillkirk) 32

Beyond TQM (exec.dev.prog) 247

Biomedical Instrumentaiton & Technology 63

Blueprints for Service Quality: The Federal Express Approach (AMA Membership Publications Division) 36–7

Bridging the Gap Between Theory & Practice (Hospital Research & Education Trust) 60

British Dental Journal 56

British Journal of Clinical Psychology 80

Building Blocks for Team Performance (video) 205

Building Customer Value for the '90s (exec.dev.prog) 240

Building Quality Software (Glass) 52

Building Self-Managed Teams and Team Leadership Skills (exec.dev.prog) 247

Building Teams (exec.dev.prog) 247

Building the High Performance Sales Force (Petrone) 50

Building the Learning Organization (exec.dev.prog) 241

Business & Economic Review 38

Business Change and Re-engineering 183

Business Education Forum 94

Business Horizons 174

Business Insurance 45

Business Marketing 30

Business Officer 86, 87, 95

Business Process Engineering: Current Perspectives and Research Directions 14

Business Process Improvement (Harrington) 135

Business Process Innovation (exec.dev.prog) 247

Business Process Redesign (exec.dev.prog) 247

Business Process Reengineering (exec.dev.prog) 247

Business Quarterly 35, 52

Business Week 12

CA Magazine 109, 110

Calibration Manager (software package) 213

Calibration Recall System (software package) 213

California Management Review 27, 162

Calming Upset Customers (Morgan) 130

Calming Upset Customers (video) 192

Candid Camera Goes to Work: Expect the Unexpected (video) 192

Candid Camera Goes to Work: Too Close to the Customer (video) 192

Cases in Total Quality Management (Butterworth-Heinemann Pub.) 20, 21, 23, 25, 30, 32–3, 38–9, 43

Cases in Total Quality Management (Oakland & Porter) 8

Catalog Age 40

Cause and Effect 97

Change 85, 90, 95, 96, 98

The Change Program (exec.dev.prog) 236

Changing Culture: New Organizational Approaches (Williams & Walters) 149

Chemical Marketing Reporter 21, 22

Chemical Week 14, 175, 176

Client-Centered Service: How to Keep Them Coming Back For More (Cottle) 128

Close to the Customer: 25 Tips from the Other Side of the Counter (Donnelly) 128

CMA Magazine 130, 160

College & Research Libraries News 103

College & University 101

College Teaching 95

Commit to Quality (Townsend & Gebhardt) 125

Communicating Change: How to Win Employee Support for New Business Directions (Larkin & Larkin) 160

Communicating Change (Quirke) 161

Companion Encyclopedia of Marketing (Routledge Pub.) 49

Compensation and Benefits Review 156

Competing in a Changing World (exec.dev.prog) 248

Computer Integrated Manufacturing: Guidelines and Applicaitons from Industrial leaders (Melnyk & Narasimhan) 137

Computers & Industrial Engineering 121

Computerworld 53

Contemporary Executive Development (exec.dev.prog) 241

Continuous General Management Programme (exec.dev.prog) 236

Continuous Improvement in Action: Eight Original In-Depth Case Studies (Society of Manufacturing Engineers) 27, 31, 32, 33

Continuous Journey: The Magazine for Continuous Improvement 183

Continuous Quality Improvement: A New Look for Education (video) 198

Continuous Quality Improvement in Health Care: Theory, Implementation and Applications (McLaughlin & Kaluzny) 73

Cooperative Approaches in the Workplace (exec.dev.prog) 236

Core Human Resources Executive Development Program (exec.dev.prog) 236

The Cornell Hotel & Restaurant Administration Quarterly 48

Corporate Cultures: The Rites and Rituals of Corporate Life (Deal & Kennedy) 141

Corrective Action: Problem Management Software for Windows (software package) 213

Cost of Quality (software package) 213

CPCI (software package) 213

CQI101: A First Reader for Higher Education 88

A CQI System for Healthcare: How the Williamsport Hospital Brings Quality to Life (Mannello) 73

Creating Quality: Concepts, Systems, Strategies and Tools (Kolarik) 136

Creating a Customer-Focused Organization (Brothers & Carson) 127

Creating and Managing High Performance Teams (exec.dev.prog) 248

Creating Corporate Culture: From Discord to Harmony (Hampden-Truner) 143

Creating the Customer-Oriented Firm (exec.dev.prog) 240

Creating the Future: The Challenge of Trans-formational Leadership (exec.dev.prog) 241

Creating the High Performance Team (Buchholz & Roth) 123

Creating the High Performance Workplace (exec.dev.prog) 241, 248

Creating Value for Customers: Designing and Implementing a Total Corporate Strategy (Band) 126

Creating World-Class Capabilities (exec.dev.prog) 245

Creating World-Class Quality: A Strategic Evaluation (exec.dev.prog) 244

Credit Union Executive 42

Crisis & Renewal: Meeting the Challenge of Organizational Change (Hurst) 144

CUPA Journal 95

Curing Health Care, New Strategies for Quality Improvement: A Report (Berwick et al.) 59

The Customer Connection: Quality for the Rest of Us (Guaspari) 129

The Customer is Always Right (video) 198

The Customer is King! (Harris) 129

Customer Satisfaction: How to Maximize, Measure and Market Your Company's "Ultimate Product" (Hanan & Karp) 129

Customer Satisfaction: Management Strategies and Tactics (exec.dev.prog) 240

Customer Service Newsletter 183

Customer Service Operations: The Complete Guide (Blanding) 127

Customer Service: Or Else! (video) 193

Customer Service Report 183

Customer Services: Building, Maintaining and Enhancing (exec.dev.prog) 240

The Customer-Driven Company: Managerial Perspectives on QFD (ASI Press) 134

Customer-Driven Service (video) 193

Customers as Partners: Building Relationships That Last (Bell) 127

Cyberquality: Quality Resources on the Internet (Clauson) 3

Database for Quality (DNQ) (software package) 214

Datamation 53, 54

The Death and Life of the American Quality Movement (Cole) 4

Delegation and the Team Effort: People and Performance (exec.dev.prog) 248

Delivering Excellent Customer Service (exec.dev.prog) 240

Delivering Knock Your Socks Service (Anderson & Zemke) 126

Deming Quality: The Right Machine (video) 205

The Deming Videotapes (video) 198

Design/IDEF (software package) 214

Designing for Quality: An Introduction to the Best Taguchi (Lochner et al) 137

Developing Quality Schools (Bayne-Jardine & Holly) 81

Developing Quality Systems in Education (Doherty) 89

Development Program for Managers (exec.dev.prog) 245

Discontinous Change: Leading Organizational Transformation (Nadler et al) 145

Discovering the Future series (video) 189

Document Manager 9000 (software package) 214

DOE-PC IV (software package) 214

EasyFlow for Windows (software package) 215

Economic Control of Quality of Manufactured Products (Shewart) 1

The Economics of Total Quality Management (Cole & Mogab) 4

Educational and Training Technology International 96

Educational Leadership 82, 83

Educational Record 90, 91, 100

Educational Technology 94

Effecting Change (exec.dev.prog) 236

The Effective Chief Executive (exec.dev.prog) 236

Effective Leadership (exec.dev.prog) 241

Electronic Business 33

Electronic Business Buyer 170, 176

Employee Relations Today 46

Employee-Driven Quality (McDermott et al.) 160

Employment Relations Today (Wilkerson & Kellogg) 140

The Empowered Manager: Positive Political Skills at Work (Block) 140

The End of Bureaucracy & the Rise of the Intelligent Organization (Pinchot & Pinchot) 146

Engineered Quality in Construction: Partnering and TQM (Kubal) 17

Engineering and Management Program (exec.dev.prog) 242

The Engineering Index 187

Enlightened Leadership: Getting to the Heart of Change (Oakley & Krug) 154

Environmental Manager 29

ERS Spectrum 83

Essentials of Cost Accounting for Health Care Organizations (Finker) 109

Essentials of SPC Computer-Based Training (software package) 215

European Quality 183

Evaluating the Performance of the Hospital CEO (American College of Healthcare Executives & American Hospital Association) 64

Evaluation Practice 117

Everyone's Problem Solving Handbook: Step-By-Step Solutions for Quality Improvement (Kelly) 136

Excellence in Government: Total Quality Management in the 1990s (Carr & Littman) 112

Executive Decisions for Self-Managed/Directed Work Teams (exec.dev.prog) 248

Executive Development Consortium (exec.dev.prog) 244

Executive Development Program (exec.dev.prog) 242, 245

Executive Development Program: The Transition from Functional to General Management (exec.dev.prog) 248

Executive Program (exec.dev.prog) 248

Executive Program for Mid-Sized Companies (exec.dev.prog) 236

Executive Program in Business Administration: Managing the Enterprise (exec.dev.prog) 236

Executive Program in International Management: Managing for Global Success (exec.dev.prog) 248

Executive Program in Organization Change (exec.dev.prog) 236

The Facilitator's Toolkit: Tools and Techniques for Generating Ideas (three–ring binder) 205

Facilities Manager 97

FACTORYnet Q/S (software package) 215

Faultless Facilitation: A Resource Guide for Group and Team Leaders (three–ring binder) 206

Faultless Facilitation: An Instructor's Manual for Facilitation Training (three–ring binder) 206

Federal Probation 119

The Fifth Discipline: The Art and Practice of the Learning Organization (Senge) 147

The Fifth Discipline Fieldbook: Strategies and Tools for Building a Learning Organization (Senge) 148

50 Activities for Self-Directed Teams (three-ring binder) 206

50 Activities for Team Building vols 1 and 2 (three-ring binder) 206

50 Ways to Keep Your Customers (video) 193

Financial Executive 18

Financial Management 77

The Financial Times 178

Flight of the Buffalo: Soaring to Excellence (video) 197

Flow Charting 4 (software package) 215

FlowChart Express (software package) 215

Flying Fox: A Business Adventure in Teams and Teamwork (Butman) 123

Food Technology 18

Four Days with Dr Deming (Latzko & Saunders) 7

Fourth Generation Management: the New Business Consciousness (Joiner) 144

From Red Tape to Results: Creating a Government that Works (Government Printing Office) 114

Front-Line Customer Service: 15 Keys to Customer Satisfaction (Carr) 127

GageTalker III Plus Real Time (software package) 216

GageTalker DataPage III (software package) 216

The Gauge Program Software (software package) 216

General Management for Mid-Sized Companies (exec.dev.prog) 236

General Management Program (exec.dev.prog) 242

German Perspectives on Total Quality (The Conference Board) 23–4, 31, 35, 117

Global Quality: A Synthesis of the World's Best Management Methods (ASQC Quality Press) 142

Global Strategy and Operations Management Program (exec.dev.prog) 246

GMP: The Greatest Management Principle in the World (LeBoeuf) 129

Good Manufacturing Practice in Transfusion Medicine (Smit *et al.*) 79

Good Old Days of Quality Service (video) 193

Government Accountants Journal 110

Government Finance Review 115, 116

Gower Handbook of Quality Management (Lock) 137

A Guide to ISO 9000: A Video Series (video) 196

Guidelines for the Organization of a Blood Transfusion Service (Gibbs & Britten) 79

Handbook of Quality Tools: The Japanese Approach (Ozeki) 138

Handbook of Software Quality Assurance (Schulmeyer & Mcmanus) 54

Harvard Business Review 13, 96, 131, 135, 147

Health Care Management Review 74, 120

Health Care Strategic Management 72

Health Care Supervisor 59

Health Services Management 119

Health Services Management Research 69

Health Systems Review 65

Healthcare Financial Management 57, 68, 69, 70, 71

Healthcare Forum 65

Healthcare Management Review 73

Helping an Organization Succeed: Using the Malcolm Baldrige National Quality Award Criteria (software package) 216

High Performance Leadership: HRD Strategies for the New Work Culture (Harris) 152

Higher Education 87, 88, 89, 92, 93

Hospital & Health Services Administration 62, 72, 76, 78

Hospital Cost Management and Accounting 77

Hospital Material Management Quarterly 69

Hospital Topics 64

Hospitality & Tourism Educator 47–8, 91

Hospitals 58, 64, 67, 70–1, 72–3, 74, 76, 77

How to Manage Teams Effectively (exec.dev.prog) 248

How To Win Customers and Keep Them For Life (LeBoeuf) 129

HR Magazine 157

Human Resource Management 160

Human Resource Management (exec.dev.prog) 244

Human Resource Management: Effecting Change Beyond the 1990s (exec.dev.prog) 249

Human Resource Management Program (exec.dev.prog) 236

I Know It When I See It (Guaspari) 129

The Idea Generator Plus (software package) 217

IEEE Proceedings of the National Aerospace and Electronics Conference 135

"I'm First": Your Customer's Message to You (Goldzimer *et al*) 129

Implementing Total Quality Management (exec.dev.prog) 244

Implementing TQM: Competing in the Nineties (Jablonski) 6–7
Implementing TQM in Health Care Videotape Series (video) 199
Implementing TQM in Small & Medium-Sized Organizations (Hodgetts) 6
Improving Government Performance: An Owner's Manual (DiIulio Jr. et al) 113
Improving Quality and Performance: Concepts, Programs and Techniques (Schroeder) 76
Improving Software Quality: An Insider's Guide to TQM (Arthur) 50
In Search of Excellence (video) 199
In Search of Quality Series (video) 199
Indiana Executive Program (exec.dev.prog) 242
Industrial & Commercial Training 157
Industrial Engineering 24, 33
Industrial Management 148
Infection Control and Hospital Epidemiology 63
Information Systems Management 55
Information Technology Management (exec.dev.prog) 240
Infotrends: The Competitive Use of Information (Keyes) 53
An Inside Job: Stuck on Quality (video) 192
Inside the Reinvention Machine: Appraising Governmental Reform (Kettl & DiIulio Jr.) 115
Inside Teams: How 20 World-Class Organizations are Winning Through Teamwork (Wellins et al.) 125
Inspiration (software package) 217
Institute for Productivity Through Quality (exec.dev.prog) 244
Integrated Management & Planning Tools: A Company Case Study Videotape (video) 209
Integrated Quality Management: The Key to Improving Nursing Care Quality (Koch & Fairly) 70
The Integrated Quality System (software package) 217
Integrating Total Quality Management in a Library Setting (Jurow & Barnard) 102
Interfaces 30
The Internal Auditor 110
Internal Auditor 172
International Journal for Quality in Health Care 183
International Journal of Quality & Reliability Management 184
International Managers Programme (exec.dev.prog) 237
International Manufacturing Programme (exec.dev.prog) 246
The International Quality Study: Best Practices Report (Ernst Young & American Quality Foundation) 31, 41, 68
International Trade Forum 174
Interpersonal Skills for Senior Managers (exec.dev.prog) 249
Introduction to Management (exec.dev.prog) 249
Introduction to Quality Control (Ishikawa) 136
An Introduction to Software Quality Control (Cho) 51

An Invented Life: Reflections on Leadership and Change (Bennis) 150
ISO 9000 Almanac: 1994–95 Edition (Peters) 169
The ISO 9000 Answer Book (Kantner) 169
ISO 9000 Made Easy (Zuckerman) 170
ISO 9000: Meeting the New International Standards (Johnson) 169
ISO 9000: Motivating the People (Huyink & Westover) 168
ISO 9000 Quality Systems Handbook (Hoyle) 168
ISO 9000: The First Step to the Future (video) 196
ISO 9001 and Software Quality Assurance (Ince) 53
ISO 14000: A Guide to the New Environmental Management Standards (Tibor) 169
ISOxPERT (software package) 217
It's About Time: A Fable About the Next Dimension of Quality (Guaspari) 129

JAMA 71
JMP (software package) 218
The Job of Managing (exec.dev.prog) 249
The Joint Commission Journal on Quality Improvement 68, 76
Journal for Healthcare Quality 62, 121
Journal for Higher Education Management 103
Journal for Quality and Participation 83, 87, 93, 97, 133, 148, 161, 177, 179, 184
Journal of Accountancy 109
Journal of Business & Psychology 159
Journal of Business Strategy 27–8, 34
Journal of College & University Foodservices 39–40
Journal of Commercial Lending 41–2
Journal of Economic Education 86
Journal of Education for Business 96, 100
Journal of European Industrial Training 162
The Journal of Family Practice 56
The Journal of Health Administration Education 97
Journal of Library Administration 101, 102, 103, 113
Journal of Management 154
Journal of Management in Engineering 105
Journal of Nursing Administration 61, 66
Journal of Nursing Care Quality 59, 60, 63
Journal of Parenteral Science and Technology 23
Journal of Productivity Analysis 184
Journal of Property Management 46–7
Journal of Quality Assurance 121
Journal of Quality Technology 184
Journal of Small Business Management 173
The Journal of State Government 112
Journal of Substance Abuse Treatment 79
Journal of the American Dietetic Association 64, 72
Journal of the Royal Society of Health 120
Journal of the Society for Health Systems 63
Juran on Leadership for Quality (Juran) 7
Juran on Planning for Quality (Juran) 7
Juran's Quality Handbook (Juran) 136
JUSE-QCAS (software package) 218
Just Change It!: Creating a Government That Works (video) 200

Kaizen: The Key to Japan's Competitive Success (Imai) 144
Keeping Customers (Sviokla & Shapiro) 131
Keeping Customers for Life (Cannie & Caplin) 127
Keeping Score: Strategies and Tactics for Winning the Quality War (Johnson) 136
Keeping Teams Together (video) 207
Kidgets: And Other Insightful Stories about Quality in Education (Cotter & Seymour) 88–9

Law Practice Management 80
A Leader's Journey to Quality (Cound) 4, 151
Leadership Across Frontiers (exec.dev.prog) 242
Leadership and Decision Making in Organizations (exec.dev.prog) 249
Leadership and Organization Development Journal 184
Leadership and Teamwork (exec.dev.prog) 249
Leadership and the New Science (video) 190
Leadership and the New Science (Wheatley) 156
The Leadership Challenge (Kouzes & Posner) 153
Leadership Competence Program (exec.dev.prog) 242
Leadership Development Programme (exec.dev.prog) 249
Leadership for Extraordinary Performance (exec.dev.prog) 242
Leadership for the Year 2000: Beyond the Team Building (exec.dev.prog) 242
Leadership in Health Services 61
Leadership in Senior Management (exec.dev.prog) 249
Leadership, Perspective and Restructuring for Total Quality (Pierce) 155
Leading and Managing People (exec.dev.prog) 237
Leading Continuous Improvement (exec.dev.prog) 242
Leading: The Art of Becoming an Executive (Cosby) 151
Leading the Human Resource Function (exec.dev.prog) 237
Leading the Nations series (video) 200
Leading Teams: Mastering the New Role (Zenger et al) 126
Leading the Team Organization (Tjosvold & Tjosvold) 125
LearnerFirst Benchmarking (software package) 219
LearnerFirst How to Implement ISO 9000 (software package) 219
LearnerFirst Process Management (software package) 219
Lessons in Teamwork: Computer-Based Training Modules (computer-based training program) 206
Liberation Management: Necessary Disorganization for the Nanosecond Nineties (Peters) 146
Library Administration & Management 104
Library Journal 53, 101
Lodging Hospitality 48–9
Logistics Management (exec.dev.prog) 247
Logistics Management Programme (exec.dev.prog) 240
Long Range Planning 55

McGill University (exec.dev.prog) 238
Magic Window (software package) 219
Making Change Work (exec.dev.prog) 237
Making Quality Happen (exec.dev.prog) 244
Making TQM Work: The Human Factor (video-integrated workbook program) 207
Manage Your Time, Manage Your Work, Manage Yourself (Douglass & Douglass) 123
Management II: A Management Development Program for Mid-Level Managers (exec.dev.prog) 250
Management Accounting 27, 36, 94, 110
Management Accounting for Healthcare Organizations (Suver et al) 77
The Management Accounting Magazine 175
Management and Measurement Software Quality (Kelly) 53
The Management of Change in Universities (Miller) 95
The Management Compass: Steering the Corporation Using Hoshin Planning (Bechtell) 132
Management Development Program (exec.dev.prog) 237, 243, 246
Management Development Program: Developing Leadership Potential (exec.dev.prog) 243
Management Development Programme (exec.dev.prog) 237, 249
Management Development Seminar (exec.dev.prog) 237
Management Effectiveness Workshop (exec.dev.prog) 250
Management for Quality Improvement: The Seven New QC Tools (Mizuno) 138
Management International Review 24, 149
Management of Managers: A Leadership Renewal Program (exec.dev.prog) 237
Management Review 12, 117, 146
Management Today 26, 32, 152
Managing Change (exec.dev.prog) 237
Managing at the Speed of Change (video) 190
Managing Customer Value: Creating Quality and Service (Gale & Wood) 129
Managing for Quality (Hunt) 6
Managing for World-Class Quality (Shecter) 8–9
Managing in the Age of Change (Ritvo et al.) 147
Managing Individual and Organizational Change (exec.dev.prog) 237
Managing Innovation (exec.dev.prog) 243
Managing Managers Institute (exec.dev.prog) 243
Managing Multinational Enterprise: The Renewal Challenge (exec.dev.prog) 237
Managing Organizational Change (Connor & Lake) 140
Managing Organizational Change (exec.dev.prog) 238
Managing People Effectively (exec.dev.prog) 250
Managing People: Effectiveness Through Individual and Group Dynamics (exec.dev.prog) 243
Managing Performance for Quality (video) 200
Managing Professional and Organizational Growth (exec.dev.prog) 246
Managing Quality (Dale) 5

Title index

Managing Quality: A Guide to Monitoring and Evaluating Nursing Services (Katz & Green) 69

Managing Quality in America's Most Admired Companies (Spechler) 9, 19, 22, 25, 26, 28–9, 30, 32, 33, 34, 35, 36, 37–8, 39, 42–3, 44, 45–6, 47, 48, 52

Managing Service Quality 184

Managing Service: Reengineering for Customer Satisfaction (exec.dev.prog) 240

Managing Strategic Innovation and Change (exec.dev.prog) 238

Managing the Closely Held Company in Changing Times (exec.dev.prog) 246

Managing the Hidden Organization (Deal & Jankins) 151

Managing the Quality of Health Care in Developing Countries (De Geyndt) 119

Managing Value for Money in the Public Sector (Bates) 111

Manufacturing Executive Program (exec.dev.prog) 244

Manufacturing Management Program (exec.dev.prog) 250

Manufacturing Solutions for Consistent Quality & Reliability (Traver) 107

Mastering Change (exec.dev.prog) 238

Mastering Revolutionary Change (video) 190

Measuring Customer Satisfaction (exec.dev.prog) 240

Measuring, Managing, and Maximizing Performance (Kaydos) 7

Measuring Software Design Quality (Card & Glass) 50–1

Medical Care 68

Medical Care Review 65

Medical Economics 56

Medical Journal of Australia 64

Medical World News 61

Meeting Customer Needs (Smith) 130

The Memory Jogger Plus+: Featuring the Seven Management and Planning Tools (Brassard) 133

The Memory Jogger Plus+ (GOAL/QPC pub.) 220

The Memory Jogger Plus+ Software: 7 M & P Tools (software package) 220

The Memory Jogger Plus+ Videotape series (video) 209

The Memory Jogger Software: 7 QC Tools (software package) 220

Michigan-IESE Global Program for Managing Development (exec.dev.prog) 240

Minitab Statistical Software (software package) 220

Minority Executive Program (exec.dev.prog) 246

MIS Quarterly 55

Modern Healthcare 60

Modular General Management Programme (exec.dev.prog) 238

Mortgage Banking 43

NASPA Journal 92

NASSP Bulletin 84

National Productivity Review 11, 12, 15, 18, 24, 30, 35–6, 38, 42, 43, 53, 91, 115, 116, 118, 135, 139, 149, 152, 155, 158, 162, 128, 175

National Real Estate Investor 46

Nation's Business 171

Network Monitor (software package) 221

New Directions for Institutional Research 93

New England Journal of Medicine 59

The New Experimental Design: Taguchi's Approach to Quality Engineering (Mori) 138

The New Partnership (video) 197

The New Workplace (video) 197

No Complaints? (video) 194

The No-Nonsense Guide to Achieving ISO 9000 (Craig) 168

Nonconformance Tracking: Reject & Failure Management Software (software package) 221

Nonprofit Management Institute (exec.dev.prog) 238

Nursing 74

Nursing Administration Quarterly 71

"...On Leadership" (exec.dev.prog) 243

On Q: Causing Quality in Higher Education (Seymour) 98

Once Upon a Campus: Lessons for Improving Quality and Productivity in Higher Education (Seymour) 99

One Company's Journey to ISO 9000 Registration (Beardsley & Schaefer) 171

One Ringy Dingy, You Are the Customer (video) 194

The Only Thing That Matters: Bringing the Power of the Customer into the Center of Your Business (Albrecht) 126

Open MBA Master Class (exec.dev.prog) 250

Optimal (software package) 221

Optimum Design of Experiments (software package) 221

Optionist (software package) 221

Organizational Architecture: Designs for Changing Organizations (Heilpern & Nadler) 88, 143

Organizational Change and Redesign: Ideas and Insights (Huber & Glick) 143

Organizational Change Skills for General Managers (exec.dev.prog) 238

Organizational Dynamics 28, 157

Organizational Excellence (exec.dev.prog) 250

Organizational Transformation: Critical Success Factors (exec.dev.prog) 238

Organizational Transformations in Health Care: A Work in Progress (Andrews *et al*) 58

Out of the Crisis (Deming) 5

The Oxford Strategic Leadership Programme (exec.dev.prog) 250

Parks & Recreation 114

The Participative Leader (Zoglio) 156

A Passion for Customers (video) 194

A Passion for Excellence (video) 200

The Path to Change series (video) 190

Patient-Centered Care: A Model for Restructuring (Parsons & Murdaugh) 75

People, Performance and Pay (Flannery *et al.*) 159

Performance and Instruction 159

Performance Through People (exec.dev.prog) 250

Personnel Journal 40, 119, 156, 157, 158

Personnel Management 14, 151, 161
The Phoenix Agenda: Power to Transform Your Workplace (Whiteside) 149
Planning for Higher Education 89
The Planning Process: Using Teamwork (exec.dev.prog) 250
Planning Review 11, 18
The Police Chief 118
Policy Deployment: Setting the Direction for Change (AT & T Quality Library) 132
Power and Leadership (exec.dev.prog) 243
Practitioner's Guide to Quality and Process Improvement (Badiru & Ayeni) 131
Prescription for Change: Total Quality in Health Care (video) 201
Prime Factor FFT (software package) 222
A Primer on the Taguchi Method (Roy) 139
Principles of Quality Costs (Campanella) 134
Proceedings of the Project Management Institute Annual Seminar Symposium 22, 106
Process Charter for Windows (software package) 222
Process Control and quality 184
Process Quality Management & Improvement Guide (AT & T Quality Library) 132
Process Reengineering: The Key to Achieving Breakthrough Success (Roberts) 8
Production and Operations Management: Total Quality and Responsiveness (Noori & Radford) 107
Productivity: Improving Productivity and Quality by Learning What's Working at Other Companies 184
Productivity Views: Solutions, Tips and Action Ideas from Service Quality Leaders 184
Profiles in Healthcare Marketing 75
Program for Manager Development (exec.dev.prog) 238
Program for Management Development: Managing Critical Issues (exec.dev.prog) 246
Program for Strategic Leadership (exec.dev.prog) 243
Project Kickstart (software package) 222
Prophets in the Dark: How Xerox Reinvented Itself and Beat Back the Japanese (Kearns & Nadler) 35
Proquis 9000 (software package) 222
Public Administration Quarterly 114
Public Administration Review 113, 117
Public Health Reports 120
Public Management 115
Public Money & Management 113
Public Productivity & Management Review 112, 114, 116
Pulp & Paper 19, 173
Purchasing 170

Q9000 Quality Manual Including 26 Operating Procedures on Disk (software package) 223
Q-Pulse (software package) 224
QC Circle 184
QC Tools (software package) 223
QFD Designer (software package) 223
QFD/Capture Software (software package) 223

QI Analyst (software package) 224
QI Analyst for Gage R & R (software package) 224
QI-TQM 184
QRC Advisor: Managing Hospital Quality, Risk & Cost 185
Quality 32
Quality and Control: An Accounting Perspective (Riahi-Belkaoui) 110
Quality and Regulation in Health Care International Experiences (Dingwall & Fenn) 119
Quality and Reliability Engineering Internaitonal 185
Quality & Risk Management in Health Care: An Information Service 185
Quality Assurance Bulletin 185
Quality Assurance for Computer Software (Dunn & Ullman) 51
Quality Assurance: Good Practice, Regulation and Law 185
Quality Assurance in Education 185
Quality Assurance in Hospitals (Graham) 67
Quality by Design (Belavendram) 132
Quality by Design: Taguchi Methods and US Industry (Ealey) 134
Quality by Experimental Design (Barker) 131
Quality Control (Besterfield) 132
Quality Control and Application (Hansen & Ghare) 135
Quality Control Handbook (Juran) 1, 7
Quality Costing (Barrie & Plunkett) 134
Quality Digest 3, 185
Quality Engineering 185
A Quality Foundation: 50 Activities for Organizational Change (three-ring binder) 191
Quality Improvement Programs in ARL Libraries (Siggins & Sullivan) 185
Quality in Action (Townsend & Gebhardt) 9
Quality in Cyberspace (Dusharme) 3
Quality in Health Care: Theory, Application and Evolution (Graham) 67
Quality in Manufacturing 185
Quality in Practice (video) 196
Quality in the Finance Function (Lynch) 109
Quality in the Office (video) 201
Quality is Free (Crosby) 2, 4
Quality is Just the Beginning (Levit) 7
Quality Management and Innovative Practices in Business (exec.dev.prog) 246
Quality Management Journal 10, 14, 142, 145, 170, 172, 177, 185
Quality Management Report (video) 201
Quality Manager's Complete Guide to ISO 9000 (Clements) 168
Quality Minutes (video) 201
Quality New Zealand 185
The Quality Professor: Implementing TQM in the Classroom (Cornesky) 88
Quality Programming: Development and Testing Software (Cho) 51
Quality Progress 3, 15, 27, 61, 82, 85, 93, 105, 126, 128, 130, 147, 152, 171, 172, 173, 174, 176, 178, 179, 186

Quality Review Bulletin 56, 63, 68, 72
The Quality Roadmap (Svenson *et al.*) 9
The Quality School: Management Students Without Coercion (Glasser) 82
The Quality School Teacher (Glasser) 82
Quality: The Magazine of Product Assurance 186
Quality: Transforming Postsecondary Education (Chaffee & Sherr) 86
Quality Today 186
Quality Up, Costs Down: A Manager's Guide to Taguchi Methods and QFD (Eureka & Ryan) 134
Quality Wars: The Triumphs and Defeats of American Business (Main) 2, 7–8
Quality Without Tears (Crosby) 4
Quality Workbench (software package) 224
Quality World: For the Quality Professional 186
Quality-Europe 185
Quantam SPC/DC (software package) 225
Quantum SPC/QA (software package) 225

The Race Without a Finish Line (Schmidt & Finnegan) 8, 88
Radiology Management 57
Randall's Practical Guide to ISO 9000: Implementation, Registration and Beyond (Randall) 169
Raosoft Survey (software package) 225
Real Estate Today 46
Records Management Quarterly 178
The Reengineering Roadmap: A How-To Approach (video) 204
Reengineering the Corporation (Hammer & Champy) 6
Reengineering the Future (video) 204
Reframing Organizations: Artistry, Choice and Leadership (Deal & Bolman) 151
Reinventing Government (video) 202
Reinventing Government: How the Entrepreneurial Spirit is Transforming the Public Sector (Osborne & Gabler) 116
Reinventing the Sales Organization (Miranda) 49
Research Technology Management 23, 111, 138
Resilience: A Change for the Better (video) 191
Restructuring Canadian Business: Strategies for Success (exec.dev.prog) 239
Return on Quality (exec.dev.prog) 245
Revitalizing Your Company: Creative Ways to Build Profits (video) 202
Risk Management 45
Root Cause Analysis (exec.dev.prog) 250
Rutgers Organizational Management Program (exec.dev.prog) 246

The SAS System (software package) 226
School Organisation 83
The School for Quality Learning: Managing the School and Classroom the Deming Way (Crawford *et al*) 81
Secrets of Software Quality: 40 Innovations from IBM (Kaplan *et al.*) 53
Seeking Customers (Sviolka & Shapiro) 131
Selling in the Quality Era (Peeler) 49–50

Seminars in Perioperative Nursing 62
Senior Executive Institute for Productivity Through Quality (exec.dev.prog) 245
Senior Executives Program (exec.dev.prog) 239
Senior Managers' Programme (exec.dev.prog) 239
The Service Edge: The Newsletter of Bottom-Line Ideas for Customer-Driven Organizations 186
The Service Era: Leadership in a Global Environment (D'Egidio) 128
The Service Industries Journal 41
Service Quality 186
Service Quality Improvement: The Customer Satisfaction Strategy for Health Care (Leebov & Scott) 72
Service Quality: New Directions in Theory and Practice (Rust & Oliver) 130
Service with Soul (video) 194
Serving them Right: Innovative and Powerful Customer Retention Strategies (Liswood) 130
SigmalPlot (software package) 226
Sloan Management Review 44, 142
Software Inspection (Gilb & Graham) 51–2
Software Inspection Process (Ebenau & Strauss) 51
Software Magazine 53
Software Quality and Reliability (Ince) 52
Software Quality Assurance: A Practical Approach (Wallmüller) 54
Software Quality Assurance and Evaluation (Dobbins) 51
Software Quality: Concepts and Plans (Dunn) 51
Software Quality Engineering: A Total Technical and Management approach (Deutsch & Willis) 51
Software Quality Management: A Pro-Active Approach (Brinkworth) 50
Software Quality Managment (Ross *et al*) 54
Software Quality: Theory and Management (Gillies) 52
Solving Quality and Productivity Problems (Staff of Goodmeasure Inc) 125
Solving the Productivity Paradox: TQM for Computer Professionals (Keyes) 53
SPC3D (software package) 227
SPC 9000 226
SPC Simplified: Practical Steps to Quality (Amsden *et al.*) 131
S.P.C. Training Simulator (software package) 227
SPC-PC IV Windows (software package) 227
SPC/PI+ Advanced SPC Software (software package) 228
SPCI+ Professional (software package) 228
SPCI+ (software package) 227
SPSS 6.1 for Windows (software package) 228
SQCpack for Windows (software package) 228
SQCpack/PLUS (software package) 228
SQCsignals (software package) 229
Standards of Care 56
Statistica/w (software package) 229
Statistical Methods for the Process Industries (McNeese & Klein) 137
Statistical Methods of Quality (Mittag & Rinne) 138
Statistical Problem Solving in Engineering (Kazmierski) 106

Statistical Process Control (exec.dev.prog) 245

STATnet/2 (software package) 229

Statselect (software package) 230

StatView (software package) 230

Straight Talk for Monday Morning: Creating Values, Visions and Vitality at Work (Cox) 123

Straight Talk on Teams (video) 207

Strategic Insights into Quality 186

Strategic Management Programme (exec.dev.prog) 239

Strategic Management in the Service Sector (exec.dev.prog) 239

Strategic Marketing (exec.dev.prog) 241

Strategic Quality Management Program (exec.dev.prog) 246

Strategies for Healthcare Excellence 59

Strategy and Strategic Management (exec.dev.prog) 239

Stuck on Quality (video) 195

Succeeding with Change: Implementing Action-Driven Strategies (Eccles) 141

The Success Paradigm: Creating Organizational Effectiveness (Friesen & Johnson) 141

Successful Team Building (Quick) 124

Supplier Management (exec.dev.prog) 245

Supplier Quality 9000 (software package) 230

Surgery 58

The Survey Manager (software package) 230

Survey Pro (software package) 231

Systems Engineering Management: Achieving Total Quality (Lacy) 106

Taguchi Methods: Applications in World Industry (Bendell & Pridmore) 132

Tallahassee Democrat 19–20

Team Building Blocks: Practicing Group Collaboration (game) 207

The Team Handbook: How to Use Teams to Improve Quality (Scholtes) 125

The Team Handbook for Educators: How to Use Teams to Improve Quality (Scholtes) 84

Team Player (video) 207

The Team Trainer: Winning Tools and Tactics for Successful Workouts (Gordon et al) 124

Team Zebra (Frangoes & Bennett) 123

Team-Based Organizations: Developing a Successful Team Environment (Shonk) 125

TeamFlow (software package) 231

The TeamNet Factor: Bringing the Power of Boundary Crossing into the Heart of Your business (Lipnack & Stamps) 124

Teams at Work: 7 Keys to Success (Zoglio) 126

Teams and Beyond (exec.dev.prog) 251

Teams for Excellence (video) 208

Teamwork and the Bottom Line: Make a Difference (Rosen) 125

Telephony 29

10 Steps to a Learning Organization (Kline & Saunders) 145

10 Steps to Improved Customer Service (video) 195

Theory Why: In Which the Boss Solves the Riddle of Quality (Guaspari) 129

Thinking about Quality (Dobyns & Crawford-Mason) 5

Time Magazine 45

Time Management for Teams (Douglass & Douglass) 123

Time: The Next Dimension of Quality (video) 202

Tom Peters on Achieving Excellence 186

Tools for Continual Improvement: Training Modules series 1 and 2 (video training modules) 209

Tools for Quality Improvement (video) 210

Tools of Total Quality on CD-ROM (CD-ROM) 210

Top Down Flowcharter (software package) 231

Topics in Health Care Financing 57

Topics in Hospital Pharmacy Management 57, 64

Topping the Network Journal 186

Total Customer Service: The Ultimate Weapon (Davidow & Uttal) 128

Total Improvement Management (Harrington) 6

Total Quality Accounting (Woods) 110

Total Quality Control (Demings) 1

Total Quality Control (Feigenbaum) 134

Total Quality Control and JIT Management in CIM (Ranky) 139

Total Quality Education: Creating Excellence in Education Using the Secrets of Japanese Quality Management (Colonna) 81

Total Quality Education: Profiles of Schools that Demonstrate the Power of Deming's Management Principles (Schmoker & Wilson) 84

Total Quality in Healthcare: From Theory to Practice (Gaucher & Coffey) 66

Total Quality in Higher Education (Lewis & Smith) 94

Total Quality in the Chemical Industry (Askey & Turner) 20

Total Quality Management 186

Total Quality Management and Employee Empowerment: The Ritz-Carlton's Success Story (video) 197

Total Quality Management and Organizational Behaviour Management (Mawhhinney) 145

Total Quality Management for Engineers (Zairi) 108

Total Quality Management for Schools (Bradley) 81

Total Quality Management Guide (Government Printing Office) 121

Total Quality Management in Academic Libraries (Association of Research Libraries) 104

Total Quality Management in Education Videotape Series (video) 202

Total Quality Management in Geriatric Care (Miller et al) 57

Total Quality Management in Government: A Practical Guide for the Real World (Cohen & Brand) 112

Total Quality Management in Higher Education: Clearing the Hurdle (Seymour) 99

Total Quality Management in Higher Education: New Directions for Institutional Research (Sherr & Teeter) 100

Total Quality Management in Human Resource Organizations (Martin) 120

*Total Quality Management in Libraries: A
Sourcebook* (O'Neill) 103
*Total Quality Management in State and Local
Government Videotape* (video) 203
*Total Quality Management: Performance and Cost
Measures* (Talley) 9
*Total Quality Management: Strategies for Local
Government* (The ICMA Training Institute) 117
*Total Quality Marketing: The Key to Regaining
Market Shares* (Reddy) 50
Total Quality Newsletter 186
*Total Quality Project Management for the Design
Firm* (Stasiowski & Burnstein) 108
The Total Quality Service Model (video) 203
Total Service: The Fizzle Factor (video) 203
TQEM Primer and Assessment Matrix (Council of
Great Lakes Industries) 29
TQM for Computer Software (Dunn & Ullman) 51
*TQM for Engineering: Applying Quality Principles to
Product Design and Development* (Sweeney) 107
TQM for Sales and Marketing Management (Cortada)
49
TQM for Small Business (video) 203
TQM in New Product Manufacturing (Menson) 106
TQM: Leadership for the Quality Transformation
(Johnson) 153
The TQM Magazine 187
TQM Toolkit (software package) 232
Training 2, 3, 12, 13, 66, 91, 159
Training & Development 11, 48, 150, 153, 154, 158,
160, 162, 174
Transaction 98
Transformational Teamwork (exec.dev.prog) 251
*Transforming the Organization: Reframing corporate
Issues* (Gouillart & Kelly) 142
Transportation & Distribution 23, 173
Transportation Program (exec.dev.prog) 247
The Trust Factor (video) 203
Trustee 74
Trusts & Estates 41
20 Training Workshops for Customer Service (three-
ring binder) 195
*21st Century Leadership: Dialogues with 100 Top
Leaders* (McFarland *et al*) 154
Type Talk at Work (Kroeger & Theusen) 159

UCLA Programs at OJAI (exec.dev.prog) 243
Understanding BS5750 and Other Quality Systems
(Brown) 168
Understanding ISO 9000 Video Tutorial Producer
(video) 196

The USC Executive Program (exec.dev.prog) 239
Using Customer Satisfaction to Improve
Organizational Performance (exec.dev.prog) 241
Using ISO 9000 to Design and Implement Your
Quality Management System (exec.dev.prog) 241
Using ISO 9000 to Improve Business Processes (AT
& T Quality Library) 132
Using Quality to Redesign School Systems (Siegel &
Byrne) 84

Variation: The Foundation for Run Charts (video
training module) 210
Visual Assessor (software package) 232
Vocational Education Journal 81

*W. Edwards Deming: Improving Quality in Colleges
and Universities* (Cornesky *et al.*) 88
Water Environment and Technology 107
What America Does Right (video) 204
What America Does Right (Waterman) 10, 204
Why Teams Don't Work: What Went Wrong (Robbins
& Finley) 124
Why TQM Fails and What to Do About It (Brown *et
al.*) 3
Win Teams (video) 208
Windows of Change (video) 191
Windsor Program (exec.dev.prog) 239
Winning Through Baldrige (video) 204
*Winning With Quality: Applying Quality Principles in
Product Development* (Wessner *et al*) 108
Winning With Quality: The FPL Story (Hudiburg) 37
*The Wisdom of Teams: Creating the High
Performance Organizations* (Katzenbach & Smith)
124
Women as Leaders: Pursuing the Challenge
(exec.dev.prog) 243
Workflow Analyzer (software package) 232
*The Working Leader: The Triumph of High
Performance* (Sayles) 155
Workplace Teams (video) 208
Workteams and the Wizard of Oz (video) 208
*World Class Quality: Design of Experiments Made
Easier* (Bhote) 133
World-Class Customer Satisfaction (Barsky) 127

Xerox: American Samurai (Jacobson & Hillkirk)
34–5

Young Managers Program (exec.dev.prog) 251

Zapp! The Lightning of Empowerment (video) 198

Subject index

Abacus Concepts Inc 223, 230
ABI Inform 187
Academics Press Inc 185
accident and health insurance (SIC 6321) 44
accounting, auditing and bookkeeping services (SIC 8721) 108–11
Action Management Associates Inc 251
Addison-Wesley Publishing Co 181
administration of public health programs (SIC 9431) 119–20
administration of social, human resource and income maintenance programs (SIC 9441) 120–1
Advanced Management Catalyst Inc 251
Advanced Quality Engineering 251
Advanced Systems & Designs Inc 227, 228
AdvanEdge Technologies Inc 221
Advent Management International Ltd 252
affinity diagrams 297
Air Force Systems Command (Dayton, Ohio) 118
air and water resource and solid waste management (SIC 9511) 121
aircraft (SIC 3721) 32–3
Alessandra & Associates 191
Alexander Research & Communications Inc 183
Allan-Bradley 225
Alligator Technologies 222
Alpha Consulting Group 195
AMACOM (American Management Association) 181
America Media Inc 207
American Health Consultants Inc 184
American Information Systems Inc 232
American Management Association (AMA) 186, 193, 201, 202, 204, 207, 208, 210
American Media Inc 193
American Productivity & Quality Center 183
American Society for Quality Control (ASQC) 26, 167, 184, 185, 186, 196, 198, 201, 203, 219, 292
analytical/statistical methods 131–40; software for 234
Apian Software 231
Applied Statistics Inc 211, 212
architectural services (SIC 8712) 108
Argyle Associates Inc 252
Ashridge Management College 237, 239, 242, 249, 250

Aspen Publishers Inc 185
ASQC Quality Press 181
Asset Development Group 252
Association for Quality and Participation 183, 184, 292
Association of British Certification Bodies 292
Association of Quality Management 292
AT & T Quality Library 181
AT & T Technical Education Center 216
A.T. Kearney Inc 268
attribute data 297
Aubuchon & Associates 252
Audio Video Campus 205
audits 233, 297
Avatar International Inc 252

Baldrige Award see Malcolm Baldrige Award
Barrier & Aids analysis 136
The Batten Group 253
Bauer & Associates 253
BBC Training Videos 196
benchmarking 233, 297; executive development programs for 244–7
'Benchmarking-Theory and Practice' workshop (1994) 139
Berritt Koehler Publishers Inc 181
Berryesa Materials Management Control 253
best practice 297
book publishing (SIC 2731) 20
brainstorming 297
Brian P. Little & Associates 270
The British Quality Association 292
British Quality Award 33
British Quality Foundation 292
British Standards Institution 167, 293
Brookings Institution 246
BS 5750 25, 89, 108
Bureau of Business Practice 185
The Business Center 254
Business Improvement Professionals 254
Business Periodicals Index 187
business process improvement (BPI) 135

calibration management 233
Calibration Manager 213

California Institute of Technology 244, 245, 247
Canada 24, 31, 32, 41, 57, 82, 95, 109
Canadian Standards Association 167
Canatech 254
capability 297
capability index 297
Carfax Publishing Co 186
Carnegie Melon University 238
Carson Research Center 254
catalog and mail-order houses (SIC 5961) 40
cause-and-effect diagrams 297
Center for Breakthrough Thinking 255
Center for Creative Leadership 236, 249
Center for Management Assistance 255
Center for Video Education 201
CFM Inc 231
Change Lab International 190
change management 298; executive development
    programs for 235–8
ChartHouse International Learning Corporation 189
check sheet 298
C.L. Carter Jr & Assoc Inc 254
classified carriers (SIC 6399) 45–6
CLEAR Software Inc 211
Clemson University 250
Clive Shearer 286
Colarelli, Meyer & Associates Inc 255
colleges, universities and professional schools (SIC
    8221) 85–101
Columbia Quality Inc 256
Columbia University 236, 237, 238, 240, 244, 247,
    248, 249
Comer School Development Program 84
commercial banks (SIC 6029) 41–2
commercial physical and biological research (SIC
    8731) 111
commercial printing (SIC 2752) 20
Commitment to Quality Award 63
communications and telecommunications industry
    (SIC 3660) 28–30
Community Television Foundation of South Florida
    202
computer and computer software stores (SIC 5734)
    39
computer industry (SIC 3571) 26–7
computer integrated manufacturing (CIM) 137, 139
computer peripheral equipment (SIC 3577) 27–8
computer processing and data preparation and
    processing services (SIC 7374) 54–5
computer related services (SIC 7379) 55
computer software (SIC 7372) 50–4
Concept III International Inc 256
conformance 298
construction industry (SIC 1500) 17
Continuous Improvement Technology 256
continuous quality improvement (CQI) 298
control charts 298
Cooperative Edge 256
Coopers & Lybrand/Sloan Management Review
    Quality Award 44
Cornell University 236, 238, 241, 244, 248, 249
Coronet/MTI 205, 207

corporate culture 3, 140–9
correctional institutions (SIC 9223) 119
corVision Media 197
cost of quality 298
Council on Hotel, Restaurant and Institutional
    Education (CHRIE) 197
The Coxe Group Inc 257
Cranfield University 238, 239, 240, 244, 247, 250
Creating and Maintaining Customer-Focused
    Organizations Conference (1992) 127
credit unions (SIC 6061) 42
Crisp Publications 192
CRM Films 190, 205, 208
The Crosby Company 216, 219
CS Consulting Group 257
CSP, Communication Structure 257
cultural change 298
customer/s 126–31, 298; executive development
    programs for 239–41
'Customers are the Center of Our Universe' program
    42
Cuthbert Productivity Concepts 213

Daniel Penn Associates 276
Dannemiller Tyson Associates Inc 257
Dartmouth Research Company 258
data collection/processing, software for 234
DeAnne Rosenberg Inc 285
Deans Hill Systems Limited 222
decision analysis 233
Decision Group 258
defect 298
Delta Systems 258
Deming Cycle 84
Deming Prize 6, 35, 37, 38
department stores (SIC 5311) 39
design of experiments 298
Development Dimensions International 181, 198
diversified financial services (SIC 6153) 42
Donnell Associates 259
Du Pont Quality Management & Technology 196
Duke University 236, 239
Dupont Quality Management and Technology 259

eating places (SIC 5812) 39–40
Eckerd College 249
Edu-Tech Industries 259
education see training
EI Compendex Plus 187
electric lamp bulbs and tubes (SIC 3641) 28
electric services (SIC 4911) 37–8
electronic connectors (SIC 3678) 30–1
elementary and secondary schools (SIC 8211) 80–5
Elsevier Science B.V. 184
Elsevier Science Ltd 183
Emory University 246
employee benefits and compensation (SIC 6400) 46
empowerment 298
engineering services (SIC 8711) 105–8
Enterprise Media Inc 191, 193, 197, 199, 200, 201,
    204, 205
ERIC 187

European Foundation for Quality Management 293
European Foundation for Quality Management Award 6, 35
European Organization for Quality 293
European Quality Publications Ltd 183
Exact Gestation et Technologies de la Qualité Inc 221
Excalibur Consulting 260
Excel Partnership Inc 260
'Executive Interview Program' 45
Executive Learning Inc 209, 210, 260
Experience in Software Inc 217, 222
experiments, design of, software for 233

fast-response organization (FRO) 107
Federal Productivity Program 110
feedback 298
Fleet & Partners Inc 212
flowcharting/diagramming 233, 299
FMI 260
FOCUS-PDCA program 61, 72
Food Agri International (North America) LLC 261
food preparation (SIC 2099) 18
force field analysis 299
Frank E. Smith & Associates 286
The Free Press 181

Gael Quality 224
GageTalker 216, 221
gauge repeatability and reproducibility (gauge R & R) 233
Gelb Consulting Group Inc 261
Gelman & Associates Inc 262
general government (SIC 9199) 111–18
general medical and surgical hospitals (SIC 8062) 57–78
George Washington University 241
Georgia State University 243
Germany 31, 41
GGI 262
GlennCo Services Inc 262
Global Conference on Management Innovation 146
GOAL/QPC 181, 199, 202, 203, 209, 220
Goldman-Nelson Group 262
good manufacturing practices (GMP) 79
Gower Publishing 181
Greenbridge Management Inc 262
group relations theory 123
Group Support Systems 94

Haddonfield Group Inc 263
Harber and Associates 263
The Harrington Group Inc 212, 213, 221, 223
Harvard University 238
Havard Business School Press 182
HavenTree Software Limited 215, 221
health and allied services (SIC 8099) 79–80
Health Management Consultants Inc 257
Health Planning and Administration Database 187
Heller, Hunt and Cuningham 263
Henley Management College 236, 238
HESTER Associates Inc 263

high velocity manufacturing (HVM) 36
Hillsdale College 248, 250
histograms 299
Hitchcock Publishing 185, 186
HJ Ford Associates Inc 261
H.J. Steudel & Associates Inc 288
Hong Kong 15
hoshin planning 83, 132, 136
hotels and motels (SIC 7011) 47–9
household furniture (SIC 2519) 19
household refrigerators and home and farm freezers (SIC 3632) 28
Howard-Lancaster & Associates Inc 264
Howick Associates 264
Huebcore Communications Inc 185
Human Dynamics 264
human resource development 156–63
Human Resource Development Press 191, 195, 205, 206, 207
H.W. Fahrlander & Associates 261
hydraulic hoses (SIC 3041) 24

IBM Total Quality Management University Competition 99
idea generation, software for 233
IdeaGen Software Limited 224
IIE (Institute of Industrial Engineers) Award for Excellence in Productivity Management 110
'In Touch' program 47
India 24
Indiana University 242
industrial inorganic chemicals (SIC 2819) 20–2
industrial organic chemicals (SIC 2869) 23–4
Information Exchange (computer-based intelligence system) 55
inorganic pigments (SIC 2816) 20
INSEAD 237, 246
Inspiration Software Inc 217
Institute of Personnel Management 182
Institute of Quality Assurance 186; 293
Insync Corporation 230
Interaction Research Institute Inc 265
Intercim Corporation 215, 229
International Institute for Management Development (IMD) 236, 242
International Management Technologies Inc 265
International Marketing Institute Boston College 246
International Organization for Standardization 167
International Quality Study (IQS) 26–7, 31, 41, 68–9, 69
International Systems Services Corporation 265
International Techne Group Inc 223
Internet 3
IQS Inc 217
Irish Management Institute 236, 249
Irwin Professional Publishing 182
ISO 9000 21, 22, 25, 49, 52, 53, 89, 108, 165–7; articles on 170–9; books on 168–70; country addresses for 167; software for implementation of 233–4, 241
ISO 9001 52, 53

Jandel Scientific Software 226
Japan 13, 15, 31, 41, 85, 138
Japanese companywide quality control 14
JCM-TECH Inc 266
Jewell Consulting Network Inc 266
J.J. Moran & Associates 273
John Wiley & Sons Ltd 182, 183, 185
The Johnson-Layton Company 266
Joiner Associates 266
Joint Commission on Accreditation of Healthcare
    Organizations (JCAHO) 57, 58, 63, 64, 79, 182
Jossey-Bass Inc 182
Juran Institute Inc 182, 218, 267
Just-in-Time (JIT) 8, 14, 140
JWA Video 193

Kaetron Software Corp 215, 231, 232
Kaizen 299
KAIZEN Institute of America 267
Karl Albrecht & Associates 203
Ken Irish Associates 265
Key Management Strategies 268
Klemm & Associates 268
Kluwer Academic Publishers Press 184
K.W. Tunnell Company Inc 291

The La Valle Group 269
Lakewood Publicataions 186
Landes Communications 269
Landis & Associates 269
Latin America 97
Latzko Associates 269
lead pencils, crayons and artists' materials (SIC
    3952) 35–6
leadership 149–56, 299; executive development
    programs for 241–3
Leadership Through Quality 34, 35
Leads-Rivers Group 270
learning organizations 145, 147
Leemak Inc 270
legal services (SIC 8111) 80
Levinson Institute 243, 251
libraries (SIC 8231) 101–4
life insurance (SIC 6311) 43–4
London Business School 235, 249
Long & Vickers Inc 271
Longman Productions 200
Lotus Inspection Data System (LIDS) 51
Louisiana State University 241, 250
LTK National Training Award 33
Luftig & Associates 271

McGill Executive Program 238
McGill University 247
McGraw-Hill 182
McNeil & Associates 271
MacQuarie University 240, 247, 249
Macro International Inc 271
Malcolm Baldrige Award 4, 5, 6, 12, 20, 21, 25, 26,
    27, 29, 30, 32, 35, 36, 37, 40, 42, 48, 49, 53, 80,
    85, 95, 96, 121, 233; criteria 133, 135
malt beverages (SIC 2082) 17–18

Management Methods Inc 272
Management Software International Inc 217
Manufacturing & Development Technology 272
Marcel Dekker Inc 182
Marilyn Manning 272
Mark M. DoMowne 259
market-perceived quality 129
Marketing Quality Assurance 49
Mass Production-Scientific Management 4
Massachusetts Institute of Technology 198, 239
Mastercard Automated Point of Sale Program
    (MAPP) 42
Mathews & Company 272
Mauch & Associates 272
MCB University Press Ltd 183, 184, 185, 186
measuring, analyzing and controlling instruments
    (SIC 3829) 33
The Media Group Inc 196
medical laboratories (SIC 8071) 78–9
Mentor Media 190, 191, 194
Meta Software Corporation 214, 232
metal cans and shipping containers (SIC 3411) 25
metals & metalworking (SIC 3334) 25
M.F. Smith & Associates Inc 287
Miami University 245
Micrografix 211
MicroMentor Inc 210
Miles Southworth 288
Millet Group Inc 273
Minitab Inc 220
M.J. Weeks Seminars 292
'Month End Closing' project 108
mortgage bankers and loan correspondents (SIC
    6166) 43
motor vehicles and passenger car bodies (SIC 3711)
    31–2
Mt Eliza Australian Management College 239, 251
Murphy Software Co 214
musical instruments (SIC 3931) 35
Myers, Marits and Associates 273

Nathan/Tyler Production 199
National Institute of Standards and Technology 293
national commercial banks (SIC 6021) 40–1
National Quality Information Centre 293
national security (SIC 9711) 121–2
National Society for Quality Through Teamwork 27,
    293
natural gas transmissions and ditribution (SIC 4923)
    38–9
Nelson & Company 273
Neuman's Systems Model 70
New Zealand Organisation for Quality Inc 185
newspapers (SIC 2711) 19–20
'Newton Success-Oriented School Model' 82
Nexus Business Communications Ltd 186
Nicholas Brealey Publishing Ltd 182
Nihon Kagaku Gijutsu Renmei 184
NIMAC Software 218
nominal group process 299
Nordill, Wilson Associates 274
Northern Ireland Quality Award 33

Northwestern University Kellogg Graduate School of
Management 240, 244, 246
nuclear fuel fabrication and metal products (SIC
3462) 25
NUTEK Inc 274

Objectives Management 230
offices and clinics of dentists (SIC 8021) 56
offices and clinics of doctors of medicine (SIC 8011)
56
OMNEO/Oliver Wright Publications Inc 182
Organization Counselors 274
organizational architecture 299
organizational behaviour management (OBM) 145
Organizational Designs in Communication Inc 274
Orr & Boss 274

P-E International 276
The Pacer Group 275
package delivery services (SIC 4513) 36–7
Panitz and Associates Inc 275
paper mills (SIC 2621) 19
Pareto analysis 24, 139, 299
'Partners for Excellence' program 45
Patton & Patton Software Corporation 215
Patton Consultants Inc 275
Paul DeBaylo Associates Inc 258
The Paul Hertz Group 263
PDCA cycle see Plan-Do-Check-Act cycle
Peak International 275
Pennsylvania State University 236, 243
pension, health and welfare funds (SIC 6371) 45
Perelmuth & Associates 276
Performance Consulting Group 276
Performex 277
performing arts (SIC 8307) 105
Periodical Abstracts 187
Perkins Award 27
Perry Johnson Inc 277
personal credit institutions (SIC 6141) 42
Personnel Journal Optimas Award 40
petrochemical industry (SIC 2860) 23
petroleum products (SIC 2900) 24
pharmaceutical preparations (SIC 2834) 22–3
Philip E. Nickerson 273
photographic equipment and supplies (SIC 3861)
34–5
The Pierce Group 277
Plan-Do-Check-Act (PDCA) 299
Plan-Test Associates 277
police protection (SIC 9221) 118–19
P.O.W.E.R. Inc 277
Powerway Inc 214, 226, 230
PQ Systems Inc 278
Practical Management Inc 278
PROACTION Management Consultants 278
process 300
Process Management International 279
process modelling, software for 234
process reengineering 297
Product Integrity Company 280
Productivity Development Group Inc 184

Productivity Improvement Program for the Federal
Government 116
Productivity Inc 184
Productivity Management Consultants 280
Productivity Network 280
Productivity Press 182
Productivity Sciences Inc 281
Productivity-Quality Systems Inc (PQ Systems) 228,
229
'Program to Improve Patient Care' program 76
Programs on Change Consulting Services 281
project planning, software for 234
public finance, taxation and monetary policy (SIC
9311) 119

Q.A.I. Limited 281
QCI International 185, 281
QFD Institute 294
Qualisoft Corp 223
Qualitran Professional Services Inc 215, 227, 228
QUALITY 3, 300
Quality & Performance Systems, Inc 282
'Quality Agenda' program 59
Quality Alert Institute 282
Quality America Inc 214, 226, 227, 232
Quality and Productivity Management Association
186
quality assurance 300; software for 235
Quality Assurance Institute 294
quality assurance/continuous quality improvement
(QA/CQI) program 62
Quality Control Institute 282
quality focus teams (QFTs) 57
Quality for American Communities 282
quality function deployment (QFD) 87, 300
Quality Groups 283
'Quality Has Value' (QHV) technique 125
quality improvement process (QIP), executive
development programs for 244—7
Quality Improvement Prototype Award 118
quality leadership process (QLP) 33, 34
Quality Learning Services, U.S. Chamber of
Commerce 203
quality management; background to 1–2; seven tools
of 300
quality management consultants 251–92
Quality Management Forum (1993) 24, 31, 35, 117
quality management program (QMP) 63
Quality Media Resources 197
Quality Resources 182, 192
quality tools, software for 234
Quality Way Inc 283
Qualtec Quality Services Inc 283
'Quantum Quality' initiative 85
Queen's University 236, 244, 245, 248

R. Breakiron and Associates 253
radio and television broadcasting and communications
equipment (SIC 3663) 30
Raosoft Inc 225
Rath & Strong Inc 284
Raymond Bedwell Associates 253

real estate agents and managers (SIC 6531) 46–7
Reddy, Traver & Woods Inc 284
reengineering 300; executive development programs for 247; software for 234
Reifler Associates Inc 284
Resource Management Consultants, Inc 284
resource material, book publishers and distributors 181–3; databases 187–8; executive development programs 235–51; Library of Congress subject headings 188–9; Malcolm Baldrige National Quality Award 294–5; periodicals 183–7; QM management consultants 251–92; software finding aid categories 233–5; software packages 211–32; TQM Associations 292–4; training materials 189–211
Rhode Island Area Coalition for Excellence 294
Richard Fudge Associates 261
R.J. Levullus & Associates 270
Roberts & Roberts Associates 285
Roberts, Curry & Company 285
root cause 300
RPM Systems Inc 283
run chart 300
Rutgers University 246

Safatech 285
Sage Publications Inc 182
St Lucie Press 182
sales and selling (SIC 7300) 49–50
SAS Institute 218, 226
scatter diagram 300
Robert H. Schaffer & Associates 285
scheduled air transportation (SIC 4512) 36
Scientific and Engineering Award 34
scientific graphing, software for 234
Scitor Corp 222
Service Excellence Inc 286
Sheldon Press 182
Shewhart Cycle see Plan-Do-Check-Act (PDCA)
Shilay Associates Inc 286
signs and advertising specialities (SIC 3993) 36
Singapaore 15
Six Sigma program 26, 39, 300
skilled nursing care facilities (SIC 8051) 56–7
soap and other detergents (SIC 2841) 23
Social Sciences Index 187
Society for Human Resource Management (SHRM) 207
Software Engineering Consultants Inc 287
Solution Finders Inc 287
Southwest Resource Development 287
SPC3D 227
SPC Press Inc 182
Spechler Associates 288
speciality outpatient facilities (SIC 8093) 79
spray equipment, industrial (SIC 3563) 25–6
SPSS Inc 224, 228
Standard Industrial Classification (SIC) 17; applications see named headings
Standards Council of Canada 167
Stanford University 236, 243
start-up 3

STAT-A-MATRIX 288
statistical process control (SPC) 25, 300; software for 234–5
StatSoft 229
steel works, blast furnaces, rolling mills (SIC 3312) 24–5
Stovall Communications 183
Strategic Planning Guild 288
supplier 300
surgical and medical instruments and apparatus (SIC3841) 33
survey tools, software for 235
The Synapse Group 289
Systems Management 289

Taguchi methods 131, 132, 134, 137, 139
Taiwan 15
Take Charge Consultants Inc 289
Team Zebra 123
team-building 300
teams 123–6, 300; software for 247–51
Technicomp 208
Templeton College 250
Texas Christian University 243
textile mills (SIC 2211) 18–19
Tomlinson Research 289
top-down flow chart 300
Total Client Satisfaction Program 29
Total Quality Care (TQC) 74
Total Quality Control (TQC) 38
Total Quality Forum 91
Total Quality Improvement (TQI) 93
total quality management (TQM) 300–1; America's involvement in 7–8; applications of see named Standard Industrial Classification (SIC) entries; basic components of 2; case studies 8, 9, 11; evolution 8; implementation of 5–6, 7, 9; in practice 2–3; problems with 12–13, 15; resistance to 11; survey of companies using 10; trends in 11
Total Quality Manufacturing 290
Total Quality Process (TQP) 65
Total Quality Project Management (TQPM) 108
Total Quality Service (TQS) 86, 118, 126
Total Quality Systems 290
Total Research Corporation 289
Tower Hill Press 182
TPG Communications 186
TQM International Ltd 182
Trade and Industry Index 187
training 156–63; audio-visual and interactive multimedia sources 189–210; software packages 211–35
tree diagram 301
Tri-Tech Services Inc 290
Triad Performance Technologies Inc 290

UCLA Extension, Anderson Graduate School of Management 243
Unique Solutions Inc 291
United Kingdom 32, 41, 75, 95, 102
United Kingdom Accreditation Service 294
University of Calgary 243

University of California 239, 242
University of Chicago 237, 240
University of Hawaii 245
University of Houston 248
University of Miami 246
University of Michigan 235, 240, 241, 246, 248
University of Minnesota 235, 237, 241
University of New Hampshire 251
University of New Mexico 245
University of New South Wales 241, 245
University of North Carolina 238, 250
University of Pennsylvania 238, 240, 243, 245, 248
University of Pittsburgh 246
University of Richmond 243
University of South Carolina 249
University of Tennessee 237, 240, 242, 244, 247
University of Texas at Austin 240, 242, 247
University of Toronto 242
University of Virginia 237, 241, 242, 243, 250
University of Washington 237, 242
University of Wisconsin-Madison 244, 247, 248

Vanderbilt University 240, 244, 245, 250
variable chart 301
variable data 301
variety stores (SIC 5311) 39
Video Arts 192, 194, 195, 198, 204
Video Publishing House Inc 192, 194, 200, 202
Video Vision 208
vision 301
Vragel & Associates 291

Warwick Daisley International 291
The Way Ahead 38
'Way of Life' program 43, 44
William & Wilkins 183
William L. Holcomb Associates Inc 264
work groups 301
World Wide Web 3

Yale University 249
Young Systems 292